XML, XSLT, Java™, and JSP™: A Case Study in Developing a Web Application

Contents At a Glance

XML, XSLT, Java™, and JSP™: A Case Study in Developing a Web Application

Westy Rockwell

www.newriders.com
201 West 103rd Street, Indianapolis, Indiana 46290
An Imprint of Pearson Education
Boston • Indianapolis • London • Munich • New York • San Francisco

XML, XSLT, Java™, and JSP™: A Case Study in Developing a Web Application

Translation from the German language edition of: XML, XSLT, Java, and JSP by Westy Rockwell © 2000 Galileo Press GmbH Bonn, Germany

FIRST EDITION: July 2001

International Standard Book Number: 0-7357-1089-9

Library of Congress Catalog Card Number: 00-110885

05 04 03 02 01 7 6 5 4 3 2 1

Interpretation of the printing code: The rightmost double-digit number is the year of the book's printing; the right-most single-digit number is the number of the book's printing. For example, the printing code 01-1 shows that the first printing of the book occurred in 2001.

Composed in Bembo and MCPdigital by New Riders Publishing

Printed in the United States of America

Trademarks

All terms mentioned in this book that are known to be trademarks or service marks have been appropriately capitalized. New Riders Publishing cannot attest to the accuracy of this information. Use of a term in this book should not be regarded as affecting the validity of any trademark or service mark. Java™ and JavaServer™ Pages (JSP) are registered trademarks of Sun Microsystems, Inc.

Warning and Disclaimer

This book is designed to provide information about XML, XSLT, Java, and JSP. Every effort has been made to make this book as complete and as accurate as possible, but no warranty or fitness is implied.

The information is provided on an as-is basis. The authors and New Riders Publishing shall have neither liability nor responsibility to any person or entity with respect to any loss or damages arising from the information contained in this book or from the use of the discs or programs that may accompany it.

Publisher
David Dwyer

Associate Publisher
Al Valvano

Executive Editor
Stephanie Wall

Managing Editor
Gina Brown

Product Marketing Manager
Stephanie Layton

Publicity Manager
Susan Nixon

Software Development Specialist
Jay Payne

Project Editor
Elise Walter

Copy Editor
Krista Hansing

Indexer
Larry Sweazy

Manufacturing Coordinator
Jim Conway

Book Designer
Louisa Klucznik

Cover Designer
Aren Howell

Proofreader
Jeannie Smith

Composition
Gina Rexrode

❖

THIS BOOK IS DEDICATED
TO MEMORIES
OF YOU,
DON ROCKWELL, SR.
YOU GAVE SO MUCH TO ME!
DID I EVER SAY ENOUGH, SOMEHOW,
FOR YOU TO KNOW HOW MUCH I LOVE YOU?
WITHOUT YOUR LOVE AND KIND
GENEROSITY,
I WOULD NOT FEEL HALF SO FORTUNATE
TO BE ALIVE TODAY. BESIDES THAT,
YOU TAUGHT ME TO ENJOY THIS LIFE,
SWIM IN THE BLUE OCEANS, AND
DIVE DOWN SO DEEPLY.
I WOULD MISS YOU FOREVER,
IF I WERE NOT SO SURE
THAT YOU ARE
HERE.

THANK YOU!

W. R.

Table of Contents

About the Author

Westy Rockwell considers himself a world citizen. Currently he is a senior developer at tarent GmbH, a Web development company in Bonn, Germany. His greatest pleasure is enjoying the company of his wife, Zamina, and their two daughters, Joaquina and Jennifer. Somehow, they tolerate his intense involvement with computers.

Westy has more than 15 years of experience as a professional software developer, but his involvement with computers dates back longer yet. In 1965, he programmed the Pythagorean theorem into an IBM 1620 with punched cards. His faculty adviser told him to stop spending so much time on programming, which had no career future. In 1970, while studying IBM 360 programming, he was considered too radical for saying that computers would one day play chess. It was not until the early 1980s, with the arrival of microcomputers, that his career and his passion could merge.

His real software education came from deeply hacking many microcomputers, including the ZX80, the Osborne, the Vic20, the C64, various Amigas, and, of course, IBM PCs. His career, meanwhile, involved him with more respectable software and hardware, including UNIX, workstations, minicomputers, mainframes, and, of course, IBM PCs. Interest in hardware design, along with C and assembly languages, culminated in 1994 when he built the prototype for an extremely successful dual-processor alcohol analyser, including the PCB design, operating system, and application software.

Soon afterward, while developing man-machine interfaces, the pre-release version of Borland Delphi turned Westy into a Windows developer. He went on to work on three-tier systems based on Windows NT, including corporate asset management, document imaging, and work management systems. For more than a year now he has refused to touch SQL or Visual tools, and he is enthusiastically pursuing Web browser- and server-based applications using Java, Tomcat, Xerces, and Xalan.

About the Technical Reviewers

These reviewers contributed their considerable hands-on expertise to the entire development process for *XML, XSLT, Java, and JSP: A Case Study in Developing a Web Application*. As the book was being written, these dedicated professionals reviewed all the material for technical content, organization, and flow. Their feedback was critical to ensuring that *XML, XSLT, Java, and JSP: A Case Study in Developing a Web Application* fits our reader's need for the highest-quality technical information.

Brad Irby holds a bachelor of computer science degree from the University of North Carolina, and he has been a programmer and system designer since 1985. He has worked with many different languages and databases over the years, but he now specializes in application development using a Microsoft SQL Server back end. A private consultant for eight years, Brad has been following the progress of the W3C and the XML specification since its inception, and he has done extensive work using the XML extensions of SQL Server to transfer data over secure internet links. He can be reached at `Brad@BradIrby.com`.

Perry Tew graduated from Georgia Institute of Technology with a degree in chemical engineering, but he has since fallen in love with computer programming. Perry began his IT career as a MCSD and currently programs with Java. He works as an integration specialist for a major contact lens producer. He spends his free time with his wife, Paula, basking in they joy of parenthood brought by the arrival of their newborn, Joshua.

Acknowledgments

Most of all, I want to thank Jennifer, Joaquina and Zamina Rockwell, who are the real treasures in my life. Without their love, understanding, playfulness and patience this book could never have been written.

There are so many others to thank, I know I will omit some here: those who toiled behind the scenes, those who taught me, worked with me, helped me come to this point in my professional career. If you are one of these, I would like to thank you as well. Please forgive the unintentional omission of your name.

Thanks are especially due to Elmar Geese, CEO of tarent GmbH, for making this book possible. Also, Manfred Weltecke, for his masterful translation of the first book version into German, to which it largely owes its success. Much credit for that success also belongs to Harald Aberfeld, Michael Klink and Florian Hawlitzek, for their technical editing of the German edition.

Thanks to all my colleagues at tarent GmbH, for their selfless support of the book project: Alex Steeg, Alexander Scharch, Boris Esser, Harald Aberfeld, Hendrik Helwich, Kerstin Weber, Markus Heiliger, Martina Hundhausen, Matthias Esken, May-Britt Baumann, Michael Klink, Robert Schuster, Thomas Mueller-Ackermann, Vanessa Haering, and Vera Schwingenheuer. My absence from their projects while working on this book created extra work for them; I appreciate that truly.

Thanks to the staff of Galileo Press, especially my editors Judith Stevens and Corinna Stefani, for making the German edition happen. Others there whose work on the book is appreciated are: proofreaders Claudia Falk and Hoger Schmidt, cover designer Barbara Thoben, illustrator Leo Leowald, producer Petra Strauch, and computer typographer Joerg Gitzelmann. Thanks also to Petra Walther and Stefan Krumbiegel of Galileo Press for supporting the German edition online.

Thanks to Lau Shih-Hor and Agnes Chin of Elixir Technologies, for adding value to the CDROM. Thanks to the developers of TextPad, so useful for a technical writer. Thanks to Jen Wilson for creating `bonForum.links2go.com`, in support of the book project.

This book depends so much upon those who make the open source projects it and its example project depend upon. Thanks to all involved with the Apache Software Foundation, especially its Jakarta and Apache XML projects. Thanks also to the staff and providers of SourceForge for making it a superb place to develop and learn about open source software. Thanks to Sun for making its JDK available for learning Java.

Many thanks to the staff of New Riders who made the English version of the book happen. Especially to Stephanie Wall (Executive Editor), who went way beyond the call of duty to keep the book alive until publication, and to Elise Walter (Project Editor), who always kept her good humor no matter how late my requests for changes came to her. The book was vastly improved by the "no-holds-barred" technical editors, including Brad Irby, Erin Mulder, and Perry Tew. Thanks to Jay Payne (Media Developer), who produced the CD-ROM. After working with words for over a year myself, I know I owe so much of this book's existence to Krista Hansing (Copy Editor), Larry Sweazy (Indexer), Gina Rexrode (Compositor). Thanks also to Susan Nixon (Public Relations).

Thanks to Jeffrey E. Northridge, whose friendship and partnership-in-programming has been so valued by me. Thanks to Jaime del Palacio, a superb software developer (and nephew). Thanks to PhoenixFire, for giving me that first, all-important chance as a professional software developer (If you read this, please contact me!). Thanks to John Haefeli of ISI, who provided so many difficult real-world problems to solve with C. Thanks to Alvaro Pastor, Glenn Forrester, and all the gang who were at Intoximeters West, especially to Doug, Iza, Petcy who helped so much to develop me as a software developer. Thanks to Paul McEvoy for his mentoring and my appreciation of cafe latte. Thanks to Elliot Mehrbach for helping me learn SQL and Delphi.

Finally, I would like to thank especially Daph, Cita and Marcos Rockwell, and all my other relatives, for their unconditional love. Thanks also to Nature and Life, for their unconditional and priceless support.

Tell Us What You Think

As the reader of this book, you are the most important critic and commentator. We value your opinion and want to know what we're doing right, what we could do better, what areas you'd like to see us publish in, and any other words of wisdom you're willing to pass our way.

As an Executive Editor at New Riders Publishing, I welcome your comments. You can fax, email, or write me directly to let me know what you did or didn't like about this book—as well as what we can do to make our books stronger.

Please note that I cannot help you with technical problems related to the topic of this book, and that due to the high volume of mail I receive, I might not be able to reply to every message.

When you write, please be sure to include this book's title and author, as well as your name and phone or fax number. I will carefully review your comments and share them with the author and editors who worked on the book.

Fax: 317-581-4663
Email: stephanie.wall@newriders.com
Mail: Stephanie Wall
Executive Editor
New Riders Publishing
201 West 103rd Street
Indianapolis, IN 46290 USA

Introduction

For more than 20 years, I have read books about software development. Many of these repeated information available to me elsewhere. Formerly, that information was often from magazines; recently its source is the Internet. A few books, refreshingly, were based instead upon the authors' "hands on" experiences with the art and science of software development.

You can now write a book about how to become a gourmet chef without ever having cooked a meal. Simply download a collection of recipes from the Web, organize and paraphrase them, and, presto! A book is born, ready to meet the market demand. Especially in the field of software development, many books seem to have been written in this way.

When I was asked to write a book about Web application development with XML and Java, I replied that the book would have to be a practical "how-to" manual, based upon real development experiences. Its target audience would be software developers trying to understand and harness those technologies. I knew that to write that book, I would have to "cook the meal" myself. My fundamental task would be to develop a functional and timely Web application project, of at least plausible utility.

Surfing the Web, I soon gathered very much information. I determined which of all the available tools and products this book would feature. Most of them were then in a state of flux, and all are still evolving. In fact, a worldwide effort is continually implementing products based on ever-evolving tools and standards related to XML and Java.

Even for an experienced software developer, putting all this information and technology to practical use was no simple task. Many of the well-documented tools were obsolete, and the more current tools were often not well documented. Extremely active mailing lists were frequented by early adopters building real Web applications; these pioneers often faced with incompatibilities between the tools and the standards.

At first, my plan was to complete the earlier chapters, which present the tools and technologies, and then to develop the book project and write the later chapters. It soon became clear that this would put the cart before the horse. I decided to first create the Web application and only then, always in the context of that project, to discuss how XML and Java-based technologies could be applied by the reader.

That is when the fun started. I designed and implemented a Web chat application called bonForum. It is based on XML and XSLT, Java servlets and applets, and JSP. It presented me with many of the most challenging tasks of Web application design. As a very popular and timely type of Web application, I trust that it will interest the reader. As an experiment and a tutorial, its design and implementation provide a framework for ongoing development by the readers of this book. It can and should morph into other types of Web applications besides a chat room.

I welcome bug reports, fixes, suggestions, feedback, and communication! Please contact me at `mail@bonforum.org`. Look for errata, version updates, mailing lists, and related information at `http://www.bonforum.org`.

Conventions Used in This Book

`Monospaced font` is used to indicate code, including commands, options, objects, and so on. It is also used for Internet addresses. *Italics* are used to introduce and define a new term. Code continuation characters are used in code listings that are too long to fit within the book's margins. They should not be used in actual implementation.

How This Book Is Organized

This book is organized so that you can easily follow along with the case study and build the Web chat application along with the author and his team. Each chapter builds on the previous one.

Chapter 1, "Introduction and Requirements," explains the goal of writing this book. It also describes why certain tools were selected for the project.

Chapter 2, "An Environment for Java Software Development," teaches you how to set up an inexpensive Java development environment. It shows you how to compile, debug and run the Web application example project.

Chapter 3, "Java Servlets and JavaServer Pages: Jakarta Tomcat," introduces Tomcat, which is an HTTP server and a container for Java Servlets and JavaServer Pages.

Chapter 4, "XML and XSLT: Xerces and Xalan," introduces Xerces, a DOM and a SAX parser, and Xalan, an XSLT and XPATH processor.

Chapter 5, "BonForum Chat Application: Use and Design," introduces you to bonForum, the Web chat application that will be the major subject of the rest of the book. It was designed as a tool to explore each of the subjects of this book, XML, XSLT, Java Servlets, Java Applets and JavaServer Pages, while solving some real Web application problems.

Chapter 6, "BonForum Chat Application: Implementation," continues the overview of bonForum that began in Chapter 5. Some tougher implementation problems are also highlighted, and suggestions for future development of the Web chat are given.

Chapter 7, "Java Servlet and Java Bean: BonForum Engine and bon Forum Store," teaches the JSP technology that the Tomcat Server supports, as JavaServer Pages are used to create a BUI, a browseable user interface, for our Web application.

Chapter 8, "Java Servlet in Charge: BonForumEngine," describes the central class in the bonForum Web application. It also illustrates some themes common to using Java Servlets in Web applications.

Chapter 9, "Java Applet Plugged In: BonForumRobot," discusses the bonForumRobot applet, which is part of the bonForum Web chat application. This chapter teaches how to create and deploy a Java Applet to control a Web application user interface and use Sun Java Plug-in to support an Applet on the client.

Chapter 10, "JSP Taglib: The bonForum Custom Tags," explains how to use a JSP Tag Library with the bonForum Web application. All the functions that are included in the multi-purpose ChoiceTag are discussed, which are used on many of the JSP documents in the Web chat example. This chapter also shows you how the Apache Xalan XSLT processor is used from the custom tag.

Chapter 11, "XML Data Storage Class: ForestHashtable," shows how data storage for the XML data in the bonForum chat application is implemented. This chapter also teaches how to add a few tricks to a descendant of the Hashtable class to optimize XML element retrieval and simulate a database program design.

Chapter 12, "Online Information Sources," provides links to XML, XSLT, Java Servlet and JSP information.

Appendices A and B provide the CD-ROM contents and copyright information. The project's source code is listed in Appendix C.

An added note: when the author uses the term "we" throughout the book, he is referring to the team that worked on the bonForum Web application.

1

Introduction and Requirements

IN THIS CHAPTER, YOU FIND OUT WHAT we want this book to provide. We also present the choices made to support the "practical" side of the book. Here we try to justify the software tools and libraries that we selected to illustrate a large subject: developing Web applications powered by XML, XSLT, Java servlets, Java applets, and JavaServer Pages.

1.1 The Goal of This Book

While writing this book, we have assumed that you, its reader, are a software developer with some Java experience and that you want to build Web applications based on XML, XSLT, Java servlets, Java applets, and JavaServer Pages. The goal of this book is to support you as you learn about using all of these increasingly important technologies together. This book will help you become familiar with a set of widely available and professional software tools that covers all these technologies. Furthermore, it will introduce you to many of the tasks that you will encounter in your own projects, by tackling these tasks within the context of a realistically large example project: a Web application named bonForum.

The examples and the Web application project for this book were developed on a PC using Windows NT 4.0. If you prefer, you can use this book together with Windows 95, 98, or 2000 instead. With a bit more effort, an experienced developer could use much of the material in this book with a Linux or UNIX operating system—we have tried to minimize any platform dependencies both in the code examples and in the case study.

Except for using Windows NT 4.0 as our operating system, we have preferred to feature freely available, platform-independent, open-source software technologies. Nevertheless, the technologies and tools that we have chosen are among the most popular ones currently in use by XML and Web application developers.

We do not intend this book to be a complete reference to XML, XSLT, Java servlets, Java applets, or JSP. Nor do we intend it to be an introduction to these topics. However, if you are an aspiring Web application developer who is new to XML technologies or new to Java server-side technologies, you can start the book with Chapter 12, "Online Information Sources." By using the many Web links there, you can find everything that is needed to understand the material in this book.

1.2 Why Use This Book?

The popularity of the Extensible Markup Language (XML) and Java server-side software technologies (servlets and JSP) is exploding as developers become aware of their power and purpose. One result is that books on these subjects are growing in number and are being translated into many languages. For example, Steve Holzner's *Inside XML*, published by New Riders (ISBN: 0-7357-1020-1), is selling extremely well. The excellent book *Core Servlets and JavaServer Pages*, by Marty Hall (ISBN: 0-1308-9340-4) and published by Prentice Hall PTR/Sun Microsystems Press, will be translated into at least eight languages from its original English. We could give many additional examples of similar books. There is something behind this popularity: XML, XSLT, Java servlets, and JavaServer Pages are quite well established in professional software development. They've now been around long enough to become extremely useful in real projects.

They are also evolving rapidly, which is illustrated by the release dates of their related proposals and recommendations published by the W3C. (The World Wide Web Consortium, an official standards body for Web technologies.) Consider some dates related to XML technologies. On February 10, 1998, the XML 1.0 specification became a recommendation of the W3C. The second edition of the specification is dated October 6, 2000. XSL was submitted as a proposal to the W3C on August 27, 1997. Version 1.0 of XSL Transformations (XSLT) is dated November 16, 1999. Version 1.0 of XSL was a candidate for official W3C recommendation by November 21, 2000.

Now consider some dates related to Java server-side Web technologies. The JavaServer Pages 0.092 specification is dated October 1998. JSP 1.0 was publicly released in June 1999. JSP 1.1, which is featured in this book, is from spring 2000. By a now robust and useful Web technology, it is based upon the Java Servlets API 2.1, which dates from April 1999.

The fast evolution of these technologies is being driven by their usefulness in the development of Web applications. Of course, you know how crucial the role of

HTML has been (and still is) within the World Wide Web. The following is a quote from the XML FAQ (`http://www.ucc.ie/xml/`), which suggests one reason for the increasing importance of XML:

> HTML is already overburdened with dozens of interesting but incompatible inventions from different manufacturers because it provides only one way of describing your information.
>
> XML allows groups of people or organizations to create their own customized markup applications for exchanging information in their domain (music, chemistry, electronics, hill-walking, finance, surfing, petroleum geology, linguistics, cooking, knitting, stellar cartography, history, engineering, rabbit-keeping, mathematics, *etcætera ad infinitum*).
>
> HTML is at the limit of its usefulness as a way of describing information, and while it will continue to play an important role for the content it currently represents, many new applications require a more robust and flexible infrastructure.

If XML is a better way of describing information (and it is), then XSLT is a better way of transforming that information from one description to another. When used to transform data into HTML, the power of XSLT becomes particularly useful in Web applications, which rely on HTML browsers for their visual presentation to a user.

Now take a look at some quotes from the Sun press release announcing JSP 1.0:

> Sun announces the immediate availability of JavaServer Pages technology, which for the first time allows Web page developers to easily build cross-platform, truly interactive Web sites.
>
> Harnessing the full power of the Java platform, JavaServer Pages technology separates the functions of content generation and page layout, providing developers with a simplified and more efficient way to create server-generated Web pages that combine content from a wide variety of enterprise data sources. Because JavaServer Pages technology encapsulates much of the functionality required to generate "dynamic," or constantly changing, content, Web page developers can concentrate on the "look" and display of the site without the need for application development expertise.

These are big promises. It is because they are more than just promises that JSP is increasingly popular. These paragraphs of PR are, in fact, a quite accurate description of JSP. For a good overall view of the increasing popularity of JSP (and servlets), visit the Industry Momentum page for JSP at Sun, at `http://java.sun.com/products/jsp/industry.html`.

The popularity of JSP and Java servlet technologies is also illustrated by the fact that more than a million downloads of Tomcat, an open-source server for Java servlets and JavaServer Pages, had occurred by the year 2001. The number of downloads of the current Java 2 software development kit from Sun (Java 2 SDK) will no doubt surpass five million by the time you are reading this. All these downloads are votes for the importance of the technologies central to our book.

This might convince you of the importance of the technologies that appear in the title of this book, if you were not convinced of that already! The question remains, though: Why should you use this book, especially with so many other resources available? The best answer is that this book is a hands-on "laboratory manual." It is meant to complement, not replace, other books on XML, XSLT, Java servlets and applets, and JSP. Like any laboratory manual, this book assumes at least a basic understanding of the subjects of its experiments. This book uses original material for learning its topics, within a context that invites experimentation and even controversial solutions. It avoids simple repetition of documentation that can be more easily and fully accessed elsewhere.

1.3 How to Use This Book

Although you might enjoy reading this book on a long airplane ride, we hope that you will read it while you are trying out its code examples and while you are online. Perhaps this book is best seen as part laboratory manual and part travel guide; its usefulness to you will depend on how much you try the examples and visit the Web links provided.

As we know too well, today you can find on the Web a "fact" related to a subject of this book, only to have it become a "fiction" (or, at least, an irrelevant fact) by the time the book is published. This is a side effect of the very popularity of our subjects; the technologies that we cover are evolving rapidly, and major changes are common. This book will provide links for you to the most relevant Internet sources and relies on your willingness to visit these for the latest information.

The quantity of information on the Internet that is related to this book is increasing rapidly. Particularly active are the various mailing lists and forums, where thousands of developers worldwide are engaged in spirited debate and information interchange. Follow our advice: Subscribe to some of these mailing lists, and take part in the online forums. You will soon experience the fast pace at which these technologies are evolving, as well as the excitement that they are generating in the worldwide community of software developers.

1.3.1 How to Stay Current

You can find some links to information relevant to this book in Chapter 12. We feel that, with evolving technology, it is vital to have sources of current information, so we will also provide some links for you here. One way to keep in touch with the entire subject of Java programming is to subscribe to related newsgroups. One important one is `comp.lang.java.programmer`.

You can also search all the newsgroups, including their archives, which is a great way to generate leads to answer just about any question that comes up. To do that, just use the search engine at `http://www.dejanews.com`.

Another way to keep current with Java, including Java servlets, Java applets, and JSP, is with the Sun mailing lists and archives, which you can find using these URLs:

http://archives.java.sun.com/cgi-bin/wa

http://archives.java.sun.com/archives/index.html

Especially relevant to this book are discussions related to Java servlets and JSP as implemented by the Jakarta project of the Apache Software Foundation. These can be found at http://jakarta.apache.org/getinvolved/mail.html.

For staying up-to-date with XML technologies, you can join another Apache mailing list by visiting http://xml.apache.org/mail.html. For a more general discussion of XML and its development, try the archives of the XML-L mailing list, at http://listserv.heanet.ie/xml-l.html.

Among the most useful sources of current information relevant to the subject of this book are the Java Technology Forums hosted by Sun Microsystems. Here are some URLs that merit your attention:

http://developer.java.sun.com/developer/community/forum.jshtml

http://forum.java.sun.com/list/discuss.sun.javaserver.pages

http://forum.java.sun.com/list/discuss.sun.java.technology.and.xml

http://forum.java.sun.com/list/discuss.sun.java.servlet.development.kit

1.3.2 Our Technology Choices in Brief

The following is a list of the technology choices that we made for developing applications based upon XML, XSLT, Java servlets and applets, and JSP:

- SDK 1.3
- Windows NT 4.0
- Jakarta Tomcat
- Xerces XML parser
- Xalan XSLT processor

The rest of this chapter discusses and attempts to justify our choices. This will be of most interest to those developers who are new to the world of Web applications.

If You Already Know These Products...

You might already be familiar with these chosen products and our reasons in support of their selection. If so, you can safely skip the rest of this chapter and proceed directly to Chapter 2, "An Environment for Java Software Development." As another alternative, some of the highlights of the following discussion are presented in italics, to allow you to quickly get the gist of the content.

It might be useful to point out that we first discuss a list of questions, without answering them. Later in the chapter, we provide our own answers to those same questions.

Some readers would no doubt prefer to have each question followed by our answer. We would rather present you with an appreciation of the fact that any discipline that can raise many questions about how to proceed will surely have room for many creative sets of answers. We do not want to leave you with the impression that our answers are the only ones that you should try.

1.4 Some Choices Facing Web Application Developers

When you want to develop Web applications, you immediately face a series of quandaries. For example, should you take advantage of all the relevant programming that is built in only on Windows and NT computers, especially considering the popularity of the Microsoft Web browser? Alternatively, should you try to conform fully to the standards and attempt a platform neutral solution? In the latter case, which versions of the standards should you adopt? Which tools should you use? Which development environments and languages should you use? Should you seek a solution that is based upon Linux, or one based on a commercial UNIX platform?

1.4.1 Client-Side Versus Server-Side Processing

Web application developers who want to take advantage of Microsoft technologies often emphasize client-side processing. They leverage library files (DLLs) that reside on the same machine as the Web browser. Many who choose this path use Microsoft developer tools, especially Visual Basic.

However, there are many advantages to emphasizing the server side when developing Web applications. One of these advantages is especially compelling to those of us who have supported widely distributed software that we had to install and configure on every last client machine!

A Web application that can change, adapt, and evolve by changing only the software on a few server machines is far easier to deploy, maintain, and support than is a Web application made up of programs that must be installed and configured on thousands of client machines.

We stated above "emphasizing the server side" because the most practical approach seems to be to allow for both server-side and client-side processing, depending upon what needs to be done. Java developers can take advantage of Java applets, which enable you to use client-side processing in a Web application while avoiding some of the software distribution problems. The Java plug-in provides a way to run Java applets transparently on differing Web browsers. According to James Gosling, the creator of Java, the closer integration of the plug-in and browser technology is an important goal for Java. That will help dispel criticisms of those who find the delays of downloading the Java plug-in and Java applets time-consuming and disruptive.

1.4.2 Which Web Server to Use

Increasingly, Web application developers prefer doing things on the server. However, they still might face a quandary, one having less to do with the Web browser than with the Web server. Three brands of Web servers are responsible for most of the traffic on the Internet. One, of course, is Microsoft Internet Information Server (IIS). Another is Netscape Enterprise Server. The third is Apache Server, which, as far back as October 2000, was credited in a Netcraft report with 59% of the server installations on the Internet. Although such statistics are controversial, there is still no doubt about the importance of more than one brand of server on the Web.

Many questions arise. Will these three popular Web servers be capable of hosting your Web application? Which implementation of the various XML and Java server-side technologies should you choose to enable these Web servers to host the application? Alternatively, should you create your Web application using one of the many commercially available Web application frameworks?

1.4.3 Which Platform(s) to Use

You face many other initial questions as a Web application developer. Which platform (operating system) will you select to host the server-side components of the Web application? You might decide to do so on Microsoft Windows NT 4.0, especially if you are already familiar with its development tools and environments, or if you decide to use Internet Information Server (IIS). As a Java programmer, on the other hand, you likely will seek a platform-independent solution and then will develop that on the platform of your choice: NT, Linux, Solaris, or whatever.

1.4.4 Which Software Language(s) and Tools to Use

Any computer language that does not try to become more useful for developing Web applications is most likely a dead language because it is one that is no longer evolving. As a developer who wants to create server-based Web applications, you have a wide choice of languages and tools to use. Some important languages are Java, C++, Visual Basic, Perl, and Python. Of course, HTML (especially now as XHTML) is crucial for controlling browser content. XML and its related languages are becoming increasingly important, especially for representing and transforming data. ASP, PHP, and Cold Fusion, specialized as they are for Web application development, are even more directly comparable to JSP and Java servlets; each of these three "languages" has many adherents among developers.

XML, XSLT, Java servlets, Java applets, and JavaServer Pages will all be crucial to our development efforts for this book. As a direct consequence of that, we have preferentially looked for tools and solutions among Java-based technologies.

1.5 Development Choices Made for This Book

This book will not even pretend to cover all the possible answers to the previous questions. Instead, we will present the one set of answers that we chose for ourselves. Our hope is that even if your answers turn out to be different, you will still find value in learning about our experience with our tools and components. In the following sections, we present the reasoning behind our strategic choices.

1.5.1 Development Platform: Microsoft NT Server 4.0

Based on the goals chosen for the book, there were many good reasons to choose Linux as the development platform. For one thing, it is freely available, and we intend to keep the cost of learning as low as possible. In addition to having its own ISP, Linux is arguably the natural choice for hosting the freely available Apache server—at least until the Windows version of this server has been as thoroughly tested and debugged as the Linux version (perhaps by the time you read this).

Regardless of these reasons, we consider that by developing our Web application project on a Windows platform, we will make it accessible to a larger audience, especially among developers who are just beginning their adventure in the world of Web application programming. We guess also that more Linux (and UNIX) developers can use information based on the Windows platform than vice versa.

The software for this book was developed on NT 4.0, while trying to remain compatible with all Win32 platforms.

We developed our examples for this book on a Windows NT Server, Version 4.0 (Build 1381: Service Pack 5). We did nothing that would not have been identical on an NT workstation of the same version, build, and service pack. We chose to use NT because, in our experience, it has been the most robust Microsoft platform for developing network applications. However, very little would have been different had we used a Windows 95 or 98 platform instead; indeed, we have often run our book project Web application on both these platforms. (If we were starting today, we would probably select Windows ME or 2000 instead, but we have not tested our software with either.)

We are assuming that most of our readers have access to a Windows platform and that they will be able to adapt our NT-based examples and discussion to their environment. Those not using Windows might need to alter the examples to use UNIX paths and naming conventions.

We have tried to minimize the impact of choosing Windows NT 4.0 as a development platform. We trust that readers will share information about using the book with other platforms, which can be done on the book project Web site at `http://www.bonforum.org`.

1.5.2 Java Development Environment: Java 2 SDK Version 1.3

We are aware that, as a reader of this book, you might already have a favorite Java development environment—perhaps VisualAge for Java from IBM, JBuilder from Inprise/Borland, Forte from Sun, or one of many others. Moreover, you surely would prefer it if we used the same tools that you want to work with.

In theory, the choice of development environment should not affect the Java Web application. That is the promise of Java, after all. However, in practice, it could affect the way that we present the information in this book. That might affect your ability to follow along with the examples by actually compiling and running them. Therefore, we will use for our development environment one that can be inexpensively installed and used by everyone.

We will try to keep our discussions and examples independent of any particular development environment. You can easily use the command-line interface to the Java 2 SDK for all examples.

We will assume that you have at least the freely available standard version of the Sun Java 2 SDK version 1.3 on your development machine. (This version is on this book's CD-ROM.) It will be possible for you to use version 1.2.2 instead, although you might find that some things work differently or look different. However, Java versions earlier than 1.2.2 will not work with the XML-related software that we will be using.

Many Java programmers reading the book will already be familiar with using the command-line interfaces to the various tools in the Java SDK. Others could benefit by becoming familiar with them. Nevertheless, window-based development environments evolved to make using the underlying SDK easier. Some readers might feel more comfortable using an integrated development environment (IDE). Indeed, those of you who have recently come to Java development from the worlds of Visual Basic or Delphi, for example, might have no experience at all with command-line interfaces. If you are shopping around for a Java IDE, you have several good choices, depending on your machine and pocketbook resources. Readers who are new to Java development will certainly want to explore both the free and the trial versions available to them, including the ones mentioned at the beginning of this section.

To provide one choice of IDE to our readers, we have arranged to include the ElixirIDE-Lite trial software on the CD-ROM accompanying this book. Note that this is a special edition provided for this book; this means that a greater number of Java files can be used than the normal trial version so that it can be used with the book project. We find that one advantage of this IDE is that it requires fewer hardware resources than most others do; this can be an attractive to those whose machines have been filled to the brim with Microsoft tools, for example. Readers will also find a second IDE on this book's CD-ROM that is worth trying: Forte for Java Community Edition, from Sun.

1.5.3 Server-Based Web Application Architecture

Another of the initial developer questions that we discussed was whether to stress client-side or server-side processing when designing a Web application. We believe that the advantage of using a server-side implementation outweighs its disadvantages.

It is often expressed that an advantage of doing things on the Web browser (client-side processing) is that you reduce network traffic. The idea is that the browser does not have to keep accessing the server for another view for the user because it has the locally available Web application to turn to for that next view. However, that depends on the application. Often, client-side processing can instead increase network traffic, requiring the download of large JavaScript files or much more data than the user will need to view.

Another commonly mentioned advantage of client-side processing is that it reduces the load on the servers, but intelligent caching can often easily offset this effect.

The Web application project for this book will lean heavily in favor of processing on the Web server rather than on the client machine.

If we were being consistent, we would try to maintain neutrality toward the choice of browsers. That would mean serving plain-vanilla HTML to the browsers, something that would work on any platform's favorite and not-so-favorite browsers. In fact, it is important for a Web application to be compatible with at least the two major browsers (Internet Explorer and Netscape). Although such cross-compatibility is preferable, we have decided to reduce the complexity of this book and its project by supporting only Internet Explorer.

The software for this book has been developed and tested using only the Internet Explorer 5.5 Web browser from Microsoft.

Note that it can be argued that because content ports more easily from Netscape to Internet Explorer than vice versa, it makes more sense to begin with Netscape compatibility. For us, the more important issue is compatibility with the more commonly used browser at an earlier date.

1.5.4 XML-Related Standards from W3C

Another question is about which XML-related standards we should apply. There is an easy answer: We will use the "real" standards, which are those decided upon by the W3C.

This book should adhere to the XML-related standards as proposed and recommended by the W3C.

You can find out all about the W3C by visiting the Web site `http://www.w3.org/`.

With new recommendations for XML-related technologies appearing often, and with rapidly evolving software that constantly pushes beyond current W3C recommendations and for newer versions of the standards, this "easy answer" turns out to be not quite so simple.

Here's how we see it: Unless you come from certain software development backgrounds, especially those that use SGML, it will probably take a fair amount of dedicated time to learn all the various things that go into making XML Web applications with Java. Thus, you might as well go for the latest standards that you can. Be aware that this means that you will sometimes be trying to learn about XML using software that is buggier than some previous stable version.

The advantage to this approach is that, when you have gathered the understanding of XML that you need to finish a project, you will be as current as possible regarding the standards. This lessens the chances that you will do what Microsoft did with its XML support for IE5.0. In other words, you will be less likely to use something that turns out to be defined only in a dialect of an XML-related technology.

Some Confusing XML Information on the Web

XML-related technologies have been changing and growing at a fast pace. This has produced some confusion in the information that you will find on the Internet. Many posts to mailing lists, for example, contain useful tips and code but do not indicate which servers, browsers, and tools (and which versions of these) were being used by the developer who posted the mailing list item.

Perhaps a greater source of confusion for the new user of Web-related XML information is that the developers of the most widely available and most advanced Web browser, Microsoft Internet Explorer, chose to extend some XML-related proposals in certain "unofficial" ways. It can be argued that this was necessary to use those XML proposals at that time. Nevertheless, the outcome was that, although a more useful browser was created, pervasive dialects of the proposals were also created. These dialects differed quite a lot from the standard XML technologies that later evolved.

More recently, version 5.5 of Internet Explorer went partway toward implementing these newer, "truer" standards, recommended by the W3C. Microsoft's intention is evidently to fully implement the W3C recommendations in some future release of Internet Explorer. Meanwhile, Microsoft has added to the mix of vendor-dependent differences in XML-related technologies.

1.5.5 XML Technologies: Xerces and Xalan

XML and its related technologies, such as XSLT, have very exciting potential to push the evolution of the Internet. This has spurred many interesting projects, each one seeking to make this potential real. Some projects are aimed at creating XML-related developer tools. Other projects are creating applications to fulfill some commercial or other user requirement. Some projects have developed products ready for real use. Others are simply experimental.

For this book, we examined projects that are creating freely available XML-related tools. The question that we faced was, which of all those XML-related tools should we select to learn about building Web applications? This book will be complex enough without trying to discuss more than a minimal set of XML-related software tools. Of course, that is part of the reason we limited our choices of tools. Indeed, we can enthusiastically recommend our two choices, which are among the most popular open-source products ever.

This book will feature two products of the Apache XML Project: Xerces and Xalan. The Java versions of these tools will be used exclusively for our XML- and XSLT-related processing.

A very strong point in favor of Xerces and Java is that both have versions written in pure Java, so both provide natural extensions for a JSP/servlet programmer to use. You can find out more about the Apache Software Foundation, the Apache XML Project, and the origins of the Apache projects with these links:

http://www.apache.org

http://xml.apache.org

http://xml.apache.org/pr/0001.txt

Let's look at other reasons for supporting these choices. Consider that both Xerces and Xalan are based partly on source code donated to the Apache Software Foundation by IBM, Sun, and other companies and individuals with XML expertise. These companies decided to take advantage of the open-source development model (the same model that has made Linux and Apache Server so successful) as a way to improve, develop, and test their own XML-related code base. They have also decided that this is the best way to create a reference code base for those standards that are evolving (through the W3C).

As an illustration of this fact, when we began our book project, the current IBM XML parser was actually just a wrapper for the Xerces XML parser. The wrapper was there only to maintain compatibility with the previous software. Sun has also been generously providing source code to the Apache XML Project, profiting no doubt from the same worldwide developer force that IBM discovered in the open-source movement. In choosing to use Xerces and Xalan as our XML parser and XSLT processor, we are actually in good company!

You can bet on one thing: Given the pace of developments in the XML world, by the time you read this, better versions of Xerces and Xalan will be available than the ones we used here. You can appreciate the difficulty of trying to keep the content of this book detailed enough to be relevant but general enough to be applicable, even after each newer version of Xerces and Xalan appears.

To be at all able to do this, we must assume that much of your learning will take place by following the Web links that we provide. Only then will your learning material be dynamic enough to keep up with the times. What you can learn from our own experience might be primarily that you will need a stubborn attitude to get software to work! You will also need a set of suitable starting points. We will attempt to help you answer these two needs in the upcoming chapters.

While you are learning about XML, undoubtedly new versions will be released of the very components that you are attempting to use. These, in turn, will often require newer versions of other components that you are also using. You will be tempted to ignore the newer versions, but, in our experience, you should jump to the newer versions as soon as possible—often great improvements in both software and documentation accompany these version changes. To try to stay with earlier versions that are more tested and known makes sense in many development situations, but not with XML-related software. This technology is simply developing in too many important, fundamental ways to ignore the changes.

1.5.6 Web Server, Servlet, and JSP Engine: Jakarta Tomcat

We mentioned earlier the three prominent Web servers (HTTP servers): IIS, Netscape, and Apache. More than likely, you will want your own Web applications to be deployable to Web hosts that use one or more of those Web servers. However, when it comes to developing Web applications with Java servlet and JSP, there is a compelling reason to look further: These Web servers must all rely upon add-on software to implement the Java servlet and JavaServer Pages technologies. Such software is known technically as a container, but it is also referred to as a servlet and JSP engine. Whatever it is called, we will need one!

The software for this book relies upon a very popular open-source product, called Tomcat, to enable the serving of Java servlets and JavaServer Pages.

Tomcat is being developed by the Jakarta Project. Like the Apache XML Project that develops Xalan and Xerces, the Jakarta Project is part of the Apache Software Foundation. You can find out more about the Jakarta Project and all its various products at `http://jakarta.apache.org`.

The intention of the Jakarta Project as it creates Tomcat is to provide a reference implementation for the Java servlet and JSP technologies. These are both defined as part of the Sun J2EE specification. If you want to learn the latest standards for these vital Web technologies, you will surely want to learn about Tomcat. Tomcat is also freely available open-source software, and it fits our low-cost development goal for this book. Furthermore, there is an unusually active developer community involved in the Tomcat project, so this is a great way to get directly involved in the excitement of building dynamic Web technology.

Unlike many other servlet and JSP container add-on modules for Web servers, Tomcat can function as a standalone Web server itself. This means that it can be used for development and testing purposes, without any reliance on another Web server. To simplify our book presentation, we use the HTTP server potential of Tomcat exclusively throughout this book.

It is important to stress that we are not using Tomcat because it is a better Web server than Apache, Netscape, or IIS servers. Later in the book we point you to the information that you will need to use Tomcat with Apache or IIS.

You can use Tomcat as a standalone Web server, as we do for the project in this book. Note, however, that deployed Web applications should use Tomcat together with another production-quality Web server.

The one compelling feature of Tomcat is that it is a Java servlet and JavaServer Pages container. In servlets and in compiled JSP pages, Java code, together with a suitable engine such as Tomcat, gives a Web server the capability to serve dynamic content to a Web browser. Such content is determined only at the time the browser makes a request to the Web server. You can find out more about this by reading Sun's white paper on JSP technology, at `http://java.sun.com/products/jsp/whitepaper.html`.

As you develop your own Web applications, you will want to examine other possible choices for a servlet and JSP container. One popular choice is Jrun, which is available for Windows, Linux, Solaris, and others. It can be run with IIS, Apache, Netscape, and other servers. You can find out about JRun at the Allaire Web site, at `http://www.allaire.com/Products/JRun/`.

Many Web-application framework products also understand servlets and JSP. Prominent among these are Netscape Application Server and iPlanet, Oracle Application Server, BEA Weblogic, and Resin.

1.6 A Note About Platform Independence

If you want to base your Web applications on the Java language, you probably know that one of its main advantages is platform independence. You should appreciate, then, that with the exception of the browser, the tools and software modules that we have selected are not bound to one particular operating system. Apache Server, Tomcat, Sun's Java Development Kit, Xalan, and Xerces can all be installed on both Windows NT and UNIX.

We hope that the next edition of this book will more explicitly cover the use of our chosen Web application tools on Linux-powered servers. In the meantime, as you are learning Web application development on an NT Server, you can rest assured that your newly acquired skills can be easily transplanted to UNIX-type operating systems.

2

An Environment for Java Software Development

In this chapter, you learn about setting up an inexpensive Java development environment. This will enable you to compile and run our Web application example project.

2.1 Java 2 Platform, Standard Edition

We will be using the Java 2 platform for all the Java code in this book. To follow along and to get the real value of hands-on programming, you should first make sure that you can compile and run Java 2 source code on your own system.

Of course, it is possible—especially because you have chosen this book—that you already are running a Java 2 development environment. Perhaps yours is one of several available products, such as JBuilder, from Inprise Corporation; Visual Age, from IBM; Forte, from Sun; or Visual Cafe 4, from Symantec. In this case, you are probably quite capable, using your present setup, of compiling and running our examples and Web application project.

Who Is This Chapter For?

If you are an experienced Java programmer, you probably know most of the information in this chapter. We are aiming the following material at those who are learning about Java. If you can develop, compile, and run Java programs already, you can safely skip this chapter. The latter half of the chapter, however, might still be useful to you if you intend to try out the ElixirIDE trial product provided on the CD-ROM accompanying this book.

2.1.1 Installing the Java 2 SDK

For readers who need some hints about setting up a Java 2 development environment or who just want to use the same one that we used as we wrote the book, we present here an overview of how to find and install the Java 2 SDK, which is available on thsis book's CD-ROM also from the Sun Web site. To download it, log on to `http://java.sun.com` and follow the product links to the download page for the Windows standard edition (J2SE) of the product. Here is the URL: `http://java.sun.com/j2se/1.3/download-windows.html`.

Version to Use

We recommend that you use version 1.3.X, unless you have a reason to use version 1.2.X. You can use either 1.2.X or 1.3.X with this book, but we assume that you have the Java 2 SDK version 1.3 on your system. If not, you will need to change the file paths in our instructions accordingly.

Installation Notes

You should start with the readme.txt file in the root of the download archive. There are also some important links on the download page itself: README, Release Notes, Features, License, and Installation Notes. We found the installation notes for version 1.3 in the Web document `http://java.sun.com/products/jdk/1.3/install-windows.html`.

This document is very useful. It will tell you about the requirements for using the SDK and also how to install it on all different Windows platforms that can use it. In addition, it has hints for troubleshooting installations that fail. It might help to know that the name for older versions of the SDK was Java Development Kit, abbreviated JDK; you will still find references to the JDK (for example, in the name of the root folder for the installation).

Be sure to read the Sun Microsystems, Inc., Binary Code License Agreement, by following the links from the download page before you get and install the Java 2 SDK. As a licensee of this product, you will be bound to the terms of this license, so you should know what you are agreeing to when you use this software.

Setting the Path in the System Environment

As mentioned in the installation notes, you will want to add the Java 2 SDK system path to your NT system path variable (or the equivalent, for other Win32 systems). In NT, you can do this by bringing up the Control Panel and using the System tool. Find the tab for the Environment settings, and edit the `Path` variable. Add a semicolon and then **c:\jdk1.3\bin** (or whatever is equivalent for your system).

Here is what our `Path` environment variable looks like:

```
Path=c:\jdk1.3\bin;c:\winnt\system32;c:\winnt
```

Setting the *JAVA_HOME* Environment Variable

While you are setting up the `Path` variable, you can also set up an environment variable needed by the Java 2 SDK. You should define the variable, `JAVA_HOME`, something like the one shown here, according to the location of the SDK on your system:

```
JAVA_HOME = c:\jdk1.3
```

Setting the *CLASSPATH* Environment

If you are looking for some clarity regarding which, if any, setting for the `CLASSPATH` environment you should use, we can think of no better place for you to find answers than `http://java.sun.com/products/jdk/1.3/docs/tooldocs/win32/classpath.html`.

2.1.2 Documentation for the Java 2 SDK

You can find a plethora of information regarding the Java 2 SDK itself, so we will certainly not try to provide all your answers about its features and use. One obvious source of answers is the SDK documentation. While you are installing the SDK, you will want to consider downloading the documentation for it. Sun makes available the documentation for version 1.3 at `http://java.sun.com/products/jdk/1.3/download-docs.html`.

Due to license restrictions, we cannot put the documentation on the book's CD-ROM. Of course, you can also browse the documentation over the Internet, so if you have an inexpensive connection to it, there is no need to download it—that can save you quite a bit of disk space. This also gives you the advantage of a using the searchable version of the documentation.

If you decide to download the documentation, try to use the same root folder for both the SDK and the documentation. The default folder choice for the version that we downloaded is c:\jdk1.3. Therefore, our documentation for the Java 2 SDK ended up in c:\jdk1.3\docs, and the SDK was installed into c:\jdk1.3\bin, c:\jdk1.3\lib, and so on.

2.1.3 The Java 2 Runtime Environment

Notice that if you want to deploy the software products that you develop with the Java 2 SDK, you can be sure that the user will be able to run your products by deploying your products together with the Java 2 Runtime Environment. This includes just the core Java classes and support files, without all the development tools. The SDK comes with its own copy of the Runtime Environment, so you do not need to install it separately to develop Java software.

You cannot redistribute the SDK itself; you can distribute only the Runtime Environment. New Riders Publishing has a special agreement with Sun to provide it to you on the book's CD-ROM. You should definitely check out the wealth of other useful material that is dynamically made available to you on the Sun Java Web site.

2.1.4 Examining the SDK

If you are new to Java, take some time to familiarize yourself with the Java 2 SDK. There is a lot there, and this should make you glad that you do not need to reinvent all those wheels!

Notice the folder c:\jdk1.3\jre. This is a Java Runtime Environment that enables you to use Java applications. Another large JAR file, called rt.jar, is in the folder c:\jdk1.3\jre\lib. That JAR file is the runtime library that we will be using. This Java Runtime Environment in the Java 2 SDK is not the same as the one that you can freely distribute; it is for use during development only.

Notice also a large file called tools.jar, which is in the folder c:\jdk1.3\lib. This JAR file is quite important because it contains the Java compiler that our Web application will use to compile JavaServer Pages. When you create a Web application that uses JSP, such as the project in this book, the container that runs that application needs to have a suitable Java compiler available; JSP pages must be compiled into Java servlets before they are useful. The standard way for you to distribute a Web application is as a Web archive (WAR file), and you commonly assume that the recipient of a WAR file has a Web server, together with a container (such as Tomcat) that can compile JSP pages and a suitable compiler for the container to use. Providing the compiler is not usually your concern as a Web application developer. However, we provide this discussion because those coming to Java from other environments will naturally think of compilation as something that happens only before distribution; it helps to see that it can be otherwise.

2.1.5 Using Internet Explorer 5.x with the SDK

We will be using Internet Explorer 5.5 as our Web browser in this book. If you have Internet Explorer 5.x on your machine, you might be tempted, as we were, to test the browser's capability to run a Java applet. For example, try browsing `file://c:\jdk1.3\demo\applets\Animator\example1.html`.

You will most likely find that the browser cannot find a Java class that it needs (`java.util.List`). Microsoft has not updated its JVM since JDK 1.1.5, and it does not contain the Swing library. Microsoft will not update it, either, because the company is competing against Java with C#. This means, for example, that any applet created with the Swing GUI will also not function with the Java virtual machine built into Internet Explorer.

In Chapter 9, "Java Applet Plugged In: BonForumRobot," we discuss using the Java plug-in from Sun, which enables you to run Java applets in most Web browsers, including those brands and versions that have no built-in capability to run applets. Using the Java plug-in is also the correct solution for running applets on Internet Explorer.

2.1.6 Other Java Development Tools

If you plan to make sizeable Java projects, you might find many freely available tools and code libraries (complete with source) that could save you time both learning and implementing software.

Bean Development Kit

For example, you might want to try downloading and testing the Bean Development Kit (when we did, it was called BDK1.1) from the Sun Web site. Here are a couple of links that will help you locate and use the BDK:

```
http://java.sun.com/products/javabeans/software/index.html
http://developer.java.sun.com/developer/onlineTraining/Beans/
Beans1/index.html
```

The BDK will give you an easier way to make those beans. As you might know already, one of the things you can do using JSP is to use Java Bean technology. This can give you advantages when you want to serialize your class instances. Additionally, it provides a good way to utilize the different scopes present in JSP. The BDK can be a useful kit to have while developing Web applications.

Note that there are two big differences between JSP JavaBeans and GUI JavaBeans. The first is that the JSP Beans are nonvisual—that is, they are server-side objects that have no graphical representation. The second difference is that JSP Beans do not interact with the `BeanContext`.

2.2 Compiling Java Programs

You have many options available when it comes time to compile your Java source files. These range from using the command-line interface to using the SDK, through some options that integrate the SDK with an editor/highlighter, to your choice of using a full-blown integrated development environment (IDE) with all the bells and whistles. We briefly discuss only two options: first the command-line interface and then a trial version of an IDE that we are including on the book's CD-ROM.

Note that the Textpad editor, which also is included on the book's CD-ROM as a trial version, covers middle-of-the range compilation options quite well. It is an excellent text editor and has some features integrating it with Java and the SDK.

2.2.1 A Useful Command Prompt Window for Compilation

We like to use the command-line interface to the Java 2 SDK because it can be a fast and simple way to do things such as compile and run programs or list JAR file contents. However, the NT command window Command Prompt must be set up differently than its default mode, which is difficult to work with. What we want to see is a window that has a scrolling display. Otherwise, we will miss many messages and outputs that are larger than the window coordinates.

In Windows NT Explorer, find the file WinNT\System32\cmd.exe. (In Windows 95 and 98, look for Windows\System32\command.com instead.) Create a shortcut to that file. Then move this new shortcut icon onto the desktop. Right-click the icon, open its Properties item, and then select the tab Layout. There, in the Screen Buffer Size panel, set Width to 128 and Height to 512. In the Window Size panel, set Width to 78 and Height to 32. You can use even larger numbers for the Window Size settings, but these work even with an 800 × 600 screen resolution. (Note that in Win9x, you can only set the number of screen lines.)

If you want, you can put this edited shortcut icon in the Start Menu folder in your Windows NT Profile and rename it Big, Scrollable Cmd.exe, or whatever. That way, you can quickly get a useable NT Command Prompt window from your Start menu. Another alternative to changing the Layout properties using a shortcut icon as described previously is to make similar changes to the Layout properties using the MS-DOS Console tool in the Control Panel. This sets set the default layout for all instances of the NT Command window.

Now that we have a more useful command window, let's see an example of a batch file used for compiling Java programs. This batch file, which we have named bonMakeIt.bat, can be used to compile the entire Web application project for this book, bonForum. We keep this batch file in the src folder, which contains the root of the bonForum package, de.tarent.forum. It expects there to be another folder named classes at the same hierarchical level as the src folder. The javac.exe compiler puts all the compiled Java class files in the proper package folders within the classes folder. At the end of the batch processing, two class files are copied explicitly into the applet folder where they are needed. This batch file assumes that your system Path variable includes the folder with the javac.exe Java compiler. Here is a listing of the batch file:

```
javac de/tarent/forum/BonForumUtils.java -d ../classes

javac de/tarent/forum/BonLogger.java -d ../classes

javac -classpath ".;c:\jakarta-tomcat\lib\servlet.jar;"
➥de/tarent/forum/BonForumTagExtraInfo.java -d ../classes

javac -classpath ".;c:\jakarta-tomcat\lib\servlet.jar;"
➥de/tarent/forum/OutputPathNamesTag.java -d ../classes
```

```
javac -classpath ".;c:\jakarta-tomcat\lib\servlet.jar;"
➥de/tarent/forum/OutputChatMessagesTag.java -d ../classes

javac -classpath ".;c:\jakarta-tomcat\lib\servlet.jar;"
➥de/tarent/forum/OutputDebugInfoTag.java -d ../classes

javac -classpath ".;c:\jakarta-tomcat\lib\servlet.jar;"
➥de/tarent/forum/NoCacheHeaderTag.java -d ../classes

javac -classpath ".;c:\xalan-j_1_2_2\xalan.jar;c:\xalan-
➥j_1_2_2\xerces.jar;c:\jakarta-tomcat\lib\servlet.jar;"
➥de/tarent/forum/Xalan1Transformer.java -d ../classes

javac -classpath ".;c:\jakarta-tomcat\lib\servlet.jar;c:\xalan-
➥j_2_0_1\bin\xalan.jar;c:\xalan-j_2_0_1\bin\xerces.jar;"
➥de/tarent/forum/Xalan2Transformer.java -d ../classes

javac -classpath ".;c:\jakarta-tomcat\lib\servlet.jar;c:\xalan-
➥j_2_0_1\bin\xalanj1compat.jar;c:\xalan-j_2_0_1\bin\xalan.jar;c:\xalan-
➥j_2_0_1\bin\xerces.jar;" de/tarent/forum/TransformTag.java -d ../classes

javac de/tarent/forum/NodeKey.java -d ../classes

javac de/tarent/forum/BonNode.java -d ../classes

javac -classpath ".;c:\jakarta-tomcat\lib\servlet.jar;"
➥de/tarent/forum/ForestHashtable.java -d ../classes

javac -classpath ".;c:\jakarta-tomcat\lib\servlet.jar;"
➥de/tarent/forum/BonForumStore.java -d ../classes

javac -classpath ".;c:\jakarta-tomcat\lib\servlet.jar;"
➥de/tarent/forum/BonForumEngine.java -d ../classes

javac BonForumRobot.java -d ../classes
copy ..\classes\BonForumRobot.class ..\..\jsp\forum\applet
copy ..\classes\BonForumRobot$RefreshThread.class ..\..\jsp\forum\applet

rem CLASS FILES MUST BE IN
rem bonForum WEBAPP CLASS FOLDERS FOR USE!
```

Do not worry if not everything in this batch file is clear at this point. You can return after reading Chapter 5, "bonForum Chat Application: Use and Design," which shows you how to install the bonForum Web application and give some hints about compiling it. You can find this batch file always on the CD-ROM in the folder bonForum\installed\webapps\bonForum\WEB-INF\src.

After you have installed the bonForum project, you will find the batch file in a folder with a path something like c:\jakarta-tomcat\webapps\bonForum\WEB-INF\src.

Note that, to be useful, the batch file must be executed in a command window after setting the current directory to the previous folder path (or its equivalent, on your Tomcat server machine).

2.2.2 Integrated Development Environments

Many developers find it a great advantage to use an integrated development environment. In fact, Sun suggests that you use its SDK via an IDE and provides links to several on its SDK download page. Be aware that some IDEs available are large, expensive, and slow on older computers, and they sometimes want a large amount of RAM. We certainly do not want our readers to think that they must own an IDE to successfully develop Web applications.

If you prefer not to depend on simple command-line tools and a good editor, there are plenty of lightweight commercial IDEs around. For example, you can investigate JBuilder Foundation or Forte. You can also try the trial version of ElixirIDE or Forte for Java Community Edition, which we have included on the book's CD-ROM for your convenience.

2.2.3 ElixirIDE

ElixirIDE, from Elixir Technology, is a useful Java Editor and IDE that is freely available in the version ElixirIDE-Lite, which you can try before buying. The Lite version available on the Elixir Web site is limited to 10 Java files per project, however, which is too limiting for our book project. The same version of ElixirIDE-Lite (2.4.2) is available on the book's CD-ROM as a special release that allows 20 Java files, which is plenty for use with our book project. You can find out more about Elixir Technology and its Java products at `http://www.elixirtech.com`.

2.2.4 Installing ElixirIDE-Lite

We will assume that you have on your machine an ElixirIDE-Lite installation file and an ElixirIDE documentation installation file, from our CD-ROM. If you purchased the full version from the Elixir Technologies Web site, these instructions should be approximately correct as well. We assume that you have these files:

ElixirIDE-2.4.2-Lite.zip

ElixirIDE-2.4.0-Docs.zip

First, unzip the documentation installation file. Browse the documentation files, starting with ElixirIDE.html. There you will find information about the requirements for using ElixirIDE, along with instructions for installing and running it. We unzipped all files into a folder called c:\Elixir, and the following discussion assumes this root path.

After unzipping both files, you will have a JAR file (ElixirIDE-2.4.2-Lite.jar) that contains all the ElixirIDE classes, plus a license file, a change log, and the HTML documentation and tutorial files.

As part of the installation, you will also need to set up an environment variable called `ELIXIR_HOME`. Here is what ours looks like:

```
ELIXIR_HOME=c:\elixir
```

2.2.5 Batch Files for Starting ElixirIDE

We found that the best way to start Elixir was to put the following into a batch file. We call ours StartElixir.bat, and we keep it in the ELIXIR_HOME folder. Here is what it contains:

```
java -mx32m -jar c:\Elixir\ElixirIDE-2.4.2-Lite.jar
```

Note that the heap size argument (`-mx`) is not displayed when typing `java` or `java -X` to see a list of arguments.

In an NT Command Prompt window, execute the new StartElixir batch file. If all goes well, you will have the initial screen of the ElixirIDE displayed. This will cause some other changes, which you can verify with the NT Explorer. Notice that Elixir added a configuration folder to your NT user folder.

The usual place to find your user folder is in the NT profiles. For example, assume that you are using version 2.4.x. If you logged in as Samuel and installed your NT Server using its default installation locations, you should be able to find an ElixirIDE configuration folder named c:\WINNT\Profiles\Samuel\.ElixirIDE\2.4.

Note that if you log into your system using different profiles—for example, to access different NT domains—you will end up with more than one ElixirIDE configuration folders, one in each profile. We solved this particular problem by copying the folder that had the latest files in it over all the other ones.

2.2.6 Elixir Plug-in Extensions

Assuming that you are using version 2.4.x of ElixirIDE, you should find Elixir's extension folder named something like c:\WINNT\Profiles\samuel\.ElixirIDE \2.4\ext.

Notice that there is a period before the ElixirIDE in one of the folder names in that path. The Ext folder is where you will place plug-in JAR extension APIs for Elixir.

A Web site makes available a worldwide community of Elixir users, plus quite a few useful plug-in extension modules. To search for plug-ins for ElixirIDE, click the Elixir Plug-ins link on the page `http://www.elixirbase.com`.

To use the plug-in extension modules, you simply unzip the JAR files from the downloadable ZIP files into Elixir's extension folder. When you restart Elixir, it will automatically load and start all extensions in this folder. We recommend using at least the two plugins described next, if not more. You will find versions of these on the book CD-ROM in the Elixir\plugins folder.

A Class Hierarchy Inspector

The plug-in file called inspector.jar will enable you to examine the class files within any Java JAR or package. You can use FTP to get the latest version of the inspector at `ftp://www.elixirbase.com/pub/elixir/plugins/inspector.zip`.

We found this plug-in to be very useful. You can add databases easily to the Elixir configuration folder so that you can examine the classes in all the Java packages that you are using in your application.

BeanShell, an Interactive Java Shell

Be sure to get the BeanShell, which is distributed under the LGPL license. This is available from the Elixir Base Web site mentioned previously as a plug-in file called bsh.jar. You can also get it with FTP at `ftp://www.elixirbase.com/pub/elixir/plugins/bsh.zip`. For more information about this cool tool, visit the BeanShell Web site at `http://www.beanshell.org`.

We have found it a great learning exercise to create scripts for the BeanShell that create Java objects. We can then interactively play with a real instance of the object, exercising its properties and methods. This experimental approach sometimes works best for answering your questions, especially if they sound like this: "I wonder what happens if I do this with that object method?"

BeanShell's Shell

Do not confuse the BeanShell plug-in with another Shell console available in ElixirIDE. The Shell console gives you access to the system shell or command processor. This means that can stay within ElixirIDE and still run GUI or text-based programs. Especially if your computer has marginally enough storage to run whatever you have running at one time, using this shell will save you time and give a history to your sequence of commands within the shell.

2.2.7 Creating the bonForum Folder Hierarchy

So that you can exercise the ElixirIDE in a realistic way, we will describe how it could be used to start our Web application project example, which is called bonForum. Later in this book, we will be discussing bonForum and developing it more fully. Right now, we will just set it up as a project in ElixirIDE.

> **Finding the Folders and Files**
>
> You can find all the folders and files for the book example project on the accompanying CD-ROM in several forms. The ones in folders named Webapps will be discussed in Chapter 5, "bonForum Chat Application: Use and Design." In the bonForum\source folder, you will find a zipped archive, named something like bonForum_0_5_1.zip, which will unzip into a folder hierarchy similar to the one that we will create later. You can also find the unzipped source archive on the CD-ROM, under thebonForum\installed\source folder. You can simply unzip the source archive file from the CD-ROM into the ELIXIR_HOME\projects folder on your own system and then use that to follow along with the book. However, it might be useful for you to know a procedure that you can use to set up a project like bonForum, so we will present that information here in addition to the source files on the CD-ROM.

Here we will use a Shell process within Elixir to create the needed folders for the bonForum project. These folders are mostly the same ones suggested for creating Web applications for the Apache Tomcat Server. Setting up our project in this way will make it easier to deploy our Web application as a WAR archive and also will make it easier to follow other Tomcat examples that use this structure.

Select the Shell item in the Process combo box in the bottom pane of the Elixir window. You should get a command-line input and, above it, a console. Enter the command `cmd`. You should get a Microsoft Windows NT copyright notice, followed by the prompt that is the name of your ELIXIR_HOME folder.

> **File Paths for Elixir**
>
> We will assume that you have Elixir installed in the folder c:\Elixir. If not, use your ELIXIR_HOME instead of ours in the file paths that we use throughout the book. We will also assume that you do not have the bonForum project folders already created.

Now that you have an NT command line, it is simple to create the following folder hierarchy using the command input line, under the NT prompt:

c:\Elixir\Projects
c:\Elixir\Projects\bonForum
c:\Elixir\Projects\bonForum\classes
c:\Elixir\Projects\bonForum\etc
c:\Elixir\Projects\bonForum\etc\docs
c:\Elixir\Projects\bonForum\lib
c:\Elixir\Projects\bonForum\src
c:\Elixir\Projects\bonForum\web
c:\Elixir\Projects\bonForum\web\images
c:\Elixir\Projects\bonForum\web\jsp
c:\Elixir\Projects\bonForum\web\mldocs

2.2.8 Creating the bonForum Project in ElixirIDE

Before creating this project, make sure that you have created the project folder hierarchy in your file system, as described previously. Also make sure that you have saved the project settings, if you made any changes to them.

If you have a preferred look and feel for your GUI components, then select the Look and Feel menu and pick your settings there. Use the Project New menu command to add our project to Elixir. Select the ELIXIR_HOME\Projects\bonForum folder and, inside it, create the new project. Elixir will automatically name the ElixirIDE project file as bonForum.

You should see a folder icon with the label bonForum appear in the Project view in Elixir. Congratulations! You now own the beginning of a Web application project.

If you leave the cursor over the Project icon for a while, the hint that appears will show you that this icon represents a file that Elixir created for you. In fact, Elixir created two files for you, with names like these:

c:\Elixir\Projects\bonForum\bonForum.project

c:\Elixir\Projects\bonForum\bonForum.project.settings

2.2.9 bonForum Project Settings in ElixirIDE

Now that we have an Elixir project, it is time to add some settings. From the Project menu, select the Settings item. You should next edit the bonForum.project.settings file that appears in the editor panel.

WorkRoot and ClassRoot Settings

In General Settings, make whatever changes are necessary so that when you are done, the following lines are there to define `WorkRoot` and `ClassRoot`. These two variables are commented out by default:

```
WorkRoot=\\Elixir\\Projects\\bonForum\\src
ClassRoot=\\Elixir\\Projects\\bonForum\\classes
```

Now Elixir knows where to look for Java source files and knows where to put compiled class files.

Refer to the following two notes after you have installed our bonForum Web application in Tomcat (see Chapter 5).

> **Copying Compiled Class File**
>
> You can avoid having to copy all but two of the compiled class files to the right Tomcat folder location by resetting this `ClassRoot` value as follows:
>
> ```
> ClassRoot=\\jakarta-tomcat\\webapps\\bonForum\\WEB-INF\\classes
> ```
>
> After you make that change, the two compiled class files for the BonForumRobot Java applet used in the bonForum project must be copied manually to a different location than the ClassRoot location for the rest of the package. This note affects the following two class files:
>
> ```
> BonForumRobot.class
> BonForumRobot$RefreshThread.class
> ```
>
> After each compilation, these two files must be copied into the folder TOMCAT_HOME\webapps\bonForum\jsp\forum\applet.

Path Setting

Now make sure that you have the `Path.Windows_NT` setting (assuming NT as operating system) set to something like our path expression here:
c:\\WinNT;c:\\jdk1.3\\bin;c:\\WinNT\\System32;

HelpPath Setting

The `HelpPath.Windows_NT` setting is another list of pathnames separated by a semicolon. Besides giving ElixirIDE access to the JDK documentation, we are adding the API documentation for the XML and XSLT packages that we will discuss in Chapter 4,"XML and XSLT: Xerces and Xalan." Notice that you will have to adjust version numbers as required if you use later versions, such as xalan-j_2_0_1, provided on the CD-ROM.

To our ElixirIDE `HelpPath.Windows_NT` variable setting, we equated a list of the following pathnames (but all in one long line, not on separate lines, as shown here for the book):

c:\\jdk1.3\\docs;

c:\\xerces-1_2_2\\docs\\apiDocs;

c:\\xalan-j_1_2_2\\docs\\apiDocs;

SourcePath Setting

The `SourcePath.Windows_NT` setting you use will enable you to browse source code files in Elixir. Again, the setting for the variable that we suggest using here includes the source paths for the source code and samples provided with both the Xerces and Xalan products, which we will tell you how to install in Chapter 4. Again, note that your version numbers might end up being different that these; if so, you will have to remember to change these settings to reflect the later versions.

We added the following pathnames to our `SourcePath.Windows_NT` variable setting (again, all in one long line, not on separate lines as shown here for the book):

c:\\jdk1.3\\src;

c:\\xerces-1_2_2\\src;

c:\\xerces-1_2_2\\samples;

c:\\xalan-j_1_2_2\\src;

c:\\xalan-j_1_2_2\\samples;

To enable Elixir to find the source code for the JDK using this variable setting, you must have the source code at the given path. It must also be unarchived, not just present in a JAR file. Therefore, we include here the following section on how to expand the SDK source files.

Expanding the SDK Source Files

If you have the space on your storage media (about 20MB), we suggest that you unpack the source code files that you get with a Java 2 SDK installation. To do so, just create a new folder for the source. We call ours c:\jdk1.3\src. Then bring up an NT Command Prompt window, using the new scrollable type display that you created earlier. Use a `jar` command, first to look at the contents and then to expand them into your new src folder. You might want to first enter just `jar` as a command to see the help information.

Here is the command to enter, from within the c:\jdk1.3 folder, to examine the contents of the JAR file:

```
jar -tvf src.jar
```

If you have the room on your drive, you can expand the source code into a file hierarchy under the current directory. To do so, just use the following command, from the c:\jdk1.3 folder, to expand the source code into the c:\jdk1.3\src folder:

```
jar -xvf src.jar
```

Debugger Setting

If you are using JDK1.3 (or JDK1.2.x, and downloaded the JPDA package for it from the Sun Web site), then you probably want to take advantage of the JPDA technology to help you debug your projects within ElixirIDE. If so, turn on the debugger with the following setting:

```
Debugger=YES
```

Other Settings

Other settings, such as those for the RCS versioning, are all documented by Elixir. We leave those up to you to use or to ignore.

> **Updating Settings**
> Remember, you must edit some of these settings when (and if) you change to a future version of the JDK.

Saving Project Settings

After making the previous edits to your bonForum.project.settings file, be sure to save them.

2.2.10 Default Project Settings in Elixir

You might want to use settings similar to some of the ones previously discussed for your other projects in ElixirIDE. If so, you can change the default project settings in another configuration file, called default.project.settings. However, you might first want to see what works for your particular situation and only then edit the defaults for all new projects.

The default.project.settings file is in the configuration folder in the NT user folder. Be careful—it is possible to use the Project Open menu item to open this file as a project (you have to change the file type to All first). If you make that mistake (as we did late one night), you will find that you have a file called default.project.settings.settings in your configuration folder, plus a whole lot of Java exception messages waiting for you when you exit ElixirIDE.

2.2.11 Adding a New Java Class to a Project

For now, we will just create one Java class source file to our new project so that you can see one way to do that. (Later, of course, we would add many more files to our new project folders.) Be careful not to go over the limit of 20 classes to an ElixirIDE-Lite project: It is not too easy to reopen the project without much wrangling. The recursive `add` function will add too many files without complaint and then will lock you out for exceeding the limit. (Hopefully, that was just on an earlier version, but we are not sure.)

Creating a Java Class in ElixirIDE

Now click the bonForum folder icon in the project tree display, to select it. Choose the menu item called Script/Java/Add Class. Add a new Java class by entering in the `CLASSNAME` script parameter this name:

```
de.tarent.forum.bonForum
```

In the messages process, a message should appear about the new Java source file just created. You will find that you now have a folder hierarchy for the Java package name that you gave to the class. Elixir created each folder for the Java package, starting inside the folder named src under the bonForum Elixir Project folder.

You now also have a Java source file with skeleton code for your class. Elixir can be used together with CVS to keep concurrent versions safely archived and available to multiple developers, if need be. We will not describe that here, but you can find out more at the Elixir Web site.

Adding a File to a Project in Elixir

Right-click the bonForum icon in the project tree display. You can see an item called New Folder on the context menu that appears. We could use that to add each folder in the Java package folder hierarchy that we just created. Then we could use the Add File item to add our new Java class source file.

Instead, let's take advantage of a faster solution. Select instead the Recursive Add menu item. In the dialog box that appears, select the folder ELIXIR_HOME\Projects\bonForum\src\de.

When you click the Add button now, you should see a new icon named Tarent appear under the bonForum icon in the project tree display panel. By clicking the icon handles, you can open the entire project folder and file hierarchy. The yellow color of the icon means that this source file needs to be compiled.

2.2.12 Compiling bonForum.java in ElixirIDE

Right-click the mouse on the bonForum.java icon in the ElixirIDE project tree display. You should be able to select Compile from the context menu that appears. After a while, the yellow color of the icon will change and a message "Done" will appear.

If you look in the file system, you should find a new bonForum.class file in the proper folder hierarchy for the project package. In other words, you should find a file with a name something like this:
c:\Elixir\Projects\bonForum\classes\de\tarent\forum\bonForum.class.

2.3 Running Java Programs

Just as with compilation of Java source files, you have a choice of methods for running the compiled class files. We present here information about running Java classes both from the command line and from the ElixirIDE, to parallel the previous compilation information.

2.3.1 Batch Files for Compilation and Running

One simple way to compile and run Java programs is to use a batch file. The following is an example of such a batch file for running the command-line XSLT processor provided with Apache Xalan. This assumes that your system `Path` variable includes the folder that contains the java.exe program. Note that this batch file contains one long line, which is wrapped here by the book margin:

```
java -classpath "c:\xalan-j_1_2_2\xerces.jar;c:\xalan-j_1_2_2\xalan.jar"
org.apache.xalan.xslt.Process -IN bonForumIdentityTransform.xml -XSL
bonForumLinks.xsl -OUT bonForumLinksTEST.html
```

For reasons that will be discussed in Chapter 4, we did not follow Sun's recommendation to put application JAR files in the extension folder. However, when we switched to release 2.0.1 of Xalan, we were able to do that by putting its xerces.jar, xalan.jar, and xalanj1compat.jar files all in the folder c:\jdk1.3\jre\lib\ext. Now java.exe would find the JARs without a classpath argument, and we could simplify our batch file as follows:

```
java org.apache.xalan.xslt.Process -IN bonForumIdentityTransform.xml
-XSL bonForumLinks.xsl -OUT bonForumLinksTEST.html
```

Of course, even more useful would be the following batch file:

```
java org.apache.xalan.xslt.Process -IN %1 -XSL %2 -OUT %3
```

You can keep a file like this one in a folder with a compiled Java class file, and you can call it xalanProc.bat or whatever you like. Then you can enter a command line like this one to run this Java program with arguments:

```
xalanProc bonForumIdentityTransform.xml bonForumLinks.xsl bonForumLinksTEST.html
```

2.3.2 Running Java Programs from ElixirIDE

Select the Show Classpath item from the Script menu in ElixirIDE. You will see that ElixirIDE has added the `ClassRoot` value from the Project Settings file to whatever `CLASSPATH` environment variable value you had when you started ElixirIDE. In the messages process display, you will see a line that begins with something like the following:

```
CLASSPATH=\Elixir\Projects\bonForum\classes;
```

The rest of the line will be the `CLASSPATH` value that existed when you started ElixirIDE, including its JAR file.

From the ElixirIDE, you can quite easily run your compiled program (assuming that it can be run). Just select the Execute item from the context menu that you get when you right-click the mouse on the Java file icon.

If the Execute item appears disabled in that context menu, check that the class you are trying to execute has a `main` method in it. The bonForum.java file that we created previously did not, for example. Double-click its icon on the Project panel, and edit it so that it has a `main` method like this:

```
public class bonForum
{
  public static void main (String[] args) {
    System.out.println("Hello, World!");
  }
}
```

Notice that when you save this change, the color of the icon changes back to yellow to indicate that the source file is newer than the compiled class file. Recompile bonForum.java, and now you should be able to execute the class. ElixirIDE creates a new process for you called de.tarent.forum.bonForum. The output from the program will go to its display panel. You should see there something close to the following:

```
java "de.tarent.forum.bonForum"
Hello, World!
Program Terminated (exit code 0) —-
```

When we tried this, we were quite surprised to see "Hello!" instead of "Hello, World!" Then we remembered that we had put a de.tarent.forum.bonForum class file under the jdk1.3\classes folder during earlier experimentation. The Java virtual machine found and executed that class file instead of our newly compiled one. If we had used "Hello, World!" in that earlier class instead of "Hello," we would never have noticed that we had executed our old class instead.

Classpaths can be a problematic thing, as this experience illustrates. We suggest that you search for a document called classpath.html at `java.sun.com`. It might help you, as it did us. For further information, see "Setting the CLASSPATH Environment," earlier in this chapter.

2.4 Debugging Java Programs

You should be able to browse the user manual for ElixirIDE by opening the file c:\Elixir\IDEManual\ElixirIDEManual.html (or its equivalent) in your browser. In that ElixirIDE manual, you can find instructions for debugging your Java programs within ElixirIDE.

ElixirIDE is capable of using the JPDA debugger from Sun. This debugger is included within the JDK1.3 (in tools.jar). However, if you are using the JDK1.2.2 instead, you will have to find and download the JPDA (jpda.jar) separately.

To use the debugger on a project, you must have the Debugger setting set to `true` in the project settings file. You must also make sure that ElixirIDE can find the JAR file. To do that with JDK1.3, we use the batch file c:\Elixir\StartElixirOnlyDebug.bat (edited here for the book page margins). Be sure to use this batch file from a command prompt window.

```
rem THIS IS FOR USE WITH JDK1.3
rem This starts ElixirIDE-2.4.2-Lite
rem together with the Sun JPDA debugger.
set JPDAJAR=c:\jdk1.3\lib\tools.jar
set ELIXIRJAR=c:\Elixir\ElixirIDE-2.4.2-Lite.jar
set CP=%CLASSPATH%;%JPDAJAR%
set CP=%CP%;%ELIXIRJAR%
java -classpath %CP% com.elixirtech.IDE
set CP=
```

In Chapter 3, "Java Servlets and JavaServer Pages: Jakarta Tomcat," and Chapter 4, we show you how to obtain and install Tomcat, Xalan, and Xerces. We could insert some Elixir-specific batch file listing into each of those two chapters, but they will be read by those who are not intending to use Elixir. Therefore, we instead present those of you reading this Elixir-specific section with a listing of our complete startup file: c:\Elixir\StartElixirDebug.bat.

This batch file gives us access to JPDA, Tomcat, and Xalan and Xerces packages while running programs from Elixir:

```
rem THIS IS FOR USE WITH JDK1.3
rem This starts ElixirIDE-2.4.2-Lite
rem together with the Sun JPDA debugger.
set JPDAJAR=c:\jdk1.3\lib\tools.jar
set ELIXIRJAR=c:\Elixir\ElixirIDE-2.4.2-Lite.jar
set JASPERJAR=c:\jakarta-tomcat\lib\jasper.jar
set SERVLETJAR=c:\jakarta-tomcat\lib\servlet.jar
set XMLJAR=c:\jakarta-tomcat\lib\xml.jar
set XERCESJAR=c:\xalan-j_1_2_2\xerces.jar
set XALANJAR=c:\xalan-j_1_2_2\xalan.jar
set CP=%CLASSPATH%;%JPDAJAR%
```

```
set CP=%CP%;%ELIXIRJAR%
set CP=%CP%;%JASPERJAR%
set CP=%CP%;%SERVLETJAR%
set CP=%CP%;%XMLJAR%
set CP=%CP%;%XERCESJAR%
set CP=%CP%;%XALANJAR%
java -classpath %CP% com.elixirtech.IDE
set CP=
```

When we were using JDK1.2.2, we made another batch file, called c:\Elixir\StartElixirDebug_jdk122.bat, which started up ElixirIDE together with the JPDA debugger. The file is the same as the previous one, except for the first few lines shown here, which change the `PATH` setting and use a different JAR file for the `JPDAJAR` variable. Again, be sure to run this batch file from a command prompt window.

```
rem THIS COMMAND IS FOR USE WITH JDK1.2.2,
rem This starts ElixirIDE-2.4.2-Lite
rem together with the Sun JPDA debugger
set PATH=%PATH%;c:\jpda\bin
set JPDAJAR= c:\jpda\lib\jpda.jar
rem CONTINUE HERE AS IN c:\Elixir\StartElixirDebug.bat!
```

2.5 Other Features of ElixirIDE

We have only touched upon the features of Elixir that are of immediate interest to a developer who is relatively new to Java. However, it would be unfair to leave the subject without at least mentioning that Elixir contains some much more powerful features that have not been described here. We will do no more than list these; if you are curious about these more advanced features, you can read about them in the HTML-based documentation provided with the product.

- Capability to custom-build processes, using the new Build Engine
- Scripting engines (Scheme interface provided)
- Version control systems (RCS interface provided)
- Syntax coloring for Java, XML, IDL, C++, HTML, OCL, and Scheme
- Novel source code collapse/expand feature (so that you can treat your source code like a tree control)
- Auto-expand capability to automate repetitive typing, incorporating dialog boxes, if required
- Project packager, which can generate obfuscated JAR files

Try the menu item Project Packager from the Project menu in ElixirIDE. It is easy to package your project Java classes into a JAR file in whatever path you want. For example, you could use this to deploy our Web application classes from Elixir project subfolders to the Tomcat Web application folders.

3

Java Servlets and JavaServer Pages: Jakarta Tomcat

THIS CHAPTER INTRODUCES A GREAT PRODUCT from the Apache Software Foundation. Tomcat is the reference implementation of the Java Servlet 2.2 and JavaServer Pages 1.1 specifications. Used together with Web servers such as Apache and IIS, it adds powerful dynamic response capabilities to their repertoire. As an HTTP server, Tomcat can also be useful alone during Web application development.

3.1 Apache Software Foundation

Most likely, you are familiar with the Apache Server. Arguably the most popular Web server in the world, it hardly needs an introduction. Along with Linux, the Apache Server has brought the efficacy and legitimacy of open-source software development to the attention of nearly everyone with an interest in computing. Hoping for similar success, some major corporate players, such as IBM and Sun, are releasing the products of their own development efforts in the open-source arena. A cast of thousands, using as a base the best code from such products, is forging some exciting and freely distributed application components.

The Apache Software Foundation is a membership-based, not-for-profit corporation that exists to take care of several of these open-source software projects, including Apache Server. Our book depends heavily upon two Apache projects: the Jakarta Project and the Apache XML Project. This chapter talks about Tomcat, which is the main product from the Jakarta Project. The next chapter talks about Xerces and Xalan, two of several products from the Apache XML Project.

If you are not already familiar with the Apache Software Foundation, we urge you to visit its Web site, which you can find at `http://www.apache.org`.

Following the links from this Web site, you can learn about the various Apache projects and also the people responsible for them. You can also find out how you can play a part in this dynamic development phenomenon.

3.2 Jakarta Tomcat

The Jakarta Project Web site is the place to find the most current official information about Tomcat Server. You can familiarize yourself with that Web site at `http://jakarta.apache.org`.

The Jakarta Tomcat project goal is to create a world-class implementation of the Java Servlet 2.2 and JavaServer Pages 1.1 specifications. Tomcat, the main product of its open-source development efforts, is, in fact, the reference implementation for those specifications.

Tomcat can be used to extend other HTTP servers, such as the popular Apache Server, enabling them to handle requests for both Java servlets and JavaServer Pages. Tomcat Server can also be used as a standalone HTTP server. We will frequently refer to Tomcat in this book simply as "the server," but keep in mind that it is usually used in tandem with another Web server.

3.2.1 Reasons to Use Tomcat

Tomcat is a great choice for learning about Java servlets, JavaServer Pages, and Web applications. First, it is freely available. Second, what you learn will become more relevant as other servlet containers match Tomcat's reference implementation. Third, this is an extremely popular product—it is being downloaded from the Jakarta Web site at a rate that is fast approaching a million copies per year!

This popularity gives Tomcat another advantage related to developer support. So many people are using and enhancing Tomcat that help requests posted to its mailing lists are answered very quickly. Support is often faster and better than it is for commercial products.

3.2.2 Tomcat Versus Apache Server

Is Tomcat a replacement for Apache Server? No—not yet, anyway. That is why Web applications that use Tomcat usually use Apache as well. Sometimes the decision to do that is obvious. One example is when an Apache Server is already being used and is configured to use other necessary software. But the best reason to use both servers is that Tomcat is not as fast as Apache Server is at serving static HTML pages.

By itself, Apache Server cannot handle Java servlets and JSPs. Usually, when you use Tomcat, it will be to provide this service to Apache (or another Web server). Used as a JSP container, Tomcat usually needs access to a Java compiler to compile the JavaServer Pages. As a developer, that is usually not your concern; you can assume that the system hosting your Web application will make available either a licensed Sun SDK or the IBM Jikes compiler.

On the other hand, Tomcat can be used in standalone mode, without Apache (or another Web server). This means that you can use Tomcat alone (as we will in this book) to develop Web applications that will later be hosted by another server plus Tomcat. This also means that you can even build Tomcat itself into a Web-enabled product as both an HTTP server and a servlet and JSP engine. Note that, in that case, you probably will want to also include with your product the Jikes compiler, which is freely redistributable.

3.2.3 Apache License for Tomcat

The Apache projects are released under the Apache license. An open source license, it basically allows any use of the software as long as several conditions are met. Mostly these deal with acknowledgement of the copyright, name protection, and legal protection. The text of the Tomcat license is included with the distribution file on the CD-ROM.

3.3 Installing Tomcat

The version of Tomcat that we are using now is 3.2.1. This release should be used instead of 3.2 because it fixed a security problem. (Earlier, the project for this book used version 3.1. If you need to use a 3.1 version for some reason, you can, but do use 3.1.1, which has the security update.) You should check the Jakarta Web site for even later releases; definitely use the latest stable version for your own projects. We cannot promise that our discussion—or the code as provided with this book—will still work with the next version of Tomcat (probably 4.0), though. When using that becomes possible, news and updates will be posted on the project Web site (`http://www.bonforum.org`).

You can get a Tomcat distribution from the CD-ROM provided with this book. Otherwise, download it from the Web. You can start at `http://jakarta.apache.org/builds/tomcat/release/`.

The following discussion assumes that you will use version 3.2.1. There are both binary and source downloads available for Tomcat. To use Tomcat, you need only the binary download. However, if you have the necessary resources, we recommend that you get both the binary and the source downloads. You can benefit from having the source code for the Tomcat servlet and the JSP container. The source download also gives you important information about running Tomcat together with Apache Server or Microsoft IIS. The download files for Windows are named jakarta-tomcat-3.2.1.zip and jakarta-tomcat-3.2.1-src.zip.

The API documentation for Java servlets and JSPs is also very useful to have on hand. Note that the basic 3.2 distributions don't include these, but you can find them on this book's CD-ROM and at `http://java.sun.com/products/servlet/2.3/javadoc/index.html` and `http://java.sun.com/products/jsp/javadoc1_1.zip`.

3.3.1 Unzipping Tomcat Distribution Files

Unzip the distribution archives into the root folder of your drive. We will assume that you are using the C drive, which will put Tomcat into the folder c:\jakarta-tomcat.

If your Java SDK is installed in c:\jdk1.3, you will have Tomcat conveniently close to it in an explorer display that is sorted alphabetically. That is a pretty good reason not to simplify jakarta-tomcat to tomcat.

3.3.2 Tomcat User Guide

Tomcat has a user manual that is gradually improving over time. Look for it with the name c:\jakarta-tomcat\doc\uguide\tomcat_ug.html.

You can also browse the user guide on the Jakarta Web site along with some other helpful Tomcat documentation. Try `http://jakarta.apache.org/tomcat/jakarta-tomcat/src/doc/index.html`.

Use its user guide to get Tomcat running on your system. We gave up trying to provide comprehensive instructions for the Apache products. A colleague said it best: "Don't try to document other peoples' software!" However, we will give some minimal instructions, as well as some advice that might help sometimes—at least until it too becomes obsolete.

3.3.3 Using Tomcat with IIS

As a Windows NT user, you are most likely familiar with the Microsoft Internet Information Server (IIS) Web server, which is included with the NT 4.0 Option Pack. For more information about IIS, you can visit the Microsoft Web site at `http://www.microsoft.com/ntserver/web/`.

It is not difficult to set up Tomcat to work together with IIS, enabling it to respond to requests for Java servlets and JSP pages. Doing so involves adding a DLL file and some registry keys to your system, and then adding an ISAPI filter to IIS and rebooting it. Complete instructions can be found in the Tomcat user guide, or online at `http://jakarta.apache.org/tomcat/jakarta-tomcat/src/doc/tomcat-iis-howto.html`.

The DLL that you need is the ISAPI redirector server plug-in isapi_redirect.dll, which is available online and also on the CD-ROM for this book in the folder Apache\jakarta\tomcat\release\v3.2.1\bin\win32\i386.

3.3.4 Using Tomcat with Apache Server

The open-source Apache Server is available for NT and various UNIX systems. It is included with most Linux distributions. You can download this free HTTP server by following the links from the Apache Software Foundation Web site at `http://www.apache.org`.

You can quite easily configure Tomcat to work with the Apache Web server. That usually means that Apache will listen to incoming requests and forward those for JSPs and Java servlets to Tomcat. Complete instructions can be found in the Tomcat user guide mentioned previously and also online at `http://jakarta.apache.org/tomcat/jakarta-tomcat/src/doc/tomcat-apache-howto.html`.

Note that this HTML file is also available in the Tomcat source distribution file. In addition, you will need a DLL file called ApacheModuleJServ.dll, which is available online. The latest version available to us is on the CD-ROM for this book, in the folder Apache\jakarta\tomcat\release\v3.2.1\bin\win32\i386.

We will not repeat here the information from the user guide and other HTML documents, but we will mention one item that confused us when we set up Apache and Tomcat together.

There is a "correct" version of ApacheModuleJServ.dll, which you can get from the Tomcat download Web page. There is another "wrong" version of this file that is for use with another program called JServ, which, like Tomcat, is also a Java servlet container. That "wrong" DLL might actually be among the Apache Server modules, which are in something like the folder c:\program files\Apache Group\Apache\modules.

Make sure that the "correct" version is in that folder to use Tomcat instead of JServ.

3.3.5 Environment Settings for Tomcat

Just in case you installed Tomcat without consulting the user guide and also skipped making the environment settings that we suggested in Chapter 2, "An Environment for Java Software Development," we are repeating the basics here. After unzipping the distribution files, you should do something to set the following values in environment variables (or similar values that are the correct ones for your own system). On Windows NT, you can use the Environment tab of the system applet in the Control Panel to set these. On other Windows platforms, use the autoconfig.bat file or a startup file. Be sure to read the tomcat.bat file in the TOMCAT_HOME\bin folder because it explains and automates these environment settings. These are the required variables:

```
set TOMCAT_HOME=c:\jakarta-tomcat
set JAVA_HOME=c:\jdk1.3
set path=c:\jdk1.3\java\bin;%path%
```

3.4 Running Tomcat

We like to keep a shortcut icon in our startup menu that launches an NT command window for using Tomcat. In the properties of the command program, we set the size of the window high and wide, and we give it a big screen buffer. Our window opens showing the current folder for running Tomcat commands, which is

TOMCAT_HOME\bin.

If you do not create a shortcut like that to click, you will have to launch your default NT command prompt window and then manually set the current folder to the bin folder with a command something like this:

```
cd c:\jakarta-tomcat\bin
```

Either way, you should now be able to set up the Tomcat environment by entering this command:

```
tomcat env
```

Start Tomcat in a separate NT command window by entering this command:

```
startup
```

When you are done with Tomcat, you can stop it with this command:

```
shutdown
```

Note that it is possible to start Tomcat so that it does not start in a separate window but instead uses the same window in which you are entering your commands. You can do that by entering the following command instead of the `startup` command shown earlier:

```
tomcat run
```

This last command is useful if you are having problems and want to be able to use your big, scrolling NT command window to view all the messages that have disappeared off the screen.

Whichever way you start Tomcat, the messages that you get on the NT command console should look somewhat like the following lines:

```
Including all jars in c:\jakarta-tomcat\lib in your CLASSPATH.

Using CLASSPATH: c:\jakarta-tomcat\classes;c:\jakarta-
tomcat\lib\ant.jar;c:\jakarta-tomcat\lib\jaxp.jar;c:\jakarta-
➥tomcat\lib\servlet.jar;c:\jakarta-tomcat\lib\parser.jar;c:\jakarta-tomcat\lib\we
➥bserver.jar;c:\jakarta-tomcat\lib\jasper.jar;c:\jakarta-
➥tomcat\lib\xalanservlet.jar;c:\jakarta-tomcat\lib\xerces.jar;c:\jakarta-
➥tomcat\lib\xalanj1compat.jar;c:\jakarta-tomcat\lib\aaxalan.jar;c:\jdk1.3\lib\too
➥ls.jar
2001-05-23 01:05:14 - ContextManager: Adding context Ctx( /examples )
2001-05-23 01:05:14 - ContextManager: Adding context Ctx( /admin )
Starting tomcat. Check the logs/tomcat.log file for errors
2001-05-23 01:05:14 - ContextManager: Adding context Ctx(  )
2001-05-23 01:05:14 - ContextManager: Adding context Ctx( /test )
2001-05-23 01:05:14 - ContextManager: Adding context Ctx( /bonForum )
2001-05-23 01:05:14 - ContextManager: Adding context Ctx( /wml )
2001-05-23 01:05:25 - PoolTcpConnector: Starting HttpConnectionHandler on 8080
2001-05-23 01:05:25 - PoolTcpConnector: Starting Ajp12ConnectionHandler on 8007
```

After all these messages appear, you can try the Tomcat examples just to see that things are working the way they should be. Browse `http://localhost:8080`.

Of course, if your browser and Tomcat are not on the same host, you will have to use a hostname instead of localhost. The browser should display a page from which you can begin exploring Tomcat documentation and trying out the Java servlet and JSP examples provided.

Note that in version 3.2, the Tomcat page incorrectly claims to be in a folder called Webpages. That was correct for version 3.0, but it's true no longer. The default Tomcat page is now the file TOMCAT_HOME/webapps/ROOT/index.html.

Another thing to note is that, unlike Web servers that register themselves as services, you will need to start up Tomcat manually to try it out (even, for example, if you have set it up as an ISAPI filter with IIS). Fortunately, it is not hard to set up Tomcat as an NT service. The instructions to do that are in the file TOMCAT_HOME\doc\NT-Service-howto.html.

As you can see in that file, you will just download jk_nt_service.exe, make two small additions to wrapper.properties, execute two commands that register it as a service, and then start it. You can optionally set it to start automatically, using the Services tool in the Control Panel. That will give you a more convenient startup, although you might still find yourself shutting down and restarting Tomcat quite often during development.

3.4.1 Problems Running Tomcat

We hope that you do not run into problems starting Tomcat on your system. If you do, we suggest that you check the FAQ lists and the archives of the mailing lists. It is likely that if you have a problem, someone has solved it for you. If neither of those options works, do not hesitate to ask the question on the Tomcat user list, where people are usually happy to help.

We will discuss a couple of problems we have encountered, just in case it helps someone with a similar problem. If you are not having problems, these next subsections might not make much sense, and you can safely skip ahead to section 3.4.2, "Tomcat Log Files." If you are trying to use these clues to solve a problem, you might have to look up any forward references to some material mentioned here but covered only later in the next chapter.

HTTP 500 "Internal Server Error"

While trying to run Tomcat, you might find that servlets work fine but that JSP produces an HTTP 500 "internal server error." When we got that error, it usually (but not always) meant that the Java compiler was not being found, which we confirmed by looking at the Tomcat log and the messages on the NT command console window.

This problem is a bit tricky because it happens only when the JSP that you are requesting is not already compiled and sitting in the Tomcat Work folder hierarchy ready to use. If you want to test that JSPs are being compiled, you can try a Tomcat JSP example, after first making sure that you delete any class files that exist for that example in the work folder for the Examples Web app. (You can read more about work folders later.) That work folder on our system is localhost_8080%2Fexamples.

When you try such a "fresh" (not compiled) Tomcat JSP example, you should end up with both the Java work file and its compiled class file in the Examples work folder. If you want to simulate the "compiler not found" problem, try repeating the previous test with the `JAVA_HOME` environment variable set to a wrong value.

The solution to this problem is to make sure that the `JAVA_HOME` environment variable is correctly set. Try the `set` command from the NT command console from which you want to start Tomcat, and check that `JAVA_HOME` has the right value. If you fix the environment variables, you must shut down Tomcat and then also use a fresh NT command console that has the new settings. Also, whenever you change versions of the Java SDK, you might need to adjust this setting.

HTTP 404 "file not found" Error

At different times, we got HTTP 404 errors that puzzled us at first. We then ran some experiments deleting files in the Examples work folder (see preceeding section). We started with a successfully working JSP and deleted its class file. That caused no problem; it just got compiled again upon the next request, which came when we clicked on the "refresh" button on the browser toolbar. (Note that the "go to" button on the browser does not compile the JSP again; it just gets the display from the cache. This also happens when you click the forward or back arrow buttons.)

We then deleted the Java work file, and again the refresh had no problem accessing the class file. Deleting both the source file and the class file was likewise not a problem for a refresh; Tomcat replaced both.

However, when we tried deleting the entire Examples Work subfolder (see preceeding section), we got the HTTP 404 error page. That is, we got that until we shut down and restarted Tomcat, which re-created the work folder for the examples and the Java servlet source and then compiled files that it needed to refresh the example.

Startup Fails, Tools.Jar Not Found

You might find that Tomcat cannot find the tools.jar file even if `TOMCAT_HOME` is set. If this is the case, try putting a copy of the tools.jar file from the JAVA_HOME\lib folder into the TOMCAT_HOME\lib folder. You'll find a FAQ link that will tell you more about this bug at `http://jakarta.apache.org/jyve-faq/Turbine/screen/DisplayQuestionAnswer/action/SetAll/project_id/2/faq_id/12/topic_id/43/question_id/414`.

Startup Fails, Explorer Starts Instead

Also make sure that the `PATH` environment you are using allows the compiler to be found. On our system, that means that it includes c:\jdk1.3\bin. If you do not have this correct, you might be surprised to find that instead of starting up Tomcat, you will have an Explorer window set to the c:\WINNT\Java folder, or something like that.

Startup Fails, Error Creating Sax Parser

When we started developing our Web application project for this book, we ran into some other very thorny problems that we have since learned to avoid. We were going to include a long section here about all these troubles, but we finally decided that it could be more confusing than helpful. Instead, we will just show you the error we were getting and tell you what the problem turned out to be. Here are the exception messages that were displayed:

```
java.lang.ClassNotFoundException: com.sun.xml.parser.Parser
at java.net.URLClassLoader$1.run(URLClassLoader.java:200)
at java.security.AccessController.doPrivileged(Native Method)
at java.net.URLClassLoader.findClass(URLClassLoader.java:188)
at java.lang.ClassLoader.loadClass(ClassLoader.java:297)
at java.lang.ClassLoader.loadClass(ClassLoader.java:253)
at java.lang.ClassLoader.loadClassInternal(ClassLoader.java:313)
at java.lang.Class.forName0(Native Method)
at java.lang.Class.forName(Class.java:120)
at org.xml.sax.helpers.ParserFactory.makeParser(ParserFactory.java:124
at org.apache.tomcat.util.xml.XmlMapper.readXml(XmlMapper.java:191)
at org.apache.tomcat.startup.Tomcat.stopTomcat(Tomcat.java:186)
at org.apache.tomcat.startup.Tomcat.execute(Tomcat.java:130)
at org.apache.tomcat.startup.Tomcat.main(Tomcat.java:163)
FATAL: configuraoion error
java.lang.Exception: Error creating sax parser
at org.apache.tomcat.util.xml.XmlMapper.readXml(XmlMapper.java:207)
at org.apache.tomcat.startup.Tomcat.stopTomcat(Tomcat.java:186)
at org.apache.tomcat.startup.Tomcat.execute(Tomcat.java:130)
at org.apache.tomcat.startup.Tomcat.main(Tomcat.java:163)
```

After coming up with some false solutions (they worked!) to this problem, we determined the real cause: We had put the xerces.jar file in the folder c:\jdk1.3\jre\lib\ext.

What we thought would be an easy way to get this JAR file in the default classpath turned out to confuse Tomcat, which needs to find its XML parser in the xml.jar file that comes with it, not in xerces.jar.

In the next chapter, we will give you instructions about the way we install Xerces so that Tomcat can still access its own XML JAR file. (We will also discuss there how we avoid some problems caused by xalan.jar when it is put in the Ext folder.) After we had solved this problem with the Xerces JAR file, our technical reviewer told us about another "gotcha" that happens when you put xerces.jar in the Ext folder, and we have also installed there the jaxp.jar file (containing the Java XML classes). Java then incorrectly tries to find certain Xerces classes in jaxp.jar because JARs are loaded alphabetically, and *jaxp* comes before *Xerces*. A solution to this problem is to rename xerces.jar to aaxerces.jar and then rename xalan.jar to aaxalan.jar A similar solution is given in the Cocoon SubProject of the Apache XML Project, where xml.jar is renamed to zzz.jar to get around a conflict between Tomcat and Cocoon. For more on this and other jar conflicts, search for "xerces" at the Cocoon Web site at the page `http://xml.apache.org/cocoon/faqs.html`.

3.4.2 Tomcat Log Files

When Tomcat starts up the first time, it creates some folders for you. Among these is TOMCAT_HOME\logs. Tomcat puts its error messages into log files inside this folder. These messages can be useful for troubleshooting problems.

Take a look at the Tomcat configuration file called server.xml. You should find it in the conf folder in the TOMCAT_HOME folder. Note that if you try to use Internet Explorer 5.x to view the file, you will get an error about a reference to an undeclared namespace (xmlmapper). To view the file in IE 5.x, you will first have to use a text editor to comment out the following line:

```
<xmlmapper:debug level="0" />
```

In server.xml, you can see how and where the log files are configured. We discuss their use later in this chapter (see Section 3.5.1, "Using Tomcat Log Files").

3.4.3 Tomcat Work Folders and Files

After Tomcat runs once, new folders will appear, something like this:

TOMCAT_HOME\work

TOMCAT_HOME\work\localhost_8080

TOMCAT_HOME\work\localhost_8080%2Fadmin

TOMCAT_HOME\work\localhost_8080%2Fexamples

TOMCAT_HOME\work\localhost_8080%2Ftest

Look again at server.xml. You will see that this XML file has a root element called server. One child element of that server element is called ContextManager. This has an attribute called workDir, which determines the folder in which Tomcat will keep its work files, such as the compiled servlets that are created from your JSP files. The default attribute setting, which you can change, if necessary, is `WorkDir="work"`.

3.4.4 Tomcat Web App Folders and WAR Files

Other folders created the first time you run Tomcat are the following:

TOMCAT_HOME\webapps\admin

TOMCAT_HOME\webapps\examples

TOMCAT_HOME\webapps\Root

TOMCAT_HOME\webapps\test

When you unzipped the downloadable installation file jakarta-tomcat.zip, there were some files in the Webapps folder that had an extension of .war; these are known as WAR files. These are their names:

admin.war

examples.war

ROOT.war

test.war

These files contain archived Web applications. When you start up Tomcat, it expands any WAR files that it finds in the Webapps folder. This is one way to deploy Tomcat Web applications. Such WAR files (Web archives) are JAR files (Java archives) with a different extension. In fact, both WAR and JAR files use the ZIP file format, so you can use zip and unzip tools on either type. This also means that you can sign Web components in a WAR file. Why not just call WAR files JAR files? Because JAR files, unlike WAR files, are meant to hold a set of class files that can be placed in the classpath and double-clicked using a GUI to launch an application.

If you add a Web application to Tomcat "automatically" by simply copying in a WAR file to the Webapps folder, Tomcat will not only expand the archive into a folder hierarchy of the same name (also under Webapps), it will also "know" that this is a Web application. You do not need to make any changes to the server.xml file, as discussed in a few paragraphs, before Tomcat can find that Web application context. However, you might sometimes need different settings for your Web application than the "automatic" ones provided, so we also will discuss how you can add a Tomcat Web application the hard way: by editing server.xml. We do that later, in the section "Editing the Server Configuration."

Tomcat Web App Contexts

The definition of a Web application is given in the Java Servlet Specification, v2.2, as follows:

> A web application is a collection of servlets, JavaServer Pages, HTML documents, and other web resources which might include image files, compressed archives, and other data. A web application may be packaged into an archive or exist in an open directory structure.

A Web application can run on containers from different vendors. A Web application also has a root, which is a path within the Web server. For example, the Web application that is the subject of most of this book is mapped to the root /bonForum. That means that every request that starts with that path as a prefix is mapped to the Web application and is handled by its `ServletContext`. As one fictitious example, a JavaServer Page resource that is part of that Web application might be located by `http://www.bonforum.org/bonforum/jsp/hello.jsp`.

3.4.5 Tomcat Web Application Contexts

Each collection of Web resources making up one Web application shares a context. Except for the Root folder that maps to an empty URI prefix, the Web application folders mentioned previously (such as examples) are each mapped to a Web application context, in the server.xml Tomcat configuration file. The `ContextManager` element in that XML file contains child elements called `Context`, for example:

```
<Context path="/examples" docBase="webapps/examples" debug="0" reloadable="true" >
```

This particular `Context` element comes included with the Tomcat installation. It sets up a Web application context mapped to the path "/examples". This path is relative to the "webapps" folder, by design. The `docBase` is instead relative to the `ContextManager` home. After a fresh installation of Tomcat, the `ContextManager` home is the same as `TOMCAT_HOME`, but that can be changed, if necessary, by adding an attribute named `home` to the `ContextManager` element in the server.xml configuration file.

Consider what happens, for example, when your browser sends a request with a URL of `http://www.servername.com/examples/jsp/snp/snoop.jsp`. Or, if you are developing Tomcat applications with both the browser and Tomcat server on the same machine, that request could be, for example, `http://localhost:8080/examples/jsp/snp/snoop.jsp`.

If Tomcat is responding to this request, it will use the path attribute of the Examples Context to transform that URL to a file system pathname. Let's assume that nobody has changed the `ContextManager` home from the default, which is `TOMCAT_HOME`. The previous URL will be mapped then, to the file TOMCAT_HOME\webapps\examples\jsp\snp\snoop.jsp.

You can try to use a local browser to open the file using a URL something like `file://c:/jakarta-tomcat/webapps/examples/jsp/snp/snoop.jsp`.

The browser will receive the source for snoop.jsp, which is text. What it does with that will depend on whether the extension has been mapped to a program on the client, such as a text editor. By default, it brings up a dialog box to ask the user what program should open the file. However, the browser does not have a servlet container. It will not be capable of compiling the JSP source to a servlet or executing such a servlet, if it already exists. To carry out those two vital functions and provide HTML to the Web browser is the job of a JSP engine, such as Tomcat.

3.4.6 Tomcat Web App Configuration Files

Every Web application installed in Tomcat has a configuration file, which contains its deployment descriptor. For an example, use Internet Explorer to examine the one for the Examples Web app, which is the file TOMCAT_HOME\webapps\examples\Web-inf\web.xml.

To understand this configuration file, you can use a text editor to read the file c:\jakarta-tomcat\conf\web.dtd, which is the `DOCTYPE` for a Web application.

A detailed discussion of everything in this file is beyond the scope of this book.

Remember, this book is meant to be a laboratory manual—it assumes that you are also relying on a textbook and class handouts. You should read web.dtd together with other material that you have for learning about servlets and JSP (such as the book *Core Servlets and JavaServer Pages*, by Marty Hall). Here we will briefly mention some of the configuration tasks that you can thus become familiar with.

One task is creating context parameters. These are used as global variables: They contain information that is visible to all the servlets, JSP pages, HTML, and so on in the Web application. For example, you could add the email address of a Webmaster to a Web app by adding the following element to its deployment descriptor in its web.xml file:

```
<context-param>
    <param-name>
        Webmaster
    </param-name>
    <param-value>
        webmaster@bonforum.org
    </param-value>
</context-param>
```

Unlike context parameters, servlet init parameters are visible only within the servlet for which you define them. You can use these init-params for many different purposes, whenever you need to be able to use a value in a servlet that can be altered by the Tomcat administrator, for example. The Tomcat Examples Web app uses the classic—and useless—"foo,bar" pair to show you how to create an init-param and set its value. You can see how this works by uncommenting (if necessary) the init-param element that appears in the snoop servlet element, which is in the web.xml file for the Examples Web app. It should look something like this when you are done:

```
<servlet>
    <servlet-name>
        snoop
    </servlet-name>
    <servlet-class>
        SnoopServlet
    </servlet-class>
    <init-param>
        <param-name>foo</param-name>
        <param-value>bar</param-value>
    </init-param>
</servlet>
```

After you have done this, you need to shut down and restart Tomcat. This means that you will obviously not be using init-params for values that need to change often. You can then access the snoop servlet example (note that this is not the same as the snoop JSP example available from the Tomcat home page), using a URL something like `http://:8080/examples/servlet/snoop`.

Near the top of the information that is displayed on the browser, you should see the name of the param and its value, as follows:

```
Servlet init parameters:
    foo = bar
```

Another configuration task useful to understand is servlet mapping. This assigns an alias to a servlet, relative to the context path for the Web application (and thus also relative to TOMCAT_HOME). For example, two servlet mappings in the examples deployment descriptor (in web.xml) enable you to request the same snoop servlet as in the last example, using either of these URLs instead of the one shown previously:

```
http://:8080/examples/snoop

http://:8080/examples/anyname.snp
```

We will return to the topic of servlet mapping again in this chapter, in the section "Editing the Web App Configuration." Meanwhile, look at those servlet mappings in the Examples deployment descriptor that allow these two variant URLs. Here is what they look like:

```
<servlet-mapping>
    <servlet-name>
        snoop
    </servlet-name>
    <url-pattern>
        /snoop
    </url-pattern>
</servlet-mapping>
<servlet-mapping>
    <servlet-name>
        snoop
    </servlet-name>
    <url-pattern>
        *.snp
    </url-pattern>
</servlet-mapping>
```

There are many more uses for the deployment descriptor in the web.xml file of a Web application. It says this in the Tomcat users guide:

> A detailed description of web.xml and the Web application structure (including directory structure and configuration) is available in Chapters 9, 10, and 14 of the Servlet API Spec, and we are not going to write about it.
>
> There is, however, a small Tomcat-related "feature" that is related to web.xml. Tomcat lets the user define default web.xml values for all contexts by putting a default web.xml file in the conf directory. When constructing a new Context, Tomcat uses the default web.xml file as the base configuration and the application-specific web.xml (the one located in the application's WEB-INF/web.xml) only to overwrite these defaults.

3.4.7 Help for Developing Tomcat Web Applications

A guide to developing Web applications for Tomcat is included with the distribution. Be sure to check the Tomcat documentation on the Jakarta Web site for newer versions because this guide will surely be updated. After we installed Tomcat, we could find the guide at `file://c:\jakarta-tomcat\doc\appdev\index.html`.

In this book, we do not follow all the procedures outlined in that guide. However, it is useful to understand how to use the Apache ant tool to build Tomcat Web apps—especially if you want to get involved with the Apache projects. Besides the hypertext guide, you can read the text file c:\jakarta-tomcat\doc\appdev\build.xml.txt, which shows how to use ant to build Web apps.

3.5 Tomcat Examples of Servlets and JSPs

One of the best ways to learn about Java servlet and JSP technologies is to study the examples that are included with Tomcat. You are urged to try all the examples. You can also study their source code, which is included in the main binary distribution in the Examples folder under jsp and WEB-INF/classes (which contains .java and .class files).

A simple way to try the examples is to browse the main Tomcat page, which will be at a URL something like `http://localhost:8080`, depending on your system.

You can also access the examples directly. For example, here is the URL that we used to access the snoop servlet on our ginkgo server, from a different host on the network: `http://ginkgo:8080/examples/servlet/snoop`.

3.5.1 Using Tomcat Log Files

After trying all the Tomcat examples, look at the files in TOMCAT_HOME\logs folder. You should be able to understand the entries now. The file jasper.log shows parameter values, query strings, and more; that can be quite useful for debugging JSP-based Web apps.

3.6 Adding Your Tomcat Web Application

Here we explain one quick way to add a new Web application to an NT machine on which Tomcat Server is available. You can follow these instructions to develop a skeleton Web application called MyApp. Feel free to change this name to something real, by the way.

3.6.1 Creating a Web Application

First, create a new folder, where you can put the files for the new Web application. The name of this folder is TOMCAT_HOME\webapps\MyApp.

Next, copy and paste all the subfolders of the TOMCAT_HOME\webapps\examples folder to the folder that you created. Your new Web application now has lots of files, including all the subfolders that you need, some vital configuration files, and copies of all the Java servlet and JSP examples for Tomcat.

You can use these new copies of the servlet and JSP examples to test your new Web application, after you change two configuration files as discussed in the next two sections. The advantage of testing is that you know that the examples were working in the Examples context, so they should also work in the new MyApp context. After you get things working right, you can delete all the example files, or just leave them there.

When editing any configuration file, such as server.xml and web.xml, you should make a backup first.

3.6.2 Editing the Server Configuration

The next step is to configure the server so that it can find your new Web application. Use your favorite text editor to edit the principal Tomcat configuration file, TOMCAT_HOME\conf\server.xml.

As we mentioned earlier, adding a Web application means adding a context element to server.xml. Again take the easy way out: Use copy and paste to clone an existing context element, such as the one for the examples context. Then change the new context element to MyApp. Here is the result:

```
<Context path="/MyApp" docBase="webapps/MyApp" debug="0" reloadable="true"
➥></Context>
```

The context path is relative to TOMCAT_HOME\webapps, and the `docBase` is relative to TOMCAT_HOME. Note that you will have to change examples to MyApp in two places within the context element. One is the value of the `docBase` attribute. The other is for the value of the `path` attribute. Leave all the other attributes alone—if it ain't broke, don't fix it. Save the new server.xml file.

3.6.3 Editing the Web App Configuration

Now edit the Web application deployment descriptor, which is in the XML file TOMCAT_HOME\webapps\MyApp\WEB-INF\web.xml.

You need to edit this deployment descriptor to define and configure all the Java servlet and JavaServer Pages that are part of the new Web application. The most common configuration task involves adding servlet and servlet-mapping tagged elements.

For each servlet and JSP that you want to use in the Web application, you can add a servlet element in this web.xml file. This element can also give your servlet or JSP an alias that is more user-friendly. Another advantage to using an alias is that it encapsulates a servlet or JSP; the application can refer to the alias, and you are free to change to a different servlet or JSP by editing only the web.xml deployment descriptor.

For each Web application servlet, you can also add a servlet-mapping element. This will give the servlet a path relative to the root of the Tomcat server space, TOMCAT_HOME. For example, assume that a compiled servlet called test.class is actually in the folder TOMCAT_HOME\webapps\MyApp\WEB-INF\classes.

If you add a servlet mapping, a client can request that servlet with a URL something like `http://localhost:8080/MyApp/test`. By using a different mapping, without moving the servlet, you can change that URL to something like `http://localhost:8080/MyApp/foo/bar/test`.

Without any mapping, the only way that the servlet can be requested is with a URL something like `http://localhost:8080/MyApp/servlet/test`.

Note that this last URL assumes that the `RequestInterceptor` prefix is set to its usual value (`/servlet/`) in the server.xml file. This prefix is a setting that applies to all Web apps under the Tomcat server configured by that file.

This web.xml file is defined by a DTD that you should take some time to investigate. You will see there many ways to set global information that will be available to all the objects that share the Web application. You can find this DTD at TOMCAT_HOME\conf\web.dtd.

3.6.4 Restarting Tomcat with the New Web App

If Tomcat is running now, you certainly will have to stop it before your changes will be effective because Tomcat processes this configuration file only during startup. Bring up an NT command window, and run this command:

```
TOMCAT_HOME\bin\shutdown.bat
```

That will bring down the server, eventually. If you look at the command window where Tomcat is running, you will see some messages. If you started Tomcat with startup.bat, you must look quickly because the command window will disappear when Tomcat stops.

Start Tomcat again, using either the `startup` or the `tomcat run` commands. While Tomcat starts up, watch its messages on its command window. This time, the context for MyApp should be among those that get initialized. Now use your browser to request the SnoopServlet copy that is in your new Web application (not the original one in the Examples Web app). For all the following tests to work, the web.xml file for your new Web application must still contain this servlet element:

```
<servlet>
    <servlet-name>
        snoop
    </servlet-name>
    <servlet-class>
        SnoopServlet
    </servlet-class>
</servlet>
```

That web.xml file should also still have these servlet-mapping elements:

```
<servlet-mapping>
    <servlet-name>
        snoop
    </servlet-name>
    <url-pattern>
```

```
            /snoop
        </url-pattern>
    </servlet-mapping>
    <servlet-mapping>
        <servlet-name>
            snoop
        </servlet-name>
        <url-pattern>
            *.snp
        </url-pattern>
    </servlet-mapping>
```

Try requesting SnoopServlet with something like each of the following URLs:

http://localhost:8080/MyApp/snoop

http://localhost:8080/MyApp/servlet/SnoopServlet

http://localhost:8080/MyApp/servlet/snoop

You should also be able to use URLs similar to these next two:

http://localhost:8080/MyApp/foo.snp

http://localhost:8080/MyApp/servlet/foo.snp

When we tried these, our Internet Explorer tried instead to download and open a "snapshot file" for the SnapView application, at least until we deleted that file extension setting from the File Types panel on the NT Explorer View Options menu item.

After each successful servlet request, look at the details about the HTTP request object in the browser display. Notice which fields change when you use different URLs.

Now also try the snoop JSP copy in your Web application. This is a JSP page that displays only some of the information that SnoopServlet displays. You can request it with the URL `http://localhost:8080/MyApp/jsp/snp/snoop.jsp`. Again, look at the resulting browser page for some details from the `Request` object.

Assuming that your web.xml file still has its original mappings from the Examples Web app, try this next exercise. Request the servletToJsp servlet (case matters!) using something like one of the following URLs:

http://localhost:8080/MyApp/servletToJsp

http://localhost:8080/MyApp/servlet/servletToJsp

To understand how this example works, look at the following two files in your text editor:

TOMCAT_HOME\webapps\MyApp\WEB-INF\classes\servletToJsp.java

TOMCAT_HOME\webapps\MyApp\jsp\jsptoserv\hello.jsp

Now try this final exercise. Request the jsptoservlet JSP using something like the URL `http://localhost:8080/MyApp/jsp/jsptoserv/jsptoservlet.jsp`.

You should get the same result as you did in the last exercise. To understand why, look at the file TOMCAT_HOME\webapps\MyApp\jsp\jsptoserv\hello.jsp in your text editor.

Congratulations! You now have a new Web application installed. As the chess saying goes, "the rest is all a matter of details." You have what you need: an example of a Java servlet calling a JSP page, and an example of another JSP page calling a Java servlet (actually, calling a servlet that calls a JSP page). You can start building upon this skeleton to develop your MyApp Web application.

3.7 Java Servlets and JSPs

At this point, we could start adding detailed information about Java servlets and JSPs to this book, and certainly we would have enough material to fill two books. However, we will not do so, for two reasons. The first is that the goal of this book is similar to that of a human anatomy class. We will provide an example of a Web application project and then thoroughly dissect it to illustrate the discussion of several popular technologies, including servlets and JSPs. You will be able to learn function as well as form because you can exercise the example that is being studied—do not try that in your human anatomy class!

The second reason we see no need to cover servlets in depth here is that many servlet resources already exist. We would rather refer you to those than reproduce their information here. The following sections will give a few suggestions and starting points for readers who want to learn more about Java servlets and JSPs. If you have a good understanding of these technologies already, you may safely skip to the next chapter and use the rest of this chapter as a reference only.

3.7.1 The Servlet API Javadoc

The Tomcat 3.1 source distribution includes the Servlet API Javadoc. This API documentation is a valuable help for the developer. With Tomcat 3.2, the servlet API documentation is available as two download files that are separate from the Tomcat distribution file. One of the files is for the binary download, and the other is for the source download. These files are called jakarta-servletapi-3.2.zip and jakarta-servletapi-3.2-src.zip. You can also find these files on this book's CD-ROM.

It is a good idea to study the servlet API documentation. One thing this will do is make the subject of Java servlets and JSPs a lot less daunting than it might otherwise seem. In fact, the design involved is quite compact and clear, and the API Javadoc is a good place to answer your own programming questions.

If you downloaded the source Tomcat 3.1 distribution, you should browse something like c:\jakarta-tomcat\src\webpages\docs\api\overview-summary.html. If you obtained the servlet API Javadoc in a separate download (for example, with version 3.2 of Tomcat), the file to browse is more like c:\jakarta-servletapi\docs\api\overview-summary.html.

Take a look at this API page, and you will see the top-level logical design of Java servlets and JSPs.

3.7.2 Learning About Java Servlets

Be sure to check Chapter 12, "Online Information Sources," for leads related to Java servlets.

One excellent way to look for anything related to servlets is to visit `http://java.sun.com/products/servlet`.

Servlet Resources

You can find a list of books, tutorials, and other learning opportunities at `http://java.sun.com/products/servlet/resources.html`.

Java Servlet Specification V2.2

All developers of Java servlets should read the Java Servlet Specification. That document, servlet2_2-spec.pdf, is available for download from the Sun Java servlet Web site. Look for a link at `http://java.sun.com/products/servlet/download.html`.

Servlet Tutorial

You are perhaps familiar with the excellent Java tutorial available online at the Sun Web site. A great way to learn the basics of servlets is by following the servlets trail, which is at `http://java.sun.com/docs/books/tutorial/servlets/index.html`.

The Java Forums

Among the most important learning resources for Java servlets, as well as all other Java topics, are the popular Java forums hosted by Sun. You can find these at `http://forum.java.sun.com/`.

3.7.3 Learning About JSP

There will be quite a few JavaServer Pages in our Web application that you can learn from. Here we provide a few suggestions to help you find more comprehensive coverage to supplement the "laboratory manual" approach of this book.

Many of our suggestions are related to useful destinations that you can reach from `http://java.sun.com/products/jsp`.

Also be sure to check Chapter 12 for other leads related to JavaServer Pages.

JSP Books and Resources

If you are looking for books about JSP, check the list at `http://java.sun.com/products/jsp/resources.html`. On that page, among many other useful resources, is a list of books. We even found there a link to information about a JSP book in German: `http://shannon.informatik.fh-wiesbaden.de/jsp/index.html`.

JSP Specification V1.1

We will use version 1.1 of JSP. The JavaServer Pages Specification is obtainable as jsp1_1-spec.pdf. You should be able to download it at `http://java.sun.com/products/jsp/download.html`.

JSP Tutorials

The JSP by Example tutorial provides a quick start to anyone who wants to create and understand JavaServer Pages. You can find that at `http://java.sun.com/products/jsp/html/jspbasics.fm.html`.

Try also a different tutorial at`http://www.builder.com/Programming/JSP/ss01.html`.

JSP Mailing List

Joining an active mailing list can be one of the best ways to get answers and gain a practical perspective on a technology. For JSP, you should send an email to `listserv@java.sun.com`. In the body of the email, write:

subscribe jsp-interest yourlastname yourfirstname

Of course, you must substitute your names for the last two items, unless your name is "yourfirstname yourlastname"!

The Java Forums

We will repeat this tip given previously because it is that important. Among the most important learning resources for Java servlets and JavaServer Pages, as well as all other Java topics, are the popular Java forums hosted by Sun. You can find these at `http://forum.java.sun.com/`.

3.7.4 The JSP Package

What is JSP? For one thing, it is a Java package, javax.servlet.jsp. A lot can be learned about JSP by studying the API document. If you took our advice and downloaded the Tomcat source code, you should be able to browse the file src\webpages\docs\api\javax\servlet\jsp\package-summary.html, which is inside your TOMCAT_HOME folder.

Some of the interfaces and classes are quite important. Two that are particularly worth studying are `HttpJspPage` and `PageContext`.

HttpJspPage

This interface is quite important because of its `_jspService` method. You will often see the statement made that a JSP is compiled into a servlet that then processes a request and produces a response according to the content of the JSP document that is not compiled. Based on that statement, you might look for a `put`, `get`, or `service` method in one of the Java files that represents a translated JSP. However, try looking in one of those Java files in a subfolder of the Tomcat Work folder. What you will find instead is a `_jspService method`.

Compare the `_jspService` method to the `service` method or any of the `doXXX` methods in a servlet. This first excerpt shows the signature of the `_jspService` method, taken from a JSP processor-generated Java file in a Tomcat Work subfolder:

```
public void _jspService(HttpServletRequest request, HttpServletResponse response)
➥throws IOException, ServletException {
```

This second excerpt shows the signature of the `doGet` method:

```
public void doGet(HttpServletRequest request, HttpServletResponse response) throws
➥ServletException, IOException {
```

The compiled JSP page is a servlet, but there is one important difference between it and other servlets. You cannot override the `_jspService` method as you can the `doGet` method, the `service` method, and so on. But you can write a JSP document, and then the containing server (Tomcat) will customize this method according to the static and dynamic content that you add to the JSP.

PageContext Class

If you want to have a way to measure your progress while learning about JSP, you can hardly find a better one than the `PageContext` class. If you can understand everything that is done by this abstract class, you will have come far in your understanding of JSP. When a JSP becomes a servlet, its `_jspService()` method calls on a `JspFactory` object to create one instance of an implementation-dependent subclass of the `PageContext` class, named `pageContext`. By using the methods of this object, the JSP servlet has access to the other objects that make up the Web application. Furthermore, the use of `JspFactory` and `pageContext` subclasses allows different JSP container implementations to provide the JSP servlet with one set of objects and methods to carry out its program. The following direct quote from the API documentation for the `PageContext` class will convince you of the central importance of this class in the JSP scheme of things:

"The `PageContext` class provides a number of facilities to the page/component author and page implementer, including these:

- A single API to manage the various scoped namespaces
- A number of convenience APIs to access various public objects
- A mechanism to obtain the JspWriter for output

- A mechanism to manage session usage by the page
- A mechanism to expose page directive attributes to the scripting environment
- Mechanisms to forward or include the current request to other active components in the application
- A mechanism to handle error page exception processing"

Some methods of `pageContext` return objects that are more conveniently accessible using "implicit" JSP variables (`out`, `request`, `response`, `session`, `application`, `config`). In Chapter 10, "JSP Taglib and Custom Tag: Choice Tag," you will see that custom JSP tags still need to use the `pageContext` methods to get these important objects. In the next section, we briefly discuss two of these objects, the `ServletContext` (`application`) and `ServletConfig` (`config`) instances related to the JSP servlet. Like all the implicit JSP objects, these two are quite useful for all servlets, not just those compiled from JSP.

3.8 The *ServletConfig* and *ServletContext* Classes

When a servlet container initializes a servlet instance, it provides it a `ServletConfig` object. That object encapsulates initialization parameters, which can be used, for example, to tailor the behavior of a servlet to the particular operating system environment that it executes in. The `ServletConfig` object also contains another important object for the servlet, which is an instance of the `ServletContext` class.

The `ServletContext` object provides a servlet a way to share objects and communicate with other components of a Web application. Here is a quote from the API documentation for the `ServletContext` class:

> There is one context per Web application per Java virtual machine. (A Web application is a collection of servlets and content installed under a specific subset of the server's URL namespace, such as /catalog, and possibly installed via a .war file.)

If a Web application is *not* marked as distributed in its deployment descriptor (web.xml file), then the `ServletContext` object is global to all the servlets in the Web application. Any object can be added to the `ServletContext` as an attribute and can be accessed by another servlet or JSP, for example. (Distributed Web applications are an advanced topic beyond the scope of this book. If you think that your Web application will end up being distributed—meaning that it will employ more than one Java virtual machine for the same instance of the application—then you will need to use a different solution, such as a database for establishing a truly global context for the servlets and JSP in the Web app.)

Another very useful object provided by the `ServletContext` to a servlet is a `RequestDispatcher` object. This can be used to pass the request that came from a browser onward to another destination such as a different servlet or JSP. This allows different components of your Web application to cooperate in creating a response for the browser.

3.9 Web Application Scopes

As a software developer, you should be aware of the importance that the concept of scope plays in programming. The scope of an object determines its visibility within the code and also determines its lifetime. To use Java servlets and JSPs to build Web applications, you need an understanding of four different scopes. Each scope is related to an object that has a certain lifetime (it might vary in duration). These objects are known to other objects within different logical contexts. These two characteristics of the scope-determining objects give different scopes to objects (such as attributes) that they contain.

3.9.1 Application Scope

Objects with application scope are contained by a `ServletContext` instance. Thus, application-scope objects are shared by servlets and JSPs within one Web app executed by a container (within one JVM). Such objects can remain available via the `ServletContext` object as long as the Web application is running.

3.9.2 Session Scope

Objects with session scope are contained by an `HttpSession` instance. A session is associated with an `HttpRequest` object. It is also associated with a particular browser (or other client), for example, through the use of a cookie and a unique identifier. A session, therefore, allows different requests to be associated with a particular client; this is very important, for example, in shopping cart applications. Session scope lasts as long as its session object, which has an indefinite life span: If the client is inactive for longer than a settable period of time (30 minutes, by default), the session object and the scope that it provides come to an end.

3.9.3 Request Scope

Objects with request scope are contained by a `ServletRequest` object. Because a request may be forwarded from one servlet or JSP to others, it is clear that objects in request scope can outlive any particular servlet within which they are available. However, after the request object has been handled, the objects that it held in request scope will no longer be available.

3.9.4 Page Scope

Objects in page scope are contained by a `PageContext` instance. Specifically, they are contained by the `pageContext` object created at the beginning of the `_jspService()` method in a compiled JSP servlet. While the JSP is handling the request object from its client, the objects in page scope are available as attributes of the `pageContext` object. A finally clause at the end of the `_jspService()` method makes sure that the `pageContext` object is released, which also means that its contained objects "go out of scope" and are no longer available.

3.9.5 Learning About Scopes

A full discussion of the important subject of Web application scopes is beyond the scope of this book (pun intended). A good resource for learning about scope is available at `http://developer.java.sun.com/developer/onlineTraining/JSPIntro/contents.html`.

Another way to start learning about scope in relation to Web applications is to read Bruce Eckel's *Thinking in Java* (ISBN: 0-1302-7363-5, published by Prentice Hall). You can even download a free trial version of that book from `http://www.mindview.net`. One section of the book that is quite relevant to our book project is "JSP Page Attributes and Scope," in the chapter "Distributed Computing."

Another useful exercise in that highly recommended book is "Manipulating Sessions in JSP." Our Web application project for this book is quite dependent on the existence of session objects. Understanding these will be useful while reading the rest of our book.

One thing to be aware of is that these four scopes are not subsets of each other. Each scope depends on the lifetime and visibility of a different object, and those objects are not nested. However, they are all dependent upon a Java virtual machine, and so, therefore, are the four scopes listed previously.

4 XML and XSLT: Xerces and Xalan

THIS CHAPTER INTRODUCES TWO MORE great offerings from the Apache Software Foundation. These two products are from the XML Project. Xerces is a DOM and SAX parser. Xalan is an XSLT and XPATH processor.

4.1 Apache XML Project

This chapter discusses two tools that will be quite important for your Web application project. Xerces and Xalan are both open source software products, and like Tomcat Server, they are being developed by projects of the Apache Software Foundation. As we did in the preceding chapter, we suggest that you visit their Web site, which you can find at the following URL:

```
http://www.apache.org
```

One overall suggestion we would like to make is that as a software developer, you will gain much from reading the source code for the Xerces and Xalan projects. Often the comments that appear with the code itself are written with more understanding than much of the secondhand material about XML that you will find elsewhere. The developers of the code, after all, had to understand the XML recommendations in a very unambiguous fashion, which can be considered quite an accomplishment!

A good, short description of the launching of the Apache XML project is available in a press release that you can get at the following URL:

```
http://xml.apache.org/pr/0001.txt
```

This document describes the software that was donated to the open source XML project, as well as the companies donating it and some of the people involved.

The home page for the Apache XML project is the following:

```
http://xml.apache.org
```

This Web site is an important destination for anyone interested in using XML. We urge you to visit it to get a good top view of the project and its various products.

4.1.1 Apache Licenses for Xerces and Xalan

The Apache projects are released under the Apache license. An open source license, it basically allows any use of the software as long as several conditions are met. Mostly, these deal with acknowledgment of the copyright, name protection, and legal protection. The text of the Apache licenses for Xerces and Xalan appears in Appendix B, "Some Copyrights and Licenses."

4.2 Installing Xerces

The XML parser that we will use is part of Xerces. During the course of writing this book, we used several versions of Xerces. Considering the ongoing evolution of XML, you will probably do the same with any XML parser that you use for a while. Changing versions inevitably seems to produce housekeeping chores for Web application development.

While we were developing the software for this book, the latest stable release of Xerces for Java was 1.2.3. Since then, release 1.3.0 has become available. Even more significantly, Xerces Java Parser 2.0 was released as the book goes to press. Although we usually recommend that you adopt the latest stable releases as soon as possible, an additional consideration applies here. As discussed later in this chapter, each Xalan XSLT processor release requires the use of a compatible Xerces release. When we developed the book project, the latest stable release of Xalan was 1.2.2, which was tested with Xerces 1.2.2. Therefore, if you use Xalan release 1.2.2, you should use it together with Xerces release 1.2.2.

As the book goes to press, Xalan 2.0.1 has just become available. This release of Xalan was tested only with Xerces 1.3.0, so if you use Xalan release 2.0.1, you should use it together with Xerces release 1.3.0. The rest of this chapter mainly discusses Xerces 1 and Xalan 1, while noting some differences you will encounter in Xerces 2 and Xalan 2. In Section 4.5, "Installing Xalan," you can find some information about using Xalan 2 with the Web application project for this book.

Please note that you do not actually have to download a Xerces distribution in order to run the Web application project for this book. This applies to the Xerces 1.2.3 distribution if you will use Xalan 1.2.2. It also applies to the Xerces 1.3.0 distribution if you will use Xalan 2.0.1. This is because every Xalan distribution includes the right Xerces JAR file to use with its Xalan JAR file. Actually, the only reason we suggest downloading a Xerces distribution in this chapter is so you can learn more about it and use all its features in your own projects.

The Xerces release we will discuss here has two installation files for Windows—one for binaries and one for sources. These installation files, totaling roughly 3MB, have the following names:

xerces-J-bin.1.2.2.zip
xerces-J-src.1.2.2.zip

You will find these installation files on the CD-ROM accompanying this book. You can also download them by following the links from the Apache XML Web site at

```
http://xml.apache.org
```

Unzip both installation files so that everything ends up in a folder named xerces-1_2_2 under your root drive. If you unzip into your root folder, be sure that the Use Folder Names checkbox is selected. Check all the pathnames in the zip files to make sure that no files will end up in the root folder.

We will assume that XERCES_HOME=C:\xerces-1_2_2. If that is not true for you, please take that into consideration as you read this book. We will note some differences we have found while using Xerces 1.3.0 with Xalan 2.0.1.

There is a lot of helpful information about Xerces in the Xerces Java Parser Readme, which you can browse starting at the following file:

C:\xerces-1_2_2\Readme.html

4.2.1 Xerces JAR File

If you are using Xerces release 1.2.2, do not put the xerces.jar file in the extension folder for the JDK runtime environment. It is true that Java automatically finds JAR files put in that folder. However, you should not put JAR files that rely upon native methods there.

When we did put the Xerces 1.2.2 JAR file in the ext folder, we had no problem until we tried to start the Tomcat Server. It would not start. It would not stop either if we put the JAR file in the ext folder after starting Tomcat. We got the following error:

```
java.lang.ClassNotFoundException: com.sun.xml.parser.Parser
```

If you are using Xerces 1.2.2 with Tomcat 3.2, the easiest way to get access to Xerces from your Tomcat Web applications is by copying C:\xerces-1_2_2\xerces.jar into the TOMCAT_HOME\lib folder. Tomcat will then automatically add this JAR file to its classpath while starting.

This did not work for us with Xerces and Tomcat 3.1. With that Tomcat version (and also with Tomcat 3.2), you can use different solution. Simply add one line to the following file:

TOMCAT_HOME\bin\tomcat.bat

After the existing line in that file that adds tools.jar to the classpath, add another line that adds the xerces.jar file, like this:

```
set CLASSPATH=%CLASSPATH%;%JAVA_HOME%\lib\tools.jar
set CLASSPATH=%CLASSPATH%;c:\xerces-1_2_2\xerces.jar
```

> **Warning**
>
> If you want to use the Xerces 1.3.0 JAR file because you are using the Xalan Java 2.0.1 JAR file, disregard the advice just given. In this case, as we found out the hard way, you SHOULD put both JAR files in the JDK extension folder (along with the Xalan 1 compatibility JAR, xalanj1compat.jar). If you put these JAR files into the tomcat lib folder, you will get an HTTP error 500 with a SAXException when our project tries to use Xalan Java 2.

4.2.2 Xerces Documentation

After you install Xerces on your system, you will have available to you a wealth of information about how to use it. The starting URL for its documentation will be something like this:

c:\xerces-1_2_2\Readme.html

If you are online, hyperlinks in this Xerces documentation will let you browse much important XML-related documentation on the Internet.

The documentation also includes the API Javadocs for DOM and SAX. As you may know, these are the two major approaches to parsing XML, both of which are implemented by Xerces. We will summarize both for you briefly.

DOM parsers are based on the Document Object Model. This approach models an XML document as a tree structure containing nodes for each part (element, attribute, text, processing instruction, and so on). DOM parsers read an entire XML document and construct a tree of node objects in memory. An application can then access and process this tree, which resides in memory, as a model of the XML document.

SAX parsers instead use an event-based model to parse XML. A SAX parser reads through an XML document and "fires" events particular to each part of the document it encounters (element, attribute, text, processing instruction, and so on). An application adds event-handling code to access and process the XML document. Note that SAX parsers can work on a file incrementally, requiring much less memory than DOM parsers, and allowing larger XML files to be parsed with a given amount of memory.

In the Xerces documentation you can also find discussions of the eight samples included with the distribution, as well as a FAQ that provides answers to some common questions.

A comprehensive discussion of XML is beyond the scope of this book. Fortunately, there exist many excellent sources of XML information, which are frequently updated. Chapter 12, "Online Information Sources," lists various Web sources that can help you begin or advance your understanding of XML. We also recommend *Inside XML* by Steven Holzner, published by New Riders.

4.3 Xerces Parses XML

We use Xerces in our Web application project, but we exercise only some of its potential. It is used as a DOM parser to parse XML in files and strings. The project also uses the Xalan XSLT processor, which in turn uses Xerces as its XML parser.

We will give a few suggestions for ways you can familiarize yourself with concepts and code that we make use of in the book project.

4.3.1 Xerces Samples

Definitely, your first experiences with Xerces should be with the sample programs provided with the distribution. Start by clicking the Samples hyperlink on the top-level page of the HTML documentation. For the purposes of understanding this book, the most important of the sample programs is DOMWriter.

Try all the samples, and be sure to look at their source code as well. You will find that using them as skeleton code will save you time when you develop your own code. Just be sure to give credit where credit is due, and follow the Apache License stipulations.

In our book project, we got a big head start by using some of the code from DOMWriter.java. We are grateful to the developers for making their sources available to the worldwide developer community, and we urge our readers to consider the advantages of open source software development. Check out the Internet links for "Open Source" in Chapter 12 to get more information about the open source movement and its guiding philosophy.

4.3.2 Studying the API Javadocs

When you browse the API Javadocs, be aware that for the purposes of this book you can concentrate your attention on the following two packages:

org.w3c.dom

org.apache.xerces.dom

The interfaces in the org.w3c.dom package give you a feel for the DOM approach to parsing and representing XML. The org.apache.xerces.dom package shows you one of the technical "hearts" of the Xerces product.

4.3.3 Studying the Source Code

One of the best ways to learn programming is to read lots of good code. If you only look at the top-level descriptions and documentation for a software project, you are looking at entities that intentionally shield you from the details. That is very useful, of course, and is a faster way to get the big picture. However, when you have to write details yourself, it is useful to have seen a lot of similar ones. The problem, then, is to decide where to begin in a project such as Xerces, which contains a wealth of code.

We suggest that if you want to study some of the source code for Xerces, begin with the files from the same two packages that we recommended for API Javadoc browsing—namely, the Java files in the following two folders (assuming the "normal" drive and top-level Xerces folder):

C:\xerces-1_2_2\src\org\w3c\dom

C:\xerces-1_2_2\src\org\apache\xerces\dom

The first of these packages sets up the interfaces that define a way to represent XML (and HTML) in software. The second package does the work of making this plan happen. The following two lists contain source code files that are good to start with. As you can see, there are many paired methods in the two packages. The first list is of source from the org.w3c.dom package:

Document.java

Node.java

Element.java

Attr.java

The next list is of source files from the org.apache.xerces.dom package that we feel should be studied initially:

DocumentImpl.java

NodeImpl.java

ElementImpl.java

AttrImpl.java

In node.java, you can see all the node types that make up the DOM view of an XML document:

```
public interface Node {
// NodeType
public static final short ELEMENT_NODE = 1;
public static final short ATTRIBUTE_NODE = 2;
public static final short TEXT_NODE = 3;
public static final short CDATA_SECTION_NODE = 4;
public static final short ENTITY_REFERENCE_NODE = 5;
public static final short ENTITY_NODE = 6;
public static final short PROCESSING_INSTRUCTION_NODE = 7;
public static final short COMMENT_NODE = 8;
public static final short DOCUMENT_NODE = 9;
public static final short DOCUMENT_TYPE_NODE = 10;
public static final short DOCUMENT_FRAGMENT_NODE = 11;
public static final short NOTATION_NODE = 12;
```

4.3.4 Compiling and Running IBM Samples

We found a useful IBM tutorial on XML programming with Java at the following Web address:

```
http://www-4.ibm.com/software/developer/education/xmljava/xmljava-6-3.html
```

It turned out to be quite easy to compile Java programs in that tutorial, such as domOne.java. All we had to do was substitute import org.apache.xerces.parsers.* for import com.ibm.xml.parsers.*. The kinship between the IBM and Apache parsers came in handy.

One important point to note is that when dealing with DOM, the natural thing is to apply a recursive method. This shows the advantage of the self-similarity property of a tree structure. The document is a node, and you call a method with that as an argument. Then you call the method with the document-element. At that point, you can iterate through its children, and to each of these apply the same method. These points are illustrated in the IBM sample domOne.java.

4.4 SAX Sees XML as Events

We will barely mention the SAX processing capabilities of the Xerces-J Java class library, because we have not made use of them in the Web application project for this book. However, when you are developing XML applications, you will definitely want to familiarize yourself with this alternative (complement?) to the DOM parsing methodology.

The most compelling reason to use SAX parsers is their reduced memory requirement relative to DOM parsers (as discussed earlier, in the section "Xerces Documentation"). Creating a DOM for very large XML files would use a vast quantity of memory, whereas a SAX parser can handle files incrementally. SAX parsing also tends to be faster. A third advantage is often the familiarity of its event-driven processing to developers.

4.4.1 Xerces and Megginson SAX

Besides the information contained in the Xerces documentation, you can also get information about the SAX parser from the Web site of David Megginson, who led its development on the XML_DEV mailing list. Try the following URL:

```
http://www.megginson.com
```

A Javadoc online there is a useful overview of SAX technology. You can find it at

```
http://www.megginson.com/SAX/Java/javadoc/index.html
```

We tried Xerces with a code example called "Quick Start for SAX Application Writers" from the Megginson Web site. The only change we had to make to adapt the code to Xerces was to the following line:

```
static final String parserClass = "com.microstar.xml.SAXDriver";
```

Here is the replacement line that allowed us to use Xerces:

```
static final String parserClass = "org.apache.xerces.parsers.SAXParser";
```

4.5 Installing Xalan

The XSL processor that we will use is part of Xalan. We have upgraded the version of Xalan that we work with several times, just as we did with Xerces. While we developed the software for this book, the latest stable release of Xerces for Java was 1.2.2.

Xalan Java 2 is now available—its latest release at press time is 2.0.1. Again, we usually recommend that you adopt the latest stable releases as soon as possible. Although Xalan Java 2 includes some major changes with respect to Xalan Java 1, these changes have had a relatively minor impact upon the book project because it only uses Xalan and Xerces for simple parsing and transformation tasks.

> **Xalan Java 1 or 2?**
> You can use either Xalan Java 1 or Xalan Java 2 with the book project. Of course, the latter has not been tested much yet—hopefully it will work as well on your system as on ours. For the latest information regarding this and other updates of Apache software as they relate to the book project, please visit the bonForum Project Web site:
>
> `http://www.bonforum.org`

We have made some late changes to the book project to allow the use of Xalan Java 2, release 2.0.1. However, little time was available for testing that, nor for changing the text. Some readers will prefer to keep using Xalan Java 1 until the bug list for version 2 gets a bit shorter. For now, we have simply put a checkbox near the beginning of the application to allow you to run the project in either its "Xalan Java 1" mode or its "Xalan Java 2" mode.

If you do want to use Xalan 2, first check on the CD-ROM, which might have more up-to-date information than here, and where you can find the latest Xalan release available to us. Basically, as we write this, you have three options with regard to Xalan and the bonForum book project Web app:

1. Use bonForum only in "Xalan Java 1" mode. First place two Xalan 1.2.2 JAR files (xalan.jar and xerces.jar) in the Tomcat lib folder (TOMCAT_HOME\lib). This is an easy choice, unless you need to use Xalan Java 2 (and its Xerces JAR). Do not put the Xalan 1.2.2 JAR files in the JDK extension folder.
2. Use bonForum in either "Xalan Java 1" or "Xalan Java 2" mode. First place three Xalan 2.0.1 JAR files (xalanj1compat.jar, xalan.jar, and xerces.jar) in the JDK extension folder (for example, C:\jdk1.3\jre\lib\ext). The Xalan 1 compatibility JAR allows you to run software designed for Xalan 1, together with Xalan 2. Do not put the Xalan 2.0.1 JARs in the Tomcat lib folder.

The only disadvantage to the second option is that the following discussion in this chapter is based on Xalan 1.2.2 and will not always apply to Xalan 2. We will note some differences.

Xalan Java 1, release 1.2.2, has only one installation file for Windows, which includes both the binaries and the sources. That installation file has the following name:

xalan-j_1_2_2.zip

This installation file is included on the CD-ROM accompanying this book. You can also download it from the Apache XML download page, which can be reached from the main Web site at

```
http://xml.apache.org
```

Unzip the installation file so that everything ends up in a folder named xalan-j_1_2_2 under your root drive. If you unzip into your root folder, be sure that the Use Folder

Names checkbox is selected. Check all the pathnames in the zip file to make sure that no files will end up in the root folder.

We will assume that XALAN_HOME=C:\xalan-j_1_2_2. If that is not true for you, please take that into consideration as you read this book.

There is a lot of helpful information about Xalan in the "Xalan Overview," which you can browse by starting at the following file:

C:\xalan-j_1_2_2\README.html

4.5.1 Xalan JAR File

Do not put the Xalan 1.2.2 JAR files in the ext folder for the JDK runtime environment. If you do put it there, you will not have any problems using the Xalan parser in some situations, such as from the command line. However, when it comes time to use it from a JSP, as we do several places in our Web application project for the book, you will get an HTTP 500 internal servlet error.

If you are using Xalan 1.2.2 with Tomcat 3.2, the easiest way to get access to Xerces from your Tomcat Web applications is by copying both C:\xalan-j_1_2_2\xalan.jar and C:\xalan-j_1_2_2\xerces.jar into the TOMCAT_HOME\lib folder. Tomcat will then automatically add these two JAR files to its classpath while starting. Note that if you added a Xerces JAR file to this lib folder earlier in this chapter, you will want to overwrite it with this Xerces JAR file from the Xalan distribution (see the next section).

This solution did not work for us with Tomcat 3.1 (as discussed in the earlier section "Xerces JAR File"). With that version (and also Tomcat 3.2), you can use a different solution—simply add one line to the following file:

TOMCAT_HOME\bin\tomcat.bat

After the existing line that puts tools.jar on the classpath, make sure there are two lines that put both xerces.jar and xalan.jar on the classpath, like this:

```
set CLASSPATH=%CLASSPATH%;%JAVA_HOME%\lib\tools.jar
set CLASSPATH=%CLASSPATH%;c:\xalan-j_1_2_2\xerces.jar
set CLASSPATH=%CLASSPATH%;c:\xalan-j_1_2_2\xalan.jar
```

This will cause some extra work when you want to access Xalan from outside of Tomcat Web applications. For example, when you run Xalan from the command line (see the later section "Using Xalan from the Command Line"), both the Xerces and Xalan JAR files must be on the classpath.

Warning

If you want to use the Xalan Java 2.0.1 JAR file, and its companion Xerces 1.3.0 JAR file, disregard the advice just given. In this case, as we found out the hard way, you SHOULD put both JAR files in the JDK extension folder (along with the Xalan 1 compatibility JAR, "xalanj1compat.jar"). If you put these JAR files into the Tomcat lib folder, you will get an HTTP error 500 with a SAXException when our project tries to use Xalan Java 2.

4.5.2 Matching Xalan and Xerces Versions

In the last batch file editing example, we made sure the folder for xerces.jar was the xalan-j_1_2_2 folder. Using the xerces.jar file that comes with the Xalan download ensures that you will still be using the correct Xerces version for the Xalan version you are using, even if someone changes the Xerces distribution.

Changing to a newer version of Xalan usually requires a newer Xerces. The xerces.jar file included with the Xalan download takes care of that in most situations, but unless you have a reason not to, it is probably best to keep the entire distribution sets for both Xalan and Xerces synchronized.

4.5.3 Xalan Documentation

Xalan is distributed with lots of information about how to use it. The documentation also includes the API Javadoc for Xalan Java, which includes two groups of packages—one for XPATH and the other for XSLT. (Note that Xalan 2 added and removed packages and rearranged everything!) Also documented are the sample applications using Xalan, which are available for you to try. In addition, a FAQ answers some common questions. The starting URL for the documentation will be something like the following:

c:\xalan-j_1_2_2\README.html

If you are online, hyperlinks on the Overview page will let you browse much important XSLT and XPATH documentation on the Internet. Comprehensive discussions of XSLT and XPATH are beyond the scope of this book. Fortunately, many excellent sources include that information. Chapter 12 lists various Web sources that can help you begin or advance your understanding of XSLT and XPATH. Again, we also recommend *Inside XML* by Steven Holzner, published by New Riders.

4.6 Xalan Transforms XML Using XSLT

We use Xalan in the Web application project with this book, but only (at the present time) for its XSLT processing capabilities. As we did for Xerces, we will give you a few suggestions to help you familiarize yourself with concepts and code that we make use of in the book project.

4.6.1 Xalan Samples

After you have Xalan installed, your next step should be to try the samples provided with the distribution. First choose Sample Apps from the documentation's menu. Although you will gain much from trying all the samples, for the purposes of this book it is sufficient to try only these two:

SimpleTransform

TransformToDom

Be sure to also read the source code for the samples. As with Xerces, you can certainly find ways to jump-start your own development efforts by taking advantage of the information that is provided with the source code. Just be sure to give credit to the developers, and follow the stipulations of the Apache License.

4.6.2 Studying the API Javadocs

When you browse the API Javadoc for Xalan Java 1, be aware that for the purposes of this book you can concentrate your attention on just one package:

org.apache.xalan.xslt

The most important Javadoc page to study in this package is the one for the `XSLTProcessor` interface. In particular, you should read about its `process` method. You can find lots of concise information about the process of transforming XML with XSL stylesheets by clicking the Description hyperlinks on two of the Javadoc pages: the Overview page for Xalan-Java and the Package page for the org.apache.xalan.xslt package.

Much has been done to shield you as a developer from the nasty details. Click the `XSLTProcessorImpl` hyperlink on the page for the `XSLTProcessor` class, and you will see what we mean!

As mentioned earlier, much is changed in Xalan 2, which handles XSLT processing using a different approach. One way to get a quick view of the changes is by following the What's New link from the Xalan 2 documentation Web page:

`http://xml.apache.org/xalan-j/index.html`

4.6.3 Studying the Source Code

If you are going to spend time studying the source code for Xalan, we recommend that you concentrate your efforts on Xalan Java 2, because it will better prepare you to join in the efforts of the Apache XML Project! If you also want a quick look at some source code for Xalan 1, begin with the files from the same package we recommended for API Javadoc browsing—namely, the Java files in the following folder (assuming the "normal" drive and top-level Xalan folder):

C:\xalan-j_1_2_2\src\org\apache\xalan\xslt

Again, as in the API documentation, you will see that considerable complexity is involved in this package. However, you can stay away from that by only examining the source files for the top-level interfaces. We suggest that you look only at the files included in the following group:

C:\xalan-j_1_2_2\src\org\apache\xalan\xslt\XSLT*.java

The code in XSLTEngineImpl.java is probably the most important in the entire package, because it is how Xalan accomplishes transformation of XML. However, it could take a while to understand everything in that one source code file!

4.7 Using Beanshell with Xalan

We had a lot of fun using the Beanshell to learn about Xalan. In Chapter 2, "An Environment for Java Software Development," we mentioned the Beanshell as a plug-in for the ElixirIDE, called bsh.jar. Look in the ElixirIDE documentation for instructions on installing the plug-in. You will then have a tabbed panel in ElixirIDE with a Beanshell console where you can interactively execute Java statements. That is how we use Beanshell, but you can also obtain, for free, a stand-alone version. Whether you use it through ElixirIDE or by itself, you'll want to check out the exciting uses for this great tool by visiting the Beanshell Web site, which is at the following URL:

```
http://www.beanshell.org
```

We highly recommend the Beanshell approach to building applications. Interactive environments are also ideal for learning about third-party software components, because they let you quickly answer questions and follow up discoveries as soon as they are made.

For example, we took some code from the Xalan 1.2.2 documentation and used the Beanshell to step through it one line at a time. The code, which is supposed to be compiled, illustrates the use of the trace facility that is built into Xalan. You can see the original code by browsing a URL something like the following:

file://C:/xalan-j_1_2_2/docs/usagepatterns.html#debugging

The following is a transcript (console command history) of our interactive Beanshell session. Note that we did have to add the last three `import` statements, which were not in the Xalan sample code:

```
import org.apache.xalan.xslt.XSLTProcessor;
import org.apache.xalan.xslt.trace.PrintTraceListener;
import org.apache.xalan.xslt.XSLTProcessorFactory;
import org.apache.xalan.xslt.XSLTInputSource;
import org.apache.xalan.xslt.XSLTResultTarget;
java.io.FileWriter fw = new java.io.FileWriter("c:\\temp\\events.log");
java.io.PrintWriter pw = new java.io.PrintWriter(fw);
PrintTraceListener ptl = new PrintTraceListener(pw);
ptl.m_traceElements = true;
ptl.m_traceGeneration = true;
ptl.m_traceSelection = true;
ptl.m_traceTemplates = true;
XSLTProcessor processor = XSLTProcessorFactory.getProcessor();
processor.addTraceListener(ptl);
String xmlFile = "c:\\temp\\foo.xml";
String xslFile = "c:\\temp\\foo.xsl";
String targetFile = "c:\\temp\\foo.out";
XSLTInputSource xmlIn = new XSLTInputSource(xmlFile);
XSLTInputSource xslIn = new XSLTInputSource(xslFile);
XSLTResultTarget targetOut = new XSLTResultTarget(targetFile);
processor.process(xmlIn, xslIn, targetOut);
pw.close();
fw.close();
```

Note that you must use \\ instead of \ in the file path strings. You will get an error if you instead try something like this:

```
java.io.FileWriter fw = new java.io.FileWriter("c:\temp\events.log");
```

If you try this example, be sure to take a look at the events.log produced by this session, as well as the target file. Of course, where the use of the Beanshell really makes sense is during the development of your own classes. The example we just gave is a rather contrived example of its use, but we selected it because it is "on topic" here. Hopefully it is less confusing out of context than some other trials we made.

4.8 Using Xalan from the Command Line

Choose the Command Line menu item in the Xalan documentation to find out how to use the Xalan command-line utility. Be sure to check out the many options available, which you can also see by entering the processing command line without any arguments at all.

This utility is a great way to set up a fast interactive session for learning XSLT and XPATH. We have made use of Xalan from the command line in several ways. One way, discussed later in the book, was to develop the XSL style sheets that we use in the Web application project for this book.

Another way we used "command-line Xalan" was to organize the many notes we took while doing online research for this book. These notes were kept in XML files, each item within paired XML tags. Our tags established a hierarchical classification system of topics based on our initial outline for the book. After the research, we wrote some style sheets to select notes for each chapter and section of the book. We used Xalan from the command line to extract the notes into separate files. This was an extremely convincing XSLT exercise!

4.9 Zvon XSL Tutorial

We found online an excellent tool for learning XSLT and XPATH. It is an interactive tutorial. You can either use it online or download it for use on your own system. The URL when we visited was as follows:

```
http://zvon.vscht.cz/HTMLonly/XSLTutorial
```

You might want to try browsing the main Web site page to see the other tutorials and information available at this interesting Web site:

```
http://zvon.vscht.cz
```

4.10 Xerces and Xalan versus XT and XP

We were curious to see how the XSLT transformation examples would work with Xerces and Xalan, instead of XT and XP, which were used in the Zvon tutorial just discussed. So we used the Xalan command-line utility to replicate some of the transformations. We found only two minor differences. This was a while ago, so the newer versions might do even better. You can expect a convergence of functionality among the leading XML parsers and XSL processors, with the possible exception of the Microsoft ones.

4.11 JSP and XML Synergy

Because the focus of our book includes JSP as well as XML, it is interesting to look for the possible synergy between the JSP technology and the XML-related technologies. We should see what support for XML there is in the JSP implementation available to us, which is version JSP1.1. We can get the best information, right from the horse's mouth, at the following Web address:

```
http://java.sun.com/products/jsp/
```

The JavaServer Pages 1.1 Specification of November 30, 1999 (JSP 1.1) only begins to deliver on two powerful planned features. The first is that XML tools will be able to create, open, and edit JSP pages in their new XML representation. The second is that JSP tools will then accept these XML "formatted" JSP files.

4.11.1 XML Compatibility of JSP

Most, but not all, of the JSP syntax is XML-compliant. Specifically, most JSP content can be contained between valid XML tags. But the "original" syntax for JSP has some other elements that are not valid XML. One example of this is the way JSP allows elements for its scripting and directives, which is for the page author to include such content within opening and closing <% and %> tokens.

There are other XML "incompatibilities" about JSP as well. One is that an XML file can have only one root element, but a JSP maintains more than one layer of information on a page by using more than one tree. An XML parser will not ignore a tag that it doesn't know, but a JSP container must do so. In order for you to use a left-angle-bracket character in an XML document without the parser seeing it as a tag-opening token, the left-angle-bracket character must be put inside a `CDATA` element. In JSP, you can put the left-angle-bracket character within the <% and %> without a problem.

The JSP 1.1 specification did not try to get rid of these differences in syntax. Instead, the step it took was to define an XML representation of a JSP page. It is therefore now possible to convert a JSP page into an XML page and to convert such an "XML" JSP page back into "real" JSP. This means that JSP-enabled servers will be able to accept JSP content represented in XML.

How does the translation of JSP into an XML-compliant form work? First, in order to satisfy the "one root" rule of XML, the process of translating a JSP page into XML begins by "encapsulating" the JSP content in a single root XML element like this:

```
<jsp:root xmlns:jsp=http://java.sun.com/products/jsp/dtd/jsp_1_0.dtd>
All the JSP stuff goes here...
</jsp:root>
```

Note that in the opening tag, a namespace is declared for the JSP prefix. The rest of the translation of "normal" JSP syntax into acceptable XML syntax uses that JSP prefix.

4.11.2 Putting Java Code in XML

We will not describe all the mechanics of the translation process just discussed. You can read about that in the specification. Here is one example, though, that shows the plan. Let's say you have scriptlet code in its JSP representation:

```
<% Code Goes Here %>
```

To translate it to an XML representation, you need to create a prefixed element as follows:

```
<jsp:scriptlet> Code Goes Here </jsp:scriptlet>
```

Note that you can therefore use JSP tags to put Java code in an XML document.

4.11.3 Creating XML with JSP

You can include XML in a JavaServer Page as part of its passive template content. It will then be output to a browser just as HTML tagged content is. Perhaps more useful is to define some custom JSP tags, or a bean object, that will put your XML into the JSPWriter output from the compiled JSP.

5 bonForum Chat Application: Use and Design

THIS CHAPTER INTRODUCES YOU TO BONFORUM, the Web chat application that will be the major subject of the rest of the book. bonForum was designed as a tool to explore each of the subjects of this book, XML, XSLT, Java servlets, Java applets, and JavaServer Pages, while solving some real Web application problems.

5.1 Installing and Running bonForum

You can understand the remainder of this book much more easily if you have installed and tried out the Web chat application that it features. Therefore, we begin this chapter with instructions for installing and running bonForum.

5.1.1 A Preview of the Rest of the Book

After helping you install and try bonForum, this chapter gives you some hints about how you can customize bonForum and develop it further yourself. After that, we discuss the design process. This chapter ends with some additional material about using XML data in Web applications.

The next chapter continues this overview of the entire bonForum project and begins by describing the implementation that our design led us to develop. That chapter ends with highlights of some of the major problems that we encountered, together with solutions found and solutions planned.

In Chapters 7–11, we cover in detail the code that we developed as we created this prototype for a multiuser, server-based Web application. Each of those chapters focuses on a different software technology that we applied to create the bonForum Web chat and uses excerpts from the source code to illustrate the discussion.

At the end of the book, you will find a listing of Web sources that might help you as you further explore the subjects of this book or as you try to fill in the gaps in its coverage of those subjects. Appendix A, "CD-ROM Contents," shows you what is on the book's accompanying CD. Finally, in the back of this book you'll find the full source code for the bonForum project, with all its warts and wrinkles.

5.1.2 Checking Tomcat Server Availability

If you have read this far in the book, you likely have realized that to develop Web applications using Tomcat Server, you will need to have one available that you are free to use as a developer. Quite a few network and machine setups exist—some quite complex—that enable you to develop and test Tomcat Web applications. Some installations, for example, might feature several Tomcat Servers being used by developers, even while other Tomcat Servers are running deployed applications over the Internet or an intranet.

To avoid introducing such complexity into the discussion, we usually assume that you have full access rights to a Tomcat Server that is on the same domain as the browsers that you will be using to test the bonForum Web application. We usually will not be giving URL examples that include domain names. We always assume that you have the freedom to stop and restart the Tomcat Server and to edit and add files to its directory space.

Instructions for getting, installing, and running Tomcat Server are covered in Chapter 3,"Java Servlets and JavaServer Pages—Jakarta Tomcat." You will need to have a suitable Java SDK installed on the Tomcat Server machine to use JSP and, therefore, to use the bonForum Web chat application.

> **Port Number for Tomcat**
>
> Throughout this book, we assume that your Tomcat Server is configured to use its default port number, port 8080. If that is not the case, you will need to change that in the examples given to the port number that you are using. If you are accessing Tomcat through another Web server, such as Apache Server, you might need no port number at all.

Trying the Tomcat Examples

First, be sure that you have a Tomcat Server installed and running on your system. You can verify this by using your browser to display the HTML document that gives access to the JSP and Java servlet examples packaged with Tomcat. If the browser is on the same host as Tomcat, first try to browse the following URL:

```
http://localhost:8080
```

If the browser that you are using is on a different host from Tomcat, you should instead use one similar to this one for a host named Freedom:

```
http://freedom:8080
```

Using IP Address Instead of Hostnames

With Internet Explorer 5.*X*, you can use a URL with the hostname even for the local host. However, we tried without success in our Netscape browser to use both of the previous address examples to browse the bonForum Web application. After that failure, we ran the ntconfig.exe program from an NT command window. That gave us the IP address for the machine on which Netscape was running, and we put that in the URL instead. That gave us an address like the following:

```
http://192.168.165.99:8080
```

That URL worked for Netscape and brought up the Examples Web page for the Tomcat Server. At least we knew then that the problem was a result of using the domain name form for the address. However, the bonForum application then ran only until it needed to use frames on a page, when it displayed instead our (nonfunctional) noframes.html link, which is for browsers that are not frames-capable or that have frames capability turned off.

To avoid wasting effort, we decided to postpone handling cross-browser compatibility issues until we had settled on a final user interface. We stayed with our plan to make Internet Explorer 5.*X* the only browser until after extensive testing of a prototype.

When Tomcat Server Is Not a Standalone Server

You might be running another Web server besides Tomcat—for example, Apache Server or Microsoft IIS. If so—and if you have configured it to use the Tomcat Server to handle JSP and Java servlet requests, and if you have also configured it to use Tomcat for requests whose paths begin with /examples—then you can test the Tomcat Server by requesting its Examples Web app through the "main" Web server. To do so, you browse a URL like one of the following:

```
http://localhost/examples
http://freedom/examples/
```

Many possible ways exist to set up Tomcat as the Java servlet container for another Web server. Therefore, the best advice that we can give you is that you should review the information about setting up Tomcat with Apache Server, found in the document "Tomcat—A Minimalistic User's Guide." That very helpful guide is supplied with the Tomcat Server download in the file TOMCAT_HOME\doc\uguide\tomcat_ug.html.

TOMCAT_HOME is the path to the folder where you installed Tomcat Server. On our system, it is c:\jakarta-tomcat. Of course, you will need to substitute your own Tomcat Server home folder path in the previous URL, as in many others in this book.

5.1.3 Installation as a Tomcat Web App

The most convenient way to install a Web application for Tomcat is as a single compressed file containing all the required files. In reality, such a file is just a .zip file, but the convention is for it to have a filename extension of .war. We have provided our chat room example on the accompanying CD in a .war file called bonForum.war.

Installing bonForum could not be simpler. First, make sure that there is not a folder with the name TOMCAT_HOME\webapps\bonForum on the server with Tomcat. If this folder exists, then it must be deleted before the new bonForum.war distribution file is used.

Copy the bonForum.war file into the Webapps folder under your TOMCAT_HOME folder. For example, if your Tomcat was installed with a TOMCAT_HOME of c:\jakarta-tomcat, then you should end up with c:\jakarta-tomcat\webapps\bonForum.war.

If the Tomcat Server is running, shut it down using the shutdown.bat command file in the TOMCAT_HOME\bin folder. When you restart Tomcat, it will find the .war file and automatically unzip it under the Webapps folder into its own folder named bonForum. On the NT command window for Tomcat Server, you now should find a line something like the following:

```
2001-03-09 02:11:55 - ContextManager: Adding context Ctx( /bonForum )
```

Tomcat assumes that a .zip archive file that it finds in its Webapps folder is an archived Web application and automatically installs the context for it to run. There is also an alternate way to install a Web application, by entering some information about it into the server.xml Tomcat configuration file, which is found in the TOMCAT_HOME\conf folder. You will need to use this nonautomatic installation method for either or both of two reasons: First, you want to install a nonarchived Web application. Second, you want to specify values for some Web application settings (such as `docBase`) that differ from the default values.

5.1.4 Running bonForum

You should now be able to begin your tour of the bonForum Web chat by browsing a URL something like one of the following (with or without the 8080 port number):

```
http://localhost:8080/bonForum
http://balderdash:8080/bonForum
http://192.168.165.99:8080/bonForum
```

That should display in your browser the default document for the bonForum Web application, the file TOMCAT_HOME\\webapps\bonForum\index.html. Click the bonForum logo to start the Web application on your browser. The bonForum user interface is simple enough, so little help is needed for you to try it out now. If you need help, you can look ahead to Chapter 7, "JavaServer Pages: The Browseable User Interface."

Here are a few tips to get you started:

- Don't expect a polished application or user interface. This is an experimental prototype, and you will find problems to solve.
- First try becoming a host by starting a chat; otherwise, you might find no chats listed for you to join.
- Start up a second browser, on the same host or another that can access the Web app. Become a guest on the chat you are hosting.
- Nicknames in bonForum must be unique. If one is rejected, try again. There are no messages yet to explain the rejection.
- You may or may not need to download or configure the Java plug-in. Enabling Java Console for Plug-in might provide help.
- Using the browser's Back arrow is not always convenient here. Exit or reenter a new nickname instead.
- You may get frequent errors regarding .gif files on the console output. This is a harmless problem often reported with Tomcat 3.2.

5.1.5 First JSP Requests Require Patience

Be patient. Especially if you are running your computer at nearly its limit for memory and machine cycle resources, be patient. You will experience user-unfriendly delays. Your computer might need to find and start up a new Java virtual machine and then load all the classes it needs to compile JSP files into Java `HTTPServlet` class files. Each new JSP file that it encounters will need to be compiled, which takes time. After compilation, JSP can output HTML to your browser at a much more exciting tempo.

Here are two thoughts to keep in mind whenever you first try using any Web application that uses JSP technology:

- Be patient! Compiling takes time, and a JavaServer Page will not thrill you with its speed the first time a browser requests it.
- Users will not experience JSP compilation delays if you make sure to visit all the JSP documents in the application when you deploy it.

5.1.6 One Java Applet and the Sun Java Plug-In

Perhaps you already have the Sun Java Plug-in installed on the machine with the browser, for example, from this book's CD-ROM. In that case, there will be some delay while it starts up the BonForumRobot Java applet that is used by bonForum. This delay happens only once—each time you start the bonForum application on the server, which happens automatically whenever Tomcat Server is restarted. Depending on how your Sun Plug-in is configured, starting up the applet can take quite some time.

However, if you do not yet have the Sun Plug-in installed on the machine on which the browser is running, you will be asked to approve its download from the Sun Web site. Before you OK that, be aware that this might require quite some time if you have a slow connection to the Internet. You will not be able to run this version of the bonForum Web chat without having the Sun Java plug-in available. For more on that, see Chapter 9, "Java Applet Plugged In: BonForumRobot."

Non-Applet Version of bonForum

Some people have objected to the use of an applet in bonForum and would rather see a purely server-side chat solution. That would require replacing our applet-based mechanism for refreshing user interface content (chat messages and so on) with different mechanisms that are not based upon an applet. In fact, our first version of bonForum did work without an applet (using the refresh Pragma), but the flashing of the refresh bothered us, so we went to the BonForumRobot applet solution.

5.1.7 Frames and Tables Required

The browser that you use to enter bonForum must be capable of displaying HTML tables and frames. Again, we "certify" bonForum use only with the IE5.X browsers, in which that is not a problem. It would be possible to have a version of bonForum that does not require tables or frames. In fact, we also began the project without either tables or frames, but we found the results to be less than satisfactory.

5.1.8 Problems Running bonForum

Perhaps the most common problem encountered while trying to install and run a new Java application is that it throws the `java.lang.NoClassDefFoundError` exception. If you did not tell Tomcat where to find the Apache Xerces XML package correctly, for example, you will not get far into bonForum before you encounter such an exception. Such exceptions should be politely shown to the user on an error page, and Tomcat has a facility for doing that. We did not add "polite" error handling to bonForum yet, so you will get the following rude message on your browser instead:

```
Error: 500
Location: /bonForum/servlet/BonForumEngine
Internal Servlet Error:
java.lang.NoClassDefFoundError: org/apache/xerces/framework/XMLParser
at java.lang.Class.newInstance0(Native Method)
at java.lang.Class.newInstance(Class.java:237)
at org.apache.tomcat.core.ServletWrapper.initServlet(
ServletWrapper.java:298)
```

The result of this error is that you cannot proceed; you must quit the application and fix the classpath problem.

5.2 Changing the bonForum Web Application

Although you might want to wait until you have read the rest of this book before editing and recompiling the source for the bonForum project, we feel certain that you will be sorely tempted to do so at some point. The software contains many loose ends and potential bugs that will no doubt aggravate you, and fixing these can be valuable learning experiences. (We would like very much to hear of these—you can email us at `email@bonforum.org`).

5.2.1 Compilation of Java Source

See Chapter 2, "An Environment for Java Programming," for help in setting up the necessary tools to compile this Web application. All the Java source code files for the de.tarent.forum package are found in the folder TOMCAT_HOME\webapps\bonForum\web-inf\src\.

You can configure your IDE to compile these and place the compiled class files into the folder where they will be used. An alternative is to run the BonMakeIt.bat command file provided in the source folder. The compiled de.tarent.forum package (but not the bonForumRobot applet class) goes in the folder TOMCAT_HOME\webapps\bonForum\web-inf \classes\.

The Java source code files can be compiled in the following order, among others:

BonForumUtils.java

BonLogger.java

BonForumTagExtraInfo.java

OutputPathNamesTag.java

OutputChatMessagesTag.java

OutputDebugInfoTag.java

NoCacheHeaderTag.java

Xalan1Transformer.java

Xalan2Transformer.java

TransformTag.java

NodeKey.java

BonNode.java

ForestHashtable.java

BonForumStore.java

BonForumEngine.java

These Java files are not all there are, however. The source for the BonForumRobot applet source file can also be found in the folder TOMCAT_HOME\webapps\bonForum\web-inf\src\. Compile it after the others, and arrange to have its two compiled class files stored in the folder TOMCAT_HOME\webapps\bonForum\jsp\applet\.

5.2.2 Editing of JSP Files

To be accessed by Tomcat Server as part of the bonForum Web application, the JSP files for bonForum must be located in the folder TOMCAT_HOME \webapps\ bonForum\jsp\forum.

We have found the Textpad editor from Helios Software Solutions to be very convenient for editing the JSP files. A trial version has been included on the CD for this book, under the \tools folder. You can find out more about this editor at the following URL:

```
http://www.textpad.com
```

If you have already requested any JSP files from Tomcat Server using a browser, you can look in its work folder, which is called work (unless this default name has been changed in its server.xml configuration file). You will find a folder there for each context. For example, for the examples that come with Tomcat, you will find the folder TOMCAT_HOME\work\localhost_8080%2Fexamples.

Inside these Work subfolders, you will see some Java class files with long, strange names, such as this one:

```
_0002fjsp_0002fsnp_0002fsnoop_0002ejspsnoop_jsp_0.java
_0002fjsp_0002fsnp_0002fsnoop_0002ejspsnoop.class
```

These are the .java files and compiled .class files created by Tomcat from the JSP files. The first time that each JSP file is requested, it gets compiled and placed here, where it can then serve requests for the JSP file. If you make any changes to the JSP file, Tomcat creates a new .java and .class file, changing the numbers that are embedded in the long filenames. It is very instructive to look at the Java files that are produced in the Work subfolder in your favorite editor because you can experiment with using JSP files. Doing so can also help you understand the error messages that you get from JSP compilation because they have line numbers that you can look up in the source here.

Some Problems Found with JSP

A few times we found that Tomcat could not compile a JSP file. Then, strangely enough, it sometimes used not the most recent successfully compiled class file, but the next older one! In these cases, stopping and restarting Tomcat fixed the problem.

Another useful trick required at times has been to stop Tomcat, delete the entire Work folder for the bonForum project, and then restart Tomcat. Sometimes it has also been necessary to restart the browser (note that you always must do that if you change and recompile an applet class). In one case, we even needed to reboot the NT Server before we could get the new JSP functioning.

You should definitely keep backups of any JSP files that you do not want to lose. For a while, our Internet Explorer was fond of changing the JSP file into an HTML file—in Unicode and full of browser-specific stuff. It somehow did so without even changing the file attributes. These JSP files became noneditable and had to be replaced by the backups that we had luckily made.

Lest you think that you are in for an unpleasant development experience, we hasten to add that the latest versions of Tomcat and the other software that we use have proven themselves very robust and stable. Hopefully, you will not need these tricks that we mention!

5.2.3 Modifying Style Sheets

The XML and XSL files for the bonForum Web application (plus a few batch files for testing things) are found in the folder TOMCAT_HOME\webapps\bonForum\mldocs (the "ml" stands for "markup language").

You can experiment quite easily with the chatItems.xsl style sheet document to change the appearance and even the functionality of the list of available chats that is displayed for a user who is looking for a chat to join. Alternatively, you can come up with a new version of chatGuests.xsl to change the way the list of guests in a chat is presented to its host for rating changes. Read the last section of Chapter 10, "JSP Taglib and Custom Tag—Choice Tag," for help with XSLT as it is applied in the bonForum Web application.

5.2.4 Using Logs to Develop and Debug

The best and most inexpensive way to debug what a servlet does is by having it create a log file for you. Our log files are built up by the accumulated results of calls to a method in our `BonLogger` class. They are created in the folder TOMCAT_HOME\webapps\bonForum\WEB-INF\logs\.

Our crude implementation of logging in the project could definitely be improved, but it helped enormously anyway. You can control its output destination by setting the logging init parameter in the web.xml configuration file to `none`, `all` or `file`.

This time-honored technique from lower-level programming practice should not be underestimated. We routinely log lots of output from our Java servlets.

Periodic Maintenance of Log Files Required

A few of the many calls to logging methods (in the source code) have been left in the source code because they give indications of errors that have occurred. Unless you have turned off logging in web.xml, the resulting log files (which, for now, are created in the TOMCAT_HOME\logs folder) will continue to grow, requiring eventual deletion by a human operator. Unlike all those Java class instances that you can leave lying around for the garbage collector, these log files will stick around until you—or someone else—delete them. In the future, the task of managing the growing log files could be assigned to a background task.

5.3 Using XML to Design Web Applications

Before we designed and developed the bonForum chat application, we spent some time using XML to model the structure, dynamics, and data that exist in a simple marketplace. The possibilities that this approach opened up were exciting. We wanted to simulate a marketplace by using that XML-based model for a Web application, but we knew that a simpler case would make a better first choice for a prototype and experimentation.

At about the same time, we stumbled upon the "Cluetrain Manifesto" on the Web, found at the following URL:

```
http://www.cluetrain.com
```

Although the entire manifesto is fascinating, it was the first statement of the manifesto that really struck us: "Markets are conversations."

We had also just been checking out a chat Web site. This simple statement instantly made clear to us that our marketplace-modeling project should be preceded by a simpler chat-modeling project. A model of a conversation would intrinsically include the essence of a market. A model of a forum could be extended into a model of a marketplace.

5.3.1 What Is Meant by an XML Design

We followed one simple design rule: The model that we built was to be representable as an XML document. The root of this document, in the case of the marketplace model, was named bonMarketPlace, where *bon* is Latin word for "root," meaning "good." The root element of the new forum project could have been bonChat, but bonForum seemed to better encompass the greater possibilities inherent in conversations, such as commerce. Conversations—that is, chats—are only one commodity of those that could be exchanged using the bonForum Web application framework.

In the succeeding months, we found that by developing an application based upon an XML-representable design, we gained both simplicity and power. This simple development model kept us from creating an architecture and implementation that were overly complex, which is a common pitfall in many software projects. Just as important, the data that our application needed to handle became active—the data participated in the design of the application from the very beginning.

These are some of the real benefits of XML-based technologies. XML is not just a way to mark up and organize data. XML also can—and should—guide the definition and design of the Web application itself.

Too often, the architecture and logic of an application determine its input and output requirements. However, just as JSP has inverted the Java servlet, XML should invert the Web application. Both of these inversions can be used for the same purpose: to enable human (or robot) interaction, in one case with the servlet and in the other case with the Web application.

In this part of this chapter, we discuss the process of designing the bonForum Web application. Some of the ideas that we cover were used in the project; others were left out for one reason or another.

5.3.2 Actors, Actions, and Things

The children of the root element in the bonMarketPlace XML model are named Actors, Actions, and Things. The Actors element has children such as `Buyer` and `Seller`. The Actions element has children such as `Sells` and `Buys`. The Things element has many children, such as `House`, `Car`, `Pizza`, and `Beer`. With this simple model, we can model such market realities as `Seller Sells Car` and `Buyer Buys Lemon`.

Let's see how a similar framework can reflect the elements to be found in a highly simplified chat forum. There are two actors in our simple forum, one a chat host and the other a chat guest. They are both engaged in one action: They talk. The thing they talk about is the topic of the chat. We can diagram this forum and its mapping in our Actors-Actions-Things XML framework, as shown in Figure 5.1.

5.3.3 XSLT in XML Web Applications

XML technologies are still evolving, and many variations and extensions of the basic idea already exist. We can say that today one central and exciting area is the use of XSLT to map XML on a server to HTML on a browser. In very simple terms, we can diagram an XML Web application based on XSLT transformation in the manner shown in Figure 5.2.

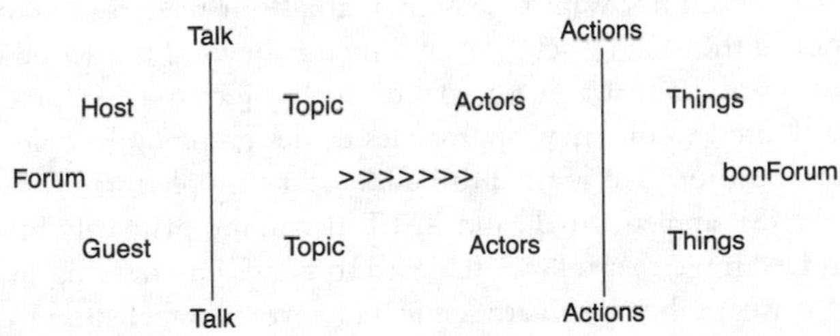

Figure 5.1 The forum and its users are reflected in the bonForum model.

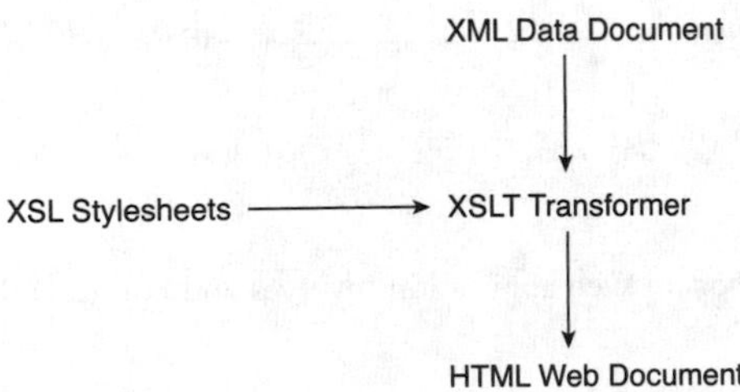

Figure 5.2 The bonForum model is transformed into the bonForum Web application.

This technology enables you to use XSL to design dynamic user interfaces. If our Actors-Actions-Things XML model has succeeded in capturing the static and dynamic elements of the Web application, it can be transformed into the HTML browser representation of the application with the help of XSLT and style sheets.

5.3.4 A Model of the Interaction Between Users

Our design must also take into consideration the interaction between the users of the application. The users of a multiuser Web application are represented in our XML-based model as children of the Actors element. Usually we think of these users as people sitting at a Web browser anywhere in the world, but they could just as easily be robots or client applications.

User interaction is obviously essential to any Web chat application. In Figure 5.3, we again include only two representative bonForum actors in this other context that our XML-to-reality mapping must encompass.

5.3.5 No UML and Data Management Tools Used

Usually at this point in the design process, we would have used a UML modeling tool to design our application. We also would have selected a database management system because handling chat data is an obvious job. We decided against that for several reasons. One is that we did not want to assume that all our readers are familiar with these professional tools, a thorough discussion of which is beyond the scope of the book. A more important reason is that a major goal of our project was exploration and experimentation. We wanted to find new approaches to designing and implementing Web applications. Furthermore, we wanted to build a learning platform for experimenting with servlets and JSP, applets, XML, and XSLT. If you are primarily interested in finding a real-world example that follows standard software engineering practice, you might think that we are being too academic. However, we feel strongly that the best way to learn about tools is to play around with them for a while.

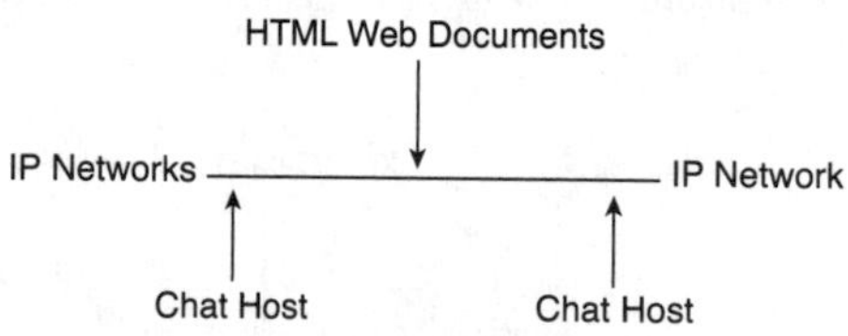

Figure 5.3 The bonForum Web application involves and connects the forum users.

5.3.6 No Interface and Class Design Used

Of course, we could not avoid at least considering the analysis of our application from an object-oriented perspective. We felt compelled to look for the Java interfaces and classes that we would build. Would not `Host` and `Guest` make good classes? Could they not share an Actor interface?

An Action interface could act as the verb in Actor-Action-Thing statements. Then `Start`, `Join`, `Execute`, and `Exit` would implement this Action interface, and their instances would handle specific types of actions. Perhaps instead it would be better to put `Start`, `Join`, `Execute`, and `Exit` methods in the Action interface. We spent some time analyzing chat forums along these lines, coming up with designs such as the one represented in Table 5.1.

Table 5.1 **Alternative Interface-and-Class Design for bonForum**

Interface	Class
Actor	`Visitor`
	`Host`
	`Guest`
	`System`
Action	`Start`
	`Stop`
	`Join`
	`Execute`
	`Exit`
Thing	`Identity`
	`Subject`
	`Chat`
	`Message`
	`Forum`

Again, however, we turned away from familiar design methodology. We decided to stay with our XML-based application design principle. The classes that we were busy identifying would instead become child elements of the Actors, Actions, and Things elements in our XML document.

We do not mean to say that we wanted to exclude objects from the application. Certainly, XML and Java representations are complimentary, not exclusive. As we will detail further, the capability of XML to model the world of a forum was to be complemented by the capability of JSP to generate servlet classes mapped to that model and to provide an extensible, Web-based view of that model.

5.3.7 A More Developed View of bonForum

We continued designing the tree that would become our XML document. Each node in the tree would become an XML element node. Actually, Figure 5.4 has been updated to resemble more closely the elements that we ended up using in the project.

As you can see, we are now including "key" nodes that related their parent elements to other nodes in the tree. To get the host that had started a chat, we used the `HostKey` child of the chat node. Not shown in this diagram is another aspect of the design: Each XML element has a "key" attribute that uniquely identified it. As we shall later discuss in detail, these keys enable us to store and retrieve the XML representation to and from a relational database.

5.3.8 An Early JSP-Based Experiment

We wanted to start experimenting with the design as something that could represent the bonForum as data that changes with the passage of time. In other words, we wanted to have a way to create events that would change the content of the XML data.

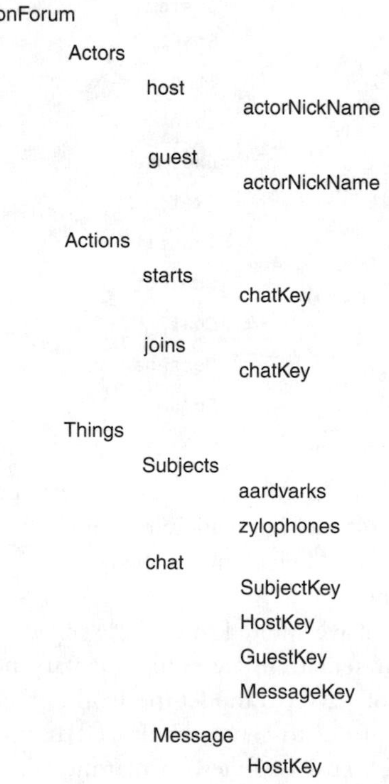

Figure 5.4 Designing bonForum XML using a tree diagram.

Using the elements of this early design, that meant being able to represent, for example, `host starts chat` as an event created by a user, which would add a `host` element, a `starts` element, and a `chat` element to our XML data and the various subelements that these required.

We decided to create a JSP document that would make this possible. The page, called choose.jsp, would display HTML on a browser to enable a user to select an Actor, an Action, and a Thing, using three select controls that were filled using the XML data. For example, the user could select `host starts chat`.

The user would have another select control available that would list all the subject items in the data. The selected subject item would become the subject of the chat. Experimenting with this simple JSP was very valuable and greatly influenced the implementation of the project.

5.3.9 Experimenting with Cookies

We needed some design-testing experiments that took into consideration the fact that bonForum was to be a multiuser application. On the Web, one way to keep track of users is with cookie objects. A cookie object packages information so that the server can send it to a browser. The browser keeps the cookie and then sends it back to the server along with its next request. Having a globally unique identifier associated with each browser allows the server to keep track of all the browsers—at least, as long as the browser user agrees to enable cookies.

Other information included in the cookie allows the server software to maintain a context that includes multiple visits by one or more browsers. The HTTP protocol by itself is "stateless." Requests coming from browsers to a server are disconnected events. One way to connect the various requests is to use information stored in the cookies that a browser includes with each request. That can connect browsers in a Web application, and it can also connect requests coming from a given browser.

Displaying Cookies in JSP

Just in case you want to experiment with cookies from a JSP page, here is some code that we used to display their name/value pairs on the browser page:

```
<%
Cookie[] cookies = request.getCookies();
Cookie cookie = null;
out.println("<H3>Cookies in request:</H3><BR>");
for (int i = 0; i < cookies.length; i++) {
cookie = cookies[i];
out.println("\t<li>"  + cookie.getName() + " = " + cookie.getValue() + "</li>");
}
%>
```

Experiments with cookies led us to create a design that was later discarded but that nevertheless began to clarify the problems that would have to be solved to deal with multiple-user contexts. This design was based on using cookies to control the XSLT process that was illustrated previously in Section 5.3.3, "XSLT in XML Web Applications."

One example can illustrate the plan. When a user started a chat in the bonForum, the browser would include in its response to that action a cookie that had two key/value pairs, one with the new user status and the other with a key to the chat that was created. That would look like this:

```
Cookie:   Status="host",  Key="8734568345"
```

When the browser sent its next request—say, to send a message to the chat—the server-side software knew from the cookie that the user's status was "host." The key value identified one element in an XML file. With that key, the application did not need to use some complex XPATH expression to find that element; it got it directly using the key. Also, the XSL to apply to the XML data using the XSLT processor was determined according to the cookie value.

It turned out that we did not use that design, but it was through experimentation such as this that we found out the real problems that we had to solve in any design. Although these problems could have been solved by manipulating cookies directly, we instead availed ourselves of the more complete, robust, and user-friendly session management offered by the Tomcat Servlet engine (which itself uses cookies and URL parameters to maintain state). If you want to explore this fascinating subject in depth, we suggest studying what the Jakarta Servlet API 3.2 documentation has to say about the cookie, `HTTPSession` class, and related interfaces and classes. Then study the source code that implements this API, which is in the package org.apache.tomcat.session in the Tomcat source.

5.3.10 And the Winner Is JSP Design

Initially, we were using JSP as a convenient way to write server-side Java code that understood the HTTP game of request and response, application contexts, and so on. Our focus was on using XSLT and cookies to design our application. Gradually, however, we started realizing that JSP could play a much more direct role in bringing our XML-based design to the Web.

The main reason for the increased role of JSP was the ease of establishing a relationship between a series of Web pages that a user traverses as they change states in the application, and between a series of JSP pages that create the HTML for those Web pages.

Sending Three-Part Commands to the Server

At first, our idea was to send our Actor-Action-Thing statements to a Java servlet, which would interpret them and control an XSLT engine. That XSLT engine would thus create HTML as an application-dependent response to each Actor-Action-Thing statement. We started calling these statements "three-part commands." We created a simple prototype Web page that could be used to send such commands to a server. It posted each of the three parts of a command in separate input fields of an HTML form element. Here are the contents of that file:

```
<html>
<body>
<h1>Test the bonForum:</h1>
<h2>Enter combinations of actor, action and thing, for testing!</h2>
<form method="POST" action="forum" >
 <input type="text" name="actor">
 <input type="text" name="action">
 <input type="text" name="thing">
 <input type="submit" name="forum">
</form>
</body>
</html>
```

To *POST* or to *GET*, That Is the Question

We would rather use a `POST` operation because we do not want to have all the parameters and values appended to the URL, especially if we start sending encoded XML parameters. The URL displayed in the browser is part of the page, and it affects the appearance. However, there is a price to pay for this aesthetic decision. `POST` operations have two very large drawbacks: They require extra user input to refresh, and they expire in the browser, limiting the user's ability to navigate with browser controls. Also, the decision to use `POST` operation was made before our project began using frames. The ugly URLs of `GET` operations are of less importance now, so perhaps we will revise that decision.

Forwarding Each Request to a JSP

At about the same time, we realized that it was easier to create a different JSP page to handle each three-part command than it was to continually revise a Java servlet so that it could parse each command and act accordingly. The servlet task could then be to simply forward the request to the correct JSP, which would be named after the three-part command. For example, if the command were `visitor creates chat`, then the servlet would forward the request that it received from the form `POST` to a JSP file named visitor_creates_chat.jsp.

We had now found the central control mechanism for the Web chat application. This seed became the `bonForumEngine` class, the "central station" of the Web application. It was the natural way to implement bonForum further, as discussed in more detail later in this chapter. However, before proceeding to create the many JSP documents that would be needed, we had a couple more problems to solve.

5.3.11 Choice of Bean or Custom Tag

Each JSP would have application-related work to do on the server side. We did not want to put that code on the JSP pages because that would obscure their function to represent the XML-inspired structure we had created. JSP documents should be kept easy to maintain and change—it is one of their strong points that they allow changes to be easily made to a Web application.

The code would go into methods in Java server-side objects. There were two possibilities to explore. To add functionality to our JSP pages in a manner that did not obfuscate the design, we could either create Java Beans and access their methods via JSP, or create a tag library and use JSP custom tags.

We liked the idea of including a JSP tag library in the project because it presents a very friendly way to add method calls to a JSP document. However there is an even more important point to consider, and that is a basic distinction between the use of beans and custom tags on JSP. A custom tag can affect the HTML that is output by the JSP, whereas a bean, by default, cannot do so. That means the decision of which to use should be based on the nature of the task at hand. Processing that does not affect the JSP page output should use a bean, whereas processing that does affect the output should use a custom tag.

To save some time, we needed a quick way to prototype the various functions that would be required by the interaction of the JSP pages with the other server-side components. We decided to temporarily house all the methods required in the one Java Servlet class that we already had, `bonForumEngine`. Then we decided to put all our JSP-side functionality, regardless of its effect upon the JSP output, into one bloated, temporary chameleon tag.

The plan was to use this setup only as a testbed. After deciding which tags and beans were to be used and what their requirements were, we would break the code out into the many files that would be required. Unfortunately, when the first edition of this book was published in Germany, we had not yet broken down those two huge classes. That is a regretful situation but nevertheless better than the alternative, which was to ship the book's project in a nonfunctioning but better designed state. Thus, our ugly testbed classes have become immortalized in print, further strengthening our opinion that most technical books are obsolete because of their slow refresh rate.

5.3.12 Original Plan: Follow the XML Design

At first, we were quite religious about having the XML data faithfully reflect both the data and the dynamics of the forum. After all, a major purpose of the project was to explore the consequences of designing software in this way. As we proceeded, we discovered that some parts of the original XML design needed to be simplified for the sake of both understandability and performance.

However, our initial strict adherence to the original plan turned out to be a valuable exercise: It helped identify the complex, unnecessary, and redundant elements in the design. We will give here one example to illustrate how our first trial implementations manipulated the XML data. This example will explain how the statement `visitor starts chat` was implemented by the software.

A user of the application would enter and become a visitor. To represent the user in that state, the software would create a `visitor` element in the XML data as a child of the Actors element. Then an `identity` element would be added as a child of the Things element. This `identity` element would contain the nickname and age given by the visitor. An `actorKey` attribute in this `identity` node would link this information with the user's `visitor` element.

If that visitor then started a chat, the software would first add a `start` element to the Actions element. Then it would add a `chat` element to the Things element. After getting the topic for the chat from the user via an HTML form, it would add a `host` element to the Actors element and change the value of the `actorKey` attribute of the user's `identity` node so that it was linked to the new `host` node. The `visitor` node and the `start` elements would then be removed from the XML data.

5.3.13 Simplifying the Grand Plan

In our initial designs, we were trying to find a kind of Lego™ set that would serve to express all possible states of the chat forum. Each Actor, Action, and Thing entity in the real chat forum would be represented by an element in the XML database. Each combination of these three types of entities would generate a "three-part statement" that would have meaning to the application. Each of these statements would be mapped to a JSP document that would create the appropriate response to the user.

However, even the very simple models that we started with quickly generated a complex matrix of "Actor-Action-Thing" statements. The steps required to dynamically modify the XML database to reflect the changing state of the forum also were numerous. It was time to simplify the design.

We started by throwing out many of the "Actor-Action-Thing" statements that were initially in the plan. One example was the statement `host joins chat`. In early plans, we included this sequence of statements:

```
visitor starts chat
visitor becomes host
host joins chat
```

This sequence of statements was replaced by just the first one, `visitor starts chat`. The visitor still becomes a host and joins the chat, but all this occurs without any formal representation in the three related architectural spheres: XML data, JSP documents, and three-part commands.

Our next major simplification involved the XML database. Although the various Action elements (`starts`, `joins`, `executes`, and `exits`) still play a part in the three-part commands and JSP filenames, they are no longer represented in the XML database. We did keep the Actions element, because in future versions of bonForum, we might add some Action elements to handle added functionality, such as a `send` element that will control a background email-sending process.

We took yet another simplifying step. We had planned to include all the features from the best of chat Web sites on the Web today. However, it was necessary to avoid doing that. The freedom to experiment and explore new models and technologies would be overwhelmed by such a long list of product requirements at such an early stage in the game.

Many of the chat programs on the Web today rely on client-side programming to achieve their complex user interfaces and feature lists. If we included similar interfaces and features as requirements in the first version of bonForum, we would probably have to rely on the same client-side, operating system code libraries that have allowed JavaScript or VBScript to create such rich Web applications. We would perhaps please the bonForum user, but we would miss our goal of prototyping a server-side Web application framework.

So, the red pencil came out, and we went to work shortening the feature list for the bonForum project. There would be no private chat rooms. The software would not remember which banner ads you clicked on the last time you were there and present you with new ones custom-picked according to your interests. The software would now have no answers to many situations that arise in real chat rooms—for example, what happens if the host of a moderated chat exits for good?

Much more needed to be done before bonForum could become a competitive Web chat solution. However, that has not been our goal. Instead, we are exploring techniques to lay down a novel framework, one that can possibly engender never-before-seen features. Best would be if the framework that we eventually develop becomes "boiled down" enough to become reusable in the context of various different Web applications, such as e-commerce, collaborative engineering, knowledge management, or online billing and product delivery. Unfortunately, the design as presented is not scalable to any of these applications, all of which would certainly need real data persistence (for example, a real database), fault-tolerant design, and so on. At this point, it may be more believable to present this as an exercise than to propose that it form the base of a future array of products.

5.3.14 Some Important Functionality Left Out

Before deploying the bonForum application, many things must be considered that we are not taking care of here in the book project. Some very important Web application features will be left out of our example project. These include some that make Web applications fast enough and scalable enough for real use.

Consider, for example, the scalability of our application. We could try to design distributed pools of bonForum components, communicating data with each other. A good reason to leave out such things in this prototype is that there are better ways of providing features like this. The new enterprise Java packages from Sun will give you much better ways to connect a large number of users to the Web application.

We will also pretend that load balancing, security, and encryption issues are all handled in some manner not discussed. The Web application that we develop will not take into account such real-world issues as speed and bandwidth. If the result is too slow for testing our hypotheses, we will try using faster hardware and fatter network connections.

The Need to Scavenge Old Chat Data

As we will discuss in detail later, one way that we simplified our programming requirements was by establishing the rule that a user client can remove an element from the XML data only if that element was added by the same client during the same HTTP session. We ensure this in a simple manner: The key of the element is made up of the session ID value followed by the element name. But what happens to all those entries in bonForum XML that are connected to sessions that are finished? According to our rule, no client can remove these orphan elements.

The bonForum Web application will thus require the addition of a background daemon thread whose sole job is to remove old elements from bonForumXML. To know which are old, the application will need to track all the session IDs that take part in bonForum. Perhaps a certain period of inactivity by a given session will be defined as sufficient reason to remove all elements connected to that session.

Persistent Data Storage

In addition, we will keep some of the data that the Web application requires in XML files. This is not the best way to do it, particularly if we want speed and scalability to be optimized. However, we will just imagine that our XML file can instead be XML-streamed from some new database, or that we have mapped the XML representation of our data into another form (say, within one or more relational database tables) that can be much more efficiently processed than XML files.

Again, this choice is related to the question of where best to learn the skills required for handling data for a server-based application. As we see it, you can find good books and sources of information that will show you how to use JBDC, for example, to persist data for a Web application in your favorite relational database tables. These resources will show you how to convert relational data into XML form. But if your favorite database does not already do that for you, it soon will. So, we will leave that work to someone else and instead focus on experimentation for the sake of learning.

Security Issues

Java has well-developed tools for ensuring the security of personal information in Web applications. These are all beyond the scope of this book. They are not necessarily beyond the scope of the Web application when it is deployed, though, depending on how much personal information it includes. Furthermore, plans to prevent the theft or destruction of data in bonForum have not received consideration and definitely should.

5.3.15 Other Uses for the bonForum Design

The JSP pages and other parts of the bonForum can be used to generate all the frames of a multipanel GUI. For example, this could be one of those extensive control panels that are found on large industrial installations. The same isolation that has been built into the Web application so that multiple users can execute commands will help establish a robust interface in other multiuser and multifunction environments.

5.4 XML Data Flows in Web Applications

We believe that passing XML data within a Web application will turn out to be as important as passing XML data between systems and applications. The latter use of XML is much discussed and heralded in particular as a great benefit in connecting legacy applications to modern Web-based applications.

Within a Web application, passing even one parameter that contains XML data can be a simple yet powerful way to pass a lot of structured information. Passing a long list of `name=value` attributes is cumbersome, by comparison. Let's look at various possibilities for creating XML data flows between the typical components of a Java-based Web application.

Please note that, unlike most of this book, this section is not based upon examples taken from our bonForum Web chat project. Although we certainly pass request parameters around in bonForum, they do not contain XML data. We are excited by our preliminary research into this use of XML. These techniques are included in our future development plans for bonForum. We think that this information may be useful to present here, even before we back it up with "real Web application experience," as we prefer.

5.4.1 Sending XML from an HTML Form

Many of the examples that follow involve putting XML data as a string into an `HTTPRequest` parameter from a browser. If you need to send XML in a request parameter from HTML documents, then you can put it in a string attribute value of an input element within a form element, as in this example:

```
<input type="hidden" name="fragment"
value="&amp;lt;tree&amp;gt;&amp;lt;topic&amp;gt;Chess Players
Chat&amp;lt;/topic&amp;gt;&amp;lt;moderator&amp;gt;Harvey
Wilkinson&amp;lt;/moderator&amp;gt;&amp;lt;/tree&amp;gt;">
```

Notice that the ampersand character (&) must be escaped twice. You have to escape the escape! The first replacement will produce the characters that are to be replaced with the "less than" character (<).

5.4.2 XML from Browser to Servlet

You can send XML from a browser to a Java servlet by putting the XML as a string into a request parameter. You can test this by putting it into an HTML form input element. Try pasting "doubly escaped" XML strings like the one used in the previous example into a form input element and posting that to your servlet.

Your Java servlet must then do something like the following to get the XML back into a string:

```
String sXML = (String)request.getParameter("paramXML");
```

In the next sections, we discuss ways to use the XML passed in from a browser, including servlet control and XSLT processing. Notice that those same ideas can be applied either to XML passed from a browser to a Java servlet, or from a browser to JSP.

5.4.3 XML from Browser to JSP

Remember that a JSP is essentially a way of turning a servlet inside-out so that its contents can be written using Java as a scripting language. A new JSP causes a servlet container, such as Tomcat, to create a newly compiled instance of an `HTTPServlet` class. This servlet will have available a `_jspService` method containing Java code that depends on the scripting elements that you put into the JSP.

The service method in a JSP servlet has access to the `HTTPRequest` object, which can have parameters. You can pass XML to the servlet via one or more of these parameters. You can process that XML using Java code that you add to the JSP script.

JSP Applies XSLT to XML from Browser

We are indebted to Steve Muench for information about passing XML from a browser to a JSP, which he posted on the xsl-list hosted by mulberrytech.com. From his mail we learned the following code fragment, needed to get the XML string transformed by an XSLT processor:

```
<%
// more code goes here…
java.io.ByteArrayInputStream bytesXML = new java.io.ByteArrayInputStream(
➥sXML.getBytes());
InputSource xmlInputSource = new InputSource(bytesXML);
// more code goes here…
%>
```

To see how to use JSP "page import" elements to access the needed Java classes, as well as how to create the XSLT processor to process this `InputSource` and an XSL style sheet, you can refer to the code we used to do that in the bonForum project. (Note that to use Xalan 2.0 with that code, you will need to make use of its "compatibility jar," as described in the Xalan 2.0 documentation.) That code is discussed in Chapter 10, " JSP Taglib and Custom Tag: Choice Tag."

5.4.4 Controlling Java from a Browser with XML

Web-based server-object control could be accomplished by passing the XML from the browser request to an XSLT processor along with an XSL document. The XML InputStream can be used to fire custom tag extensions in the XSL document. In this way, you can put the flow of processing inside Java servlet methods under the indirect control of browser-originated XML content.

Clearly, XSLT is useful to control the display of XML data streams. For this, XSL data streams are the controlling, declarative script. What is less obvious at first is that XSLT also allows XML data streams to control programs. If you can pass a data stream "into" a program at runtime (request time), then you can control that program with it. This is fertile ground for Web application designers, and not just for the ones working with embedded systems. (Think of the Internet—all that software is embedded now!)

Another similar experiment that we would like to try is feeding an XML InputSource from a browser request parameter into a SAX parser. We could then use the contents of the XML to fire Java classes via the SAX event handlers. Could these classes access the whole JSP context? What could be done within Java objects that are controllable via XML from a browser?

5.4.5 XML from Servlet to JSP

To send XML from an `HTTPServlet` to a JSP page, you can override any one of the several servlet methods that have access to the `HTTPRequest` object (`doGet`, `doPost`, or `service`). Inside the method, you get a `RequestDispatcher` to forward the request and response to the JSP page. All you need is to know the URL for the JSP. Be sure to take into consideration the Web application configuration file, (web.xml) and the Tomcat servlet container configuration file (server.xml).

To see how to do this, read the file TOMCAT_HOME\examples\jsp\jsptoserv\stj.txt. There you will find the source code of the servletToJsp servlet. As you can see, the servlet overrides the `doGet` method and adds these two relevant lines of code:

```
request.setAttribute ("servletName", "servletToJsp");
getServletConfig().getServletContext().getRequestDispatcher("/jsp/jsptoserv/hello.
➥jsp").forward(request, response);
```

So, what about passing XML? You can add that to the request object as one or more parameters, just as we did in the browser-to-servlet and browser-to-JSP examples discussed earlier.

5.4.6 XML from JSP to Servlet, or JSP to JSP

It is also possible to send XML from a JSP page either to a Java servlet or to another JSP. Simply use a form element (as shown earlier) or some other means to get the XML into a request parameter, and then use a `jsp:forward` element to send the request to the desired destination servlet or JSP.

Here is a simple example that you can try. Create a JSP page, called TOMCAT_HOME\webapps\bonForum\jsp\forwardToSnoop.jsp. Put in this file only the following lines:

```
<html>
<%
request.setAttribute("hello",
"&lt;?xml version=&quot;1.0&quot; encoding=&quot;ISO-8859-
1&quot;?>&lt;doc>Hello&lt;/doc>");
%>
<jsp:forward page="/snoop"/>
</html>
```

Find the web.xml file for the bonForum Web app, in the folder TOMCAT_HOME\webapps\bonForum\WEB-INF. Make sure that the file has a servlet element for `snoop`, like the following (if not, you can copy and edit the one in the Tomcat Examples Web app):

```
<servlet>
    <servlet-name>
        snoop
    </servlet-name>
    <servlet-class>
        SnoopServlet
    </servlet-class>
    <init-param>
        <param-name>
            fooSnoop
        </param-name>
        <param-value>
            barSnoop
        </param-value>
    </init-param>
</servlet>
<servlet>
```

Copy the SnoopServlet.class file from the Tomcat Examples Web app into the bonForum Web app. You should find the class file in the folder TOMCAT_HOME\webapps\examples\WEB-INF\classes. Copy it to the folder TOMCAT_HOME\webapps\bonForum\WEB-INF\classes.

Now try browsing (with Tomcat running) your forwardToSnoop.jsp page using this (or your similar) address:

```
http://localhost:8080/bonForum/jsp/forwardToSnoop.jsp
```

When you try this example, you should get a page full of detailed information about the HTTP request on your browser. (By the way, this works with only the `SnoopServlet`, not the snoop.jsp example.) The browser display should include the following lines:

```
Request attributes:
   hello = &lt;?xml version=&quot;1.0&quot; encoding=&quot;ISO-8859-
1&quot;?>&lt;doc>Hello&lt;/doc>;
```

Of course, this is the XML sent from JSP to the servlet:

```
hello = <?xml version="1.0" encoding="ISO-8859-1"?><doc>Hello</doc>
```

Yet, nowhere in all the `snoop` information can you see anything that would reveal the original receiver of the browser request—namely, the JSP forwardToSnoop.jsp.

5.4.7 Displaying HTML or XML Using JSP

As a final tidbit, here is a way to display an XML document using JSP. Putting this line on a JSP

```
<%= "<B><I>hello</I></B>" %>
```

displays the text in bold and italics:

hello

This second excerpt can display an XML or an HTML element. Putting this one line on a JSP

```
<%= "&lt;B>&lt;I>hello&lt;/I>&lt;/B>" %>
```

displays these tags instead:

```
<B><I>hello</I></B>
```

6

bonForum Chat Application: Implementation

THIS CHAPTER CONTINUES THE overview of bonForum that began in the last chapter. Knowing how our design turned into a working prototype will prepare you for the more detailed code analyses in the following five chapters. Some of the tougher implementation problems are also highlighted. Finally, suggestions for future development of this Web chat are given.

6.1 Building the bonForum Web Chat

While creating the implementation for bonForum, we tried to follow one main principle. The XML-based, chat-forum model that we had designed would control our implementation of the Web application. The goal was to make the XML data from the chat forum active. By "active," we mean that its form and content would drive the appearance and the dynamics of the Web application.

A pure instance of this principle's successful application can be seen in the use of XSLT to transform XML into HTML. In most cases, XSLT is used in a Web application to create a data-driven application process.

In that sense, our goal has been to make the data active. By expressing the application requirements as XML data and then developing an application implementation that "transforms" this data into a Web-browseable collection of documents, we wanted to produce in all areas of bonForum the same kind of benefits of using XSLT.

6.1.1 XML Representation of Web Applications

In Chapter 5, "bonForum Chat Application: Use and Design," we discussed the first steps of the design process. We used tree diagrams to plan an XML data structure representing a chat forum. Now we will show you what the data looks like as an XML document. You can find a more complete version of some similar XML data in Chapter 11, "XML Data Storage Class: ForestHashtable." That chapter also gives you many more details about the way the Web application uses the data.

What you see here is a *simplified version* of the real XML data document. We have left out most of the attributes so that you can more clearly see the basic design. Actually, in the real data, *every* element contains a `nodeKey` attribute, which encodes the hierarchical relationship between the elements when they are randomly stored in a `hashtable` (discussed in Chapter 11).

In the simplified version here, we have left in *only* those `nodeKey` attributes that are being referred to elsewhere in the XML document. These `nodeKey` attribute values (in the host, guest, and message elements) are matched either by an attribute value (message `hostKey`, message `guestKey`) or by the text content of an element (the `messageKey`, `hostKey`, and `guestKey` children of a chat element).

```
<?xml version="1.0"?>
<bonForum>
  <actors>
    <guest nodeKey="965506098557.965501551999.965501551959">
      <actorNickname>eve</actorNickname>
      <actorAge>40</actorAge>
      <actorRating>7</actorRating>
    </guest>
    <host nodeKey="965503119944.965501551999.965501551959">
      <actorNickname>adam</actorNickname>
      <actorAge>47</actorAge>
      <actorRating>5</actorRating>
    </host>
  </actors>
  <actions/>
  <things>
    <forums>
      <forum>
        <name>bonForum</name>
        <weblink>www.bonforum.org</weblink>
      </forum>
      <forum>
        <name>tarent</name>
        <weblink>www.tarent.de</weblink>
      </forum>
    </forums>
    <subjects>
      <Vehicles>
        <Autos>
          <BMW/>
```

```
      <Ferrari>
         <Testarossa/>
       </Ferrari>
     </Autos>
    <Trucks>
       <Mac/>
      <Other>
         <sessionID_v7iabpmzg1_992808272761
         chatTopic="my other truck is a ferrari" />
       </Other>
     </Trucks>
   </Vehicles>
  <Health>
    SPONSORED BY YOUR FRIENDLY CORPORATION
    <Prevention>
      <Headaches>
         <Migraine/>
       </Headaches>
     </Prevention>
   </Health>
 </subjects>
 <message
   nodeKey="965503142126.965501552059.965501551959"
   dateStamp="Saturday 05 09:08:09 2000"
   hostKey ="965503119944.965501551999.965501551959">
   adam::this is dynamite!
 </message>
 <message
   nodeKey="965502489387.965501552059.965501551959"
   dateStamp="Saturday 05 09:19:02 2000"
   guestKey="965506098557.965501551999.965501551959">
   eve::Is anybody there?
 </message>
 <chat>
   <guestKey>
     965506098557.965501551999.965501551959
   </guestKey>
   <messageKey>
     965503142126.965501552059.965501551959
   </messageKey>
   <messageKey>
     965502489387.965501552059.965501551959
   </messageKey>
   <hostKey>
     965503119944.965501551999.965501551959
   </hostKey>
 </chat>
</things>
</bonForum>
```

You may have noticed another long key value lost among all the triple-valued ones:

```
"sessionID_v7iabpmzg1_992808272761"
```

This is a `chatItem` element name, made from the HTTP session ID of the actor that started the chat and a time stamp. It marks a chat subject (`Vehicles.Trucks.Other`) and contains a `chatTopic` attribute value. For now, all we want to show here is the big picture.

6.1.2 Chat Information as a Hierarchy

The information that makes up one bonForum "universe" of chats, as we have seen, is structured so that it can be represented by an XML document. Let's consider further some of the implications of this design.

XML Is Representable as a Tree

One of the strengths of XML is that it is based on a tree data structure, with a node for each XML component, including elements, attributes, text, and so on. Tree structures, of course, have a long history in software development, and they have enabled many powerful algorithms.

Trees Made of Trees, Which Are Made of Trees

One of the advantages of using tree data structures is that each node of a tree can be treated as if it were the root of another tree. Some subtrees, of course, consist of only one node, a "leaf" node. This characteristic of tree structures means that you can develop methods that can be applied to a tree of data as well as to any node of that tree. The advantages of this, especially in the design of recursive algorithms, are well known.

Forests Made of Trees, Which Make Forests

One of the constraints on an XML document is that it can contain only one document node. With the exception of the information that brands the document as an XML document, all the data in an XML document, therefore, is contained in only one tree structure, with one root. To join two or more XML documents into a new document, their document nodes must be included under one new document node.

Although each instance of bonForum can be represented by one XML document, we also want to explore the dynamics of a network of distributed bonForums—on the Internet, for example. Such a network implies the existence of many XML documents. These documents are related in terms of their design and function, but they exist as separate data structures.

Inconsistencies or redundancies may exist in the data content of these XML documents. If you put such XML documents into one superdocument and then related them under one new root document node, you might not be able to conveniently process that new parent XML document in the same manner as you can process each of the child documents. For this and other reasons, we chose to consider our data as a forest and not a tree in the bonForum Web application.

A data forest can be implemented in many ways. One way is to use a collection of XML documents, which can be files, database objects, or other entities. Another way is to use the `ForestHashtable` object that we designed for bonForum. Chapter 11 provides all the details about our forest data storage class.

Meanwhile, we list here two features of forest data structures that we plan to take advantage of when we begin experimenting with many bonForum instances distributed on the Internet:

- Trees can be packaged together in a forest without this implying any relationship or compatibility between them.
- Branches can be removed from a tree in a forest and then be kept as trees in the same forest.

6.1.3 The Browsers of the bonForum Users

Let's follow our "broad brush" view of the bonForum data with a quick look at the client side of the Web application. In a Web application, the users' browsers are important components in the architecture. The variety and mutability of existing browsers is one of the most challenging aspects of making any Web application that is truly worldwide. Although ideally a Web application should be both cross-platform and cross-browser, this is too ambitious of a goal for an experimental prototype such as bonForum.

The following is a list of the requirements that a user's browser must meet before it can provide entrance into bonForum and thus become a part of the architecture of this Web application. The browser must have the capabilities to do the following:

- POST HTML forms
- Display HTML tables
- Display HTML frames
- Have HTTP cookies enabled
- Allow the Java plug-in to be installed and used

The need for a Java applet and the Sun Java plug-in has proven to be the most controversial and negatively received aspect of the bonForum Web application. You can find out much more about the issues involved in Chapter 9, "Java Applet Plugged In: BonForumRobot."

6.1.4 The Server Connects Users

Now let's take an equally brief look at the server side of our Web application. Obviously, in a server-side Web application, the software running on the server assumes a centrally important role. Although there is one Java applet in bonForum, this Web application's architecture is intended to be as "server-side" as possible. Listed here are a few of the responsibilities that the server-side software must shoulder:

- Provide various contexts for information
- Enable multiple users to simultaneously use application
- Handle and respond to requests coming from many browsers
- Provide each user with his own state in the application
- Store and retrieve data that is related to each user

This list could easily be made much longer, of course. Indeed, it would be so much longer that we must instead refer you to four out of the next five chapters (all except Chapter 9), which deal almost exclusively with server-side implementation details. At the beginning of Chapter 8, "Java Servlet in Charge: BonForumEngine," you will find a table that lists many more of the functions that server-side software must handle to make even a prototype version of a Web chat.

6.1.5 The States of the Forum

We have written quite a lot of material regarding the goals and purposes of the software design and implementation. We did so for several reasons. Knowing the history of the design can help you make sense of the current source code and its nomenclature. Our discussion also can help you appreciate the experimental nature and value of the bonForum project. Finally, we want to answer criticisms of the type that begin with, "Why was this done that way? Does the author not realize that it can be done much better this way?"

Now it is time to drop down a level in the discussion, to begin discussing the details of our actual implementation of the bonForum Web chat. We begin by detailing all the states that the application goes through for each user progressing through bonForum.

The following "states" of the bonForum Web application are abstractions. It is important to keep in mind that each state is expressed in several contexts within the implementation. Of these contexts, the three most important are the JSP documents, the three-part commands, and the XML data.

While you read the next five chapters, it may be a good idea to review this list of bonForum states, which discusses in detail all the states of bonForum.

bonForum Web Application URL

1. The URL that starts bonForum for one user on a browser takes the reader to index.html, which is the default HTML page for a Web application. The file index.html can be browsed by any Web browser. It acts as a splash screen for the Web application, giving it a wider context, for example, by displaying information about this book.
2. This page displays a logo designed by the author, which is also a link to the bonForum chat application. Clicking that link takes a user to the forum login state of the Web application.

Forum Login

1. Before we let a user enter the Web application, we might want to put that user through an authorization procedure. We do not have any authorization process in this book, but this application state is defined and reserved for this purpose.
2. In this state the application first meets a user's browser, so it is here where the application handles any initialization required. For example, this is where the session ID is checked and registered with the application. Users are not allowed into the application without going through this state.
3. In future versions, the application will recognize users who are returning after an absence and will be able to reconnect them with their previous chat context.
4. Leaving this state takes a user to the forum entry state.

Forum Entry

1. In this state each user entering the Web chat application is asked to give a nickname and an age.
2. Each nickname is registered in a nickname registry. The registry allows no duplicate values, so this state continues until the user enters a new and unique nickname.
3. The age given can be used in future versions to limit user entry to some chats by age group. However, verifying ages is not a trivial problem, and its solution is not attempted here.
4. Leaving this state takes a user to the "visitor executes choice" state of the application.

Visitor Executes Choice

1. A visitor to bonForum is greeted by nickname and asked to make a choice: start a new chat, join an existing chat, or exit bonForum.
2. Depending on the choice made, leaving this state takes a user to one of three application states: "visitor starts chat," "visitor joins chat," or bonForum.

Visitor Joins Chat

1. In this state, a visitor who has chosen to join an existing chat in the "visitor executes choice" state is now asked to choose a chat to join from a list of all the available chats.
2. By joining a chat, a visitor becomes a guest of that chat in the bonForum.
3. Leaving this state takes a visitor to the "guest executes chat" state.

Visitor Starts Chat

1. In this state, a visitor who has chosen to start a new chat in the "visitor executes choice" state is now asked to choose a chat subject category from a list. The visitor must also enter a description or topic for the chat to be created. That user can also choose whether to moderate the new chat.
2. By starting a new chat, a visitor becomes a host of that chat in bonForum.
3. Leaving this state takes a visitor to the "host executes chat" state.

Guest Executes Chat

1. In this state, a guest is in the chat joined in the "visitor joins chat" state. The chat messages entered by the guest and all others in the same chat are displayed chronologically. Each message is prefixed by the nickname of its sender. The guest can compose messages in a text input field provided.
2. A guest is here presented with a choice: send this message, exit this chat, or enter command mode.
3. If a guest sends a new message, it appears after a short delay to the chat messages display the next time this is refreshed.
4. The chat messages being displayed are intermittently refreshed so that messages entered by all chat members appear as soon as possible.
5. Depending on the choice made, leaving this state takes a guest to either of two states: "guest executes command" or "guest exits chat."

Guest Executes Command

1. In this state, a guest is presented with a choice of available commands. In the simplified book application example, there is only one: The guest can set the number of messages to display in the "guest executes chat" state.
2. Other possible commands that will be included in a full version of the bonForum Web application are listed in Section 6.8.7, "Host and Guest Commands for the Future."
3. Leaving this state takes a guest to the "guest exits command" state.

Guest Exits Command

1. In this state, the application can carry out any processing required because of choices made by a guest while in the "guest executes command" state. In the future, this will include setting up a private chat between the guest and another guest or host, for example.
2. In the simple book example, this state does nothing but forward a guest back to the chat.
3. Leaving this state takes a guest back to the "guest executes chat" state.

Guest Exits Chat

1. In this state, the Web application can make whatever changes are required by the exit of a guest from a chat. This includes, for example, removing data no longer needed and perhaps saving information that will be useful for reinstating the guest that user returns to the same chat. In the simplified book version of the Web application, this state does nothing but forward a guest to the next state.
2. In future versions of bonForum, leaving this state will take a guest to a "guest executes choice" state that will allow more complex relationships between a guest and various chats. One way to leave that new state will be to go to a "guest exits forum" state (also not yet included), where the Web application will make changes required by the exit of a guest from the bonForum (such as removing unneeded data, saving information for reinstating the guest later, and so on). Leaving that "guest exits forum" state will take a guest to the bonForum state.
3. Leaving this state (in this simple version of the Web application) takes a guest back to the "visitor executes choice" state (from where it is possible to leave to the bonForum state).

Host Executes Chat

1. In this state, a host is in the chat that he started in the "visitor starts chat" state. Chat messages entered by this host and all others who join the chat are displayed. Each message is prefixed by the nickname of its sender. The host can compose messages in a text input field provided.
2. A host is presented with a choice: send this message, exit this chat, or enter command mode.
3. If a host sends a new message, it appears after a short delay to the chat messages display the next time this is refreshed.
4. The chat messages being displayed are intermittently refreshed so that messages entered by all users appear as soon as possible.
5. Depending upon the choice made, leaving this state takes a host to either of two states: "host executes command" or "host exits chat."

Host Executes Command

1. In this state, a host is presented with a choice of available commands. In the simplified book application example, there are only three: The guest can set the number of messages to display in the "host executes chat" state, the host can increase the status of a guest, or the host can decrease the status of a guest.
2. A list of all the guests currently in the chat is displayed. Relevant details about each guest are also shown, including the guest's current rating. In future versions of this application, a status of 0 will cause the guest to be removed from the chat, while a status of 10 will cause the guest to become a co-host of the chat.
3. Other possible commands that will be included in a full version of the bonForum Web application are listed in Section 6.8.7, "Host and Guest Commands for the Future."
4. Leaving this state takes a host to the "host exits command" state.

Host Exits Command

1. In this state, the application can carry out any processing required because of choices made by the host while in the "host executes command" state. In the future, this will include setting up a private chat between the host and another guest or host, for example.
2. In the simple book example, this state does nothing but forward the host back to the chat they are hosting.
3. Leaving this state takes a host to the "host executes chat" state.

Host Exits Chat

1. In this state, the Web application can make whatever changes are required by the exit of a host from a chat. This includes, for example, removing data no longer needed and perhaps saving information that will be useful for reinstating the host if he returns to the same chat. In the simplified book version of the Web application, this state does nothing but forward a host to the next state.
2. In future versions of bonForum, leaving this state will take a guest to a "host executes choice" state that will allow more complex relationships between a host and various chats. One way to leave that new state will be to go to a "host exits forum" state (also not yet included) where the Web application will make changes required by the exit of a host from bonForum (such as removing unneeded data, saving information for reinstating the host later, and so on). Leaving that "host exits forum" state will take a host to the bonForum state.
3. Leaving this state (in this simple version of the Web application) takes a host back to the "visitor executes choice" state (from where it is possible to leave to the bonForum state).

Host Increases Rating

1. In this state, a host can increase the status of a guest in the chat. If the increased status is above a threshold, the guest will automatically become a co-host of the chat (this will be an option to select as a host command).
2. This state is left automatically in the book version of the project. It forwards a host back to the "host executes command" state.

Host Decreases Rating

1. In this state, a host will be able to decrease the status of a guest in the chat. If the decreased status is below a threshold, the guest will automatically be removed from the chat.
2. This state is left automatically in the book version of the project. It forwards a host back to the "host executes command" state.

BonForum Links

1. This state shows information about the bonForum Web-chat software and its source.
2. Links to bonForums worldwide are provided to the user.
3. One link enables the user to return to the previous bonForum.
4. Instructions remind the user that the way to exit bonForum is simply to browse a different URL.

6.1.6 Forum States and the XML Database

In the original design for the Web application, as based on the XML description of a Web chat, most of the various states described previously changed the contents of the XML data in some way. Changes in the state of the chat, as modeled with our Actor-Action-Thing method, were to be immediately reflected in the XML data.

However, as we developed the application according to that design, it became clear that in many cases we could simplify the code considerably and yet preserve the overall functionality of the application. These simplifications were departures from the original design.

In other cases, we decided to leave out some desirable functionality until some future version of the software. This was done so that we would more quickly have a working application that we could use to test the most important characteristics of the design.

The result of all these major simplifications was a great reduction in the number of interactions between the various states of the application described previously and the XML database. To fully understand the details of these interactions, you will need to read several more chapters in this book and perhaps the source code (in Appendix C, "Source Code for bonForum Web Application") as well.

Here we give only an overview of those application states that change the XML data and list the changes that they make. These listings are an excellent and very useful way to pin down exactly how the application works.

XML Effects of "Guest Executes Chat"

This application state has the following effects upon the contents of the bonForumXML database:

1. Adds a `guest` element to a bonForum/things/actors element
2. Adds an `actorNickname` element to the new guest element
3. Adds an `actorAge` element to the new guest element
4. Adds an `actorRating` element to the new guest element
5. Adds a `guestKey` element to the correct chat element
6. Adds `message` elements to a bonForum/things element
7. Adds `messageKey` elements to the correct chat element

XML Effects of "Host Executes Chat"

This application state has the following effects upon the contents of the bonForumXML database:

1. Adds a `host` element to a bonForum/things/actors element
2. Adds an `actorNickname` element to the new host element
3. Adds an `actorAge` element to the new host element

4. Adds a `chat` element to a bonForum/things element
5. Adds a `hostKey` element to the new chat element
6. Adds a session ID element to the correct subject element
7. Add an `itemKey` attribute to the new chat element
8. Adds `message` elements to a bonForum/things element
9. Adds `messageKey` elements to the new chat element

XML Effects of "Host Increases Rating"

1. This application state increments the value of an `actorRating` in a guest element.
2. The actor is optionally promoted to host when the `actorRating` reaches a settable upper-threshold value.

XML Effects of "Host Decreases Rating"

1. This application state decrements the value of an `actorRating` in a guest element.
2. The actor is optionally removed from the chat when the `actorRating` reaches a settable lower-threshold value.

6.1.7 Some Java Methods Required

We had already settled on the idea that each bonForum state described would be represented by a JSP document. Now, to take one bonForum user from one state to another, we will need a few basic methods. Our first analysis of this yielded a surprisingly short list of methods, as detailed here:

- **`addNode`**—This method simply gives us the ability to add a node anywhere in the bonForum XML data.
- **`removeNode`**—This complements the `addNode` method, allowing the removal of XML data.
- **`forwardToJSP`**—We need a way to get from one JSP to another because they represent and implement the various states through which the bonForum will transition for each user. This method turned out to be (usually!) the job of the service method of the Java servlet. For details, see Chapter 8.
- **`refresh`**—We thought we might need a method that would refresh the information displayed to a user in a certain state. It turned out to be a bit more complex than that. For details, see Chapter 9.

- **`Other Methods`**—We need a few other methods—again, surprisingly few. These are all discussed later in this chapter, as well as in the following chapters. The method `outputForumPathNames` is needed to display available chat subjects to users so that they can categorize a chat that they are starting. The method `outputForumChatMessages` is perhaps the most important one for a chat application.

6.1.8 Forum States, *bonCommands*, and JSP

We have already mentioned that one of the centrally important mechanisms in the bonForum Web application is the use of JSP pages to represent each of the various chat forum states (described in Section 6.1.5, "The States of the Forum") to each user as an HTML page. Furthermore, each JSP page is also responsible for much of the processing that is necessary in its related forum state. Transitions from state to state, therefore, are accompanied by transitions from JSP document to JSP document.

A Simple Plan Grew Complicated

We began with a rather simple mechanism: Each Web application state was related by name to one `bonCommand` and one JSP document. Here is an example:

```
Forum State: visitor joins chat
bonCommand: visitor_joins_chat
JavaServer Page: visitor_joins_chat.jsp
```

At the end of each forum state, its JSP would put the `bonCommand` for the next state in an HTML form input element and POST it to the BonForumEngine Java servlet. The servlet would take care of forwarding that HTTP request to the JSP for the next forum state. To get the filename of that next JSP, the servlet only needed to add a .jsp extension to the value of the `bonCommand` request parameter.

For reasons that will be much discussed in the rest of the book, we were not able to keep this mechanism simple for long. Among the changes that complicated this initial design were those that introduced these three characteristics:

1. More than one JSP document can exist per forum state.
2. More than one `bonCommand` can exist per forum state.
3. A JSP can be requested from a JSP in four ways.

It might take a while before the design we are describing becomes clear to you because it is comprised of several interlocking mechanisms. In fact, most of the rest of this chapter details of higher-level views of the design, and most of the next five chapters will cover the details.

More Than One JSP per Forum State

One way that the original, "simple: mechanism for bonForum application-state transitions grew complex was related to the use of HTML framesets and frames. We needed to find a way to refresh information on the Web application HTML pages—for example, to update the display of chat messages. Our first attempts to set up a "refreshing" JSP caused an unpleasant flickering effect that was clearly unacceptable. As we will later more fully discuss, our best solution for this problem involved the use of HTML frames.

The result was that most forum states are now represented on the browser by an HTML page with a frameset. Either five or six JSP documents handle the display and processing required by these forum states. This means that, for these states, two to four `bonCommands` also are involved.

Forum States and Related *bonCommand* Values

Table 6.1 lists all the forum states, together with their name-related JSP files and name-related `bonCommands`. To make sense of this table, you will have to refer also to Table 6.2 and Table 6.3, as well as the discussion about them.

Table 6.1 **Relating JSP Filenames and *bonCommand* Values to Each Forum State**

JSP Filenames (.jsp)	Forum State	`bonCommand` Values
	web-app URL	
(index.html)		(not needed)
	forum login	
forum_login		(not needed)
	forum entry	
forum_entry		`forum_entry`
	visitor executes choice	
visitor_executes_choice		`visitor_executes_choice`
	visitor joins chat	
visitor_joins_chat		`visitor_joins_chat`
visitor_joins_chat_controls		(not needed)
visitor_joins_chat_frame		`visitor_joins_chat_frame`
visitor_joins_chat_ready		`visitor_joins_chat_ready`
visitor_joins_chat_robot		`visitor_joins_chat_robot`

continues

Table 6.1 **Continued**

JSP Filenames (.jsp)	bonCommand Values
	Forum State
	visitor starts chat
visitor_starts_chat	`visitor_starts_chat`
visitor_starts_chat_controls	(not needed)
visitor_starts_chat_frame	`visitor_starts_chat_frame`
visitor_starts_chat_ready	`visitor_starts_chat_ready`
visitor_starts_chat_robot	(not needed)
	guest executes chat
guest_executes_chat	(not needed)
guest_executes_chat_console	`guest_executes_chat_console`
guest_executes_chat_controls	`guest_executes_chat_controls`
guest_executes_chat_frame	(not needed)
guest_executes_chat_ready	`guest_executes_chat_ready`
guest_executes_chat_robot	(not needed)
	guest executes command
guest_executes_command	(not needed)
guest_executes_command_controls	`guest_executes_command_controls`
guest_executes_command_frame	(not needed)
guest_executes_command_ready	`guest_executes_command_ready`
guest_executes_command_robot	(not needed)
	guest exits command
guest_exits_command	(not needed)
	guest exits chat
guest_exits_chat	(not needed)
	host executes chat
host_executes_chat	(not needed)
host_executes_chat_console	`host_executes_chat_console`
host_executes_chat_controls	`host_executes_chat_controls`
host_executes_chat_frame	(not needed)
host_executes_chat_ready	`host_executes_chat_ready`
host_executes_chat_robot	(not needed)
	host executes command
host_executes_command	(not needed)
host_executes_command_controls	`host_executes_command_controls`
host_executes_command_frame	(not needed)
host_executes_command_ready	`host_executes_command_ready`
host_executes_command_robot	(not needed)

Forum State JSP Filenames (.jsp)	`bonCommand` Values
host exits command	
host_exits_command	(not needed)
host exits chat	
host_exits_chat	(not needed)
host increases rating	
host_increases_rating	`host_increases_rating`
host decreases rating	
host_decreases_rating	`host_decreases_rating`
bonForum	
bonForum	`bonForum`

Requesting the Next JSP from the Current JSP

Table 6.2 lists the four ways in which a JSP is requested from a JSP. Each request description in the right column is associated with its request type in the left column. The type of request relates this table to Table 6.3, which lists each JSP together with all the JSP files requesting it.

Table 6.2 **Four Ways That One JSP Is Requested from Another JSP**

Type of Request	Description of Request
Frame	The requested JSP is the `src` attribute for a frame element in the requesting JSP.
bonCommand	`bonOommand` is an input element in an HTML form on the requesting JSP. The form is submitted by a user via a POST to the `BonForumEngine` Java servlet. `BonForumEngine` forwards the POST request to the requested JSP, getting its filename by adding a .jsp suffix to the `bonCommand` value.
jsp:forward	The requested JSP is the `page` attribute in a `jsp:forward` element on the requesting JSP.
BonForumRobot	The requesting JSP has a `jsp:plugin` element with its `code` attribute set to the `BonForumRobot` Java applet. Either the requesting JSP or another JSP sets a `document` session attribute value to the name of the requested JSP. `BonForumRobot` uses a `document` parameter that is set from the document session attribute.

continues

Table 6.2 **Four Ways That One JSP Is Requested from Another JSP**

Type of Request	Description of Request
	`BonForumRobot` mangles the document parameter value, suffixing a unique time value and .tfe.
	`BonForumRobot` invokes the applet `showDocument` method with the mangled name of the requested JSP. The added .tfe causes the request to go to `BonForumEngine` Java servlet due to servlet mapping in the Web application deployment descriptor (web.xml). The added unique time value prevents cached responses from being supplied by browsers.
	`BonForumEngine` unmangles the requested JSP name and forwards the request to that JSP.

A request for a JSP can have one of several effects upon the Web application, including those in the following list. Note that by "robot JSP," we mean a JavaServer page that contains the `BonForumRobot` applet in a `jsp:plugin` element. In this application, these robot JavaServer pages are "in" a frame.

- A Frame type request can display HTML in a frame and run server-side–compiled code.
- A `bonCommand` type request can cause a transition from one forum state to the next.
- A `jsp:forward` type request can cause a transition from one forum state to the next.
- A `jsp:forward` type request can request a robot JSP frame.
- A robot JSP frame can refresh the JSP for a different frame in the display.
- A robot JSP frame can request the JSP for a new forum state, which can set up a new frameset browser display.
- A JSP can request itself and thus refresh itself.

How Each JSP Is Requested

Table 6.3 lists every JSP in the bonForum Web application and also the types of requests that are used to fire that JSP. Note that a plus sign (+) before a requesting JSP name means that it sets up the `document` session attribute with the requested JSP name (see Table 6.1). A "5X" after a request type entry means that there are five separate requests in the one requesting JSP file.

Table 6.3 **Relating Each JSP to the Source(s) of Its Request(s)**

Type of Request	**Requesting JSP Files**
Requested JSP File	
(index.html)	
Default Web-app URL	(Web browser)
forum_login.jsp	
HTML link	(index.html)
forum_entry.jsp	
`bonCommand`	forum_login.jsp
visitor_executes_choice.jsp	
`bonCommand`	forum_entry.jsp
`jsp:forward`	host_exits_chat.jsp
	guest_exits_chat.jsp
visitor_joins_chat.jsp	
`bonCommand`	visitor_executes_choice.jsp
visitor_joins_chat_controls.jsp	
Frame	visitor_joins_chat.jsp
visitor_joins_chat_frame.jsp	
Frame	visitor_joins_chat.jsp
`bonCommand`	visitor_joins_chat_frame.jsp
visitor_joins_chat_ready.jsp	
`bonCommand`	visitor_joins_chat_controls.jsp
visitor_joins_chat_robot.jsp	
`jsp:forward`	visitor_joins_chat_ready.jsp
visitor_starts_chat.jsp	
`bonCommand`	visitor_executes_choice.jsp
visitor_starts_chat_controls.jsp	
Frame	visitor_starts_chat.jsp
visitor_starts_chat_frame.jsp	
Frame	visitor_starts_chat.jsp
`bonCommand`	visitor_starts_chat_frame.jsp
visitor_starts_chat_ready.jsp	
`bonCommand`	visitor_starts_chat_controls.jsp
visitor_starts_chat_robot.jsp	
`jsp:forward`	visitor_starts_chat_ready.jsp

continues

Table 6.3 **Continued**

Type of Request	Requested JSP File Requesting JSP Files
	guest_executes_chat.jsp
`BonForumRobot`	visitor_joins_chat_ready.jsp
`jsp:forward`	guest_exits_command.jsp
	guest_executes_chat_console.jsp
`bonCommand`	guest_executes_chat_controls.jsp
	guest_executes_chat_controls.jsp
Frame	guest_executes_chat.jsp
`bonCommand` (5X)	guest_executes_chat_controls.jsp
	guest_executes_chat_frame.jsp
Frame	guest_executes_chat.jsp
`BonForumRobot`	guest_executes_chat_robot.jsp + guest_executes_chat.jsp
	guest_executes_chat_ready.jsp
`bonCommand`	guest_executes_chat_controls.jsp
	guest_executes_chat_robot.jsp
Frame	guest_executes_chat.jsp
`jsp:forward`	guest_executes_chat_console.jsp
`jsp:forward`	guest_executes_chat_ready.jsp
	guest_executes_command.jsp
`BonForumRobot`	guest_executes_chat_console.jsp
	guest_executes_command_controls.jsp
Frame	guest_executes_command.jsp
`bonCommand`	guest_executes_command_controls.jsp
	guest_executes_command_frame.jsp
Frame	guest_executes_command.jsp
`BonForumRobot`	guest_executes_command_robot.jsp + guest_executes_command.jsp
	guest_executes_command_ready.jsp
`bonCommand`	guest_executes_command_controls.jsp
	guest_executes_command_robot.jsp
Frame	guest_executes_command.jsp
`jsp:forward`	guest_executes_command_ready.jsp

Type of Request	Requested JSP File Requesting JSP Files
	guest_exits_command.jsp
`BonForumRobot`	guest_executes_command_robot.jsp + guest_executes_command_ready.jsp
	guest_exits_chat.jsp
`BonForumRobot`	guest_executes_chat_robot.jsp + guest_executes_chat_ready.jsp
	host_executes_chat.jsp
`BonForumRobot`	visitor_starts_chat_ready.jsp
`jsp:forward`	host_exits_command.jsp
	host_executes_chat_console.jsp
`bonCommand`	host_executes_chat_controls.jsp
	host_executes_chat_controls.jsp
Frame	host_executes_chat.jsp
`bonCommand` (5X)	host_executes_chat_controls
	host_executes_chat_frame.jsp
Frame	host_executes_chat.jsp
`BonForumRobot`	host_executes_chat_robot.jsp + host_executes_chat.jsp
	host_executes_chat_ready.jsp
`bonCommand`	host_executes_chat_controls.jsp
	host_executes_chat_robot.jsp
Frame	host_executes_chat.jsp
`jsp:forward`	host_executes_chat_console.jsp
`jsp:forward`	host_executes_chat_ready.jsp
	host_executes_command.jsp
`BonForumRobot`	host_executes_chat_robot.jsp + host_executes_chat_console.jsp
	host_executes_command_controls.jsp
Frame	host_executes_command.jsp
`bonCommand`	host_executes_command_controls.jsp
`jsp:forward`	host_decreases_rating.jsp
`jsp:forward`	host_increases_rating.jsp

continues

Table 6.3 **Continued**

Type of Request	Requested JSP File / Requesting JSP Files
	host_executes_command_frame.jsp
Frame	host_executes_command.jsp
`bonCommand`	host_executes_command_frame.jsp
`BonForumRobot`	host_executes_command_robot.jsp + host_executes_command.jsp
	host_executes_command_ready.jsp
`bonCommand`	host_executes_command_controls.jsp
	host_executes_command_robot.jsp
Frame	host_executes_command.jsp
`jsp:forward`	host_executes_command_ready.jsp
	host_exits_command.jsp
`BonForumRobot`	host_executes_command_robot.jsp + host_executes_command_ready.jsp
	host_exits_chat.jsp
`BonForumRobot`	host_executes_chat_robot.jsp + host_executes_chat_ready.jsp
	host_increases_rating.jsp
`bonCommand`	host_executes_command_controls.jsp
	host_decreases_rating.jsp
`bonCommand`	host_executes_command_controls.jsp
	bonForum.jsp
`bonCommand`	visitor_executes_choice.jsp

6.1.9 XML Data Storage

In a later version, we will use JDBC and an SQL database to store and retrieve bonForum data. That will handle large data sets, such as those found in a chat room Web site. However, for now, we are using Java to model the database design that will be used.

All database engines of the future likely will understand XML. They will do so using highly optimized processing like that found in all major SQL database engines of today. Some XML-aware database systems already are available. Why did we not select one of these? Because we would learn more about how to process XML using Java, and because we wanted to explore our own ideas about storing XML in relational databases.

Some think that although XML may be catching on for interapplication communication, it still has a long way to go before it's competitive as a relational database. Furthermore, you might need to integrate your XML usage with a third-party RDBMS and perhaps are more interested in finding examples of XML-generating data access classes than following an experimental project. Fortunately, many other books cover these subjects—here are some links that may be useful in that regard:

- Storing XML in databases, by Uche Ogbuji: `http://www.linuxworld.com/linuxworld/lw-2001-02/lw-02-xml3databases.html`.
- XML and databases, by Ronald Bourret: `http://www.rpbourret.com/xml/XMLAndDatabases.htm`
- Modeling relational data in XML: `http://www.extensibility.com/tibco/resources.modeling.htm`

ForestHashtable Class

We called our XML data storage solution `ForestHashtable` because it extends the `hashtable` class and allows you to store and retrieve data trees. Chapter 11, "XML Data Storage Class: ForestHashtable, is devoted to a detailed explanation of this Java class. There is no need here to add to what is covered in that chapter. Instead, we will make general observations about the `ForestHashtable` data storage class.

We have used the techniques that are the basis of `ForestHashtable` for many years to optimize the storage, retrieval, and display of hierarchical data. What is new this time is that we are applying these techniques to XML data. In addition, as is usually the case, implementing the underlying algorithms in a different programming language (Java) has clarified for us both the techniques involved and their value.

The `ForestHashtable` class is a model intended for later implementations in a relational or object database system. It provides no persistent data storage for our application data (although serialization could be later employed for that purpose). Along with the rest of the bonForum project, it is a just a learning tool and a blueprint.

Not Ready for Prime Time

Until we reimplement the design of the `ForestHashtable` class using persistent objects or tables, we cannot support the deployment of a real, high-volume chat Web site. However, we can now test the bonForum Web application design. If bonForum as a prototype crawls along but functions correctly, it will be a success. The new version will be built using a relational database to handle the real data requirements of a Web chat.

6.1.10 Prototyping Custom JSP Tags

The first tag added to our JSP tag library was a multipurpose tag. It was designed to serve only as a JSP custom tag testbed, allowing the rapid prototyping of the various tag classes that we would need for bonForum. We could quickly add new commands to this one tag, without having to take the time to add new source files, attribute names, entries in the .tld file, and so on. This tag used an attribute named `type` to select from among the tag prototypes, and three generic attributes for sending any needed arguments to the tag class.

Only after we had decided which of our tag experiments were useful in the bonForum project did we break those commands out of the `ChoiceTag` class into a separate tag classes of their own.

The implementation of our chameleon tag's many methods took considerable effort. The details are the subject of Chapter 10, "JSP Taglib: The bonForum Custom Tags." In this section, we give only an overview of the implementation process using the `ChoiceTag` class. The actual tags that we ended up with are described in Chapter 10.

Calling Servlet Methods from a JSP Tag

We began by studying the `simpletag` example that comes with the Jakarta-Tomcat distribution, which gave us two tags to use as starting points. The `log` tag showed us some of the basics, such as how to output text to the HTML produced by a JSP. The `foo` tag, however, showed us something that would prove very useful: how to set up a loop structure using the tag-processing events.

We began experimenting with our `ChoiceTag` class even while our design was in its early stages. The outcome of this experimentation thus could affect the design decisions. Had we waited until more of the design was fixed, our tag implementation would have been much more constrained by pre-existing Java methods. Instead, the design of the `ChoiceTag` and the Java methods it relied upon could proceed hand in hand.

However, we did have our basic design principles in place, namely that the project would be based upon an XML definition of a chat forum. We knew that we would be using an Actor-Action-Thing command syntax. So, our first experiment was to add a `type` attribute value of `boncommand` to our `ChoiceTag` class that could be used to get actor, action, and thing values to a tag method. The following code is an example of that tag, which is not part of bonForum. It listed the attributes to the browser display, which just gave us some feedback so that we could test the command. This basically just replicated the functionality of the `foo` tag Tomcat example:

```
<ul>
<bon:choice type="bonCommand" attrOne="host" attrTwo="executes"
attrThree="command">
<li><%= member %></li>
</bon:choice>
</ul>
```

Our experiments with developing our JSP tag soon revolved around outputting our bonForum XML data and displaying it to chat users in the various formats that they would need the most:

- To start a chat, a user would need a list of subjects.
- To choose a chat, a user would need a list of available chats.
- To actually chat, a user would need to see the messages in the chat.
- To rate a chat guest, a chat host would need to see a list of guests.

Early Experiments with Xerces DOMFilter

The samples that come with the Apache Xerces download seemed a good place to start. We compiled and ran these and then studied their source code. (Doing that is a highly recommended exercise.) The DOMFilter and DOMWriter examples helped especially.

In early experiments, we took the guts of the DOMWriter and DOMFilter examples that come with the Apache XML packages and hacked them into our altered `foo` tag class. The results were two types of `ChoiceTag`, `BonWriter` and `BonFilter`, which output all our XML data or just selected attribute values from the data. These `ChoiceTag` types are not part of the application—they were just experiments that were valuable for the design process.

To have an XML representation of bonForum that we could use for developing and testing, we created a file called bonForum.xml. That was intended to be an example of what the data in our application would eventually look like. This is a very important point and one of the driving forces behind XSLT architectures: *Application logic and presentation logic can be developed in parallel with only an initial DTD and sample XML file joining the two, long before the underlying data model is complete.*

We still did not have any real data to work with. First, we would have to finish our "database"—that is, the `ForestHashtable` class. Then we would have to get it to output its contents as XML. In the meantime, our fake XML file allowed us to test our new tag types, as in the following examples:

```
<bon:choice type="bonWriter" attrOne="false" attrTwo="DEFAULT"
attrThree="..\\webapps\\bonForum\\mldocs\\bonForum.xml">
<%= "HELLO bonWriter"%>
</bon:choice>
```

The `bonWriter` tag type, shown in the previous code, output the entire XML file onto the browser display—not so useful, but it was a start. The `bonFilter` tag type, shown in the next lines, output all the attributes named `Key` with a value of `guest`. It was not used in bonForum either, but we were getting the mechanics down.

```
<bon:choice type="bonFilter" attrOne="Key" attrTwo="guest"
attrThree="..\\webapps\\bonForum\\mldocs\\bonForum.xml">
<%= "HELLO bonFilter"%>
</bon:choice>
```

Displaying Subjects and Messages

We then used `ChoiceTag` to prototype two other tag classes that are used in the bonForum Web application. When we got them working, we took the code from `ChoiceTag` and used it to fully develop these two tags for our library. Although they ended up looking quite simple on the JSP after we had them working, each one represents quite a bit of effort and code.

These two tag classes are called `OutputPathNamesTag` and `OutputChatMessagesTag`. They depend on methods that are in the `ForestHashtable` and `BonForumStore` classes. Therefore, you might need to read Chapters 8, 10, and 11 (which cover these four classes), and also Chapter 7, "JavaServer Pages: The Browseable User Interface" (which discusses many of the JSP documents), before these two seemingly simple tags will become clear to you.

The first task that we encapsulated in a tag was that of displaying all the various chat subject categories to a user about to start a new chat. These categories (we call them subjects) are initially loaded from an XML file into the `ForestHashtable` instance named `bonForumXML`. `OutputPathNamesTag` is used to access the subjects from a JSP. That happens in the JSP document named visitor_starts_chat_frame.jsp.

The second task encapsulated by `ChoiceTag` was that of displaying the messages to each host or guest in a chat. That task involved many problems, such as how to refresh the messages on each client browser and how to page the display of messages in an HTML page, among others. These problems would not have been so difficult to solve had we allowed ourselves to use client-side techniques, but we were committed by design to looking for server-side solutions whenever possible.

In the end, the `OutputChatMessagesTag` class was capable of hiding all the complex code we had created behind the simple-looking tag command that you can see on the two JSP documents named guest_executes_chat_frame.jsp and host_executes_chat_frame.jsp.

XSLT from a Tag Proves Powerful

Eventually, our tag-building efforts were concentrated predominantly on prototyping the `TransformTag` class. It gave us access to the Apache Xalan `XSLTProcessor` class from our JSP pages. We will return to that later and in Chapter 10.

As we had hoped when we began the project, this combination of XSLT and JSP turned out to be powerful and promising. We found that the `TransformTag` class was clearly the optimal tool to apply in data-display tasks, except in two tasks (displaying chat subject categories to a user starting a chat, and displaying the messages in a chat). `TransformTag` was so useful that we were able to stop adding new tags entirely!

We highly recommend the use of a JSP tag library because it very neatly packages the interfaces between the JSP pages and the Java servlets. Although developing custom tags requires some extra effort, this actually leads one to simplify those interfaces. If you use scriptlets instead of tags, it is easy to come up with a much more complex matrix of possibilities, and that can lead to a lot of undesigned contracts between the user interface (JSP) and the background processing (servlets).

6.1.11 *BonForumEngine* and *BonForumStore*

As we stated previously, the `BonForumEngine` Java servlet is the "central station" of the bonForum Web application: It handles most of the HTTP requests. It also coordinates all the JSP pages. Together with the `BonForumStore` class, it synchronizes all the users.

`BonForumEngine` has a member named `bonForumStore`, which is the one static instance of the `BonForumStore` class. One of the main functions of this bean is to encapsulate the XML database, a static `ForestHashtable` instance named `bonForumXML`. Access to the XML data from the JSP pages and from their custom tag classes is handled by methods in the one `bonForumStore` member of the `bonForumEngine`.

When we first began prototyping `bonForum`, we had only the `BonForumEngine` servlet class. It was all too convenient to try out new code ideas by adding fields and methods to `BonForumEngine`. This bloated class was criticized by many because it suffered the fate of early release in book form. Release early, release often—then hide out a while. The life of a "bottoms-up" software developer is never easy, it seems. Of course that was the wrong place for much of that code, so it now resides in `BonForumStore` (which itself will be factored someday).

A full description of these important classes is provided in Chapter 8.

All Requests Go Through the *service* Method

All of the Web application's HTTP requests to the Tomcat Server are handled by the `service` method in `BonForumEngine`. As you have seen in the previous tables (see Section 6.1.8, "Forum States, `bonCommands`, and JSP"), many JSP pages include one (or more) HTML form that is POSTed to this servlet.

In addition, the Tomcat deployment descriptor for the bonForum Web application (in the web.xml file) includes a servlet-mapping entry that causes Tomcat to send every bonForum URL that ends in .tfe to `BonForumEngine`. The `BonForumRobot` applet adds that extension to each document that it requests, via its `showDocument()` method.

The only requests for Web application URLs that are not routed through the `service()` method of `BonForumEngine` are those made by a `jsp:forward` element on a JSP page and the requests made to fill the HTML frame elements in each frameset in bonForum.

6.1.12 Forwarding from a Servlet to a JSP

In Chapter 8, we thoroughly discuss the process that `BonForumEngine` uses to forward the HTTP requests because that is one of its most important tasks in the application. In particular, read Section 8.1.13, "The `service()` Method: Forwarding HTTP Requests."

We had a problem at first trying to get `BonForumEngine` to forward a request to a JSP page. This was because of the pathname we were using. Here is an example of one that did not work: /bonForum/jsp/forum/visitor_join_chat.jsp. The correct path to use was /jsp/forum/visitor_join_chat.jsp. This path seems to imply that you can move a JSP page from one Web application to another. We have not tried that yet to find out for sure.

It was easy to fall into the problem we had. The form on the JSP page was correctly being POSTed using the following path, which was the source of our confusion:

```
<form method="POST" action="/bonForum/servlet/BonForumEngine">
```

The servlet container (Tomcat Server) will concatenate this path to the Webapps folder path. On the other hand, an instance of the `BonForumEngine` servlet, when forwarding a request, will add its path to the bonForum folder path—in other words, to the Web application folder.

6.1.13 Including Documents in a JSP

At this point in the implementation, we were running the Xalan XSLT processor from our JSP documents using our prototype for the `TransformTag` class. We had decided that during prototyping we would save the output of the XSLT processing in an HTML file (we now usually use XML output to a string variable instead). Then we made a big mistake—we confused the `include` directive with the `jsp:include` tag! We tried to use the `include` directive to display the XSLT results on the browser, something like this:

```
<%@ include file="../../mldocs/bonForumView.html"%>
```

The first time we accessed the JSP, Tomcat tried to create the Java source file for its servlet in the Work folder. However, `TransformTag` had not yet fired because that happens at request time. Therefore, Tomcat found no HTML output file because none existed yet. It gave up trying to create a Java file, much less compile it into a class file. The browser showed us the following error display:

```
Error: 500,
Internal Servlet Error
org.apache.jasper.compiler.CompileException: C:\jakarta-
➥tomcat\webapps\bonForum\jsp\forum\forum_test.jsp(23,2) Bad file argument to
➥include
```

We took out the `include` directive and then requested the JSP again. This time the page could be compiled, so `TransformTag` fired and created the HTML file. Then we put the `include` directive back in (to fix it, presumably, although it was really doing just fine). Now, because Tomcat could find the HTML file this time, it could compile the JSP again with the `include` directive. Now we got exactly the browser display that we were looking for—or so we thought. Actually, it was displaying stale content, but we had changed neither the input nor the style sheet of the XSLT transform, so there was no way for us to see that the HTML results were from the transform on the previous page (the one without any `include` directive).

Then, to see the thing work, we changed the XML input for the XSLT transform. Instead of a different browser display, as we expected, we got the same old one again! Must be a caching problem? You might think this story is getting too long, but we think it is rather funny. It is easy to see why the server-side Java forums are such busy places.

About that time, we realized our mistake: We should have used the `jsp:include` element. The `include` directive cannot be used this way for dynamic updates of the JSP output. The correct way to include a document at request time in the output of a JSP is to use the `jsp:include` action, doing something like this:

```
<jsp:include page="../../mldocs/bonForumView.html" flush="true" />
```

If you want more information about this topic, read the excellent book *Core Servlets and JavaServer Pages*, by Marty Hall, published by Prentice Hall PTR/Sun Microsystems Press.

Before we leave this topic, one more observation may be useful. Whenever you find yourself scratching your head about the behavior of a JSP, an obvious step is to look at the Java source code that the page translates into in the Work folder. Had we done that, we would have seen that our include directive produced the following source code in the servlet:

```
out.write("<html>\r\n<head>\r\n<title>bonForum</title>\r\n</head>\r\n<body
➥bgcolor=cyan>\r\n<select name=\"chatGuest\"
size=\"9\">\r\n<option>Adam age:44 rating:4</option>\r\n<option>Eve age:33
➥rating:7</option>\r\n</select>\r\n</body>\r\n</html>\r\n");
```

This would have told us something important: The display we were getting was hard-wired into the servlet. It was not dynamic; the HTML was not being read at request time.

On the other hand, here is what we would have seen in the servlet source when we (finally) used the `jsp:include` element instead:

```
{
String _jspx_qStr = "";
pageContext.include("../../mldocs/bonForumView.html" + _jspx_qStr);
}
```

Looking up the `pageContext.include` method in the Jakarta servlet API docs would have been (and still is) very educational.

6.1.14 XSLT Transform from a JSP

Being able to use the Apache Xalan XSLT processor from our JSP documents was a major goal for our project. The results are described in Chapter 10. In this chapter, we are presenting only a short chronological overview of the implementation effort. Looking back, we can see that our biggest problem was that Xalan had very little documentation available when we first began using it.

Using Xalan-Java 2 Instead of Xalan-Java 1

The bonForum release with this book was developed before a stable release of Xalan-Java 2 was available. It turned out that the part of Xalan that we use (XSLT transformation) was among the most reworked parts of the Xalan product as it went to version 2. Here is what the version 2 readme.html says:

> Given the scope of the redesign, the changes with respect to Xalan-Java 1.x are global in nature .... Xalan-Java 2 implements the TraX (Transformation API for XML) interfaces. The product of extensive open-source collaboration by members of the XML developer community, TrAX provides a conceptual framework and a standard API for performing XML transformations.

Fortunately, the changeover to Xalan-Java 2 did not have a major impact on the design of bonForum—it requires only a somewhat different way to create and use an XSLT processor—so the input and output of that processor will remain the same. For information about using either Xalan Java 1 or 2 with the bonForum project, please refer to Chapter 4, "XML and XSLT: Xerces and Xalan," Section 4.5, "Installing Xalan." Also, check for the latest bonForum information at `www.bonForum.org`.

Xalan's XSLT Servlet

At the time we were developing our XSLT custom tag, there was no XSLT servlet in Xalan. Today, we may be tempted to solve the XSLT requirements of our JSP tag by having it access the XSLT servlet that is now provided with Xalan. We recommend that you try that approach in similar situations. We tried again, with Xalan 2.0.0, but it still had the old documentation for the Xalan-Java 1.2.2 servlet, although it has changed drastically, including the name of the servlet. Now, with Xalan 2.0.1, the servlet sample is a very useful resource. Relative to the root folder for either Xalan-Java 1 or Xalan-Java 2, look for the XSLT servlet documentation at `/docs/samples.html#servlet`.

JSP Scripting with Java Code

We found some code in the Xalan sample TransformToDom that looked promising. We decided to put some similar code directly on a JSP, using scriptlets, just to test it. After it was working, we would encapsulate it in a tag class. The details of that code are discussed in section 10.6, "XSLT and the TransformTag Class," of Chapter 10.

We had hit upon perhaps the best procedure for developing the Web application. Developing and testing code directly on a JSP is fast and simple. After it works, you can move it into a separate class, which makes the JSP simpler and enables you to reuse the code elsewhere. We do this only to speed up development; the code usually doesn't belong in the JSP servlet and needs encapsulation in its own object.

XSLT from a JSP Custom Tag

Our JSP custom tag for choosing an Actor-Action-Thing command was already sending three generic attributes as arguments to a Java servlet method. It was an easy step to alter that testbed tag so that it could function also as an XSLT processor. The code that we had used to test our JSP scriptlets was further developed on our `chameleon` tag and finally found a home in the `TransformTag` class. With it, we could do the following on our JSP:

```
<bon:transform
type="XalanVersion"
inDoc="..\\webapps\\bonForum\\mldocs\\foo.xml"
styleSheet="..\\webapps\\bonForum\\mldocs\\foo.xsl"
outDoc="..\\webapps\\bonForum\\mldocs\\foo.html" >
</bon:transform>
```

Actually, the type value shown is a rather late addition. We now use type attribute values to select XSLT processes. Current acceptable values are "Xalan Java 1" and "Xalan Java 2". There is also a session attribute called "xalanVersion" which can be set to any acceptable value for the type attribute. One way you can set that session attribute is by including something like the following HTML form (JSP or otherwise) that is POSTED to the BonForumEngine:

```
<form name="forum_entry" method="POST" action="/bonForum/servlet/BonForumEngine">
<label for="xalanVersion">
Apache Xalan Version?
</label>
<input id="xalan1" type="radio" name="xalanVersion" value="Xalan-Java 1">
Xalan-Java 1
</input>
<input id="xalan2" type="radio" name="xalanVersion" value="Xalan-Java 2" CHECKED>
Xalan-Java 2
</input>
<input type="hidden" name="actorReturning" value="yes">
</input>
<input type="hidden" name="bonCommand" value="visitor_executes_choice">
</input>
<input type="submit" value="continue" name="submit">
</input>
</form>
```

The BonForumEngine servlet will set the session attribute from the request parameter. The tag class will get and use that session attribute if a value of `xalanVersion` is used for the type attribute in the custom tag on the JSP. Do not worry if the details are not clear at this point, more will be said about all this later. The output of the XSLT process need not be HTML—it can be XML, for example. It can also go to a custom scripting variable named `output`, which it does when the `outDoc` attribute is set to `output` or `outputNormalized`.

Instead of using a file for its XML `InputSource`, `TransformTag` can instead use the contents of the `ForestHashtable` XML database. It does that if the first attribute is set to the string value `bonForumXML`. This turned out to be one of our best tools for developing bonForum (see Chapter 10). Our JSP now has powerful possibilities using `TransformTag`. For example, we can dump our entire database out to the browser for debugging like this:

```
<bon:transform
type="bonTransform"
inDoc=" bonForumXML "
styleSheet="..\\webapps\\bonForum\\mldocs\\identity.xsl"
outDoc="outputNormalized" >
<%=output%>
</bon:transform>
```

6.1.15 Style Sheets

When we had `TransformTag` working, we were able to use some XSL style sheets to accomplish some of our XML data-display goals. Eventually, as the prototype is further developed, we expect that there will be many more style sheets. The ones that we have used already are discussed in Chapter 10.

All the style sheets that we used in the book version of bonForum were applied using XSLT to the entire contents of the bonForumXML `ForestHashtable`. In the future, we plan to have a more selective mechanism for determining the XML `InputSource` for the XSLT process. For that reason, we have already included in the project a second `ForestHashtable` object, named `bonBufferXML`. It will help when we want to apply XSLT to only a selected subset of the entire data contents of bonForum.

The XSL style sheet files are all found in the folder TOMCAT_HOME\webapps\bonForum\mldocs.

Here is a list of the XSL style sheet documents in use when this book went to print. They are used for getting a list of available chats, a list of the guests in a chat, and a list of links to other resources, (including other bonForums, presumably):

bonChatItems.xsl

bonChatGuests.xsl

bonForumLinks.xsl

6.1.16 Session-Based Application Information

We highly recommend to any reader interested in Java the book *Thinking in Java*, by Bruce Eckels, published by Prentice Hall. At this time, you can freely download a preview version of the entire book. Find out more about this very useful book by visiting the Web address `http://www.mindview.net`.

One chapter of that book that may be helpful for understanding bonForum is Chapter 15, "Distributed Computing." In particular, the two sections entitled "Servlets" and "JavaServer Pages" are recommended because they explain the use of the session object in servlets and the various data scopes available in JSP.

Much of the bonForum application information that is not kept in the `bonForumXML` data storage object typically ends up being kept in HTTP session attributes. We have seen, for example, that on our JavaServer pages many HTML form elements are POSTed to the `BonForumEngine` servlet. These forms include input elements whose values are visible within that servlet as HTTP request parameter values.

If one of these application variables will be required again, when a different HTTP request (from the same browser session) is being serviced, the `BonForumEngine` servlet copies it to a session attribute that it creates with the same name as the request parameter. Here is an example, from BonForumEngine.java:

```
chatTopic = normalize((String)request.getParameter("chatTopic"));
if(chatTopic.trim().length() > 0) {
session.setAttribute("chatTopic", chatTopic);
}
```

In case you are wondering what the `normalize` method does, it serves two purposes. It makes sure that strings input by the users can be legally included in the XML data, by substituting inadmissible characters with the appropriate character entities. It also replaces null values with empty strings so that we do not later have to add code to check for null values. Nor do we have to handle null-value exceptions commonly caused by passing null string values to Java methods that expect a string.

One session attribute in the application is called `bonForumStore`. It enables us to find the application interface to its XML database from anywhere, including JSP, that can access the session object with this attribute.

The use of session attributes to store information has important features and consequences that must be grasped to understand the Web application implementation:

- Each user is provided a separate variable context in the Web application.
- Each user context is tied to the existence and duration of one session, which connects all the requests made by one browser for a configurable period of activity.
- When a session expires, all information in its user context becomes inaccessible.

In addition to maintaining user-related information in storage locations with session scope, we used a user's current session ID to connect the user to important elements in the XML storage so that these could be quickly found and retrieved. That is discussed in the next section. Meanwhile, notice that when a session expires, these XML elements also become "orphans" in the application, inaccessible to the code.

Obviously, these effects of the volatility of session objects must be handled by bonForum before it is deployed. This task has been left for a future version, mostly because it involves design decisions that are better made based on the results of experimenting with the current implementation. At the very least, we will have to purge "orphan" session-related information from the data. At the other extreme, we could do what some commercial chat sites do, which is to implement a system of associating registered users with unique IDs and then track each user across all their bonForum sessions.

6.1.17 Avoiding Parsing and Searching

A major theme in the implementation of bonForum has been to find ways to optimize the application for speed. We have tried to find mechanisms that will scale up to installations handling thousands of simultaneous users. That is not to say that the prototype bonForum can do that. In fact, some of its methods will certainly need some more work before they can. Nevertheless, one of our experiments turned out promising.

Session-Unique Elements

As discussed previously, one way to know which data items are related to a particular user of the Web application is to keep those items in session attributes. However, what about all the data that we keep in an XML database? It includes items pertaining to each user, and there must be some way to know what belongs to whom.

Of course, this kind of problem is not at all new. There are obvious solutions using relational database tables. On the other hand, if we were using an XML document only to store data, the solution would most likely involve the use of XPATH. However, bonForum stores XML documents in a special `hashtable` class, `ForestHashtable`, which is a simulation for a relational database table design. Each element node of the XML is stored in a table row with a key called a `NodeKey`, which encodes the position of the node in a tree structure. We had to find our own solution to the problem of relating data to the bonForum users.

Let's use an example here. A user of the bonForum is associated with at particular chat. That chat is represented by an element node in the XML data. We could associate the user with the chat by adding a child element inside the chat element. That child element would either represent the user or point to an element elsewhere that represents the user (we did the latter).

We wanted to avoid repeated searches through our data every time the same piece of information was required. There were many places in the code where we needed to know which chat element belonged to the current user. If every time we needed that answer we had to search through all the data looking for the chat element that contained a child that was associated with that user, it was time to find a better way.

First, we made a rule. Whenever possible, we defined elements in our XML so that they would be unique for each user. That meant that they would be unique within an HTTP session. One session can "own" only one chat element. One session can own only one guest element.

The second thing we did was to create another hashtable, called a `NodeNameHashtable`. The elements that this `hashtable` holds are `NodeKey` values. The keys that it uses associate the `NodeKey`s with a user session. To use the previous example given, the key for the `NodeKey` of an XML chat node would be something like `To1012mC7576871324604071At:chat`. The key's prefix is the ID of the session that owns the chat node.

These two things together gave us a mechanism for fast access to data that is related to a particular session and, thus, the user and browser. This mechanism plays a part in quite a few places in the code. You can read more about it in Chapter 11, Section 11.5, "Caching Keys for Fast Node Access."

PathNameHashtable

In Chapter 11, section 11.5, you can also read about another mechanism we employed to prevent time-consuming processing. When a user wants to join a chat, he must choose one from a list displayed by the browser. The list shows the user the subject and topic of each available chat. Processing the user choice involves locating a particular node in the XML data—in this case, a subject node.

Instead of searching through the XML somehow, we again have a fast way to get the `NodeKey` of the node we need. This involves yet another hashtable, this time one called `PathNameHashtable`. In this case, `NodeKeys` are stored in the `hashtable` using keys that indicate the path to a subject element in the XML data tree.

As noted elsewhere, we have constrained the possible names that these elements can have. Duplicate sibling-node names are not allowed. Thus, we have a unique set of subject pathnames. When a user chooses a chat to join, the choice is associated with a unique pathname. This pathname can then be used to quickly retrieve the subject element required for the user to join the chat.

6.1.18 Synchronizing Multiple Threads

We soon had to pay more attention to the question of how our Web application would handle an environment in which it was being used by not one developer, but by many clients. One of Java's strengths is its built-in thread management. We hoped that it could solve the problem of multiple, simultaneous access to our `BonForumEngine` Java servlet.

Again, we recommend to the reader the book *Thinking in Java*, by Bruce Eckels. Especially helpful in the present context are Chapters 14 and 15: "Multiple Threads" and "Distributed Computing." That book is a good resource for learning about those two topics.

Critical Resources

Essentially, we had to find a way to use the Java mechanism of synchronization to protect access to critical resources. We could synchronize access either to methods or to blocks of code. A lot can be said about the topic of synchronization in Java by using the following two analogies:

- Synchronizing all the public methods in a class is like saying, "I'm doing this action, so you cannot do that action, nor that action, and so on."
- Synchronizing a block of code on an object is like saying, "I have this thing, so you cannot do that, nor that, and so on."

Of course, the first of the two cases is really the same as the second one, with this class instance being the object upon which code processing is being synchronized.

In any case, it is quite apparent that we must protect the bonForum data. The progress of the forum continually depends upon the current contents of its XML representation, which is what we have chosen to keep in the `bonForumXML ForestHashtable` object. This XML representation is continually being changed in response to the actions of the actors. In other words, the application data change in response to multiple asynchronous user inputs.

Typically, while interacting with one JSP-generated HTML page, each client causes more than one change to `bonForumXML`. This means that access to that XML representation must be transactional. We made sure that only one client at a time could access the `bonForumXML` object: We used the `synchronized` Java keyword.

At first, we thought that meant synchronizing all the public methods in `BonForumEngine`. These include methods that are capable of changing the `bonForumXML` object. However, if we did that, the lock being used would be on the Java servlet object. It would not be much of a servlet if only one client can access it at a time, so we knew that there must be a better way.

Instead, we synchronize any "critical code" sections on the `bonForumXML` instance. In effect, this means that whoever owns the XML representation of bonForum can access the methods that are capable of changing its contents. All the other users must wait their turn; they are blocked—in effect, queued up and buffered—by the Java synchronization mechanism.

Questions Regarding Synchronization

Certainly, the way that we have set up multiple thread access to the data is an area that needs far more testing. For one thing, it is important to minimize the number and size of synchronized code sections in the application because they constitute bottlenecks and overhead.

We also want to make sure that there are no ways to defeat the protections offered by the synchronization that we have added—for example, by accessing methods from JSP.

Getting thread synchronization right is partly an art, and we will not be surprised if problems surface. However, after we have implemented a persistent database table from our `ForestHashtable` design, we will at least be able to recover from a thread clash, which is not possible now!

6.2 Displaying and Selecting Chat Subjects

As you have read, our implementation began as a system involving many JSP documents, which used custom tags to access an XML data-interface object and an XSLT processor. At that point, we still had some major problems to solve before this system could work as a chat application.

Obviously, one of the first problems that we had to solve was how a visitor to the bonForum would start a new chat. We knew from our design that it would involve selecting one element from a subtree of subjects in our XML data. The technical question became how to display the subjects on a browser and then how to find the XML subject element using the display item that the visitor selected on the browser.

We were looking for places to apply XSLT and XPATH in bonForum. In some ways, this seemed like a good place to start, but we decided against that. It was not a simple problem on which to begin applying those technologies. Second, everything else in the project was contingent upon creating a chat, so we wanted a fast solution for that. In addition, our XML data structure was morphing and evolving in response to our attempts to find fast node-lookup mechanisms.

6.2.1 Complexities of Starting a Chat

The solutions that we created instead involved the `PathNameHashtable`, which we discussed earlier. However, starting a chat turned out to be quite a complex problem. Here we list some things involved:

- Many chats can exist that all have the same subject, with each chat belonging to a different session.
- Each chat element in the XML must somehow be connected to the XML element for its subject.
- Each chat also has a short description added by the user who starts it. This `chatTopic` must also be stored, related, and retrieved.

This chapter is not the place to describe the solution that we devised. Indeed, the solution involved working with all the various parts of our new Web application system. Therefore, again, understanding what is going on in bonForum may require reading relevant sections in several of the more technical chapter yet to come. Here we simply list the book chapters and sections that will help you the most. You might want to mark this list and refer back to it later!

- Chapter 7: "JavaServer Pages: The Browseable User Interface"
  - Section 7.2.5: "visitor_starts_chat_frame.jsp"
- Chapter 8: "Java Servlet in Charge: BonForumEngine"
  - Section 8.1.20: "The `processRequests()` Method: Handling Host Executes Chat"
  - Section 8.2.12: "Invoking Chat Methods from JSP Custom Tags"
- Chapter 10: "JSP Taglib and Custom Tag: ChoiceTag"
- Chapter 11: "XML Data Storage Class: ForestHashtable"
  - Section 11.5.2: "`NodeKeyHashtables` Cache `NodeKeys`"
  - Section 11.5.4: "`PathNameHashtable`"
  - Section 11.6.4: "Automatic Parent Node Location Retrieval"

6.3 Displaying Chat Messages

After we had a chat with a host, we were ready to tackle the problems involved in presenting the chat to a user. We decided to work on the "host executes chat" forum state before the "guest joins chat" forum state. Our solution would also apply to the "guest executes chat" forum state. In addition, it would be more challenging and more capable of positively influencing the rest of the implementation work. The problem turned out to be much more complex than we ever imagined.

Getting the job done required solving several challenging technical problems, all related to displaying the chat history for the user. Although we had foreseen some of them during the design phase of the project, we were glad that we had not tried to solve them at that time. The solutions to these problems truly required experimentation. The principles of rapid application development were vindicated in this instance. Actual experience with a prototype was worth much more than theoretical discussion of the technological possibilities.

Again, we first considered basing our solution upon XSLT and XPATH. Our reasons for not doing so are well covered elsewhere, along with the solutions that we devised. Therefore, in this chapter we will try to discuss only the implementation process itself. Here is a list of all the chapters and sections that will help you to understand the process of displaying chat messages:

- Chapter 7: "JavaServer Pages: The Browseable User Interface"
  - Section 7.2.9: "host_executes_chat.jsp"
- Chapter 8: "Java Servlet in Charge: BonForumEngine"
  - Section 8.2.12: "Invoking Chat Methods from JSP Custom Tags"
- Chapter 9: "Java Applet Plugged In: `BonForumRobot`"
  - Section 9.3: "`BonForumRobot`"
- Chapter 11: "XML Data Storage Class: `ForestHashtable`"
  - Section 11.11: "Initializing the `bonForumXML` Database"
  - Section 11.12: "Runtime `bonForumXML` Database"

6.3.1 The *outputForumChatMessages* Method

There is one very important thing to note about the method that provides the chat messages to list on the browser page. In its current implementation, it iterates through the `bonForumXML` `ForestHashtable` contents searching for elements that are named "`message`." This works for the prototype, but the results will take longer to get as the database grows. Our plan is to iterate only the message pointers that exist within a particular chat element in the XML data. We had to settle for this interim solution for this version because the real solution had a bug that was found too late to fix before writing this book. It is possible that the version on the CD-ROM does include the correct, efficient algorithm. Also, please check the project Web site at `http://www.bonforum.org` for news and new releases.

6.3.2 Session Local Data Versus Chatting

One of the rules of our system is that the code that handles one particular user can access only elements in the XML database that belong to that user's session. That means, for example, that it is not possible for one user's thread to add an `actorNickname` child to a different user's guest actor element.

We suddenly realized that by allowing a session to add elements only to parent elements that were also added by that same session, we were making chatting impossible. It seemed that the process of adding a `messageKey` element to a chat element was different from all other add operations. A guest must be allowed to add messages for any chat joined, even if the guest has not added that chat's element.

6.3.3 The Need to Refresh Chat Messages

When an actor adds a message to a chat, that message should be seen very soon by all the other actors in the chat. We needed to find a technique to do this in our bonForum. Without this, it could hardly be called a chat forum; it would be more like a message board than a chat room.

Possible Refresh Mechanisms

We considered some mechanisms for refreshing the chat history display on the browsers. Some of these were rejected for being too "client-side."

We tried using a Pragma setting to cause a refresh of the page that had the chat messages displayed on it. We got that working, but it had two problems for us. One was that it was quite browser-dependent and would not work on all browsers. Although that was not an immediate consideration because we were only testing with IE5.X, we wanted our Web application eventually to be browser-independent.

The worse problem was that there was a lot of flickering in the message's display. It seems that when IE5 repainted the display, it first erased the old one to white. We started looking for other uses of the refresh Pragma on Web sites and found some that seemed to work. An occasional refresh is not bothersome, especially if you are not always looking right at the frame that is being refreshed. In our case, we wanted one refresh every 5 seconds, so the user would be staring at the flickering messages display most of the time. That was quite bothersome.

6.3.4 *BonForumRobot* Java Applet to the Rescue

When we started the book project, we wanted to complete it without any use of client-side programming. HTML that worked on any "plain vanilla" browser was to be the ideal output from our server-side programming efforts. Had we not chosen a chat room for the Web application project, we might not have ended up creating an applet.

Therefore, after some frustrating time spent trying to solve the problem, we reluctantly turned the problem into an opportunity to have some hands-on discussion about applet use in Java Web applications. First, we made an applet that included a timer mechanism based on putting a thread to sleep. We then set it up to repeatedly call the `showDocument` method of the applet class, with the URL of the JSP that displayed the chat messages. At first, the applet was also embedded on that same JSP using a `jsp:plugin` element.

It might seem like a wrong decision not to use our applet to also display the messages, as other chat applets do. We could have perhaps avoided the caching, scrolling, and flickering problems we encountered. However, we were still hoping (and are yet) to get rid of the applet entirely, so we have minimized its role. It is our experience that without an applet, this project would be much more interesting to many who have seen it.

In any case, our own applet experiment was still not satisfactory. The JSP also had an input form field for the user to enter the next chat message. Refreshing the JSP with the applet interfered with typing in that input field. (By the way, this problem of the refresh interfering with user input had also existed with the nonapplet, Pragma-only methods of handling the refresh requirements). However, we also had a couple of other problems. We tackled the most pressing one first, which is the subject of the next section.

6.3.5 The Caching Problem with *BonForumRobot*

We were getting a refresh action due to the applet, but the browser seemed to be showing the document from the browser cache instead of from the server. We could see messages that had been added from different browsers, but always the same ones. We then tried some well-known techniques to prevent caching of the pages, but nothing worked. The browser stubbornly refused to repeatedly request the JSP from the server.

Again, we started to think that we would need even more client-side power to solve this problem. However, we finally found a smaller trick that works. The `showDocument` method in the `BonForumRobot` applet refreshes the page using a different JSP filename each time. We do that by concatenating the current time in milliseconds with the real JSP filename to get unique names. We then add a new "fake" file extension (.tfe) that we have mapped in the Tomcat Server configuration file so that it is sent to the `BonForumEngine` servlet. The servlet strips off the time and extension and forwards the request to the correct JSP.

The only problem we found with this was that the browser happily cached a page every time a refresh occurred. After a while, the browser cache was full of copies of essentially the same JSP document, such as the following series (this was before we added frames):

```
http://localhost:8080/bonForum/guest_executes_chat.jsp960816479237.tfe
http://localhost:8080/bonForum/guest_executes_chat.jsp960816479247.tfe
http://localhost:8080/bonForum/guest_executes_chat.jsp960816479257.tfe
```

6.3.6 Testing of Web Application Begins

We now had something resembling a Web application, albeit an unusable one, so we started trying to use it to foresee and forestall problems. At the same time, we were testing the wisdom of that well-known rule of rapid application development: "Get it working first, and then make it work right!"

We started up six instances of the browser and put the program through its paces. Or, rather, we put what was there of the program through its paces because we had not yet finished any but the first six or so forum states of the application. We were actually surprised by the way things were working. We were trying this on a machine with only 64MB of RAM and a 266MHz Pentium processor. Many other programs were running as well, which resulted in lots of disk thrashing.

We got things to slow down considerably this way, but only after much torturing of the application did we get our first indication of a problem: a "null pointer exception" message displayed on one of six Java consoles that were showing applet runtime information for each of the six browser instances.

6.3.7 The Need for Frames

Now that we were successfully refreshing the chat messages, we proceeded to the next biggest problem, which was the unpleasant interaction of our refresh mechanism and the users' efforts to use the application. To fix the applet solution, we broke another one of our starting rules: We used HTML frames. We needed to do that to provide a better user experience with the Web application.

We solved that by adding a frameset to our JSP output HTML. The applet, embedded in one frame, refreshes the chat messages in a different frame. A third frame holds the HTML form that lets the user input the next chat message, now without any interference at all.

6.3.8 Frames and JSP

Adding frames to our application caused a major shakeup of the design. Before we did this, our system usually had a straightforward correspondence between forum states, `bonCommands`, and JSP pages required. For example, the forum state "host executes chat" was reached by posting the `host_executes_chat bonCommand`, which caused the firing of the host_executes_chat.jsp JSP document.

Because we added frames to the application, we use several JSP documents together to create most of the forum states. One JSP page creates a frameset with two or three frames in it. Another JSP creates the content of one of the frames, which usually displays information to the user. Another JSP fills a frame that displays user input fields and controls. Yet another frame holds `BonForumRobot` in a `jsp:plugin` element. We will discuss others later in this chapter.

So as not to lose track of our design, we came up with a naming convention that retains the original JSP name for the document that creates the frameset. The other JSP documents that help to create the same forum state use the same name with additional suffixes.

This is better seen from examples. The JSP files that display and refresh the chat messages to a host and that allow the host to enter a new message are located in files named as follows:

host_executes_chat.jsp

host_executes_chat_frame.jsp

host_executes_chat_controls.jsp

host_executes_chat_robot.jsp

After we introduced frames to one of our forum states, it was natural to put them into most of the application. One of the main reasons for that was to achieve a consistent look and feel across all the browser pages. We did not need to refresh the available chat subjects in the "visitor starts chat" forum state frequently, as we did the chat messages. However, we put the display of chat subjects in its own frame anyway. Perhaps later the subjects will be added by users and need refreshing also.

The Need to Leave a Frame

Now we could load JSP-generated documents into HTML frames. These frames were also JSP-generated. Nevertheless, we had a new problem to solve. At some point, we needed to load a new part of the Web application that did not use the same frameset. We could not do that using `bonRobotApplet`, which was itself in a frame. The next document would load completely into one of the existing frames.

We needed a way to get rid of the existing frames. We tried just using the value `_top` for the second argument of the applet `showDocument` method. We tried several things. At one point, we succeeded in setting up an infinite regress of smaller framesets inside frames, like the proverbial Chinese boxes. Cute as it was, it was not exactly practical.

To make a long story short, we finally added another JSP file that also had the robot embedded in it but that was not associated with any frame or display at all. All this JSP does is load the first JSP of the next forum state. This technique proved to be useful quite a few times; some forum states have two examples of its use. One such case is the "host executes chat" forum state, which uses JSP documents in addition to the four listed previously, in this manner:

host_executes_chat_console.jsp

host_executes_chat_ready.jsp

We do need to make things a bit prettier. We can put a cute image on the robot. We can put some advertising space on the applet panel. Perhaps we can make the robot into an animated agent-like creature.

6.3.9 The Scrollbar Reset Problem

At this point, the most important remaining problem was the fact that the list of chat messages was scrolled back to the beginning after each refresh by the applet. The practical way to do this is with dynamic HTML, or other client-side solutions. Again, we rejected these to explore server-side solutions to the problem.

In fact, not only did the select list scroll unpleasantly, but as soon as there were more messages than the frame could display in the HTML select element, the frame itself would get a second scrollbar of its own, and that made the display twice as ugly. Still, it looked better now than it had without the frames.

Our solution for this problem turned out to be quite involved. The chat messages are now output one page at a time, with the page size being selectable by the user. Four buttons on the browser display, labeled First, Previous, Next, and Last, allow navigation through all the messages in the chat history. Missing is a one-message-at-a-time scrolling action, which will be added later. This solution needs more work.

The real work for all this happens in the method `bonOutputForumChatMessages` of the `BonForumStore` class. You will probably have to refer to the source code for that Java class to understand how that method works. There are also some relevant discussions in Chapters 7, 8 and 10.

6.3.10 Filtering Chat Messages by Session

When we first got some chat messages to display, we were getting all the messages in bonForum, not just the ones in the same chat as the user getting the display. Although it now displays the correct messages, the way this is accomplished is not the best way to do that. We "solved" the problem that way because we did not find until later a bug that kept guest messages from being stored in the correct chat element.

Now that we fixed the bug, there is no need to go through all the data looking for messages that are in the right chat for the current session, as is still being done now. Instead, we will iterate the children of the chat element for the current session. Among these will be the `messageKey` elements whose contents will be the `NodeKey` values of the message elements. We can use these `messageKey` elements to directly access, order, and display the message elements. This important change will be made to the source code later, hopefully in time for the CD-ROM production for the book. Please check the project Web site, `http://www.bonforum.org`, for new releases.

The next section is relevant to the problem we have been discussing: displaying the chat messages. See especially Section 6.4.1, "The `itemKey` Attribute." This next section is also important in relation to the theme of displaying and selecting a chat, which will be the topic of Section 6.5, "Displaying and Selecting Chats."

6.4 Finding the Chat Element

One problem that had not been foreseen provided somewhat of an implementation challenge. Our plan called for elements to be "attached" to the HTTP session that created them, as a way of providing user scope, albeit of short duration. The problem was that for a user to join a chat as a guest, its thread had to first find the chat. The chat was not attached to the session of the would-be guest. Rather, the chat was attached to the session of the host that created it.

The way we solved that problem is perhaps not immediately obvious. Although much is said about it in code comments and in the chapters to come, it will help to have an overview here as well. It might be that the overview is confusing without the details, and the details are confusing without the overview. If you are a software developer, you are probably accustomed to that kind of situation by now. You might want to just fold the corner of the page (unless you are reading it in the bookstore) and move on to the next book section (in this book, not the store!).

When a visitor chooses a chat to join, the selection includes both a chat subject and a chat topic. The chat subject gives the complete path to the correct chat subject element in the XML database. Each chat that exists for that subject is represented by a child element of that subject element. That child element has as its name the session ID value related to the host that created that chat. An attribute of the child element is set to the chat topic added by the chat host.

We can find the chat subject element from the would-be guest's choice by using `pathNameHashtable`. By iterating its children, searching for the one with the correct chat topic, we locate the element whose name gives us the session ID of the chat host. That enables us to find the chat element using `nodeNameHashtable`, which solves the problem. The user's thread can now add a `guestKey` to the chat element, transforming the user from a visitor to a guest.

One place to get details about this important bonForum theme is Chapter 8, in the section "Passing Information between Sessions."

6.4.1 The *itemKey* Attribute

Each time that a chat is created for a subject, the chosen subject element gets a new child element that is named after the session ID value of the visitor who creates the chat (a host session ID). This child element is known in the source code as a chat item, or `chatItem`. This unfortunate and vague term should have been avoided. Instead, it engendered another vague term, `itemKey`, which refers to the `NodeKey` for that `chatItem`. The *chat host thread* saves the value of the `itemKey` in two places. One is a session attribute (for the host's session, of course). The other is an XML attribute of the chat element in the data, named `itemKey`.

When a *chat guest thread* finds the chosen chat element, as described in the previous section, it gets the value of the itemKey attribute from it and saves it in a session attribute (for the guest's session). That is done to make it available for the guest's thread to brand messages and to display messages.

Whenever a message is sent to a chat by either a host or a guest, it is associated with the `itemKey` of the chat, which is unique in bonForum. Because that same `itemKey` is stored as an attribute of the chat element, a relationship is formed between all the message elements and the chat to which they belong. The `outputChatMessages()` method can then use this relationship to find the messages that it outputs (although, as we mentioned, that is probably not the best way to do that).

6.4.2 New XML Methods

Solving the problems that we just discussed gave us good chances to develop our XML data functionality further. We added methods to get attribute values and to find a child element with a given attribute value. We also added a method to edit a `BonNode` in a `ForestHashtable` (such as `bonForumXML`). Rather than creating an object that understands the entire official XML recommendation, we would rather let necessity dictate the evolution of the object.

If you want to see more details about finding the chat element, you can look in the source code. First, look in the file BonForumEngine.java. Look for all the code that uses term `chatItem` and the context of that code. Then look in the file ForestHashtable.java. Look at the code for these two methods:

subjectNodeKeyFromPathName

getChildNodeFromAttributeValue

6.4.3 Normalizing User Input

Another problem that we tried to solve at this time was to make sure that any input that came from a user could be used as an XML attribute value. The example that prompted that (hopefully code-wide) precaution was the `chatTopic` attribute that is added to the subject item element.

6.5 Displaying and Selecting Chats

When we could display chat messages usefully, we tackled the next major problems: the display of existing chats to a bonForum visitor wanting to become a guest, and the selection by that visitor of one of these available chats. We decided that the time was right to apply XSLT to the solution. Indeed, using XSLT had always been a major goal of the project, but this was judged the first good opportunity.

Again, in this chapter we are trying to give a quasichronological account of some of the major implementation themes we have encountered so far. Therefore, the details of how our XSLT custom JSP tag works and of the XSL style sheets that it uses in this project are left for the more technical chapters to come. We hope that this more topical account will help you digest that material more easily and will make the source code easier to read and change.

Mostly for debugging purposes, we developed early a method called `getXML()`, which output the entire contents of the `bonForumXML` (a `ForestHashtable`) as a string. Now we decided to make it the input XML stream for the Xalan XSLT processor as part of our `TransformTag` class.

Displaying the available chats would mean showing both the chat subject and the chat topic. We began with the following vague idea: We would create a style sheet that would find each chat subject item. It would accumulate the path to each such element in a variable. Then it would append the chat topic attribute to that subject path, and output that.

6.5.1 Including XSLT Output on JSP Output

As we discussed in Section 6.1.13, "Including Documents in a JSP," we had grabbed the wrong JSP `include` to display the output of the `TransformTag` prototype. Before we found our mistake (and after we had started using XML output from the XSLT processor instead of HTML), we came up with a different solution using a JSP scriptlet and a JSP expression. That is a great thing about JSP development: It is rich in possibilities. Even if one of the main reasons JSP was developed was to separate the roles of page designers and code developers, there are times when scriptlets are very handy for getting things working. Here is the code, which should really have used a `StringBuffer`:

```
<%
String selectChatGuests = "";
String optionChatGuest = "";
DataInputStream in = new DataInputStream(
                        new BufferedInputStream(
                          new FileInputStream(
"..\\webapps\\bonForum\\mldocs\\bonChatGuests.xml")));
while((optionChatGuest = in.readLine())!= null)
selectChatGuests += optionChatGuest + "\n";
in.close();
%>
[...]
```

```
<form method="POST" action="/bonForum/servlet/BonForumEngine">

<%— here we list the guests in the chat in a select box created by the
stylesheet. —%>
<p>
<%= selectChatGuests %>
</p>

[...]
```

6.5.2 Command-Line XSLT Development

If you will be doing much XSLT development, you probably will want to try out some of the many XSL design tools available for trial. For example, Excelon enables you to specify a dummy XML file and then edit your XSL in one pane while you see the transformation in another. You can find more information about Excelon at `http://www.exceloncorp.com/products/excelon_stylus.html`.

However, for a simple solution, Xalan comes with a standalone XSLT processor that can be used from the command line. It was much faster to use it to design XSL style sheets than it would have been using the XSLT JSP tag.

As an example, here is a batch file (for Xalan 1.2.2) that was used to develop the display of available chats:

```
Rem xalanTest.bat:
java org.apache.xalan.xslt.Process -IN test.xml -XSL bonChatItems.xsl -OUT
bonChatItems.xml
type bonChatItems.xml
```

Note that if you are using Xalan Java 2, you will have to update the command in this batch file. You can find information about that by reading the Xalan command line page of the Xalan 2.0.1 docs. Assuming the usual drive and installation folder, browse the following document: C:\xalan-j_2_0_1\docs\commandline.html.

The file, called test.xml, contained fake `bonForumXML` data that included just enough to test the XSLT processing. In the actual bonForum project, the XML input data for the transforms come from the `bonForumXML`. All this is described in Chapter 10, so there is no need to elaborate here.

Our XSLT solution could use some improvement. In accordance with our experimental agenda, we pressed on as soon as a minimally acceptable result was obtained. Getting a full system up and running is a higher priority than taking care of the details.

Successful Display of Available Chats

The details about displaying available chats are covered in Section 7.2.13, "visitor_joins_chat_frame.jsp," in Chapter 7. The output of the XSLT process now does not need to go to a file and then be read back into the page output, as in our prototype. Now we can output it to a scripting variable named `output`, which we can display within the `TransformTag` element. (You can read about the `TagExtraInfo` class in the Jakarta servlet API docs.) We could also change the scope of the variable to access the XSLT results from elsewhere on the page, for example. Now, we can also have output the XSLT directly into the page from the `TransformTag` class as well, and we may yet find that we do not need more than that.

6.6 Displaying Guests in Chat

When chat hosts want to change the ratings of chat guests, they need to see a list of guests. To make this happen, we simply reused the XSLT functionality that we had developed to display the available chats. To understand the code, start by looking at the JSP file host_executes_command_frame.jsp.

As you can see there, the XSLT uses a style sheet called TOMCAT_HOME\webapps\bonForum\mldocs\bonChatGuests.xsl. On the JSP file mentioned, you can see how this XML output file from the XSLT process is displayed on the HTML output file from the JSP. The chat host can then see the guest names, ages, and ratings.

6.6.1 Rating a Guest

Host actors can control the rating of the guests in their chat, incrementing or decrementing the value. New guests begin with a status of 5. If a guest reaches a rating of 10, he or she automatically becomes a co-host of the chat. (That may not yet be implemented.) If a guest reaches a rating of 0, on the other hand, that guest is automatically removed from the chat.

On the JSP pages corresponding to these two processes—namely, host_increases_rating.jsp and host_decreases_rating.jsp—we will use a `jsp:useBean` element to access the method `bonForumXML.editBonNode` in the `BonForumStore` class. We use that, along with lots of other gnarly-looking methods in the `BonForumStore` and `ForestHashtable` classes, to change the value of the `rating` attribute of the guest chosen by the host actor.

6.6.2 Displaying a Guest List to Guests

A technique similar to that used to display the guests in a chat to a host executing a command should be used again to show the guest list to each guest. That is, indeed, an expected feature of a chat room.

6.7 Outputting the bonForum Data as XML

It is useful to have the bonForum data in the form of an XML stream. This can be done two ways in the prototype version of bonForum. Eventually, this will be something that can be done by the system actor. At present, that actor does nothing.

Because these files provide overviews of the project useful for design, study, and debugging, we will show the JSP code here in this chapter. The first example provides a file that is a literal version of the simple XML contents of the `bonForumXML ForestHashtable`. It uses a so-called "identity" style sheet that simply copies the XSLT XML input to XML output. To create it, simply put the right `TransformTag` element on any JSP file (results vary accordingly). We do that from system_dumps_xml.jsp, so you should be able to find the XML output file in the mldocs folder after accessing the bonForum.jsp page in the Web application. The output file is named bonForumIdentityTransform.xml.

Here is a suitable tag command to use to "dump" the bonForum XML database:

```
<bon:transform type="Xalan Java2"
inDoc="bonForumXML"
      styleSheet="..\\webapps\\bonForum\\mldocs\\identity.xsl"
      outDoc="..\\webapps\\bonForum\\mldocs\\bonForumIdentityTransform.xml">
</bon:transform>
```

The second utility for viewing the contents of the bonForumXML data-storage object produces an emulation of an Internet Explorer view of the data. It uses a style sheet called default.xsl, which imitates Internet Explorer 5.X's default style sheet. That style sheet is provided with the Apache Xalan distribution. Here is the custom tag code to put on a JSP:

```
<bon:transform type="Xalan Java2"
inDoc=" bonForumXML "
      styleSheet="..\\webapps\\bonForum\\mldocs\\default.xsl"
      outDoc="..\\webapps\\bonForum\\mldocs\\bonForumView.html" >
</bon:transform>
```

Note that you can use another provided style sheet called default2.xsl instead, and obtain a simpler result that does not rely on JavaScript. The default.xsl style sheet uses JavaScript to produce an output that has nodes that can be collapsed and expanded by clicking on them in the browser display.

6.8 Future of bonForum Project

In this section, we discuss some things that have not been done or that have not been done right. Certainly, although writing a book about developing code might have its own benefits for a project, it also takes time away from the development process. It has often been necessary to omit some necessary features or leave in some annoying problems so that we can complete the book. The items in this section remain high on our list of priorities—and should for anyone joining the open source BonForum project on SourceForge (`http://www.bonforum.org`).

6.8.1 System Actor Functionality

From the beginning, a System actor has been planned that would function as a higher authority in bonForum. This actor would have access to all the commands and states of bonForum, plus some of its own supervisory states that would enable tuning, troubleshooting, and regulating the Web application.

6.8.2 Protecting Data from Deletion

We have built in a (very untested) `remove` method in the `BonForumStore` class that wraps the element deletion method in the `ForestHashtable` XML data class. Much more needs to be done to protect data from any deletion that adversely affects the state of the application.

For example, it will be best to prevent easy removal of `messageKeys` from a chat element. The system actor should control their removal and ensure the concurrent, transactional removal of the message element pointed to by the `messageKey` being removed.

6.8.3 Scavenging Stale Data

In a full bonForum system, there will be scavenger threads that can remove stale session objects. This might require some kind of session tracking. That would be provided, for example, by a kind of "window in time," consisting of a `hashtable` with session ID values using a datestamp as a key. If the size of the hashtable exceeds the acceptable limit in size and processor expense, any session ID older than some set number of days will be eligible for removal. Such removal would cascade throughout the bonForumXML `ForestHashtable`, removing all objects that belong to that session ID. For example, the `nodeNameHashtable` would be purged of elements having keys beginning with that session ID.

6.8.4 Tracking Stale Sessions

One of the most important additions required by bonForum is a way for a user identity to span a longer time than a session. There are various solutions to this problem of "stale" session ID values. Some sort of permanent registration is required. One simple way is to keep track of a permanent unique user nickname for each user. At the other end of the spectrum of possibilities is registration of a user using a credit card. The latter method is used by some Web sites to prevent access to adult sites by minors.

Whatever system is established will need to provide continuity for a user across different HTTP sessions. Data that is flagged with a session ID value can have the stale value replaced with a new one to keep the connection between the data and the user identity. The connection between a guest and a chat is made by referencing the session ID value of the chat's host, and these values must be updated as well when they grow stale.

Perhaps it would be better to leave the session ID values alone in the key values and to use the first one that a user gets as that user's ID. Then we only need to associate the user with a chain of session ID values that ends at the current one for that user.

It is very instructive to look over the Tomcat source code for its session-management classes. A lot of problems have been solved regarding keeping sessions in a server that are relevant to keeping users. You can find the session-management code in the Tomcat source in the package org.apache.tomcat.session.

6.8.5 Internationalization and Encoding Issues

We have been developing with a blithe disregard for a very real need: Different locations will require that different language and character encoding be used in the HTML and XML output that creates the application user interface on the browsers.

6.8.6 Host Priority over Guest

Currently, it is possible for a bonForum user to become a host by starting a chat and then re-enter the same chat as a guest. The problem is that that user then loses the capability to again be a host of that chat. Having a dual role might be an acceptable feature, if it worked. Otherwise, the user, in this case, should probably be recognized as the host and not allowed to become a guest, unless demoted with permission by another host.

6.8.7 Host and Guest Commands for the Future

As you have no doubt noticed if you tried the bonForum prototype, we have very few examples of host commands and guest commands. This is an obvious place to grow this application in terms of both utility and user interest. Here are just a few of the many possible candidates for addition as new commands:

1. Setting the refresh rate of chat messages
2. Setting the size of select lists (besides the chat messages list done now)
3. Setting the relative sizes of the various HTML frames
4. Setting properties of the applets
5. Setting color preferences
6. Setting font types and sizes
7. Selecting subsets of messages to display
8. Setting up private chat rooms

6.8.8 Better Display Method for Chat Messages

There is a more efficient way to search for the chat messages, which may not yet be in the project code that ships with this book. Check the project Web site. For more details, see Section 6.3.10, "Filtering Chat Messages by Session."

6.8.9 Unique Chat Topics per Chat Subject

It should not be possible to enter the same chat topic twice under the same subject category. Note: This problem has now been fixed.

6.8.10 Guest Promotion and Removal

The functionality to promote guests to hosts and to remove guests from chats needs to be finished. The user interface is done.

6.8.11 Displaying Guests to Each User

Each user must be able to see a list of all the guests in any chat.

6.8.12 Improvements to Use of Applets

There are ways to improve the timing used by the applets that refresh display lists and leave framesets. This involves being able to fire the action of the `BonForumRobot` applet on demand, instead of via a timer. The size of the applets can be improved and adjustable as well.

6.8.13 Dynamic Subject Reloading

The system should check the subjects.xml file datestamp and reload the list of chat subjects from it if it is newer than the last one used for that purpose.

6.8.14 User Editing of Subjects

The subjects.xml file could be made editable by hosts and perhaps guests.

6.8.15 Banning Rude Guests

There should be a way to banish guests who interfere with a chat.

6.8.16 Thread Lock Watchdog

One thing we have not addressed of is to make sure that one thread does not hold on to the synchronization lock on the `bonForumXML` object forever. One way to do that might be to add a "watchdog." We would need to calculate the maximum time a thread can hold the lock and then time out the thread if its exceeds that period. We would have to be generous with our time estimate because of the non–real-time nature of Java runtime. It is no wonder that Java comes with some license disclaimers regarding real-time application.

7 JavaServer Pages: The Browseable User Interface

IN THIS CHAPTER, YOU LEARN ABOUT HOW WE harness JavaServer pages to create a BUI, a browseable user interface, for our Web application.

7.1 JSP-Based Web Applications

The Web application example for this book will have human users, whose interface to the application will be through a Web browser. Of course, it is possible to create Web applications that do not have a user interface at all, but simply connect various client- or server-side applications together. However, the subject here is the use of JavaServer pages in the development of the bonForum Web chat application. A major promise of JavaServer pages is that they can be used to easily produce dynamic HTML pages for a browser.

We should be clear from the beginning that this chapter is not a tutorial on JSP, nor is it a JSP reference. Instead, it is a description of some of the JSP files in bonForum. We discussed in the last two chapters how we mapped these JSP files to our chat model. Now, with details from a few representative JSPs, you can understand all of them and how they relate to the other components of bonForum.

If you need to learn more about JSP technology, refer to the suggestions and resources provided in Section 3.7, "Java Servlets and JSP," in Chapter 3, "Java Servlets and JavaServer Pages: Jakarta Tomcat." We also find Marty Hall's book, *Core Servlets and JavaServer Pages*, published by Prentice Hall PTR/Sun Microsystems Press, to be very useful, and we will certainly purchase the next edition to catch up with the new JSP specification. Remember also to browse some of the JSP Web links listed in Chapter 12, "Online Information Sources," in Section 12.9.9, "JSP: Tutorials."

We also have all those Web links and more available for you on the BonForum Project Web site, `http://www.bonforum.org`.

7.1.1 Getting Input from a Web Application User

Of course, we will need to get input from users on browsers into the application. To accomplish this using an interface designed with JSP, we can simply add a `FORM` element to the HTML that the compiled JSP will produce.

That form will allow the user to input information that will be submitted to whatever destination the action of the `FORM` element dictates. In our example Web application, the `FORM` data is submitted using POST to the central Java servlet, `BonForumEngine`.

Request Parameters

When the `FORM` is submitted using POST, its fields become parameters in the HTTP request object that is an argument to the `service()` method in the `BonForumEngine` servlet. What happens then is the topic of Chapter 8, "Java Servlet and JavaBean: BonForumEngine and BonForumStore."

7.1.2 Getting Output to a Web Application User

A servlet can use the attributes of `HttpSession` objects to store information about each user. That information will then be available to display to each user, for example, in an HTML document produced by a JSP page. We have used this fact quite frequently throughout the bonForum Web application.

We will show you an example with a pair of code excerpts. The first excerpt is from the `BonForumEngine` servlet. Here a user nickname, after being stored in a `hashtable` named `nicknameRegistry`, is being made available to the current session. The "current session" means during requests made by the same browser, until the session associated with the browser expires. A session expires only when the browser is inactive longer than a set period of time: a busy browser's session will not expire, and an unused browser's session will eventually expire. Here is the code from the `BonForumEngine` servlet:

```
if(nicknameOK) {
nicknameRegistry.put(actorNickname, sessionId);
session.setAttribute("actorNickname", actorNickname);
}
```

The `actorNickname` value that is stored in the `session` attribute can thus be retrieved later by any JSP, servlet, or bean that has access to the same `HTTPSession` object. On a JSP page, you can access the session attribute by using a scriptlet such as the following:

```
<%-- greet forum actor by nickname: --%>
<%
String actorNickname = ((String)session.getAttribute("actorNickname"));
String chatWelcomeMessage = "Hello, " + actorNickname + "!";
%>
```

We have it rather easy in our example because we have decided that in the prototype application, any user will have only the same lifespan as the current session for the browser. Your application may have a requirement to create a more persistent context for each user. For example, an e-commerce venture will want to keep records of purchases made by each customer. In such cases, you will have to add the complexities of user registration and verification. You will also need to create a persistent data storage solution, perhaps using JDBC. These will also be added to bonForum in a later release; you can be involved with that at the open source project Web site `http://www.bonforum.org`.

7.1.3 Other Communication Between Servlets and JSP

Session attributes are not only good for sending data to the human users of the application. There is also communication going on between the programming in the servlet and the other code on the JSP page. When you also consider the capability of JSP tag libraries to involve other Java servlets during the runtime of a compiled JSP, you can easily comprehend the need for moving data between independent threads and modules.

Session Attributes

Here is an example of code in a bean, `BonForumStore`, setting two attributes of the current session object (accessed through a method). This makes two integer values available in the session context as string objects:

```
this.getSession().setAttribute("chatPageNumber", Integer.toString(pageNumber));
. . .
this.getSession().setAttribute("chatNumberOfPages",
Integer.toString(numberOfPages));
```

Two different JSP later use the same session attributes to access these stored String values:

```
<% String chatPageNumber =
String)session.getAttribute("chatPageNumber");%>
<% String chatNumberOfPages =
(String)session.getAttribute("chatNumberOfPages");%>
```

The values are then displayed as part of the HTML page that is output to the browser:

```
page: <%= chatPageNumber %> of <%= chatNumberOfPages %>
```

It might be argued that we could have—and probably should have—arranged for the JSP to access the data directly from the bean object instead. However, the `BonForumStore` instance is static and unique, whereas we want different values of `chatPageNumber` for each user. We would have to add a user manager to keep track of all the values for the users. That is what the session object gives us, so why not use it?

Using *jsp:useBean*

We can use the same bean in a JSP, however. Here is an example from the JSP:

```
host_increases_rating.jsp
```

First, we make the bean available with a `jsp:useBean` element:

```
<jsp:useBean id="bonForumStore" class="de.tarent.forum.BonForumStore"
scope="application"/>
```

Then a bean method is called to increase the rating of a chat guest that was previously chosen by the chat host. (The `BonForumEngine` earlier stored a copy of a request parameter from another JSP in a `chatGuest` session attribute, so the bean can find the right one there. Here is the JSP scriptlet that invokes the bean method:

```
<%
bonForumStore.changeChatActorRating("1");
%>
```

Of course, it also is possible to get data from a bean to a JSP. We will show three different ways to accomplish that (none of which is actually used in bonForum yet, by the way). First, here's the "pretty" way to get the bean:

```
<jsp:useBean id="bonForumStore" class="de.tarent.forum.BonForumStore"
scope="application"/>
```

Now that we have the bean, we can access its properties, again the "pretty" JSP way:

```
<p>
initDate: <jsp:getProperty name="bonForumStore" property="initDate"/> <BR>
</p>
```

We could also get the property via its `get` method, thus:

```
<p>
initDate: <%=bonForumStore.getInitDate()%> <BR>
```

Here is a different way to get the bean, the "ugly" way (the argument value `4` means to get an application scope attribute):

```
<%! de.tarent.forum.BonForumStore bFS; %>
<%
bFS = (de.tarent.forum.BonForumStore)pageContext.getAttribute("bonForumStore", 4);
%>
```

Finally, here is the "not-so-pretty" way to get the same property value as we did earlier:

```
<p>
initDate: <%= bFS.getInitDate()%> <BR>
</p>
```

Request Attributes

Sometimes we use a request attribute rather than a session attribute. That is not often, mostly because forwarding requests from the JSP in one frame to a JSP in another frame is not usually useful. One example, from several similar ones, in which we use request attributes, is in the communication between the two JSPs that takes a guest out of a chat. In this example, the action involves cooperation among these three JSPs:

guest_executes_chat_ready.jsp

actor_leaves_frameset_robot.jsp

guest_exits_chat.jsp

In the first of these JSPs, we can see many statements like the following:

```
request.setAttribute("target", "_top");
```

The request is then forwarded using a `jsp:forward` action to the next JSP:

```
<jsp:forward page="actor_leaves_frameset_robot.jsp"/>
```

The page receiving that request then accesses the target value from the request attribute, thus:

```
<% String target = (String)request.getAttribute("target"); %>
```

The _robot JSP then uses that target string to set the applet parameter within the `jsp:plugin` element, as follows:

```
<jsp:plugin type="applet" code="BonForumRobot.class"
codebase="/bonForum/jsp/forum/applet"
jreversion="1.3.0" width="400" height="160" >
<jsp:params>
<jsp:param name="target" value="<%=target%>"/>
. . .
</jsp:params>
. . .
</jsp:plugin>
```

In this case, using a request attribute works because the application does not need that information again—the "robot action" here is a one-shot thing. If we did need this target value again, we would be out of luck: The request object is at a dead end here because the embedded applet on the _robot JSP requests the next destination via a `showDocument` applet method invocation.

Note that session attributes would work just as well in this case as request attributes. But that would be abusing the session object because the next time a target value is needed, it is hard-wired right into the code that started off this example.

More Session Attributes

Many other situations involving communication between two JSPs in the bonForum project look very similar to this last _robot JSP example that we gave. In these cases, the purpose of the _robot JSP is to refresh the output of a JSP in a different frame of the browser display. However, here we cannot use request objects to pass information. Instead, we have used session attributes.

One example of several like this involves the following three JSPs:

guest_executes_command.jsp

guest_executes_command_robot.jsp

guest_executes_command_frame.jsp

The first JSP stuffs attributes with values destined to be applet parameters, such as this one:

```
<%
session.setAttribute("target", "display");
. . .
%>
```

The second JSP accesses those attributes, such as this one:

```
<%
String target = (String)session.getAttribute("target");
. . .
%>
```

Then the second JSP goes on to set the applet parameter inside the `jsp:plugin` element, like this:

```
<jsp:param name="target" value="<%=target%>"/>
```

If you tried to use request attributes instead of session attributes in these, as well as the other parallel pairs of JSP, you would find that the applet does not repeatedly refresh the other JSP anymore. The reason is that, in this case, there is no `jsp:forward` action being used. We cannot find a request object that is available from both the first and the second JSP. The second JSP is requested by the browser when it sets up the frameset, and we have no access to that request. That is why we use the session object instead to pass information between them.

At the end of this chapter, in Section 7.3, "Further Discussion About the JSP in bonForum," we will again discuss our use of session attributes with the _robot JSP files, when we discuss several alternatives to our present JSP-based browser interface design.

7.1.4 What Drives the Web Application?

In Chapter 8, we will claim that the `BonForumEngine` servlet is in charge of the Web application—after all, it is the communication hub in the Web application. However, viewed from the point of view of the JSP documents in the Web application, apparently the user is actually driving. The user does that by making choices using the many HTML elements displayed. The engine should just make the car go, after all, not decide where to go.

In the code shown here, another string object is being accessed on a JSP page. As you can see, the code on a JSP page can use a session attribute to communicate back to servlet code as well. In this simple case, the value received from the servlet, which sets the size of an HTML select element, is verified and corrected, if necessary, by the JSP code. In effect, this grants the designer of the JSP page the capability to overrule, or default, the values that are received from the code written by the designer of the servlet.

```
<%-- get lines per page for chat messages display --%>

<% String chatMessagesPageSize =
(String)session.getAttribute("chatMessagesPageSize");
int size = 10;
try {
size = Integer.parseInt(chatMessagesPageSize);
}
catch (NumberFormatException nFE) {
chatMessagesPageSize = "10";
}
if(size > 99) {
chatMessagesPageSize = "99";
}
else if(size < 1) {
chatMessagesPageSize = "1";
}
session.setAttribute("chatMessagesPageSize", chatMessagesPageSize);
%>
```

The verified `chatMessagesPageSize` value is used later in the page to set the size attribute of an HTML select element:

```
<select size="<%= chatMessagesPageSize %>" name="chatMessages">
. . .
</select>
```

7.1.5 Keeping the Prototype User Interface Simple

We have intentionally tried to keep the user interface created by all the JSP documents in the bonForum Web application as simple as possible. This is in keeping with the raison-d'être of JSP as we understand it; the page designers do not have to create computer code, and the software designers do not have to create page designs.

The beauty of this is that, unlike many simplified mockups of "real" software, what we end up with here should actually be easily extensible without much need to touch the existing scaffolding. Much can be done to change the appearance of the user interface, while still incorporating the fundamental message communication functionality that allows this simplified version to be as fully functional as it is.

The bonForum Web app is still evolving. It seems that we must always stress that one of its main reasons for existence is as an experimental platform for studying the use of Tomcat, Xerces, and Xalan. Getting feedback from the application is important for exploration and experimentation. While we work with the project, we find that it is very helpful to have access to as much information about it as possible. To that end, we often place the following code at the bottom of many of our JSP files. We finally put it (and more) in a custom tag:

```
<%@ page import="java.util.*" %>
<%
        out.println("<H3>Headers: </H3><BR>");
          Enumeration eh = request.getHeaderNames();
          while (eh.hasMoreElements()) {
                String name = (String)eh.nextElement();
                String value = (String)request.getHeader(name);
                out.println("\t<li>" + name + " = " + value + "</li>");
          }
        out.println("<H3>Parameters: </H3><BR>");
        Enumeration ep = request.getParameterNames();
        while(ep.hasMoreElements()) {
                String name = (String)ep.nextElement();
                String value = (String)request.getParameter(name);
                out.println("\t<li>" + name + " = " + value + "</li>");
        }
        out.println("<H3>Attributes: </H3><BR>");
        int scope;
        for(scope = 2; scope <= 3; scope++) {
                out.println("<H3>Scope: " + scope + "</H3><BR>");
                Enumeration ea = pageContext.getAttributeNamesInScope(scope);
                while(ea.hasMoreElements()) {
                        String name = (String)ea.nextElement();
                        if (name ==  null) name = "hello";
                        String value = (String)pageContext.getAttribute(name,
scope).toString();
                        out.println("\t<li>" + name + " = " +  value + "</li>");
                 }
        }
%>
```

7.1.6 Using JSP Tag Libraries Is a Good Thing

There is another way to add to the basic substructure in the bonForum prototype: by leveraging the tag classes. Creating your own custom tags is as important in a JSP-based design as having subroutines was in early BASIC programs. It furthers the separation of page design from code design, and that is the central appeal of JSP.

In this chapter, we do not discuss using tag libraries to design, but we do discuss one complex tag example: the `TransformTag` class. You can understand what we do with custom tags in the bonForum project by studying the `BonForumStore` class and all three custom tag classes: `OutputPathnamesTag`, `OutputChatMessagesTag`, and `TransformTag`. You can read about `BonForumStore` in Chapter 8, and about the custom tag classes in Chapter 10, "JSP Taglib: The bonForum Custom Tags." Refer back and forth between this chapter and those chapters to get a complete picture of what our tag commands are accomplishing.

7.1.7 JSP Files for the Example Web Application

The JSP files for this Tomcat Web application are all the files with an extension of .jsp that are found in the folder TOMCAT_HOME\webapps\bonforum\jsp\forum.

The first time that any of these JSP files is requested, Tomcat makes sure that it is translated into a servlet and compiled. That is why Tomcat requires access to a Java compiler. The Java servlet source and the compiled class files that are created from JSP are placed by Tomcat into the work folder (as determined by the server.xml Tomcat configuration file). The default work folder is TOMCAT_HOME\work.

If you look in that folder after Tomcat has compiled some JSP files that you have created, you will find that both the .java files and the .class files in the work folder for your Web application will have long, strange filenames. These are the mangled versions of the JSP page filenames, but with extensions typical of Java class files.

> **Tomcat Troubleshooting**
>
> If you are having insoluble problems with a Tomcat Web app you are developing, try down shutting Tomcat, deleting its work folder with *all* the work files it needs, and then restarting Tomcat.

Tomcat can tell when a JSP file has been modified, and it retranslates and recompiles it when necessary. This is one of the advantages of using JSP pages, in fact. It means that they are dynamic in many ways: They have a runtime behavior associated with them in their compiled form, but they also can be changed without shutting down the entire Web application.

Note that a Tomcat Web app can be set up so that changes that you make to any of its Java servlets (not just its JSP pages) will be detected and incorporated into the Web app without any requirement to stop and restart the server. Because this feature adds overhead to the processing, it is recommended that you develop and test the Web app with this feature turned on, and then turn it off afterward for better performance. You can turn it off by setting the reloadable flag to False in the Context element for the Web app in the server.xml file. You might need to add a Context element in that file, if you have been relying on the automatic Web app defaults.

7.2 Viewing bonForum from Its JSP Documents

In this section, we describe the important features of many of the most important JSP pages used in the bonForum chat application.

If you need a bird's eye view of the application as you read the rest of this chapter (and the book), refer to Section 6.1.5, "The States of the Forum," in Chapter 6, "BonForum Chat Application: Implementation."

7.2.1 Index.html

The first URL requested by a Web browser when a new user wants to enter the bonForum Web chat application is something like http://www.forums.com/bonForum.

That request, which tells Tomcat only the Web app name, must be fleshed out by Tomcat before it can be useful. The default is to assume a request for the file index.html in the document base of the Web app. (See Figure 7.1.) Section 3.6.2, "Editing the Server Configuration," in Chapter 3, contains an example of setting a document base using the Tomcat configuration file server.xml.

Our index.html file is a purely static HTML file inviting the traveler into the bonForum Web chat application. A button hyperlinks you to the first JSP "page," which is made up both of a "written" file and its compiled form as a Java servlet of a class descended from the `HTTPServlet` Java class. That first page is called forum_login.jsp.

7.2.2 forum_login.jsp

The JSP page forum_login.jsp seems superfluous. It could easily be left out of the GUI for the Web app simply by changing it so that it forwards requests to the forum_entry.jsp page. Nevertheless, it is here for two reasons. For one, it serves as a placeholder for any user login that will be added to the Web application in the future. As of this writing, Tomcat has built-in user authorization features that are subject to change. If you want to experiment with this, read the details in the Tomcat configuration file server.xml.

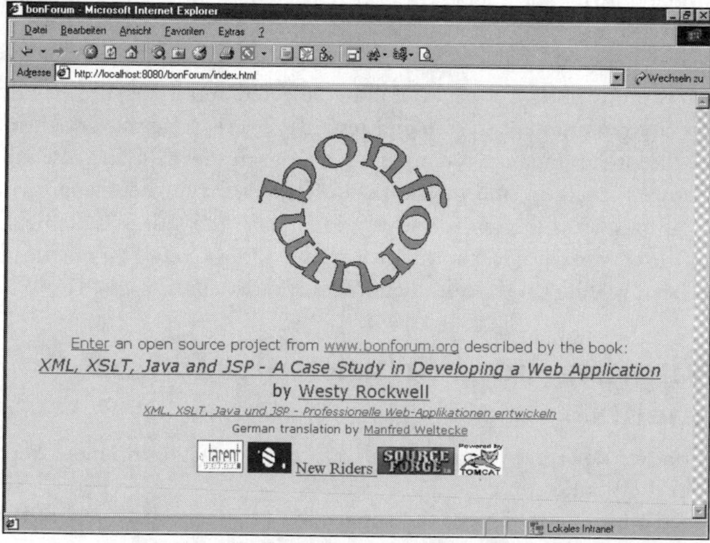

Figure 7.1 The bonForum default Web page displayed by index.html.

A button on the forum_login.jsp page only gets the user to the next page, which is forum_entry.jsp. But forum_entry.jsp should also remain in the Web application because it serves an important role as a testbed for new code. Such new code can be added as new JSP tag invocations. It can also be added in JSP scriptlets (Java code added to the text of the JSP document within the tag pairs `<%` and `%>`).

The logic behind such a test procedure is that the "shallower" into a Web application that you can do your debugging, the easier it is because it is a lengthy enough process to shut down and start up Tomcat and perhaps delete files, shut down browsers, and so on. Such a process is often required, in spite of the capability of Tomcat to allow the automatic reloading of servlets.

7.2.3 forum_entry.jsp

This JSP page has a form on it that uses an HTTP POST to send some information about you to `BonForumEngine`. The information includes your chosen nickname and age. With a `yes` value, another input value (and, thus, request parameter) named `actorReturning` tells `BonForumEngine` that the application has seen the user before (when forum_login.jsp was requested). This value is really just a convenient switch for some testing during development. A `yes` value for the resulting request parameter simply turns on the processing of other user-related form data on this (and other) JSP pages.

The most important request parameter posted by the form is the one called `bonCommand`, which tells the engine what to do and where to send you next.

In the case of the request made by forum_entry.jsp, `BonForumEngine` will take you next to visit visitor_executes_choice.jsp because the value of bonCommand is set to `visitor_executes_choice`. This simple, extensible mapping of filename to functionality is used throughout the Web application. Nevertheless, as you shall see later (especially in Chapter 9, "Java Applet Plugged In: `BonForumRobot`"), this handy method of jumping from JSP page to JSP page needed to be elaborated to complete the Web application.

7.2.4 visitor_executes_choice.jsp

On this JSP page, you can see how we use a session attribute to hold information related to one user. More accurately, it is related directly to one `HTTPSession` object and, therefore, to one browser instance for a variable period of time. The session object will continue to exist as long as the browser is reasonably active: The session will cease to exist if no requests are made by the browser for a certain period of time, the length of which can be set in the web.xml file that configures the Web application.

In the JSP file visitor_executes_choice.jsp, you can find something like this:

```
<%-- greet forum actor by nickname: --%>
<%
String actorNickname = ((String)session.getAttribute("actorNickname"));
```

```
if(actorNickname == null || actorNickname..trim().length() < 1) {
actorNickname = "&lt;unknown visitor&gt;";
}
String chatWelcomeMessage = "Hello, " + actorNickname + "! Please make a choice:";
%>

(more code was left out here)

<%= chatWelcomeMessage %>
```

The JSP expression in the last line displays a greeting containing the user nickname, entered on a different Web page. In the previous state of the Web application, forum entry, the user entered a nickname in a form element. That nickname value was POSTed to the `BonForumEngine` servlet as a request parameter. The servlet copied its value into a session attribute. There it will remain available as long as the current session lasts.

That may not seem like much, but such is the glue that holds together most of the Web applications out there today. Without something to "hold" a context for a sequence of actions by a given actor or set of actors, we can hardly have a program intelligent enough to maintain a meaningful user experience.

In the bonForum Web application, we also use another mechanism to relate different Web pages together: Each page usually determines the next page to be displayed. This is often controlled by the value of an input element in a form that is posted to the `BonForumEngine` servlet. For example, on the visitor_executes_choice.jsp page, you will find something like the following code listing. The table row elements in the original have been removed here for clarity:

```
<form name="visitor_executes_choice" method="POST"
action="/bonForum/servlet/BonForumEngine">
<label for="join">join a chat</label>
<input type="radio" id="join" name="bonCommand"
value="visitor_joins_chat"></input>
<label for="start">start a chat</label>
<input type="radio" id="start" name="bonCommand" value="visitor_starts_chat"
CHECKED></input>
<label for="exit">exit this forum</label>
<input type="radio" id="exit" name="bonCommand" value="bonForum"></input>
<input type="hidden" name="actorReturning" value="yes"></input>
<input type="submit" value="do it!" name="submit"></input>
</form>
```

The result is that in the HTML displayed by this JSP page, a choice is offered to the actor: join an existing chat, start a new chat, or exit this forum. (See Figure 7.2.) It is a simple menu action based on the one input element: `bonCommand`. Because it is in the form element on this page, it gets POSTed to `BonForumEngine` as a request parameter and causes that servlet to forward the HTTP request to the next page based on the value of whichever input element is checked by the user.

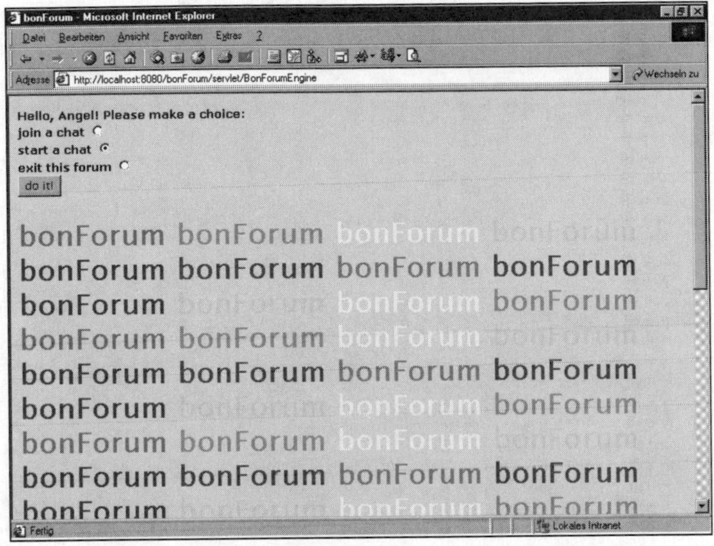

Figure 7.2 HTML displayed by visitor_executes_choice.jsp.

Of course, things are never that simple, as they say, so there must be more to it than that. Let's check out one of these three possible candidates for the next JSP page in the application. In the file visitor_starts_chat.jsp, we see the following JSP code:

```
<frameset rows="65%, 35%">

<frame src="/bonForum/jsp/forum/visitor_starts_chat_frame.jsp" name="display">

<frame src="/bonForum/jsp/forum/visitor_starts_chat_controls.jsp" name="controls"
>

</frameset>
```

We have arrived at a fork in the road. The next two JSPs that we will discuss are these frame sources. Together, they make possible the "visitor starts chat" application state.

7.2.5 visitor_starts_chat_frame.jsp

This page displays in the top display frame a list of all the available chat subject categories. The user must select and submit one of these as the chat subject when a new chat is started. (See Figure 7.3.) When the HTML form produced by this JSP is submitted to the `BonForumEngine` servlet, the subject category value that was selected by the user in the HTML select list is copied by that servlet into the `chatSubject` session attribute. This page also shows the user the current value, if any, of that `chatSubject` session attribute and also the `chatTopic` session attribute (also discussed in the next section).

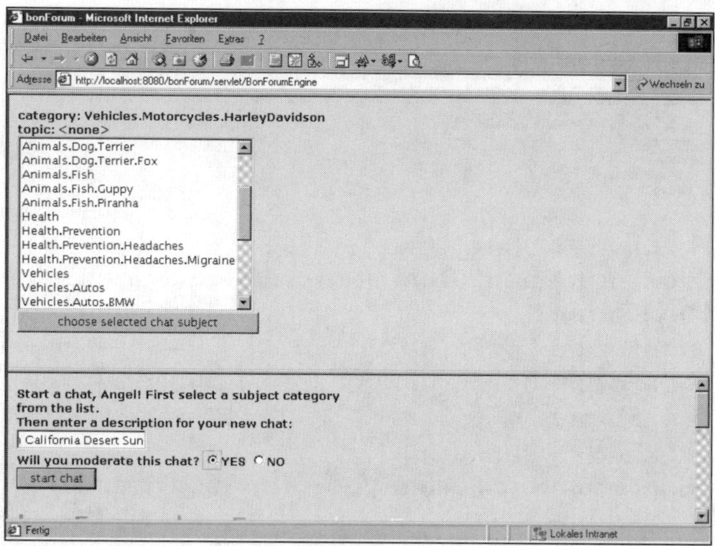

Figure 7.3 HTML displayed by visitor_starts_chat.jsp and related JSP documents.

Note that, as do all the other JSP pages in this Web application, this page needs to tell the `BonForumEngine` Java servlet what the next destination in the Web application should be. We can see that happening in the following excerpt taken from the HTML form element on this JSP file:

```
<input type="hidden" name="bonCommand" value="visitor_starts_chat_frame"></input>
<input type="submit" value="choose selected chat subject" name="submit"></input>
```

When the user clicks the Submit button, the HTML form that contains these two input elements is posted to the `BonForumEngine` servlet. The value of the `bonCommand` input element arrives at the servlet as a request parameter. It tells the servlet where the request produced by the form submission should be forwarded. The eagle-eyed reader will have noticed that, in this case, the destination is the very same JSP that produced the page making the request. The request makes a round-trip to the `BonForumEngine` servlet. Nevertheless, this does accomplish the following:

- Sets the selected subject into a session attribute
- Updates the display of the subject category on this frame
- Updates the subject categories displayed in the selection list

The last of these three effects is not currently important to the application because the list of categories is loaded at startup and is not (yet) changing. However, in similar situations, that sort of refresh action can be useful. For example, we could add another form with a Refresh Submit button on it that also did nothing but request its own JSP again.

So, the HTTP request made by the form submission is therefore caught in a loop here. It always gets forwarded to the same destination, and that simply refreshes the form's page. That means that we cannot use the standard practice of passing the values from this form to another page as request parameters because the request is never forwarded to another page. For the same reason, we cannot set anything into a request attribute hoping to send it onward to another JSP document (for example). Therefore, we use a session attribute for that instead. The session object can and does make the chat subject category selected by the user available elsewhere in the application. This `chatSubject` value can then be displayed again by other pages in the same session, as it is by the following two JSP pages:

guest_executes_chat_frame.jsp

host_executes_chat_frame.jsp

Let's get back to the page now under discussion. You can see that it also contains two examples of how to get and display a session attribute. Here is the code that gets the chat topic description from a session attribute:

```
<% String chatTopic = (String)session.getAttribute("chatTopic");
String chatTopicMessage = "topic: &lt;none&gt;";
if(chatTopic != null && chatTopic.trim().length() > 0) {
chatTopicMessage = "topic: " + chatTopic;
}
%>
```

From farther down in the JSP, here is the expression that displays that chat description:

```
<%=chatTopicMessage%>
```

The `chatTopic` contains the latest chat description (if any) that has been entered by the user into the form on the bottom frame of the frameset (see the next section). If the user submits the form that controls the frame to the `BonForumEngine` servlet before selecting and submitting a chat subject in the top display frame, the servlet will detect the missing chat subject and refuse to go on to the next application state. Instead, it will forward the request back to the JSP that creates the frameset. The user, however, will not have to re-enter the chat topic value because it has been preserved via the session attribute.

Again, notice that from the top frame we have no access to the request parameters created by the form submission on the bottom frame. The HTML in the bottom frame also cannot send a request (or have the servlet forward a request) to the JSP that creates the HTML for the top frame. That would simply create a duplicate copy of the HTML for the top frame in the bottom frame. Fortunately, by using session attributes, we can share data among two or more frames that are simultaneously being displayed.

There is another interesting thing to discuss in this JSP. The following code makes available to the user the available chat categories:

```
<select size="12" name="chatSubject">
<bon:outputPathNames docName="bonForumXML"
```

```
pathToSubTreeRootNode="bonForum.things.subjects" ancestorReplacer="COMPLETE_PATHS"
➥nodeSeparator="/">
<option><%= output %></option>
</bon:outputPathNames>
</select>
```

As you can see, this creates in the HTML result output by the JSP page a select listbox with the option value as its list item. But wait! How does that give us a list of what may be dozens of values? As we shall discuss in Chapter 10, the answer is that this option element, with the value `<% output %>`, is embedded in our own JSP tag called `bon:outputPathNames`.

Let's briefly talk about what happens here: An instance of the Java class defined by the file OutputPathNames Tag.java executes a method called `outputForumPathNames`. That method somehow causes two things to happen: The `<%= output %>` JSP expression is evaluated repeatedly in a loop, and the value of the variable named `output` contain a different one of the many available subjects in the XML data for the Web application each time through the loop.

The list of available chat subjects comes from an XML file when Tomcat is started up. That file may be freely edited to give the desired subject categories available to the tarent chat forum. You can find that chat subjects initialization file at the following location:

```
TOMCAT_HOME"\webapps\bonForum\docs\subjects.xml
```

You can browse this subjects initialization XML document by using something like the following URL:

```
http://localhost:8080/bonForum/mldocs/subjects.xml
```

As mentioned earlier in this section, submitting the HTML form element created by this JSP sends a request on a round-trip to the `BonForumEngine` servlet—and that updates the subject categories displayed in the selection list. However, as this book goes to print, a restart of the Tomcat Server still is required to load a changed subjects.xml document into bonForum, and thus to change the option items in the select element. In a future release, we plan to periodically check the file and reload it if it changes, rather than requiring a restart. That will make the chat subject selection list truly dynamic.

As you have seen, by having the select box control displayed in an HTML form that requests the same JSP that created the form itself, instead of requesting a different JSP that would remove the select box from view, we have gained these three characteristics:

- **Reusability**—The user can change a selection already submitted; we can use repeated selection events.
- **Feedback**—Submission of the form updates a separate display of the last selected option(s).
- **Dynamic content**—Submission of the form refreshes the option list; a separate "refresh only" form is possible.

In our Web application, this is the first JSP in which we find HTML frames. You may well ask why. The short answer is that there is absolutely no need for frames in this application state. We can just as easily add another HTML form element to this JSP that does request a new and excitingly different destination, and get rid of frames altogether. In fact, we previously did just that.

The real reason we use frames here is that, in a future release of bonForum, the chat actors will be able to add to the list of chat subject categories. When that happens, we will want to refresh the chat subject selection list very frequently. That will cause an annoying flicker in the list, a problem that we encountered while refreshing chat messages and that we solved elsewhere by using frames. But, we are getting ahead of our story!

We have delegated the problem of going somewhere else in the Web application to the other frame in the same HTML framework. We shall see how that happens next.

7.2.6 visitor_starts_chat_controls.jsp

This is the JSP that produces the HTML to display in the bottom (controls) frame, in the frameset created for the "visitor starts chat" state. A form on this HTML enables a visitor to input and submit a chat topic description to the Web application. The visitor is told to first select and submit a chat subject in the top (display) frame of the display, as we discussed in the previous section. The submission of a chat topic also signals the `BonForumEngine` servlet to create a new chat. The visitor becomes its host.

The chat topic description submitted here later will be shown to other visitors who are looking for a chat to join. When the form on this controls frame is submitted to the `BonForumEngine` servlet, it finds the chat topic description in a request parameter and copies its value into the `chatTopic` session attribute. As discussed in the preceding section, it is then available to JSPs and other objects that can access the current session object, including the JSP that produces HTML for the top frame of the current frameset.

The request-forwarding mechanism in the `BonForumEngine` servlet takes each user to the next JSP destination, which is the one we will discuss next. The servlet relies on the following HTML code, which you can find in the JSP file now being discussed:

```
<input type="hidden" name="bonCommand" value="visitor_starts_chat_ready"></input>
```

7.2.7 visitor_starts_chat_ready.jsp

It is the task of this JSP to get users to the next state of the Web application: the state in which they are using their new chats. It might seem that this should simply involve forwarding a request to another JSP page, just as we have been doing all along. Indeed, a request is forwarded, but this time, two things are different:

- The request is forwarded directly from this JSP page.
- The JSP destination does not create the HTML seen next on the browser screen.

In fact, the next HTML that the user sees is determined by the Java applet `BonForumRobot`. As an applet, it will be executed on the client machine, unlike our JSP and servlet classes that we have so far discussed in this chapter. In fact, this applet will be taken care of by a Java plug-in in the browser. (If the plug-in is not on the client machine already, the user automatically is given the chance to install it.)

In the next section, we discuss how that Java applet is invoked from a JSP. Let's first see how the application gets to that page from this one. In the code, examine the following lines:

```
<%
request.setAttribute("target", "_top");
request.setAttribute("document",
request.getScheme() + "://" +
request.getServerName() + ":" +
request.getServerPort() +
"/bonForum/jsp/forum/host_executes_chat.jsp");
request.setAttribute("refresh", "true");
request.setAttribute("increment", "100");
request.setAttribute("limit", "1");
request.setAttribute("message", "Preparing new chat!");
%>
<%--
attributes become applet parameters there:
--%>

<jsp:forward page="actor_leaves_frameset_robot.jsp.tfe"/>
```

What you see here is the use of the `jsp:forward` command to send the request to its next service provider, which is the JSP actor_leaves_frameset_robot.jsp, by way of the BonForumEngine servlet, which is mapped to the .tfe extension.

We also see request attributes being set; their values will be used as arguments for the Java applet `BonForumRobot`. Among these arguments is to be found the name of another JSP document file, host_executes_chat.jsp. Notice that the scheme, server name, and server port must be prefixed to the JSP filename so that the client-side applet can find it.

The robot acts as a relay station, to get a forum actor from the status of visitor to the status of host, in the action of executing a chat "thing." (About time, you say?)

You may well ask, why all the convoluted indirection? Why not just forward the request directly from this page to host_executes_chat.jsp because that is our next destination? Or, why not get the `BonForumEngine` to forward a request there? Because the destination JSP would then produce its HTML page output only within the controls frame. We would end up with a new frameset inside the bottom frame of our existing frameset. We want to create a new HTML frameset that fills the entire browser display.

Well, let's then do our forwarding, either directly or through the BonForumEngine servlet, not from this _ready page we are discussing, but instead from the _controls JSP—that is, visitor_starts_chat_controls.jsp

After all, we are using the _ready page only to get to the JSP that has the embedded robot applet. It turns out that forwarding to host_executes_chat from the _controls form fails the same way: We get a new frameset, but, again, it is entirely contained in the old controls frame.

Still, something is fishy. Let's accept that we do need the robot applet to break out of the frame. However, why not request the _robot JSP from the _controls JSP instead of requesting the _ready JSP? We can do that quite simply by changing the HTML form so that it has this line

```
<input type="radio" name="bonCommand" value="actor_leaves_frameset_robot">
```

instead of the following line:

```
<input type="radio" name="bonCommand" value="host_executes_chat_ready">
```

We would also need to set up all the robot applet's parameters on the _controls JSP just as we did on the _ready JSP.

It turns out that this last plan does work—however, not before you do these other things also:

- Set the values for the applet parameters in session attributes, not request attributes.
- Change actor_leaves_frameset_robot.jsp so that it looks for the robot parameters in session attributes, not request attributes.

So, then, something is fishy! Why didn't we do it that way, which seems simpler, after all? One justification is that, as far as we can tell, using request attributes involves less overhead than using session attributes. Request attributes should be preferred over session attributes whenever they can do the job at hand.

The actual reason, however, comes from the fact that, in later states of the bonForum Web application, we also use the robot applet class. In fact, we use it two ways. One is to break out of a frame, as we have discussed already, but with a difference: In those later states, we need to be able to break out to more than just one destination. That means that we must set up our document attribute differently for each destination JSP. The most modular, expandable, and supportable way to do that is to have a different JSP for each destination, with different suffixes on the filenames (_frame, _console, _system, and so on). Arguably, we might better have used beans than JSPs because these JSPs produce no HTML output. However, we should at least keep things as similar as possible in the various states of the application, including the "visitor starts chat" state being discussed.

Our second use of the robot applet later in the Web application is to frequently refresh the content of a display frame. We do that in several bonForum states. (To do that, it turns out that we need to use session attributes instead of request attributes to set up the applet parameters.)

The question becomes, can we use one applet to do both tasks—first to periodically fire a refresh action and second to break out of the frameset to the next application state? The answer is that we can use the same applet class, but not the same instance. We cannot simply change the session attributes, hoping that the applet's behavior will change. We need to load a new applet instance as well.

Well, that was a long section, but you asked, so we told you. (You didn't?)

7.2.8 actor_leaves_frameset_robot.jsp

As discussed more fully in Chapter 9, this JSP starts up a Java applet of the class `BonForumRobot` on the client machine. It also passes quite a few parameter values to the applet (these parameters are discussed in the following paragraphs).

In this JSP document, you can see within an HTML table element the `jsp:plugin` element that takes care of the robot applet:

```
<table>
<tr>
<img border="0" src="/bonForum/images/bonForumLogo.gif" alt="bonForum" width="112"
➥height="112">
</tr>
<tr>
<jsp:plugin type="applet" code="BonForumRobot.class"
codebase="/bonForum/jsp/forum/applet" jreversion="1.3.0" width="400" height="160"
>
<jsp:params>
<jsp:param name="target" value="<%=target%>"/>
<jsp:param name="document" value="<%=document%>"/>
<jsp:param name="refresh" value="<%=refresh%>"/>
<jsp:param name="increment" value="<%=increment%>"/>
<jsp:param name="limit" value="<%=limit%>"/>
<jsp:param name="message" value="<%=message%>"/>
</jsp:params>
<jsp:fallback>Plugin tag OBJECT or EMBED not supported by browser.
</jsp:fallback>
</jsp:plugin>
</tr>
</table>
```

Among the parameter values passed to the robot applet, two are more important here. These two are initialized using request attributes in the following JSP lines (before the table with the `jsp:plugin` element, shown previously):

```
<% String target = (String)request.getAttribute("target"); %>
<% String document = (String)request.getAttribute("document"); %>
```

You can see also, how you can display the values of these attributes right on the browser during the software development stages. This is one of the simplest and best ways to debug your development efforts. (Note that you can also use the Java console for runtime logging.)

Here is one example from the page under discussion, of the use of a JSP expression tag to get the JSPwriter to include the value of a variable into the resulting HTML document:

```
target:<%= session.getAttribute("target") %>
```

As you saw earlier, the attributes (and thus the applet parameters), for example, are set to certain values by the following JSP page:

```
visitor_starts_chat_ready.jsp
```

The value of `target` is set to this:

```
_top
```

As you probably know, the HTML definition of frames contains some preestablished values of the target into which a linked document will be displayed by the browser. The value `_top` tells the browser to display in the top-level frame, which is the highest ancestor of the frame containing the link.

The value of `document` for the robot applet to display, in our particular example, is set to a rather long Java expression:

```
request.getScheme() + "://" + request.getServerName() + ":" +
request.getServerPort() + "/bonForum/jsp/forum/host_executes_chat.jsp".
```

That expression evaluates to the very URL for the JSP document that we are going to discuss next. Before we do, we should point out that the JSP discussed in this present section does not belong to only one Web application state, as do most of the other JSP. Instead, it is shared by all the states, which rely on it to move from one frameset to the next.

7.2.9 host_executes_chat.jsp

In this JSP document, you should notice two things. The first is that you again see attributes being set with the desired applet parameter values. However, this time these are not request attributes, but session attributes. Also, nowhere on the page do we find the expected Java plug-in element that calls the applet itself. (Hint: You will find that plug-in element on another JSP page, which we discuss later: host_executes_chat_robot.jsp.) See Figure 7.4 for an example display of host_executes_chat.jsp, in the lower right frame.

The other thing you should notice is that we now are establishing a frameset within the Web application user's browser that contains three frames, not only two, as discussed previously.

```
<frameset rows="55%, 45%">
<frame src="/bonForum/jsp/forum/host_executes_chat_frame.jsp" name="display"/>
<frameset cols="77%, 23%">
<frame src="/bonForum/jsp/forum/host_executes_chat_controls.jsp" name="controls"/>
<frame src="/bonForum/jsp/forum/host_executes_chat_robot.jsp" name="robot"/>
</frameset>
</frameset>
```

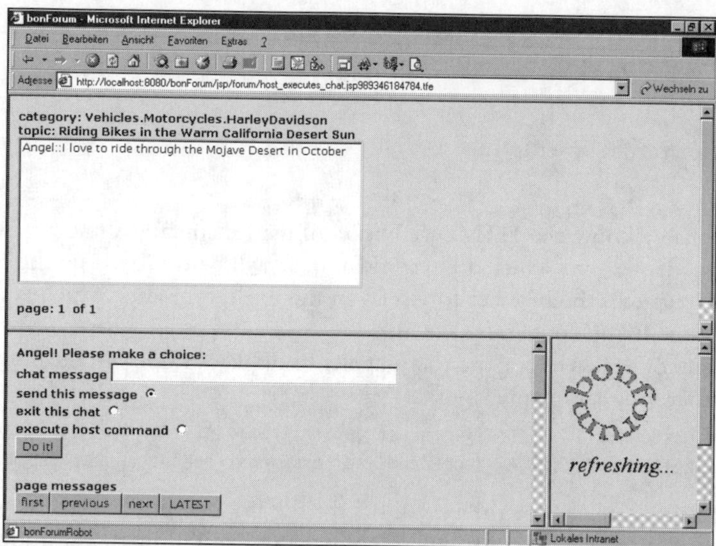

Figure 7.4 HTML displayed by host_executes_chat.jsp and related JSP documents.

We'll discuss the contents of each of these three frames next.

7.2.10 host_executes_chat_controls.jsp

On this JSP page, we create an input text box that the user can use to enter a message into the list of chat messages added by all the chat actors. That input field on the form is created as part of the following HTML form:

```
<table border="0" cellspacing="0" cellpadding="0" rows="4" cols="1" width="100%"
➥bgcolor="#00FFFF">
<form method="POST" action="/bonForum/servlet/BonForumEngine">
<tr width=100%>
<table border="0" cellspacing="0" cellpadding="0"
rows="1" cols="1" width="100%" bgcolor="#00FFFF">
<tr>
<label for="chatMessage">chat message</label>
<font face="Arial Narrow">
<input type="text" name="chatMessage" size=50></input>
</font>
</tr>
</table>
</tr>
…
</form>
…
</table>
```

This form inside a table contains, in fact, not only the previous code to set up the chat message input line, but also the following code, which contains the rest of the form innards:

```
<tr width=100%>
<table border="0" cellspacing="0" cellpadding="0"
rows="4" cols="1" width="100%" bgcolor="#00FFFF">
<tr>
<label for="bonCommand">send this message</label>
<input type="radio" name="bonCommand"
value="host_executes_chat_controls" CHECKED></input>
</tr>
<tr>
<label for="bonCommand">exit this chat</label>
<input type="radio" name="bonCommand"
value="host_executes_chat_ready"></input>
</tr>
<tr>
<label for="bonCommand">enter command mode</label>
<input type="radio" name="bonCommand"
value="host_executes_chat_console"></input>
</tr>
<tr>
<input type="hidden" name="actorReturning" value="yes"></input>
<input type="submit" value="Do it!" name="submit"></input>
</tr>
</table>
</tr>
```

By choosing one of the three available values of bonCommand, the user (a chat host) can descend into the labyrinth of JSP pages contained in this Web application. Is this needless complexity? Well, if every destination page on your Web application offers three or for further destinations, you can see that it is not hard to create considerable complexity. Anyone who does not believe that should consider the example (once famous) of the chessboard being filled with amounts of wheat that double on each successive square. The number of wheat grains soon exceeds the number of known stars in the universe—and then finally the number of atoms as well!

We are not finished yet, though. The top-level table on the resulting HTML page also contains more code. That code sets up some page-navigation buttons, labeled First, Previous, Next, and Latest. The user can use these buttons to page through the list of chat messages that are being displayed. These chat messages are in the display frame on the browser and are being displayed by the JSP document host_executes_chat_frame.jsp.

Here is the code for the navigation buttons:

```
<tr width=10%>
<table border="0" cellspacing="0" cellpadding="0"
rows="1" cols="4" width="10%" bgcolor="#00FFFF">
```

```
<%--here we display navigator buttons to page through chat messages --%>

<label for="chatMessagesNavigator">page messages</label>

<td width=10%>
<form method="POST" action="/bonForum/servlet/BonForumEngine">
<input type="hidden" name="chatMessagesNavigator" value="first"></input>
<input type="hidden" name="actorReturning" value="yes"></input>
<input type="hidden" name="bonCommand"
value="host_executes_chat_controls"></input>
<input type="submit" value=<%=chatNavigatorFirst%> name="submit"></input>
</form>
</td>
<td width=10%>
<form method="POST" action="/bonForum/servlet/BonForumEngine">
<input type="hidden" name="chatMessagesNavigator" value="previous"></input>
<input type="hidden" name="actorReturning" value="yes"></input>
<input type="hidden" name="bonCommand"
value="host_executes_chat_controls"></input>
<input type="submit" value=<%=chatNavigatorPrevious%> name="submit"></input>
</form>
</td>
<td width=10%>
<form method="POST" action="/bonForum/servlet/BonForumEngine">
<input type="hidden" name="chatMessagesNavigator" value="next"></input>
<input type="hidden" name="actorReturning" value="yes"></input>
<input type="hidden" name="bonCommand"
value="host_executes_chat_controls"></input>
<input type="submit" value=<%=chatNavigatorNext%> name="submit"></input>
</form>
</td>
<td width=10%>
<form method="POST" action="/bonForum/servlet/BonForumEngine">
<input type="hidden" name="chatMessagesNavigator"
value="last"></input>
<input type="hidden" name="actorReturning"
value="yes"></input>
<input type="hidden" name="bonCommand"
value="host_executes_chat_controls"></input>
<input type="submit" value=<%=chatNavigatorLast%>
name="submit"></input>
</form>
</td>
</table>
</tr>
```

Notice that the values of the bonCommand request parameter that will be submitted to the BonForumEngine along with the rest of one HTML form are all set to forward the request to the same page that is sending in the form submission. That means, as discussed earlier, that submitting this form is not what will take the user to the next destination in the Web application.

In fact, there are two doorways for the user to get out of the "host executes chat" frameset. These two doorways are controlled by two JSP documents, both of which we will discuss later. These two are in the following files:

host_executes_chat_ready.jsp

host_executes_chat_console.jsp

As an aside, let's continue the thread of discussion begun earlier about the complexity of JSP-based Web applications. As you are following the code to handle just one user who is becoming a host, consider that in reality we must handle hundreds of such actors simultaneously. Aren't you as glad as we are now that the able developers of the Java servlet and JSP packages have taken care of the details, and that Java hides the mechanics of multithreaded programming from our view?

Sometimes while developing and debugging a Web application, you might find it useful to insert the following JSP code, which serves to brand each browser instance with its own identifying label:

```
sessionId: <%= session.getId() %>
```

Next, we discuss the frame where the chat history appears to a chat host, which is the frame that is constructed by the compiled JSP document whose source code is called host_executes_chat_frame.jsp.

7.2.11 host_executes_chat_frame.jsp

Again, on the HTML produced by this JSP document, you see our familiar theme: how to use session attribute values to connect two otherwise stateless Web pages. Here is one example from this JSP file:

```
<%
String chatSubject = (String)session.getAttribute("chatSubject");
String chatSubjectMessage = "";
if(chatSubject != null && chatSubject.trim().length() > 0){
chatSubjectMessage = "category: " + chatSubject;
}
%>
```

A similar code section gets the `chatTopic`—that is, the description of the chat that was input by the visitor becoming a chat host. Both of these useful pieces of information are displayed to the Web application user with the following JSP elements:

```
<%=chatSubjectMessage%>
<%=chatTopicMessage%>
```

The same HTML table that contains the display of the chat category (`chatSubject` value) and description (`chatTopic` value) also contains a form like this:

```
<form method="POST" action="/bonForum/servlet/BonForumEngine">

<select size="<%= chatMessagesPageSize %>" name="chatMessages">
```

```
<font face="Fixedsys">
<bon:outputChatMessages command="bonForumXML">
<option><%= output %></option>
</bon:outputChatMessages>
</font>
</select>

</form>
```

You see here one example of many in the Web application in which we decided to use a JSP custom tag. We already discussed using a custom tag to request a list of all the available chat subjects. Now the job is to get chat messages for the user to see. More specifically, it is to get one full page of messages out of all those that have ever been sent by the host and guests. As discussed in the last section, which page of chat messages is retrieved by the custom tag is determined in part by the last navigator button that was clicked (if any). The buttons are created in the bottom frame by the JSP host_executes_chat_controls.jsp.

The default, of course, is to display the latest page of messages. The label text for the First button changes to "FIRST" whenever it was the last button clicked. The Latest button similarly changes to "LATEST." The other two buttons do not change text because they function in a "one-shot" mode.

This host_executes_chat_controls.jsp document also shows the user which of all the pages of chat messages is being currently displayed in the frame's select box. That trick is accomplished by the following line:

```
page: <%= chatPageNumber %> of <%= chatNumberOfPages %>
```

Notice that the text that is not contained within the JSP elements simply is output verbatim to the HTML result page.

How many chat messages are obtained is controlled by another variable that the chat host is free to change: Instead of sending a message to the chat, the host can select a different radio button so that the Do It! button causes the engine to forward the request to the form host_executes_chat_console.jsp.

That JSP then sets request attributes with all the right `BonForumRobot` applet parameters. The applet is used to change the state of the application to the "host executes command" bonForum state, where the user can change the setting for the number of messages to display per page. After setting the request attributes, the _console JSP simply forwards the request to the JSP actor_leaves_frameset_robot.jsp.

If you have followed the discussion thus far, you know that there are still other JSP documents awaiting discussion. (Not all—we are almost done!) However, the next one to discuss is the one that displays in the third frame of our "host executes chat" frameset. That new JSP document is in the file host_executes_chat_robot.jsp. Understanding the operation of this JSP will give you a handle on several other JSP documents that have the word *robot* in their filenames.

7.2.12 host_executes_chat_robot.jsp

We previously discussed some session attributes that are saved by the JSP document that set up the current framework visible on the user's browser, that JSP being host_executes_chat.jsp.

Those same session attributes, here in this new _robot JSP page we are discussing, are retrieved from the current session object and are used to set the various applet parameters required by any `BonForumRobot` applet. While it runs, that applet is an instance of the class that we define in the file BonForumRobot.java and that we will discuss in more detail in Chapter 10.

In addition, we have above discussed the cooperation of these two JSP documents:

visitor_starts_chat_ready.jsp

actor_leaves_frameset_robot.jsp

Working together, they manage the "breakout" from the frameset established by the JSP visitor_starts_chat.jsp.

The applet on the _robot JSP uses its `showDocument` method to cause the application to display its document to the _top target, thereby creating a new top-level frameset.

Therefore, it may seem that in the page now under discussion we have only another example of doing this same trick. In fact, we do have a parallel here, but that involves the functioning of not two, but three, JSP pages:

host_executes_chat_robot.jsp

host_executes_chat_ready.jsp

host_executes_chat_console.jsp

What is more interesting now, however, is to notice a second and more important use of the `BonForumRobot` applet.

The BonForumRobot.class file does one thing that is the real reason for its existence. It has a built-in clock that ticks at settable intervals. That interval in the pulse of the robot applet is settable by changing the value of the `interval` applet parameter.

The robot applet is set to redisplay a document in a target every time that the clock fires, up to a `limit` number of times (another applet parameter). The job for the robot here is to cause a browser to refresh a page (as fast as every 5 seconds) without causing annoying side effects for the user.

We did not embark on the task of creating the `BonForumRobot` applet lightly. We tried to use existing, simple solutions first. For example, we tried to just set a `META` tag in the HTML head element that would refresh the document periodically. What we found (with our setup, at least) is that, with a fast enough refresh rate for a chat, there was always an unacceptable amount of flicker in the browser display.

It seems that the display was being cleared to white before the new display of host_executes_chat_frame.jsp was painted on the screen. It may well be that there is some other way to control this flicker, but our idea to use an applet would kill two birds with one stone: It would solve the refresh problem and give us material for our chapter about applets, Chapter 9, "Java Applet Plugged In: bonForumRobot."

Because we also wanted to avoid using scripting languages on the client side, we decided not to pursue the experimentation with HTML pragma, buffering pages, and so on. Instead, the robot applet idea was born and provided an alternative, Java-related solution to the problems inherent in frequent refreshes of a page. For all the gory details of how it works, read Chapter 9.

We pointed out that the robot applet on the _robot JSP we are discussing gets its parameter values from session attribute values that are set on the top page in the group of pages handling the "host executes chat" phase of the Web application host_executes_chat.jsp.

If we look there again, we will see by the value used to set the `document` session attribute that this particular applet instance will continually try to display the file named host_executes_chat_frame.jsp.

This means that it is going to refresh the display of the chat messages that the host sees. That is something that we would like to do as frequently as possible, allowing for the bandwidth and physical manifestation of such a repeatedly fired Web page. When a guest in the chat adds a message, we want it to show up in the display of all the users as soon as possible.

How does the user break out of the frameset that is representing the "host executes chat" Web application phase? We saw before, in host_executes_chat_controls.jsp, that the host can do one of three things: send a message to the chat guests, exit from this chat, or enter command mode. Again, this choice is presented in the code as follows:

```
<table border="0" cellspacing="0" cellpadding="0" rows="4" cols="1" width="100%"
➥bgcolor="#00FFFF">
<tr>
<label for="bonCommand">send this message</label><input type="radio"
name="bonCommand" value="host_executes_chat_controls" CHECKED></input>
</tr>
<tr>
<label for="bonCommand">exit this chat</label><input type="radio"
name="bonCommand" value="host_executes_chat_ready"></input>
</tr>
<tr>
<label for="bonCommand">enter command mode</label><input type="radio"
name="bonCommand" value="host_executes_chat_console"></input>
</tr>
<tr>
<input type="hidden" name="actorReturning" value="yes"></input>
<input type="submit" value="Do it!" name="submit"></input>
</tr>
</table>
```

One of these Web app destinations, the "host executes command" state, will be discussed only briefly here. If you have followed the discussion so far, you will possess the information needed to understand the following seven interrelated JSP pages that are together involved in offering the chat host some commands to execute. You will have noticed that we have not provided many commands yet, but we have set up the framework and the manner in which more host (and other actor) commands will be added later.

host_executes_command.jsp
host_executes_command_frame.jsp
host_executes_command_controls.jsp
host_executes_command_ready.jsp
host_executes_command_robot.jsp
host_increases_rating.jsp
host_decreases_rating.jsp

The three commands now available for the host to execute do the following:

- Increase the status of a guest
- Decrease the status of a guest
- Change the number of messages displayed to the host

A host can select one guest in the chat from a list of guests displayed by the _frame JSP host_executes_command_frame.jsp.

That list is being produced by an XSLT transformation of the information contained in the `hashtable`-based database of the `BonForumEngine` class. For a relevant discussion, see Section 10.13, "Displaying the Guests in a Chat," in Chapter 10.

The overall idea is that the Web application will automatically remove from a chat any guest whose rating has decreased to 0. Furthermore, the Web application will automatically change the role of an actor from that of chat guest to that of chat host as soon as the rating of that guest reaches some set value, such as 10 points.

The design envisions these multihosted chats, as well as multichat forums and multiforum chat networks. However, the code for these was not considered as high of a priority as those more fleshed-out portions of the Web application.

When you are trying out this part of the Web application (you are doing that, aren't you?), you should definitely try increasing and decreasing a guest's rating, changing the number of chat messages being displayed, and exercising the navigator buttons in conjunction with smaller lists. (You may even discover that showing the first page of several is still a bit rough, although it works.) This simple exercise in user feedback in JSP should make you aware of the possibilities of control mechanisms that can be designed with similar techniques.

Notice that there is again a robot applet on a JSP: host_executes_command_robot.jsp. In a manner similar to the one discussed for the host executes chat bonForum state, this JSP works in conjunction with its top-level JSP, host_executes_command.jsp. Together, they refresh the list of chat guests on the HTML produced by the JSP host_executes_command_frame.jsp.

At this point in this chapter, you should know enough about the bonForum Web application to be able to decipher the functioning of the rest of the JSP files in the folder TOMCAT_HOME\webapps\bonForum\jsp\forum. Some of these files are better discussed in other contexts, such as the use of Java servlets in Java-and-XML–based software, so they will be visited in later chapters.

7.2.13 visitor_joins_chat_frame.jsp

We next briefly discuss visitor_joins_chat_frame.jsp, which is of considerable interest in the context of XML and XSLT. We concentrate on presenting things from the JSP point of view.

We first make sure that we can use our tag library from this page by referring to the taglib URL:

```
<%@ taglib uri="http://www.bonForum.org/taglib/bonForum-taglib" prefix="bon" %>
```

The Tomcat Server will know how to resolve this reference and will be capable of using the .tld file to find the tag classes when it translates the JSP file into a Java servlet source file. Look at one of these sometime for a JSP with a custom tag on it, to better understand how tags merge your tag class code into the code produced by a JSP.

The JSP now being discussed simply lists all the available chats to the bonForum visitor, allowing that user to select and submit a chat to join. To actually join it, the user must then click a button on the controls frame.

> **Too Many Clicks?**
>
> As an aside, this has been criticized as a stupid design—why so many clicks just to join a chat? Our answer is that we are not trying to design the simplest and best user interface now, but instead we're trying to design a prototype that will enable us to explore and solve problems. For example, we are interested in the problems encountered when several cooperating JSP reside in frames. We are essentially in the business here of creating problems! That does get criticized for being an academic exercise rather than a serious, practical example of a Web application. We would rather call it R&D than academic, but we also recognize that the way we research software technologies is not everyone's cup of tea. As to whether it is practical, that depends on whether you can learn anything practical from it (we certainly have!). As to whether it is serious, that depends on whether you are having fun yet (seriously!).

We first developed the code to display available chat topics with XSLT by writing JSP scriptlets directly on the JSP document. After we had the code working (at least, for one or two users), we moved it all into a custom tag class. The code ended up finally in the `TransformTag` class, defined by the file TransformTag.java. (See Figure 7.5.) Prototyping the XSLT custom tag to produce a chat list display is discussed in section 10.10, "XSLT and the `bonTransform` Command," in Chapter 10.

What we designed is a way to call the Apache Xalan XSLT processor to apply an XSL style sheet to the chat room data that the Web application contains at runtime. The outcome of such a process will be an XML document, which (in this case) is used to display to the user the list of chats that can be joined in bonForum. Here is how the `TransformTag` is used to generate that list:

```
<bon:transform type="bonTransform" inDoc="bonForumXML"
styleSheet="..\\webapps\\bonForum\\mldocs\\bonChatItems.xsl"
outDoc="output">
<%=output%>
</bon:transform>
```

We have already discussed the way we first put the results of the XSLT into the HTML produced by the JSP. (See section 6.1.13, "Including Documents in a JSP," and section 6.5.1, "Including XSLT Output on JSP Output," in Chapter 6.) We now output the resulting select list of available chats not to a file, but to a string named `output` that is created by the `BonForumTagExtraInfo` class. This gives us the possibility of reusing the results elsewhere, if we change the setting of the extra tag information so that it is visible outside the custom tag body.

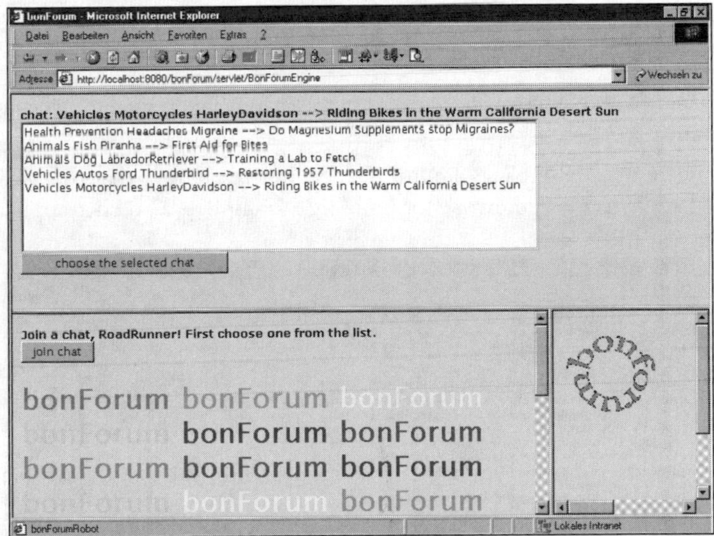

Figure 7.5 HTML displayed by visitor_joins_chat.jsp and related JSP documents.

In the following code scriptlet, you can see how this JSP page gets the value of the currently chosen `chatItem` to display to the user. When the user clicks the Submit button to choose the selected chat, the form is sent by an HTTP POST method to the `BonForumEngine` servlet. The request makes a round-trip because of the value of the `bonCommand` request parameter. That refreshes the HTML produced by the JSP and updates the selected `chatItem`—the chat that was just chosen from the selection list.

```
<%
String chatItem = (String)session.getAttribute("chatItem");
String chatItemMessage = "chat: &lt;none&gt;";
if(chatItem != null && chatItem.trim().length() > 0) {
chatItemMessage = "chat: " + chatItem;
}
%>
```

Finally, the current chat is displayed to the user using the following JSP expression:

```
<%=chatItemMessage%>
```

7.2.14 All Those Other JSP Files

By now, you should have the information required to understand all the other JSP pages in the Web application. They are just variations on the themes we have been discussing here. You can read functional descriptions of all the JSP pages in Section 6.1.5, "The States of the Forum," in Chapter 6. Figure 7.6 shows the HTML dsplayed by guest_executes_chat.jsp. Some of the JSP pages not discussed are quite simple. They only forward the request to the next page using the following JSP trick:

```
<jsp:forward page="visitor_executes_choice.jsp"/>
```

Figure 7.6 HTML displayed by guest_executes_chat.jsp and related JSP documents.

It might seem that these pages are not needed, but remember that this version of bonForum is really just a framework for building a complete Web chat application.

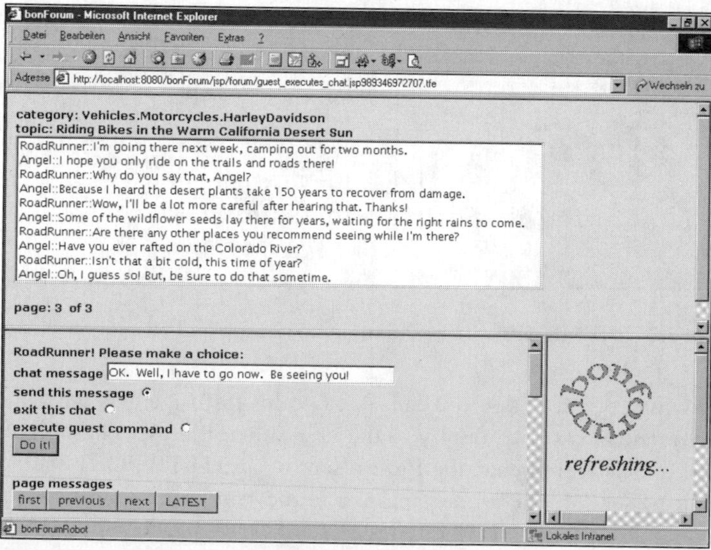

These pages that just forward the request (such as host_exits_forum.jsp) represent one Actor-Action-Thing state in the Web application. It will be far easier to add functionality later, if we have the entire design represented in the JSP pages.

For example, later we will change things so that, when a host leaves the bonForum, most of the data that was added for that host will be deleted. We can do this very conveniently from our host_exits_forum.jsp page.

Quite a bit more complex is the processing that is done by the JSP servlet compiled from the JSP page bonForum.jsp. There we use the `bon:Transform` tag command again, this time to use XSLT to get a list of available bonForum locations. The style sheet produces these in the form of a list of Web hyperlinks. We will discuss that more fully in Chapter 10 because the XSLT transform is handled by the code of the `TransformTag` class.

7.3 Further Discussion About the JSP in bonForum

Before we leave this chapter, we want to further discuss two interrelated topics:

- Using session attributes to pass data between JSPs
- Reducing versus increasing the number of JSP files

We are aware that we may be improperly using session objects when we use them to pass values for our applet parameters from one JSP to another. The criteria is whether these applet parameter values qualify as information about a specific user of the application and, thus, session information. They probably are better treated as thread-specific information instead, and we should develop a way to use beans to pass the information in a thread-safe manner between these JSPs.

Furthermore, why do we need to pass the applet parameter values into the _robot page at all? Why not just put the values directly into the applet parameters right on the _robot page? Using the same target parameter as we did in the last section as an example, that would mean doing this:

```
<jsp:param name="target" value="display"/>
```

The various other applet parameters would then also be hard-wired. Of course, that would work as well. The applet doesn't care where it gets its strings. If we did it this way, we would have no need to use the session attributes to pass values from the JSP that creates the frameset to the JSP with the embedded robot applet.

In fact, we could just put the `jsp:plugin` element in the _controls JSP and not even have a third frame. We would then get rid of all the _robot JSP files except for actor_leaves_frameset_robot.jsp.

It all comes down to a balancing act. On one hand, especially in a chat application, performance is important, and "simpler" usually means "better performance." That would argue in favor of reducing the number of frames, objects, and files—no need for all the robot session attributes, nor all the _robot JSP files.

On the other hand, a key purpose of JSP is to create dynamic Web pages that are easily expandable and customizable. We see the design of bonForum as being a lot like one of those new and empty land subdivisions that will later become an entire suburb. Each JSP can be seen as Web real estate that can later be filled in with content. The application pages could certainly use more and better content.

You will also no doubt have noticed, for example, that there is very little difference among many of the JSP files in the bonForum project. If that is so, why not just replace every group of similar JSP files with just one? We could take care of any differences that exist some other way. For example, we could replace this lot of files:

guest_executes_chat_robot.jsp

guest_executes_command_robot.jsp

host_executes_chat_robot.jsp

host_executes_command_robot.jsp

visitor_joins_chat_robot.jsp

visitor_starts_chat_robot.jsp

These six JSPs could all be replaced by one file, which we could call actor_refreshes_frame_robot.jsp.

The only other changes needed would be to the top-level JSP files in each bonForum state that uses a refresh robot, which are these files:

guest_executes_chat.jsp

guest_executes_command.jsp

host_executes_chat.jsp

host_executes_command.jsp

visitor_joins_chat.jsp

visitor_starts_chat.jsp

We would replace the entire robot frame element in all these files. Those are now all similar to this:

```
<frame src="/bonForum/jsp/forum/host_executes_chat_robot.jsp" name="robot"/>
```

They would now all contain the same robot frame element, which would be like this:

```
<frame src="/bonForum/jsp/forum/actor_refreshes_frame_robot.jsp" name="robot"/>
```

On the face of it, replacing six files with one seems like a no-brainer. However, if you look at each one of those replaceable _robot JSP files as defining a customizable piece of Web real estate that is related to a particular state of a Web application (for example, the user is joining, starting, chatting, commanding, hosting, and being a guest), then you can argue that having all those files is a better framework to build upon than having just the one file. It is a bit like biodiversity being favorable for evolution.

8 Java Servlet and Java Bean: BonForumEngine and BonForumStore

IN THIS CHAPTER, YOU LEARN ABOUT TWO classes central to the bonForum Web application. `BonForumEngine` is a servlet in charge of handling HTTP requests and responses. `BonForumStore` is a nonvisual bean that implements chat logic and encapsulates the XML chat database. You will want to have the source code and javadocs for the project—and a large cup of java—available because the discussion here will not shy away from the details. The chapter also illustrates some themes common to using Java servlets and beans in Web applications.

8.1 The *BonForumEngine* Servlet

This chapter is divided into two parts: The first covers the `BonForumEngine` servlet, and the second covers the `BonForumStore` bean. The servlet will be discussed in more detail because the problems that it solves are more universally encountered by developers of Web applications. After a brief introduction to the purposes of the servlet and its context in the Web application, we proceed to a discussion of its two major methods, the `service()` method and the `processRequest()` method. Whenever possible, code that is not dependent on the nature of the application (chatting) has been placed in the `service()` method, while code that is more related to the specific needs of the Web application (chatting) has been put in the `processRequest()` method.

8.1.1 Purpose of the *BonForumEngine* Class

The main purpose of the `BonForumEngine` class is to connect and coordinate all the JSP documents in the Web application. By extending the `HttpServlet` abstract class, it can receive the many simultaneous HTTP requests being generated by the browser user interface discussed in Chapter 7, "JavaServer Pages: The Browseable User Interface." `BonForumEngine` forwards each request it receives to a "destination" JSP. This servlet is the engine that moves every instance of bonForum from one state to the next.

Before forwarding each request, it can also process it, which it does in relation to the bonForum Web application. That "chat" processing relies heavily on the methods of the `BonForumStore` class, which is the subject of the second part of this chapter (see Section 8.2, "The `BonForumStore` Class"). Here is a listing of most of the functions of `BonForumEngine`:

- Provides multiple, simultaneous contexts for Web application
- Allows multiple simultaneous user threads to be serviced
- Prevents entry to an application except from login page
- Enforces unique nicknames within application instance
- Acts as a switchyard for different HTTP request categories
- Manages the Web application `session` objects
- Processes HTTP request objects as a Web (chat) application
- Processes and forwards applet-generated JSP requests
- Processes information from all JSPs in the Web application
- Initializes the XML data wrapper, a `BonForumStore` instance
- Sets up an application scope reference to `BonForumStore`
- Makes user input available to chat processes, by session
- Processes chat messages from JSP users to other JSP users
- Manages XML data items for multiple simultaneous users
- Forwards users from JSP to JSP with programmatic control
- Provides extension and customization mechanism for Web app
- Provides some examples of user input verification

The best way to understand any distributed application is perhaps from the point of view of the host (or hosts) that connect the clients. These connections create contracts that define the allowable transactions: between the clients, between the clients and databases, and so on. Just trying out the bonForum chat software as a chat host or as a chat guest will not reveal the mechanics of this Web application. The following discussion of the `BonForumEngine` and `BonForumStore` classes will hopefully make clear some of the Ozian wizardry behind the curtain.

8.1.2 Web Application Context for this Servlet

Although Tomcat is a complete HTTP server, its specialty is handling Java servlets and JavaServer Pages (JSP). The Tomcat configuration file web.xml determines what Tomcat does with the various requests that it gets, whether directly from a browser or from another server such as Apache. The following document type links the web.xml configuration file to a definition of what a Web application should look like:

```
<!DOCTYPE web-app PUBLIC "-//Sun Microsystems, Inc.//DTD Web Application 2.2//EN"
➥"http://java.sun.com/j2ee/dtds/web-app_2.2.dtd">
```

According to that definition, a Web application description is enclosed in a pair of matching root element tags, `<web-app>` and `</web-app>`.

Among the many element types that can exist within that Web app element are child elements enclosed within the tag pair `<servlet>` and `</servlet>`. These servlet elements enclose other elements that can contain the name, class, and parameter information for each servlet that the Web app should know about.

Web Application Deployment Descriptor for bonForum

The web.xml Web application deployment descriptor for bonForum can be found in the following file:

```
TOMCAT_HOME\webapps\bonForum\web-inf\web.xml
```

Servlet Element

This is the servlet element for the `BonForumEngine` Java servlet, as found in that configuration file:

```
<servlet>
    <servlet-name>
            BonForumEngine
    </servlet-name>
    <servlet-class>
            de.tarent.forum.BonForumEngine
    </servlet-class>
    <init-param>
            <param-name>
                    bonfoo47
            </param-name>
            <param-value>
                    bonbar47
            </param-value>
     </init-param>
</servlet>
```

This servlet element in the web.xml file tells Tomcat that within the context of the Web app that is being configured (bonForum), the name "`BonForumEngine`" will refer to the Java class:

```
de.tarent.forum.BonForumEngine
```

Servlet Initialization Parameters

To illustrate how you can pass initialization parameters to a servlet, we have included a purely illustrative parameter name, `bonfoo47`, and value `bonbar47`. To access this parameter from within the `BonForumEngine` servlet, you could use something like either of these two equivalent statements (the second is a convenient shortcut for the first):

```
String bonFoo47 = getServletConfig.getInitParameter("bonfoo47");
String bonFoo47 = getInitParameter("bonfoo47");
```

Context Initialization Parameters

You can also define initialization parameters for the entire Web application context. These are shared by all the servlets in the Web app. Here is one example from our Web application. The parameter named `Logging` has a value of `all`, which turns on the logging output both to logfiles (one for each major object) and to the console (the standard error output, actually). Here is how we make that Web app global information available:

```
<context-param>
    <param-name>
        Logging
    </param-name>
    <param-value>
        all
    </param-value>
</context-param>
```

To access context-initialization parameters from within a servlet, you can use something like either of the following equivalent statements (the second, again, is a convenient shortcut for the first):

```
String logging =
➥getServletConfig().getServletContext().getInitParameter("Logging"));
String logging = getServletContext().getInitParameter("Logging");
```

Servlet-Mapping Elements

Some other elements are present in a Web-app deployment descriptor, one or more of which can exist on the same tree level as the servlet elements. These are enclosed by the paired tags `<servlet-mapping>` and `</servlet-mapping>`. The following servlet-mapping element, together with the servlet element described previously, is critical to the behavior of the `BonForumEngine`:

```
<servlet-mapping>
    <servlet-name>
            BonForumEngine
    </servlet-name>
    <url-pattern>
            *.tfe
    </url-pattern>
```

```
</servlet-mapping>
<servlet-mapping>
    <servlet-name>
            BonForumEngine
    </servlet-name>
    <url-pattern>
            /BonForumEngine
    </url-pattern>
</servlet-mapping>
```

This is an example of mapping by using both an extension and a directory. The first servlet-mapping element in this excerpt from web.xml tells Tomcat that any request URL that has an extension of .tfe should be sent to the servlet named `BonForumEngine`. That servlet name could be a different one, but it must be the one used in the servlet tag.

The second servlet-mapping element in the web.xml file tells Tomcat that a URL pattern that matches `/BonForumEngine` should also cause Tomcat to forward the request to the servlet known as `BonForumEngine` because of the servlet tag seen earlier.

8.1.3 The *service( )* Method: An Overall View

First and foremost, the `BonForumEngine` is a descendant of `HTTPServlet`. The direct benefit that you get from that includes many things that were already taken care of for you as a developer: You simply do not have to solve some hard problems in the area of communication across the world. The best place to start examining the doings of this `HTTPServlet` is right at its heart: the `service()` method.

Servicing *HttpServletRequest* Objects

As you know already (or could guess by looking at its arguments' types), the `service()` method in an `HTTPServlet` accepts an `HttpServletRequest` object and an `HttpServletResponse` object. The servlet and the JavaServer Pages API documentation says the following about the service method:

> There's almost no reason to override the `service()` method. `service()` handles standard HTTP requests by dispatching them to the handler methods for each HTTP request type (the `doxxx` methods …).

These `doXXX` methods are `doGet()`, `doPost()`, `doPut()`, and `doDelete()`. The standard approach, when only `post` and `get` actions are to be handled (and handled in the same way), is to override `doPost()` instead of `service()`, and then to override `doGet()` to simply invoke `doPost()`. The bonForum Web app uses only the `post` action. If we were to override `doPost()` instead of `service()` and then later decided to use the `get` action also, we would have to add "and also in `doGet()`" everywhere in the book where we had written "in `doPost()`." We decided that was reason enough to override `service()`!

What *service()* Does in *BonForumEngine*

So what is in the `service()` method of `BonForumEngine`? Table 8.1 gives a brief list of its tasks.

Table 8.1 **Tasks of the *service()* Method in *BonForumEngine***

1	Entrance security	Prevent access to Web app except via the front door: forum_login.jsp.
2	Manage sessions	Make sure that each user has a valid `HttpSession` object.
3	Nickname security	Make sure that users have nicknames when they enter.
4	Classify requests from HTML forms	Route `HttpRequests` submitted to `BonForumEngine` by HTML forms—some are processed before forwarding, and others are not.
5	Classify requests mapped to servlet in deployment descriptor	Route requests mapped to `BonForumEngine`—some are processed before forwarding, and others not.
6	Invoke `processRequest()`	Calls a method that implements a request-based Web application (a chat, in this case).
7	Forward requests	Dispatch each request to a destination JSP or an error JSP, based on processing, form data, or servlet-mapped URL decoding.

Hopefully, you will now be able to make faster sense out of the source code with this information.

Pseudocode Listing for the *service()* Method

The following listing in pseudocode shows the logic of the service method in the `BonForumEngine` class. This listing can serve as a reference while you read the following sections, which discuss its concepts, terms, and details.

```
set serviceStatus to CheckForServicing

get requestUri

get boncommand request parameter

if requestUri is for BonForumEngine
      set bonForumCommand to bonCommand
      if bonCommand request parameter full
            if boncommand includes "forum entry"
                  set serviceStatus to CheckInAtEntrance
            if boncommand includes "UserMustLogin"
```

```
                set serviceStatus to UserMustLogin
            else if boncommand includes "system_executes_command"
                set serviceStatus to SystemCommands
            else
                set serviceStatus to ProcessRequest
            endif
        else
            set serviceStatus to ProcessRequest
        endif
else
        set serviceStatus to DecodeServletMappedURI
endif

if requestUri includes "forum_login"
        set serviceStatus to ForwardToLoginPage
endif
else if requestUri includes "forum_error"
        set serviceStatus to ForwardToErrorPage
endif
else if requestUri includes "UserMustLogin"
        set serviceStatus to UserMustLogin
endif

if serviceStatus is CheckInAtEntrance
        create session
        get sessionId
        // Get a servlet context attribute, or
        // if not, then an init param named,
        // "SessionMaxInactiveMinutes"
        // (default is forever).
        // Use it to set chat inactivity limit:
        set maxInactiveInterval for session
        set serviceStatus to ProcessRequest
else if serviceStatus is not ForwardToLoginPage nor ForwardToErrorPage
        // It is ProcessRequest,
        // DecodeServletMappedURI,
        // or SystemCommands!
        check for existing session
        if no session
            set serviceStatus to UserMustLogin
        else
            get sessionId
            check requested sessionId
            if requested sessionId is not valid
                set serviceStatus to UserMustLogin
            endif
        if request is from forum_entry (nickname input page)
            get input nickname from request parameter
        else
            get existing nickname from session attribute
        endif
```

```
                if nickname gotten
                    if nickname in registry
                        if nickname is for another session
                            if at forum_entry
                                // nickname is taken!
                                set serviceStatus to ForwardWithoutServicing
                                ➥set bonForumCommand to forum_entry
                                save nickname in actorNicknameNotAvailable
                                ➥session attribute
                            else
                                // existing nickname not ok,
                                // session expired?
                                set serviceStatus to UserMustLogin
                                endif
                        // else re-entered nickname is ok
                        endif
                    else
                    // nickname not in registry
                    if at forum_entry
                        // nickname unique and available
                            put nickname in registry
                            put nickname in session attribute
                    else
                            // existing nickname not ok!
                            set serviceStatus to UserMustLogin
                        endif
                    endif
                else
                    // nickname missing in request or session!
                    if at forum_entry
                        set serviceStatus to ForwardWithoutServicing
                        set bonForumCommand to forum_entry
                    else
                        set serviceStatus to UserMustLogin
                    endif
                endif
            endif
        endif

        if serviceStatus is DecodeServletMappedURI
            set serviceStatus to ForwardWithoutServicing
            if requestUri contains embedded bonForum JSP name
                set bonForumCommand to embedded JSP name
                if request needs processing (guest_executes_chat, host_executes_chat)
                    ➥set serviceStatus to ProcessRequest
                endif
            endif
        endif

        if serviceStatus is ProcessRequest, or serviceStatus is SystemCommands
            try
                save serviceStatus in a request attribute
```

```
        invoke processRequest with request, response, session, bonForumCommand
        ➥set serviceStatus from the request attribute
    catch exception
        printStackTrace
    endtry
endif

if serviceStatus is not ForwardWithoutServicing, nor ForwardAfterRequestProcessed
    ➥// service was not successful!
    if serviceStatus is ForwardToLoginPage
        set bonForumCommand to forum_login
    endif
    else if serviceStatus is ForwardToErrorPage
        set bonForumCommand to forum_error
    endif
    else if serviceStatus is SystemCommands
        set bonForumCommand to system_executes_command
    endif
    else //serviceStatus is UserMustLogin, or unknown
        if session exists
        try
                invalidate session
            catch IllegalStateException
                printStackTrace
            endtry
        endif
        create new session
        get new sessionId
        set bonForumCommand to forum_login_robot
        set robot applet parameters in session attributes
        // document is set to "forum_login.jsp"
        // target is set to "_top" frame
        // applet will restart the webapp!
    endif
endif

create JSP filename from bonForumCommand

Forward request and response to JSP using RequestDispatcher
```

Some Notes for the *service()* Method

We list here a series of items that can help you understand the functioning of the `service()` method. Rather than try to understand these items now, it is best to keep them as a reference to use while reading the sections that follow, which cover the `service()` method.

1. You can think of a `bonCommand` as a petition by one JSP to have a request forwarded to another JSP destination in the Web app. The `bonCommand` originates on a JSP-generated form and is available to the `service()` method as a request parameter.

2. You can think of `bonForumCommand` as the ticket out of the `service()` method—and, thus, out of the servlet. The value of `bonForumCommand` determines where each request gets forwarded because it generates the destination's JSP filename. The `bonForumCommand` variable is local to the `service()` method.
3. JSP-generated HTML forms in the browser interface are always posted to the `BonForumEngine` servlet, so their related `requestURI` values are always `BonForumEngine` as well.
4. A request with a URI of `BonForumEngine` and a valid `bonCommand` value automatically gets a `BonForumEngine` with the same value as the `bonCommand`. That is how a JSP form can select the next JSP in the Web application.
5. Other requests transiting the `service()` method have arrived only because of a servlet mapping for URIs that end in .tfe (as discussed in the previous section, "Servlet-Mapping elements"). For example, the `BonForumRobot` applet includes the "true" request destination (the value of its `document` parameter) as part of a mangled URI that ends in .tfe. These servlet-mapped requests are given a `BonForumCommand` that is obtained from the embedded JSP filename value.
6. To ensure that all requests pass through the `service()` method of `BonForumEngine`, we also added a .tfe suffix to the JSP filename values of all `src` attributes of HTML frame elements (for example, the frames on host_executes_chat.jsp) and the JSP filename values of all `page` attributes of the jsp:forward elements (for example, the frames on host_exits_command.jsp).
7. The only application state in which a `bonCommand` of `forum_entry` is posted as a request parameter is the `forum_login` state (created by forum_login.jsp). Therefore, if a request has a `bonCommand` value of `forum_entry`, it is correctly entering bonForum.
8. Unless a request is correctly entering bonForum, it must already have a session. Otherwise, the request gets forwarded to the forum login state, for re-entering bonForum.
9. Unless a request is correctly entering bonForum, it must already be associated with a nickname. If the request originated in the nickname input page (forum_entry.jsp), the nickname will be in a request parameter. Other nonentering requests should have a nickname stored in an attribute of a session that belongs to the request. Nonentering requests without nicknames are forwarded back so that a user can re-enter a nickname. These "bad nickname" requests are forwarded back to the nickname input page, if they originated on one. Otherwise, they are forwarded back to the `forum_login` state.
10. For normal request forwarding, either to the expected destination or back to the page that originated the request, the engine can just set `BonForumCommand` to the

JSP filename (without path or extension) and set `ServiceStatus` to `ForwardWithoutServicing` or `ProcessRequests`.

11. To handle abnormal request forwarding, the engine needs to use `BonForumRobot` to forward the request to the forum login page. Otherwise, problems can happen. (For example, if a request without a session is not correctly entering, then the usual situation is that its session has expired due to browser inactivity. If such a request originates within an HTML frame, and if the engine used the forwarding method described in item 9, the login page would end up being displayed inside the frame!) The applet came in handy here, even though its real jobs are refreshing JSP-generated HTML frames and switching application framesets, as explained in Chapter 7 and Chapter 9, "Java Applet Plugged In: BonForumRobot."

After this look at the overall tasks and design of the `service()` method, and the details of a few key characteristics, we now describe the way `BonForumEngine` classifies requests associated with the various threads "traversing" its code.

8.1.4 The *service()* Method: Classifying Requests for Processing

One of the most important tasks of the `service()` method is to classify and route each arriving request so that the processing executed by its thread is correct for the function of the request within the logical context of the application. That is the topic of this section.

Because each thread executing code within a `service()` method has its own copies of all the method variables, we can use the variables freely in the code, without worrying that one thread can affect the value of the variables for a different thread. Much of the beauty of Java lies in its built-in multithreaded processing capability. (Later, in section 8.1.20, "The `processRequest()` Method: Handling 'Host Executes Chat'" we will discuss the decidedly different situation that we face when two or more threads are sharing the same resource—for example, our database.)

The *ServiceStatus* Variable

`BonForumEngine` uses the `serviceStatus` variable to classify and route all incoming requests to the `service()` method. The value of this variable sorts the requests into various handling categories. It is used to route each request through the various processing choices in the method. Table 8.2 lists all possible values of `serviceStatus`, each with a description of its implied request category.

Table 8.2 **Request Types Handled in the *service()* Method**

Value of `serviceStatus`	Situation of Request
`CheckForServicing`	Request has just entered `service()`.
`CheckInAtEntrance`	Request is for entering the Web app and needs a session.
`SystemCommands`	Request is for access to Web app administration pages.
`ProcessRequest`	Request needs processing—invoke `processRequest()` for it.
`DecodeServletMappedURI`	Request is mapped to this servlet and needs its URL decoded.
`ForwardToLoginPage`	Request is servlet-mapped by robot applet to force relogin, so only forward it.
`ForwardToErrorPage`	Request is for error page, so only forward it.
`UserMustLogin`	Request has failed session or nickname verification, so get the `BonForumRobot` applet on the forum_login_robot JSP page to request the forum_login page.
`ForwardWithoutServicing`	Request needs to be only sent on its way (or else back where it came from), using the `bonForumCommand` to get the name of the JSP destination.
`InProcessRequestMethod`	Request is in `processRequest()` method now.
`ForwardAfterRequestProcessed`	Request is completely processed—send it on its way.

All requests entering the `service()` method are classified in the `CheckForServicing` service status:

```
String serviceStatus = "CheckForServicing";
```

Request URI

The next lines of code reclassify each request, if possible, using several criteria. An important one is obtained by the following code statement:

```
String requestUri = request.getRequestURI();
```

The URIs that are associated with requests coming to this `service()` method are of two types, as follows:

1. URI for the `BonForumEngine`
2. URI servlet-mapped to the `BonForumEngine`

The first type of request URI is always due to the following HTML code that is generated by the typical bonForum JSP:

```
<form method="POST" action="/bonForum/servlet/BonForumEngine">
```

The getRequestURI() method for any request posted by this form will, of course, return the following:

```
/bonForum/servlet/BonForumEngine
```

The second type of request URI is generated in three very different situations, each one producing a URI that ends in .tfe. One situation includes all requests used by the browser to fill frames in framesets using JSPs and is exemplified by the following HTML code taken from guest_executes_chat.jsp:

```
<frame src="/bonForum/jsp/forum/guest_executes_chat_controls.jsp.tfe"
➥name="controls"/>
```

A servlet-mapped request URI is generated also by every jsp:forward tag in the Web app, as exemplified by this one taken from host_exits_chat.jsp:

```
<jsp:forward page="visitor_executes_choice.jsp.tfe"/>
```

Finally, servlet-mapped request URIs are generated also by the BonForumRobot applet class using the following statement taken from its source file:

```
uncachedDocument = document + millis + ".tfe";
```

As discussed in the next chapter, the applet does this to produce requests with URIs, as in the following example:

```
/bonForum/jsp/forum/guest_executes_chat.jsp986480673940.tfe
```

In fact, there are four different subtypes of these "robot" request URIs. The one just shown is used to change application states, from "visitor joins chat" to "guest executes chat." A second subtype, shown next, is used to refresh the frame that displays chat messages to a guest:

```
/bonForum/jsp/forum/guest_executes_chat_frame.jsp986480680219.tfe
```

The third subtype, shown next, is used to display an error page, while ensuring that it will not display within a frame:

```
/bonForum/jsp/forum/forum_error.jsp986480474353.tfe
```

The fourth and final subtype is used to request the very first JSP of the Web app, while ensuring that it can be requested from a frame without being displayed in that frame. Here is an example:

```
/bonForum/jsp/forum/forum_login.jsp986480582348.tfe
```

Later in this chapter, in the section "Request Control and Security," we discuss what may become a fifth kind of servlet-mapped URI.

The *bonCommand*

The next criteria used by the service() method to classify and route incoming requests is obtained by this statement:

```
String bonCommand = normalize( (String)request.getParameter("bonCommand")).trim();
```

The bonCommand request parameter is sent to the servlet when a user submits an HTML form created by a compiled JSP page.

Here are some example boncommand values:

forum_entry

visitor_executes_choice

visitor_starts_chat

visitor_starts_chat_frame

visitor_starts_chat_ready

host_executes_chat_controls

visitor_joins_chat

visitor_joins_chat_frame

visitor_joins_chat_ready

guest_executes_chat_controls

system_executes_command

system_dumps_xml

bonForum

As you know, these represent both the states of the Web app and the JSP files that it uses to create its user interface. The service() method checks that the request URI for a bonCommand is for the BonForumEngine and then uses the bonCommand value to set the all-important variable bonForumEngine, which determines the next JSP page to be executed for the user of the current thread. Here is the code that sets that variable:

```
if((requestUri.indexOf("BonForumEngine") > -1)) {
if(bonCommand.length() > 0) {
bonForumCommand = bonCommand;
```

Notice that bonCommand here has an empty value whenever the request is servlet mapped to the BonForumEngine (see the previous section "Request URI"). In that case, information that is equivalent to that of bonCommand can instead be found embedded in the URI itself.)

CheckInAtEntrance

Requests that have bonCommand values end up classified in the ProcessRequest service status, unless they fall in either of two special categories. The first belong to the CheckInAtEntrance service status. By design, only the first page of the Web app creates a boncommand parameter with a value of forum_entry. The service() method uses that information to produce this category of incoming requests generated by users coming into the application through its proper entrance:

```
// Check if request came from
// the first page (forum_login.jsp).
if(bonCommand.indexOf("forum_entry") > -1) {
serviceStatus = "CheckInAtEntrance";
```

SystemCommands

The second special category of requests belong to the SystemCommands service status. These request resources that only the bonForum server administration and developers can use. This area of the Web app has a "doorway" of its own, which is created by the JSP system_executes_command. To be immediately useful, these requests need to be given a session and a nickname. After that is done, the requests are classified into a separate status and request handling of their own, as follows:

```
else if(bonCommand.indexOf( "system_executes_command" ) > -1) {
// here later add password security on system.
// for now, no security at all
// Get the session, creating it if none
session = request.getSession();
session.setAttribute("actorNickname", "system");
serviceStatus = "SystemCommands";
}
```

ProcessRequest and *DecodeServletMappedURI*

The final act of request classification at this early stage of the service() method is to throw the rest of the requests with a BonForumEngine URI into the ProcessRequest service status, and put all the servlet-mapped requests into the DecodeServletMappedURI service status.

Request Classification

We will now show the entire first part of the service() method, as much as we have discussed in this section:

```
public void service(HttpServletRequest request,
                    HttpServletResponse response)
                    throws IOException, ServletException {

HttpSession session = null;
String sessionId = "";
String serviceStatus = "CheckForServicing";
String bonForumCommand = "";

String requestUri = request.getRequestURI();

String bonCommand = normalize( (String)request.getParameter( "bonCommand"
➥)).trim();

if((requestUri.indexOf("BonForumEngine") > -1)) {
      if(bonCommand.length() > 0) {
            bonForumCommand = bonCommand;
            if(bonCommand.indexOf("forum_entry") > -1) {
                  serviceStatus = "CheckInAtEntrance";
            }
            else if(bonCommand.indexOf( "system_executes_command" ) > -1) {
```

```
                    session = request.getSession();
                    session.setAttribute( "actorNickname", "system");
                    serviceStatus = "SystemCommands";
                }
                else {
                    serviceStatus = "ProcessRequest";
                }
            }
        }
        else {
            serviceStatus = "DecodeServletMappedURI";
        }
        [the rest of the method is here. . .]
        }
```

Request Control and Security

Notice that it is part of the design that each request involved in the Web application should traverse the `service()` method of the `BonForumEngine` and thus be subject to control by whatever Java code there can accomplish. In effect, the servlet provides security within an application context. Just before this book went to print, there were still some requests that were not subject to this control. These (discussed previously in the section "Request URI") included all "frame-filling" requests made by browsers and all requests by `jsp:forward` tags. The fix for all these "out-of-control" requests turned out to be extremely simple: We only added a .tfe suffix to all the requested JSP filenames.

That left one other source of requests that were not being routed through the `service()` method of `BonForumEngine`: the error page JSP requests. Each JSP (except forum_error.jsp) has in it a page directive like this:

```
<%@ page errorPage="forum_error.jsp" %>
```

It would be a simple matter to also add .tfe to this JSP filename, which would route the request through the `service()` method. We are still debating whether it is better to gain control (and access) to all these error page requests in `BonForumEngine` or whether all JSP errors should be handled only by Tomcat.

After that fix, all the requests are sent to the `service()` method because of the servlet mapping. Without any additional changes to the code, we are ready to establish total control of all requests in the Web application. In the "if-else-if-else-if-else" construct that handles all servlet-mapped requests in the `service()` method, we can easily add new code that responds to these "frame-filling" and direct "JSP-to-JSP" transitions. (In a future release, we will use three different suffixes, not just .tfe, to provide an easy way to sort these three types of servlet-mapped requests.)

8.1.5 The *service()* Method: Requests for Engine Control

Some requests are used not to implement the Web application, but rather to control the engine that implements the Web application. As of now, the only examples in `BonForumEngine` control the error page display and reboot the application. They are described fully later in this chapter, in Section 8.1.12, "The `service()` Method: Handling Abnormal Outcomes."

These control requests need no further processing and, indeed, should not be processed. These are detected early in the `service()` method and are given a `serviceStatus` value that will route them past all the code to the request-forwarding mechanism at the end of the method. That is all done by checking the incoming request URIs, as follows:

```
if(requestUri.indexOf("forum_login") > -1) {
      serviceStatus = "ForwardToLoginPage";
}
else if(requestUri.indexOf("forum_error") > -1) {
      serviceStatus = "ForwardToErrorPage";
}
else if(requestUri.indexOf("UserMustLogin") > -1) {
      serviceStatus = "UserMustLogin";
}
```

In Section 8.1.2, "Web Application Context for this Servlet," we discuss what becomes of requests that are given these Web app control `serviceStatus` values.

8.1.6 The *service()* Method: Requests to Enter the Web Application

As discussed in Section 8.1.4, "The `service()` Method: Classifying Requests for Processing," some incoming requests get a `serviceStatus` of `CheckInAtEntrance`. The `service()` method makes sure that each of these requests has a session object (and gets its ID for later use). The maximum inactivity interval for each session is set from a user-supplied value. Finally, the `serviceStatus` is changed to `ProcessRequest`.

Until we add a user manager and chat data persistence, a chat in bonForum can last only as long as the session that creates it. (More accurately, a chat can outlive the session that created it, but it will no longer have a host, and so is not fully functional.) A session can last until it is inactive for more than a maximum inactivity interval, which can be set using the `setMaxInactiveInterval` session method. We set that to allow chats to withstand inactivity longer than they would by default. This also allows us to experiment with session timeouts and to test the code that handles session timeouts.

The `service()` method code first looks for the max inactive interval (in minutes), a `ServletContext` attribute string called `sessionMaxInactiveMinutes`. Failing that, it looks in an initialization parameter of the same name. The default, if neither is found, is `-1`, meaning that sessions persist until Tomcat shuts down.

Here is the code that handles new requests coming it at the entrance to the Web application:

```
if(serviceStatus.equals("CheckInAtEntrance")) {
      session = request.getSession();
      sessionId = session.getId();
       String sessMax = normalize((String)getServletContext().getAttribute(
            ➥"sessionMaxInactiveMinutes"));
      if(sessMax.trim().length() < 1) {
            sessMax = getServletContext().getInitParameter(
                  "sessionMaxInactiveMinutes");
            if(sessMax == null) {
                  sessMax = "-1";
            }
      }
      int minutes = -1;
      try {
            minutes = Integer.parseInt(sessMax);
      }
      catch (NumberFormatException nFE) {
            minutes = -1;
      }
      session.setMaxInactiveInterval(minutes);
      serviceStatus = "ProcessRequest";
}
```

8.1.7 The *service()* Method: Handling Normal Requests Within the Web Application

In Section 8.1.5, "The `service()` Method: Requests for Engine Control," we saw that some requests are to be routed around most of the code in the service method. Except for those login and error requests and the special Web app entrance requests that we just discussed in Section 8.1.6, "The `service()` Method: Requests to Enter the Web Application," all requests must be checked for two requirements:

- They must have a valid session object.
- They must have a valid actor nickname.

These checks are applied to all requests with the following `serviceStatus` values:

- `ProcessRequest`
- `DecodeServletMappedURI`
- `SystemCommands`

The first two are the normal requests related to users already in the Web application. Requests for system URIs also need access to all processing functionality in the servlet. Leaving the details out for now, this next code excerpt shows how requests are selected for session and nickname checking:

```
if(serviceStatus.equals("CheckInAtEntrance")) {
     //
     // Code left out here, (see Section 8.1.6).
     //
}
else if (!serviceStatus.equals("ForwardToLoginPage") &&
➥!serviceStatus.equals("ForwardToErrorPage") &&
!serviceStatus.equals("UserMustLogin")) {
     //
     // Code left out here is listed in
     // sections 8.1.8 and 8.1.9,
     // and does the following things:
     //
     // If request has no session, force relogin,
     // otherwise validate the session.
     //
     // If the session is not valid, force relogin,
     // otherwise validate nickname for request.
     //
     // If nickname is not valid, force relogin,
     // otherwise, allow further request processing.
     //
}
```

8.1.8 The *service()* Method: Validating Session Objects

The best way to give Web application pages any lasting meaning within the stateless context of an HTTP Internet world is by using session objects. These are maintained by the server, using cookies (if the browser cooperates) or rewriting the URL (if not). By using a unique identifier, a session can "brand" all the requests that come from one browser instance over a period of relative activity.

If you need to learn more about how Java handles sessions, we recommend reading Chapter 9, "Session Tracking," of Marty Hall's book, *Core Servlets and JavaServer Pages*. Another excellent and very interesting way to learn more is to study the source code in Tomcat that implements session tracking. If you have the Tomcat source code installed on your system, you will find the source code in the folder TOMCAT_HOME\src\org\apache\tomcat\session.

To continue from the last section, let's first see how the `service()` method validates the session object of each normal request. If the user entered the application through the entrance, there should be a session object (see Section 8.1.6, "The `service()` Method: Requests to Enter the Web Application"). First, it checks to see if the request has a session object. If not, something is wrong. The `serviceStatus` is set to `UserMustLogin`, which will soon take that user back to the forum login page (with a brand new session) to start all over again.

If the request does have a session, its ID is saved for later use. If the browser requested a different ID, the user must log in again. The code that accomplishes these session validation steps is shown in the following listing (for its context, see the listing in preceding section):

```
// See if session exists, but don't create one:
session = request.getSession(false);
if(session == null) {
      serviceStatus = "UserMustLogin";
}
else {
      sessionId = session.getId();
      if(!request.isRequestedSessionIdValid()) {
            serviceStatus = "UserMustLogin";
      }
      //
      // Code left out here is listed
      //in section 8.1.9, and
      // validates nickname for request.
      //
}
```

Notice that if you use the `getSession()` method without any arguments, it will make sure that you get a session. Sometimes you do not want this behavior, and you should then pass `false` as an argument. We put that argument to good use previously because a `null` return value tells us that an incoming request has no session—and that is information we need.

8.1.9 The *service()* Method: Managing Unique Nicknames

In this section, we discuss how the `service()` method ensures that every normal request that it receives has a valid and unique nickname associated with it. (This fills in more of the details that were left out of the code excerpt listed in Section 8.1.8, "The `service()` Method: Validating Session Objects.")

Except for the special nickname system, the only place that a user of the Web application gets a nickname is by filling in a form field on the HTML page produced by forum_entry.jsp. That same nickname entry form has a `bonCommand` that is unique in the application:

```
visitor_executes_choice
```

The nickname-handling code checks for that `boncommand`. If it finds it, it knows that the request came from the `forum_entry` state, and it gets a user-entered nickname from a request parameter named `actorNickname` (disallowing the restricted value of `system`). If the request did not originate in the `forum_entry` state, the code gets an existing nickname value from a session attribute also named `actorNickname`.

Whether it gets a newly input nickname or a preexisting one, the code looks it up in its nickname registry, a `hashtable` that associates each nickname in the Web app with the ID value of the session that created and registered it. The nickname is the key, so nickname values must be unique. (The special "system" nickname is again treated differently—it is always stored in the `hashtable` before the lookup is done and will always be found during the lookup.)

There are three possible outcomes of the `hashtable` lookup:

- The nickname is not found in the registry.
- The nickname is found with the current session ID.
- The nickname is found with a noncurrent session ID.

The code uses logic as expressed in Table 8.3 to decide what to do next.

Table 8.3 **Logic for handling actor nicknames in *service()***

`actorNickname`	New Input	Preexisting
Not in registry	Nickname is unique and available: Register and put it in the session attribute.	Error: User must log in again.
In registry with current session ID	Nickname is okay: The user returning, so continue processing.	Nickname for request is okay: Continue processing.
In registry with noncurrent Session ID	Nickname is taken: Return for another input by user.	Error: User must log in again.
Not in request parameter or session attribute (whichever was expected)	Nickname input was an empty string: Return for another input by user.	Error, missing nickname: User must log in again.

If the nickname is taken, it is set in a session attribute called "`actorNicknameNotAvailable`", so the user can be told the bad news.

To send a user back for another nickname, just set the `serviceStatus` to `ForwardWithoutServicing` and `bonForumCommand` to `forum_entry`. Sending a user back to relogin, when an existing nickname is not okay, is even simpler: The `serviceStatus` is set to `UserMustLogin`.

It should now be easy to follow the nickname-handling code, which is listed in the following excerpt (for its context, see the listings in the two preceding sections):

```
String actorNickname;
session.setAttribute("actorNicknameNotAvailable", "");
boolean isForumEntry = false;
// Only forum_entry allows nickname input,
// check for its bonCommand here:
if(bonCommand.indexOf("visitor_executes_choice") > -1) {
      isForumEntry = true;
      actorNickname = normalize((String)request.getParameter( "actorNickname"
➥)).trim();
      if(actorNickname.equals("system")) {
            actorNickname = "";
```

```
            }
        }
        else {
            actorNickname = normalize((String)session.getAttribute( "actorNickname"
➥)).trim();
        }
        if(actorNickname.length() > 0) {
            if(actorNickname.equals("system")) {
                nicknameRegistry.put(actorNickname, sessionId);
            }
            if(nicknameRegistry.containsKey(actorNickname)) {
                if(!(nicknameRegistry.get( actorNickname ).equals(sessionId))) {
                  ➥// registered for another session!
                    if(isForumEntry) {
                        // nickname is taken!
                        serviceStatus = "ForwardWithoutServicing";
                        bonForumCommand = "forum_entry";
                        session.setAttribute( "actorNicknameNotAvailable",
➥actorNickname);
                        actorNickname = "";
                    }
                    else {
                        // session wrong for nickname!
                        serviceStatus = "UserMustLogin";
                    }
                } // else existing nickname is OK
            }
            else {
                // nickname not in registry
                if(isForumEntry) {
                    // nickname is available!
                    nicknameRegistry.put(actorNickname, sessionId);
                    session.setAttribute("actorNickname", actorNickname);
                }
                else {
                    // nickname lost from registry!
                    serviceStatus = "UserMustLogin";
                }
            }
        }
        else {
            // nickname missing in request or session!
            if(isForumEntry) {
                // user entered empty string
                // send user back for another try:
                serviceStatus = "ForwardWithoutServicing";
                bonForumCommand = "forum_entry";
            }
            else {
                // nickname is missing!
                serviceStatus = "UserMustLogin";
            }
        }
```

8.1.10 The *service( )* Method: Handling Servlet-Mapped Requests

In this section, we describe the way that the `service()` method handles servlet-mapped requests. The following list restates what has been said so far:

- There is a servlet-mapping element in the deployment descriptor in web.xml (see the previous section "Servlet-Mapping Elements").
- Requests that do not have a URI for `BonForumEngine` can arrive at its `service()` method only by means of a servlet-mapping element. They are identified early and get `serviceStatus` values of `DecodeServletMappedURI`.

Three main types (and several subtypes) of request generators produce URIs that end in .tfe. These will all end up at the `BonForumEngine service()` method because of the mapping. (For more information on this, see "Request URI" in Section 8.1.4.)

After going through session and nickname checking (along with other normal requests), the servlet-mapped requests are handled separately. There are two tasks are to be done for each such request, as follows:

- Find the `bonForumCommand` for the request—what should be its forwarding destination?
- Determine whether the request should take part in the processing that implements the logic of the Web application (a chat, in this case).

The block of code that does these two tasks is quite long and repeats a format, so we show only a representative part of it in this next code listing:

```
if(serviceStatus.equals("DecodeServletMappedURI")) {

serviceStatus = "ForwardWithoutServicing";

if(requestUri.indexOf( "guest_executes_chat" ) > -1) {

if(requestUri.indexOf( "guest_executes_chat_frame" ) > -1) {
bonForumCommand = "guest_executes_chat_frame";
}
else if(requestUri.indexOf( "guest_executes_chat_controls" ) > -1) {
bonForumCommand = "guest_executes_chat_controls";
}
else if(requestUri.indexOf( "guest_executes_chat_robot" ) > -1) {
bonForumCommand = "guest_executes_chat_robot";
}
else if(requestUri.indexOf( "guest_executes_chat_ready" ) > -1) {
bonForumCommand = "guest_executes_chat_ready";
}
else if(requestUri.indexOf( "guest_executes_chat_console" ) > -1) {
bonForumCommand = "guest_executes_chat_console";
}
else {
bonForumCommand = "guest_executes_chat";
serviceStatus = "ProcessRequest";
```

```
}
}
else if(requestUri.indexOf( "host_executes_chat" ) > -1) {
// code left out here, follows pattern as above
}
// much code left out here:
// includes many "else if" compound
// statements like the last one shown, each
// in turn containing other "if else if"
// compound statements.
// This sieve looks for every application
// filename (without extension) embedded within
// each servlet-mapped request URI.
//
else {
bonForumCommand = "forum_error";
serviceStatus = "ForwardToErrorPage";
}
}
```

As you can see, to handle these requests we put in a whole scaffolding of if-else-if-else-if constructs that look for hardwired JSP filenames embedded in any request URIs that are not for `BonForumEngine`. The `BonForumCommand` is then set to the value of the embedded filename, without the .jsp extension and added timestamp suffix.

By default, the `serviceStatus` variable is set to `ForwardWithoutServicing` for all these URI cases. That causes their request threads to be routed around request processing. However, there are two requests (for now) that do require lots of Web application-specific (that is, chat) processing. Those two requests are for the two JSPs host_executes_chat.jsp and guest_executes_chat.jsp.

When a request being handled is for either of these two pages, the code sets the thread's `serviceStatus` variable to `ProcessRequest`. We will discuss how these two requests are processed in Section 8.1.20, "The `processRequest()` Method: Handling 'Host Executes Chat,'" and Section 8.1.21, "The `processRequest()` Method: Handling 'Guest Executes Chat.'"

Notice that this "if then else if" scaffolding makes future development very easy. It sorts requests according to names that it finds embedded in their URIs, checking for all the JSP names that exist in the bonForum Web application. We can easily add mappings for other URI extensions besides .tfe—utilizing different suffixes and prefixes can add extra meaning to requests in a structured way. We can also easily add new code processing these new types of requests. What is cool is that these requests are mapped to JSP pages and, thus, to the user interface.

Also notice that instead of checking the incoming `requestUri` values for equality, we use constructs such as the following:

```
if(requestUri.indexOf("host_executes_command") > -1)
```

That makes it easy to try out variants of a JSP by simply adding a suffix such as _test to the filename. There is no need to revise the servlet code and recompile it, as long as these JSP variants should be treated equally. In fact, earlier in the project, we had only the high-level `if` statements here (such as for `host_executes_command`), and it was easy later to add the second tier of the JSP hierarchy (such as for`host_executes_command_frame`) without changing the servlet code nearly as much as we would have otherwise.

You probably noticed that not all the JSP pages in the application are being requested via the servlet mapping, but they are nevertheless represented in this "switchyard." We added all the pages in the Web app to make experimenting easier. Working with JSP can be quite fast and interactive, and we like things that make it more so.

One final point: Instead of having a bunch of `if` statements with strings, it might look nicer to have a switch statement with "constants" for page names here. However, we would still have to compare all the `requestUri` values to strings somewhere! We could hide all this code away in another method, but we feel that having all this "broad-brush" code here, right in the middle of the method, makes us think more often about all those JSP pages, what they do, and what they could do.

Free Advice, If You Buy It

Although "hardwiring" filenames into a program is considered poor style, doing that can often let you look sooner at the fundamental questions being raised by sometimes overly ambitious plans. As long as we are waxing pedagogical, we might mention two rules of thumb that we like:

1. Get it done first, then get it done right.
2. As many problems in software stem from premature overdesign as from late under-design.

Some might disagree and say that they have always subscribed to "Do it right the first time." Our hats are off if that works for them! In our experience, computer programs get good only the third time they are developed, preferably by the same people, and preferably in different languages. Some might also like us to present statistical evidence to back up our second rule. Instead, all we did was rename them from "principles" to "rules of thumb." But we should put a survey on the bonForum Web site on SourceForge to gather some anecdotal "evidence" in support of and against these rules.

Do not start designing the details about the best way to do something until you know what you have to do. That might seem obvious, but it is amazing how many problems encountered in software projects are actually there only because some hasty, ambitious planning created the problems. Especially when you are on a steep learning curve or two, it can be better to determine the problem first and then find the solution.

Keep trying things, and keep making problems for yourself. Only when you have solved enough problems can you see a pattern emerge for some of these. If their impact upon the software is significant, they may deserve the application of a more refined design approach. Delay your cost-benefits analysis until you have a basis to determine the costs and the benefits.

8.1.11 The *service( )* Method: Invoking *processRequest( )*

We have seen that some requests are to be forwarded by BonForumEngine without further processing; these include most servlet-mapped requests, as well as some error page and login page requests. However, every other request ends up with a serviceStatus value of either ProcessRequest or SystemCommands. Either of these two values will route a request into the code that invokes the processRequest() method. Because of its size and separate functionality, we discuss that method in its own section, Section 8.1.20, "The processRequest() Method: Handling 'Host Executes Chat." In this current section, we show only how the invocation of this method is handled inside service().

Before the processRequest() method is called, a request attribute named serviceStatus is set with the current value of the serviceStatus variable. If all goes well, we expect the processRequest() method to return a value of ForwardAfterRequestProcessed in this same request attribute. The real return value of the method is a value for the bonForumCommand variable, which will determine the JSP forwarding destination at the end of the service() method.

The following excerpt is the code that takes care of invoking the processRequest() method:

```
if(serviceStatus.equals("ProcessRequest") ||
➥serviceStatus.equals("SystemCommands")) {
        try {
                request.setAttribute("serviceStatus", serviceStatus);
                bonForumCommand = processRequest(request, response, session,
➥bonForumCommand);
                serviceStatus = (String)request.getAttribute("serviceStatus");
        ➥}
        catch(Exception ee) {
                ee.printStackTrace();
        }
}
```

One way to look at the processRequest() method of bonForumEngine is that it simply moves a lot of code out of the service() method. You can tell that when you look at two of its arguments, request and response, which allow us to do the same kinds of things in processRequest() as can be done in service().

What is important about the processRequest() method is that it plugs this HttpServlet descendant into the context of a specific Web application. When this method is invoked, the service() method has already provided user verification and a session context. After `processRequest()` returns, the `service()` method takes the Web application to its next destination by forwarding the HTTP request. It is inside the `processRequest()` method that application-specific processing takes place, using the request, response, and session objects, as well any other objects within the Web application context.

8.1.12 The *service()* Method: Handling Abnormal Outcomes

After the `processRequest()` method returns (or after it is not called), the `service()` method can determine whether a particular request represents a successful transition from one Web app state to another. Success here means one of two things, as follows:

1. All Web app processing succeeded for this request.
2. The request was sent to only the engine to be forwarded.

Either way, the request will be forwarded (see the next section). All requests need to be forwarded somewhere! The engine servlet produces no HTML output itself, so if a request is not forwarded somewhere, then that user execution path through the Web app comes to a dead end. The user will have to use the back arrow, try a refresh, or try another fork in the road without knowing what happened. Unsuccessful outcomes must also take the Web app to a next state. We add four possible "non-normal" JSP destinations to the two "normal" ones listed previously. Each destination is associated with a `serviceStatus` value, as shown in Table 8.4.

Table 8.4 **Outcomes of the *service()* Method, Normal and Otherwise**

Normal	`serviceStatus`	Outcome and Destination
Yes	`ForwardWithoutServicing`	`bonForumEngine` to JSP
Yes	`ForwardAfterRequestProcessed`	`bonForumEngine` to JSP
No	`ForwardToLoginPage`	forum_login.jsp
No	`ForwardToErrorPage`	forum_error.jsp
No	`SystemCommands`	system_executes_command.jsp
No	`UserMustLogin`	forum_login_robot.jsp

The code shown in the next excerpt ignores the two normal request categories entirely. It handles the login, error, and system requests very simply: It selects the correct forwarding destination by putting its JSP filename (without an extension) into the `bonForumCommand` variable. We show what happens with that value in the next section.

All other non-normal requests are given special treatment as `UserMustLogin` requests. In case the request involved originated from HTML inside a frame on the browser, the `BonForumRobot` applet is used to call up the login page, which ensures that the page will display at the top display level, without any frameset involved. You can read more details about `BonForumRobot` in Chapter 9.

The next list shows five situations that warrant such a drastic action as a forced relogin.

1. The request is not for forum_entry, but it had no session.
2. The request's session ID is not valid for the current session.
3. The existing nickname check failed—wrong session.
4. The existing nickname check failed—not in registry.
5. The existing nickname check failed—not found in session.

Before the request can be forwarded to the robot applet, a couple things must be done. The current session, if any, has its `invalidate()` method called to clear up error conditions. Calling `invalidate()` gets rid of the session object and also all the other attributes that it holds. (It also creates "orphan nicknames" in the nickname registry which become unusable. That is a problem that will be fixed when we add a user manager.)

If a new request from the forum_login page is requested later, a new session will be created for the browser (in the `CheckInAtEntrance` service status handling). However, a new session is needed now to send parameter values to the robot applet, which receives them in session attributes. Therefore, a new session is created. Next, the `bonForumCommand` variable is set with the name of the applet, forum_login_robot, and the `session.setAttribute()` method called for each of the applet parameters, including the absolute URI for the forum_login JSP.

When the request is forwarded, that will be enough to cause a clean return to the beginning of the Web application. The robot applet will use the `showDocument()` method of its context to request the forum_login JSP, using a servlet-mapped URI ending in .tfe. That request will enter the `service()` method, where it will be given a `serviceStatus` of `ForwardToLoginPage`. That will bring the thread for that request to the same code being discussed in this section. It will then be forwarded by the `service()` method to the forum_login JSP. All that to get a clean new start after an error condition arises!

The following excerpt includes all the code that is discussed in this section:

```
if(!(serviceStatus.equals("ForwardWithoutServicing") ||
➥serviceStatus.equals("ForwardAfterRequestProcessed"))) {
if(serviceStatus.equals("ForwardToLoginPage")) {
// robot is requesting login page:
bonForumCommand = "forum_login";
}
else if(serviceStatus.equals( "ForwardToErrorPage" )) {
bonForumCommand = "forum_error";
}
else if(serviceStatus.equals( "SystemCommands" )) {
// enforce only one main system page:
bonForumCommand = "system_executes_command";
}
else {
```

```
// catch unknown serviceStatus errors:
serviceStatus = "UserMustLogin";
}
if(serviceStatus.equals( "UserMustLogin" )) {
if(session != null) {
try {
session.invalidate();
}
catch(java.lang.IllegalStateException ex) {
ex.printStackTrace();
}
}
session = request.getSession();  // creates one
sessionId = session.getId();
bonForumCommand = "forum_login_robot";
session.setAttribute("target", "_top");
session.setAttribute("document", request.getScheme() + "://" +
➥request.getServerName() + ":" + request.getServerPort() +
"/bonForum/jsp/forum/forum_login.jsp");
session.setAttribute("refresh", "true");
session.setAttribute("increment", "100");
session.setAttribute("limit", "1");
session.setAttribute("message", "Enter!");
}
}
```

In the next section, we finally arrive at the end of our detailed discussion of the `service()` method. We discuss the forwarding of requests, the mechanism that moves the user through the Web application.

8.1.13 The *service()* Method: Forwarding HTTP Requests

The only remaining task for the `service()` method is to forward the request and response objects to another JSP, which will dynamically create another piece of the bonForum browser interface. This next excerpt shows all the code used to accomplish this important task:

```
request.setAttribute ("servletName", "BonForumEngine");

getServletConfig( ).getServletContext( ).getRequestDispatcher( "/jsp/forum/" +
➥bonForumCommand + ".jsp" ).forward( request, response );
```

Identifying a Servlet in the Request

It can be useful to know where a request comes from. Therefore, although it is not used yet for anything, each request forwarded by the `service()` method is branded with the class name, as follows:

```
request.setAttribute("servletName", "BonForumEngine");
```

Forwarding Requests in *service( )* Method

The `service()` method forwards each request to a destination determined by the `bonForumCommand` value. We previously discussed the several ways that value can be determined. Here is a short summary list:

- Set from a `boncommand` request parameter
- Set from a robot-generated request URI
- Set in the `processRequest` method

The correct filename for the forwarding destination JSP page is constructed from the `bonForumCommand` value by the following expression:

```
"/jsp/forum/"+bonForumCommand+".jsp"
```

Forwarding the Request

To forward the request, we use the simplest code. Everything is included in this one long statement:

```
getServletConfig().getServletContext( ).getRequestDispatcher( "/jsp/forum/" +
➥bonForumCommand + ".jsp" ).forward(request, response);
```

Of course, if we needed to use any of the objects involved here again, we do have a choice of longer constructions that achieve the same goal. Here we show the longest way:

```
ServletConfig scfg = getServletConfig();
ServletContext sctx = scfg.getServletContext();
String NextPage = "/jsp/forum/" + bonForumCommand + ".jsp";
RequestDispatcher rd = sctx.getRequestDispatcher( NextPage );
rd.forward(request, response);
```

What to Do When Things Go Wrong: forum_error.jsp

At first, we put all the statements setting up and doing the actual forwarding of the request into a try block and tried to catch and handle all the exceptions that could be thrown by the forward method. However, while testing, we could not seem to catch the errors that interested us.

For example, what if the forwarding destination did not exist, perhaps because of a typo in a JSP page sending a request? That doesn't bother the `getRequestDispatcher()` method. It still gets a request dispatcher, without throwing an exception. Then when its `forward()` method is called with a nonexistent destination, that does not raise an exception. Instead, it generates an "HTTP 404 (Not Found)" error, which brings up that ugly page in the Internet Explorer. Okay, you might say that should not happen unless testing is inadequate; it is a programming error that should not be released.

We were trying to catch exceptions thrown by the `forward()` method, which are these three:

- **ServletException**—If the target resource throws this exception
- **java.io.IOException**—If the target resource throws this exception
- **java.lang.IllegalStateException**—If the response was already committed

However, none seems to be relevant to our situation. The first two are not because our target resources are always JSP and do not throw those exceptions. The third is not because we do nothing in the `service()` method that would commit the response.

What we really wanted was a simple way to display forum_error.jsp for any unforeseen error condition, regardless of its origin. The error page displays information that might help develop the software. It always resolves the situation by causing a new login using the robot applet. (That also allows the error page to display within a frame.) Known errors do something different—they skip the forum_error page and go directly to a new login page. (We should add a message to inform the user why it's necessary to restart the Web application.)

We got rid of the try and catch blocks, and we kept just two ways to handle errors. To handle errors generated by the applet and within the servlet, we rely on the code described in Section 8.1.12, "The `service()` Method: Handling Abnormal Outcomes." To handle errors generated within JavaServer Pages, we make sure that all the JSPs in bonForum (except forum_error.jsp) contain a page directive as follows:

```
<%@ page errorPage="forum_error.jsp" %>
```

The forum_error.jsp page itself, of course, has a different page directive, as follows:

```
<%@ page isErrorPage="true" %>
```

Now, any exceptions happening on one of our JSP pages would bring up the same error page as the applet-generated errors and the servlet-generated errors. Things were simple again!

8.1.14 The *processRequest( )* Method: Overall View

We discussed the invocation of the `processRequest` method of the `service()` method in Section 8.1.11, "The `service()` Method: Invoking `processRequest()`." In the next few sections, we discuss in detail how this method processes successive HTTP requests in the context of a Web chat application. The following discussions will be easier to follow if you have the source in an editor in front of you and an XML dump of `bonForumXML` in an XML viewer. It can also help to view bonForum.gif and subjects.gif, in the WEB-INF\docs folder.

The `processRequest()` method has access to the all-important request argument of the `service()` method. The session is passed as a convenience argument; it could be gotten from the request argument. The return string can be assigned to `bonForumCommand` in the `service()` method and determines the forwarding destination of the request. The method's signature is the following:

```
protected String processRequest(HttpServletRequest request, HttpServletResponse
response, HttpSession session, String bonForumCommand) throws IOException {. . .}
```

As mentioned before, the main general features of this method are as follows:

- It specializes the servlet (to be a chat).
- User verification can be assumed complete.
- The session object is provided.
- The request object is provided.
- The response object is available.
- Forwarding can be controlled using the method return value, which is assigned to the `bonForumCommand` variable by the calling method, `service()`, when the `processRequest()` method returns.
- A synchronized XML database wrapper object is available.

To carry out its tasks, the `processRequest()` method relies greatly upon a `BonForumStore` object called `BonForumStore`, which is a static member of `BonForumEngine`. The `BonForumStore` class is a wrapper for a `ForestHashtable` object called `bonForumXML`, which is a static member of `BonForumStore`. The `BonForumStore` class will be the last subject of this chapter. The `ForestHashtable` class will be the subject of Chapter 11 of this book.

The `BonForumEngine` servlet handles the traffic between the Web application user interface and the XML database wrapper. In this method, many string objects are being used to contain data passed back and forth from JSP pages to the servlet. That is acceptable in this prototype, but, in the future, it will be more efficient to pass grouped data in a container object or XML document.

The following list shows an overall view of the tasks that are done by the `processRequest()` method:

1. Setting serviceStatus and sessionId
2. Initializing bonForumStore
3. Getting bonForumCommand
4. Handling chat variables
5. Handling specific chat JSPs
6. Handling "host executes chat"
    - Getting Chat Subject and Topic
    - Performing thread synchronization
    - Synchronizing the XML database
        - Finding the chat and actor status in Chat
            - Rejoining existing chats
        - Starting a chat
            - Adding a host actor
            - Adding a chat element

        - Adding a chat item marker
        - Adding an itemKey to a chat
7. Handling "guest executes chat"
    - Getting chat item
    - Synchronizing the XML database
        - Finding chat and actor status in chat
            - Rejoining a chat
        - Joining a chat
            - Adding a guest actor
            - Joining a chat, continued
8. Handling chat messages
9. Setting serviceStatus for return

As you can see, most of the action takes place in handling requests to enter the "host executes chat" and "guest executes chat" bonForum states. Our discussion of the `processRequest()` method will be organized according to the major divisions of this task list.

8.1.15 The *processRequest()* Method: Setting *serviceStatus* and *sessionId*

We have seen the important role played by the `serviceStatus` variable in the `service()` method. The `processRequest()` method communicates with the `service()` method, using, in addition to its return value, a request attribute named `serviceStatus`. The `service()` method sets the attribute with the value of its `serviceStatus` variable before calling `processRequest()`, and it updates the variable with the request parameter when `processRequest()` returns. The default return value is set by the following statement:

```
request.setAttribute("serviceStatus", "InProcessRequestMethod");
```

The unique ID of the session associated with the request argument plays an important part in `processRequest()`. For convenience, it is put in the `sessionId` variable:

```
String sessionId = session.getId();
```

8.1.16 The *processRequest()* Method: Initializing *bonForumStore*

The `BonForumEngine` class contains a very important member called `bonForumStore`, which is a static object of the `BonForumStore` class. It wraps the XML data and provides access to them with its methods. It also provides other methods for use by the

BonForumEngine and the JSP-related objects in bonForum. A single instance of it is created by BonForumEngine as follows:

```
private static BonForumStore bonForumStore = new BonForumStore();
```

When we explore the BonForumStore class later, we will see that it functions in relation to a "current" session. It gets these when its initialization method is called in processRequest(), as follows:

```
bonForumStore.initialize(sessionId);
```

The bonForumStore member of a BonForumEngine instance is very useful, so access to it is made possible from anywhere in the servlet context, as follows:

```
Object temp = getServletContext().getAttribute( "bonForumStore" );
if (temp == null) {
getServletContext().setAttribute( "bonForumStore", getBonForumStore() )
};
```

In Section 8.2.12, "Invoking Chat Methods from JSP Custom Tags," and Section 8.2.13, "Invoking Chat Methods from JSP Scriptlets," you can read examples of how the value of this attribute, which has application scope, can be used to access the properties and methods of BonForumStore from JSP.

8.1.17 The *processRequest()* Method: Getting *bonForumCommand*

After a thread leaves the processRequest() method, a very important variable is the one called bonForumCommand because it will determine the next destination in the Web application. The value put into this string object comes from one of three sources, listed here in order of priority:

- The bonForumCommand method argument
- The bonCommand request parameter
- A composite of actorStatus, actionStatus, and thingStatus request parameter values

As you will recall, Actors, Actions, and Things were intrinsic to the initial design of bonForum. The entire Web application grew out of a model of a marketplace that used these three elements to describe states and organize data. The three elements also served as a vector to the next application page. Although we usually combine these three within the boncommand values passed from the JSP, the possibility of passing the command parts separately is being kept in the code because it may prove useful in the future (for one-part or two-part commands, or for commands combining parts from different sources). Here is the code that makes sure that there is a valid bonForumCommand for processRequest to later return:

```
bonForumCommand = normalize(bonForumCommand).trim();
if(bonForumCommand.length() < 1) {
    String bonCommand = normalize((String)request.getParameter( "bonCommand"
➥)).trim();
```

```
        if(bonCommand.length() > 0) {
            bonForumCommand = bonCommand;
        }
        else {
            String actorStatus = normalize((String)request.getParameter("
➥actorStatus" )).trim();
            String actionStatus = normalize((String)request.getParameter(
➥"actionStatus" )).trim();
            String thingStatus = normalize((String)request.getParameter(
➥"thingStatus" )).trim();
            if((actorStatus.length() > 0) || (actionStatus.length() > 0) ||
➥(thingStatus.length() > 0)) {
                bonForumCommand = actorStatus + "_" + actionStatus + "_" +
➥thingStatus;
                // later, trim off leading and trailing underscore chars, if any
            ➥}
            else {
                bonForumCommand = "forum_error";
                request.setAttribute("serviceStatus", "ForwardToErrorPage");
            ➥}
        }
    }
```

You can see at the end of that excerpt how `processRequest` can use a combination of `bonForumCommand` and the `serviceStatus` request attribute to control forwarding of the request later by the `service()` method.

8.1.18 The *processRequest()* Method: Handling Specific Chat JSPs

Next in the `processRequest()` method of `BonForumEngine` is an "if else if else if … else endif" construction that filters threads according to their `bonForumCommand` values. In other words, it processes requests separately, according to their intended forwarding destinations. (In this Web application these are JSPs, by design; we may later change some code in the `service()` method so that any type of URI can be used.) The `bonForumCommand` value controls what will happen next in the application. That is why we call it a "forum command" and why we call this long set of if statements a "forum command processor." Here is how it appears when simplified:

```
if(bonForumCommand.indexOf( "host_executes_chat_controls" ) > -1) ||
➥(bonForumCommand.indexOf( "guest_executes_chat_controls" ) {
    // handle chatMessagesNavigator
    // handle chatMessage
}
else if(bonForumCommand.equals( "host_executes_chat" )) {
    // start a chat
}
else if (bonForumCommand.equals( "guest_executes_chat" )) {
    // join a chat
```

```
}
else if(bonForumCommand.indexOf( "visitor_starts_chat" ) > -1) {
      if(bonForumCommand.equals( "visitor_starts_chat" )) {
            // not used yet
      }
      else if(bonForumCommand.indexOf( "visitor_starts_chat_frame" ) > -1) {
            // handle chatSubject
      }
      else if(bonForumCommand.indexOf( "visitor_starts_chat_ready" ) > -1) {
            // handle chatTopic
      }
else if(bonForumCommand.indexOf( "visitor_joins_chat" ) > -1) {
      if(bonForumCommand.equals( "visitor_joins_chat" )) {
            // not used yet
      }
      else if(bonForumCommand.indexOf( "visitor_joins_chat_frame" ) > -1) {
            // handle chatModerated
            // handle chat item
else if(bonForumCommand.indexOf( "guest_executes_command" ) > -1) {
      if(bonForumCommand.equals( "guest_executes_command" )) {
            // not used yet
      }
      else if(bonForumCommand.indexOf( "guest_executes_command_controls" ) > -1) {
      ➥ // handle chatMessagesPageSize
      }
}
else if(bonForumCommand.indexOf( "host_executes_command" ) > -1) {
      if(bonForumCommand.equals( "host_executes_command" )) {
            // not used yet
      }
      else if(bonForumCommand.indexOf( "host_executes_command_controls" ) > -1) {
      ➥// handle chatMessagesPageSize
      }
      else if(bonForumCommand.indexOf( "host_executes_command_frame" ) > -1) {
            ➥// handle chatGuest
      }
}
else if(bonForumCommand.indexOf( "visitor_executes_choice" ) > -1) {
      //actor nickname is handled in service() method,
      // handle actorAge
}
else if(bonForumCommand.indexOf( "system_sets_timeout" ) > -1) {
      // handle sessionMaxInactiveMinutes
}
else if(bonForumCommand.indexOf( "system_executes_command" ) > -1) {
      // handle xalanVersion
      // handle actorRatingType
}
else if(bonForumCommand.indexOf( "forum_entry" ) > -1) {
      // not used yet
}
else {
      // no special processing current bonForumCommand
}
```

In the `service()` method, you saw a similar "if else if else if … else endif" construct that is used to handle servlet-mapped request URIs. Both these similar constructs are good places to extend the functionality of the bonForum Web application. In each `if` statement, code has a context related to the architecture of the Web application, and it stands between one JSP document and the next intended JSP document. In the `processRequest()` method, there are "else if" clauses for many but not all of the existing `bonForumCommand` values. As each new processing is added for a given JSP destination, existing clauses should be used, or a new clause should be added if none is available for the `bonForumCommand` involved.

Again, as in the case of the servlet-mapped request processor, in the `service()` method, we have used the `indexOf()` method instead of the `equals()` method wherever possible. That allows us to create variant JSP pages without changing the servlet source code, simply by adding different suffixes to the basic filename. These variant pages share the same processing in the engine because they are all "trapped" by the `indexOf()` method.

8.1.19 The *processRequest()* Method: Handling Chat Variables

The processing of request threads depending on their `bonForumCommand` values is very much related to the many HTML forms created by the JSP of the browser interface. The value of each input element in a submitted form is available as a request parameter. In this section, we present an overall view of these bonForum variables, and give some examples of how they are handled.

Table 8.5 shows, in alphabetical order, all the bonForum variables currently used. Also shown for each is the name of the JSP where an HTML input element for the variable exists and the type of input element it is. The first column rates the priority of handling these variables based on estimated access frequency and importance to the application.

Table 8.5 **bonForum Variables: Priority, Name, Origin, Type**

	bonForum Variable	Originating JSP	HTML Input Type
14	`actorAge`	forum_entry.jsp	Text
13	`actorNickname`	forum_entry.jsp	Text
15	`actorRatingType`	None yet	—
12	`chatGuest`	host_executes_command_frame.jsp	Select (xslt gen.)
3	`chatItem`	visitor_joins_chat_frame.jsp	Select1 (xslt gen.)
1	`chatMessage`	guest_executes_chat_controls.jsp	Text
2	`chatMessage`	host_executes_chat_controls.jsp	Text
9	`chatMessagesNavigator`	host_executes_chat_controls.jsp	Hidden (on four forms)

continues

Table 8.5 **Continued**

	bonForum Variable	Originating JSP	HTML Input Type
8	`chatMessagesNavigator`	guest_executes_chat_controls.jsp	Hidden (on four forms)
11	`chatMessagesPageSize`	host_executes_command_controls.jsp	Text
10	`chatMessagesPageSize`	guest_executes_command_controls.jsp	Text
7	`chatModerated`	visitor_starts_chat_controls.jsp	Radio
4	`chatModerated`	visitor_joins_chat_frame.jsp (later)	Radio
6	`chatSubject`	visitor_starts_chat_frame.jsp	Select
5	`chatTopic`	visitor_starts_chat_controls.jsp	Text
16	`sessionMaxInactiveMinutes`	system_sets_timeout.jsp	Text
17	`xalanVersion`	system_executes_command.jsp	Radio

In Table 8.6, the same bonForum variables are shown again, each with its corresponding `bonForumCommand`. These represent the forwarding destination for the HTTP request that submits the variable to the `BonForumEngine`. The `bonForumCommand` values were determined by looking up `bonCommand` input elements in the variable's HTML forum, on its originating JSP. The rows are sorted by the `bonForumCommand` values, and the priority rankings have been transferred to the `bonForumCommand` values, using the highest bonForum variable ranking for each `bonForumCommand`.

Table 8.6 **bonForum Variables: Priority, Name, Destination**

	bonForum Variable	`bonForumCommand`
1	`chatMessage`	`guest_executes_chat_controls`
1	`chatMessagesNavigator`	`guest_executes_chat_controls`
2	`chatMessage`	`host_executes_chat_controls`
2	`chatMessagesNavigator`	`host_executes_chat_controls`
3	`chatItem`	`visitor_joins_chat_frame`
3	`chatModerated`	`visitor_joins_chat_frame`
5	`chatTopic`	`visitor_starts_chat_ready`
5	`chatModerated`	`visitor_starts_chat_ready`
7	`chatSubject`	`visitor_starts_chat_frame`
10	`chatMessagesPageSize`	`guest_executes_command_controls`
11	`chatMessagesPageSize`	`host_executes_command_controls`
12	`chatGuest`	`host_executes_command_frame`
13	`actorNickname`	`visitor_executes_choice`
13	`actorAge`	`visitor_executes_choice`

	bonForum Variable	**bonForumCommand**
15	actorRatingType	None yet
16	sessionMaxInactiveMinutes	system_sets_timeout
17	xalanVersion	system_executes_command

This is how we decided the priority of the bonForumCommand handlers described in Section 8.1.18, "The processRequest() Method: Handling Specific Chat JSPs." It's hard to say if that was worth doing, but it may allow higher-priority threads to get to shared resources first. Exercises like this have a built-in benefit: They familiarize you with the source code, which always pays dividends somewhere.

One request parameter, actorReturning, was left off the table because it is produced by virtually all the HTML forms that post to the BonForumEngine. Thus, all threads in processRequest() handle that generic variable, which does nothing now. It might be used in the future to pass extra information, options, and so on in a request, which can be associated with a particular destination and bonForumCommand processing. That will help create more complex combinations of the bonForum chat logic, by making one more variable available to each JSP-produced page of a bonForum instance.

The incoming request parameters are validated and made available to the Web application in whatever scope is appropriate. We will give two examples next.

In Section 8.1.6, "The service() Method: Requests to Enter the Web Application," you saw that whenever a new session object is created, its maximum inactivity period is set preferentially using a value that has application scope supplied by a servlet context attribute. That attribute gets the value from browser input by a bonForum administrator, as seen in the following excerpt from the processRequest() method source code:

```
sessionMaxInactiveMinutes = normalize((String)request.getParameter(
➥"sessionMaxInactiveMinutes" ));
if(sessionMaxInactiveMinutes.trim().length() > 0) {
getServletContext().setAttribute( "sessionMaxInactiveMinutes",
sessionMaxInactiveMinutes );
}
```

As a second example of request parameter handling, see how simply the age value input by a bonForum user is made available in the session scope (to JSP pages, for example). In fact, it is done so rather too simply—there are no constraints yet on the user input, which could be pizza or 11,047. The input is run through the normalize method to escape markup in the user input, so the value can safely be used as an XML attribute value, for instance. The normalize method also changes nulls to empty strings so that subsequent code need not check for null values. Here is the excerpt:

```
actorAge = normalize((String)request.getParameter( "actorAge" ));
if(actorAge.trim().length() > 0) {
session.setAttribute( "actorAge", actorAge);
}
```

In the `bonForumCommand` processor, you will find similar processing of many request parameters. For now, only two are saved to the application scope. (Besides the one shown, there is another that allows bonForum to use either Xalan-Java 1 or Xalan-Java 2 for its XSLT processing.) Those two are as follows:

```
sessionMaxInactiveMinutes
xalanVersion
```

The values of other incoming request parameters must remain persistent and also unique for each user. These are copied into session attributes. That way, the values involved are available to the `processRequest()` method later, when it is processing different request objects. (Notice that we cannot use request attributes instead of session attributes here because those subsequent requests are different objects.) The session attributes are also available to all the JSP pages and other objects in the Web application that have access to the same session object. This group of session-relative bonForum variables includes the following:

```
actorAge
actorRatingType
chatGuest
chatItem
chatMessagesNavigator
chatMessagesPageSize
chatModerated
chatSubject
chatTopic
```

Of course, the `bonForumCommand`-specific processing is not limited to setting session attribute values, and some of these variables are subject to more code than the `actorAge` example given. Specifically, the `chatSubject` handling also produces a session attribute to indicate whether the user has just selected a new subject. The `chatTopic` handler does the same. The `chatItem` handler recovers the `chatSubject` and `chatTopic` values from the `chatItem` (we will discuss why later).

Finally, one other incoming request parameter, `chatMessage`, is not now kept around in any attribute because it has not yet been needed again after processing. The `chatMessage` values are obviously quite important in a chat application. It will be easier to understand `chatMessage` handling after understanding the code that makes it possible for a bonForum visitor to start a chat or join an existing one. Therefore, we will first tackle these two themes by investigating the code in the `bonForumCommand` processor that handles requests for the "host executes chat" and "guest executes chat" bonForum destinations. The handling of `chatMessage` request parameters will be discussed later, in Section 8.1.22, "The `processRequest()` Method: Handling Chat Messages."

8.1.20 The *processRequest()* Method: Handling "Host Executes Chat"

The transition from the "visitor starts chat" bonForum state to the "host executes chat" state is brought about by a servlet-mapped request, generated using the BonForumRobot applet. As we have seen, such requests are given a serviceStatus value of DecodeServletMappedURI in the service() method and are handled according to their requestUri values. Any thread with a requestUri containing host_executes_chat (and not host_executes_chat_frame, host_executes_chat_controls, and so on) is allowed to pass into the processRequest() method by getting a serviceStatus value of processRequest. There it comes to the bonForumCommand processor, where it executes an extensive chunk of code. That is the subject of this section.

The first thing that the "host executes chat" handler does is assume some "normal" values for some flag variables that will control the program flow—and that hopefully have self-explanatory names:

```
boolean haveSubject = true;
boolean haveTopic = true;
boolean actorIsHostInChat = false;
boolean actorIsGuestInChat = false;
boolean chatExistsForSubjectAndTopic = false;
boolean actorRestartingCurrentChat = false;
```

Getting Chat Subject and Topic

The chat subject and topic, chosen by a visitor who will be a chat host, can be found in the session attributes where they were set from request parameters, also in the bonForumCommand processor, by the handlers for these bonForumCommand values:

```
"visitor_starts_chat_frame"
"visitor_starts_chat_ready"
```

For reference, refer back to Section 8.1.18, "The processRequest() Method: Handling Specific Chat JSPs," and Table 8.6, "bonForum Variables: Priority, Name, Destination."

Here is the code that gets the chat subject and topic again:

```
chatTopic = normalize((String)session.getAttribute( "chatTopic" )).trim();
chatSubject = normalize((String)session.getAttribute( "chatSubject" )).trim();
```

If a variable is empty or contains the special value of NONE, then its respective "flag" variable (haveTopic and haveSubject) will be set to false and the application will take the user back to the page where the missing value can be supplied.

The Need for Thread Synchronization

Knowing Java, you can imagine that many threads of execution in the Java Virtual Machine may be traversing this one method at close intervals from each other in time. Java takes care that they can all run the code without stepping on each other by providing each thread with its own copy of the method arguments, member objects, and so on. However, as a developer, you must be sure not to create situations in which threads can collide. That happens when more than one thread simultaneously uses a shared resource—one that does not provide a different copy for each thread to use.

Consider information accessed by more than one thread within a servlet. That is certainly going to be an important consideration while building a chat servlet. We need a way for one thread trying to edit that information to tell all the other threads trying also to edit it: "Hands off that information! It's mine until I'm done with it!" Indeed, there is a way already set up for you to do that in Java, called synchronization.

A good source of information on the hows and whys of synchronization is the chapter on multiple threads in the book *Thinking in Java*, by Bruce Eckels (Prentice Hall, 0130273635). You can also visit `http://java.sun.com/docs/books/tutorial/essential/threads/multithreaded.html` to learn more about multithreaded programming.

It turns out that applying synchronization involves a lot of art, some trial and error, and often surprises—particularly in a complex project. While prototyping, we took the brute force approach and went overboard with synchronization. It was a bit like letting only one shopper into a department store at a time! Of course, that is not the purpose of a servlet at all. It reduced the whole application to a single executing thread, and it involved extreme overhead. Performance obviously suffered. The advantage was that we could keep thread collisions out of the picture and more easily differentiate them from other errors in programming. The idea was to get things working, prove the concepts, and only then try to optimize the multithreading.

Because synchronization affects performance, there is a big incentive to reduce synchronization to the minimum. As this is being written, we are still exploring the synchronization needs of bonForum. We are using it in the `processRequest()` method, as we will discuss next. Our "database" class, `ForestHashtable`, has synchronized critical sections in its methods for adding, editing, and deleting data from its XML storage. The `TransformTag` class, which applies the Xalan XSLT processor, synchronizes its processing steps. We have no synchronization at all in the `BonForumStore` class.

Synchronizing the XML Database

There are two synchronized blocks of code in the `processRequest()` method, both using a lock on the data access wrapper object, `bonForumStore`. The first is in the "host executes chat" handler that we have been discussing. The second is in the "guest executes chat" handler, which will be discussed later. The first does something like this:

```
synchronized(bonForumStore) {
//
// 1. check if subject+topic is available
//
// 2. if so, add a chat for them to XML database
//
}
```

We must check to see if the combination of `chatSubject` and `chatTopic` chosen by a user has already been taken for an existing chat. If that particular pairing is available, then we can add a new chat for it to `bonForumXML` (the `ForestHashtable` member of the `bonForumStore` member of our `BonForumEngine` instance). However, we must enclose both these steps in a synchronized block. If we do not do so, then two threads having the same `chatSubject` and `chatTopic` values could go through the method code very close together, and the following sequence of events is possible:

1. The first thread checked its subject and topic and is about to add a chat, but it has not yet done so.
2. The second thread checks its subject and topic and finds that it is not yet taken, so it's clear to use.
3. The first thread then adds a chat with its subject and topic values.
4. The second thread adds its chat with the same subject and topic values.

Problems! When we try to use that subject and topic combination later to find a chat, we can find only one of the two that were added.

Here is how synchronization makes the problem go away. The first thread (thus session) that enters the synchronized block gets a lock on the `bonForumStore` object. The synchronized block is then closed to all other threads. Automatically blocked by Java, the other threads must wait until they can get the lock on the `bonForumStore` object so that they, too, can enter (one at a time). As you can see, the synchronization acts as a FIFO queue for the threads.

We have experimented with using a less restrictive lock for this synchronization (and for the one in the "guest executes chat" handler), as follows:

```
synchronized(bonForumStore.bonForumXML) {
     // FIFO here
}
```

For that to work, the `bonForumXML` member in `BonForumStore` must be made protected, not private. The advantage of this over the previous example is that all the threads have concurrent access to the methods and other members of `bonForumStore`. It seems to work but may require something else to be synchronized. More testing is needed.

Finding a Chat and the Actor Status in It

After executing by itself inside the first synchronized block of code, a thread in the `processRequest()` method is ready to carry out the "visitor starts chat" action leading to the "host executes chat" state. First, it looks for an existing chat with the subject and topic requested by the visiting actor. Table 8.7 gives the possible outcomes of that search (and also of the search done when the action is "visitor joins chat," which is the subject of the next section).

Table 8.7 **JSP Transitions vs. Actor-Chat Relationships**

	Chat Exists Already			**Chat DoesNot Exist**
	Actor Is Not in Chat	**Actor Is Host**	**Actor Is Guest**	
visitor starts chat	guest executes chat(1)	host executes chat(1)	guest executes chat(1)(2)	host executes chat
visitor joins chat	guest executes chat	host executes chat(3)	guest executes chat	forum error

Here are some notes for this table:

- Numbered table items are optional, to be set by user preferences in a command, with alternatives as follows:
  1. visitor starts chat
  2. host executes chat, if multihosted chat allowed
  3. guest executes chat
- If the actor is a host or a guest, the actor is rejoining the chat.

Rejoining Existing Chats

As you can see, if a chat with the requested subject and topic combination does not exist, the visitor will become the host of a new chat for that combination. If the requested chat exists already, then what happens depends upon an option setting. One option is that the user will be taken back to "visitor starts chat" to try again with a different subject, topic, or both. (Actually, in the release of bonForum for this book, this and other options listed in the notes are not yet available!)

As seen in the table cells for the "visitor starts chat" row, the outcome when a requested chat already exists can be made to depend upon whether the visitor is already a host or a guest in that chat. If not, the visitor becomes a new guest in the chat. If the visitor already a member of the chat, the visitor rejoins as a host or a guest, whichever was the case before. (Again, in the book release of bonForum, the options within the table cells are the only options!)

In a later release of bonForum, we will implement user preference settings using session attributes. Choices can be offered for the behavior of "visitor starts chat" when the requested chat already exists, as follows:

1. Always warn the user and request a new subject or new topic.
2. If the actor was in the chat, always join it with the previous status; otherwise, warn and ask again.
3. If the actor was in the chat, always join as a guest; otherwise, warn and ask again.

All these choices can be modified further according to whether the actor is restarting the current chat. Until these preference settings are added, bonForum implements only the second choice.

Looking at the table again, it is very easy to cause the various outcomes of this desired logic to happen. You simply need to set the `bonForumCommand` value to the corresponding value in the table cell (or optional value, when that is implemented).

Implementing the logic can also be quite simple. We leave the "visitor joins chat" part aside until Section 8.1.21, "The `processRequest()` Method: Handling 'Guest Executes Chat.'" Also leaving aside the numbered options (in the table notes), we could suggest the following pseudocode:

```
set bonForumCommand to host_executes_chat
if chat exists
        if actor is not host in chat
                set bonForumCommand to guest_executes_chat
        endif
endif
```

However, the code that actually exists is not that simple. Are the subject and the topic okay? If not, the user is sent back to reinput them. If the subject and the topic are okay, the code determines whether they have already been taken by an existing chat. If they are available, then a new chat will be started now. If they are taken, the code finds out even more. Is the visitor trying to restart the current chat for the session? (In the future, that information can be used for user messages or to control user preferences.) Is the actor already in the chat as a host or as a guest? If so, will the actor be joining or rejoining an existing chat? If so, the code must set some session attributes with the right values so that they reflect the chat.

Some of the methods and variables used by this code might not become clear until later in the section. Here is the code, excerpted from the `processRequest()` method, with one part of it substituted by comments that show the pseudocode for the omitted source:

```
if(haveSubject && haveTopic) {

        String fakeChatItem = chatSubject + "_[";
        fakeChatItem = fakeChatItem + chatTopic + "]";
        // '_' is separator in a chatItem
        // '.' is separator in pathNameHashtable keys
        fakeChatItem = fakeChatItem.replace('.', '_');
        // example fakeChatItem:
        //          Animals_Bird_Hawk_[Medieval falconry]

        String foundChatNodeKeyKey = getBonForumStore().getBonForumChatNodeKeyKey(
➥fakeChatItem );

        if((foundChatNodeKeyKey != null) && (foundChatNodeKeyKey.length() > 0)) {
              ➥chatExistsForSubjectAndTopic = true;
              //
```

```
                    // There is more code here, not shown!
                    // It does the following:
                    //
                    // if subject and topic are not new
                    //     (requested chat is the current chat) {
                    //     if chatNodeKeyKey exists
                    //           (current chat exists) {
                    //           if foundChatNodeKeyKey is
                    //                              chatNodeKeyKey {
                    //                 set actorRestartingCurrentChat
                    //                                    true;
                    //           } else {
                    //                 set
                    //                 chatExistsForSubjectAndTopic
                    //                                    false;
                    //                 set actorRestartingCurrentChat
                    //                                    false;
                    //           endif
                    //     endif
                    // endif
                    //
                    String actorKeyValue = normalize((String)session.getAttribute(
➥"hostKey" ));
                    if(actorKeyValue.trim().length() > 0) {
                          actorIsHostInChat = getBonForumStore().isHostInChat(
➥actorKeyValue, foundChatNodeKeyKey );
                    }
                    if(!actorIsHostInChat) {
                          actorKeyValue = normalize((String)session.getAttribute(
➥"guestKey" ));
                          if(actorKeyValue.trim().length() > 0) {
                                actorIsGuestInChat = getBonForumStore().isGuestInChat(
➥actorKeyValue, foundChatNodeKeyKey );
                          }
                    }
      }

      boolean actorWillRejoinChat = false;
      if(chatExistsForSubjectAndTopic) {
            // cannot start an existing chat
            haveTopic = false;
            if(actorIsHostInChat) {
                  bonForumCommand = "host_executes_chat";
                  actorWillRejoinChat = true;
            }
            else if(actorIsGuestInChat) {
                  bonForumCommand = "guest_executes_chat";
                  actorWillRejoinChat = true;

            else {
                  // set attribute to trigger
```

```
                    // user message that chat exists:
                    session.setAttribute( "chatSubjectAndTopicTaken", fakeChatItem
➥);
                    chatTopic = "";
                    session.setAttribute( "chatTopic", "" );
                    session.setAttribute( "newChatTopic", "no" );
                    bonForumCommand = "visitor_starts_chat";
                }
            }

            if(actorWillRejoinChat) {
                // set session attributes
                // usually set when actor starts new chat.
                //
                // nodeNameHashtable key
// for the chat node key, needed for:
                // 1. adding messages to chat later.
                // 2. seeing if a chat is the current chat
                session.setAttribute( "chatNodeKeyKey", foundChatNodeKeyKey );

                // host session doesn't need this,
                // but if rejoining chat as guest, might?
                session.setAttribute("chatItem", fakeChatItem);

                // itemKey for this chat
                // is added as message attributes later,
                // is needed for finding messages
                // (temporarily),
                // and for guest sessions to find chat.
                String foundChatItemKey =
➥getBonForumStore().getBonForumChatItemNodeKey( fakeChatItem ).toString();
                session.setAttribute( "itemKey", foundChatItemKey );
            }
        }
```

Setting `haveTopic` (or `haveSubject`) to `false` sends the user back to the "visitor starts chat" bonForum state.

Starting a Chat

In our discussion of the `processRequest()` method, we have come to a very important block of code, the one that transforms a bonForum visitor into a chat host. It adds quite a few elements to the XML data: a host element (if the visitor has none yet), a chat element, and a `chatItem` element (that relates the chat to its subject and contains its topic). The method also adds the key to the new `chatItem` as an XML attribute in the new chat element, which will relate the chat to its `chatItem` and later to its message elements. In addition, some important session attributes are set: the key to the host element, the key to the chat `nodeKey` in the `nodeNameHashtable`, and the `itemKey`.

All this sounds more complex than it is. The hardest part is showing how simple it is in this book. You can follow it with the source code to `BonForumEngine`, also in Appendix C. Finally, we suggest using an XML viewer, such as Microsoft's free XMLpad, to follow the discussion using one of the XSLT output files that contains the complete `bonForumXML` contents. First, use bonForum a while from a couple of browser instances. Start a chat in one, join it in another, and send some messages from both browsers. Then use the Output bonForum XML Data option on the System Commands page (reachable from the start of bonForum). You should then be able to view the file TOMCAT_HOME\webapps\
bonForum\mldocs\bonForumIdentityTransform.xml.

The following listing shows the entire block of code that starts a chat in `processRequest()`. After the listing, you will find a discussion of the code.

```
if(haveSubject && haveTopic) {

      // actor starts chat

      // Each actorNickname is unique in bonForum,
      // Only one host node is allowed per actorNickname

      actorNickname = normalize((String)session.getAttribute("actorNickname"));

      // Try getting key to a host node
      // for current actor's nickname

      NodeKey hostNicknameNodeKey = getBonForumStore().getActorNicknameNodeKey(
➥actorNickname, "host" );

      NodeKey hostNodeKey = null;
      if(hostNicknameNodeKey != null) {
            BonNode hostNicknameNode =
➥getBonForumStore().getBonForumXML().getBonNode( hostNicknameNodeKey);
            hostNodeKey = hostNicknameNode.parentNodeKey;
      }

      if(hostNodeKey == null) {

            // If a host node key does not exist,
            // then current actor is not yet a host,
            // so add a new host node,
            // with actorNickname,
            // actorAge and
            // actorRating children,
            // to the "actors" root-child node
            // of bonForumXML

            nameAndAttributes = "host";
```

```
            content = "";
            forestHashtableName = "bonForumXML";
            obj = bonForumStore.add( "bonAddElement", "actors", nameAndAttributes,
➥content, forestHashtableName, "nodeNameHashtable", sessionId );
            hostNodeKey = (NodeKey)obj;

            String creationTimeMillis = hostNodeKey.aKey;
            String hostNodeKeyKey = sessionId + "_" + creationTimeMillis +
➥":host";

            // Make nodeNameHashtable key
            // for the hostNodeKeyKey
            // available to session.
            // It gives quick access
            // to last host nodeKey for session

            session.setAttribute( "hostNodeKeyKey", hostNodeKeyKey );

            nameAndAttributes = "actorNickname";
            content = actorNickname;
            forestHashtableName = "bonForumXML";
            obj = bonForumStore.add( "bonAddElement", hostNodeKeyKey,
➥nameAndAttributes, content, forestHashtableName, "nodeNameHashtable", sessionId
➥);

            //NOTICE: the commented-out line below here
            // is more efficient than the above line.
            // It does not require the reconstructed
            // hostNodeKeyKey. However, we may want that
            // in a session attribute for later.
            // Also, if we use this next statement, then
            // we are using two ways to add data to the
            // XML, and it may be better to only use the
            // wrapper method.  Still trying to decide.
            // There are other similar lines below!
            // They are in "host" handling, but not in
            // "message" or "guest" handling.

            // bonForumStore.getBonForumXML(
            // ).addChildNodeToNonRootNode(
            // "actorNickname", "", content, hostNodeKey,
            // "nodeNameHashtable", sessionId);

            nameAndAttributes = "actorAge";
            content = normalize((String)session.getAttribute( "actorAge" ));
            ➥forestHashtableName = "bonForumXML";
            obj = bonForumStore.add( "bonAddElement", hostNodeKeyKey,
➥nameAndAttributes, content, forestHashtableName, "nodeNameHashtable", sessionId
➥);

            nameAndAttributes = "actorRating";
```

```
            content = normalize((String)session.getAttribute( "actorRating" ));
            ➥if(content.length() < 1) {
                content = "5";
            }
            forestHashtableName = "bonForumXML";
            obj = bonForumStore.add( "bonAddElement", hostNodeKeyKey,
➥nameAndAttributes, content, forestHashtableName, "nodeNameHashtable", sessionId
);
        }

        // Add a chat node to the "things"
        // root-child node of bonForumXML,
        // with a chatModerated attribute,
        // and no text content.

        chatModerated = normalize((String)session.getAttribute( "chatModerated" ));
        ➥if (chatModerated.equalsIgnoreCase("yes")) {
            nameAndAttributes = "chat moderated=\"yes\"";
        }
        else {
            nameAndAttributes = "chat moderated=\"no\"";
        }
        content = "";
        forestHashtableName = "bonForumXML";
        obj = bonForumStore.add( "bonAddElement", "things", nameAndAttributes,
➥content, forestHashtableName, "nodeNameHashtable", sessionId );
        NodeKey chatNodeKey = (NodeKey)obj;

        // Add a hostKey to the new chat node,
        // its text content is the key to the host node
        // example: 987195762454.987195735516.987195735486

        String creationTimeMillis = chatNodeKey.aKey;
        chatNodeKeyKey = sessionId + "_" + creationTimeMillis + ":chat";
        nameAndAttributes = "hostKey";
        content = hostNodeKey.toString();
        forestHashtableName = "bonForumXML";
        obj = bonForumStore.add( "bonAddElement", chatNodeKeyKey, nameAndAttributes,
➥content, forestHashtableName, "nodeNameHashtable", sessionId );

        // Make the hostKey available to this session.
        // It is later used for these things:
        // 1. finding out if an actor is a host in a chat
        // 2. branding messages with a host as sender

        session.setAttribute("hostKey", content);

        // Make nodeNameHashtable key
        // for the chat node key
        // available to session.
        // Example key: ofl37sijm1_987195762494:chat
```

```
// It is useful later for these things:
// 1. adding messages to chat
// 2. finding the chat node
// (to add nodes or attributes)
// 3. determining if a chat is the current chat

session.setAttribute( "chatNodeKeyKey", chatNodeKeyKey );

// Add a "chatItem" child
// to the selected chat subject element.
// That selected element is
// the chat subject category
// in bonForumXML.
// The name of the new child is "sessionID_" +
// the sessionId of
// the visitor starting the chat +
// the time the chat node was created in millis.
// The time suffix allows more than one chat
// to exist per session.
// Also add an attribute called chatTopic,
// with the (escaped) chatTopic
// input by the visitor.
// The sessionId (recoverable from
// the name of the new child) can
// be used later to quickly find the chat nodeKey.
// That is useful for example
// when a visitor joins a chat

// Note: when adding the sessionId
// element, its parent is found
// using the pathNameHashtable.
// The parent nodeKey is there
// with a key which is its pathName
// (and equal to chatSubject)

nameAndAttributes = "sessionID_";
nameAndAttributes += sessionId;
nameAndAttributes += "_";
nameAndAttributes += creationTimeMillis;
nameAndAttributes += " chatTopic=\"";
nameAndAttributes += chatTopic;
nameAndAttributes += "\"";

content = "";
forestHashtableName = "bonForumXML";
obj = bonForumStore.add( "bonAddElement", chatSubject, nameAndAttributes,
➥content, forestHashtableName, "pathNameHashtable", sessionId );
NodeKey itemNodeKey = (NodeKey)obj;

// set itemKey to itemNodeKey as a string
```

```
        String itemKey = itemNodeKey.toString();

        // Add the key to the chatItem element (itemKey)
        // to the chat element as an attribute
        // The itemKey connects a chat
        // to its subject, topic and messages!

        String attributeName = "itemKey";
        String attributeValue = itemKey;
        NodeKey nk = bonForumStore.addChatNodeAttribute( chatNodeKeyKey,
➥attributeName, attributeValue );

        // Make the itemKey available to the session

        session.setAttribute("itemKey", itemKey);
    }

    if(!(haveSubject && haveTopic)) {
    // missing information, must return to get it
    // LATER: set attribute to trigger message to user
    bonForumCommand = "visitor_starts_chat";
    }
```

Adding a Host Actor

Recall that in the bonForum XML data, a child of the root node is called `actors`. For a chat, two important children of `actors` are `host` and `guest`. When `processRequest()` handles the `host_executes_chat` `bonForumCommand`, which originates in the "visitor starts chat" state, it must decide whether to add the visitor to the XML data as a `host` element, a child of `actors`. It finds out by using the visitor's nickname, `actorNickname`.

Nicknames used by bonForum users (actors) must be unique. That is enforced by storing them as keys in a `hashtable`, the `nicknameRegistry`. Here, we make sure that each nickname has no more than one host element related to it. A user can host more than one chat, but all the chats share one host node.

The code gets the nickname for the current request from a session attribute, where it was stored after input, by `processRequest()`. To find out whether a host node exists for the current nickname, the code first invokes a method of `BonForumStore`: `getActorNicknameNodeKey()` with the nickname and `host` as arguments. The returned nickname `nodeKey`, if any, is used to get the nickname node itself, using the `getBonNode()` method of `ForestHashtable`. The `parentNodeKey` member of the nickname node is the host `nodeKey`.

Actually, if the `getActorNicknameNodeKey()` method fails to return a `nodeKey`, we know already that there is no host node for the nickname. Then why continue on to get the node itself and its `parentNodeKey`? Because we will need this host `nodeKey` as a string (`hostKey`) later, to add to the new chat and to a session attribute as well (see the section "Adding a Chat Element").

If no host `nodeKey` is found for the nickname, then a new host node is added to the `actors` child of the XML root node, using the `add()` method of `BonForumStore`, which wraps the `ForestHashtable addChildNodeToNonRootNode()` method. The `add()` method returns the `nodeKey` of the newly added host node, which is useful for the next three steps: adding the `actorNickname`, `actorAge`, and `actorRating` children of the host node. The values for these three are found in session attributes, where they were earlier set by the `processRequest` method (see Section 8.1.14, "The `processRequest()` Method: Overall View").

Note the following statements from the "add a host" part of the previous long source code listing:

```
hostNodeKey = (NodeKey)obj;
String creationTimeMillis = hostNodeKey.aKey;
String hostNodeKeyKey = sessionId + "_" + creationTimeMillis + ":host";
```

The `hostNodeKey` is obtained by casting the returned object from the `add()` method of `BonForumStore`. The next two lines re-create the `nodeNameHashtable` key for the host `nodeKey` stored there. That is needed by the next `add()` method invocation to directly add child nodes to the host node, without searching for it in the XML data.

The `aKey` is available from the return value after casting (as it is from any `NodeKey`). The `aKey` was given a value using the system clock time in milliseconds. That happened when the `NodeKey` was used to store the host node. The `NodeKey` for the host node (as a string) was then stored in the `nodeNameHashtable` with a key that looked something like this:

```
0fl37sijm1_987195762454:host
```

The first part, before the underscore character, is the session ID for the thread that added the host. The part between the underscore and the colon character is the same system clock value that was used for the `aKey` in the host `nodeKey` when the host node was stored. That happened deep in the bowels of the `ForestHashtable` class, in a statement like this:

```
nodeKeyKey = sessionId + "_" + nodeKey.aKey +":" + nodeName;
```

The `nodeKey.aKey` acts as a timestamp allowing multiple keys per session in `nodeNameHashtable`. It is used whenever we need to be able to find multiple nodes with the same name for one session. It allows bonForum to have multiple chats, hosts, and guests associated with each session object. Before this timestamp part of the `nodeKeyKey` was implemented (for this edition of the book), bonForum users could be a host or a guest in only one chat per browser instance. Now, a host and a guest can enter and leave chats at will. Before, if a user started two or more different chats in the same session, a visitor could join only the latest one, although all would appear to be available. This small change made a big difference in the usability of bonForum.

The same session ID and timestamp mechanism just described applies also to `chatNodeKeyKey` and `guestNodeKeyKey`, as you will see in the following sections. Of course, these longer timestamped keys take up memory space and entries in the `nodeNameHashtable`, so we have included an option to suppress them when they are not needed. Message nodes, for example, use a shorter `nodeNameHashtable` key such as `ofl37sijm1:messageKey` so that only the last message `nodeKey` (`messageKey`) for each session is kept in the `nodeNameHashtable`.

There is one wrinkle here that is not obvious and that you will see in several other locations in the code. (There are some comments regarding this in the source code.) It involves the use of the `BonForumStore.add()` method to add children to the host node. In this case, we could have used the method that is wrapped by that `add()` method instead. We will show and discuss the difference now. Here is the way that the `actorNickname` is actually added (the first three variables are string objects):

```
nameAndAttributes = "actorNickname";
content = actorNickname;
forestHashtableName = "bonForumXML";

obj = bonForumStore.add( "bonAddElement", hostNodeKeyKey, nameAndAttributes,
➥content, forestHashtableName, "nodeNameHashtable", sessionId );
```

As you can see, that required us to reconstruct the `hostNodeKeyKey`. Here is the way that the `actorNickname` could be added more efficiently. That substitution can be made here and in several other locations in the code, where we already have the `nodeKey` of the future parent node handy (here, the `hostNodeKey`). Therefore, there is no real need for the `nodeKey` key and the lookup in the `nodeNameHashtable`.

```
String name = "actorNickname";
String attributes = "";
content = actorNickname;
forestHashtableName = "bonForumXML";

bonForumStore.getBonForumXML().addChildNodeToNonRootNode(name, attributes,
➥content, hostNodeKey, "nodeNameHashtable", sessionId);
```

The main reason that we use only the `add()` method is so that we will have just one method adding elements to the XML data in the host threads, the guest threads, and the chat message threads. When we later discuss "visitor joins chat" handling and chat message handling, you will see why we sometimes really do need the `add()` method, with its second argument (`hostNodeKeyKey`, `chatNodeKeyKey`, and so on).

Adding a Chat Element

In the next part of the long source code listing in the previous section "Starting a Chat," a new chat element is added to the XML data. The element has an attribute to keep the user's answer to the "Will you moderate this chat?" question on the browser page. That answer is retrieved from a session attribute, where it was earlier set from a request parameter in the `visitor_joins_chat_frame` handler (see Section 8.1.18, "The `processRequest()` Method: Handling Specific Chat JSPs," and Section 8.1.19, "The `processRequest()` Method: Handling Chat Variables").

After `nameAndAttributes` has been prepared by concatenating the chat with the "moderated" attribute name and value, the new element is added with the BonForumStore add() method. As we just discussed, we can cast the return value from add() and use it to keep adding children to the new chat element. Here are the statements that re-create the very important chatNodeKeyKey:

```
NodeKey chatNodeKey = (NodeKey)obj;
String creationTimeMillis = chatNodeKey.aKey;
chatNodeKeyKey = sessionId + "_" + creationTimeMillis + ":chat";
```

Here is an example of a chatNodeKeyKey:

```
ofl37sijm1_987195762494:chat
```

The chatNodeKeyKey is immediately useful for adding the hostKey to the chat element. It is added as a string value in the text node of the chat element. That string value is also set in a session attribute named hostKey. Of course, it looks something like this:

```
987195762454.987195735516.987195735486
```

We make the hostKey available to the session so that it can later be used for two things:

- To find out if the session actor is the host in a chat
- To brand messages with the host that sent them

The first use was discussed previously in the section "Rejoining Existing Chats." The second use of hostKey is discussed later, in Section 8.1.22, "The processRequest() Method: Handling Chat Messages."

The last step in adding a chat to bonForum is to make the newly created chatNodeKeyKey available to the session as its attribute. That will come in handy for the following uses:

- To determine whether a chat is the current chat
- To find the chat node to add nodes or attributes
- To add messages to a chat

An example of the first use is described in the source code excerpt under the heading "Rejoining Existing Chats." We just saw the second use in action as we added the hostKey to the chat. The third use is discussed in Section 8.1.22, "The processRequest() Method: Handling Chat Messages."

Adding a Chat Item Marker

As you should recall, bonForum loads an XML file called subjects.xml during it startup initialization. That file contains the hierarchical list of possible chat subjects. Its XML tree is added to the bonForum XML data as the subjects subtree of the things root-child node. Now, in the processRequest() method, it is time to add another element in that subtree, one that connects a chat element to its `chatSubject` node and stores its `chatTopic` value as an attribute.

This new node is called the `chatItem`. (Note that the term `chatItem` is also used for the concatenation of the `chatSubject` and `chatTopic` that a visitor selects to join a chat, and that is sent in the request as a request parameter. That can be confusing, but they are related: One refers to them in the tree, and the other refers to them in words.)

The `nodeKey` of the new `chatItem` element, called the `itemKey`, is saved in the new chat node.

A very important part of the new `chatItem` element is its name. The name given to the new child is always something like the following example:

```
sessionID_ofl37sijm1_987195762494
```

After being concatenated with a (escaped) `chatTopic` in a `nameAndAttributes` string for the `add()` method, it comes out something like this:

```
sessionID_ofl37sijm1_987195762494 chatTopic="love"
```

The name part should look familiar, from the very similar `hostNodeKeyKey` that we discussed previously. Actually, we added the `sessionId` prefix only to fix a bug—it happened whenever the beginning of the name (the `sessionId`) started with a digit rather than a letter. It was a cute bug, and it illustrates that Murphy never sleeps. Before we added the prefix, the `chatItem` "subject marker" elements were to be like these two, in the XML data:

```
<dpwsizd7y1 nodeKey="982609718997.982609643718.982609643518" chatTopic="lizards">
➥</dpwsizd7y1>

<81tdw8d9k1 nodeKey="982610159830.982609643528.982609643518" chatTopic="bse">
➥</81tdw8d9k1>
```

However, the first one worked and the second crashed the XML database because its name is not well-formed XML—it starts with a digit.

After the fixes, the chat marker elements are like this example (they always start with a letter):

```
<sessionID_65sdwkh071 nodeKey="982619613054.982619446324.982619446314"
➥chatTopic="Magnesium supplements stop Migraines cold?">
</sessionID_65sdwkh071>
```

You probably noticed something here: This bug, and these examples, happened before we added the creation time in milliseconds to the name of the `nodeKeyKey` values and the `chatItem` element name. This next example is more current:

```
<sessionID_12rjpmlbj1_987109690411
➥nodeKey="987109690431.987109600301.987109600251" chatTopic="flying fish
recipes">
</sessionID_12rjpmlbj1_987109690411>
```

Again, adding the timestamp to the name of the `chatItem` element allowed us to provide direct access to multiple chats per session by creating unlimited unique key values for the `nodeNameHashtable`.

You will see in the next section why we have these strange names for the `chatItem` elements. The `chatNodeKeyKey` can be reverse-engineered from the element name to find a chat from a different session, as must be done when a visitor later joins a chat. Meanwhile, let's continue with the discussion of "host executes chat" handling.

After the `nameAndAttributes` string and other arguments are prepared, the `add()` method is called, as follows:

```
obj = bonForumStore.add( "bonAddElement", chatSubject, nameAndAttributes, content,
➥forestHashtableName, "pathNameHashtable", sessionId );
NodeKey itemNodeKey = (NodeKey)obj;
```

What is interesting here is that we are not using the `nodeNameHashtable` to add the `chatItem` marker element. As you see from the next-to-last argument, we use `pathNameHashtable`. The second argument, in these cases, is not the key to the parent node, but a path in the XML data (the `chatSubject`, in this case), which could be this:

```
Animals.Fish.FlyingFish
```

This brings our discussion to the last act involved in adding a chat.

Adding an *itemKey to* a Chat

The return value from the `add()` method is again cast to a `NodeKey`, as `itemNodeKey`. As a string, it becomes `itemKey`. This time we want to add it to the chat node, not as a child element, but instead as an attribute of the chat element. That is done using the `addChatNodeAttribute()` method of `BonForumStore`. It requires the very handy `chatNodeKeyKey`. No need, this time, to get it from a session attribute because we still have it from adding the chat node.

We are going to need the `itemKey` value elsewhere in this session. It connects a chat to its subject and topic. It also connects a chat to its messages and connects a message to its subject. Here then, we are finally arriving at the end of the code that handles the `host_executes_chat bonForumCommand`.

Before leaving the "host executes chat" handler, each thread checks to see if either `haveSubject` or `haveTopic` has been set to `false`; in this case, `bonForumCommand` will be set to `visitor_starts_chat`. That value will take the user back to where the missing information can be supplied.

At this point, we have also completed the two steps that need synchronization, so the next statement closes the thread-safe block of code:

```
} // end of synchronized block!
```

After this, each thread will soon be returning its `bonForumCommand` value and `serviceStatus` value back to the `service()` method, to be forwarded—hopefully not to forum_error.jsp!

8.1.21 The *processRequest( )* Method: "Handling Guest Executes Chat"

In this section, we continue with our discussion of the `processRequest()` method in `BonForumEngine`, now with the code that handles the `guest_executes_chat` `bonForumCommand` for requests that originate in the "visitor joins chat" bonForum state. We begin here with the `bonForumCommand` processor in the `processRequest()` method, beginning with the "else if" clause that begins as follows:

```
else if (bonForumCommand.equals("guest_executes_chat")) {
```

We can call this the "guest executes chat" handler. Its job is to process a visiting actor's request to join a chat, transforming the actor from a visitor to a guest. First, let's set the scene by recapitulating events up to this point. (If you think that you already know what these events must have been, you can safely skip ahead to the section "Getting the `chatItem`.")

When the thread reaches the "guest executes chat" handler, the visitor has already chosen a `chatItem`, which describes one available chat. As you can see in Table 8.5, "bonForum Variables: Priority, Name, Origin, Type," that `chatItem` variable value originated in an HTML select element displayed (using the XSLT processor) by the JSP visitor_joins_chat_frame.jsp.

That `chatItem` value included in itself both the subject and topic of the chosen chat, and arrived at the `BonForumEngine` servlet as a request parameter looking something like this example:

```
Animals_Bird_Hawk_[prehistoric falconry]
```

Furthermore, the `processRequest()` method has already processed the `chatItem` in the "visitor joins chat" frame handler within its `bonForumCommand` processor. You can look that up in Table 8.6, "bonForum Variables: Priority, Name, Destination." Notice that, in this case, the origin JSP and the destination JSP are the same! The request comes to the `BonForumEngine` servlet from the HTML produced by the _frame JSP, and the servlet forwards it back to the same _frame JSP after processing the `chatItem` request parameter (putting its value in a `chatItem` session attribute). The user can sit there all day long selecting one chat after another, without going anywhere.

Then the user clicked a button labeled Join, in the controls frame on the browser, which submitted the HTML form produced by the JSP visitor_joins_chat_controls.jsp.

That brought a new (and different) request to the `BonForumEngine` and to its `processRequest()` method. Its `boncommand`—and, thus its `bonForumCommand`—value was `visitor_joins_chat_ready`, which does not yet have (or need) a handler in the `bonForumCommand` processor. The service method then forwarded the request to the JSP visitor_joins_chat_ready.jsp.

That JSP set up some applet parameter values in its request parameters, including one for a target of _top, and another for a document with the full URI for the JSP guest_executes_chat.jsp.

Next, the _ready JSP executed this action, obviously as its last act:

```
<jsp:forward page="actor_leaves_frameset_robot.jsp.tfe"/>
```

That request was servlet-mapped, so it arrived at the `BonForumEngine`, where it was handled by the servlet-mapped request processor block discussed earlier. With the highest priority, and without being serviced by `processRequest()`, the request was forwarded to the JSP actor_leaves_frameset_robot.jsp.

The `BonForumRobot` applet in the Java plug-in on that JSP got its applet parameters from the request parameters. It dressed up the document name before asking its applet context object to have it shown in the _top frame. Now the request URI looked something like the following:

```
http://chatterbox:8080/bonForum/jsp/forum/guest_executes_chat.jsp987195879833.tfe
```

That was no static HTML document name but was yet another .tfe URI, again servlet-mapped to the `BonForumEngine`. Arriving there, its `requestURI` now looked like this:

```
/bonForum/jsp/forum/guest_executes_chat.jsp987195879833.tfe
```

The servlet-mapped request processor in the `service()` method matched the `guest_executes_chat` substring in the `requestURI` and said, "Aha! This request needs a `serviceStatus` of `ProcessRequest` and a `bonForumCommand` of `guest_executes_chat`. And that, patient reader, is how the request we are interested in arrived at the subject of this section, its `bonForumCommand` handler in the `processRequest()` method.

Getting the *chatItem*

For those of you who skipped the last section, welcome back!

The first thing done in the "guest executes chat" handler is to assume that everything is okay and that the guest will get to join a chat. A flag is set as follows:

```
boolean haveChatItem = true;
```

Next the `chatItem` is retrieved from the session attribute, where it was safely held through a chain of events involving several different request objects. Here is the statement:

```
chatItem = normalize((String)session.getAttribute("chatItem")).trim();
```

If the `chatItem` is empty or is set to the special value `NONE`, then the `haveChatItem` flag is set to `false`, which causes the request to be forwarded back to the "visitor joins chat" state for new input.

Synchronizing the XML Database for the Chat

Just as in the "host executes chat" handler discussed previously, we need for synchronization to enable thread-safe execution of code that shares a common resource: the XML data. For general information about synchronization, refer to the previous section, "The Need for Thread Synchronization". Here, we will get specific about the current need.

When a visitor joins a chat, we need to synchronize these two steps:

1. Checking to see whether a chat for `chatItem` (subject+topic) exists
2. The visitor joining that chat

At first glance, it seems that this synchronization is not necessary. Can't we just assume that the chat for `chatItem` exists because it was picked from a list generated from existing chats? The problem is that we will soon implement processes that delete existing chats, and they will do so from a different thread than any "visitor joins chat"–generated thread. The chat that is found to be okay in step 1 might have been deleted by the time that thread is ready to do step 2. Worse yet, because step 2 involves several additions to the XML data, the chat could be deleted after some of these, but not all, are completed.

If synchronization turns out to affect performance too much, we might have other possible solutions here, such as using a method that checks the integrity of a chat after it is added, together with a way to clean up "bad chat" debris caused by partially completed chat additions. The addition of a chat could loop until it is successful or exceeded a number of retries. For now, synchronization looks pretty good!

As an aside, we thought that we had a second reason to synchronize these two steps. Until we implement a user manager and data persistence, some pieces of the bonForum puzzle do not survive a session timeout. While we were adding the synchronization, we mistakenly thought that chats expire along with the session that starts them and that it could happen between the two steps listed. In fact, when the session that starts a chat times out, the chat does stay in the XML data, and it remains functional. However, it loses its host because the host's session has expired. Furthermore, a new visitor cannot get the host nickname back again, nor can any actor "reown" the host actor element, although it is still "in" the chat. Visitors can still join as guests and send messages back and forth. (Guest ratings do not survive a guest session timeout, but that is a different problem.) In any case, these problems will all go away when users can reclaim their data from session to session; that is what a user manager and data persistence will do for bonForum in a later release.

So, how do we synchronize the two steps that we listed? We would like to use the following way:

```
synchronized(bonForumStore.bonForumXML) {
        // thread-safe critical section
        // 1. step one
        // 2. step two
}
```

That way, a thread arriving at the synchronized block would get a lock on the static `ForestHashtable` member of the static `BonForumStore` member of the `BonForumEngine` instance. That would still allow multiple threads to access other nonsynchronized methods of `bonForumStore`. However, this preferred synchronization needs more testing and might require adding other synchronized methods or blocks. We are instead using the following, more severe, lock:

```
synchronized(bonForumStore) {
```

It does takes a while to rule out problems related to undersynchronization. Thread clashes are a bit like motor vehicle accidents: They're not easy to stage.

Finding a Chat and the Actor Status in It

The thread is now ready to fulfill the "visitor joins chat" action leading to the "guest executes chat" state. First, it searched for the chat with the `chatItem` that was requested by the visitor. (Does this sound familiar? This is similar to what was done in the "host executes chat" handler discussed previously, with `chatSubject` and `chatTopic` instead of `chatItem`.) There are parallels involved in joining and starting chats. We will try not to be too repetitive with things covered already. For convenience, though, we will repeat a previous table in Table 8.8 and show the possible outcomes of a chat search. This time, the last row is relevant.

Table 8.8 JSP Transitions Versus Actor-Chat Relationships

	Chat Exists Already			Chat Does Not Exist
	Actor Is Not in Chat	Actor Is Host	Actor Is Guest	
visitor starts chat	guest executes chat(1)	host executes chat(1)	guest executes chat(1)(2)	host executes chat
visitor joins chat	guest executes chat	host executes chat(3)	guest executes chat	forum error

Again, are the notes for this table:

- Numbered table items are optional, to be set by user preferences in a command, with alternatives as follows:
    1. Visitor starts chat
    2. Host executes chat, if multihosted chat allowed
    3. Guest executes chat
- If the actor is a host or a guest, the actor is rejoining a chat.

Rejoining a Chat

In the case of "visitor joins chat," if a chat with the requested subject and topic combination does not exist, the visitor will certainly not be able to join it! If the requested chat does exist, then what happens will depend upon an option setting. One option is that a visitor will join the chat as a guest, unless the visitor is already a host in the chat; in this case, that host role will resume. The other option (not yet implemented) is that the visitor will always enter the chat as a guest. This last option will allow a host in a chat to re-enter the chat as a guest.

A user preference setting can later offer a choice of options for the behavior of "visitor joins chat" when the visitor is found already in the chat as a host or guest:

1. Always join it with the previous status.
2. Always join as a guest.
3. Always offer a choice if the visitor already is a host.

At this time, the transitions given in Table 8.8 itself are implemented, and the options given in the notes are not yet implemented. We decided to tackle the harder ones first.

In the previous section "Finding a Chat and the Actor Status in It," where this table first appeared, we showed a simple way to implement the transitions for the "visitor starts chat" row. Here, we do the same for the "visitor joins chat" row:

```
if chat exists
      if actor is not host in chat
            set bonForumCommand to guest_executes_chat
      else
            set bonForumCommand to host_executes_chat
      endif
else
      set haveChatItem false  //error
endif
```

Setting the `haveChatItem` flag to `false` causes the request to be forwarded back to the "visitor joins chat" state—that is, back where it came from.

Eventually, when we are finished with the prototyping, we might decide that the visitor should always have access to both the "visitor joins chat" and "visitor starts chat" functionality on the same page. It will then be quite easy to implement all the logic in the table, as in this pseudocode:

```
if visitor starts chat or visitor joins chat
if chat exists
      if actor is not host in chat
            set bonForumCommand to guest_executes_chat
      else
            set bonForumCommand to host_executes_chat
      endif
else if visitor starts chat
      set bonForumCommand to host_executes_chat
else if visitor joins chat
      set haveChatItem false  //error
endif
endif
```

These pseudocode listings make it all look so easy. However, as is often the case, the devil is in the details. Let's start examining the actual code.

Passing Information Between Sessions

In the previous section "Adding a Host Actor," we discussed the structure of keys in the nodeNameHashtable and showed how they could be reverse-engineered in the following general manner:

```
nodeKeyKey = sessionId + "_" + nodeKey.aKey +":" + nodeName;
```

We also showed that we did not really have to do that while adding elements to a new host element because whenever we have a nodeKey to get the aKey from, we already have the key to find the node. We wanted to use only the add() method of BonForumStore, however, which requires a nodeKeyKey argument, and we also wanted the nodeKeyKey anyway, to put in a session attribute for other purposes.

However, getting back to the code for joining a chat (we can call it the guest thread), we really could use a nodeKeyKey for the chat, for two reasons: to see if the chat exists and to add elements to it. This time, we do not have the chatNodeKey, and having a chatNodeKeyKey would allow us to look up the chatNodeKey in the nodeNameHashtable. Yet, in this present situation, we cannot reconstruct the chatNodeKeyKey. One problem is this: The session ID that the chatNodeKeyKey includes as its prefix is for the session of the chat host, the actor that started the chat. That host session ID is not available to this guest thread. A second problem is this: The guest thread cannot get the aKey from the chatnodeKey to use in the reconstruction of the chatNodeKeyKey. If it had that nodeKey, it could simply use that to find the chat.

This situation is very different than the one in the section "Adding a Host Actor." There, the host node had just been added and its nodeKey had been returned by the add() method. That returned object could be cast to a NodeKey and used along with the available host session ID to reconstruct the hostNodeKeyKey.

As you no doubt know by now, this problem of passing information between sessions is the reason that we gave the chat subject marker elements in the XML (chatItem nodes) a name that is made from the chatNodeKeyKey. When a visitor chooses a chat to join (a chatItem variable), we can get from that choice the node that marks the subject and the topic (the chatItem node), that node's name, and thus the chatNodeKeyKey. Then, instead of searching through all the XML for the chat node, we can find it using its nodeKey from the nodeKeyHashtable, which we get with the chatNodeKeyKey.

Some of you who are waiting patiently for more standard ways to use XML in a Web application (a book in itself!) are perhaps saying, "Wait! Isn't that cheating?" Well, indeed it is, and for a good reason. Ensuring direct access to an object that you are going to require again in a different context looks good compared to some of the alternatives.

Here is an example of the way this cheat works. The bonForum variable called `chatItem` must get as its value the complete node path to a child element of a subject element that contains, in turn, an element whose name contains the two unique parts of the `chatNodeKeyKey` value. For example, let's say that the key to the chat `nodeKey` is as follows:

```
3vwx74igk1_987288911256:chat
```

There will be one node in the subjects XML subtree that represents the subject of the chat—for example:

```
bonForum.things.subjects.Animals.Fish.Piranhas
```

That chat subject node will have a `chatItem` child element with the following name:

```
sessionID_3vwx74igk1_987288911256
```

That `chatItem` node will have an attribute something like this:

```
chatTopic="first aid for fish breeders"
```

Like all bonForum nodes, it also will have a `nodeKey` attribute, with a value something like this:

```
nodeKey="987288999022.987288885569.987288885549"
```

That chatItem `nodeKey` value becomes the `itemKey` attribute value in the chat element and in all the messages for the chat.

Along comes a visitor who picks a chat to join from the list generated by an XSLT processor. That choice generates the following `chatItem` variable:

```
Animals_Fish_Piranhas_[first aid for fish breeders]
```

Now we can convert the `chatSubject` part of this `chatItem` string into a key for the `pathNameHashtable`. It contains `nodeKey` values for the subjects subtree that was loaded at startup from subjects.xml. That key looks like this:

```
Animals.Fish.Piranhas
```

The key gives us the Piranha `nodeKey`, and we can use that to iterate the children of the Piranha node, looking for a child that has the `chatTopic` attribute value matching the `chatTopic` part of the `chatItem`, "first aid for fish breeders." From the name of that child, we can get the `chatNodeKeyKey` and, with it, the `nodeNameHashtable` the chat node itself. Isn't it great that computers are so fast?

Of course, most of the code that takes care of all these details is not in `BonForumEngine`, but in `BonForumStore` of `ForestHashtable`. We thought that it would be difficult to understand the code in the `processRequest()` method without reviewing the details here. We are now ready to look at more code in that method. Here is all the code that looks for the chat and the actor status in it:

```
if(haveChatItem) {

        boolean chatExistsForSubjectAndTopic = false;
        boolean actorIsHostInChat = false;
```

```
        boolean actorIsGuestInChat = false;
        boolean actorWillRejoinChat = false;

        chatNodeKeyKey = getBonForumStore( ).getBonForumChatNodeKeyKey( chatItem );

        if((chatNodeKeyKey != null) && ( chatNodeKeyKey.length() > 0 )) {

              chatExistsForSubjectAndTopic = true;

              String actorKeyValue = normalize( (String)session.getAttribute(
➥"hostKey" ));

              if(actorKeyValue.trim().length() > 0) {

                    actorIsHostInChat = getBonForumStore( ).isHostInChat(
➥actorKeyValue, chatNodeKeyKey );

              }

              if(!actorIsHostInChat) {

                    actorKeyValue = normalize((String)session.getAttribute(
➥"guestKey" ));

                    if(actorKeyValue.trim().length() > 0) {

                          actorIsGuestInChat = getBonForumStore( ).isGuestInChat(
➥actorKeyValue, chatNodeKeyKey );

                    }
              }
        }

        if(chatExistsForSubjectAndTopic) {

              // needed to add messages to chat
              session.setAttribute( "chatNodeKeyKey", chatNodeKeyKey );

              if(actorIsHostInChat) {

                    bonForumCommand = "host_executes_chat";
                    actorWillRejoinChat = true;
                    haveChatItem = false;

              }
              else if(actorIsGuestInChat) {

                    actorWillRejoinChat = true;
                    haveChatItem = false;

              }
```

```
            // else join as new guest
        }

        if(actorWillRejoinChat) {

            // chatItem hasn't changed, but
            // session does need right itemKey:
            String foundChatItemKey = getBonForumStore(
➥).getBonForumChatItemNodeKey( chatItem ).toString();

            session.setAttribute( "itemKey", foundChatItemKey );

        }
    }
    else {

        // missing information, must return to get it
        // LATER: set attribute to trigger message to user
        bonForumCommand = "visitor_joins_chat";

    }
```

This "one-liner" does a lot of what we discussed previously:

```
chatNodeKeyKey = getBonForumStore( ).getBonForumChatNodeKeyKey( chatItem );
```

After that, the code just implements the logic shown in the last table. Finally, unless something has set `haveChatItem` to false, the thread proceeds with the transformation of a visitor into a chat guest.

Joining a Chat

Many parallels exist between the code that implements starting a chat and the code that implements joining a chat. After reading about the former, you will undoubtedly be able to easily understand the latter, just using the following commented excerpt `BonForumEngine.java` and referring back to the section "Starting a Chat." After the listing, we will briefly discuss this part of the `processRequest()` method and then move on to describe the process of handling chat messages. Here is the code that allows a visitor to join a chat:

```
// Check chat node OK before
// bothering to do anything else.

if(haveChatItem) {
chatNode = bonForumStore.getBonForumChatNode( chatNodeKeyKey ); // chatNode is a
➥BonNode
if(chatNode == null) {

haveChatItem = false;
bonForumCommand = "forum_error";
request.setAttribute( "serviceStatus", "ForwardToErrorPage" );
```

```
}
}

if(haveChatItem) {
      // actor joins chat

      // An actorNickname is unique in bonForum,
      // Allow only one guest node per actorNickname.
      // Get the guest nickname from session.

      actorNickname = normalize((String)session.getAttribute( "actorNickname" ));

      // Get guest nickname key

      NodeKey guestNicknameNodeKey = getBonForumStore( ).getActorNicknameNodeKey(
➥actorNickname, "guest" );

      NodeKey guestNodeKey = null;

      // If got key, get guest nickname node,
      // use its parent key to get guest node key

      if(guestNicknameNodeKey != null) {

            BonNode guestNicknameNode = getBonForumStore( ).getBonForumXML(
➥).getBonNode( guestNicknameNodeKey );

            guestNodeKey = guestNicknameNode.parentNodeKey;

      }

      // If guest node key does not exist,
      // neither does guest, so add guest node,
      // with its nickname, age and rating children
      // to the "actors" rootchild node of database.

      if(guestNodeKey == null) {

            //add guest node to actors

            nameAndAttributes = "guest";
            content = "";
            forestHashtableName = "bonForumXML";

            obj = bonForumStore.add( "bonAddElement", "actors", nameAndAttributes,
➥content, forestHashtableName, "nodeNameHashtable", sessionId );

            guestNodeKey = (NodeKey)obj;

            // add actorNickname to guest
```

```
            // the aKey in the NodeKey is
            // a timeMillis value from node addition
            // It is used also in the
            // nodeKeyHashtable key values

            String creationTimeMillis = guestNodeKey.aKey;

            String guestNodeKeyKey = sessionId + "_" + creationTimeMillis +
➥":guest";

            // Make nodeNameHashtable key
            // for the guestNodeKey
            // available to session.
            // It gives quick access to last
            // guest nodeKey for session

            session.setAttribute( "guestNodeKeyKey", guestNodeKeyKey );

            // add actorNickname to guest

            nameAndAttributes = "actorNickname";

            content = normalize( (String)session.getAttribute( "actorNickname" ));

            forestHashtableName = "bonForumXML";

            obj = bonForumStore.add( "bonAddElement", guestNodeKeyKey,
➥nameAndAttributes, content, forestHashtableName, "nodeNameHashtable",
➥sessionId);

            // Again, as discussed more fully
            // in the code for "starting a chat",
            // above, (see comment marked NOTICE:)
            // there is a more direct way
            // of adding many of these elements.
            // Here is a commented-out example:
            //
            // bonForumStore.getBonForumXML(
            // ).addChildNodeToNonRootNode(
            // "actorNickname", "", content,
            // guestNodeKey, "nodeNameHashtable",
            // sessionId);

            // add actorAge to guest:

            nameAndAttributes = "actorAge";

            content = normalize( (String)session.getAttribute( "actorAge" ));

            forestHashtableName = "bonForumXML";
```

```
            obj = bonForumStore.add( "bonAddElement", guestNodeKeyKey,
➥nameAndAttributes, content, forestHashtableName, "nodeNameHashtable",
➥sessionId);

            // add actorRating to guest

            nameAndAttributes = "actorRating";

            content = normalize( (String)session.getAttribute( "actorRating" ));

            if(content.length() < 1) {
                  content = "5";
            }

            forestHashtableName = "bonForumXML";

            obj = bonForumStore.add( "bonAddElement", guestNodeKeyKey,
➥nameAndAttributes, content, forestHashtableName, "nodeNameHashtable", sessionId
➥);

      }
      if(chatNode != null) {

            // add guestKey to chat,
            // that is how guest joins chat.

            nameAndAttributes = "guestKey";

            content = guestNodeKey.toString();

            forestHashtableName = "bonForumXML";

            //chatNodeKeyKey = normalize( (String)session.getAttribute(
➥"chatNodeKeyKey" ));

            obj = bonForumStore.add( "bonAddElement", chatNodeKeyKey,
➥nameAndAttributes, content, forestHashtableName, "nodeNameHashtable", sessionId
);

            // set the guestKey for this chat
// into a session attribute

            session.setAttribute( "guestKey", guestNodeKey.toString() );

            // set the itemKey for this chat
// into a session attribute
// for the guest's session

            String chatItemKey = bonForumStore.getBonForumAttributeValue(
➥chatNode, "itemKey" );
```

```
                session.setAttribute( "itemKey", chatItemKey );

        }
        else {

                // chatNode is null,
                // cannot add guest to chat,
                // nor set guestKey and
                // itemKey session attributes!

        }
}
```

Let's continue our discussion at the beginning of this last code excerpt. The specialized `getBonForumChatNode()` method of `BonForumStore` is used to retrieve the `chatNode`. That will not be needed until the very end of the code excerpt by the `getBonForumAttributeValue()` method of `BonForumStore`. However, we might as well get it right at the beginning because if something is wrong here, nothing else needs doing. Without a `chatNode`, there is not much point in joining a chat!

You can see here how the `chatNodeKeyKey` is what a guest thread in one session needs to have to retrieve a chat node, which belongs to a host thread with a different session.

```
chatNode = bonForumStore.getBonForumChatNode( chatNodeKeyKey ); // chatNode is a
➥BonNode
```

We expect the `chatNode` to be there because we found the `chatNodeKeyKey` earlier. If it is not there, the `haveChatItem` flag is set to `false`, sending the user back to the "visitor joins chat" bonForum state. If the `haveChatItem` flag is still `true`, the thread tries to put the visitor into the chat.

Actor nicknames are unique in bonForum. We do not want more than one guest node per nickname. The code tries to find the key of an existing one using a specialized `BonForumStore` method, `getActorNicknameNodeKey()`, and a `ForestHashtable` method, `getBonNode()`. (All this code should be later rolled into one method call.) If it cannot find a guest `nodeKey`, then it is okay to add a guest node and its children: `actorNickname`, `actorAge`, and `actorRating` elements. That should happen only if the actor has never joined a chat as a guest. (In the prototype, we can add to that during the current session.)

Adding a Guest Actor

The code for adding a guest node and its children is nearly identical to that for adding a host node. This makes you wonder if the two actions should be combined. Perhaps, but if we later want to add features specific to one or the other, it is harder to do. This is a classic dilemma in programming. When memory and storage were tight and longer source files meant more difficult editing and source code control, the tendency was to combine and shorten whenever possible. Now, with better and faster tools and compilers, it is increasingly more attractive to spread out code and let the increased redundancy and territory foster evolutionary diversity.

As when we added the host node, we used the `add()` method of `BonForumStore`, even though that meant more overhead and required the `guestNodeKeyKey`. We hope to put the key to good use later.

Joining a Chat, Continued

At this point in the code, the visitor finally is promoted to the status of guest in the chosen chat. That is done quite simply: The `nodeKey` of the guest node, as a string, becomes the content of a `guestKey` element, which is added as a child of the chat node. That relates the guest and the chat.

The same guest `nodeKey` string is also put in a session attribute, so it can be used later for two things:

- To stamp a chat message with the guest as its sender
- To find out if a visitor is already a guest in a chat

The second item is done both when a visitor wants to start a chat and it exists already, and when a visitor wants to join a chat.

Another session attribute will be needed, the `itemKey` for the chat that was just joined. To get that, we use yet another specialized `BonForumStore` method, which is the one that we got the chat node object for earlier. Here is the statement that gets the `nodeKey` of the `chatItem` so that we can put it as a string in a session attribute called `chatItem`:

```
String chatItemKey = bonForumStore.getBonForumAttributeValue( chatNode, "itemKey"
➥);
```

Before leaving the "guest executes chat" handler, each thread checks to see if the `haveChatItem` flag was set to `false`; in this case, `bonForumCommand` will be set to `visitor_joins_chat`. That value will take the user back to where the missing information can be supplied.

At this point, we have completed the two steps that need synchronization, so the next statement closes the thread-safe block of code:

```
} // end of synchronized block!
```

Again, as after each `bonForumCommand` handler, each thread will soon be returning its `bonForumCommand` value and `serviceStatus` value back to the `service()` method, to be forwarded to the next JSP.

8.1.22 The *processRequest( )* Method: Handling Chat Messages

It would not be a chat without messages! Treatment of the `chatMessage` parameter by processRequest() is more involved than that for any other parameter. We will discuss the code in this section piece by piece. It will help you to have the source code handy.

Because the processing for chatMessage parameters is lengthy and the parameters originate in two different bonForum states, the two bonForumCommand values involved are caught by their own separate if clause at the beginning of the bonForumCommand processor, as shown in the following excerpt. (The chatMessagesNavigator parameters originate on the same pages as the chatMessage ones, so they are also handled here.)

```
if(bonForumCommand.indexOf("host_executes_chat_controls") > -1) ||
➥(bonForumCommand.indexOf("guest_executes_chat_controls") {
      // handle chatMessagesNavigator
      // handle chatMessage
}
```

The first thing done is to get the message value that was input by the user in a safe form:

```
chatMessage = normalize((String)request.getParameter( "chatMessage" ));
```

Next, the chatMessage is processed, if it is not empty. Leaving out the details, this is the if statement that processes the chat message:

```
if(chatMessage.trim().length() > 0) {
// process the chat message
}
```

Let's look next at what is referred to by the simple comment process the chat message. An itemKey value relates a chat to its subject and topic. It also relates a chat to all the messages that it contains. When a message is stored in the bonForum XML data, the itemKey for the current chat is stored with it as an attribute. That itemKey value is obtained from a session attribute, where it was set when the chat was started or when it was joined. Here is the code that does that:

```
String itemKey = normalize((String)session.getAttribute( "itemKey" ));
if(itemKey.trim().length() < 1) {
logBFE.logWrite("err", "processRequest() ERROR: session has no itemKey!");
//itemKey is "";
}
```

The method in BonForumStore that adds an element to the XML chat data takes the name and attributes for the element together in one string argument. Besides the itemKey, we add the system time in milliseconds and a formatted date, both courtesy of a utility class. (Is the latter redundant, convenient, or both?) That much of the nameAndAttributes string is prepared with these statements:

```
nameAndAttributes = "message";
nameAndAttributes = nameAndAttributes + " itemKey=\"" + itemKey + "\"";
nameAndAttributes = nameAndAttributes + " timeMillis=\"" +
➥BonForumUtils.timeMillis() + "\""; JSP;BonForumEngine;chat messages
(processRequest() method)>
nameAndAttributes = nameAndAttributes + " dateStamp=\"" +
➥BonForumUtils.getLastDate() + "\"";
```

Another useful attribute for the XML element relates a message to either the chat host or the guest who added it to the chat. This `hostKey` or `guestKey` is concatenated to the `nameAndAttributes` string as a result of the following statements, which first look for a valid host or guest in that order:

```
String actorKeyValue = normalize((String)session.getAttribute( "hostKey" ));
➥if(actorKeyValue.trim().length() < 1) {
actorKeyValue = normalize((String)session.getAttribute( "guestKey" ));
if(actorKeyValue.trim().length() < 1) {
logBFE.logWrite("err", "no hostKey or guestKey for message!");
actorKeyValue = "";
}
else {
nameAndAttributes = nameAndAttributes + " guestKey=\"" + actorKeyValue + "\"";
➥}
}
else {
nameAndAttributes = nameAndAttributes + " hostKey=\"" + actorKeyValue + "\"";
➥}
```

A message element will be added to the bonForum XML as a child of the root-child "things" element. Then the string value of the message element's `nodeKey` will be added as an element of the current chat element. This messageKey will relate the message element to the chat. To find the current chat, the `add()` method needs its `chatNodeKeyKey`, which is used to look up the chat's `nodeKey` value in the `nodeKeyHashtable`. That provides direct access to the chat node. This next statement gets that important key from the session attribute where it was set when the chat was started or joined:

```
chatNodeKeyKey = normalize((String)session.getAttribute("chatNodeKeyKey"));
```

Finally, the message and its key can be added to the XML database. The actor's nickname is retrieved from a session attribute and is prefixed to the message before it is used as the content of a new `bonForum.things.message` element. The return value of the `add()` method is the `nodeKey` of the new message element, and its string value becomes the content of a new `bonForum.things.chat.messageKey` element, whose parent chat element represents the chat for the current request and session being handled in the `processRequest()` method. Here are the lines of code that accomplish all that:

```
if(!actorKeyValue.equals("") && !chatNodeKeyKey.equals("")) {
content = normalize((String)session.getAttribute( "actorNickname" ));
content += "::" + chatMessage;

forestHashtableName = "bonForumXML";
obj = bonForumStore.add( "bonAddElement", "things", nameAndAttributes, content,
➥forestHashtableName, "nodeNameHashtable", sessionId);
NodeKey messageNodeKey = (NodeKey)obj;

String messageKey = messageNodeKey.toString();
```

```
nameAndAttributes = "messageKey";
content = messageKey;
forestHashtableName = "bonForumXML";
obj = bonForumStore.add( "bonAddElement", chatNodeKeyKey, nameAndAttributes,
➥content, forestHashtableName, "nodeNameHashtable", sessionId);

session.setAttribute("messageKey", messageKey);
}
```

That completes the coverage of the details that were summed up earlier by the simple comment `process the chat message`.

8.1.23 The *processRequest()* Method: Setting *serviceStatus* for Return

Finally, before a thread leaves this long `processRequest()` method, two important steps remain to be done. One gives the okay to the `service()` method to forward the request object. The other tells it where to forward the request. These important steps can be seen in this code fragment:

```
session.setAttribute ("ServiceStatus", "ForwardAfterRequestProcessed");
return bonForumCommand;
}// end of processRequest()
```

We come here to the end of our detailed discussion of the `BonForumEngine` servlet. For the rest of this long chapter, we will discuss the `BonForumStore` class, a nonvisual bean that wraps the XML database and provides methods to implement our chat Web application.

8.2 The *BonForumStore* Class

Throughout the discussion of the `BonForumEngine` class, we have seen its dependence on the methods of the `BonForumStore` class. It is now time to look in more detail at that class. We will not go into as much detail in our discussion because the methods of `BonForumStore` are less universal in their applicability than those of `BonForumEngine`. Also, we will discuss only `BonForumStore` methods that are invoked from outside the class itself, except for a few methods that are helpful for understanding the purpose or implementation of those. The best way to find out about all the methods that are not detailed here is to look up `BonForumStore` in the Java docs for bonForum, which are provided with the Web application.

8.2.1 *BonForumStore* Is a Nonvisual Bean

For a good introduction to using beans with JSP, we recommend the chapter "Using JavaBeans with JSP" in the book *Core Servlets and JavaServer Pages*, by Marty Hall (Prentice Hall, 0130893404). As he points out, a class must have three things to qualify as a bean:

- A constructor without any arguments
- No public fields (instance variables)
- Access to persistent values through `getXXX` and `setXXX` methods (`isXXX` for Booleans)

The `BonForumStore` is a nonvisual JavaBean. It does not display anything on the screen because it is strictly a way to package properties and methods for server-side use by the bonForum application. As you probably know, the subject of JavaBeans is a large one, and many entire books are devoted to it—mostly to beans that do display something. We will certainly not try to replace any of those books for you in the remainder of this chapter.

8.2.2 Purpose of the *BonForumStore* Class

`BonForumStore` wraps the XML data for the chat Web application controlled by `BonForumEngine`, providing access to the data in the context of the application. This includes methods to get data into and out of the XML, and methods to change the data that is there. In the prototype so far implemented, we have modeled that database as an instance of the `ForestHashtable` class. The details of that class are covered in Chapter 11, "XML Data Storage Class: ForestHashtable."

`BonForumStore` also provides methods that the `BonForumEngine` servlet uses as it processes HTTP requests coming from the browser interface of the application. Other methods in `BonForumStore` are used by JavaServer Pages and custom tag classes. All these methods currently tend to be quite specialized to the purpose of implementing a chat application. Later, after more experimentation, they will be generalized to give them a wider range of application.

The following list covers most of the things that the bonForum Web application gets from the `BonForumStore` class. The rest of the chapter discusses these in terms of examples taken from the source code.

- Acts as wrapper for XML database (now a `ForestHashtable`)
- Initializes the XML database for use as a chat Web app
- Loads XML files into a database using its methods
- Dumps the content of the database as XML in a string
- Provides access to the database as a property
- Has methods to edit, add, and remove XML database nodes

- Has methods that are used by BonForumEngine processing
- Has methods for use by JSP custom tag classes
- Has methods for use by code in JSP scriptlets
- Outputs chat messages from XML with page navigation
- Outputs tree from XML as a list of pathnames to nodes

8.2.3 *ConstructorBonForumStore*

BonForumStore has only one constructor, without any arguments. It creates three objects that initialize static instance variables, as you can see here:

```
public BonForumStore() {
      super();
      bonForumXML = new ForestHashtable(5000);
      bonBufferXML = new ForestHashtable();
      outputTreeMap = new TreeMap();
}
```

In earlier chapters, we have already written quite a lot about the ForestHashtable class used by bonForum to store XML data. Often we refer to that as the "XML database" because the purpose of the class is to model a database containing XML. As you recall, a BonForumEngine object has a static member called bonForumStore. As an instance of the BonForumStore class, it contains two instances of the ForestHashtable class, both static, and therefore acts as an interface between the BonForumEngine servlet and the XML data. The data for the chat application is stored in bonForumXML.

The bonBufferXML object is still being developed and is untested; its purpose will be to hold subsets of the forum data for faster transformation processing and for more complex processing involving buffered intermediate results. It can also be used to input and output XML from the application without disturbing the working copy of the data.

As a descendant of the Hashtable class, ForestHashtable has one constructor that takes an argument for its capacity factor. We have used 5,000 for the bonForumXML capacity. For now, the XML buffer uses the default capacity value. In a future release, both ForestHashtable objects should have their capacity values taken from servlet context initialization parameters.

The outputTreeMap object is used to provide a sorted list for some methods to output. Currently, it is used to output all the messages in a chat and the list of available chat subjects.

8.2.4 Properties

As a bean, the BonForumStore should provide access to its fields only through get, is, and set methods. Two of the instance variables initialized in the constructor are available as read-only properties. These objects are accessed using their get methods even within the `BonForumStore` class itself, hopefully to make it easier to later add different data storage objects besides the `ForestHashtable` ones now used. These two members are as follows:

```
private static ForestHashtable bonForumXML;
private static ForestHashtable bonBufferXML;
```

Two other instance variables available as properties have so far been useful only to develop the software. At the end of this chapter, we show examples of accessing these from a JSP:

```
private String hitTimeMillis;
private String initDate;
```

A larger group of instance variables have property methods that have until now been used only from within the `BonForumStore` class itself. They provide access to the two top levels of the XML forum data and buffer data. The property methods for these have been kept around on the premise that they may someday be useful:

```
private NodeKey rootNodeKey;
private NodeKey actorsNodeKey;
private NodeKey actionsNodeKey;
private NodeKey thingsNodeKey;
private NodeKey bufferRootNodeKey;
private NodeKey bufferActorsNodeKey;
private NodeKey bufferActionsNodeKey;
private NodeKey bufferThingsNodeKey;
```

Finally, one other instance variable is available through `get` and `set` methods. It is used to control the log file output from a `BonForumStore` object:

```
private static String logging = "none";
```

8.2.5 Accessing *BonForumStore*

Of course, to be useful, the `BonForumStore` class must be instantiated. A `BonForumEngine` servlet object has a static `BonForumStore` member called `bonForumStore`. Here is the statement that creates that:

```
private static BonForumStore bonForumStore = new BonForumStore();
```

This "XML database" for the bonForum Web application is made available by the `BonForumEngine` as a public read-only property (unused, as yet) by the following method:

```
public BonForumStore getBonForumStore() {
        return bonForumStore;
}
```

The static `bonForumStore` member object of the `BonForumEngine` servlet can also be accessed from elsewhere in bonForum by using an attribute of application scope. Here is the statement in the `BonForumEngine` source code that sets that attribute:

```
getServletContext().setAttribute( "bonForumStore",getBonForumStore());
```

From another bean object in bonForum, for example, we could get access to the database wrapper class using a statement like the following:

```
BonForumStore bonForumStore = (BonForumStore)getServletConfig(
➥).getServletContext( ).getAttribute( "bonForumStore" );
```

We do not use any statement like that yet, but we do access `bonForumStore` often from JSP and from JSP custom tags by using their `PageContext` object (or a `jsp:useBean` tag) to get the `bonForumStore` attribute. We will discuss examples of that in Section 8.2.12, "Invoking Chat Methods from JSP Custom Tags," and 8.2.13, "Invoking Chat Methods from JSP Scriptlets."

Although the `ForestHashtable` class has thread-safe methods for changing the data within it, transactions outside that class still need thread synchronization. You can read more about that in the previous sections "The Need for Thread Synchronization," "Synchronizing the XML Database," and "Synchronizing the XML Database for the Web Chat." For now, all the critical code sections, which are in the `BonForumEngine` and `TransformTag` classes, use the static `bonForumStore` object as the lock that allows only one thread access at a time. All the examples have this form:

```
synchronized(bonForumStore) {
     // one thread at a time here
}
```

When new code is added to the project that changes the contents of `bonForumXML` using the data access methods of `bonForumStore`, the possibility that a similar synchronized block is required must be considered.

8.2.6 Initializing

For bonForum to start up, it is not enough to have an instance of `BonForumStore` that must also access the minimal data needed to function. Until data persistence is implemented in a later version, the bonForum Web application contains no chat-related data in memory when it starts up. However, it does have some XML configuration files with the minimal set of chat-related data needed for the application to function.

Every thread "passing through" the `processRequest()` method of `BonForumEngine` calls the `initialize` method of `BonForumStore`, as follows:

```
String sessionId = session.getId();
bonForumStore.initialize(sessionId);
```

The `initialize` method calls the `initXML()` method, which calls the `initializeBonForum()` method. If `bonForumXML` is empty, it gets filled with the minimal data content, including some values that are parsed from the XML configuration files using a Xerces Parser object.

Only the first thread should need to fill the data store. Ones that arrive later will find that it already contains all the initialization elements from the configuration files.

It will also contain all the chats, hosts, guests, messages, and other data that this thread and others have added since startup.

We will next show how `bonForumXML` is filled with what it needs for bonForum to successfully boot. To understand the discussion, you should know that any `ForestHashtable` like `bonForumXML` has a place to keep important node addresses, called `nodeNameHashtable`. (That is discussed in Chapter 11.) This statement clears the contents of that table:

```
getBonForumXML().getNodeNameHashtable().clear();
```

Adding the Root Node

An XML tree determines the playing field of this Web application. Its root node is the element named `bonForum`. Here we show the code that creates the first step in the XML database:

```
String rootNodeName = normalize("bonForum");
String rootNodeAttributes = "type = \"prototype\"";
String rootNodeContent = normalize("");
BonNode rootNode = getBonForumXML().addRootNode( rootNodeName, rootNodeAttributes,
➥rootNodeContent, "nodeNameHashtable" );
setRootNodeKey(rootNode.nodeKey);
```

The last statement sets one of the `BonForumStore` property values, which could be useful when we start combining more than one XML data tree in the future.

Objects of the class `BonNode` here represent the nodes of the database. This is better discussed in Chapter 11. We have not tried to make our `ForestHashtable` fulfill all the XML recommendations—that is a work in progress. For this project, it is sufficient that the data storage be capable of containing a tree of elements in a hierarchy. Each element optionally contains a list of `name=value` attribute pairs and can have content corresponding to XML `text()` nodes.

Adding Children of the Root Node

The root node in the bonForum XML database definition has three children: `actors`, `actions`, and `things`. We will show only the initialization of the `actors` element. This node serves as the parent of host, guest, and system nodes. Treating the children of the root a bit differently than their descendant nodes enables us to streamline the code for adding nodes. Here is the code to add the `actors` root child node:

```
String childNodeName = normalize("actors");
String childNodeAttributes = "type = \"READ_ONLY\"";
String childNodeContent = normalize("");
BonNode nonRootNode = getBonForumXML().addChildNodeToRootNode( childNodeName,
➥childNodeAttributes, childNodeContent, rootNode.nodeKey, "nodeNameHashtable" );
setActorsNodeKey(nonRootNode.nodeKey);
NodeKey holdNodeKey = nonRootNode.nodeKey;
```

The next-to-last statement sets the key to the `actors` node in a property to allow easy access to the root of the actors subtree in bonForumXML. The last statement only illustrates that the return value of the element addition methods often need to be kept to make addition of the next-generation nodes possible.

Adding Children of a Nonroot Node

All the varied elements that are added and removed during the operation of this Web application are at least grandchildren of the root node. Here we see the addition of the first such node, which is the actor named `system`.

```
childNodeName = normalize("system");
childNodeAttributes = "type = \"SYSTEM\"";
childNodeContent = normalize("");
nonRootNode = getBonForumXML().addChildNodeToNonRootNode( childNodeName,
➥childNodeAttributes, childNodeContent, nonRootNode.nodeKey, "nodeNameHashtable",
sessionId );
```

In fact, the system node is not very developed yet. In the future, it will provide access to the bonForum Web application in the manner of a system console, allowing the owner of the application to carry out necessary maintenance and tuning tasks.

Notice that the `addChildNodeToNonRootNode()` method takes one more argument than the `addRootNode()` and `addChildNodeToRootNode()` methods. That is because an element that is a child of a nonroot node can have its `nodeKey` put in the `nodeNameHashtable` with a key that is related to the session adding the element. That means that elements added in bonForum, such as chat messages, can "belong" to the user that added them.

After setting up the most basic XML chat document, the `initializeBonForum()` method proceeds to load some subjects and Web links into the database, which completes the initialization of bonForumXML. Because loading data from XML files is something useful that can also be done outside the initialization process, it is covered in its own section next.

8.2.7 Loading XML Data into *bonForumXML*

`BonForumStore` has some methods to load data into `bonForumXML` and `bonBufferXML` from XML files. We first describe how the `loadForumXML()` method is used during the initialization of `bonForumXML` to load a document node that is parsed from an XML file. Afterward, we expand on the method that make this possible, which you can also use by means of a wrapper method called `loadForumXMLFromURI()` that takes care of parsing its XML file argument. (The corresponding "buffer" methods are `loadBufferXML()` and `loadBufferXMLFromURI()`, which are both still untested.)

A visitor to bonForum who wants to start a new chat is offered a choice of chat subjects. In the XML representation of the chat, the subjects are a subtree of element nodes with a unique set of pathnames from the root. This subjects tree is loaded into `bonForumXML` with the `bonForum.things` element as its parent, and it provides the list of subject categories that is shown to the visitor. Here is the code that loads the subject data tree from a file named subjects.xml:

```
String pathToSubTreeRootNode = "";    // later
String parentNodeInDestination = "things";
String xmlUri = "..\\webapps\\bonForum\\mldocs\\subjects.xml";
try {
        DOMParser parser = new DOMParser();
        parser.parse(xmlUri);
        Document document = parser.getDocument();
        try {
                loadForumXML( pathToSubTreeRootNode, parentNodeInDestination,
➥document, "pathNameHashtable", sessionId );
        }
        catch(Exception ee) {
                logBFS.logWrite( "err", "exception loading subjects.xml into
➥bonForumXML:" + ee.getMessage() );
        }
}
catch(Exception ex) {
        logBFS.logWrite( "err", "exception parsing subjects.xml" +
ex.getMessage());
}
```

It is easy to see that this method can be used for far more than just getting chat subjects. As one further example, the forums.xml configuration file is loaded in a similar manner. That loads another XML subtree that represents a list of Web sites. These are later displayed as HTML links by using the XSLT processor functionality of the `TransformTag` JSP custom tag. The code that loads the forums XML file comes right after the previous code in the `BonForumStore` source file. The custom tag is discussed in Chapter 10, "JSP Taglib and Custom Tag: Choice Tag."

Meanwhile, if you get tired of the subjects that are listed in bonForum, or if you want to add some links to the exit page displayed by bonforum.jsp, simply edit the subjects.xml or forums.xml files in the mldocs folder.

Rapid Lookup of Loaded XML Elements

The `loadForumXML()` method loads XML from a DOM node into the `bonForumXML ForestHashtable`. It has the option of storing all the `nodeKeys` loaded into a `hashtable` with a `pathNameToNode` key. The `hashtable` was added to provide rapid lookup of a node using only the pathname to the node from some ancestor node in the tree. Essentially, we force some user input and program output to be connected to a sorted list of pathnames to XML nodes.

As an example, an HTML `SELECT` list of pathnames to all the available chat subject categories is shown to the visitor who is about to start a new chat. Each `OPTION` in the `SELECT` control is thus the key in the `hashtable` to the XML node that the pathname points to. Using the key to get the `nodeKey` from the `hashtable` is a lot faster than searching through all the elements looking for some matching value.

loadXMLSubTreeIntoForestHashtable( )

The `loadForumXML()` method relies on another method, `loadXMLSubTreeIntoForestHashtable()`,which loads a specified node recursively into a `ForestHashtable`. Note that it loads only element nodes with attributes and any text node children they have. This class will take some more work to meet all the recommendations for XML compatibility. This method should also probably be moved to the `ForestHashtable` class. It could then be accessed through an interface that supported other database options in addition to `ForestHashtable`.

The Java code in this method is based in part on code from an Apache Software Foundation sample. That source code is copyrighted by the Apache Software Foundation. All rights reserved.

8.2.8 Dumping XML Data from *bonForumXML*

While on the subject of `bonForumXML`, we might as well mention that as a `ForestHashtable`, it has a method called `getXMLTrees()` that can dump its entire XML contents as a string. After the `bonForumXML` initialization described previously, we write that string to the log file for the `BonForumEngine` class with the following statement:

```
logBFS.logWrite("", getBonForumXML().getXMLTrees());
```

Elsewhere, we use the `getXMLTrees()` method with the Xalan XSLT processor. The JSP custom tag for XSLT is called `TransformTag` and is discussed in Chapter 10. When its `inXML` attribute is set to `bonForumXML`, the resulting XSLT transformation gets its input from the string output of the `getXMLTrees()` method. Transforming the `bonForumXML` data onto JSP produced HTML pages has become an important part of the application.

8.2.9 Using the *bonForumXML* Property

When you read Chapter 10, you will see that to invoke the `getXMLTrees()` method as we just discussed in the last section, the `TransformTag` class must go through the `bonForumStore` member of the `BonForumEngine` servlet to get to the "official" `bonForumXML` instance, the one with the data. We show how it gets the `bonForumStore` in Section 8.2.12, "Invoking Chat Methods from JSP Custom Tags." Here, we just want to show that not all useful `ForestHashtable` members and methods are wrapped by convenient `BonForumStore` methods: Some must be accessed by getting the bonForumXML property of the `BonForumStore` object, as follows:

```
bonForumStore.getBonForumXML().getXMLTrees();
```

Here is another example of using the `bonForumXML` property, taken from the "guest executes chat" `bonForumCommand` handler code in `BonForumEngine` (see Section 8.1.21, "The `processRequest()` Method: Handling Guest Executes Chat").

```
BonNode guestNicknameNode = getBonForumStore( ).getBonForumXML( ).getBonNode(
➥guestNicknameNodeKey );
```

8.2.10 Adding, Editing, and Removing XML Elements

The purpose of `BonForumStore` is to wrap the XML database for bonForum. That implies that the Web application should add, edit, or remove XML data using `BonForumStore` methods. In this section, we discuss the current situation of these important database functions. Unfortunately, node editing has not yet been wrapped by a `BonForumStore` method; it must still be done by invoking a `ForestHashtable` method on the `bonForumXML` property.

The *add()* Method

The `add()` method is the workhorse of the `processRequest()` method in `BonForumEngine`. You will find 15 or so examples of using `add()` in `processRequest()`. This method does its work by calling the protected `addNode()` method, which wraps the database method `addChildNodeToNonRootNode()`. The following is an excerpt from the `addNode()` method source code in `BonForumEngine.java`:

```
bonNode = forestHashtable.addChildNodeToNonRootNode(name, attributes, content,
➥nonRootNodeKey, nodeKeyHashtableName, sessionId);
```

To supplement the information given here, please refer also to some examples given previously. We showed the `ForestHashtable addChildNodeToNonRootNode()` method being used to add elements to the XML data store (see the section "Adding Children of a NonRoot Node," in the context of the bonForum data design, and also see the section "Adding a Host Actor"). We described somewhat how the `pathNameHashtable` works, while describing the addition of a child element to the subject node with the `add()` method (see "Adding a Chat Item Marker"). Be forewarned that these next paragraphs repeat some of the information given previously to make it easier to find this information.

Using configuration XML files available at Web application startup time, the software adds the root and the children of the root. The `add()` method cannot be used for adding root nodes or adding children to root nodes. It is designed only for adding grandchildren to the root and their descendants.

Adding an element to one of the "intrinsic" elements in `bonForumXML` (`actors`, `actions`, or `things`) is called "fast" because the keys to these root-child nodes are kept in class properties for direct access.

When the `BonForumStore.add()` method adds a node, it finds its parent node using its `nodeKey`. How it automatically finds the parent `nodeKey` depends upon the parent node, as shown in Table 8.9.

Table 8.9 ***NodeKey Hashtable*** **Keys Versus Type of Parent Node**

Parent Node	nodeKey Hashtable	nodeKey Key	Notes
Root	nodeNameHashtable	Root name	1
Child of root	nodeNameHashtable	Parent name	2
Descendant of root-child	nodeNameHashtable	Session ID + creation time + parent name	3
Subject element	pathNameHashtable	Path from root to subject node	4

Notes:

1. The parent is the intrinsic root element (`bonForum`). You cannot use `add()` to add a child to the root node. Use the `addChildNodeToRootNode()` method of the database instead.
2. The parent is a nonroot, intrinsic element (`actors`, `actions`, `things`). The name of that element is also the key to the parent `nodeKey` in the `nodeNameHashtable`.
3. The parent is not an intrinsic element (for example, it is a chat element under the things element). (The parent is also not a subject element; the children's `nodeKeys` are put in the `pathNameHashtable`, not a `nodeNameHashtable`.) The key to the parent `nodeKey` in the `nodeKeyHashtable` is normally made up of the following:

   ```
   <sessionId> + "_" + <nodeKey.aKey> + ":" <elementName>
   ```

   The length of the session ID can vary according to encryption used. Here is an example key:

   ```
   54w5d31sq1_985472754824:chat
   ```

   Because the `aKey` of the `nodeKey` is the system time in milliseconds, the central portion of the `nodeKey` key is also referred to as the `CreationTimeInMillis` and is the time when the node was added to the data.

   There is also an option to leave out the `nodeKey.aKey` portion of the key, if the name of the parent node has been added to a selection list. That list is the `ForestHashtable` property called `UniqueNodeKeyKeyList`. This option was added to reduce the size requirements of the `nodeKeyHashtable`; for example, there is no need to store all the many message `nodeKey` keys, so `messageKey` is put on the list by default. With this option, `nodeKey` keys have the following format:

   ```
   <sessionId> + ":" <elementName>.
   ```

   Here is an example of such a "short-form" key:

   ```
   54w5d31sq1_:messageKey
   ```

4. The parent is one of certain elements loaded into the bonForumXML (such as the subjects subtree loaded with the loadForumXML command, for example), so the nodeKey is in the corresponding hashtable for that upload. For example, each subject element has its nodeKey in the pathNameHashtable with a key that is equal to the node path to that subject element node. An example of a subject nodeKey key is as follows:

```
bonForum.things.subjects.Vehicles.Motorcycles
```

Each time you call the add() method, it returns an object that can be cast to a NodeKey and kept as a reference to the nodeKey. These are useful for the following two purposes:

- To re-create the nodeKeyHashtable nodeKey key
- To recall elements by NodeKey

The *addToBuffer()* Method

The add() method works only with the bonForumXML data storage object. Another method called addToBuffer()works with bonBufferXML in a manner similar to add(). The addToBuffer() method is still under development and has not yet been tested.

The *remove()* Method

The remove() method is very similar to the add() method. It calls the removeNode() method, which, in turn, calls a ForestHashtable method, as follows:

```
forestHashtable.deleteNode((NodeKey)nodeKey, deleteLeafOnly);
```

As you can see from the argument, the deleteNode() method provides a choice between deleting elements that have no descendants (leaf nodes) and deleting elements together with any descendants that they have. That choice is made available to the remove() method by its third argument, leafOnly. If leafOnly is TRUE, uppercase, then the node is removed only if it is a leaf. Other values of leafOnly allow the method to prune branches.

The second argument to the remove() method is a string, nodeKeyKey. Currently, the remove() method can be used only to remove a descendant of a root-child whose nodeKey was put in the nodeKeyHashtable. (See the corresponding row in Table 8.9, "NodeKey Hashtable Keys Versus Type of Parent Node," and its note for details). If you want to remove a root node or a child of the root, or remove subject nodes (which have their nodeKeys in the pathNameHashtable), then you must use the ForestHashtable delete() method directly, after getting the nodeKey yourself.

The *removeFromBuffer()* Method

The remove() method works only with the bonForumXML data storage object. Another method, called removeFromBuffer(),works with bonBufferXML in a manner similar to remove().The removeFromBuffer() method is still under development and has not yet been tested.

The *edit()* and *editBonNode()* Methods

The planned edit() method in BonForumStore does not yet exist. The ForestHashtable editBonNode() method, which can edit an existing XML node, has not yet been wrapped by a BonForumStore editNode() method. When it is, that will be called by edit() and editBuffer() methods. Meanwhile, the editBonNode() method can be used for editing nodes, by first getting the ForestHashtable member (bonForumXML or bonBufferXML). This is done, for example, by the loadXMLSubTreeIntoForestHashtable() method, which is used by loadForumXML(), which is used by loadForumXMLUri(), as follows:

```
NodeKey nk = getBonForumXML().editBonNode( (NodeKey)(nextParentNodeKey ), null,
➥null, nodeContent );
```

The editBonNode() method is used also by the addChatNodeAttribute() method (see Section 8.2.11, "Invoking Chat Methods from BonForumEngine"). Yet another method that uses editBonNode() is changeActorRating(), which is used by changeChatActorRating() (see Section 8.2.13, "Invoking Chat Methods for JSP Scriptlets").

8.2.11 Invoking Chat Methods from *BonForumStore*

BonForumStore contains some methods that are quite specialized for the implementation of a chat application. These methods are used by the processRequest() method of BonForumEngine, while it processes threads whose bonForumCommand values are "host executes chat" or "guest executes chat." In the first case, the visitor is starting a chat; in the second, the visitor is joining a chat.

These BonForumStore methods are invoked when a visitor starts a chat and when visitor joins a chat:

```
getBonForumChatNodeKeyKey
isHostInChat
isGuestInChat
getBonForumChatItemNodeKey
getActorNicknameNodeKey
```

This BonForumStore method is called only when a visitor starts a chat:

```
addChatNodeAttribute
```

These BonForumStore methods are called only when a visitor joins a chat:

```
getBonForumChatNode
getBonForumAttributeValue
```

The rest of this section is one example of each of these BonForumStore chat methods being used. This section is definitely meant to be read with the source code as a ready reference. For a detailed discussion of the code that uses these `BonForumStore` methods, refer back to Section 8.1.20, "The `processRequest()` Method: Handling Host Executes Chat," and Section 8.1.21, "The `processRequest()` Method: Handling Guest Executes Chat."

The *getBonForumChatNodeKeyKey( )* Method

The `getBonForumChatNodeKeyKey()` method returns the `nodeNameHashtable` key for a chat node `nodeKey` in `bonForumXML`. That allows direct access the chat node and is used, for example, to add child elements to a chat using the `add()` method. You can see the `getBonForumChatNodeKeyKey()` method in action in the previous listings. Refer to the previous sections "Rejoining Existing Chats" and "Passing Information Between Sessions."

When a visitor joins a chat, the method is used like this:

```
chatNodeKeyKey = getBonForumStore().getBonForumChatNodeKeyKey(chatItem);
```

The `chatItem` argument is a string combining a chat subject and a topic. It could be this, for example:

```
animals_fish_piranha_[first aid for fish breeders]
```

The `getBonForumChatNodeKeyKey()` method works by invoking the `getChatItemNodeFromChatItem()` method to get the `chatItem` node. It can then recover the `chatNodeKeyKey` from the name of the `chatItem` node by removing its prefix.

The `getChatItemNodeFromChatItem()` method works by first recovering the `chatSubject` and `chatTopic` from the `chatItem` string. Next, it uses the `chatSubject` with the `subjectNodeKeyFromPathName()` method to get the `nodeKey` for the subject node. Finally it uses the `chatTopic` and the `getChildNodeFromAttributeValue()` method of the `bonForumXML` object to find the `chatItem` node, which is the only child of the subject node with the given `chatTopic` as a `chatTopic` attribute value.

The *isHostInChat( )* and *isGuestInChat( )* Methods

The `isHostInChat()` method returns `true` if a host is in a chat, given the `nodeKey` of the host (as a string) and a `chatNodeKeyKey`. The `isGuestInChat()` method returns `true` if a guest is in a chat, given similar arguments. You can see both these methods in action in the same source code listings as the method covered in the last section. Refer to the sections "Rejoining Existing Chats" and to "Passing Information Between Sessions."

An example of using one of these methods follows:

```
actorIsGuestInChat = getBonForumStore().isGuestInChat(actorKeyValue,
➥chatNodeKeyKey);
```

The `isGuestInChat()` method works by first calling the `getGuestKeysInChat()` method to get a list of `nodeKey` string values for all the guests in the chat. It then iterates the list looking for the given guest `nodeKey` value.

The getGuestKeysInChat() method works by first getting the chat node, using the chatNodeKeyKey and the getBonForumChatNode() method. It can then pass the nodeKey of the chat node and the name for chat node children that contain guest nodeKey values (guestKey) to the getChildNodeContentsFromName() method. That is a database method (for now, ForestHashtable method only) that returns an ArrayList with the combined contents of all child nodes with a given name.

The *getBonForumChatItemNodeKey()* Method

The getBonForumChatItemNodeKey() method returns a chatItem node's nodeKey from bonForumXML, given a "subject plus topic" string. You can see this method in action toward the end of the same source code listings as the methods covered in the last two sections. Refer to the sections "Rejoining Existing Chats" and "Passing Information Between Sessions."

Here is one example of the method in use:

```
String foundChatItemKey =
➥getBonForumStore().getBonForumChatItemNodeKey(fakeChatItem).toString();
```

The getBonForumChatItemNodeKey() method works by calling the getBonForumChatItemNodeKey() method. That is the same method that is called by the getBonForumChatNodeKeyKey() method. This time, the chatItem nodeKey is returned. It is used to link the chat subject and messages.

The *getActorNicknameNodeKey()* Method

The getActorNicknameNodeKey() method returns the nodeKey of an actor node for a given actorNickname. You can see this method in action in previous code listings. Refer to the sections "Starting a Chat," "Joining a Chat," and "Adding a Host Actor."

Here is an example of the method being used:

```
NodeKey hostNicknameNodeKey =
➥getBonForumStore().getActorNicknameNodeKey(actorNickname, "host");
```

The getActorNicknameNodeKey() works by calling the database method getChildNodeKeysFromName(), which returns a list of nodeKeys for all nodes with the given name that are children of a given node. In this example just given, that method call looks like this:

```
ArrayList actorNodeKeys =
➥getBonForumXML().getChildNodeKeysFromName(getActorsNodeKey(), actorNodeName);
```

The returned list therefore contains the nodeKeys of all the host children of the intrinsic actors node.

The getActorNicknameNodeKey() method continues by iterating the list of actor nodeKey values. It needs to look for one whose actorNickname child node has as its content the nickname that it is seeking. It can do that by calling the getChildNodeByNameAndContent() database method for each item in the list, which can return the (unique) actorNickname nodeKey for each actor nodeKey. When it has that, it can get the corresponding actorNickname node, compare its content to the nickname that it is seeking, and return the actorNickname nodeKey when (and if) it gets a match.

The *addChatNodeAttribute()* Method

The addChatNodeAttribute() method adds one attribute (name=value) to a chat node in bonForumXML. Currently, it works only for a ForestHashtable "database." You can see this method in action near the end of the source listing in the previous section "Starting a Chat." There is also further discussion of this method in the earlier section "Adding an itemKey to a Chat."

Here is an example of this method in use:

```
NodeKey nk = bonForumStore.addChatNodeAttribute( chatNodeKeyKey, attributeName,
➥attributeValue );
```

The addChatNodeAttribute() method works by first getting the chat nodeKey from the nodeNameHashtable using the chatNodeKeyKey argument. With the chat nodeKey, it can get the chat node itself—and, therefore, its attributes. It concatenates the new attribute with any existing ones and then calls the editBonNode() database method (which requires the chat nodeKey again as an argument). The editBonNode() method replaces the chatNode with a copy containing new string of attributes.

The *getBonForumChatNode()* Method

The getBonForumChatNode() method returns the chatNode from bonForumXML for a given chatNodeKeyKey. You can see this method in action in the previous source code listing in the section "Rejoining Existing Chats."

This method is used internally by other BonForumStore methods as well as by processRequest() in BonForumEngine, where it is called like this:

```
BonNode chatNode = null;
// . . .
chatNode = bonForumStore.getBonForumChatNode(chatNodeKeyKey);
```

The getBonForumChatNode method works by getting the nodeKey for the chat node (if any) from the nodeKeyHashtable using its argument as the key. It can then use the database method as follows to get the chat node that is returned:

```
chatNode = getBonForumXML().getBonNode(chatNodeKey);
```

It returns a null value if there is not a chat nodeKey for that nodeKeyKey in the nodeNameHashtable.

The *getBonForumAttributeValue()* Method

The getBonForumAttributeValue() method returns the value of a BonNode attribute, given the BonNode and the attribute name. You can see this method in action in the previous source code listing above in the section "Joining a Chat." There is also some discussion of the method call in both that section and in the section "Joining a Chat, Continued."

The method is called as in this example:

```
String chatItemKey = bonForumStore.getBonForumAttributeValue( chatNode, "itemKey"
➥);
```

The method works by passing the attributes of a node (the `chatNode`, in the given example) to the `getAttributeValue()` database method, which returns the value of an attribute given a string of `name=value` attributes and an attribute name (`itemKey`, in the given example).

8.2.12 Invoking Chat Methods from JSP Custom Tags

Some of the methods described previously were merely convenience methods, wrapping a bunch of lower-level code. That is definitely not the case for the methods discussed in this section, which have a major role to play in the application (at least, the ones with "forum" in their names do now—the ones with "buffer" in their names are not yet being used). Using a JSP tag library and custom tags in bonForum is the subject of Chapter 10, and the JSP custom tags invoking these methods will be fully discussed there. We will try not to repeat information here, so be sure to refer to Chapter 10 for a complete description of these methods. This section is definitely meant to be read with the source code handy.

The *outputForumPathNames()* Method

The `outputForumPathNames()` method outputs `pathNames` and `nodeKeys` from an XML subtree (for now, a `bonForumXML` subtree) into a TreeMap. The TreeMap is returned and can be used as a sorted list of the paths to all the nodes in the subtree.

The method is still under development. Currently, only one of its arguments is used, and it gives the path to the root node of the subtree to iterate. The other arguments will be used to format the output in different ways. One will provide a string (`ancestorReplacer`) that will replace all the nodes except for the last in each output node path. Another (`nodeSeparator`) will provide a string that separates each node in the node path output items. The first argument can later be used to add the `chatSubjectList` option discussed previously, as well as others.

This method is used for now only to get the list of subjects for a visitor to choose from when starting a chat. To make that easier, it skips over the `chatItems` nodes in the subjects subtree in `bonForumXML`. Doing that should be one available option, but not the default behavior, so that the method can be used for other purposes.

The `outputForumPathNames()` method iterates through the elements in the database (`bonForumXML`), starting at some element and descending through the tree hierarchy. The method uses the `pathNameFromNodeKey()` method to get a string object describing the ancestry of each node. The pathname of each visited node is output into a `TreeMap` object. That means that all the pathnames are available again but are sorted alphabetically. The code on a JSP document likes it that way.

The `OutputPathNamesTag` class essentially executes the following statements to invoke this method:

```
BonForumStore bonForumStore = null;
[. . .]
bonForumStore = (BonForumStore)(pageContext.getServletContext( ).getAttribute(
"bonForumStore" ));
[. . .]
outputTable = bonForumStore.outputForumPathNames("bonForumXML",
➥pathToSubTreeRootNode, ancestorReplacer, nodeSeparator);
```

For the details, see the source code for the custom tag and Chapter 10.

The *outputBufferPathNames()* Method

This method is still under development. It is essentially the same as the `outputForumPathNames()` method, but it's for use with the `bonBufferXML hashtable`. The two could probably be combined, but they will be called from custom tags ,and we are making it easier for their implementation to diverge widely in the future.

The *outputForumChatMessages()* Method

An actor active in a bonForum chat will see a display of chat messages posted by the host and guests of that chat. (Someday, chats will allow more than one host per chat.) The `outputForumChatMessages()` method gets for that display a `TreeMap` object full of messages from the XML chat data. It is planned that the XML source of the messages can include any XML resource with a URI. For now, it is only the `bonForumXML` data object.

This method is being developed further. For example, the attributes now unused will later select subsets of chat messages by actor, date, and so on. This method is now called only by a JSP custom tag from the two JSP documentshost_executes_chat_frame.jsp and guest_executes_chat_frame.jsp.

Simplifying the actual code, we can say that the `outputForumChatMessages()` method in `BonForumStore` is called by `OutputChatMessagesTag` using the following statements:

```
BonForumStore bonForumStore = null;
[. . .]
bonForumStore = (BonForumStore)(pageContext.getServletContext( ).getAttribute(
"bonForumStore" ));
[. . .]
outputTable = bonForumStore.outputForumChatMessages( "bonForumXML", attr1, attr2,
➥attr3, pageContext.getSession() );
```

Notice the last argument, which is the HTTP session for one particular user of the application, the one that will see the message list output by the method. The session is needed to get all the various user settings regarding message display page navigation and size, which are available in session attributes. A session attribute is also temporarily being used to provide the `itemKey` for the current chat. The `itemKey` is being used to search for all the messages that belong to a chat. This algorithm is not the correct one, and it will slow down as chat data increases. The correct way to find the `chatMessage` nodes is by iterating the `messageKey` children of the chat node. Perhaps there will be time to test the correct one before publication of the book CD-ROM, or perhaps it will await future releases on the bonForum SourceForge Web site at `www.bonforum.org`. For more about this method, see Chapter 10.

The *outputBufferChatMessages()* Method

This method is still under development. It is essentially the same as the `outputForumChatMessages()` method, but it is for use with the `bonBufferXML` `hashtable`. Again, the two could probably be combined—we are simply making it easier for their implementation to diverge widely in the future.

The *getXMLTrees()* Method

Previously discussed in Section 8.2.8, "Dumping XML Data from `bonForumXML`," and Section 8.2.9, "Using the `bonForumXML` Property," the `getXMLTrees()` method is another `BonForumStore` method that is used from a JSP custom tag, the `TransformTag` class. This method simply puts the entire contents of the `bonForumXML` data object into a string. The transform tag hands that over to another class that executes an XSLT process of the XML chat data to provide dynamic content to the browser interface. Currently, there are two such XSLT classes, one for Xalan-Java 1 and one for Xalan-Java 2.

Simplifying greatly, here are the statements called by the `TransformTag` class to get its XML database in a string:

```
private static BonForumStore bonForumStore;
String inXML; // actually, a string argument
[. . .]
bonForumStore = (BonForumStore)(pageContext.getServletContext( ).getAttribute(
➥"bonForumStore" ));
[. . .]
inXML = "<?xml version=\"1.0\" encoding=\"UTF-8\"?>"
synchronized(bonForumStore) {
inXML += bonForumStore.getBonForumXML( ).getXMLTrees();
}
```

Notice that we call the `getXMLTrees()` method from within a block that is synchronized to the `BonForumStore`. That locks out other threads from the database while dumping its contents so that they cannot change its content during the dump, perhaps changing relations between data items in the process.

Another point to mention is that dumping the XML buffer object is simply done by calling the same method on it instead of `bonForumXML`, as follows:

```
inXML = bonForumStore.getBonBufferXML().getXMLTrees();
```

In the real code, all this is a bit more involved and flexible than that because the tag is capable of transforming XML from a URI as well as from the chat database. For more about this method, see Chapter 10.

8.2.13 Invoking Chat Methods from JSP Scriptlets

In this final section of the chapter, we present the `BonForumStore` methods that are now being invoked by Java code within JSP scriptlet elements. The techniques shown here have barely been used in bonForum until now and will no doubt assume much more importance in the future of the project. First, we take a look at how a host can rate a chat guest. After that, we discuss a variety of ways to call bean methods from JSP.

The *changeChatActorRating( )* Method

A command available to chat hosts (and someday to guests as well) allows them to rate other actors in their chat. The `TransformTag` is used to display XSLT-generated lists of chat hosts and guests. When a chat host selects an actor from a list, that sends a request to the `BonForumEngine` with a parameter called either `chatHost` or `chatGuest`. That parameter contains the selected actor's name, age, and rating, and its value is set in a session attribute by the servlet. The actor doing the rating then clicks a button to increase or decrease the rating of the actor selected from the list. Clicking the button submits a request to the `BonForumEngine`, which forwards it to eitherhost_decreases_rating.jsp or host_increases_rating.jsp.

These JSPs are quite simple, for now. They contain the following tag, which allows the code after it to access methods and properties of a bean—in this case, `BonForumStore`.

```
<jsp:useBean id="bonForumStore"
class="de.tarent.forum.BonForumStore"
scope="application"/>
```

Farther down, on the first JSP you can find the following scriptlet:

```
<%
bonForumStore.changeChatActorRating("-1", session);
%>
```

To increase the rating, the other JSP uses an argument of `1` instead of `-1`. That is how simple it is to invoke the `changeChatActorRating()` method of `BonForumStore` from a JSP.

It wasn't so simple getting the `changeChatActorRating()` method to work—this turned out to be far more complex than we had anticipated. The method first gets the `chatNodeKeyKey` from a session attribute, where it was put when the host created the chat. Then the method checks for a `chatHost` session attribute (described at the beginning of this subsection). If it finds none, it looks for a `chatGuest` session attribute instead. If it finds neither, it is "game over." Otherwise, the `chatNodeKeyKey` is used as an argument to either the `getHostKeysInChat()` or the `getGuestKeysInChat()`

method, as appropriate. That returns `actorKeys`, which is an array list of `nodeKeys`, either for all host nodes or for all guest nodes in `bonForumXML`.

The `chatGuest` and `chatHost` session attribute values (`chatActor` strings) have the following format, which depends upon the XSL document used in the XSLT process that displays the lists of hosts and guests:

```
actorNickname age:actorAge rating:actorRating
```

Here is an example:

```
John Doe age:47 rating:11
```

The `actorNickname` is recovered from that string and is used as follows:

```
NodeKey actorNodeKey = getActorByNickname(actorKeys, actorNickname);
```

The `getActorByNickname()` method selects the correct actor `nodeKey` from the list for the correct one. It is then used as follows:

```
NodeKey actorRatingNodeKey = getActorRatingForActor(actorNodeKey);
```

The `getActorRatingForActor()` method gets the `nodeKey` of the `actorRating` node. That node is a child of the actor node for the actorNodeKey. The content of the actorRating node is the current rating for the actor being rated.

The final statement in the `changeChatActorRating()` method is the following:

```
return changeActorRating(actorRatingNodeKey, amount);
```

The `changeActorRating()` method gets the `actorRating` node from its key, the first argument. It then parses the `actorRating` node content and the `amount` argument as integer values. The rating value is offset by the amount value (`1` or `-1`, in our case) to get a new rating, which is converted to a string. Finally, the `actorRatingNodeKey` and the new rating value for the `actorRating` node content are both passed to the `editBonNode()` method of the database object. That method takes care of updating the actor rating in the XML data (we will spare you the details).

Accessing Bean Properties and Methods from JSP

You just saw a bean method, `changeChatActorRating()`, being called from a JSP. We will now show several ways to access bean properties and to call bean methods from JSP. The property examples will use two `BonForumStore` properties, `hitTimeMillis` and `initDate`, which are mostly useful for examples like this. For convenience, the method examples will use the `get` and `set` property access methods of these same two properties, although the techniques that we show apply to other public bean methods as well.

First, let's introduce the properties that we will use. Whenever a thread goes through the `processRequest()` `BonForumStore` method, it calls the `initialize()` method of the class. In that method, it leaves a timestamp in the `hitTimeMillis` property with the following statement:

```
setHitTimeMillis(null);
```

With a `null` argument, the `set` method uses the system clock to set the current time in the property. Both `set` and `get` methods for `hitTimeMillis` have been declared public so that we can both read and write the property from JSP in bonForum.

The thread next calls the `initializeXML()` method. If the `bonForumXML` data object is empty (normally true only after application startup), it will be filled with necessary data. When that happens, the `setInitDate()` method of `BonForumStore` is called with a `null` argument, which puts a datestamp in the `initDate` property, which shows the date and time that the database was initialized. The `getInitDate()` method is public, but the `setInitDate()` method is protected. From JSP, therefore, `initDate` is a read-only property.

One easy way to use a JavaBean from JSP is to use a `jsp:useBean` tag, as follows:

```
<jsp:useBean id="bonForumStore"
class="de.tarent.forum.BonForumStore"
scope="application"/>
```

It is important to realize that `jsp:useBean` will create a new instance of the bean only if it does not find an already existing one with the name given by the `id` attribute, in the scope given by the `scope` attribute. Because `BonForumEngine` has created a servlet context attribute called `bonForumStore` and has set it to its static `bonForumStore` data object, this tag will find the "real" data storage object, not create a new one.

You can then use a `jsp:getProperty` tag to display a property value, if you are looking for a property that is readable and that provides a value (we are, in this example):

```
initDate: <jsp:getProperty name="bonForumStore"
property="initDate"/>
```

Alternatively, you can use a JSP expression to display the same property value by using the `id` from the `jsp:useBean` tag to access the bean and its method, as follows:

```
initDate: <%=bonForumStore.getInitDate()%>
```

The `setInitDate()` method is protected, so attempts to set `initDate` from JSP will cause a compile time error. Instead, let's try to set the `hitTimeMillis` property value from a JSP, using something like this example:

```
<jsp:setProperty name="bonForumStore" property="hitTimeMillis" value="HELLO!"/>
```

Another way to set the same property is to use something like this:

```
<%
bonForumStore.setHitTimeMillis("GOODBYE!");
%>
```

Notice that this last example uses a scriptlet, not an expression, which would cause a compilation error because the `set` method returns void. Also, as you can see, we should have put some validation code in the `set` method.

These last examples illustrate some important points. Public access to a Web application—through bean properties and methods, for example—can defeat one of the main goals of JSP, which is to separate the job of the page designer from the job of the Java developer. Making writeable public properties (or readable ones with side effects) and public methods available for JSP development can create possibilities for unintentional behavior in a Web application. At the very least, changes in JSPs can then require extensive retesting of the application.

The last two examples rely on the `jsp:useBean` tag that we showed earlier. There are other ways to get the bean. One rather long one follows:

```
<%
bFS = (de.tarent.forum.BonForumStore)
pageContext.getServletContext().getAttribute( "bonForumStore" );
bFS.setHitTimeMillis(null);
%>
```

A shorter way to accomplish the same thing as this last example is to use the built-in application JSP variable, like this:

```
<%
bFS = (de.tarent.forum.BonForumStore) application.getAttribute( "bonForumStore" );
%>
hitTimeMillis: <%= bFS.getHitTimeMillis()%>
```

Yet another way to get the bean in JSP is to use the `getAttribute()` method of `pageContext`, with the appropriate scope value. (The value for an application scope attribute is `4`, session is `3`, request is `2`, and page is `1`). You must cast the object returned from the attribute to the right class before assigning it to a variable, which can then be used to access the bean and its methods, as in the JSP expression shown here:

```
<%
de.tarent.forum.BonForumStore bFS =
➥(de.tarent.forum.BonForumStore)pageContext.getAttribute( "bonForumStore", 4 );
%>
initDate: <%= bFS.getInitDate()%>
```

By the time you try using the XML versions for all the JSP tags used in the examples, you will see that lots of variations are possible here. Depending on your point of view, JSP is either a rich palette or a complicated mess!

9 Java Applet Plugged In: BonForumRobot

IN THIS CHAPTER, WE DISCUSS THE BonForumRobot applet, which is part of the bonForum Web chat application. Here you learn how to create and deploy a Java applet to control a Web application user interface. You also use the Sun Java plug-in to support an applet on the client.

9.1 Hands-on with Java Applets

As you can see by searching in a bookstore or on the Internet, much information about Java applets is available. Here we will be brief about topics that are well documented elsewhere. To find out more about applets, we suggest the Applet trail of the Sun Java Tutorial, which you can find at the following URL:

```
http://java.sun.com/docs/books/tutorial/applet/index.html
```

You can also find useful information and examples at the following URL:

```
http://java.sun.com/applets/index.html
```

If you want to use applets in your Web applications, you will certainly want to study the Java API documentation on the applet class. You may have already downloaded the documentation. It is available for browsing or downloading at the following URL:

```
http://java.sun.com/j2se/1.3/docs.html
```

As experimenters by nature, we hope that you will begin by trying out the demos and examples provided with the SDK, and we will provide the minimum help you need to get started. We will proceed from there to discuss some essentials that you will need to put your own applet programming efforts to use in your Web application. This includes telling your HTML that it should use your applet also getting the client computer to be a good applet container for your applet.

9.1.1 Try the Applet Demos

The best way to get a quick feel for what can be accomplished by adding applets to a Web application is to try some out. If you have installed the SDK for Java 1.3, you should try out the many demo applet programs provided. We will discuss only two of these here, but they all deserve study, together with their source code. You might need to compile these applet demos before trying them out.

GraphLayout

You can find the GraphLayout demo applet at something like the following location:

```
C:\jdk1.3\demo\applets\GraphLayout\example1.html
```

One of our favorites when we tried the demo applets was this visually appealing stunt that certainly takes advantage of a need for client computing power and reduces bandwidth requirements. These features are perhaps the most compelling argument for the use of applets.

MoleculeViewer

You can find the MoleculeViewer applet at something like the following location:

```
C:\jdk1.3\demo\applets\MoleculeViewer\example1.html
```

Be sure to drag the mouse pointer around on the pictures of molecules to see them from all angles. Try example2.html and example3.html as well.

9.1.2 Embedding Objects in HTML

You might be familiar with the now somewhat obsolete method of embedding an applet in an HTML document using the `APPLET` element.

The group that creates the official recommendation for HTML thought that the functionality of the Applet tag was better included into the new `Object` tag, which allows embedding of more than just applets into a document. Look up the specification for the embedded object tag in the HTML 4.01 specifications, which you can find at the following URL:

```
http://www.w3.org/TR/html401/
```

9.1.3 Using Applets with Java Plug-in

First, just for fun, try using the Java plug-in to embed one of the Sun SDK demo applets into a JSP document. You can get the details that you will need in your `jsp:plugin` element from the HTML file that is normally used to launch the applet demo.

We did this with the demo called Fractal, which we can launch using the following SDK document URL (yours may vary):

```
file://C:\jdk1.3\demo\applets\Fractal\example1.html
```

Put your new JSP document somewhere in the Tomcat Server document space. For example, we saved a file as TOMCAT_HOME\webapps\examples\bonbook\testFractal.jsp.

You must also copy the .class files. We created an Applet folder under bonbook to make things nice and neat. Copy the `CLSFractal` class as well as the supporting classes (`CLSRule`, `CLSTurtle`, and `ContextLSystem`). You should end up with all the .class files in the folder TOMCAT_HOME\webapps\examples\bonbook\applet.

Now convert the applet tag to the `jsp:plugin` as in the example that follows. Note the addition of the `type` and `jreversion` attributes, as well as the lack of the .class extension in the converted `code` attribute.

To complete the conversion from the `APPLET` element in the HTML file to a `jsp:plugin` element in the JSP file, you will need to add enclosing `<jsp:params>` and `</jsp:params>` tags. Also, each parameter tag that you have needs a few changes, especially the following:

- Change each `param` tag into a `jsp:param` tag.
- Enclose the value of each attribute in double quotation marks.
- Close the parameter tags correctly with a `/>`. (Note that the `</jsp:param>` closing tag throws a Jasper exception—you do need to use the trailing slash.)
- Change the `codebase` parameter to point to the proper location of the applet class file.

When you get done with the conversion, your JSP document will contain something like this:

```
<html>
<table>
<tr>
<jsp:plugin type="applet" code="CLSFractal.class" codebase="./applet"
jreversion="1.3.0" width="500" height="120" >
<jsp:params>
<jsp:param name="level" value="5"/>
<jsp:param name="rotangle" value="45"/>
<jsp:param name="succ1" value="F-F++F-F"/>
<jsp:param name="delay" value="1000"/>
<jsp:param name="axiom" value="F"/>
<jsp:param name="normalizescale" value="true"/>
```

```
<jsp:param name="incremental" value="true"/>
<jsp:param name="pred1" value="F"/>
<jsp:param name="border" value="2"/>
<jsp:param name="startangle" value="0"/>
</jsp:params>
<jsp:fallback>Plugin tag OBJECT or EMBED not supported by browser.</jsp:fallback>
</jsp:plugin>
</tr>
</table>
</html>
```

As you can see from our sample, we copied the CLSFractal.class file, along with its supporting class files, into a subfolder of the Examples Tomcat Web app. In other words, the class files had names similar to C:\jakarta-tomcat\webapps\examples\bonbook\applet\CLSFractal.class.

When you request the JSP page from your Tomcat Server (which should be running, obviously), you can do so using something like the following URL:

```
http://localhost:8080/examples/bonbook/testFractal3.jsp
```

If all goes well, you should be rewarded by seeing the Fractal applet demo on your browser display, this time being cared for by the Java plug-in. Now try changing some things around, such as the `codebase` attribute value and corresponding location of the `applet` class files. You will find that you can put the `applet` class in a descendant folder relative to the JSP document, but you cannot put it just anywhere at all on the system.

Debugging Applets Using the Java Console

When you deploy your applet on the browser using the Sun Java plug-in tags, you should also be aware of the Java Console setting for the plug-in. The Control Panel that comes with the Sun Java plug-in has a setting that enables or disables whether the Java Console is displayed when your applet is first initialized. You can launch the Java plug-in Control Panel by double-clicking its icon in the NT Control Panel. Make sure that Show Java Console is checked on the Basic property tab.

Notice that you can disable the Java plug-in here as well, so if a plugged-in object is not working, this is one place to troubleshoot.

Note that you can also turn on the Java Console using the Internet Properties icon in the NT Control Panel and choosing the Advanced tab. Scroll down and check the Java Console Enabled option in the Microsoft VM group.

Normally, you do not want the Java Console to appear on your system, especially because it can take quite a while to appear. For development of an applet, however, at times the Java Console will certainly help you to trace and debug your coding efforts. Simply use the Java `System.out.println()` method in your applet code to print a trace of the processing status. You can see that trace at runtime on the Java Console. Here is an example that prints out the value of one of our applet parameters:

```
System.out.println("refresh:" + this.refresh);
```

We like to use many such statements while developing. The following listing shows the contents of the Java Console taken while we were developing the BonForumRobot applet (reformatted to fit the margins of this book). It shows the normal console messages and the logging output. In production code, we should display only error codes (because logging will slow performance), but while debugging, longer messages can be useful. That certainly was true of the exception message at the end of this example:

```
Java(TM) Plug-in: Version 1.3.0rc3-Z
Using JRE version 1.3.0rc3 Java HotSpot(TM) Client VM
User home directory = C:\WINNT\Profiles\westy.001
User has overriden browser's proxy settings.
Proxy Configuration: no proxy
JAR cache enabled.
Opening
http://ginkgo:8080/bonForum/jsp/forum/applet/BonForumRobot.class with cookie
➥"JSESSIONID=To1012mC7393683872105755At".
init()
start()
refresh:true
target:_top
document:/bonForum/jsp/forum/host_executes_chat.jsp
increment:100
limit:1
message:Preparing new chat!
uncacheableDocument:/bonForum/jsp/forum/host_executes_chat.jsp963620229925.tfe
➥thisThread:Thread[963620229674,4,http://ginkgo:8080/bonForum/jsp/forum/applet/-
➥threadGroup]
top stop
thisThread:Thread[963620229674,4,http://ginkgo:8080/bonForum/jsp/forum/applet/-
➥threadGroup]
stop()
showDocument
thisThread:Thread[963620229674,4,http://ginkgo:8080/bonForum/jsp/forum/applet/-
➥threadGroup]
MalformedURLException caught in
BonForumRobot/bonForum/jsp/forum/host_executes_chat.jsp963620229925.tfe
thisThread:Thread[963620229674,4,http://ginkgo:8080/bonForum/jsp/forum/applet/-
➥threadGroup]
```

9.1.4 Converting Applet Tags to Object Tags

Because the object tags are now supposed to be used instead of applet tags, you might want to convert existing applet tags into object tags. One way to do that is by using the HTMLConverter utility from Sun. That will also mean, however, that your applets will be embedded in Java plug-in elements, and thus will be executed by the Sun Java JRE instead of the browser's default Java runtime engine.

9.2 XSLTProcessor Applet

One of the classes that comes with the Apache Xalan XSLT processor packages is an applet called XSLTProcessorApplet. As you might guess from its name, this applet encapsulates the basic XSLT transform functionality that is required to apply an XSLT style sheet to an XML document. Such a transform produces as its output a document that can be in XML, HTML, or even some other language.

This XSLT Transform applet can be found in xalan.jar in the Apache Xalan project. The applet in compiled form will be in a file with a name something like org/apache/xalan/xslt/client/XSLTProcessorApplet.class.

To use this applet, you must be sure that the applet can find xalan.jar and xerces.jar. In the object tag that declares the applet, the paths to these two important jar files are given relative to the location of the HTML that "calls" the applet.

You should be able to find an HTML file that is all set up for you to try out the Xalan XSLT applet. We found such a document at this location:

```
xalan_1_1\samples\AppletXMLtoHTML\AppletXMLtoHTML.html
```

When we tried this HTML file, we got some frames displayed on our browser but were informed by a message in the browser status bar that there was an error. The applet could not find the class `org.xml.sax.SAXException`. As so often occurs when setting up Java programs, we thought we had a classpath problem.

A file in the same Xalan samples folder, called README.html, informed us that the applet might need to be run from a server because it is restricted in what it can do by the Java "sandbox" in which it runs in a client environment. However, we found that we could get browsing of the HTML file to work by adding a `CLASSPATH` variable to our environment, with the following value:

```
c:\xalan-j_1_2_2\xalan.jar;c:\xalan-j_1_2_2\xerces.jar
```

It seemed to us that this should not be necessary. We thought that we could just set the value of the `archive` attribute in the `APPLET` element on the HTML page. Doing that should allow the applet to find the Xalan and Xerces JAR files. That did not turn out to be the case, though. As a further applet adventure, you could put the Xalan XSLTProcessor applet into a `jsp:plugin` element on a JSP page. In this next section, which is about the BonForumRobot applet, we will revisit the theme of plugging in an applet.

9.3 BonForumRobot

The BonForumRobot applet is part of the bonForum Web chat application project. How it is used in that application is discussed in Chapter 7, "JavaServer Pages: The Browseable User Interface." There you can find a description of how the applet is embedded into the JSP pages that use it. In this chapter, we discuss the design and inner workings of the applet. To follow the discussion, refer to the source code, either in the back of this book or on the accompanying CD. Note that the Java source file is not in the de.tarent.forum package. You should find the file BonForumRobot.java in the top-level bonForum source folder.

9.3.1 Problems Solved Using This Applet

The making of this robot applet was undertaken for several reasons. The most practical of these was to solve two or three problems encountered while creating the browser user interface for the bonForum Web chat application.

- Using the `jsp:forward tag` to get from one HTML frameset to another
- Refreshing HTML forms at minimum 5-second intervals
- Flickering when using the "standard" approaches to refreshing HTML
- Preventing the browser from looking for cached HTML frame content

9.3.2 Subjects Learned Using This Applet

Not the least important reason to create this applet was to have a part of our Web application project help us to learn and teach something about the following topics (at least):

- Java applet
- Object tag in HTML
- Java plug-in
- Threads
- Client-side solutions

9.3.3 Applet Life Cycles

Applets have a life cycle, which means that their container agrees to a contract to call the following methods sequentially: `init()`, `start()`, `stop()`, and `destroy()`. The names are quite self-explanatory. You take advantage of this contract by overriding the methods that you need in a subclass that you create of the `Applet` class. Here is the brief applet storyline:

The `init()` method of the applet is first called by its applet context (a browser or applet viewer) when the applet is loaded into that container system.

The `start()` method is automatically called after `init()` method and also each time the HTML client containing the applet is visited.

The `stop()` method is automatically called when the HTML page containing the applet has been replaced by another, as well as right before the `destroy()` method.

The destroy() method is called by the applet container right before it reclaims the applet, giving it a chance to destroy resources that it has allocated.

9.3.4 The *init()* Method

In our applet, this method is quite simple. We follow the standard practice of retrieving applet parameters in the init() method. The getParameter() method works for all the different types of parameters expected and helps clarify the code in the init() method.

Our applet uses these parameter value in the run() method. Retrieving init parameters in the run() method is possible but is not considered elegant.

If you are involved with client-side processing, you will sometimes need to do other things within this method, such as obtain database connections.

9.3.5 The *start()* Method

In the applet's start() method, a new RefreshThread object is created. RefreshThread is an inner class that extends Thread and will do the real work of this applet, repeating an action one or more times in a timed loop.

For debugging purposes, we also give the thread a system-unique name using the current time. Here is the code for the start() method:

```
public void start() {
  setBackground(Color.cyan);
  System.out.println("start()");
  if (refresh) {
      RefreshThread thread = new RefreshThread(
        Long.toString(System.currentTimeMillis()));
      thread.start();
  }
}
```

We also set the background color to cyan, which matches the HTML page that contains the applet. Otherwise, we might have a gray rectangle showing where the panel is located.

9.3.6 The *stop()* Method

The stop() method of the bonForumRobot applet is quite simple. It breaks what would otherwise be an endless loop, putting an end to the clocking action of the timer loop in the thread RefreshThread instance.

```
public void stop() {
System.out.println("stop()");
continueRunning = false;
}
```

The applet container can stop the looping in the `run()` method of the `RefreshThread` by using the applet's `stop()` method. However, we also need a way to end the looping from within the thread itself. That happens either because the counter has reached its maximum count or because we want to go through the loop only once. It is also useful to end error conditions. The `stopRunning` method is very simple:

```
public void stopRunning() {
stop();
}
```

You may be interested in learning about the perils of stopping threads. The Java API docs are one of your best resources for that information. Another good reference for this is the thread URL:

```
http://java.sun.com/j2se/1.3docs/api/java/lang/Thread.html
```

9.3.7 The *paint()* Method

With this method you can make the applet do something visible. In fact, several multimedia output capabilities are made available to the code in an applet. You can develop one of those Web applets that make Java famous!

We have used the `paint()` method to display a message to the user. That message is given by one of the parameters, which we can pass to the applet from the HTML object tag that contains it.

If the message parameter is set to `debug`, then the applet will graphically display the values of the current applet parameters. That is useful during development of both the applet and its surrounding application.

9.3.8 The *run()* Method

This method of the inner `RefreshThread` class contains most of the code in this applet. Much of the rest of this chapter discusses what is happening in this method. In the `run()` method, the parameters that are passed to the applet by the `jsp:plugin` element are utilized. You can find a discussion about these in Chapter 7. Here we discuss what the parameter values are used for inside the BonForumRobot applet.

9.3.9 The *jsp:plugin* Parameters

The next excerpt from visitor_joins_chat_ready.jsp shows some code that sets up the BonForumRobot applet parameters. The code then forwards the HTTP request to the actor_leaves_frameset_robot.jsp page, which contains a `jsp:plugin` element referencing the BonForumRobot applet class.

```
<%--GOING THROUGH ROBOT TO GET TO NEXT JSP PAGE ALLOWS BREAKING OUT OF A FRAMESET
--%>
➥<%
request.setAttribute("target", "_top");
```

```
request.setAttribute("document", request.getScheme() + "://" +
request.getServerName() + ":" + request.getServerPort() +
"/bonForum/jsp/forum/guest_executes_chat.jsp");
request.setAttribute("refresh", "true");
request.setAttribute("increment", "100");
request.setAttribute("limit", "1");
request.setAttribute("message", "Joining a chat!");
request.setAttribute("bonForumCommand", "visitor_joins_chat_robot");
%>
<%-- THESE PARAMETERS GOING TO AN APPLET THERE:--%>
<jsp:forward page="actor_leaves_frameset_robot.jsp"/>
```

That page where the applet receives the parameters is actor_leaves_frameset_robot.jsp. Here is the code that takes care of starting the applet with those parameters:

```
<jsp:plugin type="applet" code="BonForumRobot.class"
codebase="/bonForum/jsp/forum/applet" jreversion="1.3" width="400" height="160" >
<jsp:params>
<jsp:param name="target" value="<%=target%>"/>
<jsp:param name="document" value="<%=document%>"/>
<jsp:param name="refresh" value="<%=refresh%>"/>
<jsp:param name="increment" value="<%=increment%>"/>
<jsp:param name="limit" value="<%=limit%>"/>
<jsp:param name="message" value="<%=message%>"/>
</jsp:params>
<jsp:fallback>Plugin tag OBJECT or EMBED not supported by browser.</jsp:fallback>
</jsp:plugin>
```

In this previous example, the parameters cause the BonForumRobot applet to display in a new frameset on the browser, the document with a URL something like this:

```
http://localhost:8080/bonForum/jsp/forum/guest_executes_chat.jsp
```

It should display this document only once. Of course, because displaying the document in this case "jumps" out of the current frameset, there is no need to do that more than once.

In other circumstances, the BonForumRobot applet is programmed by its parameters to repeat its action of displaying a document. That periodically refreshes the information displayed on the browser in one target frame.

The *refresh* Parameter

This is an example of a switch in the applet that is controllable using the `refresh` parameter. This switch is rather brutal—it turns the applet on or off. In fact, it is actually just a placeholder, already conveniently present in all the many JSPs that set up the applet parameters. It is used to select the creation of different threads besides the one `RefreshThread` available now and thus will select different actions. That makes new ideas easier to try out; if any turn out well, they could then be put in their own applet class. However, to have the `refresh` parameter in the applet just to turn it on and off is not good design.

The *target* Parameter

The `target` parameter tells the applet where to display its output in a browser's HTML frameset. For example, a value of `_top` is a reserved value for the target parameter; it causes the document to display in the top frame of hierarchy of frames in the frameset. For more information, look in the HTML specification, which you can find at the following URL:

```
http://www.w3.org/TR/html401/
```

The *document* Parameter

Strangely enough, the `document` parameter tells the applet which document to display in the browser. The value of document is a URL to that document. For details on how the applet will display the URL, see the API documentation for the `Applet.showDocument()` method.

The *increment* Parameter

Of course, when the `document` parameter is set to a JSP, that document can dynamically change everything that happens next in the program. That JSP is as free as Java code allows it to be! The default action, however, is to keep repeating a loop that displays the document in that target, with a time period given by the value of the `increment` parameter, in milliseconds.

The *limit* Parameter

The `limit` parameter sets the upper bound for the number of times that the robot applet should repeat its action. In the prototype version of BonForumRobot, that action is "hardwired" to be the display of a document, using the `showDocument()` method of the `Applet` class. However, in the future, other actions could be added, including communication to the host Web application.

The *message* Parameter

While doing its robotic action, the applet should display graphically the contents of the `message` parameter. Obviously, by using a more complex object for this parameter, we could create quite sophisticated displays, control panels, and more within the applets display panel on the browser.

9.3.10 What the BonForumRobot Applet Does

In Section 9.3.1, "Problems Solved Using This Applet," we listed the reasons why we developed this applet for the bonForum project. These were also discussed in earlier chapters and will be further discussed in later sections. Here we just want to emphasize that this applet can have one of two possible behaviors. Which of the two happens depends on the value of the `target` parameter.

When *target* Is *_top*

If the target value is `_top`, it means that we are using the applet to break out of a frameset on the browser. The phrase "break out of a frameset" needs clarification. Perhaps describing one example of this will help. Consider the HTML produced by the JSP:

```
"visitor_joins_chat.jsp"
```

That sets up a simple frameset. One of its three frames (named Display) enables the user to select one of the available chats to join. Another frame (named Controls) displays a form that enables the user to join the selected chat. When this form is submitted (to the BonForumEngine servlet), we want the browser to stop displaying the current frameset and its three frames.

At first, it seemed that we could simply have the servlet "engine" forward the request to the "next" JSP (guest_executes_chat.jsp), which sets up a frameset of its own. However, when we tried that, we got a new frameset, but it was within the Controls frame of the frameset that we were trying to leave behind. In fact, we could create "Chinese boxes" (framesets within framesets ad infinitum), but we could not break out of the frameset (hence, we use this term for the applet functionality).

We could probably get around this problem if we could prevent the caching of the contents of the frames by the browser. We tried the usual methods and could succeed in only preventing the caching of visitor_joins_chat.jsp, which sets up the first frameset. But that did not turn off the caching of the contents of its frames. How can we get the browser to not cache these? We have found no way yet.

When *target* Is Not *_top*

If the target is not equal to `_top`, then for this Web application it means that we are using the applet to periodically refresh a document within one frame on the browser.

The obvious question is why an applet is needed for that. After all, there are many examples of page refreshing on the Web. That's true enough, but usually they are relying on client-side code (such as chat applets) or they are not trying to refresh the page every 5 seconds or less (required to chat).

Without a frameset, such a fast refresh led to unendurable flicker and interference with other controls on the page. With a frameset, attempts to refresh the content of one frame led to problems trying to prevent the browser from caching and reusing stale content.

Like the problem of "breaking out of frameset," this one seems like it should have a simple, ready-made solution. In fact, we have been offered several suggestions. So far, the only one that has worked is this bonForumRobot applet. Of course, we will not consider having the applet directly create and refresh the displays for the chat, using data from the server. After all, our whole point is to experiment with server-side technology for browser application.

9.3.11 Repeating an Applet Task

As discussed previously, this applet repeats an action. For the bonForum Web application, that action is to invoke the `showDocument()` method of the `Applet` object.

The action repeats at increments that are set by the value of the `increment` parameter of the applet. The maximum number of repetitions is controlled by the `limit` parameter.

However, note that if target is `_top`, no repetition of the `showDocument()` invocation can occur if the robot applet is not in the top frame of the frameset displayed on the browser.

Here is a simplified version of the loop that repeats an action. The actual code in the bonForum project is different but similar.

```
counter = 1;
while (continueRunning) {
    // put it to sleep for "increment" milliseconds
    messageLineOne = "";
    getAppletContext().showStatus("bonForumRobot");
    repaint();

    try { sleep(3*(increment/4)); }
    catch (InterruptedException e) {}

    // put it back to sleep for a "yellow light"
    messageLineOne = "refreshing...";
    repaint();

    try { sleep(increment/4); }
    catch (InterruptedException e) {}

    // are all iterations done?
    if(counter > limit) {
        System.out.println("counter:" + counter +
                                   " over limit:" + limit);
        stopRunning();
        continue;
    }

    // no, do it
    counter++;
 // NOTE: THE CODE TO PERFORM THE ACTION GOES HERE
 }
```

9.3.12 Using AppletContext to Show Documents

Each applet running is provided with an AppletContext interface, which allows the applet some functionality in its client-side runtime environment. For example, we use AppletContext to put our message in the status line at the bottom on the browser display area:

```
getAppletContext().showStatus(message);
```

As another example, this is the code that makes the robot applet display a document:

```
getAppletContext().showDocument(new URL(uncachedDocument), target);
```

That looks like it may be simple, but things are never quite simple in a real software project! That is why we created the variable named `uncachedDocument`, which you can see is the argument to the `showDocument()` method. The next section explains what it is for.

9.3.13 Circumventing Cached Documents

When we want to display a JSP page after having done it once already, its "contents" could be entirely different than they were the previous time. JavaServer Pages are dynamic. However, the name of the JSP document, its URL, can remain the same for both requests.

This can cause a problem if the browser has cached the result that it got when it first requested the JSP document. When the second request is made, the browser gets the cached result from the first request out of its cache and effectively prevents JSP from being dynamic!

We ran into this problem when we first got our robot applet working. It was making the requests for the JSP repeatedly, but the display was not changing. It should have been changing because part of it was a list of chat messages, and these were being added to from another browser acting as a guest of the same chat.

We tried to use the HTML `META` element that is supposed to suggest to the browser that it not cache a document. However, we were not able to get the applet working in this manner. The HTML that we tried was the following:

```
<META Pragma="HTTP-EQUIV" value="no-cache"> </META>
```

Later, after we had already developed the "no-cache" solution that we discuss later (generating a timestamp and affixing it to the URL), we found out that Internet Explorer will not respect cache control `META` tags unless it is shut down and restarted. After that, it obeys them. At the same time, it was suggested to us that if we wanted to prevent caching, we only needed to use the `setHeader()` method in our JSP pages to send the appropriate headers:

```
res.setHeader("Cache-Control", "no-cache");
res.setHeader("Pragma", "no-cache");
res.setDateHeader("max-age", 0);
res.setDateHeader("Expires", 0);
```

We were offered a simplified solution in the form of a custom JSP tag class called `NoCacheHeaderTag`. It really seemed like that should do the trick. However, we tried this tag in many places in the JSP. We also tried having the bonForumEngine servlet set these response headers before forwarding its requests to JSP files. Of course, we were able to prevent caching, but not everywhere—in particular, not within the frames generated by our JSP. We already discussed this problem enough (see Section 9.3.10, "What the BonForumRobot Applet Does"). It is time to discuss what *is* working instead.

In the bonForumRobot `run()` method, we fix up the JSP filename in the URL in the `document` parameter. We do that to force it to be a unique filename. Because the browser has not seen the resulting URL before, it does not look for it in its cache, even though, as we shall see, the robot may actually be requesting the very same JSP that it did the last time.

Here is an example of how the applet "fixes up" the URL for a JSP document. The original URL is shown here:

```
http://localhost:8080/bonForum/jsp/forum/visitor_joins_chat.jsp
```

After being altered, that URL becomes something like this:

```
http://localhost:8080/bonForum/jsp/forum/visitor_joins_chat.jsp.962066767851.tfe
```

The 12-digit number added to the filename is the current time in milliseconds obtained from the Java `System` object. That timestamp value creates a unique filename within the context of this session.

The fake extension .tfe that is also added to the URL acts as a signal to the Tomcat Server that it should send this request to the `bonForumEngine` object. That is because of the servlet-mapping element that we added to the web.xml Tomcat Web application deployment descriptor file.

The bonForumEngine servlet strips the timestamp and the fake extension off the altered URL. Then that servlet simply forwards the request to the JSP document that was pointed to by the original, unaltered URL. The bonForumEngine servlet is further discussed in Chapter 8, "Java Servlet in Charge: bonForumEngine."

One drawback is that although the browser will look for none of these robot-constructed and unique filenames in its cache, it will nevertheless cache the displays, and cache them, and cache them! After some time, the browser cache could contain nothing but cached bonForum refresh pages.

After we got this solution working, we were made aware of the fact that this caching problem is probably most often encountered in banner ad code and that it is usually solved just by appending a bogus parameter to the end of the URL—for example:

```
http://localhost/bonForum/jsp/forum/visitor_joins_chat.jsp?nocache=962066767851
```

This trick serves the same purpose and requires no special handling on the server side—that parameter can just be ignored. Were it not for the fact that we also need to add the .tfe extension to send our requests through the servlet "engine," we might be tempted to change our code to use the same trick.

The List of Requests That Get Mangled

The names of the JSP filenames that the BonForumRobot is watching out for are "hardwired" into this applet's code, so to speak. These JSP filenames are the ones that create documents that are to be self-refreshing through the action of the robot applet, or those that need to "break out of a frameset," as mentioned earlier.

We did not mind that we were reducing the generality of the action in the applet. By hardwiring some logic, we created a restriction that adds to the security of the bonForum game. That being said, it is nevertheless true that future versions of this robot applet should make it easier to add requests to the list or avoid its use altogether.

9.3.14 Stopping the Timer Thread

Note that to stop the timer thread in the robot applet, we use the `stop()` method of the applet. In our applet code is a loop setup that begins with this:

```
while (continueRunning) {
```

Inside the loop, to stop it, we can use the following code:

```
// are all iterations done?
if(counter > limit) {
System.out.println("counter:" + counter + " over limit:" + limit);
stopRunning();
continue;
}
```

The `stopRunning()` method simply wraps the applet `stop()` method to makes things clearer for humans:

```
public void stopRunning() {
stop();
}
```

The `stop()` method of the applet has been written to set the value of `continueRunning` to `false`:

```
public void stop() {
System.out.println("stop()");
continueRunning = false;
}
```

> **Avoiding Browser Cache Hits**
>
> If you add to the Web application and need to use the robot to avoid browser cache hits, then you will need to hard-wire the JSP name as we have the existing ones. You will also need to add code to the bonForumEngine.java file so that it appropriately handles the request received from the robot applet.

That means that the next iteration of the loop will not occur. This is the preferred way to stop the timer loop. Do not simply try to stop the thread itself; read more about the problems with stopping threads in the Java API docs for the `Thread` class.

9.3.15 Red, Yellow, Green Light

While we were developing this applet, we wanted some sort of visual feedback. By changing the color of the applet graphics background, we could tell what it was doing—and the fact that the colors changed was an indication that the applet was alive and well.

At the same time, we were curious about one thing: Would the execution of the applet code by the Java Runtime Engine have any effect upon the user's input of data (the chat message) into a form element in a different frame on the browser display? Would the user have to be instructed to do nothing while the applet was refreshing data from the bonForumXML database?

When the timer thread in the applet was sleeping, we saw the applet panel as a green rectangle. When the applet was about to awaken, we would see yellow. Finally, seeing red showed us when the `showDocument` method was being called.

It turned out that (on our system, at least) it was not difficult for the user to submit messages to the chat at any time, whether or not the applet was firing. In fact, the problem turned out to be the flashing colors there in the corner of the screen—as our traffic light cycled every 5 seconds through its colors!

Two-Phase Clock in Timer

To get the green light and yellow lights working, we put the thread to sleep twice during each iteration of the timer loop. In effect, we have two phases in our clocks ticking. That will come in handy in the future, when we need "on for *X* seconds, off for *Y* seconds" types of robotic actions. However, the catch clauses for these two sleeps should probably include `continue` statements because it's possible at some point that we might want to use an `InterruptedException` to stop the applet cold in the middle of a sleep. We would not want it to go right back to sleep again after that exception, but we would want it to do so before it gets back to the `while` and stops (that would produce a weird delayed stop effect—we stopped the applet and, 3 seconds later, it refreshed before finally stopping).

9.3.16 Implementing a Software Clock

The thread object in this applet is basically a timer. In embedded software systems that are multithreaded, it has been popular to create a clocking action in the software by putting a thread to sleep repeatedly in an endless loop. Java makes it easy to use this technique in this applet, which needs a mechanism to repeat an action indefinitely.

The *jsp:plugin* Tag and *BonRobotApplet* class

As discussed previously, we embedded our Java applet in some of our JSP documents, using the `jsp:plugin` syntax. Using JSP enabled us to pass parameters dynamically to the applet because the JSP is creating the HTML that the running applet will refer to with its `getParameter()` method.

Parameters take care of passing data from the server-side part of the application to the client-side part. What about the other direction? How can we pass dynamic information from the applet to the server? Of course, we can do that using the `showDocument()` method of the applet's context.

You might protest that `showDocument` still represents information (a document) going from the server to the client. And it does, indeed. However, the URL that is sent to the server can contain information that the applet is sending to the Web application on the server. Indeed, that URL can be mapped in Tomcat's configuration file, web.xml, so that the application data in the URL is sent to a servlet in any application context you want.

We will resist the temptation to show how that can be useful, but it does seem that it would allow us to transfer anything from one Web application to another via applets on HTML browsing clients. That raises interesting possibilities for distributed Web applications.

The `showDocument()` method can be called with just a URL or with an additional `target` argument. As you have seen, the target allows us to control the loading of documents while using frames in the HTML. Also, we can load documents into other named windows using the `target` argument.

One other thing that we can do if we use multiple applets in one context is name the applets differently. This enables us to use the `getApplet(String name)` method of the AppletContext interface for interapplet control.

Note that an applet's `isActive()` method can be used to determine whether another applet in the same applet context is running. That way, different applets can avoid running at the same time. Also, one applet can monitor the others, either to shut them down after a certain time or to recover from errors. You can make one applet act as a watchdog for the client-side of an application.

We leave it up to the reader to imagine the usefulness of having more than the one applet that we provide to our example application.

10

JSP Taglib The bonForum Custom Tags

IN THIS CHAPTER, YOU CAN LEARN ABOUT THE JSP tag library used in the bonForum Web application. First, we review the basic whys and hows of JSP tags and discuss some illustrative examples. Next, we discuss our own tags in depth, including three that display chat subjects, chat messages, and debugging information. The fourth and most powerful tag harnesses an Apache Xalan-Java XSLT processor (version 1 or 2). We describe how we used this transform tag in bonForum to display available chats, the guests in a chat, and a list of Web links.

10.1 Java Servlets, JSP, and Tag Libraries

We begin with a brief introduction to JSP 1.1 custom tags, which it is quite biased toward explaining their use in the bonForum project. This is not a comprehensive JSP custom tag reference, and it should certainly not be your only resource for this very rich subject. This is another chapter in a laboratory manual, meant to support your other resources, deepen your understanding of some aspects of tag libraries, and promote your own experimental approach to JSP technology.

10.1.1 JSP Tag Library Documentation

As you learn about JSP tag libraries, be sure to check the wealth of resources available to you at the main JSP Web site, `http://java.sun.com/product/jsp/`. You should definitely consult the excellent documentation available from the creators of JSP at `http://java.sun.com/products/jsp/docs.html`.

Especially important for learning about JSP tag libraries are the "Overview" and "Tag Extensions" chapters of the JSP 1.1 specification, which is available in portable document format as jsp1_1-spec.pdf.

While you are at the Sun Web site, you might also download the Syntax Reference Guide JSP 1.1, which can be found at `http://java.sun.com/products/jsp/tags/11/syntaxref11.html`.

Another key resource for all questions related to Java servlets and JSP is the Jakarta servlet API documentation. If you have downloaded and installed the Jakarta servlet API, you should find that at something like the following URI: `C:\jakarta-servletapi-3.2\docs\api\index.html`. To fully explore the Java basis for JSP custom tags, it is worthwhile to study the API Java docs for the package called javax.servlet.jsp.tagext.

Finally, although it is definitely not the first one to turn to, there is no deeper learning resource than the source code. Those of you who must know exactly how tag libraries work can find answers in the folder TOMCAT_HOME\src\org\apache\jasper\compiler\.

When you feel ready for such an advanced adventure, explore the Java classes that help implement tag libraries in Tomcat: the files in that folder whose filenames begin with "tag." Then search for those filenames in all the other files in the same folder, and you will have access to the nitty gritty. Such an adventure will take you to the `JspParseEventListener` class, the `Parser` class, and its static final `Tag` class. You will see that a deep understanding of tag libraries requires an understanding of the rest of JSP, which requires an understanding of servlets. This is all very interesting, and all way beyond the scope of this book!

10.1.2 What Are JSP Custom Tags?

To see where JSP taglibs and custom tags fit in, it helps to take a lightning tour of JavaServer Pages. In JSP 1.1, a page is made up of elements and template data. An element is something whose meaning is understood and that the JSP container responds to. Everything that is not an element is template data, such as static HTML content for a browser to display. An element belongs to one of three types: it can be a directive element, a scripting element, or an action.

A directive element directs the JSP container in a global manner, such as by controlling aspects of page translation, or by providing a URL to locate a needed resource. These elements use syntax based on `<%`, as follows:

```
<%@ directive ...%>
```

Scripting elements makes it possible to use scripting languages on the page (in JSP 1.1, only Java). A scripting element can be a declaration, a scriptlet, or an expression. Scripting elements also use syntax based on `<%`:

```
<%! declaration %>
<% scriptlet %>
<%= expression %>
```

A declaration element creates something that is available to all other scripting elements (such as an instance variable in the compiled page). A scriptlet enables you to put any code into the compiled page, allowing its logic to control and affect other page content. An expression is a complete Java expression that can be evaluated at response time, usually providing a string to be included in the JSP output stream.

An action encapsulates useful functionality. Standard actions are always available in JSP, while custom actions are added to JSP by means of the tag extension mechanism provided. Actions are expressed using an XML-based syntax, as follows:

```
<x:foo attr1="..." attr2="..." attr3="..." />
```

Actions can have a body and be expressed as follows:

```
<x:foo attr1="..." attr2="..." attr3="..." >
body
</x:foo/>
```

We have thus arrived at our goal of positioning the subject of this chapter within the wider context of JSP. JSP custom tags are used for adding actions to the built-in ones available in JSP. The JSP 1.1 Specification, Section 2.11, has this to say about actions:

> *Actions* may affect the current *out* stream and use, modify and/or create objects. Actions may, and often will, depend on the details of the specific request object received by the JSP page. The JSP specification includes some action types that are *standard* and must be implemented by all conforming JSP containers. New action types are introduced using the taglib directive. The syntax for action elements is based on XML; the only transformation needed is due to quoting conventions (see Section 7.5).

Elsewhere, the Specification also says the following:

> Actions permit the *encapsulation* of useful functionality in a convenient form that can also be manipulated by tools.

JSP custom tags can be added to the built-in JSP tags to extend JSP in a portable manner. Each custom tag packages Java code into a reusable "action" element, which can easily be added to JSP documents. A group of one or more custom tags is made available to JSP documents as a tag library. This component technology extends JSP, furthering its aims of portability, reusability, separation of static and dynamic Web content, and a wide choice of development tools.

10.1.3 How Do Custom Tags Differ from Beans?

This question is a bit of a trick. A custom tag is used to express a custom action. That action encapsulates some Java-based functionality, made possible by a Java class called a tag handler. This is, in fact, a server-side JavaBean. This bean implements either the `Tag` or the `BodyTag` interface. So, here we have one answer to the question posed in our heading.

But we can say that a JSP developer faces the choice of using a bean or using a tag. He can take advantage of the standard action, `jsp:useBean`, to access a JavaBean from a JSP. Or, he can subclass the convenient `TagSupport` or `BodyTagSupport` classes provided by JSP, to take advantage of the taglib protocol, which allows a feature-rich connection between JSP and Java server-side components. We will explore this latter choice in this chapter. And in this sense, we will often make a distinction between custom tags and beans.

10.1.4 How Do JSP Custom Tags Work?

In this section, we give a brief overview of the mechanics of JSP custom tag extensions. It should be sufficient to give you a framework to understand the rest of the chapter.

The Tag Handler Class

The behavior of a tag is determined by a JavaBean known as a Tag Handler class. It must implement either the `javax.servlet.jsp.tagext.Tag` interface or its `BodyTag` extension. Two classes in the servlet API do that for you already: `TagSupport` and `BodyTagSupport`. Usually, you can extend one of these to define a Tag Handler class.

The Tag Library Descriptor

Tags are always part of a tag library, which is defined by an XML file called a tag library descriptor, or TLD, file. Its main purpose is to connect the Tag Handler class with a tag name that will appear in the JSP document. It also gives the JSP container more information about the tags that it describes. For example, it declares the tag attributes that can be used with the tag and tells whether they are required or optional.

The Name of a Tag

A JSP tag is approximately an XML tag. Some come standard with all JSP implementations. The name of a tag is in the form prefix:suffix. The prefix is defined in a taglib directive in the JSP file. The directive associates the tags with that prefix and with a particular tag library descriptor file. The suffix is the name that the TLD file associates with a tag handler class.

Tag Attributes and Tag Handler Properties

A tag can also have attributes, like an XML tag. (There are some differences in how quotes are used, however.) These enables the JSP page author to pass values to the Tag Handler class. Each tag attribute corresponds to a property within the bean that implements the `Tag` (or `BodyTag`) interface.

The *BodyContent* Class and Body Content Processing

Body content can exist between a start tag and an end tag. The TLD description of the tag can enforce empty content or allow JSP or tag-dependent content. Tags that implement only the `Tag` interface, usually by extending `TagSupport`, can only ignore or include body content in the JSP. Tags that implement `BodyTag`, usually by extending `BodyTagSupport`, can manipulate and iteratively process body content. The `BodyContent` class is a special `JspWriter` object that encapsulates the body content while a tag is manipulating it.

Tag Action Methods in a Tag Handler

The methods within the Tag Handler class are related to the various parts of the tag. Thus, there is a method to handle the opening tag, called `doStartTag()`. Another method, `doEndTag()`, handles the closing tag. If a tag has attributes, then each one requires a property-setter method in the Tag Handler class and can have a `get` method. If the tag has a body, two other methods handle that: `doInitBody()` and `doAfterBody()`. Each method returns certain final static constants to control the sequential execution of these methods.

Context and Nesting of Tag Handler Instances

When a JSP is translated into source code for a servlet, the Tag Handler class for any custom tags on the JSP is instantiated within the `_jspService()` method of the servlet. The Tag Handler instance has properties set to refer to the powerful `pageContext` object of the JSP. Tags can nest. If a tag is nested in another, its parent property contains a reference to the tag it is nested in. Tags can find each and share objects in any Web application scope. `BodyContents` can form a stack, to facilitate nested manipulation of body content.

Translation-Time Tag Extension Methods

The javax.servlet.jsp.tagext package contains classes that implement JSP custom tags. Besides the ones mentioned previously, there are others that give the JSP container information at JSP translation time about tags and the variables they use. These classes are `TagAttributeInfo`, `TagData`, `TagExtraInfo`, `TagInfo`, `TagLibraryInfo`, and `VariableInfo`.

The *doStartTag()* Method

Implementing the `Tag` interface implies defining a `doStartTag()` method. A tag handler class can either do that or extend the `TagSupport` class and override its `doStartTag()` method to begin the action. When the method begins, the JSP container will have set the `pageContext` property and also the parent property (null, if the tag is not nested). It will also have set all the tag attribute properties provided in the start tag. As the developer, you control whether the body content is processed next, by returning the appropriate constant. Here is what a `doStartTag` looks like when you want to ignore body content:

```
public int doStartTag() throws JspException {
// do something, or nothing
return SKIP_BODY;
}
```

This means that everything between the opening and closing tags of the custom JSP element will be ignored. If that is not the desired behavior, you can return a different value, as follows:

```
public int doStartTag() throws JspException {
// do something, or nothing
return EVAL_BODY_INCLUDE
}
```

This means that everything between the opening and closing tags of the custom JSP element will be evaluated into the current output stream object for a simple, non-nested tag that starts out being the `JspWriter` object named "out." The tag element in the TLD for the tag must not have a value of `empty`, of course. `SKIP_BODY` and `EVAL_BODY_INCLUDE` are the only return values for `doStartTag()` if only `Tag` is implemented. If `BodyTag` is implemented, a new `BodyContent` output stream will be created, and returning `EVAL_BODY_TAG` will throw a `JspException`. Tags that implement `BodyTag` should return either `SKIP_BODY` or `EVAL_BODY_TAG`, as follows:

```
public int doStartTag() throws JspException {
// do something, or nothing
return EVAL_BODY_TAG;
}
```

After this last example of `doStartTag()`, the JSP container can invoke two other methods to process the body content: `doInitBody()` and `doAfterBody()`, discussed next.

The *doInitBody()* Method

The `doInitBody()` method can be used to do some processing before any body content is evaluated (into the `BodyContent` output stream). After the invocation of `doInitBody()`, the tag body content is evaluated and the `doAfterBody()` method is invoked.

The *doAfterBody()* Method

The `doAfterBody()` method is invoked after the first evaluation of the body content (if it is not empty). By returning `SKIP_BODY`, the `doAfterBody()` method can tell the JSP container that the processing of the body content is finished:

```
public int doAfterBody() throws JspException {
// do something, or nothing
return SKIP_BODY;
}
```

Sometimes the Tag Handler class must continually process the body content of a custom tag in a loop. You can tell the JSP container to repeatedly evaluate the body content and `doAfterBody()` invocation by returning `EVAL_BODY_TAG` from `doAfterBody()`. Note that because processing can change the body content or its context, each body content evaluation can have differing results.

```
public int doAfterBody() throws JspException {
//do something, or nothing
return EVAL_BODY_TAG;
}
```

The *doEndTag()* Method

Whether only the `Tag` interface or the `BodyTag` interface is implemented by a Tag Handler class, the `doEndTag()` method is invoked by the container. It can be used for any final processing in the action, whether body content has been evaluated or not. The container will call the `release()` method to release tag state.

10.1.5 Why Use Custom Tags?

In Chapter 8, "Java Servlet and Java Bean: BonForumEngine and BonForumStore," we discussed `BonForumStore`, a server-side Java bean that makes actions available to the JSP documents in bonForum. Our example was just complex enough to show that by using the `jsp:useBean` action, much dynamic content could be created for a Web application. The minimum requirements for a custom tag are greater than those for a JavaBean. It takes less work to create a bean than a custom tag. Why should a developer use custom tags? The reasons include the following:

- JSP tags are more integrated than beans into JSP. By default, they have access to the implicit JSP `pageContext` object. That gives tags easy access to the other implicit JSP objects. These include the request, response, page, application, session, and config objects. It also includes the `JSPWriter` object out, which makes it easy for tags to write into the output stream of the JSP. Furthermore, the JSP exception handling, using an error page and its implicit exception object, is readily available to custom tags.
- Using JSP tags provides the developer with ready-made mechanisms for nesting actions and for passing object references between actions. A mechanism for nesting output stream objects make it easy to use a hierarchical set of tags to incrementally construct content to be sent to a client, such as a browser.
- JSP tags can be more compact to express in the JSP document. The single tag `<my:foo bar="47"/>` could handle lots of processing. To handle it with a bean would require at least a tag to get the bean and another to call a method. That might not seem like much, but it keeps it simple for the page designer and also facilitates the separation of static and dynamic Web content design and creation.
- A developer should consider using custom tags whenever output to the browser from the processing will be involved because that is simpler to accomplish from a custom tag than from a bean. For processing without any JSP output, a bean is simpler and preferable.

One thing to be aware of is that JSP custom tags do not work with JSP 1.0, so if that version is a requirement, you must use beans.

10.1.6 Tag Libraries

Loosely speaking, a collection of custom tags is known as a tag library. Technically, a tag library is all the Java classes for a set of custom JSP actions, plus a tag library descriptor file that describes their tags to the JSP container. A tag library can be packaged in a JAR file, as the following definition explains. It comes from the document type definition for a tag library descriptor:

> A tag library is a JAR file containing a valid instance of a tag library descriptor (taglib.tld) file in the META-INF subdirectory, along with the appropriate implementing classes and other resources required to implement the tags defined therein.

JSP custom tags define actions in a manner that is accessible to tools as well as developers. The official way to deliver a tag library to a tool that can use it is to place it as a JAR file in the TOMCAT_HOME\lib folder. A JSP container, such as Tomcat, can also use tag libraries by finding the appropriate implementing classes in its default or other class locations and locating the tag library descriptor file in a default or other configurable location.

10.1.7 Taglib Directives

A JSP directive is a type of element that provides global information to the JSP container. Being global, it applies for all the requests that the JSP will service. Most directive information is useful to the container at page translation or compilation time. The syntax of a directive is as follows:

```
<%@ directive { attr="value" }* %>
```

The curly brackets and the asterisk simply mean that 0 to *N* attributes may be present. There may be optional whitespace after `<%@` and before `%>`.

A taglib directive in a JSP document links it to an XML document that describes a set of custom JSP tags and determines which tag-handler class implements the action of each tag. Here is an example of a taglib directive, taken from the Jakarta-taglibs project:

```
<%@ taglib uri="http://jakarta.apache.org/taglibs/datetime-1.0" prefix="dt" %>
```

Here is another taglib directive, the one used by the bonForum Web application:

```
<%@ taglib uri="http://www.bonForum.org/taglib/bonForum-taglib-0.5"
prefix="bon" %>
```

A taglib directive uses a URI to uniquely identify a tag library to the JSP container (in our case, Tomcat). The directive also tells the JSP container something important: the prefix that the tags in the library will use on this particular JSP document. The given prefix must appear before the tag name that appears in the descriptor file. You can see an example of a prefix in use in section 10.1.9, "Tag Library Descriptor File." Prefixes enable you to use tags from different tag libraries without problems arising from clashing names. You use different prefixes (of your choice) in the taglib directives for different libraries on the same JSP.

10.1.8 Taglib Element in Web App Descriptor

The container uses the URI in the taglib directive to locate an XML file containing the tag library descriptor. Although a relative URI can be used to locate that file, the preferred method is the use of a taglib element in the Web application descriptor file (WEB-INF\web.xml). The next listing shows the taglib element for the bonForum Web app. It maps the URI from the bonForum taglib directive shown previously to the bonForum tag library descriptor file. Note that the filename in the URI and for the file need not be the same. Here is the bonForum taglib element:

```
<taglib>
    <taglib-uri>
        http://www.bonForum.org/taglib/bonForum-taglib-0.5
    </taglib-uri>
    <taglib-location>
       /WEB-INF/jsp/bonForum-taglib-0.5.tld
    </taglib-location>
</taglib>
```

10.1.9 Tag Library Descriptor File

We sometimes refer to the tag library descriptor file as a TLD file, or as a .tld file, after its conventional file extension. This XML file contains information for the JSP container about a set of tags that can appear in the JSP. To be a TLD file, an XML file needs to have the right `DOCTYPE` declaration at the beginning, after the usual XML declaration, as follows:

```
<?xml version="1.0" encoding="ISO-8859-1" ?>
<!DOCTYPE taglib
    PUBLIC "-//Sun Microsystems, Inc.//DTD JSP Tag Library 1.1//EN"
    "http://java.sun.com/j2ee/dtds/web-jsptaglibrary_1_1.dtd">
```

The root of the TLD XML document is a taglib element. It contains child elements to contain the versions of the tag library and the minimum JSP version that it requires. There are also elements for a short name, a URI, and an "info" string for the tag library. Also in the XML, and the reason for its existence, are tag elements for each JSP custom action in the library.

The tag elements contain different types of elements to describe aspects of each action tag, including its name, its tag-handler class, information about what the tag body can contain, information about any attributes it uses, and more. One way to get the whole picture in an official way, is to look at the DTD defining the JavaServer Pages 1.1 tag library descriptor (.tld) (XML) file. We found a copy of it in the file TOMCAT_HOME\src\org\apache\jasper\resources\web-jsptaglib_1_1.dtd.

10.1.10 Empty Custom Tag Without Attributes

Let's look next at a very simple custom tag. The tag library corresponding to the first taglib directive shown in Section 10.1.6, "Tag Libraries"), describes an action for a tag named `currenttime`. That description is in the following XML element in the TLD file:

```
<tag>
<name>
currenttime
</name>
<tagclass>
org.apache.taglibs.datetime.CurrentTimeTag
</tagclass>
<bodycontent>
empty
</bodycontent>
<info>
Gets the current time in milliseconds since Jan 1, 1970 GMT.
</info>
</tag>
```

The info tag should tell you what action to expect from adding the tag to a JSP. In any page that contains the `datetime` taglib directive that we showed previously, each of the action elements belonging to the datetime tag library must appear with a "dt" prefix, as follows:

```
<dt:currenttime/>
```

A JSP custom tag can hardly get any simpler than this example. As you see in the tag element in the TLD file for the `currenttime` action, this tag has an empty body content. That is equivalent to having a body with nothing in it; note that because whitespace here is ignored, the last tag example can also be written on a JSP using both a start tag and an end tag, without element content, like this:

```
<dt:currenttime>
</dt:currenttime/>
```

Custom tags take on more complex actions in two ways:

- Using attributes to pass information from the JSP to the Tag Handler class
- Processing body content, whatever is between the start tag and the end tag

We will illustrate both of these mechanisms in the descriptions of the bonForum tags in Section 10.2, "bonForum Tag Library."

10.1.11 Custom Tag Attributes

Custom tags can have zero to many attributes, which are in the familiar name-value pairs format, separated by whitespace, and appear after the tag name, like this:

```
<mylib:mytag attr1="value1" attr2="value2"/>
```

Attributes provide a way for the custom tag user to pass information into the Tag Handler class at request time. Note also that if a custom tag attribute is given a name of "id," then it is special. If a tag with this ID attribute creates a runtime object, that object can be identified to other tags, for example, by the value of that attribute (see Section 10.1.12, "Custom Tag with Body Content").

Here is an example of a custom tag with attributes, one we used to test Xalan-Java 2 with its birds example files:

```
<bon:transform type="xalanVersion"
inXML="..\\webapps\\bonForum\\mldocs\\birds.xml"
inXSL="..\\webapps\\bonForum\\mldocs\\birds.xsl"
outDoc="..\\webapps\\bonForum\\mldocs\\birds.html"> </bon:transform>
```

All four attributes in this example are required because of the way they are described in the TLD (and because the Tag Handler class needs them). Another tag used in bonForum illustrates that this can be otherwise. Here are three different ways to add the `outputDebugInfo` action to a JSP in bonForum:

```
<bon:outputDebugInfo type="init"/>
<bon:outputDebugInfo/>
<bon:outputDebugInfo force="yes"/>
```

To coordinate the Tag Handler of a tag that has attributes with the JSP document and its container, we need to add some attribute elements to the tag element in the TLD file. Abbreviating the actual info element content for simplicity, the `outputDebugInfo` tag element in the bonForum TLD file is as follows:

```
<tag>

<name>
outputDebugInfo
</name>
<tagclass>
de.tarent.forum.OutputDebugInfoTag
</tagclass>
<bodycontent>
JSP
</bodycontent>
<info>
Outputs debug information.
</info>
<attribute>
<name>type</name>
<required>false</required>
</attribute>
```

```
<attribute>
<name>force</name>
<required>false</required>
</attribute>
</tag>
```

10.1.12 Custom Tag with Body Content

Anything besides comments and ignorable whitespace that appears between the start and end tags of an action element is referred to as "body content." A tag can be designed to ignore such content or to include it in the JSP output. Alternatively, the tag handler class can process, or "manipulate," the body content. The possible effects of that upon the JSP runtime result are endless. For example, the body content can be read as a string and used by the tag class. Another possibility is for the tag class to create entirely new content based on the existing body content and then append it to the output stream of the JSP. In a simple case, the tag can simply validate the body content and optionally include it in the output. In the next section, we show an example that is at the more complex end of the spectrum.

The content of a custom action element can be simple text, as shown here using the log tag featured in the Tomcat JSP examples, which you can try from its index HTML page:

```
<eg:log>
Remember to check for new release of bonForum!
</eg:log>
```

You can do much more with body content made up of JSP actions, scriptlets, and expressions, or of XML, HTML, or anything that JSP allows.

10.1.13 Nested Custom Tags

Of particular importance is the fact that you can nest JSP custom tags within other JSP custom tags. You can design such nested tags so that they share a context and a design. The inner tags can find the Tag Handler class instances representing the outer tags, and they can share variable data from these enclosing tags. Various Tag Handler classes can work in concert. A tree of nested tags can accomplish a coordinated custom action, much as many HTML tags do (such as form element tags). Our book project does not use any nested tags yet, but this is an important topic that you should not ignore.

We will illustrate the richness that markup in body content makes possible by reproducing here a complete example JSP from the Jakarta Taglib Project. The example is provided under the Apache Software License which is reproduced in Appendix B, "Some Copyrights and Licenses." It is quite valuable to download the Jakarta Taglib Project. You can find links to it at the Apache XML Web site `http://xml.apache.org/`. It is also included on this book's CD-ROM.

The Taglib Project download is also available from the Sun Developer Connection Web site (www.sun.com/developers/). After installing the download, you can find the following SQL tag library example in something like the file C:\jakarta-taglibs\sql\examples\web\test.jsp.

Using the SQL and other tag libraries, you can learn more about JSP custom tags than we could ever cover in this chapter. By the way, an appendix of the JSP 1.1 specification also features SQL tags as an example. Here is the JSP file we mentioned, showing nested tags with body content:

```
<%@ taglib uri="http://jakarta.apache.org/taglibs/sql-1.0" prefix="sql" %>

<html>
<head>
<title>Examples of JSPSPEC SQL Tag Library Tag Usage</title>
</head>
<body bgcolor="white">

<sql:connection id="conn1" >
  <sql:dburl><%= request.getParameter("dburl") %></sql:dburl>
  <sql:driver><%= request.getParameter("driver") %></sql:driver>
  <sql:userid><%= request.getParameter("userid") %></sql:userid>
  <sql:password><%= request.getParameter("password") %></sql:password>
</sql:connection>

<sql:query id="getBoxen" connection="conn1" visibility="table">
SELECT * FROM <%= request.getParameter("table") %>
<% if( request.getParameter("where") != null && request.getParameter("where") !=
➥"" ) { %>
WHERE <%= request.getParameter("where") %>
<% } %>
</sql:query>

</body>
</html>
```

As you can see, all six custom tags work together to display data from a database using an SQL query. All the tags have body content, which in different places includes text, JSP scriptlets, JSP expressions, and nested tags. We will not discuss the entire SQL tag library, but we will show you the primary mechanism by which the nested tags here work together.

Let's take a look at the `dburl` tag, nested within the `connection` tag. At request time, the expression in the `dburl` tag body was replaced by the value of the `dburl` request parameter, which could be from an HTML form. In the source code for the `dburl` Tag Handler class, `DburlTag.java`, we can find the following:

```
connectionTag.setDburl( bodyContent.getString() );
```

It appears that the `dburl` tag handler is capable of calling a "setter" method on the enclosing connection tag's handler, to set its `dburl` property to the body content of the dburl tag (that is, the request parameter value). But how does the dburl tag handler find the connection tag handler? It uses the findAncestorWithClass() method of the TagSupport class. This is a mechanism of choice in the nested-tag arsenal of the JSP taglib API:

```
ConnectionTag connectionTag = (ConnectionTag) TagSupport.findAncestorWithClass(
➥this, org.apache.taglibs.sql.ConnectionTag.class );
```

Another important mechanism for nesting JSP tags is provided by the BodyContent class, which allows each nesting level to have its own JspWriter object, with the JSP container taking care of a runtime execution stack of such objects. We will return to that topic in the section "The *BodyContent* Class and Body Content Processing."

Also important to the nesting capability of JSP tags is the parent property of the Tag interface, which is what makes nesting possible. If a tag is nested in another, the child tag gets this property set to its parent very soon after being instantiated in the JSP servlet's _jspService() method. Only the pageContext property is set before that.

10.1.14 Tomcat's Not-so-Simple *SimpleTag*

For an overview of how custom tags work in JSP and of what you must do to get custom tags to do something, you can study the SimpleTag example provided in the Tomcat 3.1 distribution. In fact, the example is not such a simple tag; it illustrates quite a few aspects of custom tags. The tag in the example, called foo, creates in the HTML produced by a JSP an unordered list element whose list items contain the values of the attributes of the tag itself. Studying all the files involved with this example tag will help you to understand how the tag works.

With Tomcat running, you should be able to try the simple tag example, either by finding it from the Tomcat default index.html page or by requesting it directly using something like the URL http://localhost:8080/examples/jsp/simpletag/foo.jsp (depending on your host and port number settings). Look for that JSP file for this simple tag example in a folder with the name TOMCAT_HOME\webapps\examples\jsp\simpletag. The Java source code and compiled class files for this JSP Tag example are found in the folder TOMCAT_HOME\webapps\examples\WEB-INF\classes\examples.

Another vital part of this tag example is the tag library descriptor file for the example Web application, which is an XML document named example-taglib.tld, in the folder TOMCAT_HOME\webapps\examples\WEB-INF\jsp.

10.2 The bonForum Tag Library

After the basic information about JSP tag libraries covered in the first part of this chapter, you should be more than ready to understand the rest of the chapter, which concentrates on the bonForum tag library developed to explore the use of custom tags in building a browser interface for a multiuser Web application. Of course, you have already seen and read about the bonForum tags from several perspectives, including the more historical presentation of the application design considerations, the JSP page descriptions, and the discussions of the various bean methods invoked by the various tag handlers to provide content for their actions to display on a browser page. Because some of the tags to be discussed use similar methods and techniques, we will try to avoid repetitive discussion by first covering topics that apply to more than one tag and then discussing only what is unique about each tag.

We would like to point out here that these tags, and the methods underlying their functionality, owe a debt to the generosity of open source developers, especially of those contributing to the Apache Software Foundation's Jakarta Tomcat and Apache XML projects. The `normalize()` method that we grabbed from open source is covered by the Apache License reproduced in Appendix B. But, as helpful as a ready-made method or two might be, what really helps is to see lots of working code, the kind where the details were really sweated over. It gives something that no simple tutorial examples can give. A favorite book of ours was the complete source code for CP/M. It is in that spirit that we will include lots of source code in this chapter.

10.2.1 Tag Library Descriptor for BonForum

The Tag Library Descriptor for the bonForum Web application is in the file TOMCAT_HOME\webapps\bonForum\WEB-INF\jsp\bonForum-taglib.tld. You can also find the contents of that file reproduced in Appendix C, "Source Code for bonForum Web Application." Of course, it might have other tags added to it soon, so check the bonForum Web site for later releases.

10.2.2 Custom JSP Tags Available in bonForum

Table 10.1 shows the custom tags that are currently available in bonForum:

Table 10.1 **Available JSP Custom Tags in bonForum**

Tag	Functionality
`outputDebugInfo`	Used only for debugging Web applications. Outputs values of request headers and parameters, servlet context init parameters, and attribute values in all scopes (page, request, session, and application).
`outputPathNames`	Outputs all successive sorted node paths from a `bonForumXML` or `bonBufferXML` subtree.
`outputChatMessages`	Outputs sequential chat messages from `bonForumXML` or `bonBufferXML`.
`transform`	XML + XSL = XML | HTML applied by Xalan XSLT processor to a file or to `bonForumXML`. Output is a file or a string page attribute.
`noCacheHeader`	Sets headers in the response object to prevent browsers from caching the result of requesting a JSP.

The first four tags are used in bonForum and will be discussed in detail later in this chapter in individual sections named after each tag. The `noCacheHeader` tag is in the project by permission of Perry Tew, its author, who suggested its use in the place of the `BonForumRobot` timestamp suffixes, to prevent caching on browsers from interfering with page refreshes. Unfortunately, we have not yet found a place to place the tag where it could accomplish that function. Perhaps a reader can provide that solution.

10.2.3 Finding Bean Methods from JSP Tags

In Section 8.2.11, "Invoking Chat Methods from BonForumEngine" in Chapter 8, we discussed the methods of the nonvisual JavaBean class `BonForumStore`, used by the custom JSP actions in bonForum. It is very useful to be able to execute methods on a server-side bean from Tag Handler classes, and there are different ways to manage that. A bean can even be made into a tag handler itself, simply by implementing the `Tag` interface. We make our bean available to the tags by setting a reference to it in an attribute of the `ServletContext` (application) object. We have shown elsewhere how we set that attribute, but perhaps a brief overview here will be convenient.

The bean whose methods we want to invoke from Tag Handler classes is a special case: There is only one instance of the `BonForumStore` class, called `bonForumStore`, that is a static member of the `BonForumEngine` servlet. We use the `getBonForumStore()` method of `BonForumEngine` to get `bonForumStore` and then set it in an application attribute. This happens in the `processRequest()` method of `BonForumEngine`, as shown in the following code. This sets the attribute only if it is not there already:

```
Object temp = getServletContext( ).getAttribute( "bonForumStore" );
if(temp == null) {
getServletContext( ).setAttribute( "bonForumStore", getBonForumStore() );
}
```

We also must be able to get the `bonForumStore` application attribute from inside the tag-handler classes for the `outputPathNames`, `outputChatMessages`, and transform tags. We do that only once per Tag Handler class using a static variable and the method `findBonForumStore()`, which is defined in handler classes for each of these tags and is shown in the following excerpt. Of course, we can then invoke any available `BonForumStore` methods to support these custom tag actions. Here is the declaration of the object variable and the method that turns it into a reference to the database wrapper:

```
private static BonForumStore bonForumStore = null;

private void findBonForumStore() {
if(bonForumStore == null) {
if ( pageContext.getServletContext( ).getAttribute( "bonForumStore" ) != null) {
bonForumStore = (BonForumStore)( pageContext.getServletContext( ).getAttribute(
➥"bonForumStore" ));
}
else {
```

```
log("err", "ERROR? OutputPathNamesTag DID NOT GET bonForumStore. Session ID:" +
➥pageContext.getSession( ).getId( ));
}
}
}
```

10.2.4 Using *TreeMap* for Sorted Output

Two of the bonForum custom tags, `outputPathNames` and `outputChatMessages`, get some string results returned from a `BonForumStore` method in a `TreeMap` object. They then use an iterator to process the items in the `TreeMap` object. We will discuss the use of `TreeMap` once here instead of twice later, where these tags are discussed.

Using `TreeMap` is an easy way to provide a sorted list of strings. Each tag handler for the two tags involved here declares a `TreeMap` as follows:

```
TreeMap outputTable = null;
Iterator iterator = null;
```

At first, we worried about using instance variables here. Wouldn't that be dangerous in a multithreaded situation? Also, `TreeMap` and `Iterator` are not synchronized—wouldn't we have to do something about that?

First, we do need to have access to the `outputTable` object from two different methods in the Tag Handler class: `doInitBody()` and `doAfterBody()`. For that reason, we could not create a local `TreeMap` variable inside a method, but we had to declare it outside of both methods as an instance variable of the Tag Handler class.

Second, the `TreeMap` instance on the `bonForumStore` bean does need to be synchronized because it is created new as a local method variable for each thread.

Third, the situation is not as dangerous as it looks. When a JSP with the tag is translated into a Java source file by the JSP container, the Tag Handler class is instantiated within a `_jspService()` method in a servlet. If you have requested any JSP with a custom tag in it, you can see that for yourself by finding its translated JSP Java servlet source file in the Tomcat work folder. For example, if you have already started a chat in bonForum, view the Java work file for the JSP visitor_starts_chat_frame.jsp.

It will have one of those long, funny-looking filenames, but you can find all the words of the JSP filename in its name and a .java file extension. You should find it in something like the folder TOMCAT_HOME\work\localhost_8080%2FbonForum, (depending on your server and port, and work folder configuration).

Look inside the `service` method, which starts like this:

```
public void _jspService(HttpServletRequest request, HttpServletResponse response)
throws IOException, ServletException {
```

Find the statement that looks like this:

```
de.tarent.forum.OutputPathNamesTag _jspx_th_bon_outputPathNames_0 = new
➥de.tarent.forum.OutputPathNamesTag();
```

Each thread executing the code in the `service` method is getting its own instance of the Tag Handler class. So, only one thread will be accessing the instance variables within that instance. Our `outputTable` and iterator do not need to be thread-safe after all!

In fact, for the same reason the tag attribute property variables in a tag handler class are safe for each thread. Clearly, a tag would have to be thread-safe to be useful. It does help to understand why they are safe, however.

10.2.5 Static Variables of Tag Handler Classes

The static class variables within our Tag Handler are a different story! Only one copy of these exists for all the instances of the Tag Handler class. We have some in our Tag Handler classes, defined like this:

```
private static BonForumStore bonForumStore = null;
private static boolean loggingInitialized = false;
private static BonLogger logOCMT = null;
private static String logging = null;
```

That means that every Tag Handler instance is getting access to the same object here. These are shared objects, so we need to consider synchronization if more than one thread is going to change their value. The first question, in a situation like this, should be: Do we need to share these at all?

The `bonForumStore` object wraps our database, and obviously all threads need access to that. We certainly do not want a copy of the database for each thread, so that must be shared. In the prototype bonForum, the database is a `ForestHashtable`, which extends the `Hashtable` class, which is synchronized (thread-safe) already. But `ForestHashtable` also uses other `Hashtable` objects to cash some keys, so we have added our own synchronization to the add, edit, and delete methods of `ForestHashtable` so that the entire transaction involving all its `Hashtables` is also thread-safe.

In a later version of bonForum, `BonForumStore` will be a database connection pool, handing out available JDBC connections to an SQL database. That setup will be thread-safe by virtue of the database application at the other end of the connections.

10.2.6 Initializing the *BonLogger* Object

Now for the other three static variables, which all deal with logging output from the tag-handler classes. The `BonLogger` class just writes strings out to standard out, error out, and a log file for each class. We certainly do not want a different log file for each session. And there is only one `out` and one `err`. So, we want one static `BonLogger` instance per Tag Handler class, and it will be shared. It is thread-safe because `PrintWriter`, `System.out`, and `System.err` are thread-safe, as well as because of the way it is created.

For each Tag Handler class, one static BonLogger instance is created by the first thread that "fires" the tag on any JSP in the Web application. It happens as the first tag attribute is being set (we make sure that it is a required attribute). Here is the code:

```
public void setType(String value) {
if(!loggingInitialized) {
logging = pageContext.getServletContext( ).getInitParameter( "Logging" );
logTT = new BonLogger( "TransformTagLog.txt", logging );
loggingInitialized = true;
System.err.println( "TransformTag init logging:" + logging);
}

[rest of method left out here...]

}
```

Is there a chance that more than one BonLogger instance gets created? If that mattered, we could synchronize the block of code shown. But when you are first starting up the Web application, you should visit every page so that it gets compiled (unless it is all compiled in a JAR). That means that there will most likely be only one thread accessing each tag handler class that first time. Also, if two BonLogger instances were created before one thread locks the block with the static flag, that should be innocuous: One gets garbage-collected as an orphan, and the other gets the static variable.

10.2.7 Using *TagExtraInfo* for Scripting Variables

As you can see wherever we use them, three of the bonForum tags, outputPathNames, outputChatMessages, and transform, use a variable named output. It appears within a JSP expression in the body content of the tag, as in this example, where the expression appears between HTML option elements:

```
<option><%= output %></option>
```

You can find that example in the JSP visitor_starts_chat_frame.jsp.

That expression results in the value of the output variable appearing in the HTML produced by the JSP. You might have looked in vain for the place where the output variable was defined. We will discuss how it comes to exist once here, instead of doing it three times later (once for each tag that uses it).

The trick involved here is a bonForum class so small that we might as well list the entire source here:

```
package de.tarent.forum;
import javax.servlet.jsp.tagext.*;
public class BonForumTagExtraInfo extends TagExtraInfo {
    public VariableInfo[] getVariableInfo(TagData data) {
        return new VariableInfo[] {
            new VariableInfo("output",
                             "String",
                             true,
```

```
                    VariableInfo.NESTED),
        };
    }
}
```

As you see, we extend TagExtraInfo. That means that the JSP container will be capable of using this class at translation or compilation time to get information about variables that are used in the Web application. It will assume as it translates the tag that these variables are available as page attributes. Later, when we look at the translated Java code for a Tag Handler instance, you can see where the value of the attribute is "loaded" into a local variable for use by the tag processing.

In our case, we have only one such scripting variable, and it is a String, so this is an extremely simple use of the class. The last argument of the VariableInfo constructor is the scope that you want the variable to have. It can be AT_BEGIN, AT_END, or NESTED. AT_BEGIN means that the variable with be available from the doBeginTag() method onward to the end of page processing. AT_END means that the variable appears in the doEndTag() method. NESTED variables are defined only while the tag is being processed. If you use a value other than NESTED for a tag, you will not be able to put that tag on the same page twice because you will get an exception when the container tries to create a variable that exists. Also, consider synchronization issues with such variables.

We leave it up to you to further explore TagExtraInfo use. You can see another example of TagExtraInfo use in the SQL tag library that we discussed in Section 10.1.13, "Nested Custom Tags." The variables declared here, of course, could be other classes besides String. When you put that together with the fact that the compiler can check that they exist at translation time, you can see that this mechanism adds great potential to JSP tag libraries.

To use the TagExtraInfo class, we had to do one more thing besides compile the class. That was to add a line to the tag element in the TLD file for the bonForum tag library, as in the following abbreviated listing of one example:

```
<tag>
<name>
outputPathNames
</name>
<tagclass>
de.tarent.forum.OutputPathNamesTag
</tagclass>
<teiclass>
de.tarent.forum.BonForumTagExtraInfo
</teiclass>
<bodycontent>
JSP
</bodycontent>
[info and attribute elements omitted for brevity]
</tag>
```

The `teiclass` element tells the JSP container about our `TagExtraInfo` descendant class, which tells the container about our `output` variable.

What does the container do with that information? Again, the best way to answer questions like this is to look at the translated JSP file—that is, the corresponding Java servlet source file in the Tomcat work folder. The next listing shows the result seen there, having a `TEI` class and the TLD tag element as shown previously, and the example body content shown at the beginning of this section:

```
do {
    String output = null;
    output = (String) pageContext.findAttribute("output");
    out.write("\r\n\t\t<option>");
    out.print( output );
    out.write("</option>\r\n\t");
} while (_jspx_th_bon_outputPathNames_0.doAfterBody() == BodyTag.EVAL_BODY_TAG);
```

We have simplified this excerpt greatly to show only the relevant statements. Also, all we are showing here is the loop that iterates the `doAfterBody` method in the tag handler. The `output` page attribute is what is called a scripting variable. The code inside the `do` block is what is referred to often in the documentation by phrases such as "the tag handler evaluates the body content into the existing output stream of the JSP." The HTML option tag and the JSP expression with the output scripting variable are the body content here, and the `out.write` and `out.print` method invocations are processing the body content. You can find this excerpt in a container translation of the same JSP file that we used as an example in the last section (after you requested that JSP at least once while using the Web app): visitor_starts_chat_frame.jsp.

What we have, in this case, is just a fancy way of using a `page` attribute. It is informative to look at the translated JSP. That is how we realized that we could do the following `page` attribute setting, in the `outputPathNames` tag handler class, inside the `doAfterBody()` method:

```
if(iterator.hasNext()) {
pageContext.setAttribute( "output", (String)iterator.next() );
return EVAL_BODY_TAG;
}
else {
bodyContent.writeOut( bodyContent.getEnclosingWriter());
return SKIP_BODY;
}
```

But, wait! Instead of going to all the trouble of setting up the output `variable` with the `TagExtraInfo` class and the TLD file, why not just do something like this in our tag handler class:

```
bodyContent.println( "<option>" + (String)iterator.next() + "</option>");
```

The answer is that we *could* do that. If so, then we would also want to print the `<select>` and `</select>` tags in the `doInitBody()` and `doAfterBody()` methods. We would lose the flexibility of being able to use the same tag to get different results. For example, with the `output` variable, we could create something besides a select list by using a tag something like this:

```
<ul>
<prefix:tagname attr="value">
<li><%= output %></li>
<prefix:tagname>
</ul>
```

Perhaps most importantly, we would lose this opportunity to play with the `TagExtraInfo` class. We demystified it in the playing more than its sparse documentation ever could. But using the scripting variable causes extra string copying and attribute setting to happen. That is probably too expensive, especially with many threads in a chat, so it could be argued that we should get rid of the `output` variable and write the new body content directly from the tag handler methods involved.

Better yet is to make both behaviors into available options based on the value of an attribute. In fact, we have already done that with the `TransformTag` tag handler class, as you shall see when we discuss its output in section 10.6, "XSLT and the `TransformTag` Class."

10.3 The *OutputDebugInfoTag* Class

As mentioned in Table 10.1, the `outputDebugInfo` action is used to provide information via the browser display during the development of Web applications. It can also serve as an educational tool. To turn on the debug output, simply enter the system commands state of bonForum from the main entrance. If the check box is checked and the Set button is clicked, you will see the debug information there and in succeeding pages visited. We have put the `outputDebugInfo` tag on every JSP that displays anything in bonForum.

You might notice that as it stands today, this tag did not really need to implement BodyTag (by extending `BodyTagSupport`). It could have gotten the information that it displays and used the `JspWriter` (out) to add it to the JSP output, instead of using the `BodyContent` writer object. The body content processing support was added to the tag to provide more potential for future expansion of this tag.

10.3.1 The *outputDebugInfo* Descriptor

The following listing shows the `Tag` element in the bonForum TLD that describes the `outputDebugInfo` custom action tag:

```
<!-- outputDebugInfo tag -->
<tag>
  <name>outputDebugInfo</name>
  <tagclass>de.tarent.forum.OutputDebugInfoTag</tagclass>
  <bodycontent>JSP</bodycontent>
  <info>
    Outputs request header and parameter values.
```

```
    Outputs attributes values for all scopes.
    Attribute type="init" turns tags on for entire
      session,  if a request parameter exists called
      "output_debug_info" with a value of "yes".
      Afterwards, a tag but no attribute
      is required to output debug info on page.
    Attribute type="init" turns tags off,
      if no request parameter exists called
      "output_debug_info" that is equal to "yes".
    Attribute force ="yes" turns that tag on only.
  </info>
  <attribute>
    <name>type</name>
    <required>false</required>
  </attribute>
  <attribute>
    <name>force</name>
    <required>false</required>
  </attribute>
</tag>
```

The text in the `info` element should be sufficient to tell you how the tag behaves in a JSP. Instead of repeating all that, we will describe how the tag accomplishes that behavior.

10.3.2 The *outputDebugInfo* Tag Handler

The following listing shows the source code, stripped of lots of its javadoc comments, for the `OutputDebugInfoTag` class:

```
package de.tarent.forum;

import java.util.*;
import javax.servlet.http.*;
import javax.servlet.jsp.*;
import javax.servlet.jsp.tagext.*;

/** Tag Handler outputs debugging info.
  */
public class OutputDebugInfoTag
        extends BodyTagSupport {
    private static BonLogger logODI = null;
    private static boolean loggingInitialized = false;
    private static String logging = null;
    private String type="";
    private String force="";

    private void log( String where, String what ) {
        if( logging != null ) {
            logODI.logWrite( System.currentTimeMillis( ), pageContext.getSession(
➥).getId( ), where, what );
```

```
        }
    }

    /** Sets value of the type attribute,
      * and initializes logging once.
      */
    public void setType( String value ) {

        if( !loggingInitialized ) {
            logging = pageContext.getServletContext( ).getInitParameter( "Logging"
➥);
            logODI = new BonLogger( "OutputDebugInfoTagLog.txt", logging );
            loggingInitialized = true;
            System.err.println( "OutputDebugInfoTag init logging:" + logging );
        ➥}

        if ( value.equals( null )) {
            value = "";
        }
        type = value;
    }

    /** Sets value of the force attribute.
      */
    public void setForce( String value ) {
        if ( value.equals( null ) ) {
            value = "";
        }
        force = value;
    }

    /** Sets "output_debug_info" request parameter
      * value to session attribute
      * @returns EVAL_BODY_TAG
      * constant that causes tag body to be evaluated.
      */
    public int doStartTag( )
            throws JspException {
        if( type.equals( "init" ) ) {
            if( pageContext.getRequest( ).getParameter( "output_debug_info" ) !=
➥null ) {
                if( ( ( String )( pageContext.getRequest( ).getParameter(
➥"output_debug_info" ) ) ).equals( "yes" ) ) {
                    pageContext.setAttribute( "output_debug_info", "yes", 4 );
                      ➥// 4 is application scope
                }
            }
            else {
                pageContext.setAttribute( "output_debug_info", "no", 4 );
            }
        }
```

```
        if( force.equals( "yes" ) ) {
            return EVAL_BODY_TAG;
        }
        if( pageContext.getAttribute( "output_debug_info", 4 ) != null ) {
            if( ( ( String )( pageContext.getAttribute( "output_debug_info", 4 ) )
➥).equals( "yes" ) ) {
                return EVAL_BODY_TAG;
            }
        }
        return SKIP_BODY;
    }

    /** Outputs values of headers, parameters,
      * attributes, etc. and ends tag processing.
      * @returns SKIP_BODY  constant that causes
      * tag body to NOT be evaluated (again)
      */
    public int doAfterBody( )
            throws JspException, JspTagException {
        try {
            HttpServletRequest req = ( HttpServletRequest )
➥pageContext.getRequest( );

            bodyContent.println( "<H4>Request Headers: </H4>" );
            Enumeration eh = req.getHeaderNames( );
            while( eh.hasMoreElements( ) ) {
                String name = ( String )eh.nextElement( );
                String value = ( String ) req.getHeader( name );
                bodyContent.println( "\t<li>" + normalize( name ) + " = " +
➥normalize( value ) + "</li>" );
            }

            bodyContent.println( "<H4>Request Parameters: </H4>" );
            Enumeration ep = req.getParameterNames( );
            while( ep.hasMoreElements( ) ) {
                    String name = ( String ) ep.nextElement( );
                    String value = ( String ) req.getParameter( name );
                    bodyContent.println( "\t<li>" + normalize( name ) + " = " +
➥normalize( value ) + "</li>" );
            }

            bodyContent.println( "<H4>Application Initialization Parameters:
➥</H4>" );
            Enumeration eip = pageContext.getServletContext(
➥).getInitParameterNames( );
            while( eip.hasMoreElements( ) ) {
                    String name = ( String ) eip.nextElement( );
                    String value = ( String ) pageContext.getServletContext(
➥).getInitParameter( name );
                    bodyContent.println( "\t<li>" + normalize( name ) + " = " +
➥normalize( value ) + "</li>" );
```

```
            }

            int scope;
            String title = null;
            for( scope = 4; scope >= 1; scope-- ) {
                switch( scope ) {
                case 1:
                    title = "Page Attributes:";
                    break;
                case 2:
                    title = "Request Attributes:";
                    break;
                case 3:
                    title = "Session Attributes:";
                    break;
                case 4:
                    title = "Application Attributes:";
                    break;
                }
                bodyContent.println( "<H4>" + title + "</H4>" );
                Enumeration ea = pageContext.getAttributeNamesInScope( scope );
                    ➥while(ea.hasMoreElements( )) {
                        String name = ( String ) ea.nextElement( );
                        String value = ( String ) pageContext.getAttribute( name,
➥scope ).toString( );
                        bodyContent.println( "\t<li>" + normalize( name ) + " = "
➥+ normalize( value ) + "</li>" );
                    }
            }

            bodyContent.writeOut( bodyContent.getEnclosingWriter( ) );
            return SKIP_BODY;
        }
        catch( java.io.IOException ex ) {
            log( "err", "OutputDebugInfoTag doInitBody caught IOException" );
            throw new JspTagException( "OutputDebugInfoTag doInitBody caught
➥IOException" );
        }
    }

    /** Normalizes the given string,
      * replacing chars with entities.
      * NOTE: replaces null string with empty string.
      * Based on Apache Software Foundation sample!
      */
    protected String normalize(String s) {
        StringBuffer str = new StringBuffer();
        str.append("");
        int len = (s != null) ? s.length() : 0;
        for (int i = 0; i < len; i++) {
            char ch = s.charAt(i);
```

```
            switch (ch) {
                case '<': {
                    str.append("&lt;");
                    break;
                }
                case '>': {
                    str.append("&gt;");
                    break;
                }
                case '&': {
                    str.append("&amp;");
                    break;
                }
                case '"': {
                    str.append("&quot;");
                    break;
                }
                case '\r':
                case '\n': {
                    str.append("&#");
                    str.append(Integer.toString(ch));
                    str.append(';');
                    break;
                }
                default: {
                    str.append(ch);
                }
            }
        }
        return str.toString();
    }
}
```

Code common to more than one Tag Handler class was already explained. For that, refer to Section 10.2.3, "Finding Bean Methods from JSP Tags"; Section 10.2.5, "Static Variables of Tag-Handler Classes"; and Section 10.2.6, "Initializing the `BonLogger` Object." With the help of those sections and Section 10.3.1, "The `outputDebugInfo` Descriptor," most of the code in this class should be quite simple to follow. Here we will discuss only a few highlights.

10.3.3 Attribute-Setter Methods

As you see, each tag attribute is represented by a private variable with a public `setter` method in the Tag Handler bean. These two property methods, `setType()` and `setForce()`, replace any null values with empty strings to simplify code that uses the attributes later. Of course, other argument validation steps are often useful in setter methods.

10.3.4 The *doStartTag()* Method

Notice in the `doStartTag()` method that the `init` attribute turns the tag output on or off. A request parameter named `output_debug_info` with a value of `yes` can turn it on by setting the `output_debug_info` session parameter to `yes`; any other situation turns tag output off by setting the session parameter to `no`. If that session attribute or the `force` attribute has a value of `yes`, then the `doStartTag()` method will return `EVAL_BODY_TAG`; otherwise, the method returns `SKIP_BODY`. These constants determine whether the tag handler executes the methods that process the body content `doInitBody()` and `doAfterBody()` or goes instead directly to the `doEndTag()` method, skipping the body.

10.3.5 The *doAfterBody()* Method

In this tag, we do not need to override the `doInitBody()` method because we can do all our work in the `doAfterBody()` method. (In fact, we could have done all we do in a `doEndTag` method.) You can see now how useful it is that the JSP container gives the `pageContext` object to the Tag Handler instance created within the `_jspService()` method. (You can see where that happens by viewing the Java translation file for any JSP with a custom tag in it, which you find in the Tomcat work folder. We also show it in a listing in Section 10.5.8, "The Translated Tag Handler in a JSP Servlet.")

Looking up the `PageContext` class in the Jakarta servlet API documentation will convince you how much power having the `pageContext` object gives to a Tag Handler class. With that object, the tag action can use all the implied variables of its JSP (`out`, `page`, `request`, `response`, `session`, `application`) and also has access to headers, parameters, attributes, and so on in all Web application scopes. It can participate in the HTTP game, forwarding and including requests. Custom tags can do a lot quite easily. We will return to the discussion of the `pageContext` object after first looking briefly at how the tag handler outputs to the browser.

The *BodyContent* Output Stream

You can see from the code that the `doAfterBody()` method uses the `bodyContent.println()` method to "send" HTML to the browser, as it does first in this statement:

```
bodyContent.println( "<H4>Request Headers: </H4>" );
```

The `BodyContent` class can be confusing at first; we will discuss it more fully in Section 10.5.7, "A Stack of `BodyContent` Writers." For now, just note that, if the tag implements `BodyTag`, you can print to the `BodyContent` output stream and everything will be buffered. The buffer will not autoflush—in fact, you cannot flush it, either. You can discard it or write it into the enclosing writer, which could be the `JspWriter`, if the tag is not nested in another, or it could be another `BodyContent` instance, if the tag does have a parent tag. The `doAfterTag()` method returns `SKIP_BODY` to keep the body content loop from repeating. Before it does that, though, you can see it passing the bodyContent back out.

```
bodyContent.writeOut( bodyContent.getEnclosingWriter( ) );
return SKIP_BODY;
```

The Mighty *pageContext* Object

Way before that, we have some work to do! The method uses the pageContext object to get the implicit request object:

```
HttpServletRequest req = ( HttpServletRequest ) pageContext.getRequest( );
```

It can then output the "header headers" and get the request header names in an enumeration. Then it is easy to enumerate the header names, printing these with the header values in HTML list item element content, as follows:

```
        try {
                bodyContent.println( "<H4>Request Headers: </H4>" );
                Enumeration eh = req.getHeaderNames( );
                while( eh.hasMoreElements( ) ) {
                    String name = ( String )eh.nextElement( );
                    String value = ( String ) req.getHeader( name );
                    bodyContent.println( "\t<li>" + normalize( name ) + " = " +
➥normalize( value ) + "</li>" );
                }
```

That pretty much explains the mechanics of the tag. The rest of the output of information in the doAfterBody() method features some different ways to get stuff to print from the servlet context (application), for example:

```
                        String value = ( String ) pageContext.getServletContext(
➥).getInitParameter( name );
```

Another trick used is a for loop to get the attributes in all four Web application scopes, using the following handy method to get four successive enumerations of attribute names for each scope:

```
                Enumeration ea =
pageContext.getAttributeNamesInScope( scope );
```

Having the attribute names gives the values also, courtesy of yet another pageContext method:

```
                            String value = ( String ) pageContext.getAttribute( name,
➥scope ).toString( );
```

10.4 The *OutputPathNamesTag* Class

In the sections "The outputForumPathNames() Method" and "The outputBufferPathNames() Method" in Chapter 8, we discussed the JavaBean methods created to support the outputPathNames JSP custom tag action.

The `outputPathNames` tag can be seen in use on the JSP page visitor_starts_chat_frame.jsp, which presents the chat visitor with available chat subjects for a new chat. Here is the custom tag as it appears on the JSP:

```
<select size="12" name="chatSubject">
<bon:outputPathNames
docName="bonForumXML"
pathToSubTreeRootNode="bonForum.things.subjects"
ancestorReplacer="COMPLETE_PATHS"
nodeSeparator="/">
<option><%= output %></option>
</bon:outputPathNames>
</select>
```

One of the strengths of custom tags is their reusability. It might seem strange, therefore, that the `outputPathNames` tag is used only in one place in bonForum, to output node paths to chat subject elements from the XML database. The project is a prototype, and so is the tag. The tag design attempts to include features that will make it useful in other situations when hierarchical information kept in XML needs to be transformed into sorted lists of node paths.

We will start by showing the descriptor and the code for the tag. We'll continue with brief discussions of its attributes and methods, and finally we'll include some notes on its design.

10.4.1 The *outputPathNames* Descriptor

The following listing shows the `Tag` element in the bonForum TLD that describes the `outputPathNames` custom action tag:

```
<!-- outputPathNames tag -->
<tag>
  <name>outputPathNames</name>
  <tagclass>de.tarent.forum.OutputPathNamesTag</tagclass>
  <teiclass>de.tarent.forum.BonForumTagExtraInfo</teiclass>
  <bodycontent>JSP</bodycontent>
  <info>
    Outputs pathNames (node paths)
    from subTree of XML tree or forest.
    (Note: ignores chatItem nodes in bonForumXML.)
  </info>
  <attribute>
    <name>docName</name>
    <required>true</required>
  </attribute>
  <attribute>
    <name>pathToSubTreeRootNode</name>
    <required>true</required>
  </attribute>
  <attribute>
```

```
      <name>ancestorReplacer</name>
      <required>true</required>
    </attribute>
    <attribute>
      <name>nodeSeparator</name>
      <required>true</required>
    </attribute>
  </tag>
```

Note that the only attribute that does anything in this book release of bonForum is `docName`.

10.4.2 The *outputPathNames* Tag Handler

The following listing shows the source code for the `OutputPathNamesTag` class (stripped of its Javadoc comments, to save space):

```
package de.tarent.forum;

import java.util.*;
import javax.servlet.jsp.*;
import javax.servlet.jsp.tagext.*;

/** Outputs pathNames from subTree of an XML tree
  * or forest ( except chatItems! )
  */
public class OutputPathNamesTag extends BodyTagSupport
{
    TreeMap outputTable = null;
    Iterator iterator = null;

    private static BonForumStore bonForumStore = null;

    private static BonLogger logOPNT = null;
    private static boolean loggingInitialized = false;
    private static String logging = null;

    private String docName = "";
    private String pathToSubTreeRootNode = "";
    private String ancestorReplacer = "";
    private String nodeSeparator = "";

    private void log( String where, String what ) {
        if( logging != null ) {
            logOPNT.logWrite( System.currentTimeMillis( ), pageContext.getSession(
➥).getId( ), where, what );
        }
    }

    /** locates bonForumStore in application
     */
```

```
    private void findBonForumStore( ) {
        // code omitted here is in appendix,
        // and in Section 10.2.3,
        // "Finding Bean Methods from JSP Tags "
    }

    /** Sets value of the docName attribute;
      * also initializes logging.
      */
    public void setDocName( String value ) {
        if( !loggingInitialized ) {
            logging = pageContext.getServletContext( ).getInitParameter( "Logging"
➥);
            logOPNT = new BonLogger( "OutputPathNamesTagLog.txt", logging );
            ➥loggingInitialized = true;
            System.err.println( "OutputPathNamesTag init logging:" + logging );
        ➥}

        if ( value.equals( null ) ) {
            value = "bonForumXML";
        }
        docName = value;
    }

    /** Sets value of the pathToSubTreeRootNode attribute.
      */
    public void setPathToSubTreeRootNode( String value ) {
        if( value.equals( null ) ) {
            value = "";
        }
        pathToSubTreeRootNode = value;
    }

    /** Sets value of the ancestorReplacer attribute.
      */
    public void setAncestorReplacer( String value ) {
        if( value.equals( null ) ) {
            value = "";
        }
        ancestorReplacer = value;
    }

    /** Sets value of the nodeSeparator attribute.
      */
    public void setNodeSeparator( String value ) {
        if( value.equals( null ) ){
            value = "";
        }
        nodeSeparator = value;
    }
```

```
    /** Makes sure the body of the tag is evaluated.
      */
    public int doStartTag( ) throws JspException {
        return EVAL_BODY_TAG;
    }

    /** Gets bonforumStore,
      * and outputTable with pathnames;
      * gets iterator.and outputs first pathname.
      */
    public void doInitBody( ) throws JspException, JspTagException {

        findBonForumStore( );

        if( bonForumStore != null ) {
            try {
                outputTable = new TreeMap( bonForumStore.outputForumPathNames(
➥docName, pathToSubTreeRootNode, ancestorReplacer, nodeSeparator ) );
                if ( outputTable != null ) {
                    iterator = outputTable.keySet( ).iterator( );
                    if( iterator.hasNext( ) ) {
                        pageContext.setAttribute( "output", ( String
➥)iterator.next( ) );
                    }
                }
            } catch ( Exception ex ) {
                log( "err",  "caught Exception in OutputPathNamesTag doInitBody"
➥);
                throw new JspTagException( "caught Exception in OutputPathNamesTag
➥doInitBody" );
            }
        }
    }

    /** Iterates outputTable into "output" page attribute until done.
      */
    public int doAfterBody( ) throws JspException, JspTagException {
        if( bonForumStore != null && outputTable != null && iterator != null ) {
            ➥try {
                if( iterator.hasNext( ) ) {
                    pageContext.setAttribute( "output", ( String )iterator.next( )
➥);
                    return EVAL_BODY_TAG;
                } else {
                    bodyContent.writeOut( bodyContent.getEnclosingWriter( ) );
                   ➥return SKIP_BODY;
                }
            } catch ( java.io.IOException ex ) {
                log( "err",  "caught IOException in OutputPathNamesTag
➥doAfterBody" );
                throw new JspTagException( "caught IOException in
```

```
➥OutputPathNamesTag doAfterBody" );
            }
        }
        else {
            //log( "",  "ERROR: OutputPathNamesTag doAfterBody no store | no
➥table | no iterator" );
            return SKIP_BODY;
        }
    }
}
```

Code that is common to more than one Tag Handler class was already explained. For that, refer to the following sections:

- Section 10.2.3, "Finding Bean Methods from JSP Tags"
- Section 10.2.4, "Using `TreeMap` for Sorted Output"
- Section 10.2.5, "Static Variables of Tag Handler Classes"
- Section 10.2.6, "Initializing the `BonLogger` Object"
- Section 10.2.7, "Using `TagExtraInfo` for Scripting Variables"

With the help of those sections and Section 10.4.1, "The `outputPathNames` Descriptor," you should be able to follow the code in this class. We will now discuss a few highlights.

The `outputPathNames` Tag Handler class implements the `BodyTag` interface by extending `BodyTagSupport`, which means that it can override the `doInitBody()` and `doAfterBody()` methods and set up a looping construct. It takes advantage of that to output a list of node paths that will contain a variable number of items.

10.4.3 Attribute-Setter Methods

As usual, each tag attribute is represented by a private variable with a public property `setter` method in the tag handler bean. The first property method, `setDocName()`, replaces any null incoming value with a default value so that later code will not have to check for nulls. The other attribute methods involved are `setPathToSubTreeRootNode()`, `setAncestorReplacer()`, and `setNodeSeparator()`. These set nulls to empty strings for now because they are not yet used by the bean method that will someday do so. For the meaning and allowable values of the tag attributes, we refer you to the references given in the first paragraph of Section 10.4, "The `OutputPathNamesTag` Class."

10.4.4 The *doStartTag()* Method

The `doStartTag()` method is overridden only to return `EVAL_BODY_TAG`; otherwise, the method returns `SKIP_BODY`. We want to always execute the methods that process the body content, `doInitBody()` and `doAfterBody()`. This would be the place to switch off these methods, for example, depending upon some state or initialization parameters in the Web application.

10.4.5 The *doInitBody()* Method

The first body content-handling method starts off by making sure that the reference to the `bonForumStore` XML data wrapper object is valid, by calling `findBonForumStore()`. When and if it is valid, the method invokes its `outputForumPathNames` method, passing the tag attributes as arguments. The bean method returns a `TreeMap` object filled with the items to use sequentially for each body content evaluation in the Tag Handler. The `TreeMap` returned is used to create a new one in the Tag Handler. (That a new one is created here might be left over from attempts to use a synchronized `TreeMap` instance variable on the bean. A reference to the local `TreeMap` method variable used on the bean might work now, but it needs to be tested first.)

As an aside, note that the iterator here is of the keys in the `TreeMap` because these contain the sorted node paths to each chat subject node in the XML data. The values in the `TreeMap` object each contain the `nodeKey.aKey` for the node at the end of the path in the key. Perhaps these should be included in the JSP output stream. They would be useful to locate the subject node directly, rather than using a method that takes the node path as an argument.

To return to the business at hand, the `doInitBody()` method continues by setting the first `TreeMap` key value in its iterator (if it is not empty) in the `output` page attribute, which is the scripting variable known to the JSP container at JSP translation time. We could just as easily simply output the key value as a string into the `bodyContent` output stream, which would make it show up on the browser page (after the `bodyContent` was written to the `out JspWriter` of the JSP and was flushed, if necessary). We discuss why that is not done in Section 10.2.7, "Using `TagExtraInfo` for Scripting Variables."

Because we are invoking a bean method that might throw an exception, we put all this in a `try` block. Any exceptions caught cause an entry to the log for the Tag Handler class and result in throwing a new `JspTagException`, passing the buck to the surrounding JSP code, which should display the Web application JSP error page.

10.4.6 The *doAfterBody()* Method

As described in Section 10.1.4, "How Do JSP Custom Tags Work?", the `doAfterBody()` method is invoked after the `doInitBody()` method whenever the Tag Handler class implements the `BodyTag` interface and returns `EVAL_BODY_TAG` from the `doStartTag()` method. When the `doAfterBody()` method is invoked, the body content has already been evaluated into the output stream. Let's see what that means.

In the case of the Tag Handler instance being discussed here, the body content, as shown in Section 10.4, is this:

```
<option><%= output %></option>
```

Therefore, the body content evaluation in the output stream in this instance of the Tag Handler involves execution of the following statements, which appear in the translation of the JSP document into a servlet class source-code file in the Tomcat work folder:

```
String output = null;
output = (String) pageContext.findAttribute("output");
out.write("\r\n\t\t<option>");
out.print( output );
out.write("</option>\r\n\t");
```

Again, these statements have already executed by the time the doAfterBody() method begins. You might well ask what happens if the iterator obtained is empty. The option tag would get a null in it if the page attribute did not exist. We take care of that in a kludgy manner by making sure that no empty TreeMap can be returned at the end of the outputForumPathNames() method in BonForumStore:

```
if(outputTreeMap.size()<1) {
outputTreeMap.put(".", "0");
}
```

Worse yet, the HTML select option might get the last value left over from a previous invocation of the Tag Handler earlier on the same page. That will not happen in this case, where there is no change in output from one outputForumPathNames() method call to the next, but in are general case that could happen. It would be far better to take care of both output problems by initializing the page attribute in the doInitBody() method and resetting it in the doEndTag() method or when the iterator is found empty in the doAfterBody() method. Perhaps when you download a new release of bonForum from the www.bonforum.org Web site we will have made those changes!

Unless the iterator was empty or contained just one value, the doAfterBody() method returns EVAL_BODY_TAG, which ensures that the body content will be evaluated again and that the doAfterBody() method will be invoked again. That loop will continue until the iterator is empty, in which case the doAfterBody() method returns SKIP_BODY, to signal that the looping should end. Before doing that, it writes the buffer contents of the BodyContent non-autoflushing output stream into the enclosing output stream for the tag instance, which in this non-nested tag is the original JspWriter instance out. That ensures that all the hard work of repeatedly evaluating the tag body content will actually reach the JSP client (browser).

The doEndTag() method will be called by the container next. It could be used to do anything that should be done whether doStartTag() returns SKIP_BODY or EVAL_BODY_TAG (or, in the case of a Tag Handler with only a Tag interface, EVAL_BODY_INCLUDE). The doStartTag() method can also be used to return SKIP_PAGE, which terminates the JSP page by executing a return statement from the jspService() method. In our tag, we have not overridden the doEndTag() method, so it returns the default EVAL_PAGE, and the rest of the _jspService() method is executed next.

Because the output stream can throw a `java.io.IOException`, we wrap the processing in a `try` block. If we catch the exception, we log the problem and throw a new `JspTagException`, which will hopefully show up on the JSP error page for the Web application. We should probably also throw a new exception if `bonForumStore`, `outputTable`, or `iterator` is null when `doAfterBody` begins; instead, we just end the body content processing with an unhealthy "it can't happen here" attitude.

10.4.7 Where Is the *OutputTable* Tag?

Software often starts out solving one problem but turns out to have a wider utility. In that case, the software tends to evolve toward a design that can solve the general-case problem. In the case of two of our tag handler classes, `OutputPathNamesTag` and `OutputChatMessagesTag`, the opposite occurred. We began by developing an `OutputTable` tag to solve the general case problem of outputting tables based on XML data. (Actually, as readers of the German version of this book know, it was really an option called `bonOutputTable` of our `ChoiceTag` prototype Tag Handler class.) As it turned out, that tag was never used in the project because the `TransformTag` XSLT solution turned out to be so flexible that it solved the table output problem with far less work and code duplication. (See Section 10.6, "XSLT and the `TransformTag` Class.") Ironically, the `transform` tag itself certainly exemplifies the rule that software evolves toward solving a general problem!

The work we did on `OutputTable` was not wasted, however. What began as an attempt at a general solution ended up being applied to some more specific problems. The code lives on in these two heavily used bonForum Tag Handler classes:

- `OutputForumPathNamesTag`
- `OutputForumChatMessages`

10.4.8 Unique Pathnames for Speed Optimization

If you skipped some chapters, you might wonder how we can be use node paths (pathnames) from an XML document as keys in a `TreeMap` because keys must have unique values. What if there are two sibling nodes with the same name? The answer is that, as an optimization, we built a restriction into the design of the bean method: It can be used only with an XML subtree that has unique node paths starting from the root node of the subtree. We can select the subtree rooted at `bonForum.things.subjects` and know that there are no descendant sibling nodes with the same name. One further assumption was made: It always outputs all the elements in that subtree, including all its leaves.

Why not just use the `TreeMap` values for the pathnames and use the always unique `nodeKey.aKey` values for the keys? Because we used the `TreeMap` to sort the pathnames. To make the tag more widely useable, it does seem now that it would be better to follow this alternative and use a different method (perhaps the `Collections.sort` method) to sort the pathnames for the select list of available chat subjects.

10.5 The *OutputChatMessagesTag* Class

In the sections "The `outputForumChatMessages()` Method" and "The `outputBufferChatMessages()` Method" in Chapter 8, we discussed the JavaBean methods created to support the `outputChatMessages` JSP custom tag action.

The `outputChatMessages` custom action tag can be seen in action (pun intended) on the following two JSPs from the bonForum Web application:

guest_executes_chat_frame.jsp

host_executes_chat_frame.jsp

Here is an excerpt from one of those files, showing the custom action tag being used to display a page full of chat messages from the chat history:

```
<form method="POST"
      action="/bonForum/servlet/BonForumEngine">
<select size="<%= chatMessagesPageSize %>"
      name="chatMessages">
      <font face="Arial Narrow">
      <bon:outputChatMessages
            command="bonForumXML">
            <option><%= output %></option>
      </bon:outputChatMessages>
      </font>
</select>
</form>
```

As do all the bonForum tags that we will discuss, the `outputChatMessages` Tag Handler class implements the `BodyTag` interface by extending `BodyTagSupport`. That means that it can override the `doInitBody()` and `doAfterBody()` methods and set up a looping construct. In this action, that loop is used to output a list of chat messages that will certainly vary in number, even as we display them.

We will once again first show the TLD tag element for this action and then show the edited source code for its Tag Handler class. After that, we discuss attribute and action methods of the Tag Handler class. Then we take a deeper look at what really happens by dissecting some of the code produced by the JSP container when it translates a JSP in which this tag has been used. We wrap up the discussion of this tag with some notes about its design.

10.5.1 The *outputChatMessages* Descriptor

The following listing shows the `Tag` element in the bonForum TLD that describes the `outputChatMessages` custom action tag:

```
<!-- outputChatMessages tag -->
<tag>
  <name>outputChatMessages</name>
  <tagclass>de.tarent.forum.OutputChatMessagesTag</tagclass>
  <teiclass>de.tarent.forum.BonForumTagExtraInfo</teiclass>
```

```
  <bodycontent>JSP</bodycontent>
  <info>
    Outputs chatMessages from subTree of XML tree or forest.
    Attributes are reserved for future use selecting messages.
  </info>
  <attribute>
    <name>command</name>
    <required>true</required>
  </attribute>
  <attribute>
    <name>attr1</name>
    <required>false</required>
  </attribute>
  <attribute>
    <name>attr2</name>
    <required>false</required>
  </attribute>
  <attribute>
    <name>attr3</name>
    <required>false</required>
  </attribute>
</tag>
```

10.5.2 The *outputChatMessages* Tag Handler

The following listing shows the source code, minus its javadoc comments, for the `OutputChatMessagesTag` class:

```
package de.tarent.forum;

import java.util.*;
import javax.servlet.jsp.*;
import javax.servlet.jsp.tagext.*;

/** Outputs chat messages from a bonForum
  * XML Document or ForestHashtable.
  */
public class OutputChatMessagesTag
    extends BodyTagSupport
{
    TreeMap outputTable = null;
    Iterator iterator = null;

    private static BonForumStore bonForumStore = null;

    private static boolean loggingInitialized = false;
    private static BonLogger logOCMT = null;
    private static String logging = null;

    private String command = "";
```

```
    private String attr1 = "";
    private String attr2 = "";
    private String attr3 = "";

    private void log( String where, String what ) {
        if( logging != null ) {
            logOCMT.logWrite( System.currentTimeMillis( ), pageContext.getSession(
).getId( ), where, what );
        }
    }

    /** locates bonForumStore in application
     */
    private void findBonForumStore( ) {
        // code omitted here is in appendix,
        // and similar code is in Section 10.2.3,
        // "Finding Bean Methods from JSP Tags "
    }

    /** Sets value of the command attribute; also initializes logging.
     */
    public void setCommand( String value ) {

        if( !loggingInitialized ) {
            logging = pageContext.getServletContext( ).getInitParameter( "Logging"
➥);
            logOCMT = new BonLogger( "OutputChatMessagesTagLog.txt", logging );
            ➥loggingInitialized = true;
        }

        if ( value.equals( null ) ) {
            value = "bonForumXML";
        }
        command = value;
    }

    /** Sets value of the attr1 attribute.
     */
    public void setAttr1( String value ) {
        if( value.equals( null ) ) {
            value = "";
        }
        attr1 = value;
    }

    // NOTE: Two similar setter methods,
    // setAttr2() and setAttr3(),
    // were omitted in book for brevity!

    /** Makes sure the body of the tag is evaluated.
     */
```

```
    public int doStartTag( ) throws JspException {
        return EVAL_BODY_TAG;
    }

    /** Gets chat messages from bonForumStore,
        outputs the first one, if any.
      */
    public void doInitBody( ) throws JspException, JspTagException {

        findBonForumStore( );

        if( bonForumStore != null ) {
            try {

                outputTable = new TreeMap( bonForumStore.outputForumChatMessages(
➥command, attr1, attr2, attr3, pageContext.getSession( ) ) );

                if ( outputTable != null ) {
                    iterator = outputTable.values( ).iterator( );
                    if( iterator.hasNext( ) ) {

                        pageContext.setAttribute( "output", ( String
➥)iterator.next( ) );

                    }
                }
            } catch ( Exception ex ) {

                log( "err",  "caught Exception in OutputChatMessagesTag
➥doInitBody" );

                throw new JspTagException( "caught Exception in
➥OutputChatMessagesTag doInitBody" );

            }
        }
    }

    /** Outputs rest of chat messages, if any.
      */
    public int doAfterBody( ) throws JspException, JspTagException {

        if( bonForumStore != null && outputTable != null && iterator != null ) {

            try {

                if( iterator.hasNext( ) ) {

                    pageContext.setAttribute( "output", ( String )iterator.next( )
➥);
```

```
                        return EVAL_BODY_TAG;

                    } else {

                        bodyContent.writeOut( bodyContent.getEnclosingWriter( ) );

                        return SKIP_BODY;

                    }

                } catch ( java.io.IOException ex ) {

                    log( "err",  "caught IOException in OutputChatMessagesTag
➥doAfterBody" );

                    throw new JspTagException( "caught IOException in
➥OutputChatMessagesTag doAfterBody" );

                }
            }
            else {

                log( "err",  "ERROR: OutputChatMessagesTag doAfterBody no store | no
➥table | no iterator" );

                return SKIP_BODY;

            }
        }
    }
```

Code that is common to more than one Tag Handler class has been already explained. For that, refer to the following sections:

- Section 10.2.3, "Finding Bean Methods from JSP Tags"
- Section 10.2.4, "Using `TreeMap` for Sorted Output"
- Section 10.2.5, "Static Variables of Tag Handler Classes"
- Section 10.2.6, "Initializing the `BonLogger` Object"
- Section 10.2.7, "Using `TagExtraInfo` for Scripting Variables"

With the help of those sections and Section 10.5.1, "The `outputChatMessages` Descriptor," you should be able to follow the code for this class.

10.5.3 Attribute-Setter Methods

Each tag attribute is represented by a private variable with a public `setter` method in the Tag Handler bean. Three of the property methods, `setAttr1()`, `setAttr2()`, and `setAttr3()`, are not currently used and set any `null` argument to an empty string. Two are omitted for brevity. If the `setCommand()` setter method gets a `null` argument, it sets the command property to `bonForumXML`, the default value. A command with this value means that messages from the bonForum XML database of that name should be displayed. The messages from the data that are displayed are currently controlled by the values of some session attributes. Notice that the command is the only required attribute in the custom tag.

10.5.4 The *doStartTag()* Method

The `doStartTag()` method is overridden only to return `EVAL_BODY_TAG`; otherwise, the method would return `SKIP_BODY`. We want to always execute the methods that process the body content, `doInitBody()` and `doAfterBody()`. This would be the place to switch off these methods, for example, depending upon some state or initialization parameters in the Web application.

10.5.5 The *doInitBody()* Method

The `doInitBody()` method of the `outputChatMessages` tag handler is very similar to that of the `outputPathNames` tag handler, which we discussed in Section 10.4.5, "The `doInitBody` Method." One major difference is that the `BonForumStore` method that is invoked by `outputChatMessages` is different, as shown here:

```
outputTable = new TreeMap( bonForumStore.outputForumChatMessages( command, attr1,
➥attr2, attr3, pageContext.getSession( ) ) );
```

This method returns a `TreeMap` object with `nodeKey.aKey` values as keys and chat messages (prefaced by the chat actor name) as the values. As you know, the keys are made from unique system clock times in milliseconds, so when the `TreeMap` keeps them sorted, it is effectively sorting them chronologically—important for displaying a page of chat messages. Because we want to display the messages, not the keys, there is another subtle difference in this `doInitBody()` method, compared to the one for the `outputPathName` tag. The iterator is on the `TreeMap` values, not its keys, as shown here:

```
iterator = outputTable.values( ).iterator( );
```

Besides using a different message in case of an exception, the rest of the method is the same as for `outputPathNames`. The first (if any) value the iterator has available is put in the `output` scripting variable, where the upcoming tag body evaluation will find it as it evaluates the JSP expression used in the tag: `<%= output %>`.

10.5.6 The *doAfterBody()* Method

There were few differences between the `outputChatMessages` and the `outputPathNames` `doInitBody()` methods. There are almost none between their `doAfterBody()` methods. The only one, until now, is the message that gets logged and thrown in case of an exception. That means that you can here simply refer to the equivalent section for `outputPathNames`, which is Section 10.4.6, "The `doAfterBody()` Method."

Only one thing would need to change if we were to clone that section here. That is the kludge for making sure that no empty `TreeMap` can be returned, which in this case is at the end of the `outputForumChatMessages()` method in `BonForumStore`:

```
if(outputTreeMap.size()<1) {
outputTreeMap.put( "0", "::::::::::::empty chat::::::::::::::::::");
}
```

As in the case of `outputPathNames`, the scripting variable should be initialized and reset within the Tag Handler class; it should not rely on the method that it calls to keep it from outputting wrong results.

10.5.7 A Stack of *BodyContent* Writers

We promised previously that we would return sometime to the subject of `BodyContent` on a deeper level. There has not been much new to discuss about this tag, so now is the time. The API docs have this definition of `BodyContent`:

> A `JspWriter` subclass that can be used to process body evaluations so they can re-extracted later on.

Another clue is found in the comment given for its constructor, which says:

> Protected constructor. Unbounded buffer, no autoflushing.

Recall also that JSP custom tags can nest. How does JSP keep track of all the output from tags, even nested ones? Simple: It uses a stack of unbounded, nonflushing output buffers. Actually, even a single isolated tag is nested, if it implements the `BodyTag` interface in the JSP `service` method. At least, its output stream object is nested, and the tag itself will have a null parent property.

It works like local variables on a stack. Each nested level of code can do what it wants with its `BodyContent`. That does not affect the next outer level or the resulting output stream of the JSP, unless that `BodyContent` is explicitly written out to the enclosing writer before being popped off the stack. If an exception occurs, the `BodyContent` is simply discarded, which preserves intact the content of the output stream that is one level farther out. Look again at one of the translated JSP files with a custom tag. You should be able to see now what purpose the `bodyContent` subclass of `JspWriter` serves. In fact, we are going to look at one such file next.

10.5.8 The Translated Tag Handler in a JSP Servlet

This next listing represents all the code generated by the `outputChatMessagesTag` tag. We took it from the `_JspService()` method of a translated JSP file (guest_executes_chat_frame.jsp), or, in other words, from the servlet source code for that JSP, which we found in the Tomcat work folder. We have shortened the tag name to `output` in this listing, to make it easier to reproduce in the book. We also added some blank lines for clarity, added some spaces here and there to promote better wrapping at the book margin, and removed some comments. After this listing, we discuss the code while showing again related statements from this listing:

```
/* ---- bon:output ---- */

de.tarent.forum.OutputTag _jspx_th_bon_output_0 = new de.tarent.forum.OutputTag(
➥);

_jspx_th_bon_output_0.setPageContext( pageContext );

_jspx_th_bon_output_0.setParent( null );

_jspx_th_bon_output_0.setCommand( "bonForumXML" );

try {

    int _jspx_eval_bon_output_0 = _jspx_th_bon_output_0.doStartTag(  );

    if ( _jspx_eval_bon_output_0 == Tag.EVAL_BODY_INCLUDE )
        throw new JspTagException( "Since tag handler class
➥de.tarent.forum.OutputTag implements BodyTag, it can't return
Tag.EVAL_BODY_INCLUDE" );

    if ( _jspx_eval_bon_output_0 != Tag.SKIP_BODY ) {

        try {

            if ( _jspx_eval_bon_output_0 != Tag.EVAL_BODY_INCLUDE ) {

                out = pageContext.pushBody(  );

                _jspx_th_bon_output_0.setBodyContent( ( BodyContent ) out );

            }

            _jspx_th_bon_output_0.doInitBody(  );

            do {

                String output = null;

                output = ( String ) pageContext.findAttribute( "output" );

                out.write( "\r\n\t\t\t<option>" );

                out.print(  output  );

                out.write( "</option>\r\n\t\t" );
```

```
            } while ( _jspx_th_bon_output_0.doAfterBody(  ) ==
➥BodyTag.EVAL_BODY_TAG );

        } finally {

            if ( _jspx_eval_bon_output_0 != Tag.EVAL_BODY_INCLUDE )
                out = pageContext.popBody(  );

        }

    }

    if ( _jspx_th_bon_output_0.doEndTag(  ) == Tag.SKIP_PAGE )
        return;

} finally {

    _jspx_th_bon_output_0.release(  );

}
```

How the Java Code for a Tag Works

First, an instance of the output tag Tag Handler class is created (for each thread). The name of the object includes a prefix from the container (`jspx_th`), the prefix from the taglib directive (`bon`), the tag name from the TLD (`output`), and a suffixed number. The number is incremented each time the custom tag appears on the JSP (although it is possible to reuse available tag-handler instances). Here is the statement, taken from the previous "fixed-up" listing:

```
de.tarent.forum.OutputTag _jspx_th_bon_output_0 = new de.tarent.forum.OutputTag(
➥);
```

The all-important `pageContext` object, from the JSP containing the tag, is put in a property of the Tag Handler. This tag is not nested, so the parent property is set to `null`. The only attribute that appeared in the tag action (the only *required* attribute) is set to the value in the action (`bonForumXML`). Here are the three statements that do all that:

```
_jspx_th_bon_output_0.setPageContext( pageContext );
_jspx_th_bon_output_0.setParent( null );
_jspx_th_bon_output_0.setCommand( "bonForumXML" );
```

After this point, the entire tag action will be handled next inside a try block, with a final clean-up when it's done. It looks like this:

```
try {

    //handles the tag action here!

} finally {
```

```
        _jspx_th_bon_output_0.release( );

    }
```

The first method called handles the start tag. In particular, it has access to its attribute values, if any. All tags have a start tag; this method is always called in a Tag Handler. As you saw in Section 10.5.4, "The `doStartTag()` Method," our tag does nothing in this method except return `EVAL_BODY_TAG` to ensure that the `doInitTag()` method will be called. Here is the method invocation:

```
int _jspx_eval_bon_output_0 = _jspx_th_bon_output_0.doStartTag( );
```

As you know, some static `int` constants are used to control the execution flow within a Tag Handler. The `doStartTag()` method, in any Tag Handler implementing the `BodyTag` interface, can return `SKIP_BODY` to skip over the `doInitBody()` and `doAfterBody()` method invocations and proceed immediately with the `doEndTag()` method invocation. It looks like anything else returned by `doStartTag()`, except `EVAL_BODY_INCLUDE`, will cause body content processing to take place (although for that one it is supposed to return `EVAL_BODY_TAG`). The next statement checks that the developer who wrote the `doStartTag()` method did not mistakenly return `EVAL_BODY_INCLUDE`, which is allowed only when one does not implement `BodyTag`. (See the previous section "The `doStartTag()` Method.") If that mistake is made, an exception will be thrown. Here is that insurance statement:

```
    if ( _jspx_eval_bon_output_0 == Tag.EVAL_BODY_INCLUDE )
        throw new JspTagException( "Since tag handler class
➥de.tarent.forum.OutputTag implements BodyTag, it can't return
Tag.EVAL_BODY_INCLUDE" );
```

Because the class we are discussing here extends the `BodyTagSupport` class, it implements the `BodyTag` interface. If we had instead defined a Tag Handler that descends from `TagSupport`, we would not be able to have a `doInitBody()` or `doAfterBody()` method. The `if` statement we just showed would have been different then, as would the contents of the next `if` statement after that. This is what the previous one would have looked like then:

```
    if ( _jspx_eval_bon_Date_0 == BodyTag.EVAL_BODY_TAG )
        throw new JspTagException( "Since tag handler class
➥de.tarent.forum.DateDisplay does not implement BodyTag, it can't return
BodyTag.EVAL_BODY_TAG" );
```

Let's continue with the analysis of the `output` tag, which does implement the `BodyTag` interface. The next `if` statement, paraphrased in this next listing, uses the return value of `doStartTag()` to control access to the body content processing:

```
    if ( _jspx_eval_bon_output_0 != Tag.SKIP_BODY ) {
        try {
            // save the old "out" writer.
            // get a new "out" writer,
            // and make it the bodyContent writer
```

```
        //
        // invoke doInitBody() method
        //
        // 1. evaluate body content into out.
        // 2. invoke doAfterBody() method.
        // repeat 1 and 2
        // as long as doAfterBody()
        // returns EVAL_BODY_TAG.
    } finally {
        // get the old "out" writer back
    }
```

You can now see what we got by extending `BodyTagSupport` instead of `TagSupport`. You might wonder what this `if` statement would have looked like with a `Tag` interface, not `BodyTag` interface, implementation. Here it is:

```
if (_jspx_eval_bon_Date_0 != Tag.SKIP_BODY) {
do {
// evaluate body content into out.!
} while (false);
}
```

You can see why, without implementing `BodyTag`, you can return `EVAL_BODY_INCLUDE` from the `StartTag()` method to get the Tag Handler to evaluate the body content of the tag into the current `out` output stream (a `JspWriter` instance, unless the tag itself is nested). The tag body content could be anything that JSP allows. However, you will not have that useful initialized `do` loop available for repeated body content evaluations, nor the stacking `BodyContent` output stream objects.

In the paraphrased `BodyTagSupport if` statement that we just showed, you can see that before the `doInitBody()` method is called, the output stream switching takes place. Here is the actual code that does that:

```
out = pageContext.pushBody( );
jspx_th_bon_output_0.setBodyContent( ( BodyContent ) out );
```

Now the API Javadoc on the `PageContext` class makes sense when it says what the `pushBody()` method does (behind the scenes):

> Return a new `BodyContent` object, save the current `out JspWriter`, and update the value of the `out` attribute in the page scope attribute namespace of the `PageContext`.

The final clause will be executed no matter what happens in the `doInitBody()` method and the (possibly) looping `doAfterBody()` method. In that finally clause, you can see the code that restores the output stream to the enclosing writer object:

```
out = pageContext.popBody( );
```

Because the `popBody()` call is restoring the outer-level `JspWriter`, it is not cast to `BodyContent`, which it would have to be if this were happening deeper in the stack.

You can see why you must write the `BodyContent` buffer out to the enclosing writer object in the `doAfterBody()` method for it to make a difference to the JSP's resulting output stream. Finally, here is what the API docs say the `popBody()` method of `PageContext` does:

> Return the previous `JspWriter out` saved by the matching `pushBody()`, and update the value of the `out` attribute in the page scope attribute namespace of the `PageConxtext`.

You do not need to call the `print` method of `BodyContent` or `JspWriter` in a tag action method. You can do something like the following instead, and the `popBody()` and `pushBody()` methods take care that you get the right object when you get the `out` page attribute:

```
pageContext.getOut().print(new java.util.Date());
```

After the final clause, the `doEndTag()` method is invoked, your last chance to do something in the action. The `release()` method makes sure that properties and scripting objects are cleaned up—unless you use a `TagExtraInfo` subclass to tell the container to keep a variable around until the end of the JSP service method. But that, as they say, is another story, and we are done with our tour of tag handling in a JSP. Hopefully, we got some of it right; we're still learning more each time we look into JSP.

10.5.9 Another Aside on the Project Goals

The task of displaying chat history seemed at first to be the best place in bonForum for us to use the XSLT transformation capabilities that were we were planning for the transform custom JSP action. We decided against using XSLT for this action, for the following reasons:

- We wanted to refresh the chat messages on each browser as frequently as possible, and we decided that XSLT would be slower than an optimized procedure.
- We also wanted to add a way for the user to navigate through the chat history a page at a time. It seemed that developing a style sheet to do that might be quite time-consuming.
- We had an `outputTable` tag prototype that was working and could be adapted for chat messages. Getting the entire system up fast was a priority. XSLT could wait until later to display a list of available chats.

In the original XML-based design, connections between data items were maintained by matching key values in related elements. The connection between a message and its chat was based on matching key values in two XML elements called `chatKey` and `chatMessageKey` (or something like that).

Key values were kept not in XML attribute values, but in XML `text()` nodes. When we tackled the problem of displaying chat messages, that design made a big difference!

Trying to output chat messages with Java, we found ourselves getting deeper into successive, nested iterations of the entire XML database. These iterations nested four or five levels deep—very expensive in terms of processor time. We stopped, knowing that such complexity should eliminate such code from contention.

We changed the XML design underlying the Web application design. The key values are now kept as XML attributes, not element content. We revisited the Java code and created the `outputForumChatMessages()` bean method that the `outputChatMessages` custom tag utilizes.

Given all that, it might have been easier after all to use XSLT to transform the XML data. That is what it's for, after all! Certainly, it would have been easier to keep all the data in an SQL database and use JDBC connections and SQL queries (tag library are already available). But we would not have gained the insight into the difference that putting a value in attributes rather than element content could make in processing complexity. The bonForum project is for exploration and experimentation. It has been soundly criticized as being "just an academic exercise, without practical application." So were the first rockets. Try going to the moon with a train. Practicality, like so much else, depends upon context. If you must get your company Web site out next week, this might not be the book to read right now. But if your company's Web site looks like every other Web site next year, they didn't let you play enough.

10.6 XSLT and the *TransformTag* Class

If you have not already done so, you should definitely visit the most important documents about XSLT, the recommendations at the Web site `http://www.w3.org/TR/xslt`.

In addition to assuming a basic familiarity with XSLT, the discussion that follows assumes that you have spent some time with the Xalan-Java 1 or Xalan-Java 2 processing library from the Apache XML Project. Certainly, that is the case if you have read Chapter 4, "XML and XSLT: Xerces and Xalan." You will certainly want to keep in touch with the "real" authority on Xalan questions: `http://xml.apache.org`.

For the rest of this chapter, we will be discussing how we put Xalan to work on our JSP-based browser interface. You already read about that from the browser point of view in Chapter 7, "JavaServer Pages: The Browseable User Interface." Here, we explore the details of the `transform` tag and its tag handler class. Of course, no understanding of an XSLT-based process would be complete without a look at the XSL style sheet that controls it, the XML input expected, and the output, so we will examine all that as well.

It might help to note one thing regarding the output of the XSLT processing. It can be set, as you know, using a `method` attribute of the `xsl:output` element, as in the following example from one of the bonForum style sheets:

```
<xsl:output method="xml" omit-xml-declaration="yes" indent="no"/>
```

In bonForum, we set the output to `xml`. However, the output of the transformations that we use to build the browser interface is actually quite simple XHTML. This is a small point, but it's another potential source of confusion out of the way.

The `transform` action in the bonForum tag library is designed to be a flexible JSP to Xalan processor interface. As such, it can be used with various input and output combinations, which are controllable using the tag attributes.

10.6.1 Using the *transform* Custom JSP Tag

The `transform` tag has four attributes named `type`, `inXML`, `inXSL`, and `outDoc`. You can use it as follows:

```
<bon:transform
type="..."
inDoc="..."
styleSheet="..."
outDoc="..." />
```

That is equivalent to using the tag with empty content, as follows:

```
<bon:transform
type="..."
inDoc="..."
styleSheet="..."
outDoc="..." >
</bon:transform>
```

The tag can also have body content, which will be evaluated as follows:

```
<bon:transform
type="..."
inDoc="..."
styleSheet="..."
outDoc="...">
<H1>JSP body content</H1>
</bon:transform>
```

Here is what the attributes can do:

- The `type` attribute selects the XSLT processor and currently can have three values: `Xalan Java 1`, `Xalan Java 2`, or `xalanVersion`. If type is `xalanVersion`, the Tag Handler object looks for an attribute in application scope, also named `xalanVersion`, and uses its value to select the processor. At present, only `Xalan Java 1` and `Xalan Java 2` are valid values for `xalanVersion`.
- The `inXML` attribute can be a URI for an XML input source to the XSLT processor. Otherwise, `inXML` can be set to `bonForumXML` or `bonBufferXML`, in which case the tag handler will use the XML content of the bonForum database object (currently a `ForestHashtable`).
- The `inXSL` attribute can be a URI for an XSL input source to the XSLT processor. Otherwise, it can be a string containing a valid XSL style sheet.
- The `outDoc` attribute can be the URI of the file to which the output of the XSLT process should be written. Otherwise, it can be set to `print`, in which case the output of the XSLT process will be written into the JSP output stream

to the client. An alternative `outDoc` value to `print` is `printNormalized`, which normalizes the XSLT output before it goes into the JSP output stream. Yet another choice is to set `outDoc` to `output`, in which case the output of the XSLT process is put in a page attribute named `output`. An `outDoc` value of `outputNormalized` behaves the same, except that it normalizes the XSLT output first.

In the section "The `getXMLTrees()` Method" in Chapter 8, we discussed a JavaBean method that supports the transform JSP custom tag action. Using an `inDoc` value of `bonForumXML` causes this `getXMLTrees()` method to be invoked internally, dumping the `bonForumXML` object content to a string, which becomes the input source of XML for the XSLT processor. That means that we can output the contents of the chat database to an XML file, as follows:

```
<bon:transform type="xalanVersion"
inXML = "bonForumXML"
inXSL =
"..\\webapps\\bonForum\\mldocs\\identity.xsl"
outDoc =
"..\\webapps\\bonForum\\mldocs\\bonForumIdentical.xml"/>
```

Notice that you can find all these transform action examples in the system_dumps_xml.jsp file, which is requested from a form on the system_executes_command.jsp page, accessible from the entrance to the bonForum Web application. All you have to do to try the examples is to edit the system_dumps_xml.jsp file, removing comments where necessary and refreshing the browser display.

The example action shown previously assumes that you have set an application attribute to the Xalan processor of your choice. You can set the Xalan version from the form on system_executes_command.jsp. Note that if you have `Xalan-Java-2`, you can also set `xalanVersion` to `Xalan Java 1`, as long as the compatibility JAR file is accessible, for example, as TOMCAT_HOME\lib\xalanj1compat.jar.

Let's do something with that new XML file with all the chat data in it:

```
<bon:transform type="xalanVersion"
inXML =
"..\\webapps\\bonForum\\mldocs\\bonForumIdentical.xml"
inXSL =
"..\\webapps\\bonForum\\mldocs\\identity.xsl"
outDoc =
"..\\webapps\\bonForum\\mldocs\\bonForumTest.xml"/>
```

Hello, Dolly! We have a clone. Successful processing also tells you that the input is well-formed XML. We can view the bonForumTest.xml file on Internet Explorer 5.x, for example. Now let's transform the new bonForum XML data dump file to an

HTML file that can be viewed on a browser. We use the `default2.xsl` style sheet, which produces a view of the XML that looks like the Internet Explorer display of the XML we just saw. Note that `default2.xsl` is a simplified version of `default.xsl`—the `default.xsl` generated output files that have nodes that can be collapsed and expanded by clicking on them with the mouse. Here is the tag command:

```
<bon:transform type="xalanVersion"
inXML =
"..\\webapps\\bonForum\\mldocs\\bonForumIdentical.xml"
inXSL =
"..\\webapps\\bonForum\\mldocs\\default2.xsl "
outDoc =
"..\\webapps\\bonForum\\mldocs\\bonForumTest.html "/>
```

That covers using XSLT with output to a file. Now what about some XSLT with output into the JSP-generated browser page? No problem. Use a value of `print` for `outDoc`, and you have it. Here is the example action:

```
<bon:transform type="xalanVersion"
inXML =
"..\\webapps\\bonForum\\mldocs\\bonForumIdentical.xml"
inXSL =
"..\\webapps\\bonForum\\mldocs\\default2.xsl "
outDoc = "print" />
```

Compare the viewing of the HTML file in the previous example with this direct writing of the HTML to the browser. The `print` value of `outDoc` saves time and also wear and tear on your browser buttons. Sometimes it's nice to see the source behind the display, and we can do that by using the `printNormalized` value of `outDoc`, which gets a display with all the active characters entitized (`<` , `&`, and so on). All we have to do is replace the `outDoc` attribute setting in the last example with the following one:

```
outDoc = "printNormalized" />
```

Our next example uses the `output` page attribute variable controlled by the `TagExtraInfo` class (see Section 10.2.7, "Using `TagExtraInfo` for Scripting Variables"). If we want to see anything, we will have to include within the tag body content a JSP expression for the `option` variable. We can put other XHTML code in there, as shown here in this example:

```
<bon:transform type="xalanVersion"
inXML =
"..\\webapps\\bonForum\\mldocs\\bonForumIdentical.xml"
inXSL =
"..\\webapps\\bonForum\\mldocs\\default2.xsl "
outDoc="output" >
<HR/><%= output %><HR/>
</bon:transform>
```

Of course, there is also the option to get the output into the `output` variable, but normalize that XML document in a string first. That means only substituting the `outDoc` command with the following:

```
outDoc="outputNormalized" >
<HR/><%= output %><HR/>
</bon:transform>
```

All the various ways of using the `transform` tag, discussed here, are made available by the `TransformTag` class. It relies on other classes to carry out the actual transform processing. Currently, there are two such classes, whose sources are the following files:

Xalan1Transformer.java

Xalan2Transformer.java

We first show and discuss the `TransformerTag` class source code, and then we show the source for the two Xalan processor encapsulation classes.

10.6.2 The *transform* Descriptor

The following listing shows the `Tag` element in the bonForum TLD that describes the `transform` custom action tag:

```
!-- transform tag -->
<tag>
  <name>transform</name>
  <tagclass>de.tarent.forum.TransformTag</tagclass>
  <teiclass>de.tarent.forum.BonForumTagExtraInfo</teiclass>
  <bodycontent>JSP</bodycontent>
  <info>
    XSLT processing (type) applies inXSL to inXML.

    If inXML = "bonForumXML"
        transforms entire forum content.

    If inXML = "bonBufferXML"
        transforms buffer content.

    Else inXML is a URL for an XML document.

    If outDoc is URL produces XML file.

    If outDoc = "print"
        calls out.println with the output.

    If outDoc = "printNormalized"
        does same as for "print", normalizes first.

    If outDoc = "output"
        puts output in "output" page variable.

    If outDoc = "outputNormalized"
        does same as for "output", normalizes first.
```

```
    Transform uses one stylesheet parameter
    called "param1", which it looks for
    in a session attribute of the same name.
  </info>
  <attribute>
    <name>type</name>
    <required>true</required>
  </attribute>
  <attribute>
    <name>inXML</name>
    <required>true</required>
  </attribute>
  <attribute>
    <name>inXSL</name>
    <required>true</required>
  </attribute>
  <attribute>
    <name>outDoc</name>
    <required>true</required>
  </attribute>
</tag>
```

10.6.3 The *transform* Tag Handler

In this next listing, we show the source code for the TransformTag class. To shorten the listing, we removed Javadoc comments. Also, some methods are repeated in other classes, so their bodies were replaced here with comments pointing to the code in other previous listings. Here is the listing:

```
package de.tarent.forum;

import java.text.*;
import java.io.*;
import java.net.*;
import java.util.*;
import javax.servlet.jsp.*;
import javax.servlet.jsp.tagext.*;

/** JSP custom tag class for XSLT processing.
 */
public class TransformTag extends BodyTagSupport
{
    private static BonForumStore bonForumStore;
    private static BonLogger logTT = null;
    private static boolean loggingInitialized = false;
    private static String logging = null;
    private String type = "";
    private String inXML = "";
    private String inXSL = "";
```

```
    private String outDoc = "";

    private void log( String where, String what ) {
        if(logging != null) {
            logTT.logWrite(System.currentTimeMillis(),
➥pageContext.getSession().getId(), where, what);
        }
    }

    /** locates bonForumStore in application
     */
    private void findBonForumStore( ) {
        // code omitted here is in appendix,
        // and similar code is in Section 10.2.3,
        // "Finding Bean Methods from JSP Tags "
    }

    /** Sets type attribute to select XSLT processor.
      */
    public void setType( String value ) {
        if( !loggingInitialized ) {
            logging = pageContext.getServletContext( ).getInitParameter( "Logging"
➥);
            logTT = new BonLogger( "TransformTagLog.txt", logging );
            loggingInitialized = true;
        }

        if( value.indexOf( "xalanVersion" ) > -1 ) {
            try {
                value = ( String )pageContext.getAttribute( "xalanVersion", 4
➥).toString( );  // 4 is application scope
            }
            catch( java.lang.NullPointerException ex ) {
                value = "Xalan-Java 1";
            }
        }
        if( value.equals( null ) ) {
            value = "Xalan-Java 1";
        }
        type = value;
    }

    /** Sets inXML attribute; determines input to XSLT.
      */
    public void setInXML( String value ) {
        inXML = value;
    }

    /** Sets inXSL attribute; determines XSLT stylesheet.
      */
    public void setInXSL( String value ) {
```

```
        inXSL = value;
    }

    /** Sets outDoc attribute, determines XSLT output.
      */
    public void setOutDoc( String value ) {
        outDoc = value;
    }

    /** Makes sure the body of the tag is evaluated
      */
    public int doStartTag( ) throws JspException {
        return EVAL_BODY_TAG;
    }

    /** Apply XSLT to XML with XSL stylesheet.
      * input XML database | file; XSL is string | file
      * output to browser | page attribute | file.
      */
    public void doInitBody( ) throws JspException {
        if ( ( inXML != null ) && ( inXSL != null ) && ( outDoc != null ) ) {
            if( inXML.equals( "bonForumXML" ) ) {

                findBonForumStore( );

                if( bonForumStore != null ) {
                    synchronized( bonForumStore ) {
                        inXML = "<?xml version=\"1.0\" encoding=\"UTF-8\"?>" +
➥bonForumStore.getBonForumXML( ).getXMLTrees( );
                    }
                }

            }
            else if( inXML.equals( "bonBufferXML" ) ) {

                findBonForumStore( );

                if( bonForumStore != null ) {
                    synchronized( bonForumStore ) {
                        inXML = "<?xml version=\"1.0\" encoding=\"UTF-8\"?>" +
➥bonForumStore. getBonBufferXML ( ).getXMLTrees( );
                    }
                }

            }

            String param1 = ( String )pageContext.getSession( ).getAttribute(
➥"param1" );
            if( param1 == null || param1.trim( ).length( ) < 1 ) {
                param1 = " ";
            }
```

```
                if( type.equals( "Xalan-Java 1" ) ) {

                    try {
                        synchronized( bonForumStore ) {
                            Xalan1Transformer transformer = new Xalan1Transformer( );
                            ➥if( outDoc.equals( "print" ) ) {
                                bodyContent.println( transformer.transform( inXML,
➥inXSL, outDoc, param1 ) );
                            }
                            else if( outDoc.equals( "printNormalized" ) ) {
                                bodyContent.println( normalize( transformer.transform(
➥inXML, inXSL, outDoc, param1 ) ) );
                            }
                            else if( outDoc.equals( "output" ) ) {
                                pageContext.setAttribute( "output",
➥transformer.transform( inXML, inXSL, outDoc, param1 ) );
                            }
                            else if( outDoc.equals( "outputNormalized" ) ) {
                                pageContext.setAttribute( "output", normalize(
➥transformer.transform( inXML, inXSL, outDoc, param1 ) ) );
                            }
                            else {
                                transformer.transform( inXML, inXSL, outDoc, param1 );
                            ➥}
                        }
                    }

                    catch ( Exception ex ) {
                        log( "err", "Exception in TransformTag, Xalan1Transformer
➥process failed!" );
                        throw new JspException( "Exception in TransformTag,
➥Xalan1Transformer process failed! " + ex.getMessage( ) );
                    }

                }
                else if ( type.equals( "Xalan-Java 2" ) ) {

                    try {
                        synchronized( bonForumStore ) {
                            Xalan2Transformer transformer = new Xalan2Transformer( );
                            ➥if( outDoc.equals( "print" ) ) {
                                bodyContent.println( transformer.transform( inXML,
➥inXSL, outDoc, param1 ) );
                            }
                            else if( outDoc.equals( "printNormalized" ) ) {
                                bodyContent.println( normalize( transformer.transform(
➥inXML, inXSL, outDoc, param1 ) ) );
                            }
```

```
                        else if( outDoc.equals( "output" ) ) {
                            pageContext.setAttribute( "output",
➥transformer.transform( inXML, inXSL, outDoc, param1 ) );
                        }
                        else if( outDoc.equals( "outputNormalized" ) ) {
                            pageContext.setAttribute( "output", normalize(
➥transformer.transform( inXML, inXSL, outDoc, param1 ) ) );
                        }
                        else {
                            transformer.transform( inXML, inXSL, outDoc, param1 );
                        ➥}
                    }
                }

                catch ( Exception ex ) {
                    String mess = "Exception in TransformTag, Xalan2Transformer
➥process failed!" + ex.getMessage( );
                    log( "err", mess );
                    throw new JspException( mess );
                }

            }
            else {
                log( "err",  "Unsupported XSLT transformer type arg in
➥TransformTag!" );
            }

        }
        else {
            log( "err",  "Error: null arg( s ) in TransformTag!" );
        }
    }

    /** Puts XSLT results out to JSP, and ends processing.
      */
    public int doAfterBody( ) throws JspException {
        try {
            bodyContent.writeOut( bodyContent.getEnclosingWriter( ) );
            return SKIP_BODY;
        }
        catch ( Exception ex ) {
            String mess = "TransformTag doAfterBody caught Exception!" +
➥ex.getMessage( );
            log( "err", mess );
            throw new JspException( mess );
        }
    }

    /** Normalizes the given string, replacing chars
      * with entities, null with empty string.
```

```
        */
        protected String normalize( String s ) {
            StringBuffer str = new StringBuffer( );
            //
            // code omitted here can be seen in appendix, or in
            // Section 10.3.2, "The outputDebugInfo Tag Handler"
            //
            return str.toString( );
        }
    }
```

Code that is common to more than one Tag Handler class was already explained. For that, refer to the following sections:

- Section 10.2.3, "Finding Bean Methods from JSP Tags"
- Section 10.2.5, "Static Variables of Tag-Handler Classes"
- Section 10.2.6, "Initializing the `BonLogger` Object"
- Section 10.2.7, "Using `TagExtraInfo` for Scripting Variables"

With the help of those sections and Section 10.6.1, "The `transform` Descriptor," you should be able to follow the code in this class. As usual, we will discuss a few highlights.

10.6.4 Attribute-Setter Methods

The `transform` tag has four attributes named `type`, `inXML`, `inXSL`, and `outDoc`. You can use it as follows:

```
<bon:transform
type="..."
inDoc="..."
styleSheet="..."
outDoc="..." />
```

As usual, there is a method to set each tag attribute as a property of the tag handler. The previous section about how to use the `transform` tag also explains the use of the attributes. Here we will just add some notes regarding the source code for the setter methods.

The `setType()` method is the first one to be invoked by the container, so we use it to make sure that the logging for the class is ready to go if it is enabled by an application-initialization parameter. Next, the `setType()` method looks for an application attribute called `xalanVersion` and, if found, uses it to set the version of the Xalan XSLT processor that will be used by the `transform` tag. The default for the version setting is `Xalan-Java 1`.

The `inXML()`, `inXSL()`, and `outDoc()` methods are completely simple. Although there are various possible ways to use these attributes with the tag, the setter methods for these properties simply set them to the incoming string values from the tag attributes. It is up to the doInitBody() method and the XSLT processing wrapper classes to know what to do with these values.

10.6.5 The *doStartTag( )* Method

The doStartTag() method returns EVAL_BODY_TAG, to ensure that the Tag Handler will execute the methods that process the body content, doInitBody() and doAfterBody().

10.6.6 The *doInitBody( )* Method

The doInitBody() method applies an XSLT transformation to an XML document using an XSL style sheet. The input XML can be from the database or a file. The XSL is either a string or a file. The output is to one of three destinations: the JSP output stream, the output page attribute, or a file.

If the inXML value is bonForumXML or bonBufferXML, that means that the data to be transformed is from the bonForum database, so the findBonForumStore() method is called to set a reference variable to the JavaBean that wraps the database. The inXML value is then replaced by an XML declaration plus the XML contents of the database by the following statement (or a similar one, for the bonBufferXML data):

```
synchronized( bonForumStore ) {
    inXML = "<?xml version=\"1.0\" encoding=\"UTF-8\"?>" +
➥bonForumStore.getBonForumXML( ).getXMLTrees( );
}
```

The XSL style sheet used by the transform tag can be passed one parameter (in the current version). The doInitBody() method looks for it as a session attribute named param1, as follows:

```
String param1 = ( String )pageContext.getSession( ).getAttribute( "param1" );
➥if( param1 == null || param1.trim( ).length( ) < 1 ) {
param1 = " ";
}
```

The next step is to invoke a method to carry out the XSLT. We have created two classes to encapsulate the steps required for either Xalan-Java 1 or Xalan-Java 2. The classes are called Xalan1Transformer and Xalan2Transformer. Each has one method called transform, which returns a string containing the results of the XSLT process. What is done with that string depends upon the value of the outDoc attribute, as we detailed in Section 10.6.1, "Using the transform Custom JSP Tag." With that information, it should be easy to follow the code in the doInitBody() method. (Much of the code is repeated exactly for the two Xalan versions; other arrangements are made awkward by the need to synchronize some of the steps.)

You have already seen how the output scripting variable can be set to a value using the setAttribute() method of the pageContext Tag Handler property. Here you can see a more direct way of putting a string from a Tag Handler instance into the output stream of the JSP that contains the tag action. We used the println() method of the bodyContent object for that, although, as we have seen, the out variable will do as well.

It is also possible to use the `transform` tag with input from an XML file. In that case, the `bonForumStore` object still serves in this code to provide a synchronization lock for the block that creates the processor class instance and invokes the process method. In this case, nothing needs to be done with the returned string from the process method because the output is put in a file, whose name is given by the `outDoc` attribute of the `transform` tag action.

The `doInitBody()` method carries out its XSLT in a `try` block and throws a new `JspException` after logging a message that is useful for remote debugging purposes.

One last thing to mention here is that the use of `transform` with the `bonBufferXML` object is under development and has not been tested. The idea here is that data can be put into the buffer object from different sources and the `transform` tag then can be used to dynamically use this data in the context of the Web application.

10.6.7 The *doAfterBody()* Method

The `doAfterBody()` method, as usual, is invoked after the `doInitBody()` method. In the case of the `transform` tag, it is invoked only once because it always returns `SKIP_BODY`, which means that it will not be invoked again. The only task of `doAfterBody()` in the `transform` tag is to pass the XSLT results to the JSP. Remember, the body content evaluation, if any, and the creation of new body content, if any, have both taken place using a nested output stream. For anything done there to have any effect upon the JSP output stream, the contents must be written out from the current inner stream to the containing outer stream. That is done quite simply, with the following statement:

```
bodyContent.writeOut( bodyContent.getEnclosingWriter( ) );
```

Again, this happens within a `try` block. If an exception is caught, a message is logged before a new `JspException`, also with that message, is thrown.

10.6.8 The *Xalan1Transformer* Class

The following listing comes of the source code for the `Xalan1Transformer` class, which encapsulates the steps necessary to carry out an XSLT process using the Xalan-Java 1 processor from the Apache XML project.

```
package de.tarent.forum;

import java.text.*;
import java.io.*;
import java.net.*;
import java.util.*;
import javax.servlet.jsp.*;
import javax.servlet.jsp.tagext.*;

import org.w3c.dom.*;
```

```
import org.xml.sax.*;
import org.apache.xerces.dom.*;
import org.apache.xerces.parsers.*;
import org.apache.xalan.xslt.*;

/** XSLT processing using Xalan-Java 1.
 */
public class Xalan1Transformer {

    /** XSLT of inXML to outDoc using inXSL
      * stylesheet, with Xalan-Java 1.
      */
    public String transform( String inXML, String inXSL, String outDoc, String
➥param1 )
    throws org.xml.sax.SAXException, Exception {
        XSLTProcessor processor = null;
        XSLTInputSource inputXML = null;
        XSLTInputSource inputXSL = null;
        XSLTResultTarget outputDoc = null;
        StringWriter stringWriter = null;

        try {
            processor = org.apache.xalan.xslt.XSLTProcessorFactory.getProcessor(
➥);
        }
        catch ( org.xml.sax.SAXException ex ) {
            System.err.println( "SAXException in Xalan1Transformer, cannot create
➥processor!" );
            throw ex;
        }

        try {
            // Set a param named "param1",
            // that the stylesheet can obtain.
            processor.setStylesheetParam( "param1", processor.createXString(
➥param1 ) );
        }
        catch ( Exception ex ) {
            System.err.println( "SAXException in Xalan1Transformer, cannot set
➥param1!" );
            throw ex;
        }

        try {
            if( inXML.indexOf( "<?xml" ) == 0 ) {
                inputXML = new XSLTInputSource( new StringReader( inXML ) );
            ➥}
            else {
                inputXML = new XSLTInputSource( inXML );
            }
            if( inXSL.indexOf( "<?xml" ) == 0 ) {
```

```
                if( inXSL.indexOf( "<xsl:stylesheet" ) > -1 ) {
                    inputXSL = new XSLTInputSource( new StringReader( inXSL ) );
                ➥}
            }
            else {
                inputXSL = new XSLTInputSource( inXSL );
            }
            if( outDoc.indexOf( "output" ) == 0 || outDoc.indexOf( "print" ) == 0
➥) {
                stringWriter = new StringWriter( );
                outputDoc = new XSLTResultTarget( stringWriter );
            }
            else {
                outputDoc = new XSLTResultTarget( outDoc );
            }

        }
        catch ( Exception ex ) {
            System.err.println( "Exception in Xalan1Transformer, processor prep
➥failed!" );
            throw ex;
        }

        try {
            processor.process( inputXML, inputXSL, outputDoc );
            if( outDoc.indexOf( "output" ) == 0 || outDoc.indexOf( "print" ) == 0
➥) {
                return outputDoc.getCharacterStream( ).toString( );

            }
            else {
                return null;
            }
        }
        catch ( org.xml.sax.SAXException ex ) {
            System.err.println( "SAXException in Xalan1Transformer, processing
➥failed!" );
            throw ex;
        }
    }
}
```

The steps to execute an XSLT process here are taken from the simple transformation examples given in the documentation and examples that come with Xalan-Java 1. A major improvement is to use compiled style sheets. Because bonForum uses only a few style sheets, it would be easy to compile these and make them available to the class; this would allow the XSLT to proceed more quickly.

As you can see in the code, the single XSL parameter that currently can be used is hardwired with the not-very-imaginative name of param1. As we find the need to use more than the single parameter that we have so far (see Section 10.9.3, "XSLT Style

Sheet for chatGuests"), we should design a more flexible means of indicating to the transform classes where and what those parameters are. Here is the statement that makes the param1 argument available for use within the style sheet:

```
processor.setStylesheetParam( "param1", processor.createXString( param1 ) );
```

We mentioned before that the inXML and inXSL arguments could be either URI values or strings containing XML data or an XSL style sheet, respectively. Notice here how these cases are differentiated by searching within the argument values for the beginning signature of an XML declaration (<?xml). In the case of the inXSL, success at this is followed up by a second search for the signature of an XSL style sheet (<xsl:stylesheet). The implication with either argument is that if the value is not an XML string, then the value must be a URI pointing to the correct type of XML or XSL file resource available to the transformer.

One more thing to note here is that a string can be "fed" into the Xalan-Java 1 processor. It expects an object of the XSLTInputSource class. That class is quite flexible and takes several types of arguments, among them any StringReader object. That enables us to get the XML chat data into the XSLT processor using the following statement:

```
inputXML = new XSLTInputSource(new StringReader(inXML));
```

A similar thing is done to get the output of the XSLT process into a string that can be either put into the scripting variable or written out to the JSP output stream:

```
outputDoc = new XSLTResultTarget(stringWriter);
```

Later improvements considered for this class include being able to output the transform results to DOM, as well as having a SAX, event-driven processing ability.

10.6.9 The *Xalan2Transformer* Class

The Xalan2Transformer class was designed to encapsulate XSLT using the Xalan-Java 2 processor from the Apache XML project. In terms of what we have done, as opposed to what was done by that project, there is very little different between this class and the Xalan1Transformer class that was just described. By combining the previous discussion with the appropriate documentation from the Xalan-Java 2 release, it should be quite easy to follow the listing of the source code for our class:

```
package de.tarent.forum;

import java.text.*;
import java.io.*;
import java.net.*;
import java.util.*;
import javax.servlet.jsp.*;
import javax.servlet.jsp.tagext.*;

// Imported TraX classes
```

```
import javax.xml.transform.TransformerFactory;
import javax.xml.transform.Transformer;
import javax.xml.transform.stream.StreamSource;
import javax.xml.transform.stream.StreamResult;
import javax.xml.transform.TransformerException;
import javax.xml.transform.TransformerConfigurationException;

/** XSLT processing using Xalan-Java 2.
 */
public class Xalan2Transformer {

    /** XSLT of inXML to outDoc using inXSL
      * stylesheet, with Xalan-Java 2.
     */
    public String transform( String inXML, String inXSL, String outDoc, String
➥param1 )
    throws TransformerException,
           TransformerConfigurationException,
           FileNotFoundException,
           IOException {

        String output = "";

        try {
            TransformerFactory factory = TransformerFactory.newInstance( );

            Transformer transformer = null;

            if( inXSL.indexOf( "<?xml" ) == 0 ) {
                if( inXSL.indexOf( "<xsl:stylesheet" ) > -1 ) {
                    transformer = factory.newTransformer( new StreamSource( new
➥StringReader( inXSL ) ) );
                    transformer.setParameter( "param1", param1 );
                }
                System.err.println( "ERROR: Xalan2Transformer No stylesheet for
➥inputXSL, thus no transformer!" );
            }
            else {
                transformer = factory.newTransformer( new StreamSource( inXSL ) );
                ➥transformer.setParameter( "param1", param1 );
            }

            StreamSource inputXML = null;

            if( inXML.indexOf( "<?xml" ) == 0 ) {
                inputXML = new StreamSource( new StringReader( inXML ) );
            }
            else {
                inputXML = new StreamSource( inXML );
            }
```

```
            StreamResult outputDoc = null;

            if( outDoc.indexOf( "output" ) == 0 || outDoc.indexOf( "print" ) == 0
➥) {
                outputDoc = new StreamResult( new StringWriter( ) );
            }
            else {
                outputDoc = new StreamResult( new FileOutputStream( outDoc ) );
           ➥ }

            transformer.transform( inputXML, outputDoc );

            if( outDoc.indexOf( "output" ) == 0 || outDoc.indexOf( "print" ) == 0
➥) {
                return outputDoc.getWriter( ).toString( );
            }
            else {
                return null;
            }
        }
        catch ( TransformerConfigurationException ex ) {
            System.err.println( "Xalan2Transformer transform caught
➥TransformerConfigurationException" );
            throw ex;
        }
        catch ( TransformerException ex ) {
            System.err.println( "Xalan2Transformer transform caught
➥TransformerException" );
            throw ex;
        }
        catch ( FileNotFoundException ex ) {
            System.err.println( "Xalan2Transformer transform caught
➥FileNotFoundException" );
            throw ex;
        }
        catch ( IOException ex ) {
            System.err.println( "Xalan2Transformer transform caught IOException"
➥);
            throw ex;
        }
    }
}
```

As you can see, the `Transform` method itself is unchanged from the `Xalan1Transformer` class. It has the same four string arguments: `inXML`, `inXSL`, `outDoc`, and `param1`. Underneath the hood, however, things look very different, reflecting the major changes in this area of the Apache product. Unlike our version 1 class, the version 2 class uses compiled style sheets for the XSLT. Gone are the `XSLTInputSource` objects, replaced by the newer `StreamSource` objects.

First we use the static `TransformerFactory.newInstance()` method to instantiate a

TransformerFactory. The javax.xml.transform.TransformerFactory system property setting determines the actual class to instantiate:

```
org.apache.xalan.transformer.TransformerImpl
```

Our instance of the TransformerFactory class uses the style sheet to create an instance of the Transformer class, which includes the compiled style sheet as a Templates object. The Transformer instance can then be used repeatedly for XSLT processing, without any need to repeatedly parse the style sheet. That is the same advantage available in Xalan-Java 1 with compiled style sheets, but, in this case, style-sheet compilation is assumed to be the normal procedure.

The Transformer object has a Transform() method that takes only two arguments: one for the XML data input and the other for the output of the XSLT processing. Our method uses the same signature tricks as we described in our discussion of the Xalan-Java 1 transformer class. It decides whether to prepare a string containing XML or XSL by feeding it first to a StringReader object, before feeding it to the StreamSource object expected by the transformer. For example, in the case of the input XML data, this statement gets executed if the data is in a string, not a file:

```
inputXML = new StreamSource( new StringReader( inXML ) );
```

If the argument was a URI for an XML file resource, the statement is instead this simpler one:

```
inputXML = new StreamSource( inXML );
```

If the outDoc argument contains either output or print, this indicates that the XSLT result will be needed in a string object. The calling class can put it into either the scripting variable or the JSP output stream. We get the transformer to output into a string by giving it the proper type of StreamSource, which is created as follows:

```
outputDoc = new StreamResult( new StringWriter( ) );
```

If the outDoc argument was a URI, then the situation is again different. Here is that way to get the transform results into the file resource indicated by the URI:

```
outputDoc = new StreamResult( new FileOutputStream( outDoc ) );
```

In Xalan-Java 2, making a style-sheet parameter available to the XSL document is done by calling a method on the Transformer instance, as follows:

```
transformer.setParameter( "param1", param1 );
```

When everything is in place, carrying out the XSLT processing is as simple as the following statement:

```
transformer.transform( inputXML, outputDoc );
```

Of course, some exceptions can occur and must be dealt with, including the new ones, TransformerException and TransformerConfigurationException.

The calling class expects the result of the XSLT to be returned in a string if the `outDoc` attribute of the `transform` tag was set to `output`, `outputNormalized`, `print`, or `printNormalized`. That is accomplished by the following statement, which executes after the successful XSLT process is done:

```
return outputDoc.getWriter( ).toString( );
```

10.6.10 An XSLT Processing Method on a JSP

We believe that one of the most exciting things about working with JavaServer Pages is that you can quickly and very interactively develop Java methods by scripting Java code directly in the JSP document. The Tomcat Server automatically recompiles your efforts when it finds a newer JSP file. Developing Java on a JSP page, using short compilations of minimum amounts of new code, turned out to be a positive experience. Even with the added effort of later moving the tested code into another server-side component, we found that we had a net savings in development time.

Much of the code for doing XSLT from a JSP was originally developed using scriptlets on a JSP page. After testing, we moved the code into a custom tag handler. Besides helping to simplify the JSP document and further the JSP objective of separating page design from dynamic content production and processing, replacing the scriptlet code with a much simpler custom action also allowed us to change the visibility of some of the server-side objects that were used in the scriptlet code from public to protected. A custom tag helps things not only from the JSP side, but also from the bean side, by reducing to one place (the tag handler class) some common and important programming requirements, such as handling security or data validation.

10.7 Displaying the Available Chats

The capability to do XSLT processing with the `transform` custom tag is a powerful way to continue building the Web application user interface. We have been aiming toward this since the beginning of the project. An early foundation of the bonForum project was that XSLT processing could help achieve a major goal of JSP-based development: separating the presentation layer from the business logic.

Therefore, we intentionally left the HTML content of the JSP pages extremely simple, hoping that all the hype about XSLT and JSP would prove correct. We can expect future bonForum versions to have page content created by Web designers, using the tools and tags that we develop while experimenting with the prototype.

10.7.1 The Input XML Data from *bonForumXML*

Here is a fragment of the `bonForumXML` contents at runtime. It represents one chat in the bonForum. We removed all other nodes of the XML, leaving only those related to what we call one `chatItem` element in the project.

```
<?xml version="1.0" encoding="UTF-8"?>
<bonForum nodeKey="987930397948.987930397948.987930397948" type="prototype">
```

```
➥<things nodeKey="987930398299.987930397948.987930397948" type="READ_ONLY">
<subjects nodeKey="987930400301.987930398299.987930397948">
<Animals nodeKey="987930400522.987930400301.987930398299">
<Fish nodeKey="987930400572.987930400522.987930400301">
<Piranha nodeKey="987930400582.987930400572.987930400522">
<sessionID_iee898dwc2_987947695230
➥nodeKey="987947695250.987930400582.987930400572" chatTopic="pet piranha
stories"/>
</Piranha>
</Fish>
</Animals>
</subjects>
</things>
</bonForum>
```

Depending on the level of encryption on the machine running Tomcat, the session ID could be longer than the one shown. In this case, the previous example `chatItem` name would have been something like the following:

```
<sessionID_To1012mC3112047861890935 3At_987947695230
```

Remember that there can be many such `chatItems` present at once in the `bonForumXML` data object. We have left out all the other subjects, all the other things, and all the other children of the bonForum root node.

The pathname to a node in the bonForum XML tree is a string made up of the concatenated node names in order from the root node to the node whose pathname it is. The pathname for the previous `chatItem` is as follows:

```
bonForum.things.subjects.Animals.Fish.Piranha.sessionID_iee898dwc2_987947695230
```

The innermost node is the element for the `chatItem`. It has a name that contains five parts, as follows:

1. A prefix, `sessionID`, to prevent names starting with digits
2. An underscore character, _
3. The session ID of the visitor who started the chat and thus became its host
4. An underscore character, _
5. A suffix, the system time in millis when the chat node was created, which is also the `nodeKey.aKey` of the chat node

The session ID is used as part of the name of any `chatItem` node because it links the host to the chat via the session ID. It also forms part of the key for the chat element `nodeKey` in the `nodeNameHashtable`. That allows a fast lookup of the chat node using its `nodeKey` instead of the slower process of looking at all the chat elements in the database for the one with an `itemKey` value equal to the `nodeKey` of the `chatItem`.

Before we added the prefix to the `chatItem` names, we had a problem—which, of course, we found only after releasing the software the first time. If a session ID started with a digit instead of a letter, it created an invalid XML element name. That produced a runtime error when running visitor_joins_chat.jsp. It also corrupted the XML contents of `bonForumXML` so that all other XSLT processes failed also.

The only solution was to restart bonForum.

The timestamp suffix makes the `chatItem` name unique, which allows more than one chat to exist per session object. That is all you need to know for this custom tag discussion, so feel free to skip the next heading, which is definitely an "aside."

An Aside: Session ID, *nodeKey.aKey*, and *nodeNameHashtable*

Notice that the timestamp is also a unique `nodeKey.aKey` in the database. Therefore, by itself it would give direct access to the `chatnode`, without having the session ID. It seems that there is no need to use the `nodeNameHashtable` if you have the `nodeKey.aKey`, which is unique in the entire XML database. Why the extra complexity of using the `nodeNameHashtable`, you might ask?

The answer to that question is partly due to the development history and partly due to its planned future. Look at the session ID as being a "stand-in" for a user ID. In earlier versions, the `nodeNameHashtable` keys had no timestamp suffixes and consisted only of a session ID and an element name, as in these examples:

```
iee898dwc2:chat
iee898dwc2:host
iee898dwc2:message
```

These connected one element of a particular name with one particular user. The intent was to allow that user fast access to that element by stashing its `nodeKey` in the `nodeNameHashtable`. Remember, nodes in the XML are unordered, and to look through all of them every time you need that chat that Joe started is expensive. At that time, the `chatItem` names also had no timestamp suffix. The `chatItem` naming scheme came about as a way for a visitor thread to determine the session ID for a chat's `nodeNameHashtable` key and, therefore, find the chat knowing only its subject and topic. That all worked fine, except that it allowed a user to be a host or a guest of only one chat at a time. Clearly, hosts and guests should be able to go in and out of chats without losing their connection to the chat.

So, the timestamp was added as a way of having multiple host and guest items in the `nodeNameHashtable` for each session. Using the unique `nodeKey.aKey` was a natural choice because `BonForumEngine` was already getting that back from the database whenever any node was added. Then the timestamp had to be put in the `chatItem` name also because it was used to get the `nodeNameHashtable` key for a chat with that subject and topic. At that point. it became obvious that the timestamp itself pointed to the chat node. Should we throw out the `nodeNameHashtable` or the session ID part of the `chatItem` name? That seems like a simplification, but it is also an impoverishment. The session ID (later, user ID) connects the chat to the user, which the `nodeKey.aKey` of the chat does not directly do. (To find all the chat nodes for a particular user would take quite a bit of searching, but to do that with a user ID is fast.)

So, there is more method to this madness than is at first apparent. In a future release, a user's first session ID (perhaps encrypted) will become his user ID, which authorization will make available. Then when the user says, "Give me a list of all my chats for April, fast!", this will not bring the server to its knees.

The *chatTopic* Attribute

A `chatItem` element must also have an attribute with the name `chatTopic`, whose value is the description of the chat given by the actor that started the related chat. The contents of `chatTopic` must be different than for all other `chatItems` with the same parent subject element. That is enforced by the software that adds `chatItems`. The parent element of a `chatItem` element can be called a `subjectItem` element.

10.7.2 The Desired HTML Output

The following is an example of the HTML `select` element that we create via the XSLT processing of the `bonForumXML`. The `select` element is filled with options, which are its child elements. Each option identifies a `chatItem` (an available chat). Here is an example, with two chats:

```
<select name="chatItem" size="9">
<option value="Animals_Dog_LabradorRetriever_[Teaching your dog to fetch!]">
➥Animals Dog LabradorRetriever --> Teaching your dog to fetch!
</option>
<option value=" Vehicles_Motorcycles_Honda_[Fixing vintage dirt bikes]">
Vehicles Motorcycles Honda --> Fixing vintage dirt bikes
</option>
</select>
```

The XSL style sheet that we use is shown next. The style sheet produces "prettier" visible option content than the "uglier" subject-plus-topic string, and it hides that away from the user (as the value of the option's `value` attribute).

10.7.3 Using an XSL Style Sheet: *bonChatItems.xsl*

Our first real application use of XSLT from a custom tag was to display to a potential chat guest this pick list of available chats. We have described everything except the XSL style sheet that is processed together with the XML chat data to create the HTML code for the `select` list. You can find that style sheet, `bonChatItems.xsl`, in the folder TOMCAT_HOME\webapps\bonForum\mldocs.

Indeed, it took us a while to create a style sheet that would produce approximately what we wanted. Creating prettier option content than the option value strings was quite a recent addition. You might find some older information elsewhere in the book describing the previous version. Here is the latest XSL file, at this point in time:

```
<?xml version="1.0"?>

<xsl:stylesheet xmlns:xsl="http://www.w3.org/1999/XSL/Transform" version="1.0">
```

```
<xsl:output method="xml" omit-xml-declaration="yes" indent="no"/>

<xsl:template match="/">
    <select size="9" name="chatItem">
    <xsl:apply-templates select="/bonForum/things/subjects/descendant::*[
➥@chatTopic ]"/>
    </select>
</xsl:template>

<xsl:template match="text()">
</xsl:template>

<xsl:template match="*">

<xsl:variable name="option-value">
    <xsl:for-each select="ancestor::*">
        <xsl:choose>
            <xsl:when test="name()='bonForum'">
            </xsl:when>
            <xsl:when test="name()='things'">
            </xsl:when>
            <xsl:when test="name()='subjects'">
            </xsl:when>
            <xsl:otherwise>
                <xsl:value-of select="name()"/>
                <xsl:if test="child::node()">
                <xsl:text>_</xsl:text>
                </xsl:if>
            </xsl:otherwise>
        </xsl:choose>
    </xsl:for-each>

    <xsl:choose>
        <xsl:when test="self::node()[@chatTopic]">
            <xsl:text>[</xsl:text>
                <xsl:value-of select="@chatTopic"/>
            <xsl:text>]</xsl:text>
        </xsl:when>
        <xsl:otherwise>
            <xsl:value-of select="name()"/>
        </xsl:otherwise>
    </xsl:choose>
</xsl:variable>

<xsl:variable name="subject">
    <xsl:value-of select=" substring-before( string( $option-value ), string(
➥&quot;[&quot; ) )"/>
</xsl:variable>

<xsl:variable name="topic">
    <xsl:value-of select=" substring-before( substring-after( string( $option-
```

```
➥value ), string( &quot;[&quot; ) ), string( &quot;]&quot; ) )"/>
</xsl:variable>

<option>
    <xsl:attribute name="value">
        <xsl:value-of select="$option-value"/>
    </xsl:attribute>

    <xsl:value-of select="translate( $subject, string( &quot;_&quot; ), string(
➥&quot; &quot; ) )"/>

    <xsl:text> --> </xsl:text>

    <xsl:value-of select="$topic"/>
</option>

</xsl:template>

</xsl:stylesheet>
```

If you think that XSL document is hard to follow, you should have seen the first version. At that time, the Xalan processor insisted on including all the whitespace in the file, so we had to wrap most of the file lines into one big mess, without using any tabs or spaces! Thankfully, that bug seems to be gone now—at least, while using the Xalan-Java 1 compatibility JAR or the Xalan-Java 2 JAR.

10.8 Displaying the Available bonForums

We decided to display on the browser a list of Web links. The original idea was that there could be many bonForum Web sites in the world, and each would display links to all the others on the HTML page created by bonforum.jsp. That is why, in the bonForumXML data design, these Web links are each kept in a `forum` element that is a child of `bonForum.things.forums`. Later we decided that because there were no other bonForum Web sites, we would keep some real Web sites there so that the links would be functional and related to the book. Essentially, this was another opportunity to try out the XSLT `transform` custom tag.

10.8.1 *bonTransform* Applies *XSLTProcessor*

If it is clear to you from the previous discussion how we used the transform tag to display available chats in a `select` list, then it will be easy to understand how we use the same tag to create a list of link elements. The discussion here is therefore short. We simply display the relevant XML data, the XML output that we require, and the XSL style sheet, and repeat the `transform` action element as it appears on the JSP document.

10.8.2 XML Fragment with Link to Forum

The following listing shows the `bonForum.things.forums` XML subtree from some `bonForumXML` data. We have left out all other things descendants, as well as the actor and actions subtrees.

```
<?xml version="1.0" encoding="UTF-8"?>
<bonForum nodeKey="987930397948.987930397948.987930397948" type="prototype">
  <things nodeKey="987930398299.987930397948.987930397948" type="READ_ONLY">
  ➥<forums nodeKey="987930400922.987930398299.987930397948">
    <forum nodeKey="987930400932.987930400922.987930398299">
      <name nodeKey="987930400942.987930400932.987930400922">
        Galileo Press
      </name>
      <weblink nodeKey="987930400952.987930400932.987930400922">
        http://www.galileocomputing.de
      </weblink>
    </forum>
    <forum nodeKey="987930400992.987930400922.987930398299">
      <name nodeKey="987930401002.987930400992.987930400922">
        tarent
      </name>
      <weblink nodeKey="987930401012.987930400992.987930400922">
        http://www.tarent.de
      </weblink>
    </forum>
    <forum nodeKey="987930400962.987930400922.987930398299">
      <name nodeKey="987930400972.987930400962.987930400922">
        New Riders Publishing
      </name>
      <weblink nodeKey="987930400982.987930400962.987930400922">
        http://www.newriders.com
      </weblink>
    </forum>
   </forums>
  </things>
</bonForum>
```

The `forums` content is loaded at startup by the `initForumXML()` method from the XML configuration file TOMCAT_HOME\webapps\bonForum\mldocs\forums.xml.

It should also be possible to use the `loadForumXmlFromURI()` method of the `BonForumStore` bean to overwrite the `forums` subtree at runtime, although that is as yet untested.

10.8.3 XSLT Style Sheet for bonForum

Here is the XSL style sheet that we use in bonForum to transform the `forums` XML data into a list of Web links. The style sheet creates an HTML table element containing as rows the names and links from each `forum` element.

```
<?xml version="1.0"?>
```

```
<xsl:stylesheet xmlns:xsl="http://www.w3.org/1999/XSL/Transform" version="1.0">
<xsl:output method="xml" omit-xml-declaration="yes" indent="no"/>

<xsl:template match="/">
<table width="100%" name="bonForums">
<tr>
<A>
<xsl:attribute name="href">
http://www.bonForum.org/
</xsl:attribute>
bonForum.org
</A>
</tr>
<tr>
<xsl:text> </xsl:text>
</tr>
<xsl:apply-templates select="/bonForum/things/forums//*"/>
</table>
</xsl:template>

<xsl:template match="text()">
</xsl:template>

<xsl:template match="forum">
<tr>
<A>
<xsl:attribute name="href">
<xsl:value-of select="weblink"/>
</xsl:attribute>
<xsl:value-of select="name"/>
</A>
</tr>
</xsl:template>

<xsl:template match="*">
</xsl:template>

</xsl:stylesheet>
```

The first template makes sure that at least one Web link is always available in the table of links, which is the Web site for the SourceForge open source bonForum project: `http://www.bonforum.org`.

10.8.4 Making a Table of Links with XSLT

Here is how the result of the `bonTransform ChoiceTag` command turned out on one occasion, a bit rearranged on the page for clarity:

```
<table name="bonForums" width="100%">
<tr>
<A href="http://www.bonForum.org/">
```

```
bonForum.org
</A>
</tr>
<tr> </tr>
<tr>
<A href="http://www.galileocomputing.de">
Galileo Press
</A>
</tr>
<tr>
<A href="http://www.tarent.de">
tarent
</A>
</tr>
<tr>
<A href="http://www.newriders.com">
New Riders Publishing
</A>
</tr>
</table>
```

10.9 Displaying the Guests in a Chat

Another type of select list used in the bonForum browser interface contains actorNickname values, of either all the guests or all the hosts in the chat for the current session. (Of course, until we implement multihosted chats, there is only one member in a host list). Each nickname item contains other actor information (the actorRating and actorAge, for now). To increase or decrease a guest rating, a chat host can now pick a guest from such a list. These select lists of actors in a chat will also be used in a future release in the "host executes chat" and "guest executes chat" application states so that users can tell who is in their current chats. The XSL style sheet shown next makes two lists: one of hosts in the chat and the other of guests in the chat.

10.9.1 The XML Data for a Chat Guest

Here is an excerpt of the bonForumXML, showing the data for only one host in a chat. We have simplified the XML considerably by leaving out all other actors node descendants, as well as the entire things and actions subtrees.

```
<?xml version="1.0" encoding="UTF-8"?>
<bonForum nodeKey="988064756730.988064756730.988064756730" type="prototype">
<actors nodeKey="988064756850.988064756730.988064756730" type="READ_ONLY">
<host nodeKey="988065011617.988064756850.988064756730">
<actorAge nodeKey="988065011637.988065011617.988064756850">
74
</actorAge>
<actorNickname nodeKey="988065011627.988065011617.988064756850">
```

```
adam
</actorNickname>
<actorRating nodeKey="988065011647.988065011617.988064756850">
5
</actorRating>
</host>
</actors>
</bonForum>
```

10.9.2 Select List for *chatGuests*

The following is one example of the kind of output that we need. This HTML creates a select list of all the guests that are currently in a host's chat. The XSLT must be capable of producing something like this, at a minimum:

```
select name="chatGuest" size="6">
<option>larry age:49 rating:7</option>
<option>curly age:47 rating:1</option>
<option>moe age:45 rating:9</option>
</select>
```

10.9.3 XSLT Style Sheet for *chatGuests*

This is the style sheet that we used to produce the previous HTML snippet. In the design of this and the other style sheets in this Web application project, there is great room for additional creativity.

```
<?xml version="1.0"?>

<xsl:stylesheet xmlns:xsl="http://www.w3.org/1999/XSL/Transform" version="1.0">

<xsl:output method="xml" omit-xml-declaration="yes" indent="no"/>

<xsl:param name="param1" select="'error in param1'"/>

<xsl:template match="/">
  Guests in your chat:<BR/>
  <select size="6" name="chatGuest">
  <xsl:apply-templates select="/bonForum/things/*"/>
  </select>
</xsl:template>

<xsl:template match="text()">
</xsl:template>

<xsl:template match="chat[@itemKey=$param1]">
  <xsl:for-each select="*">
    <xsl:if test="name()='guestKey'">
      <xsl:variable name="guestKey-value">
```

```
            <xsl:value-of select="."/>
          </xsl:variable>
          <xsl:for-each select="/bonForum/actors/guest">
            <xsl:variable name="guest-value">
              <xsl:value-of select="@nodeKey"/>
            </xsl:variable>
            <xsl:if test="$guest-value=$guestKey-value">
              <option>
              <xsl:value-of select="actorNickname"/>
              <xsl:text> age:</xsl:text>
              <xsl:value-of select="actorAge"/>
              <xsl:text> rating:</xsl:text>
              <xsl:value-of select="actorRating"/>
              </option>
            </xsl:if>
          </xsl:for-each>
        </xsl:if>
      </xsl:for-each>
    </xsl:template>

    <xsl:template match="*">
    </xsl:template>

    </xsl:stylesheet>
```

10.9.4 *TransformTag* Uses a Style Sheet Parameter

As you can see, the previous style sheet relies on a parameter that is passed before the XSLT processing takes place. The parameter "tells" the style sheet the value of the `itemKey` for the current session, which can be used to uniquely identify its chat. However, we call the parameter `param1` because we will use it also for other style sheets where it has different meaning.

To use this style-sheet parameter, we had to add code in other places, of course. (Note that these changes were made close to the publication date and might not be reflected in other chapters of this book.) One place needing a change was the JSP that has the `transform` tag in it, which is host_executes_command_frame.jsp.

Here is the code that we added to that JSP:

```
<%
String itemKey = (String)session.getAttribute("itemKey");
if(itemKey == null || itemKey.trim().length() < 1) {
    itemKey = "000000000000.000000000000.000000000000";
}
session.setAttribute("param1", itemKey);
%>
```

This scriptlet gets the `itemKey` identifying the chat for the current session, which the host is in, and puts it in another session attribute called `param1`. Later in the same JSP, the `transform` tag is called, invoking the methods of its handler class. The following code in that handler, from TransformTag.java, takes care of getting the style-sheet parameter:

```
String param1 = (String)pageContext.getSession( ).getAttribute( "param1" );
if( param1 == null) {
param1 = "";
}
```

The `TransformTag` class invokes an XSLT processing method in one of several ways, depending on the tag attribute values. Every such invocation, whether for Xalan-Java 1 or Xalan-Java 2, passes the style-sheet parameter as an argument, like this:

```
transformer.transform(inXML, inXSL, outDoc, param1)
```

10.9.5 How the Style Sheet works

The first template in the style sheet matches the root node. It begins an HTML `select` element and then applies templates to all the `bonForum.things` nodes. A chat element is found whose `itemKey` value matches the `param1` value passed by the JSP tag action. That is the current chat for the session. The children of that chat element are iterated looking for any `guestKey` elements. Whenever one is found, its value (a `nodeKey` string) is saved in the `guestKey-value` variable, and the processing jumps to a different place altogether in the bonForum XML data: Guest elements (children of the bonForum.actors node) are iterated. When a guest element `nodeKey` value matches the saved `guestKey` value, that element is a guest in the chat. Its nickname, age, and rating element contents can now be concatenated as an HTML option for the `select` that is being built by this style sheet. The iteration of the `guestKeys` in the chat continues until all the HTML option strings have been output. The closing tag for the HTML select is output as well.

Why the Style Sheet Is Used

As we discussed in the section "The `changeChatActorRating()` Method" in Chapter 8, a chat host has commands available to raise or lower the rating of any guest in the "current" chat. (That functionality will later be extended to allow any chat actor to rate any other one in its chat.) Now you know how that host gets a list of the guests in its chat so that it can pick one to promote or demote.

10.9.6 JSP Tags and XSLT in the Future

One of the main goals of our Web application design is that it should be extensible and customizable using technologies designed for such purposes. The two most powerful ways to turn the bonForum prototype into a chat that is visually appealing and full of features are JSP custom tags and XSLT processing.

10.9.7 Sending Feedback to the Author

We hope that you enjoy altering and improving the JSP documents and the XSL style sheets as much as we enjoyed creating the ones shown here. To send your own solutions, improvements, donations, and flames, or to discuss the contents of this book, feel free to email the author of this book at `email@bonforum.org`, or use the forums and mailing lists provided by SourceForge to reach the bonForum project Web site: `http://www.bonforum.org`.

11 XML Data Storage Class: ForestHashtable

IN THIS CHAPTER, YOU CAN LEARN HOW we implemented data storage for the XML data in the bonForum chat application. A descendant of the `Hashtable` class adds a few tricks to optimize XML element retrieval, as it simulates our design for a relational database schema.

11.1 Overview of bonForum Data Storage

One of the more controversial aspects of the bonForum project has been its data storage implementation. Throughout this chapter, we will include some of the objections that have been raised. Perhaps the most common question is why did we not use a relational database. Certainly, that would not have been as difficult as creating the `ForestHashtable` class in Java, right? Questions are also raised about the way we designed our objects. These questions deserve an answer, so here are three:

- We are not against using a database—in fact, we will. However, we wanted to design ours (and experiment with its design) without using a database tool. As you read this chapter, be aware that we are not trying to replace the use of a database engine—or to reinvent, one either.
- Our objective was never to design the best way of storing, manipulating, and retrieving XML data using Java objects. Instead, we were using Java objects to simulate and test a table design for a relational database.

- We did it this way because we believe that putting a problem into a different context than its usual one often stimulates insights into the problem that would otherwise go unseen. Paradoxically, doing it the hard way first can help you find the best way sooner.

The `de.tarent.ForestHashtable` class extends the `java.util.Hashtable` class. In this chapter, we assume that you are familiar with the `Hashtable` class. If you are not, or if you have questions about it, consult the API documentation for the Java SDK you are using.

Briefly, a `Hashtable` instance keeps track of a number of objects called elements. When you add an element to a `Hashtable`, you associate it with another object called a key. You can later use this key to find the element again. Because our `ForestHashtable` class is a descendant of a `Hashtable`, it can serve as the object storage facility for our Web application example project.

Note that the term *element* is used in this chapter with two different definitions: an object held by a `Hashtable`, and a type of XML node. Hopefully, each time the term appears, context will differentiate between the two meanings.

11.1.1 *ForestHashtable* Stores Simple XML

A `ForestHashtable` caches XML documents for fast processing. Each element in a `ForestHashtable` is an object that can be cast to a `BonNode` object, and each key is an object that can be cast to a `NodeKey` object. The `BonNode` objects are mappable to the element nodes in one or more XML documents. The NodeKey objects are designed to keep track of the hierarchical tree relationship that exists between the XML nodes. How this all works is the first subject of this chapter.

11.1.2 *ForestHashtable* Is an Experiment

Please note that `ForestHashtable` is still in a primitive state of development and should be considered an experiment rather than an attempt to provide a comprehensive XML storage object. In fact, in the version discussed in this book and used in its Web application project, a `ForestHashtable` stores only XML element nodes and any of their children that are either attribute nodes or text nodes. Other XML node types besides these are ignored.

11.1.3 A Preview of This Chapter

By reading this far in the book, you have already learned enough theory about the `ForestHashtable` class used in the bonForum Web application. These are the major points that should be familiar as we proceed:

- The `ForestHashtable` is a customized `Hashtable` whose elements are `BonNode` objects and whose keys are `NodeKey` objects.

- The BonNode objects can represent XML elements together with their attributes and text content.
- The NodeKey objects, which simulate three "key columns" in a database table, can map the hierarchical relationships between the XML elements and facilitate some optimized data-access operations.

In the rest of this chapter, our discussion of ForestHashtable will focus less on its theoretical aspects and more on its practical aspects. Here is a list of some major areas we will cover:

- Access to BonNode objects in a ForestHashtable can be optimized by caching some of the keys that are used to store them. We will discuss two such optimization mechanisms that we have developed.
- To make it useful, we added some methods to the ForestHashtable class. These methods include those for adding, deleting, and editing the BonNode objects kept in a ForestHashtable. Here as elsewhere, we find techniques for optimizing the performance of these common tasks.
- To apply other XML technologies, especially XSLT, to our ForestHashtable data, we develop a way to retrieve these data in a manner that obeys the rules of XML.
- The bonForum Web chat application uses an instance of the ForestHashtable class, called bonForumXML. We will show you how the data in bonForumXML is initialized, and we also will discuss an example of bonForumXML data after a couple chats were started.

11.2 The *NodeKey* Class

The following excerpt from the file NodeKey.java is the definition of the NodeKey class:

```
class NodeKey {
   String aKey;
   String bKey;
   String cKey;
   public NodeKey() {
        this.aKey = "";
        this.bKey = "";
        this.cKey = "";
   }
   public String toString() {
        return aKey + "." + bKey + "." + cKey;
   }
}
```

As you can see, a NodeKey instance simply encapsulates three strings, which together form a three-part key. The three parts are known as aKey, bKey, and cKey. Its constructor initializes these to empty strings, so we never need to check for a null value in any part of the triple-key value.

11.2.1 Using Unique Triple-Key Values

A `NodeKey`, when converted to a string by the `toString()` method, is simply the three strings separated by period characters. An example of a `NodeKey` as a string is the following:

```
"963539545905.963539545895.963539545885"
```

`NodeKeys` such as these are used to represent the hierarchical relationships between `BonNodes` in a `ForestHashtable`. This is explained next, together with a discussion of the reasons for using these triple keys.

11.2.2 Timestamps for Order and Uniqueness

The important thing to note for now is that the first string of 12 digits (the `aKey`) is different for each `NodeKey` instance, something that allows each `NodeKey` object to function as a unique key for a `BonNode` object in the `ForestHashtable`. The `aKey` is derived from the system time in milliseconds, which gives a way to order `NodeKeys` in time and also ensures that each `NodeKey` can be given a unique value, as long as only one source of `NodeKey` values is present.

11.3 The *BonNode* Class

Here is the definition of the `BonNode` class, from the file BonNode.java:

```
class BonNode {
   NodeKey nodeKey;
   NodeKey parentNodeKey;
   boolean deleted;    // flag as deleted, for quick deletes
   boolean flagged;    // general purpose state flag
   String nodeName;    // name of element
   String nodeAttributes;  // attributes of element
   String nodeContent;  // text between opening and closing tags
}
```

11.3.1 *NodeKey* in a *BonNode*

The `NodeKey` that is used to retrieve a `BonNode` from the `ForestHashtable` is also kept inside the `BonNode` instance itself, as the `NodeKey` member. If a `BonNode` is a child of another `BonNode`, then the `NodeKey` of the parent is kept in the `parentNodeKey` member. From these two `NodeKeys` kept in the `BonNode`, we can determine hierarchical relationships between `BonNode` objects from the objects themselves.

11.3.2 *parentNodeKey* in a *BonNode*

Note that the `BonNode` string member known as `parentNodeKey` is not needed for representing the hierarchical position of a node, as long as the `NodeKey` member is a multipart key object, such as the triple-key values that we use in the bonForum project and which are discussed fully later.

Why is the `parentNodeKey` in the `BonNode` class, then? There are two reasons for that. (Hint: You might want to revisit these two items after reading about forest tables.)

1. You could use the `BonNode` class with different types of keys that are not multiple-valued, like the double and triple-key examples. In that case, the two members `NodeKey` and `parentNodeKey` determine the hierarchical position of the node.
2. If you have used a triple-valued key (discussed later) in each of the two members `NodeKey` and `parentNodeKey`, then you will have fast access to the parent, grandparent, and great-grandparent above the current node that is represented by any `BonNode`. Of course, this would be done through methods, such as `node.getParent().getGrandParent()`.

11.3.3 Name of a *BonNode*

A `BonNode` is designed to represent a node in a tree. Sometimes in this book, you might find the term *node* used rather loosely to refer to a `BonNode`. A `BonNode` is used in the bonForum project to represent three types of XML nodes. An XML element is mappable to the name that appears in an opening tag and its matching closing tag (if any) of an XML document. The only thing that the `BonNode` must keep to faithfully map an XML element node is its hierarchical position (in the `NodeKey` member) and its name (in the `nodeName` string member).

11.3.4 Attributes of a *BonNode*

From a low-level XML programming view, it is advantageous to access the attributes of an element as child nodes of the element node that they are attributes of. So, attributes are best represented as nodes in their own right, so to speak. Such "attribute nodes" would have to be specialized in some fashion, of course, to distinguish them from true children and ensure that the original XML could be reproduced. However, for the purposes of the bonForum Web application, all that is needed is to keep the list of name=value items associated with the associated XML element. A `BonNode` object keeps such a list as a single string member of itself, which is called `nodeAttributes`.

11.3.5 Content of a *BonNode*

The third thing that a `BonNode` can represent from an XML document is a concatenation of all the text nodes that are children of the element named by the `nodeName` string member. The concatenated text is kept in the `nodeContent` string member of the `BonNode`.

11.3.6 Background Deletion of a *BonNode*

By using the flag called `deleted`, we intend to implement delayed deletion of nodes. The `deleteNode()` method will have to be changed so that it sets this flag value to `true` in a node instead of deleting the node. A background task could periodically purge nodes marked for deletion. As an added advantage, we could implement an `unDoNodeDeletion()` method.

Node deletion comes in two "flavors." In the first, or "leaf-only" version, it can avoid deletion of nodes that have children. In the second, or "recursive" version, it can delete all descendants (if any) of any node deleted. Note that in the `ForestHashtable` design (as opposed to a simple Java object hierarchy), it is necessary to explicitly check for `parentNode` references to the deleted object to carry out either type of deletion. For a fuller discussion as it relates to foreground instead of background deletion, see Section 11.7.4, "Deleting Descendants or Only Leaf Nodes."

11.3.7 Flagging Visits to a *BonNode*

Another flag in each node is called `flagged`. This is used by the `getXMLForest()` method that converts the data in a `ForestHashtable` into XML trees. This conversion requires repeated iterations of the `Hashtable` contents, first to get the root nodes, then to get their children, and finally to recursively visit all the other nodes. We "hide" each node that has already been processed by setting its `flagged` member to a value of `True`. This enables us to simplify the code that we use to test the depth of a node in the hierarchy.

Someone might raise the objection that this is mixing procedural with OOP and can introduce multithreading and data integrity problems, and that it would be much safer to have this method keep its own separate list of `nodeKeys` visited and check against that. We hope that this objection will no longer hold when our simulation (the `ForestHashtable` class) is implemented in a relational database. The `getXMLForest()` method should be seen as a convenience for the simulation and not essential to the design.

11.4 *ForestHashtable* Maps Data Trees

The `ForestHashtable` class is designed to simulate a database table that uses three columns as key values. You can implement the same functionality as the `ForestHashtable` class by creating such a table within any one of the many available databases together with some methods that can also be programmed as stored procedures within the database or within one or more Java classes. The `ForestHashtable` class is simply a simulation of such a database setup.

11.4.1 Design of the *ForestHashtable*

Many of the advantages of using a database table with three keys to represent hierarchical data structure are not utilized by the Web application project in this book. Therefore, you might wonder why such a design was implemented at all. We will briefly discuss the reasons in this section.

11.4.2 Hierarchical Data Representation

A hierarchy, or tree structure, is commonly implemented in software by using just one variable to create links between the node objects of the tree. Each node object contains a member that acts as a pointer or key to its parent node. Because each node has only one parent node, such an arrangement can represent the entire tree, and methods can be created to add, edit, delete, traverse, and otherwise manipulate its node objects.

11.4.3 Forest Tables Using Two Keys

A database table can be used to hold such hierarchical data. Each row represents a data node. Each node uses one column to contain a primary key that uniquely identifies that node. A second key column contains the primary key of a different row in the table, the one that represents that node's parent.

If a node has no parent, then it is a root node. The parent key of a root node is set to point to the root node itself. Therefore, if the values of the node and parent key are equal, the node in question is a root node. Usually, in Java APIs, the parent of a root node is null—that is, it represents the absence of a parent. Notice that making the parent equal to the node means that to traverse a tree, you cannot use this "usual" phrase:

```
for (node = someNode; node.getParent() != null; node = node.getParent()){…}
```

Neither can you use this stock phrase:

```
while ((node = node.getParent()) != null){…}
```

Instead, for tree traversal, you would use this:

```
while (node != node.getParent()) {…}
```

These examples were cited as a source of potential confusion stemming from our design. However, it does seem to us that the third example is simpler, at least.

Let's use an example to help you visualize such a table. We call the two keys `node` and `parent`, and we give each node just two columns for a name and type. For primary key values we will use sequential integers. First we will display part of the table in Table 11.1.

Table 11.1 **Tree of Life in a Double-Key Table**

Node	Parent	Name	Type
1	1	Animalia	Kingdom
2	1	Mollusca	Phylum
3	1	Chordata	Phylum
4	3	Mammalia	Class
5	4	Carnivora	Order
6	2	Gastropoda	Class
7	4	Primates	Order
8	7	Hominidae	Family
9	3	Reptilia	Class
10	8	Homo	Genus
11	11	Plantae	Kingdom
12	10	Sapiens	Species
13	10	Hacker	Species

Next we display the contents of the example table fragment as a hierarchical structure. We constructed the tree using the two key values for each node, and we use them separated by a period as a prefix in each node label:

```
1.1 Kingdom Animalia
   2.1 Phylum Mollusca
         6.2 Class Gastropoda
   3.1 Phylum Chordata
         4.3 Class Mammalia
               5.4 Order Carnivora
               7.4 Order Primates
                     8.7 Family Hominidae
                           10.8 Genus Homo
                                 12.10 Species sapiens
                                 13.10 Species hacker
         9.3 Class Reptilia
11.11 Kingdom Plantae
```

11.4.4 Forest Tables Using Three Keys

The table that is simulated by the `Hashtable` in our `ForestHashtable` class uses three key columns. In each row, we keep track of both the node's parent and its grandparent.

We should point out here that some might think that the grandparent key is superfluous and redundant and that it promotes bad design/coding practices. Normalized database design would use either the two-key approach (for single-parent trees) or a single key and a mapping table (for multiparent relationships).

Here is the same partial table example, this time with an additional key called `grandparent`. Note that in the `NodeKey` used by the `ForestHashtable`, the three keys are called `aKey`, `bKey`, and `cKey` instead of `node`, `parent`, and `grandparent`.

Table 11.2 **Tree of Life in a Triple-Key Table**

Node	Parent	Grandparent	Name	Type
1	1	1	Animalia	Kingdom
2	1	1	Mollusca	Phylum
3	1	1	Chordata	Phylum
4	3	1	Mammalia	Class
5	4	3	Primates	Order
6	2	1	Gastropoda	Class
7	4	3	Carnivora	Order
8	7	4	Hominidae	Family
9	3	1	Reptilia	Class
10	8	7	Homo	Genus
11	11	11	Plantae	Kingdom
12	10	8	Sapiens	Species
13	10	8	Hacker	Species

Again we display the contents of the example table fragment as a hierarchical structure. We constructed the tree using the triple-key values for each node. In fact, as you have seen, we need only the first two keys to make the tree. This time, we use all three values, separated by periods as a prefix in each node label:

```
1.1.1 Kingdom Animalia
   2.1.1 Phylum Mollusca
         6.2.1 Class Gastropoda
   3.1.1 Phylum Chordata
         4.3.1 Class Mammalia
               5.4.3 Order Carnivora
               7.4.3 Order Primates
                     8.7.4 Family Hominidae
                           10.8.7 Genus Homo
                                  12.10.8 Species sapiens
                                  13.10.8 Species hacker
         9.3.1 Class Reptilia
11.11.11 Kingdom Plantae
```

11.4.5 Advantages of a Triple-Key Forest Table

The simpler "double-key" table can provide all the functionality that we required for the Web chat application project in this book. Why then did we use a solution that uses three keys? The reason is that we wanted our simplified chat application to become the basis for a full Web e-commerce application. Using "three-key" tables to hold hierarchical data enables some additional methods that provide superior performance and simplified programming requirements.

Table 11.3 lists some of the methods that are especially easy and efficient to implement using a triple-key table to contain nodes. We will discuss these methods and others as well. For further elucidation, try to implement these methods using only a double-key table design, and then use a triple-key table design.

Table 11.3 **Methods Made Easy by Triple-Key Table Design**

Method of Node	Key Relation to Implement Method
`isNodeAChildOfRoot()`	`aKey <> bKey and bKey = = cKey`
`hasNodeAGrandParent()`	`bKey <> cKey`
`getGrandParentOfNode()`	`cKey = = Grandparent's aKey`
`getGrandChildrenOfNode()`	`aKey = = Grandchildren's cKey`

Some might say that if these methods are necessary to obtain sufficient speed from a tree, the tree is not well-designed in the first place. The argument is that putting in extended family methods defeats the purpose of the structure and draws arbitrary, nonintuitive boundaries between objects. (To take this to an extreme, why not have a `getGreatGrandparent()` or a `getGreatGreatGrandparent()`?)

Well, as mentioned before, `getGreatGrandparent` is `getParent().getGrandParent()` (or do you really like `getParent().getParent().getParent()` better?). Also, `getGreatGreatGrandparent()` is `getGrandParent().getGrandParent()`, instead of `getParent().getParent().getParent().getParent()`. In Section 11.4.10, "Prefetching to Save Time and Bandwidth," we will discuss some scenarios in which we do think the triple-key design has merit.

11.4.6 *isNodeAChildOfRoot()*

Finding the result of this method that returns a Boolean value is intrinsic to the design of the `ForestHashtable`. As the second column in Table 11.3 shows, you need to determine only that the first two key values of the three-valued key are not equal and that the last two of the same three values are equal.

Doing the same thing using only two-valued keys instead for a node at an arbitrary depth in a tree could take many, many iterations of getting the parent node, seeing if it has a parent, and so on.

11.4.7 *hasNodeAGrandParent()*

If the last two of the three values in the triple key differ from each other, then the node has parent and grandparent nodes at least, although maybe more direct ancestors as well. This information is thus also intrinsic to the design of the `ForestHashtable`'s triple-key table data storage (remember, although this is stored here in a `Hashtable`, it could as well be in a relational or object-oriented database table).

Again, trying to find the Boolean return value for this method is more difficult with a double-valued key system. You have to access the parent node keys and determine whether the parent has a parent, which is equivalent to determining whether the parent is a root node. The information is not intrinsic to the node, in other words.

Remember, a node can be big and expensive to request over a network. You might want to just get the parents' keys, not all the objects in the node. But then, if you are asking this question, you probably will access the rest of the node as well, which means that you have a choice of either two object retrievals sometimes or one object retrieval always.

11.4.8 *getGrandParentOfNode()*

If you use triple-key tables, then you can directly index the grandparent node of any node in a forest. Besides getting the value of the `hasNodeAGrandparent()` method, the triple key gives you the index for the nodes row in the table. As the second column in Table 11.3 shows, you only need to find the row in the table with a primary key value equal to the third value in the triple key of the current node (that is, the grandchild node).

With double-key tables, you must retrieve the keys from the parent node of a given node to find and retrieve the grandparent of the given node. Again, how big a deal that is depends on what the nodes are and where they are, among other things. But it certainly will not be faster access than with a three-key table.

11.4.9 *getGrandChildrenOfNode()*

Getting all the child nodes of a given node using a triple-key table requires only a single pass through all the primary key values. As the second column in Table 11.3 hints, you need to grab only the nodes whose third key is equal to the first key of the current node (that is, the grandparent node).

To implement this method with a double-key table, you must first get each child node and then find all its child nodes, which you retrieve. If you realize that the rows in the table are not ordered by tree order but by insertion order, you can appreciate that it could take much longer to retrieve all the grandchildren and that it will require more than one pass through the rows of the table.

11.4.10 Prefetching to Save Time and Bandwidth

In e-commerce, user interfaces are often tied to large databases that have hierarchical data structures. The user interface often requires that these data structures receive input from a user and provide values to be displayed to the user.

11.4.11 Linking List Controls

Frequently, in such user interfaces, the need arises to link two or more lists of items. For this discussion we assume that the need exists to link two list box controls.

One of the controls contains values from one level of a hierarchical data structure—in other words, values from a set of sibling tree nodes. The second control contains values from the children of whichever tree node corresponds to the selected value in the first list. When the user picks a parent node by selecting its value in the first list, the second list should automatically show the values of all its children.

After that, the next step is often to drill down or up in the hierarchy. This procedure applies, for example, to the "explorer" type of user interface designs, such as those used to traverse and display filesystem contents in a user interface display.

Drilling Down the Hierarchy

When it becomes necessary to drill down into a tree data structure, the selected child becomes the new parent, and its child nodes, if any, must now be found by the software and displayed in the user interface. Would it not be advantageous to have already retrieved the required child nodes? Of course, we do not mean that we should try to guess successfully which new parent node will be selected by the user ahead of time.

Using a `ForestHashtable`, we can easily prefetch and cache all the "next-generation" nodes in an XML data store. We can do this using the `getGrandchildrenOfNode()` method, discussed previously. This way, we can search through a much smaller data set that is guaranteed to contain all the new child nodes that we must find instead of making many new requests from a database.

Climbing Up the Hierarchy

In the opposite direction, the `ForestHashtable` can more quickly find the parent of a node (if available) and the grandparent of a node (if available). This might not be important if the parent can be retrieved quickly and used in turn to find the grandparent. However, there may be cases in which small savings add up over time. Try iterating cousin nodes with two-valued versus three-valued keys to see the difference that the grandparent key can make.

11.4.12 Faster Response and Reduced Bandwidth

As you have seen, this capability of the `ForestHashtable` to prefetch grandchildren of a node comes from the fact that it simulates a database table that uses three keys. The advantages of this design show themselves in two ways: faster response to user actions and reduced bandwidth requirements with remote databases. Although our simple chat application does not take full advantage of this design, an e-commerce application based on the same architecture would certainly do so.

11.4.13 Keeping XML Documents in a Table

As you can see, there can be any number of root nodes in either the double-key or the triple-key tables discussed. That is why the Java class that we use to simulate this table was named `ForestHashtable`, not `TreeHashtable`.

XML documents, on the other hand, can have only one root node. This means that we can store multiple XML documents in either of these types of table, and each XML document root will have a separate root node in the table. The `ForestHashtable` can also store more than one XML document.

11.4.14 The Animal Kingdom as an XML Document

Here is what the animal kingdom data in our example table might look like if it were in an XML document. Of course, we could add more attributes to the element start tags, as well as some text content between the start and end tags, to make a more informative document. We are keeping it simple, though, to better show how XML can be stored in a database table.

```
<?xml version="1.0"?>
<Kingdom name=" Animalia">
      <Phylum name="Mollusca">
            <Class name="Gastropoda">
            </Class>
      </Phylum>
      <Phylum name=" Chordata">
            <Class name=" Mammalia">
                  <Order name="Carnivora">
                  </Order>
                  <Order name="Primates">
                        <Family name="Hominidae">
                              <Genus name="Homo">
                                    <Species name="sapiens">
                                    </Species>
                                    <Species name="hacker">
                                    </Species>
                              </Genus>
                        </Family>
                  </Order>
            </Class>
            <Class name=" Reptilia">
            </Class>
      </Phylum>
</Kingdom>
```

The plant kingdom classification would have to be in a different XML document, unless we added another higher-level root element (for example, using the tag pair `<Life></Life>`. That would then be the parent of both the animal kingdom and the plant kingdom nodes.

11.4.15 Some XML Nodes Not Handled Yet

What about all the other types of XML nodes? As we stated at the beginning of the chapter, the ForestHashtable is an experiment in progress. As such, it has been intentionally kept simple, with just enough functionality to illustrate its potential and fulfill the needs of the bonForum Web application example.

11.4.16 Future XML Capabilities Are Planned

The BonNode class actually represents three different types of XML nodes together in one object. Therefore, a BonNode object can contain an XML element node, plus its attribute nodes and its text nodes. In a future design, every node in an XML document would be mapped to a single row in a table, including attribute nodes and text nodes.

Because an XML document can be fully described as a tree of nodes, there is no reason why the design used in this simplified ForestHashtable cannot be extended to include all the other XML node types as well.

11.5 Caching Keys for Fast Node Access

Because a ForestHashtable extends the Hashtable class, obviously it has access to itself as a Hashtable, and that is where it contains the nodes of data. However, it also contains two other Hashtable member objects that it uses to optimize the processing of the BonNode objects that it stores.

11.5.1 *NodeKey* Gives Direct Access to a *BonNode*

As we have seen, NodeKey objects are used as Hashtable keys for keeping the BonNodes objects in a ForestHashtable. Therefore, having a NodeKey allows direct access to its associated BonNode. If you do not have a NodeKey for a BonNode, you have to search the entire ForestHashtable using an Enumeration to find that particular BonNode, and that can be a very time-consuming search procedure. In fact, for some searches, you must iterate several enumerations in nested loops, which is very expensive in terms of both memory and processor time.

11.5.2 *NodeKeyHashtables* Cache *NodeKeys*

To have fast and more direct access to BonNode objects, the ForestHashtable has two different ways of caching their associated NodeKey objects. These cached NodeKey objects can then later be quickly found and used in turn to find their associated BonNode objects in the ForestHashtable. The two NodeKey caches, both java.util.Hashtable objects, are named nodeNameHashtable and pathNameHashtable. We discuss each of these in separate subsections.

There are two different `NodeKey` caches because each uses a different type of key object to store its `NodeKey` objects. The `Hashtable` key used by `nodeNameHashtable` contains the `nodeName` value for the `BonNode` whose `NodeKey` is being cached (sometimes with a prefix identifying the HTTP session, and optionally the node-creation time). The `pathNameHashtable` object uses instead a key that describes the path in the data tree from a root node to the `BonNode` whose `NodeKey` is being cached.

The two different caches for `NodeKey` objects are referred to generically as `NodeKeyHashtables`. Some methods that use them have an argument to select which one to use by its specific name, and the argument is named `nodeKeyHashtableName`. It is anticipated that other types of caches might be useful, so some of the code was written with an eye to the future.

11.5.3 *nodeNameHashtable*

The first `Hashtable` objects, named `nodeNameHashtable`, is created by the following statement from the file ForestHashtable.java:

```
public NodeNameHashtable nodeNameHashtable = new NodeNameHashtable();
```

Notice that a class called `NodeNameHashtable` has been defined that extends `java.util.Hashtable` but that adds nothing to that class. This has been done solely to make the variable available from JSP tags.

Users Only Add Children of Nonroot Nodes

In Section 8.6, "The `add()` Method," of Chapter 8, "Java Servlet in Charge: BonForumEngine," we discuss the `add()` method of the `BonForumEngine` class. There we point out that it eventually depends on the `addChildNodeToNonRootNode()` method in the `ForestHashtable` class, which will be discussed in the section "Session-Visible Children of Nonroot Nodes." You should see by now that to get a full understanding of how a `nodeKeyHashtable` works, you will need to understand both the `BonForumEngine` and the `ForestHashtable` classes. That will most likely require studying their source code, as well as Chapter 8.

The *addNode()* Method's *nodeKeyHashtable* Cache

In the `ForestHashtable` class, the public classes that add data nodes all call a private class called `addNode()`. The `addNode()` method uses the `nodeNameHashtable` to cache the `NodeKey` of the `BonNode` being added, whenever its `nodeKeyHashtableName` argument is set to the value `nodeNameHashtable`.

The code excerpt shown in the next subsection is from the `addNode()` method of the `ForestHashtable` class. You can see how the `NodeKey` for a `BonNode` being added to the `ForestHashtable` is saved in the `nodeKeyHashtable` cache.

Application Global versus HTTP Session-Dependent Caching

The `addNode()` method has another argument called `nodeKeyKeyPrefix` that is set to the value `NO_NODEKEY_KEY_PREFIX` when the root node and its children are added to initialize the Web application database. The same argument is set instead to the value `SESSION_ID` or `SESSION_ID_AND_CREATION_TIME` whenever a node is added that is at least a grandchild of the root node.

```
if(nodeKeyHashtableName.equals("nodeNameHashtable")) {
  // Hashtable is synchronized, but we need to sync two together here:
  String nodeKeyKey = null;
  synchronized(this) {
    try {
      this.put(nodeKey, node);
    }
    catch(Exception ee) {
      log(sessionId, "err", "EXCEPTION in addNode():" + ee.getMessage());
      ee.printStackTrace();
    }
    if(nodeKeyKeyPrefix == SESSION_ID) {
      // allows only one key per session
      // use this option to reduce size of table
      // by not storing key to nodeKeys not needed
      // (examples: message keys, messageKey keys).
      nodeKeyKey = sessionId + ":" + nodeName;
    }
    else if(nodeKeyKeyPrefix == SESSION_ID_AND_CREATION_TIME) {
      // the nodeKey.aKey acts as a timestamp
      // allowing multiple keys per session in nodeNameHashtable
      // use to find multiple nodes with same name for one session
      // (example: chat keys, guest keys, host keys)
      nodeKeyKey = sessionId + "_" + nodeKey.aKey +":" + nodeName;
    }
    else if(nodeKeyKeyPrefix == NO_NODEKEY_KEY_PREFIX) {
      // use no prefix for elements global to all sessions
      nodeKeyKey = nodeName;
    }
    else {
      nodeKeyKey = nodeName;  // unknown arg value, could complain
    }
    this.nodeNameHashtable.put(nodeKeyKey, nodeKey);
  }
}
```

Elements Branded by HTTP Session and Creation Time

If the parent is not one of the intrinsic system elements (for example, a "message" element inside the "things" element) then the key in the nodeKeyHashtable is made up of the following:

```
<sessionId> + "_" + <nodeKey.aKey> + ":" <elementName>.
```

An example of such a key is `54w5d31sq1_985472754824:message`. There is also an option to leave out the `nodeKey.aKey` portion of the key for a selected list of node names (see `ForestHashtable`, property `UniqueNodeKeyKeyList`). That option reduces the size requirements of the `nodeKeyHashtable` (for example, by not storing all the message `nodeKey` keys).

```
String hostNodeKeyKey = sessionId + "_" + creationTimeMillis + ":host";
session.setAttribute( "hostNodeKeyKey", hostNodeKeyKey );
nameAndAttributes = "actorNickname";
content = actorNickname;
forestHashtableName = "bonForumXML";
obj = bonForumStore.add( "bonAddElement", hostNodeKeyKey, nameAndAttributes,
content, forestHashtableName, "nodeNameHashtable", sessionId );
```

11.5.4 *PathNameHashtable*

The other `Hashtable` that a `ForestHashtable` uses, besides itself and the `nodeNameHashtable`, is called the `pathNameHashtable`. The source code that creates that variable is shown here:

```
public  PathNameHashtable pathNameHashtable = new PathNameHashtable();
```

As with the `NodeNameHashtable` class, you can see that this cache is an instance of a class (`PathNameHashtable`) that has been defined to extend `java.util.Hashtable`, but it adds nothing else to that class. Again, this has been done only to make the `pathNameHashtable` variable available from JSP tags.

BonForumEngine Uses *pathNameHashtable*

The `ForestHashtable` class contains only a definition of the `pathNameHashtable` member at present. All the code that uses this second `NodeKey` cache facility is now in the `BonForumEngine` class, although it will later be moved into the `ForestHashtable` class. Therefore, it is convenient to say more about the `pathNameHashtable` in this chapter. To fully understand the `pathNameHashtable`, however, you should also refer to the information in Chapter 8.

Hashtable Key Used by *pathNameHashtable*

The `pathNameHashtable` uses a key for each `NodeKey` stored in it that is made by concatenating the names of all the data nodes starting from the root node and ending with the node whose `NodeKey` is being cached, with a period separating each node name used. An example of one of these keys is the following string value:

```
bonForum.things.Subjects.Animals.Fish.Piranha
```

PathNameHashtable and Chat Subjects

At present, the `pathNameHashtable` is used only when adding the tree of subject categories to the `bonForumXML` `ForestHashtable`. We have adopted a rule that no duplicate pathNames are allowed in this tree of subjects. This means, for example, that you cannot have two sibling nodes named Piranha or two sibling nodes named Fish.

A pathName, such as the example just given for the Piranha subject node, is used as the key in the pathNameHashtable to store the NodeKey object that is associated with the node "pointed to" by the pathName. In the case of the example, the Piranha BonNode is stored in the bonForumXML ForestHashtable with a triple-valued NodeKey. That NodeKey is immediately put into the pathNameHashtable (as an element this time) with a key that is a string containing the pathName that was just given as an example.

Mapping User Choices to *PathName* Keys

We can now display to the user any list of chat subjects that are mapped to the pathName keys. (This is a good place to apply XSLT.) When the user selects a chat subject, the associated pathName key can be used to get immediate access to the BonNode for the subject—for example, to add a child element to it. For example, here is the code (from the BonForumEngine class) that adds an element named after the user's session ID to the chat subject element that the user has selected it:

```
obj = bonForumStore.add("bonAddElement", chatSubject, nameAndAttributes, content,
forestHashtableName, "pathNameHashtable sessionId");
NodeKey itemNodeKey = (NodeKey)obj;
```

The last argument of the add() method in BonForumEngine tells it to use the pathNameHashtable because that is where subject NodeKeys are cached. The nameAndAttributes argument contains the session ID from the user's HTTP request. The chatSubject argument provides a pathName key (such as the example given previously) to find the subject node (which in our example case is the Piranha element).

HTTP Session Branding in bonForum Web Chat

Here is what the equivalent XML for a chat item with a subject category of Animals.Fish.Piranha and a topic of pet piranha stories would look like after the SessionID and the chatTopic child elements have been added, using the pathNameHashtable to avoid searching for the Piranha subject parent node.

```
<Piranha nodeKey="965501558519.965501558509.965501558459">
<sessionID_v7iabpmab1_9928478272761
➥nodeKey="965503120084.965501558519.965501558509" ➥chatTopic="pet piranha
stories" />
</Piranha>
```

Filling the *pathNameHashtable*

You might wonder how the subject NodeKeys got into the pathNameHashtable in the first place. That also happens in the BonForumEngine class, as shown by the following excerpt from its Initialize() method:

```
String xmlUri = "..\\webapps\\bonForum\\docs\\subjects.xml";
try {
```

```
        DOMParser parser = new DOMParser();
        parser.parse(xmlUri);
        Document document = parser.getDocument();
        try {
           loadForumXML(pathToSubTreeRootNode,
           parentNodeInDestination, document, "pathNameHashtable");
        }
        catch(Exception ee) {
           logTFE.logWrite("err", "bonLog1.txt", "caught exception
           trying to load subjects.xml into bonForumXML");
        }
     }
     catch(Exception ex) {
        logTFE.logWrite("caught exception trying to parse subjects.xml");
     }
```

If we follow the trail of the `loadForumXML()` method, we find that we must continue on to a poorly named `loadXMLSubTreeIntoForestHashtable()` method, which is called from `loadForumXML()` as follows:

```
loadXMLSubTreeIntoForestHashtable(node, parentNodeKey, bonForumXML,
nodeKeyPathName, nodeKeyHashtableName);
```

It is in `loadXMLSubTreeIntoForestHashtable` that the real job of filling the `pathNameHashtable` takes place:

```
if(nodeKeyHashtableName.equals("pathNameHashtable")) {
   // here save nodeKey with a pathName key
   // only save descendants of bonForum.things.subjects
   if (nodeKeyPathName.equals("")) {
        if((!(nodeName.equals("bonForum"))) &&
              (!(nodeName.equals("things"))) &&
              (!(nodeName.equals("subjects"))) )  {
           nodeKeyPathName = nodeName;
        }
   }
   else {
      // build the pathName by concatenating node just added
      nodeKeyPathName = nodeKeyPathName + "." + nodeName;
   }
   if(!nodeKeyPathName.equals("")) {
      forestHashtable.pathNameHashtable.put(nodeKeyPathName, nextParentNodeKey);
   }
}
```

11.5.5 Dependencies on *bonForumEngine*

Most of the code in `bonForumEngine` that relates to `pathNameHashtable` should really be moved into the `ForestHashtable` class. In fact, that is not the only dependency between the two classes.

Originally the `ForestHashtable` was defined within the `bonForumEngine` source file, and it has only partially been extracted as a freestanding class. Our first goal was to get enough code working to experiment with the concepts behind the Web application project. The results of these experiments will undoubtedly change the requirements of both classes, so there is no point in getting too stuck in perfecting the definition of either class now.

11.6 Adding *ForestHashtable* Nodes

To simplify the methods that manipulate its nodes, the `ForestHashtable` class distinguishes among three different kinds of nodes, as follows:

Root nodes

Children of root nodes

Children of nonroot nodes

A separate public method is provided for adding nodes in each of these categories, as follows:

`addRootNode()`

`addChildNodeToRootNode()`

`addChildNodeToNonRootNode()`

Each of these three methods depends upon a protected method called `addNode()`, which we shall discuss before the three public methods. However, as you have seen, all the nodes in a `ForestHashtable` require a `NodeKey`, so let's first look at the method that provides the three public node addition methods with a unique key to store their new nodes.

11.6.1 Creating a New, Unique *NodeKey*

The `ForestHashtable` has a private long variable named `lastCurrentTimeMillis`. You can see how it uses this to provide a new, unique `NodeKey` instance by examining the method that returns a `NodeKey` to use for storing each newly created `bonNode`:

```
private NodeKey getNextAvailableNodeKey() {
  long temp = 0;
  long lastCurrentTimeMillis = System.currentTimeMillis();
  NodeKey nodeKey = new NodeKey();
  while (temp <= lastCurrentTimeMillis) {
    temp = System.currentTimeMillis();
  }
  nodeKey.aKey = Long.toString(temp);
  // initialize other keys to first,
  // that makes node a root node by default
  nodeKey.bKey = nodeKey.aKey;
  nodeKey.cKey = nodeKey.aKey;
  return nodeKey;
}
```

By initializing the second and third keys to the same value as the primary key, we are effectively making a `NodeKey` for a root node, by default. We discussed why this is so in Section 11.4.1, "Design of the `ForestHashtable`."

11.6.2 The *addNode()* Method

As mentioned previously, the public methods to add nodes at various levels of the `ForestHashtable` hierarchy all depend upon the `addNode()` method, which is shown in the following excerpt from the source code:

```
private BonNode addNode(String nodeName, String nodeAttributes, String
nodeContent, NodeKey nodeKey, NodeKey parentNodeKey, String nodeKeyHashtableName,
int nodeKeyKeyPrefix, String sessionId) {
  BonNode node = new BonNode();
  node.deleted = false;
  node.flagged = false;
  node.nodeName = nodeName;
  if(nodeAttributes != null && nodeAttributes.length() > 0) {
    node.nodeAttributes = "nodeKey=\""+ nodeKey + "\" " + nodeAttributes;
  }
  else {
    node.nodeAttributes = "nodeKey=\""+ nodeKey + "\"";
  }
  node.nodeContent = nodeContent;
  node.nodeKey = nodeKey;
  node.parentNodeKey = parentNodeKey;
  // put in this ForestHashtable
  // also optionally put nodeKey in nodeNameHashtable
  // but not if it is a subject element, etc.
  if(nodeKeyHashtableName.equals("nodeNameHashtable")) {
    // Hashtable is synchronized, but we need to sync two together here:
    String nodeKeyKey = null;
    synchronized(this) {
      try {
        this.put(nodeKey, node);
      }
      catch(Exception ee) {
        log(sessionId, "err", "EXCEPTION in addNode():" + ee.getMessage());
        ee.printStackTrace();
      }
      if(nodeKeyKeyPrefix == SESSION_ID) {
        // allows only one key per session
        // use this option to reduce size of table
        // by not storing key to nodeKeys not needed
        // (examples: message keys, messageKey keys).
        nodeKeyKey = sessionId + ":" + nodeName;
      }
      else if(nodeKeyKeyPrefix == SESSION_ID_AND_CREATION_TIME) {
        // the nodeKey.aKey acts as a timestamp
        // allowing multiple keys per session in nodeNameHashtable
        // use to find multiple nodes with same name for one session
```

```
          // (example: chat keys, guest keys, host keys)
          nodeKeyKey = sessionId + "_" + nodeKey.aKey +":" + nodeName;
        }
        else if(nodeKeyKeyPrefix == NO_NODEKEY_KEY_PREFIX) {
          // use no prefix for elements global to all sessions
          nodeKeyKey = nodeName;
        }
        else {
          nodeKeyKey = nodeName;  // unknown arg value, could complain
        }
        // else ifs and/or else can add other prefixes here.
        // Note: it replaces older table entries, if any
        this.nodeNameHashtable.put(nodeKeyKey, nodeKey);
      }
    }
    // else ifs here can add other hashtables later
    else {
      // Hashtable is synchronized, so if you change ancestor class for this,
      // be sure to sync addition to this here also.
      this.put(nodeKey, node);
    }
    return node;
  }
```

You might want to read again two relevant sections earlier in this chapter: Section 11.2, "The `NodeKey` Class," and Section 11.3, "The `bonNode` Class." The `addNode()` method creates a new `bonNode` and then uses argument values to set its name, attributes, and content.

NodeKey: Key, Node Member, Child Element

Notice that the `addNode()` method adds an additional attribute that keeps the `NodeKey` string value with the `BonNode`. That must be done because when `ForestHashtable` elements are converted into an XML document, its nodes can have attribute or child element values that "point" to the `NodeKey` of another nodes. For example, in the `bonForumXML ForestHashtable` used in the bonForum Web chat application, each chat element contains a child called `hostKey`. This `hostKey` points to the host of the chat by having the string value of a host element `NodeKey` as its text content.

Putting the *bonNode* in This *ForestHashtable*

After filling in the `node.nodeKey` and `node.parentNodeKey` members of the new `bonNode`, the `addNode()` method uses the `NodeKey` passed in as an argument again, this time to put the new `bonNode` into the `ForestHashtable` with the following statement:

```
this.put(nodeKey, node);
```

Caching the *bonNode*'s *Hashtable* Key

Before returning the new `bonNode`, the method checks to see if it should cache its `NodeKey` in a `NodeKeyHashtable`. The reasons for doing this, and the details of how it works, were discussed in Section 8.1.20, "Adding a Host Actor." At the time we wrote this, only the `nodeKeyHashtable` was handled inside the `addNode()` method. The `pathNameHashtable` is still being handled in the `bonForumEngine` class, but it should be moved here also. Other `Hashtables` can be added for specific optimization tasks in the future.

The `nodeKeyKeyPrefix` argument value determines whether the `NodeKey` being cached is for a globally available `BonNode` or whether it is associated with an HTTP session-dependent `BonNode`. We have discussed this optimization already and will add more to that later.

The `addNode()` method caches a `NodeKey` object in the `nodeKeyHashtable` with the following statement:

```
this.nodeNameHashtable.put(nodeKeyKey, nodeKey);
```

The `nodeKeyKey` can be used later to quickly retrieve the `nodeKey`, which in turn allows fast retrieval of the `BonNode` associated with it.

11.6.3 Adding Root Nodes

The simplest type of node to add to a `ForestHashtable` is a root node. Here is the source code for the public `addRootNode()` method that does that:

```
public BonNode addRootNode(String rootNodeName, String rootNodeAttributes, String
➥rootNodeContent, String nodeKeyHashtableName) {
NodeKey nodeKey = getNextAvailableNodeKey();
NodeKey emptyParentNodeKey = new NodeKey();
return addNode(rootNodeName, rootNodeAttributes, rootNodeContent, nodeKey,
➥emptyParentNodeKey, nodeKeyHashtableName,NO_NODEKEY_KEY_PREFIX, "");
}
```

The `NodeKey` returned by `getNextAvailableNodeKey` has all three keys set to the same value, which means that the `BonNode` we are adding with that `NodeKey` will be a root node, by definition. Therefore, we do not have to set the values of the `aKey`, `bKey`, and `cKey` in the `NodeKey` to make our newly added node be a root node.

Because a root node has no parent, we set the `parentNodeKey` to a new `NodeKey` that has empty key values. The value of `emptyParentNodeKey` as a string will be two period characters (..). We could have instead used a null `parentNodeKey` value, but then we would have to be more careful not to cause exceptions when we use it in other methods.

ForestHashtable Root Nodes Are Global

This method calls `addNode()` with the right arguments for adding a root node. The next-to-last argument value is `NO_NODEKEY_KEY_PREFIX`. As you can tell from the previous discussion about the `addNode()` method, this means that a root node in a `ForestHashtable` can never "belong" to one HTTP session; it is always global to the users of the `ForestHashtable`. In terms of the bonForum Web chat application, this means that there is only one cached `NodeKey` object for the primary XML data elements such as `bonForum`.

11.6.4 Automatic Parent Node Location Retrieval

If the node being added to a `ForestHashtable` object is to have a parent node, then the `addNode()` method must somehow "know" the location of this parent node. Because of the way that data is stored in a `ForestHashtable`, it must get the `NodeKey` object corresponding to that parent node. In fact, the correct parent `nodeKey` is found in one of the following three ways:

1. The parent's `NodeKey` is retrieved from the `nodeKeyHashtable` using as a key the parent `nodeName`.
2. The parent's `NodeKey` is retrieved from the `nodeKeyHashtable` using a key made from the session ID (and optionally a timestamp) plus a colon prefixed to the parent `nodeName`.
3. The parent's `NodeKey` is retrieved from the `pathNameHashtable` using as a key the complete path to the parent node in the data hierarchy.

Adding Children to Global Nodes

In the first case, the node that will be the parent of a newly added node may be globally available to all the users of the `ForestHashtable`. This means that when this parent node was itself added to the `ForestHashtable`, its `NodeKey` was also added to the `nodeKeyHashtable` with a key consisting of only the name of the parent node, without a session ID prefix. Thus, the name of the parent node can be used as the key in the `nodeKeyHashtable` to find the key in the `ForestHashtable` for the parent node itself.

Global *BonNodes* in bonForum Web Chat

This is easier to see with an example. In the bonForum Web chat application, the global nodes are the one and only root element (`bonForum`) and all three of its child elements (`actors`, `actions`, `things`). As you have just seen (in Section 11.6.3, "Adding Root Nodes"), a root node added to the `ForestHashtable` will always be a global node.

If you want to add a child to any of these global elements, then you do not need to search the `ForestHashtable` using an enumeration. You simply use the element name to find the element's `NodeKey` in the `nodeKeyHashtable`, and then you use that `NodeKey` to find the element in the `ForestHashtable`.

Adding Children with *nodeKeyHashtable*

In the second case, the parent node of the newly added node will "belong" to one user. As implemented in the Web application example for this book, one user means one HTTP session. It also means one browser and one thread.

For the addition of a node to fall in this case, the parent-node-to-be must itself have been added by the same user that is now adding a child to it. Also, as you shall see, it must be at least a grandchild of a root node. When a user adds a node in this second category to a `ForestHashtable`, its `NodeKey` is stored in the `nodeKeyHashtable` using a key that is made up of the HTTP session ID (and optionally a timestamp), followed immediately by a colon plus the `nodeName` of the node being added.

Example from bonForum Web Chat

Let's illustrate this with an example from the bonForum Web chat application. Consider the addition of a chat message by a user. It is stored in the `bonForumXML` `ForestHashtable` belonging to the `bonForumEngine` Java servlet. Within the XML data structure, the message is stored as a `message` element inside the global `bonForum.things` element. The key in `bonForumXML` for the newly added message will be a `NodeKey` object. This `NodeKey` object will also be stored in the `nodeKeyHashtable` belonging to `bonForumXML` using a key looking something like `To1010mC1859245324354153At:message`.

Adding Children with *pathNameHashtable*

The third way to find the parent node's key when adding a new node is to find it in the `pathNameHashtable` of the `ForestHashtable` using a key that represents the path to the parent node from its root node in the data. An example of such a `pathName` key is this:

```
bonForum.things.subjects.Vehicles.Motorcycles
```

The `pathNameHashtable` has already been extensively discussed in this chapter and also in Chapter 8, so there is little need to add more here.

Chat Subjects Cached in *pathNameHashtable*

The technique of using a node path to find a cached node key is currently being used for only the Subjects configuration subtree in `bonForumXML`. However, it is a technique that can be applied easily to the additional dynamic XML application-data sets that are envisioned for other Web applications (for example, an e-commerce application named bonMarketPlace).

NodeKeys for Node Access and Reuse

Each of the `ForestHashtable` methods that add a node return the node as well. (Note that the `BonForumEngine add()` method, which wraps the `ForestHashtable` `addChildNodeToNonRootNode()` method returns, instead an object that can be cast to a `NodeKey`.)

The return value can be important if you have more than one sibling with the same name, and the `add()` method uses `nodeNameHashtable`. Using `nodeNameHashtable`, you can recall only the last node added for a given `NodeKey` key.

Multiple Elements per HTTP Session

If you need to access more than one sibling node with the same name, then you can use `NameHashtable` keys that have both the session ID and the timestamp in their prefix, (`SESSION_ID_AND_CRATION_TIME`).

11.6.5 Adding a Node to a Root Node

Here is the source code for the method that can add a node to any root node:

```
public BonNode addChildNodeToRootNode(String childNodeName, String
childNodeAttributes, String childNodeContent, NodeKey rootNodeKey, String
➥nodeKeyHashtableName) {
NodeKey childNodeKey = getNextAvailableNodeKey();
childNodeKey.bKey = rootNodeKey.aKey;
childNodeKey.cKey = rootNodeKey.bKey;
// when the second and third key are equal, it is child of a root
return addNode(childNodeName, childNodeAttributes, childNodeContent, childNodeKey,
➥rootNodeKey, nodeKeyHashtableName, NO_NODEKEY_KEY_PREFIX, "");
}
```

Setting the Keys to Add the Node

Recall that the `NodeKey` returned by the `getNextAvailableNodeKey()` method is by default a root `NodeKey`. However, this method changes the `bKey` and `cKey` values to that of the `aKey` in the `NodeKey` of the desired parent root node. After these changes, the invocation of the `addNode()` method will have the correct `childNodeKey` argument for a child of a root node.

Children of Root Nodes Are Also Global

Notice that the next-to-last argument of the `addNode()` method call (`nodeKeyKeyPrefix`) is set to `NO_NODEKEY_KEY_PREFIX`. As discussed previously, this means that the newly added node will be available to all HTTP sessions using the `ForestHashtable`.

11.6.6 Adding a Node to a Nonroot Node

Here is the source code for the method that can add a node to any nonroot node:

```
protected BonNode addChildNodeToNonRootNode(String childNodeName, String
childNodeAttributes, String childNodeContent, NodeKey nonRootNodeKey, String
nodeKeyHashtableName, String sessionId) {
  NodeKey childNodeKey = getNextAvailableNodeKey();
  // when no keys are equal, its a root grandchild or deeper
  childNodeKey.bKey = nonRootNodeKey.aKey;
  childNodeKey.cKey = nonRootNodeKey.bKey;
```

```
  // Assume multiple keys per nodeKey allowed in "nodeNameHashtable"
nodeKeyHashtable
  int nodeKeyKeyPrefix = SESSION_ID_AND_CREATION_TIME;
  // unless node name to be added is in the "list".
  if(uniqueNodeKeyKeyList.trim().length() > 0) {
    if(uniqueNodeKeyKeyList.indexOf(childNodeName) > -1) {
      nodeKeyKeyPrefix = SESSION_ID;
    }
  }
  return addNode(childNodeName, childNodeAttributes, childNodeContent,
childNodeKey, nonRootNodeKey, nodeKeyHashtableName, nodeKeyKeyPrefix, sessionId);
}
```

Setting the Keys to Add the Node

This method is very similar to the `addChildNodeToRootNode()` method discussed previously. The first of two differences is that the new node's `NodeKey` has its `bKey` and `cKey` values set to the `aKey` and `bKey` values of the `NodeKey` of its parent node. Remember, when no two of its "triple keys" have matching values, a node is three or more levels deep in the data hierarchy—that is, it is a child of a nonroot node.

Session-Visible Children of Nonroot Nodes

The second difference is that the `nodeKeyKeyPrefix` argument value in the `addNode()` method invocation is set to `SESSION_ID_AND_CREATION_TIME` or `SESSION_ID`. These values mean that, if the `nodeKeyHashtableName` argument value used when the `addChildNodeToNonRootNode()` method is invoked is set to `nodeKeyHashtable`, then the newly added node will "belong" to the HTTP session that is making the node addition.

Note that, in the current version of `ForestHashtable`, this means that the `nodeKeyHashtable` can be used for global nodes only when these are root nodes, or children of root nodes. It may be a good idea to change that by passing the `nodeKeyKeyPrefix` argument to the `addChildNodeToNonRootNode()` method.

Sharing Session Nodes Between Users

Note also that the connection between an HTTP session and a node relates only to the use of the `nodeKeyHashtable` as a fast node-access mechanism. You can still arrange to "share" nodes between different HTTP sessions (users) by keeping their `NodeKey` values in another location that is available to all sessions, or passing the `NodeKey` from one session to another.

11.7 Deleting *ForestHashtable* Nodes

Have you wondered what happens to nodes in a data tree whose visibility is tied to an HTTP session when that session ceases to exist? Such nodes would never normally be accessed again, so they must be either be deleted from the tree or associated with another HTTP session that is tied to the same user (for example). The lifetime of a session is of a variable length of time and depends upon both some settings in the server environment and some client factors.

Here is the source code for the `doDeleteNode()` method of `ForestHashtable`. This is the lower-level private method that actually does the work of deleting the node. Notice that changing this method is part of the future scenario of `ForestHashtable`; it might become a data storage class with a persistent data store.

```
private boolean doDeleteNode(NodeKey keyOfNodeToDelete) {
   if (this.containsKey(keyOfNodeToDelete)) {
         this.remove(keyOfNodeToDelete);
         return true;
   }
   else {
         return false;
   }
}
```

Another planned optimization is to implement the code that uses the `deleted` flag in the `NodeKey` class to carry out virtual node deletion with a background system thread that scavenges older dead nodes. That would mean that the `doDeleteNode` would simply mark nodes as deleted and could be implemented with different XML data storage solutions at a later date. Some limited undo facilities could also be implemented using this scheme.

11.7.1 *doDeleteNodeRecursive()*

The `doDeleteNodeRecursive()` method of `ForestHashtable` uses an enumeration of that class as a `Hashtable`, finds a node to delete using its `NodeKey`, and calls itself for each child of that node. It then removes the node from the `ForestHashtable` as a `Hashtable`. This recursion effectively deletes the first node and all its descendants.

```
private boolean doDeleteNodeRecursive(NodeKey keyOfNodeToDelete) {
   String parentAKey = keyOfNodeToDelete.aKey;
   NodeKey nodeKey = new NodeKey();
   BonNode bonNode = null;
   Enumeration enumeration = this.elements();
   if(!(enumeration.hasMoreElements())) {
      return false; // no elements to delete
   }
   while(enumeration.hasMoreElements()) {
      bonNode = (BonNode)enumeration.nextElement();
      nodeKey = bonNode.nodeKey;
      if(nodeKey.bKey.equals(parentAKey)) {  // found a child
         doDeleteNodeRecursive(nodeKey);
      }
   }
   //bonNode = this.getBonNode(keyOfNodeToDelete);
   this.remove(keyOfNodeToDelete);
   return true;
}
```

11.7.2 *getBonNode()*

The `getBonNode()` method of `ForestHashtable` is a simple utility method to get a `BonNode` element in the `ForestHashtable`, given its key, which is a `NodeKey`. Here is the code:

```
public BonNode getBonNode(NodeKey nodeKey) {
   if(nodeKey == null) {
      return null;
   }
   if(this.containsKey(nodeKey)) {
      return (BonNode)this.get(nodeKey);
   }
   else {
     return null;
   }
}
```

The `doDeleteNodeRecursive()` method can be changed to invoke the `getBonNode` method before removing a node by its key from the `ForestHashtable`. If that change is made, then the `getBonNode()` method can be overridden to provide some kind of event that is caused by node deletion. That can often be useful, but a price will be paid for it, so the invocation of this method appears commented out in the `doDeleteNodeRecursive` source code shown before.

However, perhaps a better alternative is to create some kind of `preDelete()` or `beforeDelete()` method in the nodes that can do any required cleanup and perhaps return a Boolean allowing or disallowing the delete.

11.7.3 *deleteNode()*

You have seen how the optionally recursive node deletion works. Now let's look at the public method by which a user application deletes a `BonNode` from a `ForestHashtable`. Here is the source code for its `deleteNode()` method:

```
public boolean deleteNode(NodeKey keyOfNodeToDelete, boolean leafOnly) {
   if(this.containsKey(keyOfNodeToDelete)) {
      if(leafOnly) {
         if(hasAtLeastOneChild(keyOfNodeToDelete)) {
            return false;// was not a leaf node, so not deleted
         }
      }
      return doDeleteNodeRecursive(keyOfNodeToDelete);
   }
   else {
      return false;  // no such node
   }
}
```

You can see how easy node access is when you have the `NodeKey`. Of course, this does not require the three keys in the `NodeKey`, as discussed at the beginning of this chapter.

But it is rather nice to have one key encoding both order in a table and hierarchy in a tree at the same time. It would be more expensive to keep these two potentially independent factors in separate objects.

11.7.4 Deleting Descendants or Only Leaf Nodes

If `leafOnly` is `true`, then the `BonNode` is not deleted if it has (one or more) child nodes. This would allow you, for example, to not delete a folder that still had files or folders in it, in a typical computer file system.

On the other hand, if `leafOnly` is `false`, then the `BonNode` and all of its descendants are deleted. This allows you to prune branches off a data tree by deleting the node at the base of the branch to delete.

11.7.5 *hasAtLeastOneChild()*

Now let's display the Java source code for the `hasAtLeastOneChild()` method of `ForestHashtable`. It is used by the `deleteNode()` method to determine whether a `BonNode` is a leaf node when the `leafOnly` argument of the `hasAtLeastOneChild()` method is set to a value of `true`. Feel free to use this public method for other purposes.

```
public boolean hasAtLeastOneChild(NodeKey parentNodeKey) {
    BonNode bonNode = null;
    String parentAKey = parentNodeKey.aKey;
    Enumeration enumeration = this.elements();
    while(enumeration.hasMoreElements()) {
        bonNode = (BonNode)enumeration.nextElement();
        if(bonNode.nodeKey.bKey.equals(parentAKey)) {
            return true;
        }
    }
    return false;
}
```

In a `ForestHashtable`, children have a `nodeKey.bKey` equal to the parent's `nodeKey.aKey`. Therefore, when the enumeration of the `ForestHashtable` contents finds a single node that passes that test, it can return a value of `true` for the `hasAtLeastOneChild()` method.

11.8 Editing *ForestHashtable* Nodes

Changing a `BonNode` can be done with a `delete()` method plus an `add()` method, of course. More convenient is the `editBonNode()` method. It finds a `BonNode` using its `NodeKey` and then replaces any or all of the `nodeName`, `nodeAttributes`, and `nodeContent` items that are passed in as arguments.

11.8.1 *editBonNode()*

```
public NodeKey editBonNode(NodeKey nodeKey, String newNodeName, String
newNodeAttributes, String newNodeContent) {
    NodeKey retval = null;
    synchronized(this) {
        BonNode bonNode = getBonNode(nodeKey);
        if(bonNode != null) {
            boolean putNew = false;
            if(newNodeName != null) {
                bonNode.nodeName = newNodeName;
                putNew = true;
            }
            if(newNodeAttributes != null) {
                bonNode.nodeAttributes = newNodeAttributes;
                putNew = true;
            }
            if(newNodeContent != null) {
                bonNode.nodeContent = newNodeContent;
                putNew = true;
            }
            if(putNew) {
                try {
                    doDeleteNode(nodeKey);
                }
                catch(Exception ee) {
                    logFH.logWrite("editBonNode() exception deleting node!:"
                    ➥+ ee.getMessage());
            }
                try {
                    retval = (NodeKey)this.put(nodeKey, bonNode);
                }
                catch(Exception ee) {
                    logFH.logWrite("editBonNode() exception putting node!:"
                    + ee.getMessage());
                }
            }
            else {
                logFH.logWrite("editBonNode() no edits to make!");
            }
        }
            else {
                logFH.logWrite("editBonNode() no bonNode.with this nodeKey!");
            }
        }
        return retval;
}
```

The `editBonNode()` method is used in the `BonForumEngine` servlet for two purposes. One is to get content into nodes that have been loaded from XML documents by the `LoadXMLSubTreeIntoForestHashtable()` method. The other is to add an `itemKey` attribute to a chat element. We will also try using it to allow a chat host to change the rating of a guest in a chat.

> **Warning**
>
> The `BonNodes` in a `ForestHashtable` are insufficiently protected from editing at this point. Of course, for one user to get the session ID of another to edit the other's nodes is hard to do without it being planned that way. But the global nodes (root and its children) are editable by any user now. That is hardly a situation that should be tolerated in a real Web application.

11.9 Getting *ForestHashtable* as XML

The primary purpose of the `ForestHashtable` class is to contain XML data to experiment with Web application-dependent node-access optimizations. It obviously is convenient to get the content of a `ForestHashtable` instance as an XML document, to allow compatibility with other XML tools in the software development arsenal. Such convenience is supplied by methods of `ForestHashtable`.

In this section we discuss the `getXMLTree()` public method and the various lower-level, private methods that make it possible. However, we first look at the source code for the `getXmlNode()` method:

```
public String getXmlNode(NodeKey nodeKey) {
    String xml = "";
    BonNode bonNode = getBonNode(nodeKey);
    String name = bonNode.nodeName;
    String attributes = bonNode.nodeAttributes;
    String content = bonNode.nodeContent;
    if (attributes != null && attributes.trim().length() > 0) {
      xml = xml + "<" + name + " " + attributes;
    }
    else {
      xml = xml + "<" + name;
    }
    if (content != null && content.trim().length() > 0) {
      xml = xml + ">" + content + "<\\" + name + ">";
    }
    else {
      xml = xml + "\\>";
    }
    return xml;
}
```

As you can see, the `getXmlNode()` simply unwraps the name, attributes, and content of a `BonNode` instance and puts it into the tagged XML format in a string object. All this method needs is the `NodeKey` associated with a `BonNode` in the `ForestHashtable`, and it will return a valid XML element as a string. Of course, in the future it will need to deal with other types of XML nodes.

Also note that it could be a good idea to check that the key used in the `ForestHashtable` as a `Hashtable` (the `nodeKey` argument) is the same as the key that is stored in the node's `nodeKey` member itself (`bonNode.nodeKey`). Such a test has been omitted for speed.

11.9.1 *getXMLTrees()*

The `getXMLTrees()` method of the `ForestHashtable` returns a string containing all the trees in the `ForestHashtable`. Depending on the application and its state, that can be a large string object, so it should not be used casually. In future versions of the class, more selectivity is to be desired in extracting XML subsets of the entire content, including perhaps XPATH functionality.

This method assumes that `ForestHashtable` includes zero or more well-formed XML subtrees—more specifically, that it contains zero or more elements each either a leaf node or the root of a well-formed tree of elements. The method reads this content as a forest tree and provides the opening and the closing tags to format the contents as valid XML, although without the opening XML programming instruction node.

```
public String getXMLTree() {
   BonNode bonNode;
   String xml = "";
   long elementCount;
   String nameRootNode = "";
   String nameChildOfRootNode = "";
   String name = "";
   String attributes = "";
   String content = "";
   elementCount = unFlagAllFlaggedElements();
   Enumeration enumerationRN = this.elements();
   lastRootNodeFound = false;
   while (!lastRootNodeFound) {
      bonNode = getNextRootNode(enumerationRN);
      if (bonNode == null) {
      lastRootNodeFound = true;
      break;
   }
   name = bonNode.nodeName;
   nameRootNode = name;
   attributes = bonNode.nodeAttributes;
   content = bonNode.nodeContent;
   // OUTPUT A ROOTNODE
   if (attributes != null && attributes.trim().length() > 0) {
       xml = xml + "<" + name + " " + attributes;
   }
   else {
       xml = xml + "<" + name;
   }
   if (content != null && content.trim().length() > 0) {
       xml = xml + ">" + content;
   }
```

```
        else {
              xml = xml + ">";
        }
        Enumeration enumerationCRN = this.elements();
        lastChildOfRootNodeFound = false;
        while (!lastChildOfRootNodeFound) {
           bonNode = getNextChildOfRootNode(enumerationCRN);
           if (bonNode == null) {
              lastChildOfRootNodeFound = true;
              break;
           }
           name = bonNode.nodeName;
           nameChildOfRootNode = name;
           attributes = bonNode.nodeAttributes;
           content = bonNode.nodeContent;
           // OUTPUT A CHILD OF A ROOTNODE
           if (attributes != null && attributes.trim().length() > 0) {
              xml = xml + "<" + name + " " + attributes;
        }
        else {
           xml = xml + "<" + name;
        }
        if (content != null && content.trim().length() > 0) {
           xml = xml + ">" + content;
        }
        else {
           xml = xml + ">";
        }
           xml = getNextChildOfNonRootNodeRecursively(xml, bonNode.nodeKey);
           xml = xml + "</" + nameChildOfRootNode + ">";
        }
           xml = xml + "</" + nameRootNode + ">";
        }
        elementCount = unFlagAllFlaggedElements();
        return xml;
   }
```

In accordance with the node classification that the class design used for optimization, the getXMLTrees() method uses different methods to get the root nodes, their children, and then recursively the other descendants of the roots. The methods that are used to retrieve nodes of the three types (root node, child of a root node, and child of a nonroot node) are each discussed later.

Using String Buffers

Note that we have used concatenation operations throughout this method (and, in fact, throughout the bonForum project) because they are easier to visualize in the code listings. However, these should be replaced by using a string buffer, which offers a big improvement in the speed and the memory usage of the application. Using strings as we have previously creates many very large temporary strings and buffers, and is thus expensive and inefficient.

unFlagAllFlaggedElements()

When nodes have been selected for inclusion in the output returned by any of the private methods that get nodes from a `ForestHashtable`, these "used" nodes are flagged by setting their `flagged` member to `true`. Then further processing of the `Hashtable` can simply skip used nodes rather than test them again. We thus need a way to clear all the `flagged` flags, which is provided by the `unFlagAllFlaggedElements()` method shown here:

```
protected long unFlagAllFlaggedElements() {
   Enumeration enumerationALL;
   BonNode bonNodeALL = null;
   NodeKey nodeKeyALL = null;
   long count = 0;
   boolean foundNextRootNode;
   foundNextRootNode = false;
   enumerationALL = this.elements();
   while(enumerationALL.hasMoreElements()) {
      bonNodeALL = (BonNode)enumerationALL.nextElement();
      nodeKeyALL = bonNodeALL.nodeKey;
      if(nodeKeyALL != null) {
         count++;
         bonNodeALL.flagged = false;
      }
   }
   return count;
}
```

> **Warning**
>
> Obviously, as the size of the `ForestHashtable` contents grows, there is a reduced efficiency to most of its methods because of the frequent use of enumerations to iterate all the nodes in the contents. Again, we reiterate that this software is for experimentation. Handling large numbers of data elements will be addressed more fully when we reimplement this design using a commercial or open source database. We envision our `Hashtable` methods as operating on cached subsets of a larger relational database. This large intended grouping of `Hashtables` and caches with its triple keys IS a relational database, not a pure XML database. We do not want to reinvent the wheel.

11.9.2 *getNextRootNode()*

The `getNextRootNode()` method of `ForestHashtable` requires as its only argument an `Enumeration` object to be processed. It finds the first nonhidden root node, hides it, and returns it. When it cannot find a root node using the `Enumeration`, it returns a null value and sets a class flag called `lastRootNodeFound`. You should have enough information from reading the previous material here to be able to understand the source code for the method, which is reproduced here:

```
protected BonNode getNextRootNode(Enumeration enumerationRN) {
   BonNode bonNodeRN = null;
   NodeKey nodeKeyRN = null;
   boolean foundNextRootNode;
   foundNextRootNode = false;
   while(enumerationRN.hasMoreElements()) {
      bonNodeRN = (BonNode)enumerationRN.nextElement();
      nodeKeyRN = bonNodeRN.nodeKey;
      // this is a test for a root node
   if((!bonNodeRN.flagged) &&
   (nodeKeyRN.aKey.equals(nodeKeyRN.bKey)) &&
   (nodeKeyRN.bKey.equals(nodeKeyRN.cKey))) {
         foundNextRootNode = true;
         // hide this node, so we get it only once
         bonNodeRN.flagged = true;
         if(nodeKeyRN != null) {
            currentRootNodeAKey = nodeKeyRN.aKey;
            currentRootNodeBKey = nodeKeyRN.bKey;
         }
         break;
      }
   }
      if (!foundNextRootNode) {
      lastRootNodeFound = true;
      bonNodeRN =  null;
   }
   return bonNodeRN;
}
```

Note that several top-level class member variables keep track of the current triple-key values of the last root node found. These variables allow the coordination of the various methods that are used by the `getXMLTrees()` method. Some of the variables, including the `currentRootNodeCKey` variable in the `getNextRootNode()` method, are needed only for debugging.

11.9.3 *getNextChildOfRootNode()*

The `getNextChildOfRootNode()` method of `ForestHashtable`, like the `getNextRootNode` method, requires as its only argument an `Enumeration` object to be processed. It finds the first nonhidden child of a root node, hides it, and returns it. When it cannot find a node that is a child of a root node using the `Enumeration`, it returns a null value and sets a class flag called `lastChildOfRootNodeFound`. You should have enough information from reading the material here to be able to understand the source code for the method, which is reproduced here:

```
protected BonNode getNextChildOfRootNode(Enumeration enumerationCRN) {
   BonNode bonNodeCRN =  null;
```

```
    NodeKey nodeKeyCRN = null;
    boolean foundNextChildOfRootNode;
    foundNextChildOfRootNode = false;
    while(enumerationCRN.hasMoreElements()) {
       bonNodeCRN = (BonNode)enumerationCRN.nextElement();
    nodeKeyCRN = bonNodeCRN.nodeKey;
    // this is a test for child of current root node
    if((!bonNodeCRN.flagged) &&
    (nodeKeyCRN.aKey != nodeKeyCRN.bKey) &&
    (nodeKeyCRN.bKey = = currentRootNodeAKey) &&
    (nodeKeyCRN.cKey = =       currentRootNodeBKey)) {
        foundNextChildOfRootNode = true;
        // hide this node, so we get it only once
        bonNodeCRN.flagged = true;
        if(nodeKeyCRN != null) {
           currentChildOfRootNodeAKey = nodeKeyCRN.aKey;
           currentChildOfRootNodeBKey = nodeKeyCRN.bKey;
        }
        break;
      }
    }
    if (!foundNextChildOfRootNode) {
       lastChildOfRootNodeFound = true;
       bonNodeCRN =  null;
    }
    return bonNodeCRN;
}
```

Again, note that several top-level class variables keep track of the current triple-key values of the last child of a root node found. These variables allow the coordination of the various methods that are used by the `getXMLTrees()` method. Some of the variables, including the `currentChildOfRootNodeCKey` variable of the `getNextChildOfRootNode()` method, are needed only for debugging.

11.9.4 *getNextChildOfNonRootNodeRecursively()*

The `getNextChildOfNonRootNodeRecursively()` method of `ForestHashtable` invokes the `getNextChildOfNonRootNode()` to get the next nonhidden node that is at least a grandchild of a root node. Then it invokes itself recursively. The result, after some addition of tags in XML format, is a string containing an XML subtree starting at the node whose key it began with.

This method requires two arguments. One is the recursion variable that is the string that accumulates the final XML subtree. When no more nodes that are descendants of a nonroot node are found, the method sets a class flag called `lastChildOfNonRootNodeFound`. You should have enough information from reading the material here to be able to understand the source code for the method, which is reproduced here:

```
protected String getNextChildOfNonRootNodeRecursively(String xml, NodeKey
nonRootNodeKey) {
```

```
        String nameChildOfNonRootNode;
        String name;
        String attributes;
        String content;
        boolean lastChildOfNonRootNodeFound;
        BonNode bonNode = null;
        nameChildOfNonRootNode = "";
        Enumeration enumerationCNRN = this.elements();
        lastChildOfNonRootNodeFound = false;
        while (!(lastChildOfNonRootNodeFound)) {
           bonNode = getNextChildOfNonRootNode(enumerationCNRN, nonRootNodeKey);
           if (bonNode == null) {
              lastChildOfNonRootNodeFound = true;
              break;
           }
           name = bonNode.nodeName;
           nameChildOfNonRootNode = name;
           attributes = bonNode.nodeAttributes;
           content = bonNode.nodeContent;
           // OUTPUT A CHILD OF A NON-ROOTNODE
           if (attributes != null && attributes.trim().length() > 0) {
               xml = xml + "<" + name + " " + attributes;
           }
           else {
              xml = xml + "<" + name;
           }
           if (content != null && content.trim().length() > 0) {
              xml = xml + ">" + content;
           }
           else {
              xml = xml + ">";
           }
              xml = getNextChildOfNonRootNodeRecursively(xml, bonNode.nodeKey);
              xml = xml + "</" + nameChildOfNonRootNode + ">";
        }
        return xml;
    }
```

11.9.5 *getNextChildOfNonRootNode()*

The `getNextChildOfNonRootNode()` method of `ForestHashtable`, like the other node-getting methods, requires as its first argument an `Enumeration` object to be processed. Unlike those other node-getting methods, it also requires a second argument, which is used as a recursion variable (see Section 11.9.4, "`getNextChildOfNonRootNodeRecursively()`"). The method finds the first nonhidden child of a nonroot node and then hides it and returns it.

This method also differs a bit from other similar methods in that it is called recursively by another method. That method sets a class flag called `lastChildOfNonRootNodeFound`. You should have enough information from reading the material here to be able to understand the source code for the method, which is reproduced here:

```
protected BonNode getNextChildOfNonRootNode(Enumeration enumerationCNRN, NodeKey
nonRootNodeKey) {
   BonNode bonNodeCNRN =  null;
   NodeKey nodeKeyCNRN = null;
   boolean foundNextChildOfNonRootNode;
   foundNextChildOfNonRootNode = false;
   while(enumerationCNRN.hasMoreElements()) {
      bonNodeCNRN = (BonNode)enumerationCNRN.nextElement();
      nodeKeyCNRN = bonNodeCNRN.nodeKey;
      // this is a compound test for child of current non-root node
      String currentChildOfNonRootNodeAKey = nonRootNodeKey.aKey;
      String currentChildOfNonRootNodeBKey = nonRootNodeKey.bKey;
      String currentChildOfNonRootNodeCKey = nonRootNodeKey.cKey;
      boolean isChildOfNonRootNode = false;
      if(currentChildOfNonRootNodeAKey != null &&
      ➥currentChildOfNonRootNodeAKey.length() < 1) {
          // node is grandchild of a root node
          if((!bonNodeCNRN.flagged) && (nodeKeyCNRN.bKey ==
          ➥currentChildOfRootNodeAKey) && (nodeKeyCNRN.cKey ==
          ➥currentChildOfRootNodeBKey)) {
              isChildOfNonRootNode = true;
          }
      }
      else {
         // node is great-grandchild or greater of a root node
         if((!bonNodeCNRN.flagged) && (nodeKeyCNRN.bKey ==
         currentChildOfNonRootNodeAKey) ➥&& (nodeKeyCNRN.cKey ==
         currentChildOfNonRootNodeBKey)) {
            isChildOfNonRootNode = true;
         }
      }
      if (isChildOfNonRootNode) {
          foundNextChildOfNonRootNode = true;
         // hide this node, so we get it only once:
         bonNodeCNRN.flagged = true;
         if(nodeKeyCNRN != null) {
             currentChildOfNonRootNodeAKey = nodeKeyCNRN.aKey;
             currentChildOfNonRootNodeBKey = nodeKeyCNRN.bKey;
         }
         break;
       }
     }
    if (!foundNextChildOfNonRootNode) {
    bonNodeCNRN = null;
   }
   return bonNodeCNRN;
}
```

Again, note that several top-level class variables keep track of the current triple-key values of the last child of a nonroot node found. These variables allow the coordination of the various methods that are used by the `getXMLTrees()` method. Some of the variables, such as the `currentChildOfNonRootNodeCKey` variable of the `getNextChildOfNonRootNode()` method, are needed only for debugging.

11.10 More Public *ForestHashtable* Methods

A few other public methods in `ForestHashtable` can be helpful with the handling of nodes. We will present these methods in this section.

11.10.1 *countChildren()*

In a `ForestHashtable`, children have the value of `nodeKey.bKey` equal to the parent's `nodeKey.aKey`. That makes it easy to count the children of a node given its `NodeKey`. Here is the source for the `countChildren()` method:

```
public long countChildren(NodeKey parentNodeKey) {
   long counter = 0;
   BonNode bonNode = null;
   String parentAKey = parentNodeKey.aKey;
   Enumeration enumeration = this.elements();
   while(enumeration.hasMoreElements()) {
      bonNode = (BonNode)enumeration.nextElement();
      if(bonNode.nodeKey.bKey.equals(parentAKey)) {
         counter++;
      }
   }
   return counter;
}
```

11.10.2 *getChildNodeFromAttributeValue()*

Again, because in a `ForestHashtable` children have a value of `nodeKey.bKey` equal to the parent's `nodeKey.aKey`, we can iterate the children of a node to find one child that has a certain attribute value. For this project, we knew that there would be only one child with the given attribute value, so the method we wrote gets only the first child that satisfies the search criteria (`value=name`). The method can be easily changed to return a list of nodes when needed.

```
public BonNode getChildNodeFromAttributeValue(NodeKey parentNodeKey, String
➥attributeName, String attributeValue) {
   BonNode bonNode = new BonNode();
   if(parentNodeKey != null && attributeName != null && attributeValue != null) {
      String parentAKey = parentNodeKey.aKey;
      Enumeration enumeration = this.elements();
      while(enumeration.hasMoreElements()) {
         bonNode = (BonNode)enumeration.nextElement();
```

```
            if(bonNode.nodeKey.bKey.equals(parentAKey)) {
               // node is a child
               if(attributeValue.equals(getAttributeValue(
               bonNode.nodeAttributes, attributeName))) {
                  return bonNode;
               }
            }
         }
      }
      return null;
   }
```

The `getChildNodeFromAttributeValue()` method is used in the BonForumEngine servlet to locate the session ID of the chat host from the chat guest's HTTP session by looking for one child of a subject element using an attribute value. Section 8.4.9, "Passing Information between Sessions," in Chapter 8, discusses how this is done.

11.10.3 *attributeExists()*

Sometimes it is convenient to test for the presence of an attribute with a given name in a `BonNode`. You can use the following method, which takes the argument `allAttributes`, which is compatible with the `nodeAttributes` member of a `BonNode` object. This method is a bit rough and assumes that no spaces are allowed between an attribute name and the following equals sign in a `name=value` pair. It would also be fooled if the value of any attributes value included the name being sought followed by an equals sign.

```
public boolean attributeExists(String allAttributes, String attributeName) {
   if(allAttributes.indexOf(attributeName+"=\"") > -1) {
      return true;
   }
   else {
      return false;
   }
}
```

11.10.4 *getAttributeValue()*

To get the value of a `BonNode` attribute, you can use `getAttributeValue()` method, whose source is shown next. This method takes the argument `allAttributes`, which is compatible with the `nodeAttributes` member of a `BonNode` object.

As in the case of the `attributeExists()` method discussed previously, this method is a bit rough and assumes that no spaces are allowed between an attribute name and the equals sign following it in a `name=value` pair. We also must ensure elsewhere that no whitespace exists between the equals sign and the `attributeValue`.

We do allow escaped quotes characters within an attribute value. Adding that capability made the code somewhat complex, so it can probably be redesigned. It was tested for escaped quotes and also catches some errors such as no closing quotes in an attribute value and an attributeName argument that cannot be found. But, as with all the code in this book, use this at your own risk!

In the source code file ForestHashtable.java, we added some comments based on one of the allAttributes argument values that we used to design and test the method. That test argument was a string that included three attributes called type, itemKey, and dateStamp, as shown here:

```
type="tes\"ti\"ng" itemKey="961755688708.961755643923.961755643913" dateStamp="Fri
Jun 23 12:21:39 2000"
```

We used these arguments to help visualize the test argument as the code finds the desired attribute value while checking for escaped quotes characters in the allAttributes argument value. We also had to log many messages to a file to debug and test this method. It might help you to look at the commented-out log messages in the source code file as well, if you care to follow this code.

```
public String getAttributeValue(String allAttributes, String attributeName) {
   String str1 = null;
   int inx1 = allAttributes.indexOf(attributeName+"=\"");
   if(inx1 > -1) { // found name
      int inx2 = inx1 + (attributeName+"=\"").length();
      // remove all up through name, equals and opening quote
      str1 = allAttributes.substring(inx2);
      String str2 = new String(str1);
   boolean findingClosingQuote = true;
   int inxAcc = 0;
   while(findingClosingQuote) {
     // find next quotation mark
     int inx3 = str2.indexOf("\"");
     if(inx3 < 0) {
         //ERROR no closing quotation mark after value
       str1 = null;
       break;
     }
    // find next escaped quotation mark (if any)
    int inx4 = str2.indexOf("\\\"");
    if(inx4 > -1) {
       // found an escaped quotation mark
       if(inx3 == inx4 + 1) {
           // same one again, accumulate index relative to beginning of attribute
           value
           inxAcc += inx3 + 1;
           // remove all up to and including escaped quote
           str2 = str2.substring(inx3 + 1);
           }
           else {
           if(inxAcc > 0) {
                 inx3 = inxAcc + ++inx3;
           }
```

```
            str1 = str1.substring(0, inx3);
            break; // success
        }
    }
    else {
        if(inxAcc > 0) {
        inx3 = inxAcc + ++inx3;
        }
        str1 = str1.substring(0, inx3);
        break; // success
    }
        }
    }
    else {
        logFH.logWrite("ERROR? attributeName not found!");
    }
    return str1;
}
```

11.11 Initializing the *bonForumXML* Database

Here we display a shortened sample version of the initial XML data contents of the bonForum project's `ForestHashtable`, which is called `bonForumXML`. This XML document is equivalent to the contents of the triple-key table contents and is produced by the `getXML()` method in the `ForestHashtable` class.

To dump the data from the `bonForumXML ForestHashtable` into an XML file at any stage of the Web application, see the instructions in Section 6.7, "Outputting the bonForum Data as XML." A complete bonForum data sample printed with the source code also appears at the end of this book, as well as on the accompanying CD installation image. You should be able to view it by browsing the following file under the \bonforum\installed folder on the CD, or under the TOMCAT_HOME folder if you installed bonForum on your machine:

```
webapps\bonForum\docs\bonForumIdentityTransform.xml
```

As you can see, a root node called `bonForum` contains `actors`, `actions`, and `things` nodes. At initialization, one child of `actors`, called `system`, is added. A bonForum's XML database also contains initially a list of links to other bonForum Web sites, plus a complete subjects catalog (ours is just an incomplete sample for testing and is shortened here to save space).

You will notice that every element in the XML has one attribute called `nodeKey`, which is set to the value of the `nodeKey` for that element in the `ForestHashtable` (`bonForumXML`). When we output the contents of the `bonForumXML`, we put the value of the `NodeKeys` in these `NodeKey` attributes.

```
<?xml version="1.0"?>
<bonForum nodeKey="963539545855.963539545855.963539545855"
```

```
type="prototype">
<actors nodeKey="963539545885.963539545855.963539545855" type="READ_ONLY">
<system nodeKey="963539545895.963539545885.963539545855" type="SYSTEM">
</system>
</actors>
<things nodeKey="963539545945.963539545855.963539545855" type="READ_ONLY">
<forums nodeKey="965501558629.965501552059.965501551959">
<forum nodeKey="965501558669.965501558629.965501552059">
<weblink nodeKey="965501558689.965501558669.965501558629">
http://www.websitename.de/bonForum
</weblink>
<name nodeKey="965501558679.965501558669.965501558629">
Germany
</name>
</forum>
<forum nodeKey="965501558699.965501558629.965501552059">
<name nodeKey="965501558709.965501558699.965501558629">
India</name>
<weblink nodeKey="965501558719.965501558699.965501558629">
http://www.websitename.in/bonForum
</weblink>
</forum>
</forums>
<subjects nodeKey="963539548248.963539545945.963539545855">
<Animals nodeKey="963539548458.963539548248.963539545945">
<Dog nodeKey="963539548539.963539548458.963539548248">
<Terrier nodeKey="963539548559.963539548539.963539548458">
<Fox nodeKey="963539548569.963539548559.963539548539" />
</Terrier>
<LabradorRetriever nodeKey="963539548549.963539548539.963539548458"
/>
</Dog>
<Bird nodeKey="963539548468.963539548458.963539548248">
<Hawk nodeKey="963539548488.963539548468.963539548458"
/>
<Parrot nodeKey="963539548478.963539548468.963539548458"
/>
<Chicken nodeKey="963539548498.963539548468.963539548458"
/>
</Bird>
</Animals>
<Vehicles nodeKey="963539548308.963539548248.963539545945">
<Trucks nodeKey="963539548428.963539548308.963539548248">
<Mac nodeKey="963539548438.963539548428.963539548308" />
</Trucks>
<Autos nodeKey="963539548318.963539548308.963539548248">
<Rover nodeKey="963539548368.963539548318.963539548308">
<LandRover nodeKey="963539548378.963539548368.963539548318"
/>
</Rover>
<Subaru nodeKey="963539548388.963539548318.963539548308"
```

```
/>
</Autos>
<Motorcycles nodeKey="963539548398.963539548308.963539548248">
<Honda nodeKey="963539548418.963539548398.963539548308"
/>
<HarleyDavidson nodeKey="963539548408.963539548398.963539548308"
/>
</Motorcycles>
</Vehicles>
</subjects>
</things>
<actions nodeKey="963539545935.963539545855.963539545855" type="READ_ONLY" />
</bonForum>
```

11.12 Runtime *bonForumXML* Database

Here we show one example of the contents of `bonForumXML` at runtime from one imaginary simple instance. You can refer to this while reading this chapter to follow the discussion. Note that we shortened the contents of the subjects and forums elements to save space. The `nodeKeys` differ from the previous example because this is a different instance of the bonForum Web application.

To dump the data from the `bonForumXML ForestHashtable` into an XML file at any state of the Web application, see the instructions in Section 6.7, "Outputting the `bonForum` Data as XML." A complete bonForum data sample printed with the source code also appears at the end of this book, as well as on the accompanying CD installation image. You should be able to view it by browsing the following file under the \bonforum\installed folder on the CD, or under the TOMCAT_HOME folder if you installed bonForum on your machine:

```
webapps\bonForum\docs\bonForumIdentityTransform.xml
<?xml version="1.0"?>
<bonForum nodeKey="965501551959.965501551959.965501551959" type="prototype">
<actors nodeKey="965501551999.965501551959.965501551959" type="READ_ONLY">
<guest nodeKey="965506098557.965501551999.965501551959">
<actorAge nodeKey="965506098577.965506098557.965501551999">
32
</actorAge>
<actorNickname nodeKey="965506098567.965506098557.965501551999">
wally
</actorNickname>
<actorRating nodeKey="965506098587.965506098557.965501551999">
5
</actorRating>
</guest>
<test nodeKey="965501552039.965501551999.965501551959" type="TEST" />
<host nodeKey="965502388382.965501551999.965501551959">
<actorNickname nodeKey="965502388392.965502388382.965501551999">
adam
```

```
</actorNickname>
<actorAge nodeKey="965502388402.965502388382.965501551999">
123
</actorAge>
</host>
<system nodeKey="965501552009.965501551999.965501551959" type="SYSTEM">
</system>
<host nodeKey="965503119944.965501551999.965501551959">
<actorNickname nodeKey="965503119974.965503119944.965501551999">
charlie
</actorNickname>
<actorAge nodeKey="965503119984.965503119944.965501551999">
99
</actorAge>
</host>
</actors>
<actions nodeKey="965501552049.965501551959.965501551959" type="READ_ONLY"
/>
<things nodeKey="965501552059.965501551959.965501551959" type="READ_ONLY">
<forums nodeKey="965501558629.965501552059.965501551959">
<forum nodeKey="965501558639.965501558629.965501552059">
<name nodeKey="965501558649.965501558639.965501558629">
Mexico
</name>
<weblink nodeKey="965501558659.965501558639.965501558629">
http://www.websitename.mx/bonForum
</weblink>
</forum>
<forum nodeKey="965501558729.965501558629.965501552059">
<name nodeKey="965501558739.965501558729.965501558629">
United Kingdom
</name>
<weblink nodeKey="965501558749.965501558729.965501558629">
http://www.website.uk/bonForum
</weblink>
</forum>
</forums>
<subjects nodeKey="965501558198.965501552059.965501551959">
<Vehicles nodeKey="965501558308.965501558198.965501552059">
<Autos nodeKey="965501558318.965501558308.965501558198">
<BMW nodeKey="965501558328.965501558318.965501558308" />
<Ford nodeKey="965501558348.965501558318.965501558308">
<Thunderbird nodeKey="965501558359.965501558348.965501558318"
/>
</Ford>
</Autos>
<Trucks nodeKey="965501558429.965501558308.965501558198">
<Mac nodeKey="965501558439.965501558429.965501558308" />
<Other nodeKey="965501558449.965501558429.965501558308">
<sessionID_v7iabpmzg1_992808272761
➥nodeKey="965502388482.965501558449.965501558429" chatTopic="my other truck is
a ferrari"
```

```
/>
</Other>
</Trucks>
</Vehicles>
<Animals nodeKey="965501558459.965501558198.965501552059">
<Fish nodeKey="965501558509.965501558459.965501558198">
<Piranha nodeKey="965501558519.965501558509.965501558459">
<sessionID_47iabpmz11_992808274711
➥nodeKey="965503120084.965501558519.965501558509" chatTopic="pet piranha
stories"
/>
</Piranha>
<Guppy nodeKey="965501558529.965501558509.965501558459" />
</Fish>
</Animals>
<Health nodeKey="965501558258.965501558198.965501552059">
SPONSORED BY YOUR FRIENDLY CORPORATION
<Prevention nodeKey="965501558268.965501558258.965501558198">
<Headaches nodeKey="965501558278.965501558268.965501558258">
<Migraine nodeKey="965501558298.965501558278.965501558268" foo="this is foo!"
type="TESTING THIS NOW">
MORE STUFF CAN GO HERE
</Migraine>
</Headaches>
</Prevention>
</Health>
</subjects>
<message nodeKey="965502489387.965501552059.965501551959"
itemKey="965502388482.965501558449.965501558429" timeMillis="965502489287"
dateStamp="Saturday 05 09:08:09 2000"
hostKey="965502388382.965501551999.965501551959">
adam::this is dynamite!
</message>
<message nodeKey="965503142126.965501552059.965501551959"
itemKey="965503120084.965501558519.965501558509" timeMillis="965503141685"
dateStamp="Saturday 05 09:19:02 2000"
hostKey="965503119944.965501551999.965501551959">
charlie::Is anybody there?
</message>
<chat nodeKey="965502388412.965501552059.965501551959" moderated="yes"
itemKey="965502388482.965501558449.965501558429">
<hostKey nodeKey="965502388432.965502388412.965501552059">
965502388382.965501551999.965501551959
</hostKey>
<messageKey nodeKey="965502489397.965502388412.965501552059">
965502489387.965501552059.965501551959
</messageKey>
</chat>
<message nodeKey="965506175077.965501552059.965501551959"
itemKey="965503120084.965501558519.965501558509" timeMillis="965506174967"
dateStamp="Saturday 05 10:09:35 2000"
guestKey="965506098557.965501551999.965501551959">
```

```
wally::Hey! I'm here charlie. Are you there?
</message>
<chat nodeKey="965503120064.965501552059.965501551959" moderated="no"
itemKey="965503120084.965501558519.965501558509">
<guestKey nodeKey="965506098637.965503120064.965501552059">
965506098557.965501551999.965501551959
</guestKey>
<messageKey nodeKey="965503142136.965503120064.965501552059">
965503142126.965501552059.965501551959
</messageKey>
<hostKey nodeKey="965503120074.965503120064.965501552059">
965503119944.965501551999.965501551959
</hostKey>
</chat>
</things>
</bonForum>
```

11.12.1 Chat Data in the XML Data Example

At the time the bonForum data was dumped to an XML file, two chats had been started. The nicknames and ages of the two chat hosts are stored inside `host` elements as children of the `actors` element. Only one guest has joined a chat, and that guest's nickname and age are stored in a `guest` element also as a child of the `actors` element.

Adam is the host of a topic with the subject Vehicles.Trucks.Other and the topic "my other truck is a ferrari." Adam is still awaiting his first guest, and only his own single message appears in the chat. It could be displayed as follows:

```
[Saturday 05 09:08:09 2000]  adam::this is dynamite!
```

Charlie is the host of a chat with the subject Animals.Fish.Piranhas and the topic "pet piranha stories." Charlie and his guest, Wally, have each entered one message to the chat, which could be displayed as follows:

```
[Saturday 05 09:19:02 2000]  charlie::Is anybody there?
[Saturday 05 10:09:35 2000]  wally::I'm here, charlie.
```

11.13 More *ForestHashtable* Considerations

In this last part of this chapter, we will mention a few final things that are important to the understanding and future development of the `ForestHashtable` class.

11.13.1 Some Important Data Characteristics

In the example of bonForum XML data content at runtime shown previously, you can notice the following two characteristics of the way the chat data is kept in the `ForestHashtable`:

1. The objects stored in a `Hashtable` have no order. Therefore, the order of sibling elements in the XML document has no meaning. For human readability, if that is needed, some XML elements could be sorted by modifying the XSLT style sheet. Sorting could also be implemented by changing the underlying data structure to a `SortedMap` implementer, such as `TreeMap`, or by keeping an external sorted index in the manner of an RDB.
2. The `NodeKey` values are referred to by other key attributes, to relate the information in different elements together. For example, a chat element has a `hostKey` child that contains the value of the chat's host's `NodeKey`. That is why we preserve the `NodeKey` values in `NodeKey`" attributes within each element when the XML is output from the `ForestHashtable`.

11.13.2 Setting *ForestHashtable* Capacity

By reading the API documentation on the `java.util.Hashtable` class, you can learn about the issue of the capacity of a `Hashtable` object. The only way we have dealt with this so far is to provide a constructor for the class that takes an argument called **`capacity`**, which (surprise!) sets the capacity of a `ForestHashtable`.

The idea is that this capacity setting can be determined by the Web application, perhaps by having it saved as a parameter in the Web app deployment descriptor (web.xml) of the application. For the bonForum Web chat application example, we set the capacity to 5000. This number was selected by estimating 200 bytes per node. More testing is necessary to tune this factor, which is very important for the experience of using the Web application. Setting the capacity correctly can minimize the inevitable rehashing time.

11.13.3 XPATH Modeling Planned

One premise behind the design of `ForestHashtable` is that is could be easier or faster to manipulate a triple-valued key than to work with the (infinitely) long path expressions that can be present in an XML data document. The hierarchy of nodes can be modeled as a forest of trees by a table with a double- or triple-valued key.

A plan for the future is to see if we can create methods that fulfill all the XPATH functionality solely by processing the keys in the table.

11.13.4 Self-Healing XML Documents

Another idea of ours is to create an XML document representation that would create, by default, any "missing" set of nodes. These nodes that would be supplied form a node path connection between a "disconnected" XML fragment and the "closest" existing related node.

Why do that? Because that means you can put a tree-fragment into empty space in the forest. Then you could either tell or ask the forest to "decide" which tree the fragment belongs in. This would cause the forest to "grow" any necessary branches to connect the fragment with the tree, thus creating one new tree that can be expressed as a valid XML document.

Two practical outcomes appear here. First, if the keys for the forest are globally unique identifiers, you can throw together two or more forests of data, and they will still function as a forest (that is, the keys will not clash). That would be great for mixing data from laptops and servers, for example. Second, the self-sticking tree fragment addition to the forest means that relations among combined data sets can be "patched" by using default values, which preserves displayability and processability, in many cases. It might even keep your browser from choking!

11.13.5 Improvement of Algorithms

Much of the code in this class, as in the bonForum project in general, is intentionally written in a "dumb" style, leaving much room for optimization. Rather than trying to get too smart and doing many things in one statement, we think that it is easier to debug code that is spread out over smaller steps. Our motto is, "First get it working, and then get it working right!"

moveNode()

Further optimization will include addition of new methods. One candidate, for example, is a `moveNode()` method that would have the following signature:

```
moveNode(NodeKey KeyOfNodeToMove, NodeKey KeyOfNewParentNode, Boolean IfLeafOnly);
```

The `moveNode()` method would also have a `leafOnly` argument, as the `deleteNode()` method does. If `IfLeafOnly` is `true`, then the node would not be moved if it has one or more child nodes. If `IfLeafOnly` is `false`, then the node and all its descendants would be moved.

Another argument called `NewParentNode` would tell the method the destination to which it should move a node. If the `NewParentNode` is null, then the `NodeToMove` would be made a root node in the forest.

11.13.6 Enforcing Uniqueness Among Nodes

In the `addNode()` method of `ForestHashtable`, uniqueness is enforced for `nodeNameHashtable` entries. When we remove an "old" cached `NodeKey` from the `nodeNameHashtable`, we cannot simultaneously remove the node in the `ForestHashtable` because it may be in use in other thread.

However, we need to enforce unique sibling names in some situations—for example within descendant levels of the Subjects subtree in the bonForum Web chat application XML data. Also, at least in that application of the `ForestHashtable`, we would like to somehow enforce unique `chatTopic` values and `nickName` values by using a mechanism intrinsic to the `ForestHashtable`. This is left as a task for a future time.

11.13.7 Usability of the *ForestHashtable* Class

Without having tested the ForestHashtable experimental class sufficiently, it is not yet possible to characterize its runtime performance versus the quantity of data and thread loading. Certainly, processing will slow down at some point, but that depends on many factors, including the hardware on which it is running.

ForestHashtable Is a Design Laboratory

The ForestHashtable class is primarily a design laboratory. We will be implementing some of the ideas tried out there in a relational database system. You are invited to bring your comments and participation to http://www.bonforum.org, our open source site for the bonForum project on SourceForge.

12 Online Information Sources

THESE INTERNET LINKS ARE MOSTLY to XML, XSLT, Java servlet, and JSP information. Some cover what was left out of this book, intentionally or otherwise. Some link to topics that were discussed in this book. To keep current with all these technologies, you might want to subscribe to some mailing list groups and search and surf the Web frequently. This list does not pretend to be complete or fair—it simply offers some starting points on the Internet. It also is available on the CD-ROM accompanying this book and online at `www.bonForum.org`, where you can click on the links. Our apologies go out to all the developers who have been ignored—we promise that it was not done intentionally!

12.1 Always Useful Sites

Web site for the bonForum Web application project
`http://www.bonForum.org`

A fun and smart way to search the Web
`http://www.links2go.com/`

A huge number of Java links from Cetus Links
`http://www.cetus-links.org/oo_java.html`

XML-based information retrieval
`http://www.goxml.com`

A great multilingual text editor

`http://www.textpad.com`

The World Wide Web Consortium

`http://www.w3c.org/`

W3C recommendations

`http://www.w3.org/TR/#Recommendations`

Internet Engineering Task Force

`http://www.ietf.org/`

Mailing lists and archives

`http://archives.java.sun.com/cgi-bin/wa`

`http://archives.java.sun.com/archives/index.html`

Sun Java Forums

`http://forum.java.sun.com/`

12.2 Apache Software Foundation

Apache Software Foundation

`http://www.apache.org/`

Apache Conference

`http://apachecon.com/`

Apache mailing lists

`http://xml.apache.org/mail.html`

`http://jakarta.apache.org/getinvolved/mail.html`

News about Apache

`http://slashdot.org/index.pl?section=apache`

12.3 Big Corporations

IBM

`http://www.ibm.com`

IBM Alphaworks

`http://www.alphaworks.ibm.com/`

IBM DeveloperWorks

`http://www.ibm.com/developer/`

Microsoft

`http://www.microsoft.com/`

MSDN

`http://msdn.microsoft.com/`

Sun Microsystems

`http://www.sun.com`

Sun Developers
http://www.sun.com/developers/

12.4 CSS

Cascading Style Sheets information
http://www.w3.org/TR/REC-CSS2/

CSS and XSL overview
http://www.w3.org/Style/Activity

12.5 DOM Information

Recommendations
http://www.w3.org/TR/#Recommendations

DOM Scripting WebRing
http://nav.webring.org/hub?ring=domscript;list

XML via the Document Object Model
http://wdvl.com/Authoring/Languages/XML/DOM/Intro/

12.6 HTML

Recommendations
http://www.w3.org/TR/html401/
http://www.w3.org/TR/REC-html32

HTML reformulated as XML
http://www.w3.org/TR/xhtml1/

Web Developers Library links for HTML
http://wdvl.com/Authoring/HTML/

The HTML Guide
http://www.webfrontier.org/html/index.html

12.7 HTTP

Description of HTTP
http://www.ietf.org/rfc/rfc2068.txt

12.8 Java

12.8.1 Java: Compilers and SDKs

Java 2 SDK, Standard Edition, download
`http://java.sun.com/j2se/1.3/download-windows.html`

12.8.2 Java: Books, Articles, and Magazines

Thinking in Java, free downloadable book
`http://www.bruceeckel.com/TIJ2/index.html`

Java Developer's Journal
`http://www.sys-con.com/java/newjava.cfm`

JBuilder Developer's Journal
`http://www.sys-con.com/jbuilder/index.html`

The Swing Connection
`http://java.sun.com/products/jfc/tsc/articles/index.html`

12.8.3 Java: Information

Sun BluePrints design guidelines for J2EE
`http://java.sun.com/j2ee/blueprints/`

Enterprise JavaBeans technology
`http://java.sun.com/features/1999/12/ejb.html`

Information on setting the class path
`http://java.sun.com/products/jdk/1.2/docs/tooldocs/win32/classpath.html`

About three-tier distributed architecture at Java Report Online
`http://www.javareport.com/html/features/archive/9804/reese.shtml`

Tomcat servlet and JSP development with VisualAge for Java
`http://www7.software.ibm.com/vad.nsf/data/document2389?OpenDocument`

Java extensions FAQ
`http://java.sun.com/products/jdk/1.2/docs/guide/extensions/ext_faq.html`

Bridging Java and Active X with Java plug-in scripting
`http://java.sun.com/products/plugin/1.2/docs/script.html`

12.8.4 Java: Language

The Java Language Specification: Gosling
`http://java.sun.com/docs/books/jls/html/index.html`
`http://java.sun.com/docs/books/jls/html/1.1Update.html`

Code conventions for the Java Programming Language contents
`http://java.sun.com/docs/codeconv/html/CodeConvTOC.doc.html`

12.8.5 Java: Resources

Bruce Eckel's MindView, Inc., OOP resources
`http://www.bruceeckel.com/`

Java programming resources at Gamelan.com
`http://www.gamelan.com/`

12.8.6 Java: Tools

JavaBeans and BDK1.1
`http://java.sun.com/products/javabeans/`

Forte for Java, free Community Edition
`http://www.sun.com/forte/ffj/ce/`

ElixirIDE
`http://elixirtech.com`

Java Beanshell: interactive Java shell
`http://www.beanshell.org`

JPython
`http://www.jpython.org/`

IBM alphaWorks Bean Scripting Framework
`http://www.alphaworks.ibm.com/tech/bsf`

Java for Linux
`http://blackdown.org/`

12.8.7 Java: Tutorials

The Java Tutorial
`http://java.sun.com/docs/books/tutorial/index.html`

12.9 JavaServer Pages

12.9.1 JSP: Main Web Site

JavaServer Pages technology
`http://java.sun.com/products/jsp/`

12.9.2 JSP: Specifications

JavaServer Pages (JSP) Specfication, Version 1.1
`http://java.sun.com/products/jsp/download.html`

12.9.3 JSP: Books

JavaServer Pages book
`http://www.browsebooks.com/Fields/`

Group writing a JSP book online
`http://www.esperanto.org.nz/jspbook`
`http://www.aptura.com/technology/jspBook_Architectures.html`

12.9.4 JSP: Companies

Information about commercial products supporting JSP
`http://java.sun.com/products/jsp/industry.html`

tarent GmbH
`http://www.tarent.de`

12.9.5 JSP: FAQ

Sun JSP FAQ
`http://java.sun.com/products/jsp/faq.html`

Good FAQ for JSP, maintained by Richard Vowles
`http://www.esperanto.org.nz/jsp/jspfaq.html`

12.9.6 JSP: Hosting

Free server space on the Internet, including Java servlet and JSP support
`http://www.mycgiserver.com`

12.9.7 JSP: Information

JSP syntax cards, tutorials, a technical FAQ, and various presentations
`http://java.sun.com/products/jsp/technical.html`

JavaServer Pages technology: white paper
`http://java.sun.com/products/jsp/whitepaper.html`

Chat about JavaServer Pages
`http://developer.java.sun.com/developer/community/chat/JavaLive/2000/jl0222.html`

JSP versus ASP
http://java.sun.com/products/jsp/jsp-asp.html

Introduction to JavaServer Pages
http://www.builder.com/Programming/JSP/

12.9.8 JSP: Taglibs

Example
http://www.orionserver.com/examples/jsp/taglib/loop/index.html

12.9.9 JSP: Tutorials

JavaServer Pages tutorial
http://java.sun.com/products/jsp/docs.html

Servlet and JSP short courses
http://courses.coreservlets.com/Servlet-Courses.html

Basic JSP tutorial
http://java.sun.com/products/jsp/pdf/talks/WebLayer.pdf

IBM tutorial on JSP
http://www.software.ibm.com/developer/education/java/online-courses.html

12.10 Java Servlets

12.10.1 Servlets: Main Web Site

Servlet Web site at Sun
http://java.sun.com/products/servlet/

12.10.2 Servlets: Specifications

Servlet implementations and specifications
http://java.sun.com/products/servlet/download.html

Servlet API Javadoc online
http://java.sun.com/products/servlet/2.2/javadoc/index.html

12.10.3 Servlets: Books, Articles, and Magazines

Server-side Java magazine online
http://www.servletcentral.com

12.10.4 Servlets: Companies

JRun developer Web Site

`http://www.allaire.com/developer/jrunreferencedesk/`

tarent GmbH

`http://www.tarent.de`

12.10.5 Servlets: Hosting

Free server space on the Internet, including Java servlet and JSP support

`http://www.mycgiserver.com`

Servlet hosting

`http://www.wantjava.com/`

`http://www.coolservlets.com/hosts.html`

`http://www.servlets.net/index.html`

12.10.6 Servlets: Information

Good overview of servlets

`http://java.sun.com/docs/books/tutorial/servlets/overview/index.html`

Information about servlets

`http://www.javasoft.com/products/servlet/index.html`

12.10.7 Servlets: Mailing Lists

Archives of `SERVLET-INTEREST@JAVA.SUN.COM`

`http://archives.java.sun.com/archives/servlet-interest.html`

12.10.8 Servlets: Resources

Jason Hunter's Web site

`http://www.servlets.com`

Free, open source Java servlets

`http://www.coolservlets.com`

Servlets Taverne, with links to information in French

`http://www.interpasnet.com/JSS/textes/xml.htm`

Information on XML, Java, JDBC, and servlets by Nazmul Idris

`http://developerlife.com/`

12.10.9 Servlets: Tutorials

Servlets tutorial
`http://java.sun.com/docs/books/tutorial/servlets/`

12.11 Linux

Linux Open Source Magazine
`http://www.linux.com/`

Java Programming on Linux, the book
`http://www.javalinux.net/`

12.12 Open Source

Online book: *Open Sources: Voices from the Open Source Revolution*
`http://www.oreilly.com/catalog/opensources/book/toc.html`

Eric S. Raymond's *The Cathedral and the Bazaar*
`http://www.tuxedo.org/~esr/writings/cathedral-bazaar/`

SourceXchange
`http://www.sourcexchange.com/`

The Open Source Page
`http://www.opensource.org/`

The Techie-Hacker's Case for Open Source
`http://www.opensource.org/for-hackers.html#marketing`

Ask Tim at O'Reilly
`http://www.oreilly.com/ask_tim/index.html`

ExoLab.org Open Source & Enterprise Java
`http://www.exolab.org/`

Free support for Open Source projects
`http://sourceforge.net/docs/site/services.php`

Licensing Open Source Software: Jason Hunter's license
`http://www.servlets.com/resources/com.oreilly.servlet/license.html`

ClueTrain Manifesto
`http://www.cluetrain.com`

Mozilla
`http://www.mozilla.org/`

Open source version control software
`http://www.sourcegear.com/CVS`

Open XML
`http://www.openxml.org/`

Open Source Enhydra Java-XML Application Server Home
http://www.enhydra.org/

Free XML software
http://www.garshol.priv.no/download/xmltools/

12.13 RDF

Resource description framework
http://www.w3.org/TR/REC-rdf-syntax/

12.14 Web Applications

Open Source Enhydra Java-XML Application Server Home
http://www.enhydra.org/

IBM white paper, "The Web Application Programming Model"
http://www.software.ibm.com/ebusiness/pm.html

XML: The Key to E-Business
http://www.washingtontechnology.com/news/14_10/tech_features/723-5.html

IBM white papers
http://www3.ibm.com/e-business/

12.15 Web Browsers

Microsoft Internet Explorer 5.5
http://www.microsoft.com/downloads/

MSDN Online Voices: Extreme XML
http://msdn.microsoft.com/voices/xml.asp

Information about IE5.5 XML
http://xmlhack.com/read.php?item=402
http://xmlhack.com/read.php?item=806

Mozilla (open source Netscape Web browser)
http://www.mozilla.org/

12.16 Web Servers

Apache Server
http://www.apache.org/httpd.html

Jigsaw Web Server (W3C)
http://www.w3.org/Jigsaw/
http://www.w3.org/Jigsaw/User/Introduction/wp.html

Jakarta Tomcat main Web site

http://jakarta.apache.org/

FAQ index for Tomcat

http://jakarta.apache.org/faq/faqindex.html

Latest Tomcat Users Guide

http://jakarta.apache.org/cvsweb/index.cgi/jakarta-tomcat/src/doc/tomcat-ug.html

12.17 XML

12.17.1 XML: Specs and Recommendations

W3C recommendation

http://www.w3.org/TR/REC-xml

XML.com: The Annotated XML Specification

http://www.xml.com/xml/pub/axml/axmlintro.html

Specifications of all XML-related technologies

http://java.sun.com/xml/docs/tutorial/overview/2_specs.html

12.17.2 XML: Articles, Books, and Magazines

XML Developer's Journal

http://www.sys-con.com/xml/index2.html

XML Books: Mastering XML from Sybex

http://www.extensibility.com/xml_resources/XML_books_mastering.htm

Writings of Benoit Marchal

http://www.pineapplesoft.com/site/focus/writings.html

Articles by Jon Bosak

http://www.ibiblio.org/bosak/

XML Developers Conference proceedings

http://metalab.unc.edu/bosak/conf/xmldev99/tauber/tauber.pdf

An Introduction to XML for Java Programmers

http://www.xmlmag.com/upload/free/features/xml/1999/01win99/pmwin99/pmwin99.asp

Fatbrain.com: books about XML

http://www.fatbrain.com/

12.17.3 XML: Companies

Bluestone Software, Inc.
`http://www.bluestone.com`

tarent GmbH
`http://www.tarent.de`

12.17.4 XML: Editors and Tools

Links and information for many XML editors
`http://www.xmlsoftware.com/editors/`

Free XML software
`http://www.garshol.priv.no/download/xmltools/`

XMLwriter
`http://xmlwriter.net/`

XMetal
`http://www.softquad.com/`

XML Spy
`http://www.icon-is.com/`

Xeena and visual XML tools from IBM
`http://www.alphaworks.ibm.com/tech/`

Visual XML
`http://www.pierlou.com/visxml/index.html`

12.17.5 XML: Examples

All Shakespeare works in XML
`http://metalab.unc.edu/`

An XML-based project for instant messaging
`http://jabber.org/`

XMLBinder and XSLServlet projects
`http://downloads.dyomedea.com/java/examples/`

12.17.6 XML: Information

Anything related to XML
`http://tecfa.unige.ch/guides/xml/pointers.html`

XML Global
`http://www.xmlglobal.com`

XML Search Engine People
`http://www.goxml.com`

Cafe con Leche XML news and resources
`http://metalab.unc.edu/xml/`

Extensible Markup Language (XML)
`http://www.oasis-open.org/cover/xml.html`

Chinese XML Now (English home page)
`http://www.ascc.net/xml/en/utf-8/index.html`

MSDN Online XML Developer Center
`http://msdn.microsoft.com/xml/default.asp`

XMLHack: great way to keep current on XML
`http://xmlhack.com`

Pineapplesoft Online Java, XML from Belgium (Benoit Marchal)
`http://www.pineapplesoft.com/`

IBM developerWorks XML Standards: Describing Data
`http://www2.software.ibm.com/developer/standards.nsf/xml-describing-byname`

XML APIs for databases
`http://developer.java.sun.com/developer/technicalArticles/xml/api/`

Activity in the XML world
`http://www.xml.org/xmlorg_catalog.htm`

XML in Spanish
`http://www.ramon.org`

XML, Java, JDBC, and servlets information
`http://developerlife.com/`

12.17.7 XML: Mailing Lists

Apache XML Project mailing lists
`http://xml.apache.org/mail.html`

XML-DEV for XML developers around the world: To subscribe to this list, send an email message to `majordomo@ic.ac.uk` with "subscribe xml-dev your@email.address" in the body.

XML-DEV archive
`http://www.lists.ic.ac.uk/hypermail/xml-dev/`

The xmlhack Daily News Digest
`http://xmlhack.com/`

12.17.8 XML: Microsoft

XML-related product downloads
`http://msdn.microsoft.com/downloads/`

Information about MSXML
`http://xmlhack.com/read.php?item=806`

An XML manifesto
`http://msdn.microsoft.com/workshop/xml/articles/xmlmanifesto.asp`

MSDN Online XML Developer Center
`http://msdn.microsoft.com/xml/default.asp`

XML Magazine
`http://www.xmlmag.com/`

12.17.9 XML: Namespaces

W3C recommendation
`http://www.w3.org/TR/REC-xml-names/`

12.17.10 XML: Organizations

Oasis XML and SGML organization
`http://www.oasis-open.org`

XML.ORG: The XML Industry Portal, hosted by OASIS
`http://www.xml.org/`

Biztalk.org
`http://www.biztalk.org/`

12.17.11 XML: Parsers

Apache XML Project
`http://xml.apache.org/`

Open XML
`http://www.openxml.org/`

XML Parser for Java, another alphaWorks technology
`http://www.alphaworks.ibm.com/tech/xml4j`

XP
`http://www.jclark.com/xml/xp/index.html`

Expat
`http://www.jclark.com/xml/expat.html`

Python XML parser
`http://www.python.org/topics/xml/`

TclXML
`http://www.zveno.com/zm.cgi/in-tclxml/`

Fxp, a parser written in SML
`http://www.informatik.uni-trier.de/~aberlea/Fxp/`

12.17.12 XML: SAX API

Megginson Technologies, Ltd.
http://www.megginson.com/

SAX: The simple API for XML
http://www.megginson.com/SAX/Java/index.html

12.17.13 XML: SVG

W3C Scalable Vector Graphics (SVG)
http://www.w3.org/Graphics/SVG/

The SVG viewer applet demos
http://sis.cmis.csiro.au/svg/demo.html

12.17.14 XML: Tutorials

Very complete XML tutorial, based on JAXP
http://java.sun.com/xml/docs/tutorial/index.html

Tutorial on XML and Java
http://www.developer.com

Zvon tutorials
http://zvon.vscht.cz/ZvonHTML/Zvon/zvonTutorials_en.html

IBM developerWorks XML Education: online courses
http://www-4.ibm.com/software/developer/education/transforming-xml/transforming-xml-to-html/index.html

Introduction to XML
http://www-4.ibm.com/software/developer/education/xmlintro/

XML and Java
http://www-4.ibm.com/software/developer/education/xmljava/

XML for Linux
http://www-4.ibm.com/software/developer/library/xml-for-linux1.html

The Foundation XML, XSL, X-Link
http://www.webreference.com/xml/column2/

Good online XML guide slanted toward Microsoft version of XML
http://xmlwriter.net/xml_guide/

12.17.15 XML: XHTML

HTML reformulated as XML
http://www.w3.org/TR/xhtml1/

12.17.16 XML: XLINK

Proposed W3C recommendation

http://www.w3.org/TR/xlink/

Good description of XLINK and XPOINTER

http://www.xml.com/pub/2000/02/xtech/tutorials.html

12.17.17 XML: XPOINTER

Proposed W3C recommendation

http://www.w3.org/TR/xptr

12.18 XSL

12.18.1 XSL: Recommendations

W3C recommendations for XSL, XSLT, and XPATH

http://www.w3.org/TR/#Recommendations

Extensible Stylesheet Language (XSL)

http://www.w3.org/TR/xsl/

XML Path Language (XPath)

http://www.w3.org/TR/xpath

XSL Transformation (XSLT)

http://www.w3.org/TR/xslt

12.18.2 XSL: Articles, Books, and Magazines

XSL Transformations: book chapter

http://metalab.unc.edu/xml/books/bible/updates/14.html

XSL Programming for Teams

http://developer.iplanet.com/viewsource/marchal_xml2/marchal_xml2.html

Validate Data with Regular Expressions and XSL

http://www.inquiry.com/techtips/xml_pro/10min/10min1199/10min1199.asp

12.18.3 XSL: Information

Style sheets

http://www.w3.org/Style/Activity

XSL in developerWorks XML library

http://www-4.ibm.com/software/developer/library/hands-on-xsl/

12.18.4 XSL: Mailing Lists

XSL-List: Send mail to majordomo@mulberrytech.com with "subscribe xsl-list" as the body of your message, or visit http://www.mulberrytech.com/xsl/xsl-list/index.html.

XSL-List archive indexed by thread
http://www.mulberrytech.com/xsl/xsl-list/archive/

12.18.5 XSL: Resources

Crane Softwrights, Ltd.
http://www.CraneSoftwrights.com/s/

XMLBinder and XSLServlet projects
http://downloads.dyomedea.com/java/examples/

Resources for XT
http://4xt.org/

XML- and XSLT-driven Web site
http://www.ctvsportsnet.com

12.18.6 XSL: Tools

Xalan overview
http://xml.apaohe.org/xalan/overview.html

SAXON processor
http://users.iclway.co.uk/mhkay/saxon/index.html

12.18.7 XSL: Tutorials

Zvon XSL tutorial
http://www.zvon.org/xxl/XSLTutorial/Books/Book1/index.html

XML online course
http://www-4.ibm.com/software/developer/education/transforming-xml/transforming-xml-to-html/index.html

XPathTutorial-General-examples.html
http://zvon.vscht.cz/HTMLonly/XPathTutorial/General/examples.html

Online XSLT-XSL Tutorials at XSLINFO
http://xslinfo.com/tutorials/

A
CD-ROM Contents

THIS APPENDIX DISCUSSES WHAT YOU can find on the CD-ROM that comes with this book.

At this time, all software developed by this book's author on the CD-ROM has been tested *only* with Windows NT 4.0 (Service Pack 5). Of course, much of the software should be portable to other operating systems, because it is all written in Java, JSP, HTML, XML, and so on, but no guarantees of any kind can be given. Please check the Web site at `http://www.bonforum.org` for possible information about using the software with operating systems other than Windows NT 4.0. That Web site also lists known problems, fixes, and updates for the software featured in this book and CD-ROM.

Please be aware that all the software files on this CD-ROM, whether created by this book's author or other parties, are licensed and have associated copyrights. You can find the appropriate licenses and distribution files in Appendix B, "Some Copyrights and Licenses." Please use and distribute the software products on this CD-ROM only in accordance with the provisions of their respective licenses!

Chapter 12, "Online Information Sources," is in the root folder of the CD-ROM so that you can load it into your Web browser. Please take advantage of its many Web links to find information related to the topics covered in this book. We especially recommend the links related to the Open Source software movement.

There are five folders in the root of the CD-ROM. The following text describes their contents in a general way, without listing all the subfolders or their contents in detail.

\Sun

The Sun folder contains the distributable Java Runtime Environment (JRE) installation files. It also contains the Java 2 SDK and the Forte for Java Community Edtion. In order to use and modify the Web applications featured in this book, you need the Sun Java SDK. Information about obtaining and installing the Java SDK is given in the first two chapters of this book, as well as at `http://java.sun.org`, from where you may download the SDK.

\Apache

The Apache folder and its subfolders contain three open source product releases from the Apache Software Foundation, which are fully discussed in the book and are used by the bonForum Web application (discussed in a moment). These products include the Jakarta Tomcat Server (release 3.2.1), the Xerces XML parser for Java (release 1.3.0), and the Xalan XSLT processor for Java (release 2.0.1). Note that these releases are the latest ones now tested with the software for this book.

You will also find on the CD-ROM some later releases of these three products—the latest that were available when this CD-ROM was produced. These have *not* been tested with the book or with the bonForum project software! We will post information about using these, and later releases that become available, at the bonForum open source project Web site at `http://www.bonforum.org`.

In addition, the CD-ROM contains other open source products released by Apache Software Foundation projects, which should interest readers of this book. These other products (Cocoon, ant, xang, and jakarta-taglibs) are not discussed in this book. You can find further information about them on the Apache Software Foundation Web site at `http://www.apache.org`.

\bonForum

The bonForum folder contains files related to the bonForum open source Web application project, which is thoroughly discussed in this book. It is a prototype for a Web chat application that is intended to test design concepts for Web applications of various types. In its present state, it is *not* intended for public deployment on the Internet as a chat application! None of the necessary security provisions for it are provided for in the design and implementation of the bonForum Web application, because its intent is purely and solely instructional and experimental.

Unless covered by another license, all the software (in both binary and source form) found in the bonForum folder and its subfolders has been released by the author under an open source license called the "bonForum license." A copy of it is included on the CD-ROM and appears in Appendix B. Distribution and use of the bonForum Web application software is covered by that license, so please read it if you use or distribute the software.

The bonForum project files are supplied in three forms, which are described next.

\bonForum\webapp\bonForum.war

This is a ready-to-install Jakarta Tomcat webapp (bonForum.war). You can copy this zipped archive file into a Tomcat webapps folder and restart Tomcat to install the chat application project. Chapter 5, "bonForum Chat Application: Use and Design," gives you the details.

\bonForum\source\bonForum\Projects_bonForum_001107_0503.zip

Note that the date and time at the end of this name may vary. This is a zipped archive of all the source code for the chat application, ready to add to the ElixirIDE projects folder, or wherever you want to use it. The pathnames of the zipped files all begin with "bonForum."

You are encouraged to experiment with it, fix it, hack it, and generally do whatever is consistent with the included copyrights, disclaimers, notices, and warnings. This is tutorial software without warranties of any kind. A few parts of the source are based on demonstration code that is supplied with various Apache Software Foundation projects (Xalan, Xerces, and Tomcat). We have included their license information in the source files involved and in Appendix B. You should check these to see if and how they apply to any code you derive from us or them.

> **Note**
>
> Any changes you make to files here must first be copied to the Tomcat webapps bonForum hierarchy before you see any change to the application. That includes HTML, JSP, XSL, class, image, and other files used by bonForum.

If you are not using an IDE, you can use the batch file provided. It will compile the Java files into the same folders where they are kept. The resulting class files must be used to overwrite the class files in the Tomcat application folders before the changes will appear in bonForum. Note that the BonForumRobot.class file is in two locations in the Tomcat webapps bonForum hierarchy.

> **Note**
>
> It is best *not* to copy the zipped file to your TOMCAT_HOME\webapps folder and unzip it there. If you want the source there, it is better to unzip into a temp folder and then move the bonForum\src folder hierarchy where you want it. Any zip file in TOMCAT_HOME\webapps will create a webapp when Tomcat starts up. Also, depending on your configuration of Tomcat, files might end up being browseable that should not be.

\bonForum\installed\

This folder has copies of two directory subtrees taken from the author's development machine. More details about these appear in the following sections.

\bonForum\installed\webapps\bonForum

This contains the bonForum Web application as installed in TOMCAT_HOME\webapps. You should be able to see from these files how the files in the source tree and webapp tree are related. Note that a few files appear in two locations in the webapp but only once in the source. This is true of the gif image files and of BonForumRobot.class. If you change these on your machine, be sure you change both copies.

\bonForum\installed\source\bonForum

This contains the complete source code hierarchy as it was installed in the C:Elixir\Projects folder on the author's machine. It was zipped to create the source code archive provided separately as something like bonForum_O_S1.zip. You can copy this to a projects folder for your IDE, if you want. Note that the source was also copied into an src folder under WEB-INF folder in the bonForum WAR file (discussed earlier).

\tools

The tools folder contains trial versions of three products from Elixir Technologies. This book discusses only ElixirIDE, but the other products (ElixirCASE and ElixirReport) look interesting and have been included for you to try. Chapter 2, "An Environment for Java Software Development," discusses the use of ElixirIDE, a Java Integrated Development Environment. You may use it to compile the Web application project example (bonForum) upon which this book is based. Alternatively, you may use your own familiar tools or the Java SDK command-line environment. Also in the tools folder are some plug-in modules that can be used with ElixirIDE. See its manual for details.

Also in the tools folder is a trial version of the TextPad editor, which I have found to be very useful for development. I usually put all the JSP files in one workspace and open that with one instance of TextPad. I put all the Java files in another workspace and open that in another instance of TextPad. A third instance and workspace makes all other project files (XSL, HTML, etc.) available. The "Find in Files" command in the Search menu is particularly useful.

E-Book

The E-Book folder contains this book in PDF format. This is copyrighted material and permission is required for commercial use and reproduction.

B

Some Copyrights and Licenses

THIS APPENDIX CONTAINS COPYRIGHT and license information for some of the various software products that have been discussed in this book and used in bonForum.

BonForum License

BonForum Software License, version 1.0.

Redistribution and use in source and binary forms, with or without modification, are permitted provided that the following conditions are met:

1. Redistributions of source code must retain the above copyright notice, these conditions, and the following disclaimer and note(s).
2. Redistributions in binary form must reproduce the above copyright notice, these conditions, and the following disclaimer and note(s) in the documentation and/or other materials with the distribution.
3. The end-user documentation included with the redistribution, if any, must include the following acknowledgment:

   "This product includes software developed by Westy Rockwell (`http://www.bonForum.org/`)."

   Alternately, this acknowledgment may appear in the software itself, if and wherever such third-party acknowledgments normally appear.

4. The names "bonForum," "BonForum," "BonForumEngine," and "BonForumRobot" must not be used to endorse or promote products derived from this software without prior written permission. Permission info is at `http://www.bonForum.org/`.
5. Products derived from this software may not be called by the names listed in item 4, nor may these names appear in their names without written permission. Permission info is at `http://www.bonForum.org/`.

DISCLAIMER: THIS SOFTWARE IS PROVIDED "AS IS," AND ANY EXPRESSED OR IMPLIED WARRANTIES, INCLUDING, BUT NOT LIMITED TO, THE IMPLIED WARRANTIES OF MERCHANTABILITY AND FITNESS FOR A PARTICULAR PURPOSE, ARE DISCLAIMED. IN NO EVENT SHALL THE AUTHORS OR CONTRIBUTORS TO THIS SOFTWARE, NOR ITS PUBLISHERS IN WHATEVER FORM, BE LIABLE FOR ANY DIRECT, INDIRECT, INCIDENTAL, SPECIAL, EXEMPLARY, OR CONSEQUENTIAL DAMAGES (INCLUDING, BUT NOT LIMITED TO, PROCUREMENT OF SUBSTITUTE GOODS OR SERVICES; LOSS OF USE, DATA, OR PROFITS; OR BUSINESS INTERRUPTION), HOWEVER CAUSED AND ON ANY THEORY OF LIABILITY, WHETHER IN CONTRACT, STRICT LIABILITY, OR TORT (INCLUDING NEGLIGENCE OR OTHERWISE) ARISING IN ANY WAY OUT OF THE USE OF THIS SOFTWARE, EVEN IF ADVISED OF THE POSSIBILITY OF SUCH DAMAGE.

NOTE: This software is provided for tutorial use! It is part of bonForum, a Web chat application that is fully discussed in a book by Westy Rockwell called XML, XSLT, Java, and JSP: A Case Study in Developing a Web Application," published by New Riders Publishing (`http://www.newriders.com/`). This book is published in German as "XML, XSLT, Java, und JSP: Eine Professionelle Webapplikation Programmieren" by Galileo Press (`http://galileo-press.de/`). For further information, please visit `http://www.bonforum.de/`.

Apache Xerces License

The Apache Software License, version 1.1.

Copyright ©1999 The Apache Software Foundation. All rights reserved.

Redistribution and use in source and binary forms, with or without modification, are permitted provided that the following conditions are met:

1. Redistributions of source code must retain the above copyright notice, this list of conditions, and the following disclaimer.
2. Redistributions in binary form must reproduce the above copyright notice, this list of conditions, and the following disclaimer in the documentation and/or other materials provided with the distribution.
3. The end-user documentation included with the redistribution, if any, must include the following acknowledgment:

Apache Xalan License

3. The end-user documentation included with the redistribution, if any, must include the following acknowledgment: "This product includes software developed by the Apache Software Foundation (`http://www.apache.org/`)." Alternately, this acknowledgment may appear in the software itself, if and wherever such third-party acknowledgments normally appear.
4. The names "Xalan" and "Apache Software Foundation" must not be used to endorse or promote products derived from this software without prior written permission. For written permission, please contact `apache@apache.org`.
5. Products derived from this software may not be called "Apache," nor may "Apache" appear in their name, without prior written permission of the Apache Software Foundation.

THIS SOFTWARE IS PROVIDED "AS IS," AND ANY EXPRESSED OR IMPLIED WARRANTIES, INCLUDING, BUT NOT LIMITED TO, THE IMPLIED WARRANTIES OF MERCHANTABILITY AND FITNESS FOR A PARTICULAR PURPOSE, ARE DISCLAIMED. IN NO EVENT SHALL THE APACHE SOFTWARE FOUNDATION OR ITS CONTRIBUTORS BE LIABLE FOR ANY DIRECT, INDIRECT, INCIDENTAL, SPECIAL, EXEMPLARY, OR CONSEQUENTIAL DAMAGES (INCLUDING, BUT NOT LIMITED TO, PROCUREMENT OF SUBSTITUTE GOODS OR SERVICES; LOSS OF USE, DATA, OR PROFITS; OR BUSINESS INTERRUPTION), HOWEVER CAUSED AND ON ANY THEORY OF LIABILITY, WHETHER IN CONTRACT, STRICT LIABILITY, OR TORT (INCLUDING NEGLIGENCE OR OTHERWISE) ARISING IN ANY WAY OUT OF THE USE OF THIS SOFTWARE, EVEN IF ADVISED OF THE POSSIBILITY OF SUCH DAMAGE.

This software consists of voluntary contributions made by many individuals on behalf of the Apache Software Foundation and was originally based on software copyright © 1999, Lotus Development Corporation, `http://www.lotus.com`. For more information on the Apache Software Foundation, please see `http://www.apache.org/`.

Jakarta Tomcat License

The Apache Software License, version 1.1.

Copyright © 1999 The Apache Software Foundation. All rights reserved.

Redistribution and use in source and binary forms, with or without modification, are permitted provided that the following conditions are met:

1. Redistributions of source code must retain the above copyright notice, this list of conditions, and the following disclaimer.
2. Redistributions in binary form must reproduce the above copyright notice, this list of conditions, and the following disclaimer in the documentation and/or other materials provided with the distribution.

3. The end-user documentation included with the redistribution, if any, must include the following acknowledgment: "This product includes software developed by the Apache Software Foundation (`http://www.apache.org/`)." Alternately, this acknowledgment may appear in the software itself, if and wherever such third-party acknowledgments normally appear.
4. The names "The Jakarta Project," "Tomcat," and "Apache Software Foundation" must not be used to endorse or promote products derived from this software without prior written permission. For written permission, please contact `apache@apache.org`.
5. Products derived from this software may not be called "Apache," nor may "Apache" appear in their names without prior written permission of the Apache Group.

THIS SOFTWARE IS PROVIDED "AS IS," AND ANY EXPRESSED OR IMPLIED WARRANTIES, INCLUDING, BUT NOT LIMITED TO, THE IMPLIED WARRANTIES OF MERCHANTABILITY AND FITNESS FOR A PARTICULAR PURPOSE, ARE DISCLAIMED. IN NO EVENT SHALL THE APACHE SOFTWARE FOUNDATION OR ITS CONTRIBUTORS BE LIABLE FOR ANY DIRECT, INDIRECT, INCIDENTAL, SPECIAL, EXEMPLARY, OR CONSEQUENTIAL DAMAGES (INCLUDING, BUT NOT LIMITED TO, PROCUREMENT OF SUBSTITUTE GOODS OR SERVICES; LOSS OF USE, DATA, OR PROFITS; OR BUSINESS INTERRUPTION), HOWEVER CAUSED AND ON ANY THEORY OF LIABILITY, WHETHER IN CONTRACT, STRICT LIABILITY, OR TORT (INCLUDING NEGLIGENCE OR OTHERWISE) ARISING IN ANY WAY OUT OF THE USE OF THIS SOFTWARE, EVEN IF ADVISED OF THE POSSIBILITY OF SUCH DAMAGE.

This software consists of voluntary contributions made by many individuals on behalf of the Apache Software Foundation. For more information on the Apache Software Foundation, please see `http://www.apache.org/`.

C

Source Code for bonForum Web Application

C.1 Filename: TOMCAT_HOME\webapps\bonForum\WEB-INF\web.xml

```
<?xml version="1.0" encoding="ISO-8859-1"?>
<!DOCTYPE web-app
    PUBLIC "-//Sun Microsystems, Inc.//DTD Web Application 2.2//EN"
    "http://java.sun.com/j2ee/dtds/web-app_2.2.dtd">
<web-app>
    <display-name>
        bonForum
    </display-name>
    <context-param>
        <param-name>
            Webmaster
        </param-name>
        <param-value>
            email@bonforum.org
        </param-value>
    </context-param>
    <!-- Logging output can be none, all, std, file -->
    <context-param>
        <param-name>
            Logging
        </param-name>
        <param-value>
```

```
            all
        </param-value>
    </context-param>
    <servlet>
        <servlet-name>
            BonForumEngine
        </servlet-name>
        <servlet-class>
            de.tarent.forum.BonForumEngine
        </servlet-class>
        <init-param>
            <param-name>
                bonfoo47
            </param-name>
            <param-value>
                bonbar47
            </param-value>
        </init-param>
    </servlet>
    <servlet>
        <servlet-name>
            snoop
        </servlet-name>
        <servlet-class>
            SnoopServlet
        </servlet-class>
        <init-param>
            <param-name>
                bonFooSnoop
            </param-name>
            <param-value>
                bonBarSnoop
            </param-value>
        </init-param>
    </servlet>
    <servlet>
      <servlet-name>
          servletToJsp
      </servlet-name>
      <servlet-class>
          servletToJsp
      </servlet-class>
    </servlet>
    <servlet-mapping>
        <servlet-name>
            BonForumEngine
        </servlet-name>
        <url-pattern>
            *.tfe
        </url-pattern>
    </servlet-mapping>
```

```
<servlet-mapping>
    <servlet-name>
        BonForumEngine
    </servlet-name>
    <url-pattern>
        /BonForumEngine
    </url-pattern>
</servlet-mapping>
<servlet-mapping>
    <servlet-name>
        snoop
    </servlet-name>
    <url-pattern>
        /snoop
    </url-pattern>
</servlet-mapping>
<servlet-mapping>
    <servlet-name>
        snoop
    </servlet-name>
    <url-pattern>
        *.snp
    </url-pattern>
</servlet-mapping>
<servlet-mapping>
    <servlet-name>
        servletToJsp
    </servlet-name>
    <url-pattern>
        /servletToJsp
    </url-pattern>
</servlet-mapping>

<taglib>
    <taglib-uri>
    http://www.bonForum.org/taglib/bonForum-taglib
    </taglib-uri>
    <taglib-location>
       /WEB-INF/jsp/bonForum-taglib.tld
    </taglib-location>
</taglib>
<session-config>
    <session-timeout> -1 </session-timeout>
</session-config>

<!— Define the context-relative URL(s) to be protected —>
<!— If you list http methods, only those methods are protected —>
<!— Anyone with one of the listed roles may access this area —>
<!—
<security-constraint>
  <web-resource-collection>
```

```
        <web-resource-name>Protected Area</web-resource-name>
        <url-pattern>/jsp/security/protected/*</url-pattern>
     <http-method>DELETE</http-method>
        <http-method>GET</http-method>
        <http-method>POST</http-method>
     <http-method>PUT</http-method>
     </web-resource-collection>
     <auth-constraint>
        <role-name>tomcat</role-name>
     <role-name>role1</role-name>
     </auth-constraint>
   </security-constraint>
   —>
   <!— Default login configuration uses BASIC authentication —>
   <!—
   <login-config>
     <auth-method>BASIC</auth-method>
     <realm-name>Example Basic Authentication Area</realm-name>
   </login-config>
   —>
   <!— If you want to experiment with form-based logins, comment
        out the <login-config> element above and replace it with
        this one.  Note that we are currently using a nonstandard
        authentication method, because the code to support form
        based login is incomplete and only lightly tested.  —>
   <!—
   <login-config>
     <auth-method>EXPERIMENTAL_FORM</auth-method>
     <realm-name>Example Form-Based Authentication Area</realm-name>
     <form-login-config>
       <form-login-page>/jsp/security/login/login.jsp</form-login-page>
       <form-error-page>/jsp/security/login/error.jsp</form-error-page>
     </form-login-config>
   </login-config>
   —>

</web-app>
```

C.2 Filename: TOMCAT_HOME\webapps\bonForum\WEB-INF\jsp\bonForum-taglib.tld

```
<?xml version="1.0" encoding="ISO-8859-1" ?>
<!DOCTYPE taglib
     PUBLIC "-//Sun Microsystems, Inc.//DTD JSP Tag Library 1.1//EN"
    "http://java.sun.com/j2ee/dtds/web-jsptaglibrary_1_1.dtd">
<!— Tag library descriptor for bonForum —>
<!— as described in the book: —>
<!— XML, XSLT, Java and JSP - A Case Study in Developing a Web Application —>
<!— by Westy Rockwell —>
```

```
<!— For further information visit www.bonForum.org—>
<taglib>
  <!— after this the default space is
    "http://java.sun.com/j2ee/dtds/jsptaglibrary_1_2.dtd"
  —>
  <tlibversion>1.0</tlibversion>
  <jspversion>1.1</jspversion>
  <shortname>forumTags</shortname>
  <!—
  <urn></urn>
   —>
  <info>
    Tag library for bonForum
  </info>
  <!— outputDebugInfo tag —>
  <tag>
    <name>outputDebugInfo</name>
    <tagclass>de.tarent.forum.OutputDebugInfoTag</tagclass>
    <bodycontent>JSP</bodycontent>
    <info>
      Outputs request header and parameter values.
      Outputs attributes values for all scopes.
      Attribute type="init" turns tags on for entire session,
          if a request parameter exists called
          "output_debug_info" that is equal to "yes".
          Afterwards, a tag but no attribute
          is required to output debug info on page.
      Attribute type="init" turns tags off,
          if no request parameter exists called
          "output_debug_info" that is equal to "yes".
      Attribute force="yes" turns that tag on only.
    </info>
    <attribute>
      <name>type</name>
      <required>false</required>
    </attribute>
    <attribute>
      <name>force</name>
      <required>false</required>
    </attribute>
  </tag>
  <!— outputChatMessages tag —>
  <tag>
    <name>outputChatMessages</name>
    <tagclass>de.tarent.forum.OutputChatMessagesTag</tagclass>
    <teiclass>de.tarent.forum.BonForumTagExtraInfo</teiclass>
    <bodycontent>JSP</bodycontent>
    <info>
      Outputs chatMessages from subTree of XML tree or forest.
      Attributes are reserved for future use selecting messages.
    </info>
```

```
    <attribute>
      <name>command</name>
      <required>true</required>
    </attribute>
    <attribute>
      <name>attr1</name>
      <required>false</required>
    </attribute>
    <attribute>
      <name>attr2</name>
      <required>false</required>
    </attribute>
    <attribute>
      <name>attr3</name>
      <required>false</required>
    </attribute>
  </tag>
  <!— outputPathNames tag —>
  <tag>
    <name>outputPathNames</name>
    <tagclass>de.tarent.forum.OutputPathNamesTag</tagclass>
    <teiclass>de.tarent.forum.BonForumTagExtraInfo</teiclass>
    <bodycontent>JSP</bodycontent>
    <info>
      Outputs pathNames from subTree of XML tree or forest
      (Note: ignores chatItem nodes in bonForum forests.)
    </info>
    <attribute>
      <name>docName</name>
      <required>true</required>
    </attribute>
    <attribute>
      <name>pathToSubTreeRootNode</name>
      <required>true</required>
    </attribute>
    <attribute>
      <name>ancestorReplacer</name>
      <required>true</required>
    </attribute>
    <attribute>
      <name>nodeSeparator</name>
      <required>true</required>
    </attribute>
  </tag>
  <!— transform tag —>
  <tag>
    <name>transform</name>
    <tagclass>de.tarent.forum.TransformTag</tagclass>
    <teiclass>de.tarent.forum.BonForumTagExtraInfo</teiclass>
    <bodycontent>JSP</bodycontent>
    <info>
```

```
      XSLT processing (type) applies inXSL to inXML.
      If inXML = "bonForumXML" transforms entire forum content.
      If inXML = "bonBufferXML" transforms buffer content.
      Else inXML is a URL for an XML document.
      If outDoc is URL produces XML file.
      If outDoc = "print" calls out.println with the output.
      If outDoc = "printNormalized" does same, normalizes first.
      If outDoc = "output" puts output in "output" page variable.
      If outDoc = "outputNormalized" does same, normalizes first.
      Transform uses one stylesheet parameter called "param1",
      which it looks for in a session attribute of the same name.
    </info>
    <attribute>
      <name>type</name>
      <required>true</required>
    </attribute>
    <attribute>
      <name>inXML</name>
      <required>true</required>
    </attribute>
    <attribute>
      <name>inXSL</name>
      <required>true</required>
    </attribute>
    <attribute>
      <name>outDoc</name>
      <required>true</required>
    </attribute>
  </tag>
  <!— noCacheHeader tag —>
    <tag>
      <name>noCacheHeader</name>
      <tagclass>de.tarent.forum.NoCacheHeaderTag</tagclass>
      <info>
        Sets headers in the response object to prevent
        a browser from keeping jsp content in cache.
        This tag contains no attributes, body, or end tag.
        The four headers set are: Cache-Control: no-cache,
        Pragma: no-cache, max-age: 0, Expires: 0.
        Returns SKIP_BODY always. Since JDK1.3.
        This tag must be placed before any output is
        sent to the web browser, or an
        IllegalStateException will occur.
        Used by permission of its author, Perry Tew
      </info>
  </tag>
</taglib>
```

C.3 Filename: TOMCAT_HOME\webapps\bonForum\index.html

```
<html>
<head>
<title>bonForum</title>
</head>
<body bgcolor=cyan>
<table border="0" rows="6" width="100%">
<tr>
<td align="center"><H1><a href="/bonForum/UserMustLogin.tfe"><img border="0"
src="images/bonForumLogo.gif" alt="Enter bonForum"></a></H1></td>
</tr>
<tr><td align="center">
<font  face="Verdana" size="2" color="#000099">
<a href="/bonForum/jsp/forum/forum_login.jsp">Enter</a> an open source project
from <a href="http://www.bonforum.org">www.bonforum.org</a>
described by the book:
</font>
</td></tr>
<tr><td align="center">
<font face="Verdana" size="3" color="#FF0000">
<a href="http://www.newriders.com">
<I>XML, XSLT, Java and JSP - A Case Study in Developing a Web Application</I>
</a>
</font>
</td></tr>
<tr><td align="center">
<font face="Verdana" size="3" color="#000099">
by
<a href="mailto://email@bonforum.org">Westy Rockwell</a>
</font>
</td></tr>
<tr><td align="center">
<font face="Verdana" size="1" color="#000099">
<a href="http://www.galileocomputing.de">
<I>XML, XSLT, Java und JSP - Professionelle Web-Applikationen entwickeln</I>
</a>
</font>
</td></tr>
<tr><td align="center">
<font face="Verdana" size="1" color="#000099">
German translation by
<a href="mailto:weltecke@eircom.net">Manfred Weltecke</a>
</font>
</td></tr>
</table>
<table border="0" width="100%">
<tr>
<td align="center">
```

```
<a href="http://www.tarent.de"><img src="images/tarent.gif" alt="tarent GmbH"
width="50" height="35" border="1"></a>
<a href="http://www.galileocomputing.de"><img src="images/galileo_logo_anim2.gif"
alt="Galileo Press"  width="50" height="35" border="0"></a>
<a href="http://www.newriders.com">New Riders</a>
<a href="http://sourceforge.net"> <img src="images/sflogo.png" alt="SourceForge
Logo"
width=88 height=31 border="0"></a>
<a href="http://jakarta.apache.org"><img src="images/tomcat-power.gif" alt="Tomcat
Logo" width="50" height="35" border="0"></a>
</td>
</tr>
</table>
</body>
</html>
```

C.4 Filename: TOMCAT_HOME\webapps\bonForum\docs\subjects.xml

```
<?xml version ="1.0"?>
<subjects>
    <Health>
    Element_content_test_string_1
        <Prevention>
            <Headaches>
                <Migraine type="Test_Attribute" foo="This is foo!">
                Element_content_test_string_2
                </Migraine>
            </Headaches>
        </Prevention>
    </Health>
    <Vehicles>
        <Autos>
            <BMW />
            <Fiat />
            <Ford>
                <Thunderbird/>
            </Ford>
            <Rover>
                <LandRover/>
            </Rover>
            <Subaru />
        </Autos>
        <Motorcycles>
            <HarleyDavidson/>
            <Honda />
        </Motorcycles>
        <Trucks>
            <Mac />
```

```
                <Other />
            </Trucks>
        </Vehicles>
        <Animals>
            <Bird>
                <Parrot />
                <Hawk />
                <Chicken />
            </Bird>
            <Fish>
                <Piranha />
                <Guppy />
            </Fish>
            <Dog>
                <LabradorRetriever />
                <Terrier>
                    <Fox>
                    </Fox>
                </Terrier>
            </Dog>
        </Animals>
</subjects>
```

C.5 Filename: TOMCAT_HOME\webapps\bonForum\docs\bonChatItems.xsl

```
<?xml version="1.0"?>
<xsl:stylesheet xmlns:xsl="http://www.w3.org/1999/XSL/Transform" version="1.0">
<xsl:output method="xml" omit-xml-declaration="yes" indent="no"/>
<xsl:param name="param1" select="'000000000000.000000000000.000000000000'"/>
<xsl:template match="/">
     <select size="9" name="chatItem">
     <xsl:apply-templates select="/bonForum/things/subjects/descendant::*[
@chatTopic ]"/>
     </select>
</xsl:template>
<xsl:template match="text()">
</xsl:template>
<xsl:template match="*">
<xsl:variable name="option-value">
     <xsl:for-each select="ancestor::*">
          <xsl:choose>
               <xsl:when test="name()='bonForum'">
               </xsl:when>
               <xsl:when test="name()='things'">
               </xsl:when>
               <xsl:when test="name()='subjects'">
               </xsl:when>
               <xsl:otherwise>
```

```
                <xsl:value-of select="name()"/>
                <xsl:if test="child::node()">
                <xsl:text>_</xsl:text>
                </xsl:if>
            </xsl:otherwise>
        </xsl:choose>
    </xsl:for-each>
    <xsl:choose>
        <xsl:when test="self::node()[@chatTopic]">
            <xsl:text>[</xsl:text>
                <xsl:value-of select="@chatTopic"/>
        <xsl:text>]</xsl:text>
        </xsl:when>
        <xsl:otherwise>
            <xsl:value-of select="name()"/>
        </xsl:otherwise>
    </xsl:choose>
</xsl:variable>
<xsl:variable name="subject">
    <xsl:value-of select=" substring-before( string( $option-value ), string(
&quot;[&quot; ) )"/>
</xsl:variable>
<xsl:variable name="topic">
    <xsl:value-of select=" substring-before( substring-after( string( $option-
value ), string( &quot;[&quot; ) ), string( &quot;]&quot; ) )"/>
</xsl:variable>
<option>
    <xsl:attribute name="value">
        <xsl:value-of select="$option-value"/>
    </xsl:attribute>
    <xsl:value-of select="translate( $subject, string( &quot;_&quot; ), string(
&quot; &quot; ) )"/>
    <xsl:text> —> </xsl:text>
    <xsl:value-of select="$topic"/>
</option>
</xsl:template>
</xsl:stylesheet>
```

C.6 Filename: TOMCAT_HOME\webapps\bonForum\docs\bonChatItemsTEST.html

```
<select name="chatItem" size="9"><option value="Vehicles_Autos_Subaru_[Four Wheel
Drive Tips]">Vehicles Autos Subaru  —&gt; Four Wheel Drive Tips</option><option
value="Animals_Bird_Hawk_[Medieval Falconry]">Animals Bird Hawk  —&gt; Medieval
Falconry</option></select>
```

C.7 Filename: TOMCAT_HOME\webapps\bonForum\docs\bonChatGuests.xsl

```
<?xml version="1.0"?>
<xsl:stylesheet xmlns:xsl="http://www.w3.org/1999/XSL/Transform" version="1.0">
<xsl:output method="xml" omit-xml-declaration="yes" indent="no"/>
<xsl:param name="param1" select="'error in param1'"/>
<xsl:template match="/">
     <!— for debugging, can display the xsl parameter like this: —>
     <!— <p><xsl:value-of select="$param1"/></p> —>

     Guests in your chat:<BR/>
     <select size="6" name="chatGuest">
     <xsl:apply-templates select="/bonForum/things/*"/>
     </select>

</xsl:template>
<xsl:template match="text()">
</xsl:template>
<xsl:template match="chat[@itemKey=$param1]">
     <xsl:for-each select="*">
          <xsl:if test="name()='guestKey'">
               <xsl:variable name="guestKey-value">
                    <xsl:value-of select="."/>
               </xsl:variable>
               <xsl:for-each select="/bonForum/actors/guest">
                    <xsl:variable name="guest-value">
                         <xsl:value-of select="@nodeKey"/>
                    </xsl:variable>
                    <xsl:if test="$guest-value=$guestKey-value">
                         <option>
                         <xsl:value-of select="actorNickname"/>
                         <xsl:text> age:</xsl:text>
                         <xsl:value-of select="actorAge"/>
                         <xsl:text> rating:</xsl:text>
                         <xsl:value-of select="actorRating"/>
                         </option>
                    </xsl:if>
               </xsl:for-each>
          </xsl:if>
     </xsl:for-each>
</xsl:template>
<xsl:template match="*">
</xsl:template>
</xsl:stylesheet>
```

C.8 Filename: TOMCAT_HOME\webapps\bonForum\docs\forums.xml

```
<?xml version ="1.0"?>
<forums>
<forum>
<name>Galileo Press</name>
<weblink>http://www.galileocomputing.de</weblink>
</forum>
<forum>
<name>New Riders Publishing</name>
<weblink>http://www.newriders.com</weblink>
</forum>
<forum>
<name>tarent</name>
<weblink>http://www.tarent.de</weblink>
</forum>
</forums>
```

C.9 Filename: TOMCAT_HOME\webapps\bonForum\docs\bonForumLinks.xsl

```
<?xml version="1.0"?>
<xsl:stylesheet xmlns:xsl="http://www.w3.org/1999/XSL/Transform" version="1.0">
<xsl:output method="xml" omit-xml-declaration="yes" indent="no"/>
<xsl:param name="param1" select="'000000000000.000000000000.00000000000'"/>
<xsl:template match="/">
    <table width="100%" name="bonForums">
    <tr><A><xsl:attribute
name="href">http://www.bonForum.org/</xsl:attribute>bonForum.org</A></tr><tr><xsl:
text> </xsl:text></tr>
    <xsl:apply-templates select="/bonForum/things/forums//*"/>
    </table>
</xsl:template>
<xsl:template match="text()">
</xsl:template>
<xsl:template match="forum">
<tr>
<A>
<xsl:attribute name="href"><xsl:value-of select="weblink"/></xsl:attribute>
<xsl:value-of select="name"/>
</A>
</tr>
</xsl:template>
<xsl:template match="*">
</xsl:template>
</xsl:stylesheet>
```

C.10 Filename: TOMCAT_HOME\webapps\bonForum\docs\bonForumLinksTEST.html

```
<table name="bonForums" width="100%"><tr><A
href="http://www.bonForum.org">bonForum.org</A></tr><tr> </tr><tr><A
href="http://www.galileocomputing.de">Galileo Press</A></tr><tr><A
href="http://www.newriders.com">New Riders Publishing</A></tr><tr><A
href="http://www.tarent.de">tarent</A></tr></table>
```

C.11 Filename: TOMCAT_HOME\webapps\bonForum\docs\identity.xsl

```
<?xml version="1.0"?>
<xsl:stylesheet xmlns:xsl="http://www.w3.org/XSL/Transform/1.0" version="1.0">
<xsl:output method="xml" indent="no"/>
<xsl:template match="@*¦node()">
  <xsl:copy>
    <xsl:apply-templates select="@*¦node()"/>
  </xsl:copy>
</xsl:template>
</xsl:stylesheet>
```

C.12 Filename: TOMCAT_HOME\webapps\bonForum\docs\bonForumIdentityTransform.xml

```
<?xml version="1.0" encoding="UTF-8"?>
<bonForum nodeKey="989940500081.989940500081.989940500081"
type="prototype"><things nodeKey="989940500211.989940500081.989940500081"
type="READ_ONLY"><chat nodeKey="989940725325.989940500211.989940500081"
moderated="yes" itemKey="989940725365.989940501233.989940501213"><messageKey
nodeKey="989941076119.989940725325.989940500211">989941076109.989940500211.9899405
00081</messageKey><guestKey
nodeKey="989940808505.989940725325.989940500211">989940808445.989940500151.9899405
00081</guestKey><messageKey
nodeKey="989940892075.989940725325.989940500211">989940892065.989940500211.9899405
00081</messageKey><messageKey
nodeKey="989940940595.989940725325.989940500211">989940940585.989940500211.9899405
00081</messageKey><hostKey
nodeKey="989940725355.989940725325.989940500211">989940725275.989940500151.9899405
00081</hostKey><messageKey
nodeKey="989940792722.989940725325.989940500211">989940792712.989940500211.9899405
00081</messageKey></chat><message nodeKey="989940892065.989940500211.989940500081"
itemKey="989940725365.989940501233.989940501213" timeMillis="989940891714"
dateStamp="mar may 15 05:34:52 2001"
guestKey="989940808445.989940500151.989940500081">Eve::I am!  But mostly in the
```

```
use of hawks as symbols in medieval paintings.</message><subjects
nodeKey="989940500912.989940500211.989940500081"><Vehicles
nodeKey="989940501022.989940500912.989940500211"><Motorcycles
nodeKey="989940501133.989940501022.989940500912"><Honda
nodeKey="989940501153.989940501133.989940501022"/><HarleyDavidson
nodeKey="989940501143.989940501133.989940501022"/></Motorcycles><Trucks
nodeKey="989940501173.989940501022.989940500912"><Mac
nodeKey="989940501183.989940501173.989940501022"/><Other
nodeKey="989940501193.989940501173.989940501022"/></Trucks><Autos
nodeKey="989940501033.989940501022.989940500912"><Ford
nodeKey="989940501063.989940501033.989940501022"><Thunderbird
nodeKey="989940501073.989940501063.989940501033"/></Ford><Subaru
nodeKey="989940501123.989940501033.989940501022"/><BMW
nodeKey="989940501043.989940501033.989940501022"/><Fiat
nodeKey="989940501053.989940501033.989940501022"/><Rover
nodeKey="989940501083.989940501033.989940501022"><LandRover
nodeKey="989940501113.989940501083.989940501033"/></Rover></Autos></Vehicles><Health
nodeKey="989940500962.989940500912.989940500211">Element_content_test_string_1<Pre
vention nodeKey="989940500972.989940500962.989940500912"><Headaches
nodeKey="989940500982.989940500972.989940500962"><Migraine
nodeKey="989940501012.989940500982.989940500972" foo="This is foo!"
type="Test_Attribute">Element_content_test_string_2</Migraine></Headaches></Preven
tion></Health><Animals nodeKey="989940501203.989940500912.989940500211"><Fish
nodeKey="989940501263.989940501203.989940500912"><Piranha
nodeKey="989940501273.989940501263.989940501203"/><Guppy
nodeKey="989940501283.989940501263.989940501203"/></Fish><Bird
nodeKey="989940501213.989940501203.989940500912"><Chicken
nodeKey="989940501243.989940501213.989940501203"/><Hawk
nodeKey="989940501233.989940501213.989940501203"><sessionID_8g4vezxgi1_98994072532
5 nodeKey="989940725365.989940501233.989940501213" chatTopic="Medieval
Falconry"/></Hawk><Parrot
nodeKey="989940501223.989940501213.989940501203"/></Bird><Dog
nodeKey="989940501293.989940501203.989940500912"><Terrier
nodeKey="989940501313.989940501293.989940501203"><Fox
nodeKey="989940501323.989940501313.989940501293"/></Terrier><LabradorRetriever
nodeKey="989940501303.989940501293.989940501203"/></Dog></Animals></subjects><mess
age nodeKey="989940940585.989940500211.989940500081"
itemKey="989940725365.989940501233.989940501213" timeMillis="989940940544"
dateStamp="mar may 15 05:35:40 2001"
hostKey="989940725275.989940500151.989940500081">Adam::That's interesting, Eve.
Tell me more.</message><forums
nodeKey="989940501483.989940500211.989940500081"><forum
nodeKey="989940501523.989940501483.989940500211"><weblink
nodeKey="989940501543.989940501523.989940501483">http://www.newriders.com</weblink
><name nodeKey="989940501533.989940501523.989940501483">New Riders
Publishing</name></forum><forum
nodeKey="989940501493.989940501483.989940500211"><name
nodeKey="989940501503.989940501493.989940501483">Galileo Press</name><weblink
nodeKey="989940501513.989940501493.989940501483">http://www.galileocomputing.de</w
eblink></forum><forum nodeKey="989940501553.989940501483.989940500211"><weblink
nodeKey="989940501573.989940501553.989940501483">http://www.tarent.de</weblink><name
```

```
nodeKey="989940501563.989940501553.989940501483">tarent</name></forum></forums><me
ssage nodeKey="989940792712.989940500211.989940500081"
itemKey="989940725365.989940501233.989940501213" timeMillis="989940792391"
dateStamp="mar may 15 05:33:12 2001"
hostKey="989940725275.989940500151.989940500081">Adam::Hello! Is anyone interested
in Medieval Falconry besides me?</message><message
nodeKey="989941076109.989940500211.989940500081"
itemKey="989940725365.989940501233.989940501213" timeMillis="989941076069"
dateStamp="mar may 15 05:37:56 2001"
guestKey="989940808445.989940500151.989940500081">Eve::Sure, but first I have to
let the cat out.  I'll be right back.</message></things><actions
nodeKey="989940500201.989940500081.989940500081" type="READ_ONLY"/><actors
nodeKey="989940500151.989940500081.989940500081" type="READ_ONLY"><system
nodeKey="989940500161.989940500151.989940500081" type="SYSTEM"><system2
nodeKey="989940500171.989940500161.989940500151" type="SYSTEM"><test
nodeKey="989940500181.989940500171.989940500161"
type="TEST"/></system2></system><host
nodeKey="989940725275.989940500151.989940500081"><actorNickname
nodeKey="989940725285.989940725275.989940500151">Adam</actorNickname><actorRating
nodeKey="989940725305.989940725275.989940500151">5</actorRating><actorAge
nodeKey="989940725295.989940725275.989940500151">123</actorAge></host><test
nodeKey="989940500191.989940500151.989940500081" type="TEST"/><guest
nodeKey="989940808445.989940500151.989940500081"><actorNickname
nodeKey="989940808475.989940808445.989940500151">Eve</actorNickname><actorAge
nodeKey="989940808485.989940808445.989940500151">121</actorAge><actorRating
nodeKey="989940808495.989940808445.989940500151">5</actorRating></guest></actors><
/bonForum>
```

C.13 Filename: TOMCAT_HOME\webapps\bonForum\docs\xalanTest.bat

```
rem java -classpath "c:\xalan_1_2_2\xerces.jar;c:\xalan_1_2_2\xalan.jar"
org.apache.xalan.xslt.Process -IN bonForumIdentityTransform.xml -XSL
bonChatItems.xsl -OUT bonChatItemsTEST.html
rem bonChatGuests.xsl cannot be tested from command line as it requires a runtime
parameter
rem java -classpath "c:\xalan_1_2_2\xerces.jar;c:\xalan_1_2_2\xalan.jar"
org.apache.xalan.xslt.Process -IN bonForumIdentityTransform.xml -XSL
bonChatGuests.xsl -OUT bonChatGuestsTEST.html
rem java -classpath "c:\xalan_1_2_2\xerces.jar;c:\xalan_1_2_2\xalan.jar"
org.apache.xalan.xslt.Process -IN bonForumIdentityTransform.xml -XSL
bonForumLinks.xsl -OUT bonForumLinksTEST.html
java -classpath "c:\jakarta-tomcat\lib\xalanj1compat.jar;c:\jakarta-
tomcat\lib\xerces.jar;c:\jakarta-tomcat\lib\xalan.jar"
org.apache.xalan.xslt.Process -IN bonForumIdentityTransform.xml -XSL
bonChatItems.xsl -OUT bonChatItemsTEST.html
rem bonChatGuests.xsl cannot be tested from command line as it requires a runtime
```

```
parameter
rem java -classpath "c:\jakarta-tomcat\lib\xalanj1compat.jar;c:\jakarta-
tomcat\lib\xerces.jar;c:\jakarta-tomcat\lib\xalan.jar"
org.apache.xalan.xslt.Process -IN bonForumIdentityTransform.xml -XSL
bonChatGuests.xsl -OUT bonChatGuestsTEST.html
java -classpath "c:\jakarta-tomcat\lib\xalanj1compat.jar;c:\jakarta-
tomcat\lib\xerces.jar;c:\jakarta-tomcat\lib\xalan.jar"
org.apache.xalan.xslt.Process -IN bonForumIdentityTransform.xml -XSL
bonForumLinks.xsl -OUT bonForumLinksTEST.html
```

C.14 Filename: Projects\bonForum\src\bonMakeIt.bat

```
rem path c:\jdk1.3\bin;%PATH%
rem set JAVA_HOME=c:\jdk1.3
rem set JAVAC=c:\jdk1.3\bin\rem javac.exe
javac de/tarent/forum/BonForumUtils.java -d ../classes
javac de/tarent/forum/BonLogger.java -d ../classes
javac -classpath ".;c:\jakarta-tomcat\lib\servlet.jar;"
de/tarent/forum/BonForumTagExtraInfo.java -d ../classes
javac -classpath ".;c:\jakarta-tomcat\lib\servlet.jar;"
de/tarent/forum/OutputPathNamesTag.java -d ../classes
javac -classpath ".;c:\jakarta-tomcat\lib\servlet.jar;"
de/tarent/forum/OutputChatMessagesTag.java -d ../classes
javac -classpath ".;c:\jakarta-tomcat\lib\servlet.jar;"
de/tarent/forum/OutputDebugInfoTag.java -d ../classes
javac -classpath ".;c:\jakarta-tomcat\lib\servlet.jar;"
de/tarent/forum/NoCacheHeaderTag.java -d ../classes
javac -classpath ".;c:\xalan-j_1_2_2\xalan.jar;c:\xalan-
j_1_2_2\xerces.jar;c:\jakarta-tomcat\lib\servlet.jar;"
de/tarent/forum/Xalan1Transformer.java -d ../classes
javac -classpath ".;c:\jakarta-tomcat\lib\servlet.jar;c:\xalan-
j_2_0_1\bin\xalan.jar;c:\xalan-j_2_0_1\bin\xerces.jar;"
de/tarent/forum/Xalan2Transformer.java -d ../classes
javac -classpath ".;c:\jakarta-tomcat\lib\servlet.jar;c:\xalan-
j_2_0_1\bin\xalanj1compat.jar;c:\xalan-j_2_0_1\bin\xalan.jar;c:\xalan-
j_2_0_1\bin\xerces.jar;" de/tarent/forum/TransformTag.java -d ../classes
javac de/tarent/forum/NodeKey.java -d ../classes
javac de/tarent/forum/BonNode.java -d ../classes
javac -classpath ".;c:\jakarta-tomcat\lib\servlet.jar;"
de/tarent/forum/ForestHashtable.java -d ../classes
javac -classpath ".;c:\jakarta-tomcat\lib\servlet.jar;"
de/tarent/forum/BonForumStore.java -d ../classes
javac -classpath ".;c:\jakarta-tomcat\lib\servlet.jar;"
de/tarent/forum/BonForumEngine.java -d ../classes
javac BonForumRobot.java -d ../classes
copy ..\classes\BonForumRobot.class ..\..\jsp\forum\applet
copy ..\classes\BonForumRobot$RefreshThread.class ..\..\jsp\forum\applet
rem CLASS FILES MUST BE IN bonForum WEBAPP CLASS FOLDERS FOR USE!
```

C.15 Filename: Projects\bonForum\src\BonForumRobot.java

```
/*<Imports>*/
import java.io.*;
import java.net.*;
import java.util.*;
import java.applet.*;
import java.awt.Font;
import java.awt.Color;
import java.awt.Graphics;
import java.awt.Component;  // temp
/*</Imports>*/
/** BonForumRobot repeatedly invokes showDocument method of applet.
 * It can be used from a frame display to request a different frameset.
 * It can also be used to continually refresh one frame from another.
 * The applet parameters are:
 * target, document, increment, limit, message and refresh.
 * <p>For further information visit the open source
 * <A HREF="http://www.bonForum.org">BonForum Project on SourceForge</A>
 * @author <A HREF="mailto://email@bonforum.org">Westy Rockwell</A>
 */
public class BonForumRobot extends Applet {
    URL codeBase = null;
    String document = "";
    String target = "";
    String messageLineOne = "";
    String messageLineTwo = "";
    String message = "";
    boolean refresh = false;
    boolean continueRunning = true;
    int increment = 0;
    int limit = 0;
    int counter = 0;
    Font font = new Font("TimesRoman", Font.ITALIC,24);
    public void init() {
        System.out.println("init()");
        // get other plugin parameters
        target = getParameter("target", "_self");
        document = getParameter("document", "");
        increment = getParameter("increment", 20000);
        limit = getParameter("limit", 10000);
        message = getParameter("message", "BonForumRobot applet");
        refresh = getParameter("refresh", false);
        // see these debugging messages on the Java Console
        codeBase = this.getCodeBase();
        System.out.println("documentBase:" + this.getDocumentBase().toString());
        System.out.println("codeBase:" + codeBase.toString());
```

```
        System.out.println("refresh:" + this.refresh);
        System.out.println("target:" + this.target);
        System.out.println("document:" + this.document);
        System.out.println("increment:" + this.increment);
        System.out.println("limit:" + this.limit);
        System.out.println("message:" + this.message);
        // forces application global error displays not to be in a frame:
        if(document.indexOf("forum_error") > -1) {
            if(!target.equals("_top")) {
                target = "_top";
                System.out.println("changed to forum_error target:" +
this.target);
            }
        }
    }
    public void start() {
        // kick off thread to do the dirty work
        setBackground(Color.cyan);
        System.out.println("start()");
        if (refresh) {
            RefreshThread thread = new
RefreshThread(Long.toString(System.currentTimeMillis()), codeBase);
        thread.start();
        }
    }
    public void stopRunning() {
        stop();
    }
    public void stop() {
        System.out.println("stop()");
        continueRunning = false;
    }
    public void paint(Graphics graphics) {
        graphics.setFont(font);
        graphics.setColor(Color.black);
        if(message.equalsIgnoreCase("debug")) {
            graphics.drawString(messageLineOne,10,20);
            graphics.drawString(messageLineTwo,10,40);
            graphics.drawString(target,10,60);
            graphics.drawString(document,10,80);
            graphics.drawString(new Boolean(refresh).toString(), 10, 100);
            graphics.drawString(Integer.toString(increment), 10, 120);
            graphics.drawString(Integer.toString(limit), 10, 140);
        }
        else {
            graphics.drawString(messageLineOne,10,20);
            graphics.drawString(messageLineTwo,10,40);
        }
```

```
}
private String getParameter(String name, String defaultValue){
String retval = getParameter(name);
     if (retval == null || retval.trim() == ""){
          retval = defaultValue;
     }
     return retval;
}
private int getParameter(String name, int defaultValue){
int retval = defaultValue;
     String tmp = getParameter(name);
     if (tmp != null && tmp.trim() != ""){
          try {
               retval = Integer.parseInt(tmp);
          } catch (NumberFormatException nfe) {
               // don't do anything.
               // it's still assigned to the defaultValue!
          }
     }
     return retval;
}
private boolean getParameter(String name, boolean defaultValue){
     boolean retval = defaultValue;
     String tmp = getParameter(name);
     if (tmp != null){
          if (tmp.equalsIgnoreCase("true")) retval = true;
          if (tmp.equals("1")) retval = true;
          if (tmp.equalsIgnoreCase("false")) retval = false;
          if (tmp.equals("0")) retval = false;
     }
     return retval;
}
public class RefreshThread extends Thread {
     private URL codeBase;
     public RefreshThread(String s, URL cb){
          super(s);
          codeBase = cb;
     }
    public void run() {
          String uncachedDocument = "";
          String errorDocument = codeBase.toString() + "../forum_error.jsp";
          messageLineOne = "";
          messageLineTwo = "";
          // These are two behaviors that depend on the "target" parameter:
          //
          // 1. target = "_top"
          //
          // This means we are using the applet to break out of a frameset on
the browser.
          //
          // 2. target <> "_top"
```

```
            //
            // This means we are using the applet to periodically refresh a
document within a frame
            //
//
            // The code below here makes this applet repeat an action
(showDocument)
            // roughly every increment seconds, with a maximum controlled by
the limit parameter.
            // However, note that if target is "_top" no repetition of
showDocument occurs.
            counter = 1;
          while (continueRunning) {
                // put it to sleep for "increment" milliseconds
                messageLineOne = "";
                getAppletContext().showStatus("bonForumRobot");
                repaint();
                try { sleep(3*(increment/4)); } catch (InterruptedException e)
{continue;}
                // put it back to sleep for a "yellow light"
                messageLineOne = "refreshing...";
                repaint();
                try { sleep(increment/4); } catch (InterruptedException e)
{continue;}
                // are all iterations done?
                if(counter > limit) {
                    System.out.println("counter:" + counter + " over limit:"
+ limit);
                    stopRunning();
                    continue;
                }
                // no, do it
                counter++;
                String millis = Long.toString(System.currentTimeMillis());
                // LATER: we will somehow refresh content only if stale
                if(    (document.indexOf("forum_error") > -1)
                    || (document.indexOf("forum_login") > -1)
                    || (document.indexOf("visitor_joins_chat") > -1)
                    || (document.indexOf("visitor_starts_chat") > -1)
                    || (document.indexOf("guest_executes_chat") > -1)
                    || (document.indexOf("guest_exits_chat") > -1)
                    || (document.indexOf("guest_executes_command") > -1)
                    || (document.indexOf("guest_exits_command") > -1)
                    || (document.indexOf("host_executes_chat") > -1)
                    || (document.indexOf("host_exits_chat") > -1)
                    || (document.indexOf("host_executes_command") > -1)
                    || (document.indexOf("host_exits_command") > -1)) {
                    //
                    // We fixup the filename as a unique filename to prevent
 browser from
                    // retrieving the last result for a jsp uri request from
```

```
its cache.
                              //
                              // For example,
                              //
"http://localhost:8080/bonForum/jsp/forum/visitor_joins_chat.jsp#entry47"
                              // will become something like this:
                              //
"http://localhost:8080/bonForum/jsp/forum/visitor_joins_chat.jsp#entry47.962066767
851.tfe"
                              //
                              // The "millis" value added will create a unique
filename, so the browser will fetch the jsp
                              //
                              // The ".tfe" at the end of the uncached URL will map to
the BonForumEngine servlet.
                              //
                              // One drawback is that although the browser will look
for none of these unique names in the cache,
                              // it will nevertheless cache them, and cache them, and
cache them! Filling the cache with them!
                              //
                              uncachedDocument = document + millis + ".tfe";
                              System.out.println("Created name for uncachedDocument:" +
uncachedDocument);
                    }
                    else {
                              // NOTE: applet code must be in subfolder (e.g.,
"applet") of folder with forum_login.jsp
                              // so this creates something like
"http://freedom:8080/bonForum/jsp/forum/forum_login.jsp"
                              uncachedDocument = errorDocument + millis + ".tfe";
                              System.out.println("Document not in list, using an error
document:" + uncachedDocument);
                              target = "_top";
                              message = "Unknown destination, new login required!";
                    }
                    if(target.equals("_top")) {
                              stopRunning(); // after this loop
                              getAppletContext().showStatus(message);
                    }
                    messageLineOne = "loading...";
                    messageLineTwo = message;
                    repaint();
                    try {
                              getAppletContext().showDocument(new
URL(uncachedDocument), target);
                    } catch(MalformedURLException ee) {
                              System.out.println("MalformedURLException:" +
ee.getMessage());
                              System.out.println("MalformedURLException,
uncachedDocument:" + uncachedDocument);
```

```
                        document = ""; // force errorDocument next time
                    }
                    messageLineTwo = "";
                }
        }
        }  //End of Inner Class
}
```

C.16 Filename: Projects\bonForum\src\de\tarent\forum\BonForumEngine.java

```
package de.tarent.forum;
/*<Imports>*/
import java.io.*;
import java.util.Hashtable;
import javax.servlet.*;
import javax.servlet.http.*;
/*</Imports>*/
/** BonForumEngine is the central servlet of bonForum web application.
 * At present, it implements a chat. Its purpose is experimentation.
 * It is described fully in the book:
 * <i>XML, XSLT, Java and JSP - A Case Study in Developing a Web Application</i>,
 * by Westy Rockwell, published by <A HREF="http://www.newriders.com">New
Riders</A>.
 * Translation to German published by <A
HREF="http://www.galileocomputing.de">Galileo Press</A>.
 * <p>For further information visit the open source
 * <A HREF="http://www.bonForum.org">BonForum Project on SourceForge</A>
 * @author <A HREF="mailto://email@bonforum.org">Westy Rockwell</A>
 */
public class BonForumEngine extends HttpServlet {
     // holds and gives access to the data for the forum
     private static BonForumStore bonForumStore = new BonForumStore();
     // ensures nicknames are unique
     private static Hashtable nicknameRegistry = new Hashtable();
     // logs debugging information
     private static BonLogger logBFE = null;
     // controls logger output
     private static String logging = null;
     // false until logger ready
     private static boolean loggingInitialized = false;
    /** Initializes a BonForumEngine instance.
     *  Also sets its logging value from application init param.
     *  Also creates its logger if not done before.
     *
     */
     public void init() throws ServletException {
          System.err.println("ENTERING BonForumEngine init");
          if(!loggingInitialized) {
```

```
                System.err.println("BonForumEngine init loggingInitialized:" +
loggingInitialized);
                logging = getServletContext().getInitParameter("Logging");
                System.err.println("BonForumEngine init logging:" + logging);
                if(logging != null) {
                     logBFE = new BonLogger("BonForumEngineLog.txt", logging);
                     System.err.println("BonForumEngine init logBFE:" + logBFE);
                     loggingInitialized = true;
                     System.err.println("BonForumEngine init loggingInitialized:" +
loggingInitialized);
                     getBonForumStore().setLogging(logging);
                     System.err.println("BonForumEngine init
getBonForumStore().setLogging(logging)");
                }
           }
           System.err.println("LEAVING BonForumEngine init");
      }
     /** Gets the BonForumStore from this BonForumEngine.
      *
      * @return BonForumStore
      */
      public BonForumStore getBonForumStore() {
           return bonForumStore;
      }
      private void log(String sessionId, String where, String what) {
           if(logging != null) {
                logBFE.logWrite(System.currentTimeMillis(), sessionId, where,
what);
           }
      }
      /** Processes requests in context of web application rules.
       *  Called from BonForumEngine service method.
       *  Customizes the HttpServlet based engine as a web application
       *  (a chat in this case).
       *
       * @param request              HttpServletRequest argument from service method
       * @param response             HttpServletResponse  argument from service
method
       * @param session              HttpSession current
       * @param bonForumCommand      String routes request to next destination
       * @return String bonForumCommand parameter, maybe changed by this method,
maybe not.
       *
       * @throws IOException
       */
     protected String processRequest(HttpServletRequest request,
                                              HttpServletResponse response,
                                              HttpSession session,
                                              String bonForumCommand)
                                              throws IOException {
          BonNode chatNode = null;
```

```
        Object obj = null;
        String actorNickname = "";
        String actorAge = "";
        String xalanVersion = "";
        String sessionMaxInactiveMinutes = "";
        String actorRatingType = "";
        String chatModerated = "";
        String chatTopic = "";
        String chatSubject = "";
        String chatItem = "";
        String chatGuest = "";
        String chatMessage = "";
        String chatMessagesNavigator = "";
        String chatMessagesPageSize = "";
        String nameAndAttributes = "";
        String content = "";
        String forestHashtableName = "";
        String chatNodeKeyKey = "";
        request.setAttribute("serviceStatus", "InProcessRequestMethod");
    String sessionId = session.getId();
        // using sessionId for now, later it will be
        // replaced with userId, when user manager is implemented.
        bonForumStore.initialize(sessionId);
        // See if bonForumStore instance is bound to this ServletContext
        // If not, bind bonForumStore so it can be found elsewhere in web app
        // Then, you can use code like the following from other classes, to
        // have access to the methods of the bonForumStore:
        //
        // BonForumStore bonForumStore =
        // (bonForumStore)application.getAttribute("bonForumStore");
        //
        // Or, from a JSP page:
        //
        //   if (pageContext.getServletContext().getAttribute("bonForumStore")
!= null) {
        //              BonForumStore bFS =
        //
(bonForumStore)(pageContext.getServletContext().getAttribute(
        //                "bonForumStore"));
        //  }
        //
        // Of course, to use properties, it is simpler to do this:
        //
        // <jsp:useBean id="bonForumStore"
        //          class="de.tarent.forum.BonForumStore"
       //      scope="application"/>
       //
        Object temp = getServletContext().getAttribute("bonForumStore");
        if (temp == null) {
            getServletContext().setAttribute("bonForumStore",
getBonForumStore());
```

```
            }
            // bonForumCommand selects the next state of the application
            // Its value will be used to create a JSP filename.
            // If it has no value here, construct one from bonCommand
            // request parameter, or else, from other request parameters.
            bonForumCommand = normalize(bonForumCommand).trim();
            if(bonForumCommand.length() < 1) {
                 // As a second alternative the engine uses
                 // the bonCommand request parameter
                 // to tell where to forward the request
                 String bonCommand =
normalize((String)request.getParameter("bonCommand")).trim();
                 if(bonCommand.length() > 0) {
                      bonForumCommand = bonCommand;
                 }
                 else {
                      // As a third alternative, the engine can use any combination
                      // of one to three other parameters (actor, action, thing)
                      // to construct the bonForumCommand described above
                      String actorStatus =
normalize((String)request.getParameter("actorStatus")).trim();
                      String actionStatus =
normalize((String)request.getParameter("actionStatus")).trim();
                      String thingStatus =
normalize((String)request.getParameter("thingStatus")).trim();
                      if((actorStatus.length() > 0) ||
                         (actionStatus.length() > 0) ||
                         (thingStatus.length() > 0)) {
                           bonForumCommand = actorStatus + "_" + actionStatus + "_"
+ thingStatus;
                           // later, trim off leading and trailing underscore chars,
if any
                      }
                      else {
                           bonForumCommand = "forum_error";
                           request.setAttribute("serviceStatus",
"ForwardToErrorPage");
                           log(sessionId, "err", "No bonForumCommand! Forwarding To
Error Page!");
                      }
                 }
            }
            // used for debugging only:
            session.setAttribute("bonForumCommand", bonForumCommand);
            //
            // NOTES: ADDING ELEMENTS to bonForumXML ForestHashtable using
BonForumStore
            //
            // The BonForumStore.add() method automatically finds parent nodeKey
three ways:
            //
```

```
        // 1. If the parent is one of the intrinsic system elements then that
        // element's name ("bonForum", ""actors", "actions", "things", "system",
etc.)
        // is the key in the nodeNameHashtable for the parent nodeKey.
        //
        // 2. If the parent is not one of the intrinsic system elements
        // (for example, a "message" element inside the "things" element)
        // then the key in the nodeKeyHashtable is made up of the following:
        //  <sessionId> + "_" + <nodeKey.aKey> + ":" <elementName>.
        // (for example: "54w5d31sq1_985472754824:message")
        // NOTE: there is also an option to leave out the nodeKey.aKey portion
of
        // the key, for a selected list of node names (see ForestHashtable,
property
        // UniqueNodeKeyKeyList. That reduces the size requirements of the
        // nodeKeyHashtable (for example, by not storing all the message nodeKey
keys).
        //
        // 3. If the parent is one of certain elements that are loaded into
        // the bonForumXML (like the "subjects" subtree loaded with the
        // loadForumXML command, for example), then the nodeKey is in the
        // corresponding hashtable for that upload.
        // (For example, subjects elements are in the pathNameHashtable with
        // a key made from the path from root to the node whose nodeKey is
saved.
        // An example of a subject key is
"bonForum.things.subjects.Vehicles.Motorcycles")
        // NOTE: EACH add() method call also returns an object
        // that can be cast to a NodeKey
        //
        // 1) YOU CAN USE THESE TO RE-CREATE THE nodeKeyHashtable nodeKey key.
        //
        // 2) YOU CAN ALSO USE THESE TO RECALL ELEMENTS BY NodeKey.
        //
        // With the cast returned object, you can keep a reference to any
        // nodeKey around. For the message element just added, we could keep
        // its nodeKey as follows:
        //
        //          NodeKey messageNodeKey = (NodeKey)obj;
        //
        // Then, using the aKey member of the NodeKey, together with the
sessionId
        // and the name of the node, you can recreate the key for the NodeKey in
the
        // nodeKeyHashTable, and use it to add children to the node.  For an
example,
        // see below how we add hostKey to chat. That example uses two different
        // cast returned objects, one to get the hostNodeKey as a String,
        // the other to get the chatNodeKeyKey for adding a node (hostKey) with
that
        // String as content to the chat node. That same hostKey value will be
```

```
used
            // to stamp all messages from that host to that chat.
            //
            // We also use the NodeKey cast return object to get access to its
contents
            //
            // Notice, however, that the add() method involves extra overhead in the
            // example just cited, where hostKey is added to chat, and elsewhere.
            // The add() method in BonForumStore wraps the addChildNodeToNonRootNode
            // method in ForestHashtable, which can be used instead, if parent
nodeKey
            // is known.  Having just one method adding nodes does have advantages
though.
            // PROCESSING OF MANY FORUM COMMANDS IS NEXT
            // This extra bonForum variable is available on most JSP form,
            // It can be used later for setting options for bonForumCommand, or
whatever.
            String actorReturning =
normalize((String)request.getParameter("actorReturning"));
            if(actorReturning.trim().length() > 0) {
                  session.setAttribute("actorReturning", actorReturning);
            }
            else {
                  session.setAttribute("actorReturning", "");
            }
            // Incoming request parameters are used as "bonForum variables"
            // (including actor data, GUI settings, chat messages, etc.).
            // The parameter values are processed and/or set in attributes.
            // Most are set in session attributes, but at least two in application
attributes.
            // They can also be added to the bonForumXML "database" (chat messages
are, for example)
            // These if clauses are roughly prioritized by frequency of access,
            // and grouped by application state, (except for "_executes_chat"
commands)
            if(bonForumCommand.indexOf("host_executes_chat_controls") > -1 ||
                  bonForumCommand.indexOf("guest_executes_chat_controls") > -1) {
                  //handle chatMessagesNavigator
                  chatMessagesNavigator =
normalize((String)request.getParameter("chatMessagesNavigator"));
                  if(chatMessagesNavigator.trim().length() > 0) {
                        session.setAttribute("chatMessagesNavigator",
chatMessagesNavigator);
                  }
                  // handle chatMessage
                  // If we have a message save it as child of things,
                  // and the messageKey to the chat element.
                  chatMessage =
normalize((String)request.getParameter("chatMessage"));
                  if(chatMessage.trim().length() > 0) {
                        // add message child to things element
```

```
                // get itemKey from session Attribute
                String itemKey =
normalize((String)session.getAttribute("itemKey"));
                if(itemKey.trim().length() < 1) {
                    itemKey = "";
                    log(sessionId, "err", "processRequest() ERROR: session
has no itemKey!");
                }
                // NOTE: make sure attribute name=value items are separated by
a space
                //       and that there are no spaces next to the "=" between
name and value
                //       You can have quotes inside the value string, but only
using \" to escape them
                // to optimize speed, attributes ordered by frequency of
access using getAttributeValue()
                nameAndAttributes = "message";
                nameAndAttributes = nameAndAttributes + " itemKey=\"" +
itemKey + "\"";
                // date and time stamp for message
                nameAndAttributes = nameAndAttributes + " timeMillis=\"" +
BonForumUtils.timeMillis() + "\"";
                nameAndAttributes = nameAndAttributes + " dateStamp=\"" +
BonForumUtils.getLastDate() + "\"";
                // Try to get hostKey from session Attribute
                // If it is not there get guestKey instead
                // LATER: add systemKey to this also!
                String actorKeyValue =
normalize((String)session.getAttribute("hostKey"));
                if(actorKeyValue.trim().length() < 1) {
                    actorKeyValue =
normalize((String)session.getAttribute("guestKey"));
                    if(actorKeyValue.trim().length() < 1) {
                        log(sessionId, "err", "no hostKey or guestKey for
message!!!!!!!!!!");
                        actorKeyValue = "";
                }
                else {
                        nameAndAttributes = nameAndAttributes + "
guestKey=\"" + actorKeyValue + "\"";
                    }
                }
                else {
                    nameAndAttributes = nameAndAttributes + " hostKey=\"" +
actorKeyValue + "\"";
                }

                chatNodeKeyKey =
normalize((String)session.getAttribute("chatNodeKeyKey"));
                /* THESE ARE DEBUGGING TESTS
                // test value with escaped quote (xml error)
```

```
                    nameAndAttributes = nameAndAttributes + "
type=\"te\\\"st\\\"ing\"";
                    // test unclosed quotes in value (xml error)
                    nameAndAttributes = nameAndAttributes + " test1=\"" + "hello
test1!";
                    */
                    // if no actor key or no chatNodeKeyKey just silently omits
message
                    if(!actorKeyValue.equals("") && !chatNodeKeyKey.equals("")) {
                        // who said what in message
                        content =
normalize((String)session.getAttribute("actorNickname"));
                        content += "::" + chatMessage;
                        // add message element as child of "things" in
bonForumXML, a ForestHashtable
                        forestHashtableName = "bonForumXML";
                        obj = bonForumStore.add("bonAddElement", "things",
nameAndAttributes, content, forestHashtableName, "nodeNameHashtable", sessionId);
                        NodeKey messageNodeKey = (NodeKey)obj;
                        // get messageKey as String
                        //String messageKey = messageNodeKey.aKey + "." +
messageNodeKey.bKey + "." + messageNodeKey.cKey;
                        String messageKey = messageNodeKey.toString();
                        // add messageKey to chat
                        nameAndAttributes = "messageKey";
                        //content = messageKey;
                        content = messageKey;
                        forestHashtableName = "bonForumXML";
                        obj = bonForumStore.add("bonAddElement", chatNodeKeyKey,
nameAndAttributes, content, forestHashtableName, "nodeNameHashtable", sessionId);
                        session.setAttribute("messageKey", messageKey);
                    }
                }// end of chat message processing
            }
            else if(bonForumCommand.equals("host_executes_chat")) {
                boolean haveSubject = true;
                boolean haveTopic = true;
                boolean actorIsHostInChat = false;
                boolean actorIsGuestInChat = false;
                boolean chatExistsForSubjectAndTopic = false;
                boolean actorRestartingCurrentChat = false;
                // get chat topic chosen by host
                chatTopic =
normalize((String)session.getAttribute("chatTopic")).trim();
                // if no topic, prevent chat start
                if(chatTopic.length() < 1) {
                    log(sessionId, "err", "ERROR: SESSION HAS NO chatTopic,
forwarding back to get it!");
                    haveTopic = false;
                }
                else if(chatTopic.equalsIgnoreCase("NONE")) {
```

```
log(sessionId, "err", "ERROR: SESSION HAS chatTopic=NONE,
forwarding back to get it!");
                haveTopic = false;
            }
            // get chat Subject chosen by host
            chatSubject =
normalize((String)session.getAttribute("chatSubject")).trim();
            // if no subject, prevent chat start
            if(chatSubject.length() < 1) {
                log(sessionId, "err", "ERROR: SESSION HAS NO chatSubject,
forwarding back to get it!");
                haveSubject = false;
            }
            else if(chatSubject.equalsIgnoreCase("NONE")) {
                log(sessionId, "err", "ERROR: SESSION HAS chatSubject=NONE,
forwarding back to get it!");
                haveSubject = false;
            }
            // Note: here we must synchronize two things:
            // 1. the check to see subject+topic is taken
            // 2. the addition of new chats.
            // If we do not do that, two threads with same subject+topic
            // can go through here very close together, and this can happen:
            // - The first checked subject+topic and is about to add chat, but
hasn't.
            // - The second checks it subject+topic and finds it clear to use.
            // - The first adds its chat with the same subject+topic.
            // - The second adds its chat with the same subject+topic
            // Problems!  Using subject+topic to find chat again can only find
one!
            //
            // The first thread (thus session) that enters the synchronized
block
            // gets a lock on bonForumStore object.
            // The synchronized block is then closed to all other threads.
            // Automatically blocked by Java, they must wait until they can
            // get the lock on the bonForumStore object before they can enter.
            // Thus the synchronization functions as a FIFO for the threads.
            //
            // this almost works, needs something else synchronized?
            //synchronized(bonForumStore.bonForumXML) {
            synchronized(bonForumStore) {
            // If subject and topic are ok, see if that chat exists.
            // If so, check for two things:
            // 1. Is it the current chat for session and actor is trying to
restart it,
            // 2. Is it a chat the actor is already in either as host or as
guest.
            // (The third alternative is that it is a new chat to start.)
            if(haveSubject && haveTopic) {
                // see if subject+topic combination exists as a chat
```

```
                    String fakeChatItem = chatSubject + "_[" + chatTopic + "]";
                    // replace all '.' with '_' which is separator in chatItem
                    // '.' is separator in pathNameHashtable
                    fakeChatItem = fakeChatItem.replace('.', '_');
                    String foundChatNodeKeyKey =
getBonForumStore().getBonForumChatNodeKeyKey(fakeChatItem);
                    if((foundChatNodeKeyKey != null) &&
(foundChatNodeKeyKey.length() > 0)) {
                         // a chat exists with chosen subject and topic
                         chatExistsForSubjectAndTopic = true;
                         // see if actor wants to restart current chat for session
                         // (that information may come in useful later for user
messages, preferences
                         String newChatSubject =
normalize((String)session.getAttribute("newChatSubject"));
                         String newChatTopic =
normalize((String)session.getAttribute("newChatTopic"));
                         if(!newChatTopic.equals("yes") &&
!newChatSubject.equals("yes")) {
                              // actor trying to re-start current chat for this
session
                              // see if current chat for session exists
                              chatNodeKeyKey =
normalize((String)session.getAttribute("chatNodeKeyKey"));
                              if(chatNodeKeyKey.trim().length() > 0) {
                                   // session has a chat
                                   // see if it is the right one for subject and
topic
                                   if(chatNodeKeyKey.equals(foundChatNodeKeyKey)) {
                                        actorRestartingCurrentChat = true;
                                   }
                                   else {
                                        //CHAT GONE! WILL RESTART ONE FOR SUBJECT &
TOPIC
                                        chatExistsForSubjectAndTopic = false;
                                        actorRestartingCurrentChat = false;
                                   }
                              }
                         }
                         // see if actor is a host in chat found with requested
subject and topic
                         String actorKeyValue =
normalize((String)session.getAttribute("hostKey"));
                         if(actorKeyValue.trim().length() > 0) {
                              actorIsHostInChat =
getBonForumStore().isHostInChat(actorKeyValue, foundChatNodeKeyKey);
                         }
                         if(!actorIsHostInChat) {
                              // if not, see if actor is a guest in current chat
                              actorKeyValue =
normalize((String)session.getAttribute("guestKey"));
```

```
                    if(actorKeyValue.trim().length() > 0) {
                        actorIsGuestInChat =
getBonForumStore().isGuestInChat(actorKeyValue, foundChatNodeKeyKey);
                    }
                }
            }
            // If actor will rejoin existing chat,
            // route actor there using a bonForumCommand,
            // which determines next JSP destination.
            // when engine forwards request.
            boolean actorWillRejoinChat = false;
            if(chatExistsForSubjectAndTopic) {
                // cannot start chat, it exists already
                haveTopic = false;
                // Here later implement a user preference, using session
attributes.
                // Choices can be offered for behavior of "visitor starts
chat" when chat exists
                // 1. always warn user and ask again for new subject
and/or new topic
                // 2  if actor was in it, always join with previous
status, else warn and ask again
                // 3. if actor was in it, always join as guest, else warn
and ask again
                // All these choices can be modified re
actorRestartingCurrentChat value
                // For now, we implement choice #2
                if(actorIsHostInChat) {
                bonForumCommand = "host_executes_chat";
                    actorWillRejoinChat = true;
                else if(actorIsGuestInChat) {
                    bonForumCommand = "guest_executes_chat";
                    actorWillRejoinChat = true;
                }
                else {
                    // cannot start existing chat
                    // set attribute for using on
visitor_starts_chat.jsp
                    // to trigger user message that chat exists:
                    session.setAttribute(
                        "chatSubjectAndTopicTaken", fakeChatItem);
                    chatTopic = "";
                    session.setAttribute(
                        "chatTopic", "");
                    session.setAttribute(
                        "newChatTopic", "no");
                    bonForumCommand = "visitor_starts_chat";
                }
            }
            // If actor will rejoin existing chat,
            // need to set session attributes that
```

```
                // are usually set when actor starts new chat.
                //
                if(actorWillRejoinChat) {
                    // nodeNameHashtable key for the chat node key is needed
for:
                    // 1. adding messages to chat later.
                    // 2. seeing if a chat is the current chat
                    session.setAttribute("chatNodeKeyKey",
foundChatNodeKeyKey);
                    // host session doesn't need this,
                    // but if rejoining chat as guest, might?
                    session.setAttribute("chatItem", fakeChatItem);
                    // set the itemKey for this chat into a session attribute
                    // item key is added as a message attribute later
                    // it is needed for finding messages (temporarily)
                    // and for any guest session to find chat
                    String foundChatItemKey =
getBonForumStore().getBonForumChatItemNodeKey(fakeChatItem).toString();
                    session.setAttribute("itemKey", foundChatItemKey);
                }
            }
            if(haveSubject && haveTopic) {
                // actor starts chat
                // Each actorNickname is unique in bonForum,
                // Only one host node is allowed per actorNickname
                actorNickname =
normalize((String)session.getAttribute("actorNickname"));
                // Try getting key to a host node
                // for current actor's nickname
                NodeKey hostNicknameNodeKey =
getBonForumStore().getActorNicknameNodeKey( actorNickname, "host" );
                NodeKey hostNodeKey = null;
                if(hostNicknameNodeKey != null) {
                    BonNode hostNicknameNode =
getBonForumStore().getBonForumXML().getBonNode( hostNicknameNodeKey);
                    hostNodeKey = hostNicknameNode.parentNodeKey;
                }
                if(hostNodeKey == null) {
                    // If a host node key does not exist,
                    // then current actor is not yet a host,
                    // so add a new host node,
                    // with actorNickname,
                    // actorAge and
                    // actorRating children,
                    // to the "actors" root-child node
                    // of bonForumXML
                    nameAndAttributes = "host";
                    content = "";
                    forestHashtableName = "bonForumXML";
                    obj = bonForumStore.add( "bonAddElement", "actors",
nameAndAttributes, content, forestHashtableName, "nodeNameHashtable", sessionId );
```

```
                        hostNodeKey = (NodeKey)obj;
                        String creationTimeMillis = hostNodeKey.aKey;
                        String hostNodeKeyKey = sessionId + "_" +
creationTimeMillis + ":host";
                        // Make nodeNameHashtable key
                        // for the hostNodeKeyKey
                        // available to session.
                        // It gives quick access to last host nodeKey for session
                        session.setAttribute( "hostNodeKeyKey", hostNodeKeyKey );
                        nameAndAttributes = "actorNickname";
                        content = actorNickname;
                        forestHashtableName = "bonForumXML";
                        obj = bonForumStore.add( "bonAddElement", hostNodeKeyKey,
nameAndAttributes, content, forestHashtableName, "nodeNameHashtable", sessionId );
                        //NOTICE: the commented-out line here is more efficient
than the above line.
                        // and does not require the hostNodeKeyKey to be
reconstructed!
                        // However, we may want the hostNodeKeyKey in a session
attribute for later?
                        // Also, if we use this next statement, then we are using
two ways to add
                        // data to the XML. It may be better if all adding goes
throught the
                        // wrapper method? Still trying to decide. Performance
difference may decide this?
                        // There are other similar lines that could be faster.
                        // They are in host handling, but not in message or guest
handling.

//bonForumStore.getBonForumXML().addChildNodeToNonRootNode("actorNickname", "",
content, hostNodeKey, "nodeNameHashtable", sessionId);
                        nameAndAttributes = "actorAge";
                        content = normalize((String)session.getAttribute(
"actorAge" ));
                        forestHashtableName = "bonForumXML";
                        obj = bonForumStore.add( "bonAddElement", hostNodeKeyKey,
nameAndAttributes, content, forestHashtableName, "nodeNameHashtable", sessionId );
                        nameAndAttributes = "actorRating";
                        content = normalize((String)session.getAttribute(
"actorRating" ));
                        if(content.length() < 1) {
                            content = "5";
                        }
                        forestHashtableName = "bonForumXML";
                        obj = bonForumStore.add( "bonAddElement", hostNodeKeyKey,
nameAndAttributes, content, forestHashtableName, "nodeNameHashtable", sessionId );
                    }
                    // Add a chat node to the "things"
                    // root-child node of bonForumXML,
                    // with a chatModerated attribute,
```

```
                    // and no text content.
                    chatModerated = normalize((String)session.getAttribute(
"chatModerated" ));
                    if (chatModerated.equalsIgnoreCase("yes")) {
                         nameAndAttributes = "chat moderated=\"yes\"";
                    }
                    else {
                         nameAndAttributes = "chat moderated=\"no\"";
                    }
                    content = "";
                    forestHashtableName = "bonForumXML";
                    obj = bonForumStore.add( "bonAddElement", "things",
nameAndAttributes, content, forestHashtableName, "nodeNameHashtable", sessionId );
                    NodeKey chatNodeKey = (NodeKey)obj;
                    // Add a hostKey to the new chat node,
                    // its text content is the key to the host node
                    String creationTimeMillis = chatNodeKey.aKey;
                    chatNodeKeyKey = sessionId + "_" + creationTimeMillis +
":chat";
                    nameAndAttributes = "hostKey";
                    content = hostNodeKey.toString();
                    forestHashtableName = "bonForumXML";
                    obj = bonForumStore.add( "bonAddElement", chatNodeKeyKey,
nameAndAttributes, content, forestHashtableName, "nodeNameHashtable", sessionId );
                    // Make the hostKey available to this session.
                    // It is later used for these things:
                    // 1. finding out if an actor is a host in a chat
                    // 2. branding messages with a host as sender
                    session.setAttribute("hostKey", content);
                    // Make nodeNameHashtable key
                    // for the chat node key
                    // available to session.
                    // It is useful later for these things:
                    // 1. adding messages to chat
                    // 2. finding the chat node
                    // (to add nodes or attributes)
                    // 3. determining if a chat is the current chat
                    session.setAttribute( "chatNodeKeyKey", chatNodeKeyKey );
                    // Add a "chatItem" child
                    // to the selected chat subject element.
                    // That selected element is
                    // the chat subject category
                    // in bonForumXML.
                    // The name of the new child is "sessionID_" +
                    // the sessionId of
                    // the visitor starting the chat +
                    // the time the chat node was created in millis.
                    // The time suffix allows more than one chat
                    // to exist per session.
                    // Also add an attribute called chatTopic,
                    // with the (escaped) chatTopic
```

```
                    // input by the visitor.
                    // The sessionId (recoverable from
                    // the name of the new child) can
                    // be used later to quickly find the chat nodeKey.
                    // That is useful for example
                    // when a visitor joins a chat
                    // Note: when adding the sessionId
                    // element, its parent is found
                    // using the pathNameHashtable.
                    // The parent nodeKey is there
                    // with a key which is its pathName
                        // (and equal to chatSubject)
                        nameAndAttributes = "sessionID_";
                        nameAndAttributes += sessionId;
                        nameAndAttributes += "_";
                        nameAndAttributes += creationTimeMillis;
                        nameAndAttributes += " chatTopic=\"";
                        nameAndAttributes += chatTopic;
                        nameAndAttributes += "\"";
                        content = "";
                        forestHashtableName = "bonForumXML";
                        obj = bonForumStore.add( "bonAddElement", chatSubject,
nameAndAttributes, content, forestHashtableName, "pathNameHashtable", sessionId );
                        NodeKey itemNodeKey = (NodeKey)obj;
                        // set itemKey to itemNodeKey as a string
                        String itemKey = itemNodeKey.toString();
                        // Add the key to the chatItem element (itemKey)
                        // to the chat element as an attribute
                        // The itemKey connects a chat
                        // to its subject, topic and messages!
                        String attributeName = "itemKey";
                        String attributeValue = itemKey;
                        NodeKey nk = bonForumStore.addChatNodeAttribute(
chatNodeKeyKey, attributeName, attributeValue );
                        // Make the itemKey available to the session
                        session.setAttribute("itemKey", itemKey);
                    }
                    if((!chatExistsForSubjectAndTopic) && (!haveSubject ||
!haveTopic)) {
                        // missing information, must return to get it
                        // LATER: set attribute to trigger message to user
                        bonForumCommand = "visitor_starts_chat";
                    }
                    } // end of synchronized block!
                }// end of host_executes_chat processing
                else if (bonForumCommand.equals("guest_executes_chat")) {
                    // assume visitor will join chat
                    boolean haveChatItem = true;
                    boolean chatExistsForSubjectAndTopic = false;
                    // get chat Subject/Topic pair chosen by guest
                    chatItem =
```

```
normalize((String)session.getAttribute("chatItem")).trim();
                    if(chatItem.length() < 1) {
                         haveChatItem = false;
                         log(sessionId, "err",
                         "processRequest() ERROR: session has no chatItem, going
back for it!");
                    }
                    if(chatItem.equalsIgnoreCase("NONE")) {
                         haveChatItem = false;
                         log(sessionId, "err",
                         "processRequest() ERROR: session has chatItem=NONE, going
back for it!");
                    }
                    // For a guest to join a chat, we need to get sessionId of HOST
                    // that started that chat! To find chat for that visitor to
join,
                    // we will need the key to its nodeKey in the nodeNameHashtable.
                    // We call that key the chatNodeKeyKey, and can use it to add
                    // elements, etc. directly to the chat. Note that we CANNOT just
                    // make a new "<sessionId>_<creationTimeMillis>:chat" key
string,
                    // because the chat was created by the host's sessionId and we
                    // have only the guest's sessionId now! So we get the right
                    // chatNodeKeyKey for the chat, which is
                    //           <hostSessionId>_<creationTimeMillis>:chat
                    // directly from the nodeName of the chosen chatItem element
which
                    // was saved when the chat was started. This way there is no
need
                    // to iterate the chats looking for the one with the right
itemKey.
                    // Instead, we will be able to use:
                    //           chatNodeKeyKey =
session.getAttribute("chatNodeKeyKey");
                    //
                    // NOTE: chatItem must be the path to sessionId child element of
                    // subject element. That must be generated from a more
meaningful
                    // chat selection list presented to user. We use XSLT to
generate
                    // that more meaningful chat selection list.
                    // NOTE: we must disallow '>[' in subject node names for this to
work!
                    // NOTE: For now, separator in incoming chat subject path is
wired as '_'
                    // e.g. Animals_Fish_Piranha_[first aid for fish breeders]
                    // NOTE: the creationTimeMillis portion of the nodeNameHashtable
keys
                    // allows hosts and guests to be in more than one chat,
                    // and allows actors to host and guest multiple chats.
                    // NOTE: there is also an option to leave out the nodeKey.aKey
```

```
portion of
                    // the key, for a selected list of node names (see
ForestHashtable, property
                    // UniqueNodeKeyKeyList. That reduces the size requirements of
the
                    // nodeKeyHashtable (for example, by not storing all the message
nodeKey keys).
                    // It can also be used for security, for example, to insure that
there is
                    // only one host node per session, etc.
                    // As in the case of "visitor starts chat"
                    // (see the note before synchronize block above),
                    // we synchronize here two things:
                    // 1. the check for existence of chat for subject+topic
(chatItem)
                    // 2. the joining of a chat by visitor
                    // - We assume that the chat for chatItem exists, since it was
picked
                    // from a list generated by the webapp from existing chats.
                    // - When chat deletion is implemented,
                    // (and even now, because chats expire with their session),
                    // we need to guard against adding part of the elements, etc.
                    // required for joining a chat, and then not being able to
complete all
                    // the additions required. If synchronization turns out to
affect
                    // performance too much, we could make a background task to
clean up
                    // such debris?
                    // almost works, needs something else synchronized?
                    //synchronized(bonForumStore.bonForumXML) {
                    synchronized(bonForumStore) {
                    if(haveChatItem) {
                          boolean actorIsHostInChat = false;
                          boolean actorIsGuestInChat = false;
                          boolean actorWillRejoinChat = false;
                          // See if chatItem (i.e., subject+topic) exists already as
a chat:
                          chatNodeKeyKey =
getBonForumStore().getBonForumChatNodeKeyKey(chatItem);
                          if((chatNodeKeyKey != null) && (chatNodeKeyKey.length() >
0)) {
                                // Being able to find a chatNodeKeyKey from chatItem
                                // means that a chat exists with chosen subject and
topic.
                                chatExistsForSubjectAndTopic = true;
                                // see if actor is a host in chat found
                                String actorKeyValue =
normalize((String)session.getAttribute("hostKey"));
                                if(actorKeyValue.trim().length() > 0) {
                                      actorIsHostInChat =
```

```
getBonForumStore().isHostInChat(actorKeyValue, chatNodeKeyKey);
                                        }
                                        if(!actorIsHostInChat) {
                                                // if not, see if actor is a guest in chat
found
                                                actorKeyValue =
normalize((String)session.getAttribute("guestKey"));
                                                if(actorKeyValue.trim().length() > 0) {
                                                        actorIsGuestInChat =
getBonForumStore().isGuestInChat(actorKeyValue, chatNodeKeyKey);
                                                }
                                        }
                                }
                                // see if visitor will rejoin chat
                                // because already a host or guest,
                                // or will join chat becoming a new guest
                                if(chatExistsForSubjectAndTopic) {
                                        // set the chatNodeKeyKey for this chat into a
session attribute
                                        session.setAttribute("chatNodeKeyKey",
chatNodeKeyKey);
                                        // if visitor already in chat as host or guest, will
re-join it.
                                        if(actorIsHostInChat) {
                                                bonForumCommand = "host_executes_chat";
                                                actorWillRejoinChat = true;
                                                haveChatItem = false;
                                        }
                                        else if(actorIsGuestInChat) {
                                                //bonForumCommand = "guest_executes_chat";
                                                actorWillRejoinChat = true;
                                                haveChatItem = false;
                                        }
                                        else {
                                                // visitor not in chat yet, so will join as
guest
                                                //bonForumCommand = "guest_executes_chat";
                                        }
                                }
                                // set session attributes for message handling
                                if(actorWillRejoinChat) {
                                        // not needed, hasn't changed?
                                        // session.setAttribute("chatItem", chatItem);
                                        // set the itemKey for this chat into a session
attribute
                                        // it is needed for finding messages (temporarily)
                                        // and for any guest session to find it
                                        String foundChatItemKey =
getBonForumStore().getBonForumChatItemNodeKey(chatItem).toString();
                                        session.setAttribute("itemKey", foundChatItemKey);
                                }
```

```
            }
            // check chat node OK before doing anything else
                chatNode =
bonForumStore.getBonForumChatNode(chatNodeKeyKey);
                if(chatNode == null) {
                    haveChatItem = false;
                    bonForumCommand = "forum_error";
                    request.setAttribute("serviceStatus",
"ForwardToErrorPage");
                    log(sessionId, "err",
                    "ERROR! No chatNode in guest_executes_chat handler!
Forwarding To Error Page!");
                }
            }
            // actor joins chat
            if(haveChatItem) {
                // actorNickname is unique in bonForum,
                // Allow only one guest node per actorNickname
                // Get the guest nickname from session
                actorNickname =
normalize((String)session.getAttribute("actorNickname"));
                // Get guest nickname key
                NodeKey guestNicknameNodeKey =
getBonForumStore().getActorNicknameNodeKey(actorNickname, "guest");
                NodeKey guestNodeKey = null;
                // If got key, get guest nickname node,
                // use its parent key to get guest node key
                if(guestNicknameNodeKey != null) {
                BonNode guestNicknameNode =
getBonForumStore().getBonForumXML().getBonNode(guestNicknameNodeKey);
                    guestNodeKey = guestNicknameNode.parentNodeKey;
                }
                // If guest node key does not exist,
                // neither does guest, so add guest node,
                // with its nickname, age and rating children
                // to the "actors" rootchild node of database.
                if(guestNodeKey == null) {
                    //add guest node to actors
                    nameAndAttributes = "guest";
                    content = "";
                    forestHashtableName = "bonForumXML";
                    obj = bonForumStore.add("bonAddElement", "actors",
nameAndAttributes, content, forestHashtableName, "nodeNameHashtable", sessionId);
                    guestNodeKey = (NodeKey)obj;
                    // add actorNickname to guest
                    // the aKey in the NodeKey is a timeMillis value
from node addition
                    // It is used also in the nodeKeyHashtable key
values
                    String creationTimeMillis = guestNodeKey.aKey;
                    String guestNodeKeyKey = sessionId + "_" +
```

```
creationTimeMillis + ":guest";
                                // Make nodeNameHashtable key
                                // for the guestNodeKey
                                // available to session.
                                // It gives quick access to last guest nodeKey for
session
                                session.setAttribute( "guestNodeKeyKey",
guestNodeKeyKey );
                                // add actorNickname to guest
                                nameAndAttributes = "actorNickname";
                                content =
normalize((String)session.getAttribute("actorNickname"));
                                forestHashtableName = "bonForumXML";
                                obj = bonForumStore.add("bonAddElement",
guestNodeKeyKey, nameAndAttributes, content, forestHashtableName,
"nodeNameHashtable", sessionId);
                                // see the NOTICE above, in comment when adding
actorNickname to host
                                // add actorAge to guest
                                nameAndAttributes = "actorAge";
                                content =
normalize((String)session.getAttribute("actorAge"));
                                forestHashtableName = "bonForumXML";
                                obj = bonForumStore.add("bonAddElement",
guestNodeKeyKey, nameAndAttributes, content, forestHashtableName,
"nodeNameHashtable", sessionId);
                                // add actorRating to guest
                                nameAndAttributes = "actorRating";
                                content =
normalize((String)session.getAttribute("actorRating"));
                                if(content.length() < 1) {
                                        content = "5";
                                }
                                forestHashtableName = "bonForumXML";
                                obj = bonForumStore.add("bonAddElement",
guestNodeKeyKey, nameAndAttributes, content, forestHashtableName,
"nodeNameHashtable", sessionId);
                        }
                        // add guestKey to chat, that is how guest joins chat.
                        nameAndAttributes = "guestKey";
                        content = guestNodeKey.toString();
                        forestHashtableName = "bonForumXML";
                        //chatNodeKeyKey =
normalize((String)session.getAttribute("chatNodeKeyKey"));
                        obj = bonForumStore.add("bonAddElement", chatNodeKeyKey,
nameAndAttributes, content, forestHashtableName, "nodeNameHashtable", sessionId);
                        // set the guestKey for this chat into a session attribute
                        session.setAttribute("guestKey", guestNodeKey.toString());
                        // set the itemKey for this chat into a session attribute
for the guest's session
                        String chatItemKey =
```

```
bonForumStore.getBonForumAttributeValue(chatNode, "itemKey");
                        session.setAttribute("itemKey", chatItemKey);
                        //LATER: here add status attribute to guest
                } // end if haveChatItem (#3)
                if((!chatExistsForSubjectAndTopic) && (!haveChatItem)) {
                        // missing information, must return to get it
                        // LATER: set attribute to trigger message to user
                        bonForumCommand = "visitor_joins_chat";
                }
                } // end of synchronized block!
        }// end of guest_executes_chat processing
        else if(bonForumCommand.indexOf("visitor_starts_chat") > -1) {
                //if(bonForumCommand.equals("visitor_starts_chat")) {
                        // not used yet
                //}
                //else
                if(bonForumCommand.indexOf("visitor_starts_chat_frame") > -1) {
                        //chat subject
                        chatSubject =
normalize((String)request.getParameter("chatSubject"));
                        // strip off some leftmost nodes, there during development
only
                        if(chatSubject.indexOf("bonForum.") == 0) {
                                chatSubject =
chatSubject.substring("bonForum.".length());
                        }
                        if(chatSubject.indexOf("things.") == 0) {
                                chatSubject =
chatSubject.substring("things.".length());
                        }
                        if(chatSubject.indexOf("subjects.") == 0) {
                                chatSubject =
chatSubject.substring("subjects.".length());
                        }
                        if(chatSubject.trim().length() > 0) {

if(chatSubject.equals(normalize((String)session.getAttribute("chatSubject")))) {
                                        session.setAttribute("newChatSubject", "no");
                                }
                                else {
                                        session.setAttribute("newChatSubject", "yes");
                                        session.setAttribute("chatSubject",
chatSubject);
                                }
                        }
                }
                //else
if(bonForumCommand.indexOf("visitor_starts_chat_controls") > -1) {
                //}
                //else if(bonForumCommand.indexOf("visitor_starts_chat_robot") >
-1) {
```

```
                    //}
                    else if(bonForumCommand.indexOf("visitor_starts_chat_ready") > -
1) {
                        //chat moderated flag
                        chatModerated =
normalize((String)request.getParameter("chatModerated"));
                        if(chatModerated.trim().length() > 0) {
                            session.setAttribute("chatModerated",
chatModerated);
                        }
                        //chat topic
                        chatTopic =
normalize((String)request.getParameter("chatTopic"));
                        if(chatTopic.trim().length() > 0) {
                            if(chatTopic.equals(

normalize((String)session.getAttribute("chatTopic")))) {
                                session.setAttribute("newChatTopic", "no");
                            }
                            else {
                                session.setAttribute("newChatTopic", "yes");
                                session.setAttribute("chatTopic", chatTopic);
                            }
                        }
                    }
                    // else {
                    // NOTE: test which ones?
                    // NOTE: change this so it checks indexOf not equals,
                    //   then looks for equals(xxxxx_ready, etc.)
                    //   e.g., _ready here will make sure subject and topic have
values
                    //   and if not, will change bonForumCommand to send user
                    //   back to visitor_starts_chat
                    // ALSO: use constants not strings here?
                    // NOTE: also, move the processing of request parameters into
                    //   these blocks as methods, so more than one block can
                    //   share them (e.g., nickname).
                    //
                    // NOTE: Then move chat processing code out to new class
BonForumChat.java
                    // }
            }// end of visitor_starts_chat processing
              else if(bonForumCommand.indexOf("visitor_joins_chat") > -1) {
                    //if(bonForumCommand.equals("visitor_joins_chat")) {
                        // not used yet
                    //}
                    //else
                    if(bonForumCommand.indexOf("visitor_joins_chat_frame") > -1) {
                        //chat moderated flag
                        chatModerated =
normalize((String)request.getParameter("chatModerated"));
```

```
                    if(chatModerated.trim().length() > 0) {
                         session.setAttribute("chatModerated",
chatModerated);
                    }
                    //chat item
                    chatItem =
normalize((String)request.getParameter("chatItem"));
                    // strip off some leftmost nodes, there during development
only
                    if(chatItem.indexOf("bonForum.") == 0) {
                         chatItem = chatItem.substring("bonForum.".length());
                    }
                    if(chatItem.indexOf("things.") == 0) {
                         chatItem = chatItem.substring("things.".length());
                    }
                    if(chatItem.indexOf("subjects.") == 0) {
                         chatItem = chatItem.substring("subjects.".length());
                    }
                    if(chatItem.trim().length() > 0) {
                         session.setAttribute("chatItem", chatItem);
                    }
                    //take chatItem apart to get subject and topic from guest
session
                    //we cannot get it from session attribute, because that
was saved by a host
                    if(chatItem.trim().length() > 0) {
                         // e.g. animals_fish_piranha_[first aid for fish
breeders]
                         int inxTopic = chatItem.indexOf("[");
                         // temp kludge until xsl to remove the '_' char
before '[' is found!
                         int adjust = 1;
                         int inxTopic2 = chatItem.indexOf("_[");
                         if(inxTopic2 == inxTopic - 1) {
                              inxTopic = inxTopic2;
                              ++adjust;
                         }
                         chatSubject = chatItem.substring(0, inxTopic);
                         // replace all '_' with '.' which is separator in
pathNameHashtable
                         chatSubject = chatSubject.replace('_', '.');
                         inxTopic += adjust;
                         chatTopic = chatItem.substring(inxTopic,
chatItem.length() - 1);
                         session.setAttribute("chatSubject", chatSubject);
                         session.setAttribute("chatTopic", chatTopic);
                    }
               }
               //else if(bonForumCommand.indexOf("visitor_joins_chat_controls")
> -1) {
               //}
```

```
                    //else if(bonForumCommand.indexOf("visitor_joins_chat_robot") >
-1) {
                    //}
                    //else if(bonForumCommand.indexOf("visitor_joins_chat_ready") >
-1) {
                    //}
                }
                else if(bonForumCommand.indexOf("guest_executes_command") > -1) {
                    //if(bonForumCommand.equals("guest_executes_command")) {
                        // not used yet
                    //}
                    //else
                    if(bonForumCommand.indexOf("guest_executes_command_controls") >
-1) {
                        //chatMessagesPageSize
                        chatMessagesPageSize =
normalize((String)request.getParameter("chatMessagesPageSize"));
                        if(chatMessagesPageSize.trim().length() > 0) {
                            session.setAttribute("chatMessagesPageSize",
chatMessagesPageSize);
                        }
                    }
                }
                else if(bonForumCommand.indexOf("host_executes_command") > -1) {
                    //if(bonForumCommand.equals("host_executes_command")) {
                        // not used yet
                    //}
                    //else
                    if(bonForumCommand.indexOf("host_executes_command_controls") > -
1) {
                        //chatMessagesPageSize
                        chatMessagesPageSize =
normalize((String)request.getParameter("chatMessagesPageSize"));
                        if(chatMessagesPageSize.trim().length() > 0) {
                            session.setAttribute("chatMessagesPageSize",
chatMessagesPageSize);
                        }
                    }
                    else if(bonForumCommand.indexOf("host_executes_command_frame") >
-1) {
                        //chat guest
                        chatGuest =
normalize((String)request.getParameter("chatGuest"));
                        if(chatGuest.trim().length() > 0) {
                            session.setAttribute("chatGuest", chatGuest);
                        }
                    }
                }
                else if(bonForumCommand.indexOf("visitor_executes_choice") > -1) {
                    //actor nickname is handled in service() method,
                    //actor age
```

```
                    actorAge = normalize((String)request.getParameter("actorAge"));
                    if(actorAge.trim().length() > 0) {
                          session.setAttribute("actorAge", actorAge);
                    }
              }
              else if(bonForumCommand.indexOf("system_sets_timeout") > -1) {
                    //sessionMaxInactiveMinutes "-1" or "dddddddd" (set in
application attribute!)
                    sessionMaxInactiveMinutes =
normalize((String)request.getParameter("sessionMaxInactiveMinutes"));
                    if(sessionMaxInactiveMinutes.trim().length() > 0) {

getServletContext().setAttribute("sessionMaxInactiveMinutes",
sessionMaxInactiveMinutes);
                    }
              }
              else if(bonForumCommand.indexOf("system_executes_command") > -1) {
                    //xalanVersion "Xalan-Java 1" or "Xalan-Java 2" (set in
application attribute!)
                    xalanVersion =
normalize((String)request.getParameter("xalanVersion"));
                    if(xalanVersion.trim().length() > 0) {
                          getServletContext().setAttribute("xalanVersion",
xalanVersion);
                    }
                    //actorRatingType will set differenct options for actor rating
(not yet implemented)
                    actorRatingType =
normalize((String)request.getParameter("actorRatingType"));
                    if(actorRatingType.trim().length() > 0) {
                          session.setAttribute("actorRatingType", actorRatingType);
                    }
              }
              else if(bonForumCommand.indexOf("forum_entry") > -1) {
                    // not used yet
              }
              else {
              // processRequest does not special process bonForumCommand
              }// end of bonForumCommand processing
              // ************YOU can add new commands here*********
              // announce success, unless other result was announced in method

if(request.getAttribute("serviceStatus").equals("InProcessRequestMethod")) {
                    request.setAttribute("serviceStatus",
"ForwardAfterRequestProcessed");
              }
              return bonForumCommand;
        }// end of processRequest()
        /** Classifies and forwards chat requests, and optionally invokes their
processing,
         * while managing security and sessions.
```

```
     *  (See chapter "Java Servlet and Java Bean - BonForumEngine and
BonForumStore"
     *   in the book: XML, XSLT, Java and JSP - A Case Study in Developing a Web
Application).
     *
     * @param request                    HttpServletRequest
     * @param response                   HttpServletResponse
     * @throws IOException
     */
    public void service(HttpServletRequest request,
                        HttpServletResponse response)
                        throws IOException, ServletException {
        HttpSession session = null;
        String sessionId = "0000000000";
        String serviceStatus = "CheckForServicing";
        String bonForumCommand = "";
        // Some request URI's are servlet-mapped to this servlet
        // and others are posted directly to this servlet.
        String requestUri = request.getRequestURI();
        //log(sessionId, "out", "requestUri: " + requestUri);
        // A bonCommand parameter asks for a destination JSP
        String bonCommand = normalize(
          (String)request.getParameter("bonCommand")).trim();
        if((requestUri.indexOf("BonForumEngine") > -1)) {
            // Get forwarding destination from request parameter
            if(bonCommand.length() > 0) {
                bonForumCommand = bonCommand;
                if(bonCommand.indexOf("forum_entry") > -1) {
                    // request came from first page (forum_login.jsp).
                    serviceStatus = "CheckInAtEntrance";
                }
                else if(bonCommand.indexOf("UserMustLogin") > -1) {
                    // request is for drastic recovery of webapp
                    serviceStatus = "UserMustLogin";
                }
                else if(bonCommand.indexOf("system_executes_command") > -
1) {
                    // request is for access to system administration
                    // (Later add password security on system nickname,
                    // for now, there is no security at all.)
                    // Get the session, creating it if none exists:
                    session = request.getSession();
                    session.setAttribute("actorNickname", "system");
                    serviceStatus = "SystemCommands";
                }
                else {
                    // these are normal requests from jsp forms:
                    serviceStatus = "ProcessRequest";
                }
            }
            else {
```

```
                    // these requests need bonForumCommand value
                    // set by processing before forwarding.
                    // e.g., by specific actor, action, thing parameters
                    serviceStatus = "ProcessRequest";
                }
            }
            else {
                // these requests are here due to servlet-mapping
                serviceStatus = "DecodeServletMappedURI";
            }
            // route some error handling request destinations
            // through the method without any processing:
            if(requestUri.indexOf("forum_login") > -1) {
                serviceStatus = "ForwardToLoginPage";
            }
            else if(requestUri.indexOf("forum_error") > -1) {
                serviceStatus = "ForwardToErrorPage";
            }
            else if(requestUri.indexOf("UserMustLogin") > -1) {
                serviceStatus = "UserMustLogin";
            }
            // handle non-error requests here:
            if(serviceStatus.equals("CheckInAtEntrance")) {
                // Is request for forum_entry from forum_login.
                // Get the session, creating it if none there.
                session = request.getSession();
                // Get the session identification
                sessionId = session.getId();
                // TEMP, Remove later (see "LATER" below)
                // We sidestep the issue of user management for now!
                // That means a chat lasts only as long as the session that
created it!
                // So, make sessions last a long time for now, by
                // Specifying the time, in seconds, between client requests
                // before the servlet container will invalidate this session.
                // A negative time indicates the session should never timeout.
                // look for max chat inactivity interval in application
attribute:
                String sessMax =
normalize((String)getServletContext().getAttribute(
                    "sessionMaxInactiveMinutes"));
                if(sessMax.trim().length() < 1) {
                    // if not found, look for it in web.xml
                    sessMax = getServletContext().getInitParameter(
                        "sessionMaxInactiveMinutes");
                    if(sessMax == null) {
                        sessMax = "-1";
                    }
                }
                int minutes = -1;
                try {
```

```
                    minutes = Integer.parseInt(sessMax);
                }
                catch (NumberFormatException nFE) {
                    log(sessionId, "err",
                    "ERROR! service(), cannot parse maxInactiveInterval app
attr as int: " + sessMax);
                    minutes = -1;
                }
                session.setMaxInactiveInterval(minutes);  // default to forever
                //session.setMaxInactiveInterval(30);       // chats last 30
secs, for testing
                //session.setMaxInactiveInterval(24*60*60); // chats last a day
                //session.setMaxInactiveInterval(-1);      // chats last until
tomcat shutdown
                serviceStatus = "ProcessRequest";
            }
            else if (!serviceStatus.equals("ForwardToLoginPage") &&
                    !serviceStatus.equals("ForwardToErrorPage") &&
                    !serviceStatus.equals("UserMustLogin")) {
                // Request is not for forum_entry page from forum_login,
                // and not a robot applet request for forum_login.jsp,
                // and not a request for forum_error.jsp,
                // and not a request for robot applet to request login
                //
                // serviceStatus is ProcessRequest,
                // or is DecodeServletMappedURI,
                // or is SystemCommands!
                // See if we have an existing session, but don't create one if
not
                session = request.getSession(false);
                // Prevent new session from entering except from entrance page.
                // Also send expired sessions to beginning (with new session).
                if(session == null) {
                    log(sessionId, "err", "Not entering, but session is null.
UserMustLogin");
                    serviceStatus = "UserMustLogin";
                }
                else {
                    // request came with a session
                    sessionId = session.getId();
                    // validate session for each request.
                    // 1. valid sessions: enable further processing.
                    // 2. stale sessions: give new session and update session-
related data,
                    // (Note: #2 is not implemented yet, so stale session must
re-login.)
                    //See if requested session is still valid (testing this)
                    String requestedSessionId =
request.getRequestedSessionId();
                    if(request.isRequestedSessionIdValid()) {
                        //requestedSessionId is valid
```

```
                        }
                        else {
                              //    LATER: May add code here to update
nodeNameHashtable contents
                              //           by replacing old sessionId with
currrent (or new) sessionId?
                              //           For now, just forward requests for
wrong sessions
                              //           to the web application entrance.
                              log(sessionId, "err",
"request.getRequestedSessionId() NOT VALID, UserMustLogin:" + requestedSessionId);
                              serviceStatus = "UserMustLogin";
                        }
                        // make sure user has a valid, unique nickname:
                        String actorNickname;
                        // clear any previous unavailable names
                        session.setAttribute("actorNicknameNotAvailable", "");
                        boolean isForumEntry = false;
                        // Only web-app state that allows nickname input
                        // is forum_entry.  Check for its bonCommnand here:
                        if(bonCommand.indexOf("visitor_executes_choice") > -1) {
                              isForumEntry = true;
                              // get user's nickname choice ("system" not allowed)
                                    actorNickname = normalize(

(String)request.getParameter("actorNickname")).trim();
                              String aN = normalize(

(String)session.getAttribute("actorNickname")).trim();
                              if(actorNickname.equals("system") &&
!(aN.equals("system"))) {
                                    actorNickname = "";
                              }
                        }
                        else {
                              // get pre-existing nickname
                              actorNickname = normalize(

(String)session.getAttribute("actorNickname")).trim();
                        }
                        if(actorNickname.length() > 0) {
                              if(actorNickname.equals("system")) {
                                    nicknameRegistry.put(actorNickname,
sessionId);
                              }
                              //check for nickname in registry
                              if(nicknameRegistry.containsKey(actorNickname)) {
                                    if(!(nicknameRegistry.get(

actorNickname).equals(sessionId))) {
                                          // nickname is registered for another
```

```
session!
                                        if(isForumEntry) {
                                            // send user back for another one:
                                            serviceStatus =
"ForwardWithoutServicing";
                                            bonForumCommand = "forum_entry";
                                            // set attribute for using on
forum_entry.jsp
                                            // to trigger user message that
name is taken:
                                            session.setAttribute(
                                                "actorNicknameNotAvailable",
actorNickname);
                                            // nickname choice is not unique,
disallow it:
                                            actorNickname = "";
                                            log(sessionId, "err",
                                                "actorNickname rejected as
duplicate:" +
                                                 actorNickname);
                                        }
                                        else {
                                            // pre-existing nickname registered
for another session!
                                            // is this reachable? missed
session expired?
                                            // if so, maybe later here we can
keep user,
                                            // but switch data to new session?
                                            serviceStatus = "UserMustLogin";
                                            log(sessionId, "ERR", "Pre-existing
nickname registered for another session! UserMustLogin:" + actorNickname);
                                        }
                                    } // else existing nickname is OK
                                }
                                else {
                                    // nickname not in registry
                                    if(isForumEntry) {
                                        // add new nickname, unique and
available
                                        nicknameRegistry.put(actorNickname,
sessionId);
                                        session.setAttribute("actorNickname",
actorNickname);
                                        log(sessionId, "out", "New nickname
added to registry:" + actorNickname);
                                    }
                                    else {
                                        // pre-existing nickname is no longer in
registry
                                        serviceStatus = "UserMustLogin";
```

```
                                        log(sessionId, "err", "Pre-existing
nickname is no longer in registry! UserMustLogin:" + actorNickname);
                                    }
                              }
                        }
                        else {
                              // nickname missing in request or session!
                              if(isForumEntry) {
                                    // user entered empty string
                                    // send user back for another try:
                                    serviceStatus = "ForwardWithoutServicing";
                                    bonForumCommand = "forum_entry";
                                    log(sessionId, "err", "New nickname is missing
in request!! ForwardWithoutServicing to forum_entry ");
                              }
                              else {
                                    // nickname is needed!
                                    serviceStatus = "UserMustLogin";
                                    log(sessionId, "err", "Expected nickname is
missing in session!! UserMustLogin");
                              }
                        }
                  }
            }
            if(serviceStatus.equals("DecodeServletMappedURI")) {
                  // Requests that are not addressed to this BonForumEngine
                  // come to its service method due to a servlet-mapping
                  // in the web-app deployment descriptor (web.xml) file.
                  // It maps the file extension, ".tfe", to this servlet.
                  // Some JSP in the web-app forward their requests
                  // to a BonForumRobot applet in another JSP.  That applet
                  // uses its showDocument method to send a (different)
                  // request for a URL with a file extension of ".tfe".
                  // That indirect requesting is done for one of two
                  // reasons, as follows:
                  // 1. to continually request a JSP that displays its
                  //    output in a different frame than one the robot is in.
                  //    Doing that provides a frequent refresh of its content.
                  //
                  // 2. to request a JSP that sets up a different frameset
                  //    than the one containing the frame the robot is in.
                  //    This indirect requesting prevents the new frameset
                  //    from displaying within a frame of the old frameset.
                  // There are also other servlet-mapped requests that
                  // are handled here.  All "frame-filling" JSP files
                  // have ".tfe" added.  Also, all "jsp:forward" filenames
                  // have ".tfe" added.  One can also request any resource
                  // "through" the BonForumEngine, and this block of code,
                  // by suffixing ".tfe" to the resource name and then
                  // dispatching a request.
                  // In this next code section, this servlet tries to
```

```
                    // find any of this web application's JSP filenames
                    // embedded in the URL that the robot applet requested.
                    // If it finds one, it will forward the current request
                    // and response to that JSP.  If serviceStatus equals
                    // "ForwardWithoutServicing", which is its default,
                    // the forwarding happens without the processRequest
                    // method being called.
                    // Some pages do need processRequest called, so for these,
                    // serviceStatus is set to "ProcessRequest". These are
                    // host_executes_chat and guest_executes_chat.  Each has
                    // a related processing block in the processRequest method,
                    // with much application related code there.
                    // Note: you can set serviceStatus to "ProcessRequest"
                    // for any request URL here, in order to send it through
                    // the processRequest method before the request is
                    // forwaded.  But you must also add new code to process
                    // that request in the processRequest method. We suggest
                    // you put the code there inside a new and similar if
                    // statement as the ones used for host_executes_chat and
                    // guest_executes_chat.
                    // Note: For easier expansion, most JSP in webapp are here,
                    // even if not now being requested via a servlet-mapping.
                    // Arrange these if blocks in the order of their access
frequency.
                    serviceStatus = "ForwardWithoutServicing";
                    if(requestUri.indexOf("actor_leaves_frameset") > -1) {
                         if(requestUri.indexOf("actor_leaves_frameset_robot") > -1)
{
                              bonForumCommand = "actor_leaves_frameset_robot";
                         }
                         else {
                              bonForumCommand = "forum_error";
                              serviceStatus = "ForwardToErrorPage";
                         }
                    }
                    else if(requestUri.indexOf("guest_executes_chat") > -1) {
                         if(requestUri.indexOf("guest_executes_chat_frame") > -1) {
                              bonForumCommand = "guest_executes_chat_frame";
                         }
                         else if(requestUri.indexOf("guest_executes_chat_controls")
> -1) {
                              bonForumCommand = "guest_executes_chat_controls";
                         }
                         else if(requestUri.indexOf("guest_executes_chat_robot") >
-1) {
                              bonForumCommand = "guest_executes_chat_robot";
                         }
                         else if(requestUri.indexOf("guest_executes_chat_ready") >
-1) {
                              bonForumCommand = "guest_executes_chat_ready";
                         }
```

```
                    else if(requestUri.indexOf("guest_executes_chat_console")
> -1) {
                          bonForumCommand = "guest_executes_chat_console";
                    }
                    else {
                          bonForumCommand = "guest_executes_chat";
                          serviceStatus = "ProcessRequest";
                    }
              }
              else if(requestUri.indexOf("host_executes_chat") > -1) {
                    if(requestUri.indexOf("host_executes_chat_frame") > -1) {
                          bonForumCommand = "host_executes_chat_frame";
                    }
                    else if(requestUri.indexOf("host_executes_chat_controls")
> -1) {
                          bonForumCommand = "host_executes_chat_controls";
                    }
                    else if(requestUri.indexOf("host_executes_chat_robot") > -
1) {
                          bonForumCommand = "host_executes_chat_robot";
                    }
                    else if(requestUri.indexOf("host_executes_chat_ready") > -
1) {
                          bonForumCommand = "host_executes_chat_ready";
                    }
                    else if(requestUri.indexOf("host_executes_chat_console") >
-1) {
                          bonForumCommand = "host_executes_chat_console";
                    }
                    else {
                          bonForumCommand = "host_executes_chat";
                          serviceStatus = "ProcessRequest";
                    }
              }
              else if(requestUri.indexOf("visitor_joins_chat") > -1) {
                    if(requestUri.indexOf("visitor_joins_chat_frame") > -1) {
                          bonForumCommand = "visitor_joins_chat_frame";
                    }
                    else if(requestUri.indexOf("visitor_joins_chat_controls")
> -1) {
                          bonForumCommand = "visitor_joins_chat_controls";
                    }
                    else if(requestUri.indexOf("visitor_joins_chat_robot") > -
1) {
                          bonForumCommand = "visitor_joins_chat_robot";
                    }
                    else if(requestUri.indexOf("visitor_joins_chat_ready") > -
1) {
                          bonForumCommand = "visitor_joins_chat_ready";
                    }
                    else {
```

```
                                        bonForumCommand = "visitor_joins_chat";
                                    }
                              }
                              else if(requestUri.indexOf("visitor_starts_chat") > -1) {
                                    if(requestUri.indexOf("visitor_starts_chat_frame") > -1) {
                                          bonForumCommand = "visitor_starts_chat_frame";
                                    }
                                    else if(requestUri.indexOf("visitor_starts_chat_controls")
> -1) {
                                          bonForumCommand = "visitor_starts_chat_controls";
                                    }
                                    else if(requestUri.indexOf("visitor_starts_chat_robot") >
-1) {
                                          bonForumCommand = "visitor_starts_chat_robot";
                                    }
                                    else if(requestUri.indexOf("visitor_starts_chat_ready") >
-1) {
                                          bonForumCommand = "visitor_starts_chat_ready";
                                    }
                                    else {
                                          bonForumCommand = "visitor_starts_chat";
                                    }
                              }
                              else if(requestUri.indexOf("host_executes_command") > -1) {
                                    if(requestUri.indexOf("host_executes_command_frame") > -1)
{
                                          bonForumCommand = "host_executes_command_frame";
                                    }
                                    else
if(requestUri.indexOf("host_executes_command_controls") > -1) {
                                          bonForumCommand = "host_executes_command_controls";
                                    }
                                    else if(requestUri.indexOf("host_executes_command_robot")
> -1) {
                                          bonForumCommand = "host_executes_command_robot";
                                    }
                                    else if(requestUri.indexOf("host_executes_command_ready")
> -1) {
                                          bonForumCommand = "host_executes_command_ready";
                                    }
                                    else {
                                          bonForumCommand = "host_executes_command";
                                    }
                              }
                              else if(requestUri.indexOf("guest_executes_command") > -1) {
                                    if(requestUri.indexOf("guest_executes_command_frame") > -
1) {
                                          bonForumCommand = "guest_executes_command_frame";
                                    }
                                    else
if(requestUri.indexOf("guest_executes_command_controls") > -1) {
```

```
                        bonForumCommand = "guest_executes_command_controls";
                    }
                    else if(requestUri.indexOf("guest_executes_command_robot")
> -1) {
                        bonForumCommand = "guest_executes_command_robot";
                    }
                    else if(requestUri.indexOf("guest_executes_command_ready")
> -1) {
                        bonForumCommand = "guest_executes_command_ready";
                    }
                    else {
                        bonForumCommand = "guest_executes_command";
                    }
                }
                else if(requestUri.indexOf("host_exits_") > -1) {
                    if(requestUri.indexOf("host_exits_chat") > -1) {
                        bonForumCommand = "host_exits_chat";
                    }
                    else if(requestUri.indexOf("host_exits_command") > -1) {
                        bonForumCommand = "host_exits_command";
                    }
                    else {
                        bonForumCommand = "host_exits_forum";
                    }
                }
                else if(requestUri.indexOf("guest_exits_") > -1) {
                    if(requestUri.indexOf("guest_exits_chat") > -1) {
                        bonForumCommand = "guest_exits_chat";
                    }
                    else if(requestUri.indexOf("guest_exits_command") > -1) {
                        bonForumCommand = "guest_exits_command";
                    }
                    else {
                        bonForumCommand = "guest_exits_forum";
                    }
                }
                else if(requestUri.indexOf("visitor_executes_choice") > -1) {
                    bonForumCommand = "visitor_executes_choice";
                }
                else {
                    bonForumCommand = "forum_error";
                    serviceStatus = "ForwardToErrorPage";
                }
            }
            // Now process each request,
            // unless only to be forwarded,
            // or user being sent to login or error page.
            // Also, allow system parameters to set attributes, etc.
            if(serviceStatus.equals("ProcessRequest") ||
               serviceStatus.equals("SystemCommands")) {
                try {
```

```
                        request.setAttribute("serviceStatus", serviceStatus);
                        bonForumCommand = processRequest(request, response,
session, bonForumCommand);
                        serviceStatus =
(String)request.getAttribute("serviceStatus");
                        // The processRequest() method should "return" a
                        // serviceStatus request attribute which has been
                        // set to "ForwardAfterRequestProcessed", or to
                        // another value that will forward the request below.
                  }
                  catch(Exception ee) {
                        // handle this better.
                        log(sessionId, "err", "Caught Exception calling
processRequest()!");
                        log(sessionId, "err", ee.getMessage());
                        ee.printStackTrace();
                  }
            }
            // Now see if we will need to forward to an error page
            // because request processing failed.
            // These are the possible successful outcomes:
            // 1. all processing is done for this request
            // 2. request was only sent to engine to be forwarded
            if(!(serviceStatus.equals("ForwardWithoutServicing") ||
                 serviceStatus.equals("ForwardAfterRequestProcessed"))) {
                 // unsuccesful outcome!
                 if(serviceStatus.equals("ForwardToLoginPage")) {
                        // request was already sent to start over,
                        // using a UserMustLogin serviceStatus, and
                        // now the robot is requesting login page:
                        bonForumCommand = "forum_login";
                  }
                  else if(serviceStatus.equals("ForwardToErrorPage")) {
                        // request is for error page
                        // it was routed around all processing, etc.
                        bonForumCommand = "forum_error";
                  }
                  else if(serviceStatus.equals("SystemCommands")) {
                        // request is for system only page
                        // enforce only one main page here:
                        bonForumCommand = "system_executes_command";
                  }
                  else {
                        // catch unknown serviceStatus errors:
                        serviceStatus = "UserMustLogin";
                  }
                  // drastic recovery time:
                  if(serviceStatus.equals("UserMustLogin")) {
                        // Send user to start the web application over again!
                        // 1. request is not for forum_entry, has no session
                        // 2. request sessionId is not for current session
```

```
                    // 3  existing nickname is for wrong session
                    // 4  existing nickname is not in registry
                    // 5. existing nickname not found in session attribute
                    // These conditions will arise until we
                    // add a user manager and persistent data store
                    // because of session expiration, and server restarts.
                    // After these new features, the conditions still
                    // need to be handled as error states, although
                    // some will no longer occur normally.
                    // For now, we deal with conditions 2 thru 5
                    // by getting rid of the current request's session,
                    // as well as its attributes, etc.
                    // (That makes orphan nicknames, a problem for later fix)
                    log(sessionId, "err", "Forcing Login!:" + sessionId);
                    if(session != null) {
                         log(sessionId, "err", "Invalidating session:" +
session.getId());
                         try {
                              session.invalidate();
                         }
                         catch(java.lang.IllegalStateException ex) {
                              log(sessionId, "err", "IllegalStateException
invalidating session!");
                              ex.printStackTrace();
                         }
                    }
                    // Need a session to send applet its parameters
                    // so we get a new one here:
                    session = request.getSession();  // creates new session
                    sessionId = session.getId();
                    log(sessionId, "out", "NEW LOGIN sessionId:"+sessionId);
                    // Here, we use the BonForumRobot applet,
                    // running in client, to request the login page,
                    // because if the unsuccessful request originated
                    // from HTML inside a frame, using the robot
                    // prevents forum_login.jsp from displaying its
                    // output in that frame.
                    bonForumCommand = "forum_login_robot";
                    session.setAttribute("target", "_top");
                    session.setAttribute("document", request.getScheme() +
"://" +

request.getServerName() + ":" +

request.getServerPort() +

"/bonForum/jsp/forum/forum_login.jsp");
                    session.setAttribute("refresh", "true");
                    session.setAttribute("increment", "100");
                    session.setAttribute("limit", "1");
                    session.setAttribute("message", "Please enter bonForum!");
```

```
                }
            }
            // identify our servlet to the next page or servlet
            request.setAttribute ("servletName", "BonForumEngine");
            // The forwarding destination filename
            // (without jsp extension) is the value of
            // bonForumCommand, which was set in one of three ways:
            // 1. from an incoming bonCommand request parameter,
            //    if the Request URI was BonForumEngine.
            // 2. from a JSP filename embedded in a request URI,
            //    when that was not BonForumEngine.
            // 3. inside processRequest(), e.g., from other request
            //    parameters. That can alter values set as in #1.
            // ready for takeoff
            getServletConfig().getServletContext().getRequestDispatcher(
                    "/jsp/forum/"+bonForumCommand+".jsp").forward(
                    request, response);
    }
    /* Code below here is based on Apache Software Foundation samples
    (see notice at file beginning)
    */
/** Normalizes the given string, replacing chars with entities.
 * (less than, greater than, ampersand, double quote, return and linefeed).
 * Note: this replaces null string with empty string.
 *
 * @param s String
 * @return normalized string (not null)
 */
protected static String normalize(String s) {
    StringBuffer str = new StringBuffer();
        str.append("");
            int len = (s != null) ? s.length() : 0;
            for (int i = 0; i < len; i++) {
                char ch = s.charAt(i);
                switch (ch) {
                        case '<': {
                            str.append("&lt;");
                            break;
                        }
                        case '>': {
                            str.append("&gt;");
                            break;
                        }
                        case '&': {
                            str.append("&amp;");
                            break;
                        }
                        case '"': {
                            str.append("&quot;");
                            break;
                        }
```

```
                    case '\r':
                    case '\n': {
                        str.append("&#");
                        str.append(Integer.toString(ch));
                        str.append(';');
                        break;
                    }
                    default: {
                        str.append(ch);
                    }
                }
            }
        return str.toString();
    }
}// end class BonForumEngine
```

C.17 Filename: Projects\bonForum\src\de\tarent\forum\BonForumStore.java

```
package de.tarent.forum;
/*<Imports>*/
import java.io.*;
import java.util.Collections;
import java.util.ArrayList;
import java.util.Iterator;
import java.util.Enumeration;
import java.util.TreeMap;
import java.util.Hashtable;
//import javax.servlet.*;
import javax.servlet.http.*;
import org.w3c.dom.Attr;
import org.w3c.dom.Document;
//import org.w3c.dom.Element;
//import org.w3c.dom.NamedNodeMap;
import org.w3c.dom.Node;
import org.w3c.dom.NodeList;
//import org.apache.xerces.readers.MIME2Java;
import org.apache.xerces.dom.*;
import org.apache.xerces.parsers.*;
/*</Imports>*/
/** BonForumStore is the central bean of the bonForum web application.
 * It wraps the XML database used by the chat controlled by BonForumEngine.
 * It provides methods that can be used by JSP pages and custom tag classes.
 * It is described fully in the book:
 * <i>XML, XSLT, Java and JSP - A Case Study in Developing a Web Application</i>,
 * by Westy Rockwell, published by
 * <A HREF="http://www.newriders.com">New Riders</A>.
 * Translation to German published by
 * <A HREF="http://www.galileocomputing.de">Galileo Press</A>.
```

```
 * <p>For further information visit the open source
 * <A HREF="http://www.bonForum.org">BonForum Project on SourceForge</A>
 * @author <A HREF="mailto://email@bonforum.org">Westy Rockwell</A>
 */
public class BonForumStore {
      // these cache important nodeKey instances, for fast access:
      private NodeKey rootNodeKey;
      private NodeKey actorsNodeKey;
      private NodeKey actionsNodeKey;
      private NodeKey thingsNodeKey;
      private NodeKey bufferRootNodeKey;
      private NodeKey bufferActorsNodeKey;
      private NodeKey bufferActionsNodeKey;
      private NodeKey bufferThingsNodeKey;
      private String hitTimeMillis;
      private String initDate;
      // holds forum data, in proprietary, rudimentary XML format
      private static ForestHashtable bonForumXML;
      // buffers transformations and I/O of forum data
      private static ForestHashtable bonBufferXML;
      // logs debugging information
      private static BonLogger logBFS = null;
      // controls logger output
      private static String logging = null;
      // false until logger ready
      private static boolean loggingInitialized = false;
      // for logging output
      private static String sessionId = "0000000000";
    /** Creates a BonForumStore.
      */
      public BonForumStore() {
            super();
            bonForumXML = new ForestHashtable(5000);
            bonBufferXML = new ForestHashtable();
      }
      private void log(String sessionId, String where, String what) {
            if(logging != null) {
                  logBFS.logWrite(System.currentTimeMillis(), sessionId, where,
what);
            }
      }
    /** Gets logging setting.
      *
      * @return String logging
      */
      public String getLogging() {
            return logging;
      }
    /** Sets logging setting.
     *
     * @param newLogging String setting for logger logtype
```

```
("none","all","std","file")
     */
      public void setLogging(String newLogging) {
            logging = newLogging;
            if(!loggingInitialized) {
                  System.err.println("BonForumStore init loggingInitialized:" +
loggingInitialized);
                  System.err.println("BonForumStore init logging:" + logging);
                  if(logging != null) {
                        logBFS = new BonLogger("BonForumStoreLog.txt", logging);
                        System.err.println("BonForumStore init logBFS:" + logBFS);

                        logBFS.setLogging(newLogging);
                        loggingInitialized = true;
                        System.err.println("BonForumStore init
loggingInitialized:" + loggingInitialized);
                  }
            }
            getBonForumXML().setLogging(newLogging);
            bonBufferXML.setLogging(newLogging);
      }
    /** Gets bonForumXML, the forum datastore.
     *
     * @return ForestHashtable bonForumXML (static)
     */
      protected ForestHashtable getBonForumXML() {
            return bonForumXML;
      }
    /** Gets bonBufferXML, a buffer for the forum datastore.
     *
     * @return ForestHashtable bonBufferXML (static)
     */
      protected ForestHashtable getBonBufferXML() {
            return bonBufferXML;
      }
    /** Gets nodeKey of root element (in "bonForumXML" ForestHashtable member).
     *
     *      which is "bonForum" root element global to all HTTP Sessions.
     *            (This property caches the key for faster node retrieval).
     *
     * @return NodeKey for the global "bonForum" element
     */
      protected NodeKey getRootNodeKey() {
            return rootNodeKey;
      }
    /** Gets nodeKey of "actors" element (in "bonForumXML" ForestHashtable
member).
     *
     *      which is child of "bonForum" root and global to all HTTP Sessions.
     *            (This property caches the key for faster node retrieval).
     *
```

```
	 * @return NodeKey for the global "actors" element
	 */
	protected NodeKey getActorsNodeKey() {
		return actorsNodeKey;
	}
	/** Gets nodeKey of "actions" element (in "bonForumXML" ForestHashtable
member).
	 *
	 *	which is child of "bonForum" root and global to all HTTP Sessions.
	 *		(This property caches the key for faster node retrieval).
	 *
	 * @return NodeKey for the global "actions" element
	 */
	protected NodeKey getActionsNodeKey() {
		return actionsNodeKey;
	}
	/** Gets nodeKey of "things" element (in "bonForumXML" ForestHashtable
member).
	 *
	 *	which is child of "bonForum" root and global to all HTTP Sessions.
	 *		(This property caches the key for faster node retrieval).
	 *
	 * @return NodeKey for the global "things" element
	 */
	protected NodeKey getThingsNodeKey() {
		return thingsNodeKey;
	}
	/** Sets nodeKey of root element (in "bonForumXML" ForestHashtable member).
	 *
	 *	which is "bonForum" root element global to all HTTP Sessions.
	 *		(This property caches the key for faster node retrieval).
	 */
	protected void setRootNodeKey(NodeKey value) {
		rootNodeKey = value;
	}
	/** Sets nodeKey of "actors" element (in "bonForumXML" ForestHashtable
member).
	 *
	 *	which is child of "bonForum" root and global to all HTTP Sessions.
	 *		(This property caches the key for faster node retrieval).
	 */
	protected void setActorsNodeKey(NodeKey value) {
		actorsNodeKey = value;
	}
	/** Sets nodeKey of "actions" element (in "bonForumXML" ForestHashtable
member).
	 *
	 *	which is child of "bonForum" root and global to all HTTP Sessions.
	 *		(This property caches the key for faster node retrieval).
	 */
	protected void setActionsNodeKey(NodeKey value) {
```

```
        actionsNodeKey = value;
    }
    /** Sets nodeKey of "things" element (in "bonForumXML" ForestHashtable
member).
     *
     *      which is child of "bonForum" root and global to all HTTP Sessions.
     *           (This property caches the key for faster node retrieval).
     */
     protected void setThingsNodeKey(NodeKey value) {
          thingsNodeKey = value;
     }
    /** Gets nodeKey of root element  (in "bonBufferXML" ForestHashtable member).
     *
     *      which is "bonForum" root element global to all HTTP Sessions.
     *           (This property caches the key for faster node retrieval).
     *
     * @return NodeKey for the global "bonForum" element
     */
     protected NodeKey getBufferRootNodeKey() {
          return bufferRootNodeKey;
     }
    /** Gets nodeKey of "actors" element  (in "bonBufferXML" ForestHashtable
member).
     *
     *      which is child of "bonForum" root and global to all HTTP Sessions.
     *           (This property caches the key for faster node retrieval).
     *
     * @return NodeKey for the global "actors" element
     */
     protected NodeKey getBufferActorsNodeKey() {
          return bufferActorsNodeKey;
     }
    /** Gets nodeKey of "actions" element  (in "bonBufferXML" ForestHashtable
member).
     *
     *      which is child of "bonForum" root and global to all HTTP Sessions.
     *           (This property caches the key for faster node retrieval).
     *
     * @return NodeKey for the global "actions" element
     */
     protected NodeKey getBufferActionsNodeKey() {
          return bufferActionsNodeKey;
     }
    /** Gets nodeKey of "things" element  (in "bonBufferXML" ForestHashtable
member).
     *
     *      which is child of "bonForum" root and global to all HTTP Sessions.
     *           (This property caches the key for faster node retrieval).
     *
     * @return NodeKey for the global "things" element
     */
```

```
        protected NodeKey getBufferThingsNodeKey() {
              return bufferThingsNodeKey;
        }
      /** Sets nodeKey of root element (in "bonBufferXML" ForestHashtable member).
       *
       *     which is "bonForum" root element global to all HTTP Sessions.
       *            (This property caches the key for faster node retrieval).
       */
        protected void setBufferRootNodeKey(NodeKey value) {
             bufferRootNodeKey = value;
        }
      /** Sets nodeKey of "actors" element (in "bonBufferXML" ForestHashtable
member).
       *
       *      which is child of "bonForum" root and global to all HTTP Sessions.
       *            (This property caches the key for faster node retrieval).
       */
        protected void setBufferActorsNodeKey(NodeKey value) {
              bufferActorsNodeKey = value;
        }
      /** Sets nodeKey of "actions" element (in "bonBufferXML" ForestHashtable
member).
       *
       *      which is child of "bonForum" root and global to all HTTP Sessions.
       *            (This property caches the key for faster node retrieval).
       */
        protected void setBufferActionsNodeKey(NodeKey value) {
              bufferActionsNodeKey = value;
        }
      /** Sets nodeKey of "things" element (in "bonBufferXML" ForestHashtable
member).
       *
       *      which is child of "bonForum" root and global to all HTTP Sessions.
       *            (This property caches the key for faster node retrieval).
       */
        protected void setBufferThingsNodeKey(NodeKey value) {
              bufferThingsNodeKey = value;
        }
      /** Gets hitTimeMillis, time of last user initialization.
       *
       * @return String hitTimeMillis
       */
        public String getHitTimeMillis() {
              return hitTimeMillis;
        }
      /** Sets hitTimeMillis.
       *
       * @return void
       */
        public void setHitTimeMillis(String newHitTimeMillis) {
              if(newHitTimeMillis == null) {
```

```
                hitTimeMillis = BonForumUtils.timeMillis();
            }
            else {
                hitTimeMillis = newHitTimeMillis;
            }
        }
    /** Gets initDate, date of XML data initialization.
     *
     * @return String formatted date and time
     */
        public String getInitDate() {
            return initDate;
        }
    /** Sets initDate.
     *
     * @return void
     */
        protected void setInitDate(String newInitDate) {
            if(newInitDate == null) {
                initDate = BonForumUtils.getLastDate();;
            }
            else {
                initDate = newInitDate;
            }
        }
    /** initializes BonForumStore.
     *
     * @return void
     */
        protected void initialize(String initSessionId) {
            // Later: replace session attribute use with local user manager ala
session mgr
            setHitTimeMillis(null);
            sessionId = initSessionId;
            // Initialize new "database" or get the old one back
            initializeXML(sessionId);
            // Initialize a "database" buffer
            //bonForumStore.initializeBuffer(sessionId);
        }
    /** Loads XML from URI into "bonForumXML" ForestHashtable member.
     *
     *
     * @param pathToSubTreeRootNode      String
     * @param xmlUri                           String
     * @param nodeKeyHashtableName       String
     * @param sessionId                        String
     */
        protected void loadForumXMLFromURI(String pathToSubTreeRootNode, String
parentNodeInDestination, String xmlUri, String nodeKeyHashtableName, String
sessionId) {
            pathToSubTreeRootNode = pathToSubTreeRootNode.trim();
```

```
            if(pathToSubTreeRootNode == null || pathToSubTreeRootNode.length() <
1) {
                  pathToSubTreeRootNode = "";
            }
            parentNodeInDestination = parentNodeInDestination.trim();
            if(parentNodeInDestination == null || parentNodeInDestination.length()
< 1) {
                  parentNodeInDestination = "things";
            }
            // parse document
            try {
                  DOMParser parser = new DOMParser();
                  parser.parse(xmlUri);
                  Document document = parser.getDocument();
                  try {
                        loadForumXML(pathToSubTreeRootNode,
parentNodeInDestination, document, "pathNameHashtable", sessionId);
                  }
                  catch(Exception ee) {
                        log(sessionId, "err", "caught exception trying to load
into bonForumXML: "+ xmlUri);
                  }
            }
            catch(Exception ex) {
                  log(sessionId, "err", "caught exception trying to parse: " +
xmlUri);
            }
      }
    /** Loads XML from URI into "bonBufferXML" ForestHashtable member.
     *
     *
     * @param pathToSubTreeRootNode      String
     * @param xmlUri                     String
     * @param nodeKeyHashtableName       String
     * @param sessionId                        String
     */
      protected void loadBufferXMLFromURI(String pathToSubTreeRootNode, String
parentNodeInDestination, String xmlUri, String nodeKeyHashtableName, String
sessionId) {
            pathToSubTreeRootNode = pathToSubTreeRootNode.trim();
            if(pathToSubTreeRootNode == null || pathToSubTreeRootNode.length() <
1) {
                  pathToSubTreeRootNode = "";
            }
            parentNodeInDestination = parentNodeInDestination.trim();
            if(parentNodeInDestination == null || parentNodeInDestination.length()
< 1) {
                  parentNodeInDestination = "things";
            }
            // parse document
            try {
```

```
                DOMParser parser = new DOMParser();
                parser.parse(xmlUri);
                Document document = parser.getDocument();
                try {
                      loadBufferXML(pathToSubTreeRootNode,
parentNodeInDestination, document, "pathNameHashtable", sessionId);
                }
                catch(Exception ee) {
                      log(sessionId, "err", "caught exception trying to load
into bonBufferXML: "+ xmlUri);
                }
          }
          catch(Exception ex) {
                log(sessionId, "err", "caught exception trying to parse: " +
xmlUri);
          }
     }
    /** Loads XML from DOM node into "bonForumXML" ForestHashtable member.
     *
     *
     * @param pathToSubTreeRootNode      String
     * @param parentNodeInDestination    String
     * @param node                                 Node
     * @param nodeKeyHashtableName             String
     * @param sessionId                          String
     */
     protected void loadForumXML(String pathToSubTreeRootNode, String
parentNodeInDestination, Node node, String nodeKeyHashtableName, String sessionId)
{
          Object parentNodeKey = null;
          String nodeKeyPathName = "";
          boolean foundParentNodeKey = true; // assume success
          if(parentNodeInDestination.equals("actors")) {
                parentNodeKey = (Object)getActorsNodeKey();
          }
          else if(parentNodeInDestination.equals("actions")) {
                parentNodeKey = (Object)getActionsNodeKey();
          }
          else if(parentNodeInDestination.equals("things")) {
                parentNodeKey = (Object)getThingsNodeKey();
          }
          else {
                if
(getBonForumXML().getNodeNameHashtable().containsKey(parentNodeInDestination)) {
                      parentNodeKey =
getBonForumXML().getNodeNameHashtable().get(parentNodeInDestination);
                }
                else {
                      foundParentNodeKey = false;
                }
          }
```

```
            if(parentNodeKey != null && foundParentNodeKey) {
                  try {
                        // needs test and finishing, especially
pathToSubTreeRootNode argument
                        loadXMLSubTreeIntoForestHashtable(node, parentNodeKey,
bonForumXML, nodeKeyPathName, nodeKeyHashtableName, sessionId);
                  }
                  catch(Exception ee) {
                        log(sessionId, "err", "loadForumXML() caught Exception
invoking loadXMLSubTreeIntoForestHashtable()");
                  }
            }
      }
      /** Loads XML from DOM node into the bonBufferXML ForestHashtable.
       *
      *
      * @param pathToSubTreeRootNode      String
      * @param parentNodeInDestination    String
      * @param node                                   Node
      * @param nodeKeyHashtableName       String
      * @param sessionId                            String
      */
      protected void loadBufferXML(String pathToSubTreeRootNode, String
parentNodeInDestination, Node node, String nodeKeyHashtableName, String sessionId)
{
            Object parentNodeKey = null;
            String nodeKeyPathName = "";
            boolean foundParentNodeKey = true; // assume success
            if(parentNodeInDestination.equals("actors")) {
                  parentNodeKey = (Object)getBufferActorsNodeKey();
            }
            else if(parentNodeInDestination.equals("actions")) {
                  parentNodeKey = (Object)getBufferActionsNodeKey();
            }
            else if(parentNodeInDestination.equals("things")) {
                  parentNodeKey = (Object)getBufferThingsNodeKey();
            }
            else {
                  if
(bonBufferXML.getNodeNameHashtable().containsKey(parentNodeInDestination)) {
                        parentNodeKey =
bonBufferXML.getNodeNameHashtable().get(parentNodeInDestination);
                  }
                  else {
                        foundParentNodeKey = false;
                  }
            }
            if(parentNodeKey != null && foundParentNodeKey) {
                  try {
                        // needs test and finishing, especially
pathToSubTreeRootNode argument
```

```
                    loadXMLSubTreeIntoForestHashtable(node, parentNodeKey,
bonBufferXML, nodeKeyPathName, nodeKeyHashtableName, sessionId);
                }
                catch(Exception ee) {
                    log(sessionId, "err", "loadBufferXML() caught Exception
invoking loadXMLSubTreeIntoForestHashtable()");
                }
            }
        }
        /** Loads the specified node, recursively, into a ForestHashtable.
         *  NOTE: only loads element nodes with attributes, and any text node
children.
         *
         * @param node                          Node
         * @param parentNodeKey                 Object
         * @param forestHashtable               ForestHashtable
         * @param nodeKeyPathName               String
         * @param nodeKeyHashtableName          String
         * @param sessionId                     String
        */
        protected void loadXMLSubTreeIntoForestHashtable(Node node, Object
parentNodeKey, ForestHashtable forestHashtable, String nodeKeyPathName, String
nodeKeyHashtableName, String sessionId) {
            String nodeName = "";
            String nodeAttributes = "";
            String nodeContent = "";
            Object nextParentNodeKey = parentNodeKey;
            String pathName = "";
            if ( node == null ) {
            return;
            }
            // the ForestHashtable instance must exist for this method to work
        int type = node.getNodeType();
            switch(type) {
          // process document node
          case Node.DOCUMENT_NODE: {

loadXMLSubTreeIntoForestHashtable(((Document)node).getDocumentElement(),
parentNodeKey, forestHashtable, nodeKeyPathName, nodeKeyHashtableName, sessionId);
            break;
            }
          // process element with attributes, and also get text nodes for content
          case Node.ELEMENT_NODE: {
                  nodeName  = node.getNodeName();
                    // LATER: here can wait for element named by
pathToSubTreeRootNode, ignoring ancestors
                    Attr attrs[] =
BonForumUtils.sortAttributes(node.getAttributes());
                    nodeAttributes = "";
                    for ( int i = 0; i < attrs.length; i++ ) {
                          Attr attr = attrs[i];
```

```
                        nodeAttributes += (" ");
                        nodeAttributes += (attr.getNodeName());
                        nodeAttributes += ("=\"");
                        nodeAttributes += (normalize(attr.getNodeValue()));
                        nodeAttributes += ("\"");
                    }
                    // adds node and gets its nodeKey
                    BonNode bonNode;
                    bonNode = forestHashtable.addChildNodeToNonRootNode(nodeName,
nodeAttributes, nodeContent, (NodeKey)parentNodeKey, nodeKeyHashtableName,
sessionId);
                    nextParentNodeKey =
(Object)forestHashtable.nodeKeyFromBonNode(bonNode);
                    // optionally save nodeKey in a hashtable to use for fast
lookups, pathname sorting, etc.
                    if(nodeKeyHashtableName != null && nodeKeyHashtableName != "") {
                        if(nodeKeyHashtableName.equals("pathNameHashtable")) {
                            // here optionally save nodeKey with a pathName key
                            // only save descendants of bonForum.things.subjects
                            if (nodeKeyPathName.equals("")) {
                                if(    (!(nodeName.equals("bonForum"))) &&
                                    (!(nodeName.equals("things"))) &&
                                    (!(nodeName.equals("subjects"))) )  {
                                    nodeKeyPathName = nodeName;
                                    }
                            }
                            else {
                                // build the pathName by concatenating node
just added
                                nodeKeyPathName = nodeKeyPathName + "." +
nodeName;
                            }
                            if(!nodeKeyPathName.equals("")) {

forestHashtable.getPathNameHashtable().put(nodeKeyPathName, nextParentNodeKey);
                            }
                        }
                        else {
                            // later we can add other types of hashtables here
                        }
                    }
                    // here we get text nodes for our content, and recursively visit
element descendants
                    // we are ignoring ENTITY_REFERENCE_NODE, CDATA_SECTION_NODE,
PROCESSING_INSTRUCTION_NODE
                    NodeList children = node.getChildNodes();
                    if ( children != null ) {
                    int len = children.getLength();
                  for ( int i = 0; i < len; i++ ) {
                            // get text if any, else recursively visit element
children
```

```
                        int nodeType = children.item(i).getNodeType();
                    if(nodeType == Node.TEXT_NODE) {
                            nodeContent += " " +
normalize(children.item(i).getNodeValue().trim());
                        }
                        else if(nodeType == Node.ELEMENT_NODE) {
                            // recursion to visit all subnodes
                    loadXMLSubTreeIntoForestHashtable(children.item(i),
nextParentNodeKey, forestHashtable, nodeKeyPathName, nodeKeyHashtableName,
sessionId);
                        }
                }
        }
                // edit the node to add content from text node
                nodeContent = nodeContent.trim();
                if(nodeContent.length() > 0) {
                    NodeKey nk =
getBonForumXML().editBonNode((NodeKey)(nextParentNodeKey), null, null,
nodeContent);
                }
            break;
            }  // end case Node.ELEMENT_NODE
            }  // end switch
        }
        /** Adds a node to "bonForumXML" ForestHashtable member.
         *
         * @param command = "bonAddElement"  (others could follow)
         * @param parentNodeKeyKey                String
         * @param nameAndAttributes               String
         * @param content                         String
         * @param forestHashtableName             String
         * @param nodeKeyHashtableName            String
         * @param sessionId                       String
         * @return Object that can be cast to a NodeKey
        */
        protected Object add(String command, String parentNodeKeyKey, String
nameAndAttributes, String content, String forestHashtableName, String
nodeKeyHashtableName, String sessionId) {
            BonNode bonNode = new BonNode();
            NodeKey nonRootNodeKey = new NodeKey();
                nonRootNodeKey = (NodeKey)addNode(bonNode, nonRootNodeKey,
command, parentNodeKeyKey, nameAndAttributes, content, forestHashtableName,
nodeKeyHashtableName, sessionId);
            return (Object)(nonRootNodeKey);
        }
        /** Adds a node to "bonBufferXML" ForestHashtable member.
         *
         * @param command = "bonAddElement"  (others could follow)
         * @param parentNodeKeyKey                String
         * @param nameAndAttributes               String
         * @param content                         String
```

```
     * @param forestHashtableName          String
     * @param nodeKeyHashtableName           String
     * @param sessionId                        String
     * @return Object that can be cast to a NodeKey
    */
    protected Object addToBuffer(String command, String parentNodeKeyKey, String
nameAndAttributes, String content, String forestHashtableName, String
nodeKeyHashtableName, String sessionId) {
            BonNode bonNode = new BonNode();
            NodeKey nonRootNodeKey = new NodeKey();
                   nonRootNodeKey = (NodeKey)addNode(bonNode, nonRootNodeKey,
command, parentNodeKeyKey, nameAndAttributes, content, forestHashtableName,
nodeKeyHashtableName, sessionId);
            return (Object)(nonRootNodeKey);
    }
    /** Adds a node to "bonForumXML", or "bonBufferXML", or other
ForestHashtable.
     *
     * @param bonNode                                              BonNode
     * @param nonRootNodeKey                               NodeKey
     * @param command                                              String ="bonAddElement"
(others could follow)
     * @param parentNodeKeyKey                             String
     * @param nameAndAttributes                            String
     * @param content                                      String
     * @param forestHashtableName                  String
     * @param nodeKeyHashtableName                         String
     * @param sessionId                                            String
     * @return Object that can be cast to a NodeKey
    */
    protected Object addNode(BonNode bonNode, NodeKey nonRootNodeKey, String
command, String parentNodeKeyKey, String nameAndAttributes, String content, String
forestHashtableName, String nodeKeyHashtableName, String sessionId) {
            boolean fast = false;
            ForestHashtable forestHashtable;
            if(forestHashtableName.equals("bonForumXML")) {
                   forestHashtable = bonForumXML;
                   if (parentNodeKeyKey.equals("actors")) {
                          nonRootNodeKey =  getActorsNodeKey();
                          fast = true;
                   }
                   else if (parentNodeKeyKey.equals("actions")) {
                          nonRootNodeKey =  getActionsNodeKey();
                          fast = true;
                   }
                   else if (parentNodeKeyKey.equals("things")) {
                          nonRootNodeKey =  getThingsNodeKey();
                          fast = true;
                   }
            }
            else if(forestHashtableName.equals("bonBufferXML")) {
```

```
                forestHashtable = bonBufferXML;
                if (parentNodeKeyKey.equals("actors")) {
                     nonRootNodeKey =  getBufferActorsNodeKey();
                     fast = true;
                }
                else if (parentNodeKeyKey.equals("actions")) {
                     nonRootNodeKey =  getBufferActionsNodeKey();
                     fast = true;
                }
                else if (parentNodeKeyKey.equals("things")) {
                     nonRootNodeKey =  getBufferThingsNodeKey();
                     fast = true;
                }
           }
           else {
                forestHashtable = null;
           }
           if (command.equals("bonAddElement")) {
                try {
                     if(!fast) {  // not a "fast" parent nodeKey
                          //
                          // There are two possibilities (more later):
                          //
                          //   1. The parentNodeKey is saved in
nodeNameHashtable.
                          //      The parentNodeKeyKey format has one of two
formats:
                          //
                          //      The first format is:
                          //
sessionID_creationTimeMillis:parentElementName
                          //      (e.g.,
"To1012mC7576871324604071At:985400336097:chat")
                          //
                          //      The second format is:
                          //      sessionID:parentElementName
                          //      (e.g.,
"To1012mC7576871324604071At:messageKey")
                          //
                          //   2. The parentNodeKey is saved in
pathNameHashtable.
                          //      The parentNodeKeyKey used is the pathName to
the
                          //      subject node (e.g.,
"Vehicles.Motorcycles.Triumph").
                          //
                          //   If the parentNodeKeyKey is not "actors",
"actions", "things",
                          //   then the parentNodeKeyKey is a key into a
Hashtable
                          //   with the name nodeKeyHashtableName
```

```
                        //
                        if(nodeKeyHashtableName.equals("pathNameHashtable"))
{

if(forestHashtable.getPathNameHashtable().containsKey(parentNodeKeyKey)) {
                                    nonRootNodeKey =
(NodeKey)forestHashtable.getPathNameHashtable().get(parentNodeKeyKey);
                              }
                              else {
                                    log(sessionId, "err", "add() DID NOT FIND
parentNodeKeyKey IN pathNameHashtable: " + parentNodeKeyKey);
                              }
                        }
                        // The key should be in <sessionId:nodeName> format
                        // we could later check the incoming sessionId
prefix is valid
                        // using isRequestedSessionIdValid(prefix)
                        else if
(nodeKeyHashtableName.equals("nodeNameHashtable")) {
                              String temp = "" +
forestHashtable.getNodeNameHashtable().size();
                              if
(forestHashtable.getNodeNameHashtable().containsKey(parentNodeKeyKey)) {
                                    nonRootNodeKey =
(NodeKey)forestHashtable.getNodeNameHashtable().get(parentNodeKeyKey);
                              }
                              else {
                                    log(sessionId, "err", "add() DID NOT
FIND parentNodeKeyKey IN nodeNameHashtable: " + parentNodeKeyKey);
                              }
                        }
                        else {
                              log(sessionId, "err", "UNRECOGNIZED
nodeKeyHashtableName in add(): " + parentNodeKeyKey);
                        }
                  }
                  try {
                        if(nonRootNodeKey != null) {
                              if(nonRootNodeKey.aKey != null &&
nonRootNodeKey.aKey.length() > 0) {
                                    String name = "";
                                    String attributes = "";
                                    if(nameAndAttributes == null) {
                                          nameAndAttributes = "";
                                    }
                                    int inx =
nameAndAttributes.trim().indexOf(' ');
                                    if (inx > -1) { // space between name and
attributes
                                          name =
nameAndAttributes.substring(0, inx);
```

```
                                                                    attributes =
nameAndAttributes.substring(inx).trim();
                                                            }
                                                            else {
                                                                    name = nameAndAttributes;
                                                            }
                                                            bonNode =
forestHashtable.addChildNodeToNonRootNode(name, attributes, content,
nonRootNodeKey, nodeKeyHashtableName, sessionId);
                                                    }
                                            }
                                    }
                                    catch (Exception ex) {
                                            log(sessionId, "err", "addChildNodeToNonRootNode()
caused exception in add()");
                                    }
                            }
                            catch (Exception ee) {
                                    log(sessionId, "err", "Exception in add()");
                            }
                    }
                    return (Object)(bonNode.nodeKey);
            }
            /** Removes a (session-dependent) node from "bonForumXML" ForestHashtable
member.
             * @param command                String = "bonRemoveElement" (others later)
             * @param nodeKeyKey      String
             * @param leafOnly               String if uppercased is "TRUE" nodes with
children not removed
             * @param forestHashtableName  String
            */
            protected void remove(String command, String nodeKeyKey, String leafOnly,
String forestHashtableName) {
                    removeNode (command, nodeKeyKey, leafOnly, forestHashtableName);
            }
            /** Removes a (session-dependent) node from "bonBufferXML" ForestHashtable
member.
             * @param command                String = "bonRemoveElement" (others later)
             * @param nodeKeyKey      String
             * @param leafOnly               String if uppercased is "TRUE" nodes with
children not removed
             * @param forestHashtableName String
             */
            protected void removeFromBuffer(String command, String nodeKeyKey, String
leafOnly, String forestHashtableName) {
                    removeNode (command, nodeKeyKey, leafOnly, forestHashtableName);
            }
            /** Removes a node from a ForestHashtable.
             *             (for now: only non-global nodes removed)
             * @param command                String = "bonRemoveElement" (others later)
             * @param nodeKeyKey      String
```

```
     * @param leafOnly          String if uppercased is "TRUE" nodes with
children not removed
     * @param forestHashtableName     String
    */
    protected void removeNode (String command, String nodeKeyKey, String
leafOnly, String forestHashtableName) {
        NodeKey nonRootNodeKey = new NodeKey();
        boolean fast = false;
        // For now: just a choice between existing ForestHashtable instances
        ForestHashtable forestHashtable = null;
        if(forestHashtableName.equals("bonForumXML")) {
            forestHashtable = bonForumXML;
            if (nodeKeyKey.equals("actors")) {
                nonRootNodeKey =  getActorsNodeKey();
                fast = true;
            }
            else if (nodeKeyKey.equals("actions")) {
                nonRootNodeKey =  getActionsNodeKey();
                fast = true;
            }
            else if (nodeKeyKey.equals("things")) {
                nonRootNodeKey =  getThingsNodeKey();
                fast = true;
            }
        }
        else if(forestHashtableName.equals("bonBufferXML")) {
            if (nodeKeyKey.equals("actors")) {
                nonRootNodeKey =  getBufferActorsNodeKey();
                fast = true;
            }
            else if (nodeKeyKey.equals("actions")) {
                nonRootNodeKey =  getBufferActionsNodeKey();
                fast = true;
            }
            else if (nodeKeyKey.equals("things")) {
                nonRootNodeKey =  getBufferThingsNodeKey();
                fast = true;
            }
        }
        NodeKey nodeKey = new NodeKey();
        if (command.equals("bonRemoveElement")) {
            try {
                if(!fast) {
                    // does not have a "fast" global parent nodeKey
                    // For now, only non-fast nodes can be removed!
                    //
                    // Each NodeKey instance is saved in
nodeNameHashtable.
                    // "fast" nodes have a nodeKeyKey of
                    //       "actors", "actions", or "things",
                    // "non-fast" nodes hava a nodeKeyKey
```

```
                    // (a key into the nodeNameHashtable)
                    // with a key format that is either:
                    //        sessionId_creationTimeInMillis:nodeName
                    // or, optionally:
                    //        sessionId:nodeName
                    // We could later check the incoming sessionId
prefix
                    // is valid using isRequestedSessionIdValid(prefix)
                    if
(forestHashtable.getNodeNameHashtable().containsKey(nodeKeyKey)) {
                        nodeKey =
(NodeKey)forestHashtable.getNodeNameHashtable().get(nodeKeyKey);
                    }
                }
                try {
                    if(nodeKey.aKey != null && nodeKey.aKey.length() >
0) {
                        boolean deleteLeafOnly = false;
                        if(leafOnly.equalsIgnoreCase("TRUE")) {
                            deleteLeafOnly = true;
                        }
                        forestHashtable.deleteNode((NodeKey)nodeKey,
deleteLeafOnly);
                    }
                }
                catch (Exception ex) {
                    log(sessionId, "err", "deleteNode() caused exception
in remove()");
                }
            }
            catch (Exception ee) {
                log(sessionId, "err", "Exception in remove()");
            }
        }
    }
    /** Gets the NodeKey for a pathName in a pathNameHashtable.
     *  (The NodeKey for each element in the "subjects" subtree
     *  is also in a pathNameHashtable, with a pathName key).
     *
     * @param pathName              String
     * @param pathNameHashtable   PathNameHashtable
     * @return NodeKey for the pathName
     */
    protected NodeKey subjectNodeKeyFromPathName(String pathName,
PathNameHashtable pathNameHashtable) {
        return (NodeKey)pathNameHashtable.get(pathName);
    }
    /** Returns the BonNode for a subject from a ForestHashtable.
     *  (The subject pathName is a key value for a NodeKey in a
PathNameHashtable).
     *
```

```
	 * @param pathName			String
	 * @param pathNameHashtable	PathNameHashtable
	 * @param forestHashtable	ForestHashtable
	 * @return NodeKey for the pathName
	 */
	protected BonNode subjectBonNodeFromPathName(String pathName,
PathNameHashtable pathNameHashtable, ForestHashtable forestHashtable) {
		NodeKey nodeKey = subjectNodeKeyFromPathName(pathName,
pathNameHashtable);
		if(forestHashtable.getNodeNameHashtable().contains(nodeKey)) {
			return (BonNode)forestHashtable.get(nodeKey);
		}
		else {
			return(null);
		}
	}
	/** Returns the pathName to a NodeKey in a ForestHashtable.
	 *
	 * @param nodeKey NodeKey
	 * @param forestHashtable	ForestHashtable
	 * @return The pathName for the nodeKey as a String
	 */
	public String pathNameFromNodeKey(NodeKey nodeKey, ForestHashtable
forestHashtable)
	{
		String temp = "";
		BonNode bonNode;
		NodeKey parentNodeKey;
		try {
			bonNode = forestHashtable.getBonNode(nodeKey);
			temp = bonNode.nodeName;
			parentNodeKey = bonNode.parentNodeKey;
			boolean done = false;
			while (!done) {
				if(bonNode.parentNodeKey.aKey.equals("")) {
					done = true;
					break;
				}
				else {
					bonNode = forestHashtable.getBonNode(parentNodeKey);
					temp = bonNode.nodeName + "." + temp;
					parentNodeKey = bonNode.parentNodeKey;
				}
			}
		}
		catch(Exception ee) {
			log(sessionId, "err", "Exception caught in
pathNameFromNodeKey()");
		}
		return temp;
	}
```

```
    /** Returns the pathKey to a NodeKey in a ForestHashtable.
     *  A pathKey is made up of the combined nodeKeys of all the nodes from the
root
     *  to the nodeKey argument.
     *  Each nodeKey is a triple-valued key used by a ForestHashtable.
     *  An Example of a pathKey is:
     *  238493049323-384930493039-584954059453.463748293847-564738473623-
827347382374
     *  The nodeKeys is a pathKey are separated by a period, '.', and the
     *  AKey, BKey and CKey in each nodeKey are separated by a dash, '-'.
     *
     * @param nodeKey NodeKey
     * @param forestHashtable    ForestHashtable
     * @return The pathKey for the nodeKey as a String
     */
    public String pathKeyFromNodeKey(NodeKey nodeKey, ForestHashtable
forestHashtable) {
        String temp = "";
        BonNode bonNode;
        NodeKey parentNodeKey;
        try {
            bonNode = forestHashtable.getBonNode(nodeKey);
            temp = bonNode.nodeKey.aKey + "-" + bonNode.nodeKey.bKey + "-" +
bonNode.nodeKey.cKey;
            parentNodeKey = bonNode.parentNodeKey;
            boolean done = false;
            while (!done) {
                bonNode = forestHashtable.getBonNode(parentNodeKey);
                temp = bonNode.nodeKey.aKey + "-" + bonNode.nodeKey.bKey +
"-" + bonNode.nodeKey.cKey + "." + temp;
                if(bonNode.parentNodeKey.aKey.equals("")) {
                    done = true;
                    break;
                }
                else {
                    parentNodeKey = bonNode.parentNodeKey;
                }
            }
        }
        catch(Exception ee) {
            log(sessionId, "err", "Exception caught in
pathKeyFromNodeKey()");
        }
        return temp;
    }
    /** Outputs pathNames and nodeKeys from a bonForumXML subTree as a TreeMap.
     * (except for chatItems!).
     *  The TreeMap can be used as a sorted list of the paths to all the nodes.
     *
     *        NOTE: if you need method to output chatItem elements,
     *        You can add an option arg to do that!
```

```
	 *	(chatItem elements have names that are equal to:
	 *	"sessionID_" + chatCreatorHostSessionId +
chatNodeCreationTimeInMillis),
	 *
	 * @param command			String (unused, available argument)
	 * @param pathToSubTreeRootNode	String
	 * @param option1			String (reserved argument)
	 * @param option2			String (reserved argument)
	 * @return TreeMap
	 */
	protected TreeMap outputForumPathNames(String command, String
pathToSubTreeRootNode, String option1, String option2) {
		// the command argument can later be used to provide tag-visible sub-
types of this method
		if(!command.equals("bonForumXML")) {
			if(command.equals("bonBufferXML")) {
				return outputBufferPathNames(command,
pathToSubTreeRootNode, option1, option2);
			}
			else {
				TreeMap errorTreeMap = new TreeMap();
				errorTreeMap.put("0", "::::::::::::error in
command:::::::::::::");
				return errorTreeMap;  // later this error causes
exception?
			}
		}
		log(sessionId, "err", "Hello, outputForumPathNames!");
		BonNode bonNode = null;
		NodeKey nodeKey = new NodeKey();
		TreeMap outputTreeMap = new TreeMap();
		Enumeration enumeration = getBonForumXML().elements();
		while(enumeration.hasMoreElements()) {
			bonNode = (BonNode)enumeration.nextElement();
			nodeKey = bonNode.nodeKey;
			// LATER: pass option2 to pathNameFromNodeKey to replace all but
last nodeName with nbsp, for example
			// LATER: pass option3 to pathNameFromNodeKey as the separator
			String pathName = pathNameFromNodeKey(nodeKey, bonForumXML);
			// ASSUMPTION: if element has chatTopic attribute it is
chatItem,
			// and we want to suppress these in users display of forum
pathNames (e.g., chat subjects)
			if (pathToSubTreeRootNode != null &&
pathToSubTreeRootNode.length() > 0) {
				if(bonNode.nodeAttributes.indexOf("chatTopic=\"") < 0) {
					if(pathName.indexOf(pathToSubTreeRootNode) == 0) {
						// strip off leftmost nodes
						pathName =
pathName.substring(pathToSubTreeRootNode.length());
						// strip off period separator
```

```
                                        if(pathName.indexOf(".") == 0) {
                                                pathName = pathName.substring(1);
                                        }
                                        if(pathName.length() > 0) {
                                                outputTreeMap.put(pathName,
nodeKey.aKey);
                                        }
                                }
                        }
                }
                else {
                        if(pathName.length() > 0) {
                                outputTreeMap.put(pathName, nodeKey.aKey);
                        }
                }
        }
        if(outputTreeMap.size()<1) {
                outputTreeMap.put(".", "0"); // these are empty output return
values
        }
        log(sessionId, "err", "Goodbye, outputForumPathNames!");
        return outputTreeMap;
    }
    /** Outputs pathNames and nodeKeys from a bonBufferXML subTree as a TreeMap.
     *  The TreeMap can be used as a sorted list of the paths to all the nodes.
     *
     * @param command                   String (reserved argument, available from
ChoiceTag)
     * @param pathToSubTreeRootNode     String
     * @param option1                   String (reserved argument, available from
ChoiceTag)
     * @param option2                   String (reserved argument, available from
ChoiceTag)
     * @return TreeMap
     */
    protected TreeMap outputBufferPathNames(String command, String
pathToSubTreeRootNode, String option1, String option2) {
        // the command argument can later be used to provide tag-visible sub-
types of this method
        BonNode bonNode = null;
        NodeKey nodeKey = new NodeKey();
        TreeMap outputTreeMap = new TreeMap();
        Enumeration enumeration = bonBufferXML.elements();
        while(enumeration.hasMoreElements()) {
                bonNode = (BonNode)enumeration.nextElement();
                nodeKey = bonNode.nodeKey;
                // LATER: pass option2 to pathNameFromNodeKey to replace all but
last nodeName with nbsp, for example
                // LATER: pass option3 to pathNameFromNodeKey as the separator
                String pathName = pathNameFromNodeKey(nodeKey, bonBufferXML);
                // LATER: add pathToSubTreeRootNode processing here (see
```

```
outputForumPathNames)
                        outputTreeMap.put(pathName, nodeKey.aKey);
                }
                if(outputTreeMap.size()<1) {
                        outputTreeMap.put(".", "0"); // these are empty output return
values
                }
                return outputTreeMap;
        }
        /** Outputs the messages in the session's current chat from bonForumXML as a
TreeMap.
         *  The TreeMap can be used as a sorted list of the messages for that
session's chat.
         *
         * @param command                        String (reserved argument, available from
ChoiceTag)
         * @param option1                        String (reserved argument, available from
ChoiceTag)
         * @param option2                        String (reserved argument, available from
ChoiceTag)
         * @param option3                        String (reserved argument, available from
ChoiceTag)
         * @param session                        HttpSession (e.g.,
pageContext.getSession())
         * @return TreeMap
         */
        protected TreeMap outputForumChatMessages(String command, String option1,
String option2, String option3, HttpSession session) {
                // the command argument can later be used to provide tag-visible sub-
types of this method
                // the optionN arguments are available, also from ChoiceTag as attrN
                if(!command.equals("bonForumXML")) {
                        if(command.equals("bonBufferXML")) {
                                return outputBufferChatMessages(command, option1, option2,
option3, session);
                        }
                        else {
                                TreeMap errorTreeMap = new TreeMap();
                                errorTreeMap.put("0", "::::::::::::error in
command:::::::::::::");
                                return errorTreeMap;  // later this error causes
exception?
                        }
                }
                String messageTimeMillis = "";
                BonNode bonNode = null;
                TreeMap outputTreeMap = new TreeMap();
                TreeMap tempTreeMap = new TreeMap(Collections.reverseOrder());
                Enumeration enumeration = getBonForumXML().elements();
                // get this session's itemKey (chat subject category) from session
Attribute
```

```
        String itemKey = normalize((String)session.getAttribute("itemKey"));
        if(itemKey.trim().length() < 1) {
            log(sessionId, "err", "outputForumChatMessages() ERROR: session
has no itemKey!");
        }
        else {
            // get all messages that have this chat's itemKey
            while(enumeration.hasMoreElements()) {
                // get bonNode and its name, attributes and content
                bonNode = (BonNode)enumeration.nextElement();
                String name = bonNode.nodeName;
                String attributes = bonNode.nodeAttributes;
                String content = bonNode.nodeContent;
                // if the bonNode is a message
                if(name.equals("message")) {
                    /* THESE WERE DEBUGGING TESTS FOR getAttributeValue
                    // test value with escaped double quote in it (xml
error!)
                    String testStr =
getBonForumXML().getAttributeValue(attributes, "type");
                    //log(sessionId, "", "outputForumChatMessages(),
testStr: " + testStr);
                    // test attribute value not there (programming
error)
                    testStr =
getBonForumXML().getAttributeValue(attributes, "notThere");
                    //log(sessionId, "", "outputForumChatMessages(),
testStr: " + testStr);
                    // test value without closing double quote (xml
error)
                    testStr =
getBonForumXML().getAttributeValue(attributes, "test1");
                    //log(sessionId, "", "outputForumChatMessages(),
testStr: " + testStr);
                    */
                    // get itemKey attribute value
                    String messageItemKey =
getBonForumXML().getAttributeValue(attributes, "itemKey");
                    if(messageItemKey == null) {
                        // error, handle later
                        log(sessionId, "err",
"outputForumChatMessages(), ERROR! NO ItemKey found in message attributes!");
                        continue;
                    }
                    // if its this session's itemKey, it is also this
session's chat
                    if(messageItemKey.equals(itemKey)) {
                        // get message timeMillis attribute value
                        messageTimeMillis =
getBonForumXML().getAttributeValue(attributes, "timeMillis");
                        if(messageTimeMillis == null) {
```

```
                                        // error, handle later
                                        log(sessionId, "err",
"outputForumChatMessages(), ERROR! NO timeMillis found in message attributes!");
                                        continue;
                                    }
                                }
                                else {
                                    continue;
                                }
                                // assume content is "<normalized actorNickname>:: "
followed by chatMessage
                                // put content in TreeMap with timeMillis as key
                                tempTreeMap.put(messageTimeMillis, content);
                            } // end if
                        } // end while
                    } // end else
                    // keep track of last message by its time
                    session.setAttribute("lastMessageTimeMillis", messageTimeMillis);
                    // should we make sure here that currentTimeMillis is > largest
messageTimeMillis?
                    // the TreeMap chatHistoryTreeMap now contains the sorted chat lines
                    // ready to be put into the "output" choiceTag attribute,
                    // in a manner analogous to that use in the "bonOutputTable" choiceTag
command.
                    // Here we get a sorted subset of the messages according to session
attributes.
                    // This allows user to set size of output and page through messages
                    // messages array gets sorted message times in reverse order
                    String[] messages = (String[]) tempTreeMap.keySet().toArray(new
String[0]);
                    // keep track of how many there were at this output time
                    int numberOfMessages = messages.length;
                    String quantity =
(String)session.getAttribute("chatMessagesPageSize");
                    if (quantity == null) {
                        log(sessionId, "err", "outputForumChatMessages(), quantity ==
null");
                        quantity = "10"; // initialize
                    }
                    int numberPerPage = -1;
                    try {
                        numberPerPage = Integer.parseInt(quantity);
                    }
                    catch (NumberFormatException nFE) {
                        log(sessionId, "err", "outputForumChatMessages(), cannot parse
quantity requested as int: " + quantity);
                        numberPerPage = 10;
                    }
                    if(numberPerPage > numberOfMessages) {
                        numberPerPage = numberOfMessages;
                    }
```

```
            int numberOfPages = 0;
            try {
                  numberOfPages = (numberOfMessages / numberPerPage);
                  if((numberOfMessages % numberPerPage) != 0) {
                        ++numberOfPages;
                  }
            }
            catch(Exception ee) {
                  numberOfPages = 0;
            }
            session.setAttribute("chatNumberOfPages",
Integer.toString(numberOfPages));
            String pagesFromEnd = (String)session.getAttribute("pagesFromEnd");
            int pagesToSkip = -1;
            try {
                  pagesToSkip = Integer.parseInt(pagesFromEnd);
            }
            catch (NumberFormatException nFE) {
                  log(sessionId, "err", "outputForumChatMessages(), cannot parse
session attribute pagesFromEnd: " + pagesFromEnd);
                  pagesToSkip = -1;
            }
            if(pagesToSkip >= numberOfPages) {
                  pagesToSkip = numberOfPages - 1;
            }
            int pageNumber = numberOfPages - pagesToSkip;
            if(pageNumber > numberOfPages) {
                  pageNumber = numberOfPages;
            }
            session.setAttribute("chatPageNumber", Integer.toString(pageNumber));
            String navigation;
            try {
                  navigation =
(String)session.getAttribute("chatMessagesNavigator");
                  if(!navigation.equals("same") && !navigation.equals("first") &&
!navigation.equals("previous") && !navigation.equals("next") &&
!navigation.equals("last")) {
                        navigation = "last";
                  }
            }
            catch(Exception ee) {
                  log(sessionId, "err", "outputForumChatMessages(), no session
attribute chatMessagesNavigator, using \"last\"");
                  navigation = "last";
                  session.setAttribute("chatMessagesNavigator", "last");
            }
            // We have reversed the sort order of messages in tempTreeMap,
            // therefore these navigation cases will seem to be backwards!
            // Also, it means that if there are more than one page of messages,
            // then the first page of messages may be less than full,
            // while the last will stay full. (This is more convenient, since the
```

```
usual
            // case is to display the last page after each refresh, and this
            // way the user sees more messages most of the time.  Later we could
            // implement scrolling by the message instead of by the page.)
            if(navigation.equalsIgnoreCase("previous")) {
                  ++pagesToSkip;
                  if(pagesToSkip >= numberOfPages) {
                        pagesToSkip = numberOfPages - 1;
                  }
                  session.setAttribute("chatMessagesNavigator", "same");
            }
            else if(navigation.equalsIgnoreCase("next")) {
                  —pagesToSkip;
                  if(pagesToSkip < 0 ) {
                        pagesToSkip = 0;
                  }
                  session.setAttribute("chatMessagesNavigator", "same");
            }
            else if(navigation.equalsIgnoreCase("last")) {
                  pagesToSkip = 0;
            }
            else if(navigation.equalsIgnoreCase("first")) {
                  pagesToSkip = numberOfPages - 1;
            }
            // If we are not showing last page of messages, we do not want list to
refresh
            // because messages coming into chat from other guests or host will
scroll
            // the messages.  That is ok only when user is looking at last message
in
            // display.  Otherwise, it is confusing and irritating!
            // So, let's control the robot applet's refresh action here:
            String noScrolling = "same;first;previous;next";
            if(noScrolling.indexOf(navigation) > -1) {
                  session.setAttribute("refresh", "false");
            }
            else {
                  session.setAttribute("refresh", "true");
            }
            session.setAttribute("pagesFromEnd", Integer.toString(pagesToSkip));
            int numberToSkip = numberPerPage * pagesToSkip;
            if(navigation.equalsIgnoreCase("same")) {
                  String lastNumOfMessages =
normalize((String)session.getAttribute("numberOfMessages"));
                  try {
                        int lastNumberOfMessages =
Integer.parseInt(lastNumOfMessages);
                        int numberOfNewMessages = numberOfMessages -
lastNumberOfMessages;
                        numberToSkip += numberOfNewMessages;
                  }
```

```
                catch(Exception ee) {
                }
            }
            if(numberToSkip > numberOfMessages) {
                numberToSkip = numberOfMessages;
            }
            session.setAttribute("numberOfMessages",
Integer.toString(numberOfMessages));
            int ii;
            for(ii = 0; ii < numberToSkip; ++ii);
            if((numberOfMessages - numberToSkip) < numberPerPage) {
                numberPerPage = numberOfMessages - numberToSkip;
            }
            int jj;
            for(jj = ii; jj < ii + numberPerPage; ++jj) {
                outputTreeMap.put(messages[jj], tempTreeMap.get(messages[jj]));
            }
            String lastMNO = Integer.toString(jj-1);
            session.setAttribute("lastMessageNumberOutput", lastMNO);
            if(outputTreeMap.size()<1) {
                outputTreeMap.put("0", ":::::::::::empty
chat::::::::::::::::::");
            }
            return outputTreeMap;
        }
        /** Outputs the messages in the session's current chat from bonBufferXML as
a TreeMap.
         *  The TreeMap can be used as a sorted list of the messages for that
session's chat.
         *
         * @param command                   String (reserved argument, available from
ChoiceTag)
         * @param option1                   String (reserved argument, available from
ChoiceTag)
         * @param option2                   String (reserved argument, available from
ChoiceTag)
         * @param option3                   String (reserved argument, available from
ChoiceTag)
         * @param session                   HttpSession (e.g.,
pageContext.getSession())
         * @return TreeMap
         */
        protected TreeMap outputBufferChatMessages(String command, String option1,
String option2, String option3, HttpSession session) {
            // the command argument can later be used to provide tag-visible sub-
types of this method
            // the optionN arguments are available, also from ChoiceTag as attrN
            String messageTimeMillis = "";
            BonNode bonNode = null;
            TreeMap outputTreeMap = new TreeMap();
            TreeMap tempTreeMap = new TreeMap(Collections.reverseOrder());
```

```
            Enumeration enumeration = bonBufferXML.elements();
            // get this session's itemKey (chat subject category) from session
Attribute
            String itemKey = normalize((String)session.getAttribute("itemKey"));
            if(itemKey.trim().length() < 1) {
                  log(sessionId, "err", "outputBufferChatMessages() ERROR: session
has no itemKey!");
            }
            else {
                  // get all messages that have this chat's itemKey
                  while(enumeration.hasMoreElements()) {
                        // get bonNode and its name, attributes and content
                        bonNode = (BonNode)enumeration.nextElement();
                        String name = bonNode.nodeName;
                        String attributes = bonNode.nodeAttributes;
                        String content = bonNode.nodeContent;
                        // if the bonNode is a message
                        if(name.equals("message")) {
                              /* THESE WERE DEBUGGING TESTS FOR getAttributeValue
                              // test value with escaped double quote in it (xml
error!)
                              String testStr =
bonBufferXML.getAttributeValue(attributes, "type");
                              //log(sessionId, "", "outputBufferChatMessages(),
testStr: " + testStr);
                              // test attribute value not there (programming
error)
                              testStr = bonBufferXML.getAttributeValue(attributes,
"notThere");
                              //log(sessionId, "", "outputBufferChatMessages(),
testStr: " + testStr);
                              // test value without closing double quote (xml
error)
                              testStr = bonBufferXML.getAttributeValue(attributes,
"test1");
                              //log(sessionId, "", "outputBufferChatMessages(),
testStr: " + testStr);
                              */
                              // get itemKey attribute value
                              String messageItemKey =
bonBufferXML.getAttributeValue(attributes, "itemKey");
                              if(messageItemKey == null) {
                                    // error, handle later
                                    log(sessionId, "err",
"outputBufferChatMessages(), ERROR! NO ItemKey found in message attributes!");
                                    continue;
                              }
                              // if its this session's itemKey, it is also this
session's chat
                              if(messageItemKey.equals(itemKey)) {
                                    // get message timeMillis attribute value
```

```
                                        messageTimeMillis =
bonBufferXML.getAttributeValue(attributes, "timeMillis");
                                        if(messageTimeMillis == null) {
                                            // error, handle later
                                            log(sessionId, "err",
"outputBufferChatMessages(), ERROR! NO timeMillis found in message attributes!");
                                            continue;
                                        }
                                    }
                                    else {
                                        continue;
                                    }
                                    // assume content is "<normalized actorNickname>:: "
followed by chatMessage
                                    // put content in TreeMap with timeMillis as key
                                    tempTreeMap.put(messageTimeMillis, content);
                                } // end if
                            } // end while
                        } // end else
                        // keep track of last message by its time
                        session.setAttribute("lastMessageTimeMillis", messageTimeMillis);
                        // should we make sure here that currentTimeMillis is > largest
messageTimeMillis?
                        // the TreeMap chatHistoryTreeMap now contains the sorted chat lines
                        // ready to be put into the "output" choiceTag attribute,
                        // in a manner analogous to that use in the "bonOutputTable" choiceTag
command.
                        // Here we get a sorted subset of the messages according to session
attributes.
                        // This allows user to set size of output and page through messages
                        // messages array gets sorted message times in reverse order
                        String[] messages = (String[]) tempTreeMap.keySet().toArray(new
String[0]);
                        // keep track of how many there were at this output time
                        int numberOfMessages = messages.length;
                        String quantity =
(String)session.getAttribute("chatMessagesPageSize");
                        if (quantity == null) {
                            log(sessionId, "err", "outputBufferChatMessages(), quantity ==
null");
                            quantity = "10"; // initialize
                        }
                        int numberPerPage = -1;
                        try {
                            numberPerPage = Integer.parseInt(quantity);
                          }
                          catch (NumberFormatException nFE) {
                                log(sessionId, "err", "outputBufferChatMessages(), cannot
parse quantity requested as int: " + quantity);
                            numberPerPage = 10;
                        }
```

```
            if(numberPerPage > numberOfMessages) {
                  numberPerPage = numberOfMessages;
            }
            int numberOfPages = 0;
            try {
                  numberOfPages = (numberOfMessages / numberPerPage);
                  if((numberOfMessages % numberPerPage) != 0) {
                        ++numberOfPages;
                  }
            }
            catch(Exception ee) {
                  numberOfPages = 0;
            }
            session.setAttribute("chatNumberOfPages",
Integer.toString(numberOfPages));
            String pagesFromEnd = (String)session.getAttribute("pagesFromEnd");
            if(pagesFromEnd.equals("null")) {
                  pagesFromEnd = "0";
            }
            int pagesToSkip = -1;
            try {
                  pagesToSkip = Integer.parseInt(pagesFromEnd);
            }
            catch (NumberFormatException nFE) {
                  log(sessionId, "err", "outputBufferChatMessages(), cannot parse
session attribute pagesFromEnd: " + pagesFromEnd);
                  pagesToSkip = -1;
            }
            if(pagesToSkip >= numberOfPages) {
                  pagesToSkip = numberOfPages - 1;
            }
            int pageNumber = numberOfPages - pagesToSkip;
            if(pageNumber > numberOfPages) {
                  pageNumber = numberOfPages;
            }
            session.setAttribute("chatPageNumber", Integer.toString(pageNumber));
            String navigation;
            try {
                  navigation =
(String)session.getAttribute("chatMessagesNavigator");
                  if(!navigation.equals("same") && !navigation.equals("first") &&
!navigation.equals("previous") && !navigation.equals("next") &&
!navigation.equals("last")) {
                        navigation = "last";
                  }
            }
            catch(Exception ee) {
                  log(sessionId, "err", "outputBufferChatMessages(), exception
getting session attribute chatMessagesNavigator, using \"last\"");
                  navigation = "last";
            }
```

```
        // We have reversed the sort order of messages in tempTreeMap,
        // therefore these navigation cases will seem to be backwards!
        // Also, it means that if there are more than one page of messages,
        // then the first page of messages may be less than full,
        // while the last will stay full. (This is more convenient, since the
usual
        // case is to display the last page after each refresh, and this
        // way the user sees more messages most of the time.  Later we could
        // implement scrolling by the message instead of by the page.)
        if(navigation.equalsIgnoreCase("previous")) {
            ++pagesToSkip;
            if(pagesToSkip >= numberOfPages) {
                pagesToSkip = numberOfPages - 1;
            }
            session.setAttribute("chatMessagesNavigator", "same");
        }
        else if(navigation.equalsIgnoreCase("next")) {
            --pagesToSkip;
            if(pagesToSkip < 0 ) {
                pagesToSkip = 0;
            }
            session.setAttribute("chatMessagesNavigator", "same");
        }
        else if(navigation.equalsIgnoreCase("last")) {
            pagesToSkip = 0;
        }
        else if(navigation.equalsIgnoreCase("first")) {
            pagesToSkip = numberOfPages - 1;
        }
        session.setAttribute("pagesFromEnd", Integer.toString(pagesToSkip));
        int numberToSkip = numberPerPage * pagesToSkip;
        if(navigation.equalsIgnoreCase("same")) {
            String lastNumOfMessages =
normalize((String)session.getAttribute("numberOfMessages"));
            try {
                int lastNumberOfMessages =
Integer.parseInt(lastNumOfMessages);
                int numberOfNewMessages = numberOfMessages -
lastNumberOfMessages;
                numberToSkip += numberOfNewMessages;
            }
            catch(Exception ee) {
            }
        }
        if(numberToSkip > numberOfMessages) {
            numberToSkip = numberOfMessages;
        }
        session.setAttribute("numberOfMessages",
Integer.toString(numberOfMessages));
        int ii;
        for(ii = 0; ii < numberToSkip; ++ii);
```

```
                if((numberOfMessages - numberToSkip) < numberPerPage) {
                        numberPerPage = numberOfMessages - numberToSkip;
                }
                int jj;
                for(jj = ii; jj < ii + numberPerPage; ++jj) {
                        outputTreeMap.put(messages[jj], tempTreeMap.get(messages[jj]));
                }
                String lastMNO = Integer.toString(jj-1);
                session.setAttribute("lastMessageNumberOutput", lastMNO);
                if(outputTreeMap.size()<1) {
                        outputTreeMap.put("0", ":::::::::::empty
chat:::::::::::::::::::");
                }
                return outputTreeMap;
        }
        /** allows using bonBufferXML from other classes including JSP code and JSP
tags.
         *   NOTE: This is experimental! Could it be problematic?
         *
         * @param sessionId String
         */
        protected void initializeBuffer(String sessionId) {
                initializeBonForum("bonBufferXML", sessionId);
        }
        /** allows using bonForumXML from other classes including JSP code and JSP
tags
         *   NOTE: This is experimental! Could it be problematic?
         *
         * @param sessionId String
         */
        protected void initializeXML(String sessionId) {
                initializeBonForum("bonForumXML", sessionId);
        }
        /** Initializes "bonForumXML" or "bonBufferXML" ForestHashtable member.
         *          (until more cases added).
         *   When initializing, bonForumXML either gets new default or existing one is
not changed.
         *   When initializing, bonBufferXML is cleared as are its nodeKey tables.
         *   The sessionId is required to add nodes to ForestHashtable (children of
non-root nodes)
         *
         * @param forestHashtableName String ("bonForumXML" or "bonBufferXML", for
now)
         * @param sessionId String
         */
        protected void initializeBonForum(String forestHashtableName, String
sessionId) {
                if(forestHashtableName.equals("bonForumXML")) {
                        if(getBonForumXML().size()<1) {
                                log(sessionId, "out", "<<<INITIALIZING NEW
bonForumXML>>>");
```

```
                    // Here we create the minimal XML content for the bonForum
to boot up.
                    // We will do that in a ForestHashtable object:
bonForumXML.
                    // There is only one per BonForumStore bean instance
                    getBonForumXML().getNodeNameHashtable().clear();
                    //Element bonForum is the root node.
                    String rootNodeName = normalize("bonForum");
                    String rootNodeAttributes = "type = \"prototype\"";  // do
not normalize yet, handle &quot;
                    String rootNodeContent = normalize("");
                    BonNode rootNode =
getBonForumXML().addRootNode(rootNodeName, rootNodeAttributes, rootNodeContent,
"nodeNameHashtable");
                    // This will give faster access to root
                    setRootNodeKey(rootNode.nodeKey);
                    // Then actors element is a child of the root node.
                    String childNodeName = normalize("actors");
                    String childNodeAttributes = "type = \"READ_ONLY\"";
                    String childNodeContent = normalize("");
                    BonNode nonRootNode =
getBonForumXML().addChildNodeToRootNode(childNodeName, childNodeAttributes,
childNodeContent, rootNode.nodeKey, "nodeNameHashtable");
                    // This will give faster access to actors
                    setActorsNodeKey(nonRootNode.nodeKey);
                    // This is used to demonstrate adding element after the
first, to the same parent
                    NodeKey holdNodeKey = nonRootNode.nodeKey;
                    // Here we add the system actor, which is a child of a
non-root node.
                    childNodeName = normalize("system");
                    childNodeAttributes = "type = \"SYSTEM\"";
                    childNodeContent = normalize("");
                    nonRootNode =
getBonForumXML().addChildNodeToNonRootNode(childNodeName, childNodeAttributes,
childNodeContent, nonRootNode.nodeKey, "nodeNameHashtable", sessionId);
                    // Here we add the system2 actor, which is a child of a
non-root node.
                    childNodeName = normalize("system2");
                    childNodeAttributes = "type = \"SYSTEM\"";
                    childNodeContent = normalize("");
                    nonRootNode =
getBonForumXML().addChildNodeToNonRootNode(childNodeName, childNodeAttributes,
childNodeContent, nonRootNode.nodeKey, "nodeNameHashtable", sessionId);
                    // JUST TESTING NEXT LEVEL
                    // Here we add a test element, which is a child (and
grandchild) of a non-root node.
                    childNodeName = normalize("test");
                    childNodeAttributes = "type = \"TEST\"";
                    childNodeContent = normalize("");
                    nonRootNode =
```

```
getBonForumXML().addChildNodeToNonRootNode(childNodeName, childNodeAttributes,
childNodeContent, nonRootNode.nodeKey, "nodeNameHashtable", sessionId);
                        // Here we add element using a saved nodeKey
                        nonRootNode =
getBonForumXML().addChildNodeToNonRootNode(childNodeName, childNodeAttributes,
childNodeContent, holdNodeKey, "nodeNameHashtable", sessionId);
                        // Another child of the root node: actions
                        childNodeName = normalize("actions");
                        childNodeAttributes = "type = \"READ_ONLY\"";
                        childNodeContent = normalize("");
                        nonRootNode =
getBonForumXML().addChildNodeToRootNode(childNodeName, childNodeAttributes,
childNodeContent, rootNode.nodeKey, "nodeNameHashtable");
                        // This will give faster access to actions
                        setActionsNodeKey(nonRootNode.nodeKey);
                        // Another child of the root node: things
                        childNodeName = normalize("things");
                        childNodeAttributes = "type = \"READ_ONLY\"";
                        childNodeContent = normalize("");
                        nonRootNode =
getBonForumXML().addChildNodeToRootNode(childNodeName, childNodeAttributes,
childNodeContent, rootNode.nodeKey, "nodeNameHashtable");
                        // This will give faster access to things
                        setThingsNodeKey(nonRootNode.nodeKey);
                        // load the subjects sub-tree into the bonForumXML from a
file
                        log(sessionId, "out", "loading subjects tree into
bonForumXML");
                        String pathToSubTreeRootNode = "";  // later
                        String parentNodeInDestination = "things";
                        String xmlUri =
"..\\webapps\\bonForum\\mldocs\\subjects.xml";
                        // parse and load document
                        try {
                              DOMParser parser = new DOMParser();
                              parser.parse(xmlUri);
                              Document document = parser.getDocument();
                              // note: for now this command works only with
bonForumXML, it could work with bonBufferXML, etc.
                              try {
                                    loadForumXML(pathToSubTreeRootNode,
parentNodeInDestination, document, "pathNameHashtable", sessionId);
                              }
                              catch(Exception ee) {
                                    log(sessionId, "err", "exception loading
subjects.xml into bonForumXML:" +
                                    ee.getMessage());
                              }
                        }
                        catch(Exception ex) {
                              log(sessionId, "err", "exception parsing
```

```
subjects.xml" +
                            ex.getMessage());
                    }
                    // load the forums sub-tree into the bonForumXML from a
file
                    log(sessionId, "out", "loading forums tree into
bonForumXML");
                    pathToSubTreeRootNode = "";   // later
                    parentNodeInDestination = "things";
                    xmlUri = "..\\webapps\\bonForum\\mldocs\\forums.xml";
                    // parse document
                    try {
                        DOMParser parser = new DOMParser();
                        parser.parse(xmlUri);
                        Document document = parser.getDocument();
                        // note: for now this command works only with
bonForumXML, it could work with bonBufferXML, etc.
                        try {
                            loadForumXML(pathToSubTreeRootNode,
parentNodeInDestination, document, "", sessionId);
                        }
                        catch(Exception ee) {
                            log(sessionId, "err", "caught exception trying
to load forums.xml into bonForumXML");
                        }
                    }
                    catch(Exception ex) {
                        log(sessionId, "err", "caught exception trying to
parse forums.xml");
                    }
                    // Here we could load more stuff into the bonForum later.
                    // This debugging output dumps ForestHashtable contents.
                    //log(sessionId, "", getBonForumXML().getXMLTrees());
                    // Announce success of bonForumXML initialization!
                    setInitDate(null);
                    log(sessionId, "out", "NEW bonForumXML IS READY,
initDate:" + getInitDate());
                }
                else {
                    // This debugging output dumps ForestHashtable contents.
                    //log(sessionId, "", getBonForumXML().getXMLTrees());
                    // Announce finding of existing bonForumXML
ForestHashtable instance!
                    //log(sessionId, "", "FOUND EXISTING bonForumXML");
                }// end of initialize forum or get old forum
            }
            else if(forestHashtableName.equals("bonBufferXML")) {
                // NOTE: ALL BonBufferXML code in the project is under
development and untested!
                bonBufferXML.clear();
                bonBufferXML.getNodeNameHashtable().clear();
```

```
                    bonBufferXML.getPathNameHashtable().clear();
                    if(bonBufferXML.size()<1) {
                        log(sessionId, "out", "<<<INITIALIZING NEW
bonBufferXML>>>");
                        // Here we create the minimal XML content for the
bonBuffer to boot up.
                        // We will do that in a ForestHashtable object:
bonBufferXML.
                        // There is only one per BonForumStore bean instance
                        // bonBufferXML.nodeNameHashtable.clear();
                        //Element bonForum is the root node.
                        String rootNodeName = normalize("bonForum");
                        String rootNodeAttributes = "type = \"buffer\"";  // do
not normalize yet, handle &quot;
                        String rootNodeContent = normalize("");
                        BonNode rootNode = bonBufferXML.addRootNode(rootNodeName,
rootNodeAttributes, rootNodeContent, "nodeNameHashtable");
                        // This will give faster access to root
                        setBufferRootNodeKey(rootNode.nodeKey);
                        /* Maybe bonBufferXML should have nothing?
                        But it needs a root at least (see above).
                        Should it perhaps shadow the default bonForumXML?
                        The code to do so is here, commented out:
                        */
                        /* Commented-out code begins here!
                        // Then actors element is a child of the root node.
                        String childNodeName = normalize("actors");
                        String childNodeAttributes = "type = \"READ_ONLY\"";
                        String childNodeContent = normalize("");
                        BonNode nonRootNode =
bonBufferXML.addChildNodeToRootNode(childNodeName, childNodeAttributes,
childNodeContent, rootNode.nodeKey, "nodeNameHashtable");
                        // This will give faster access to actors
                        setBufferActorsNodeKey(nonRootNode.nodeKey);
                        // Here we add the system actor, which is a child of a
non-root node.
                        childNodeName = normalize("system");
                        childNodeAttributes = "type = \"SYSTEM\"";
                        childNodeContent = normalize("");
                        nonRootNode =
bonBufferXML.addChildNodeToNonRootNode(childNodeName, childNodeAttributes,
childNodeContent, nonRootNode.nodeKey, "nodeNameHashtable", sessionId);
                        // Another child of the root node: actions
                        childNodeName = normalize("actions");
                        childNodeAttributes = "type = \"READ_ONLY\"";
                        childNodeContent = normalize("");
                        nonRootNode =
bonBufferXML.addChildNodeToRootNode(childNodeName, childNodeAttributes,
childNodeContent, rootNode.nodeKey, "nodeNameHashtable");
                        // This will give faster access to actions
                        setActionsNodeKey(nonRootNode.nodeKey);
```

```
                        // Another child of the root node: things
                        childNodeName = normalize("things");
                        childNodeAttributes = "type = \"READ_ONLY\"";
                        childNodeContent = normalize("");
                        nonRootNode =
bonBufferXML.addChildNodeToRootNode(childNodeName, childNodeAttributes,
childNodeContent, rootNode.nodeKey, "nodeNameHashtable");
                        // This will give faster access to things
                        setThingsNodeKey(nonRootNode.nodeKey);
                        // load the subjects sub-tree into the bonBufferXML from a
file
                        String pathToSubTreeRootNode = "";   // later
                        String parentNodeInDestination = "things";
                        String xmlUri =
"..\\webapps\\bonForum\\mldocs\\subjects.xml";
                        // parse document
                        try {
                              DOMParser parser = new DOMParser();
                              parser.parse(xmlUri);
                              Document document = parser.getDocument();
                              try {
                                    loadBufferXML(pathToSubTreeRootNode,
parentNodeInDestination, document, "pathNameHashtable");
                              }
                              catch(Exception ee) {
                                    log(sessionId, "err", "caught exception trying
to load subjects.xml into bonBufferXML");
                              }
                        }
                        catch(Exception ex) {
                              log(sessionId, "err", "caught exception trying to
parse subjects.xml");
                        }
                        // load the forums sub-tree into the bonBufferXML from a
file
                        pathToSubTreeRootNode = "";   // later
                        parentNodeInDestination = "things";
                        xmlUri = "..\\webapps\\bonForum\\mldocs\\forums.xml";
                        // parse document
                        try {
                              DOMParser parser = new DOMParser();
                              parser.parse(xmlUri);
                              Document document = parser.getDocument();
                              try {
                                    loadBufferXML(pathToSubTreeRootNode,
parentNodeInDestination, document, "");
                              }
                              catch(Exception ee) {
                                    log(sessionId, "err", "caught exception trying
to load Forums.xml into bonBufferXML");
                              }
```

```
                    }
                    catch(Exception ex) {
                         log(sessionId, "err", "caught exception trying to
parse forums.xml");
                    }
                    // Here we could load more stuff into the bonBuffer later.
                    */ //commented out section of code ends above
                    // This debugging output dumps ForestHashtable contents.
                    //log(sessionId, "", bonBufferXML.getXMLTrees());
                    // Announce success of bonBufferXML initialization!
                    log(sessionId, "out", "<<<NEW bonBufferXML IS READY>>>");
               }
          }
     }
    /** Adds one attribute (name=value) to a chat node in bonForumXML
ForestHashtable.
     *
     * @param chatNodeKeyKey String ("<hostSessionId>:<creationTimeMillis>:chat")
     * @param attrName String
     * @param attrValue String
     *
     * @return NodeKey of chat node affected, or null if key no good
     */
     public NodeKey addChatNodeAttribute(String chatNodeKeyKey, String attrName,
String attrValue) {
          NodeKey chatNodeKey = null;
          if
(getBonForumXML().getNodeNameHashtable().containsKey(chatNodeKeyKey)) {
               chatNodeKey =
(NodeKey)getBonForumXML().getNodeNameHashtable().get(chatNodeKeyKey);
          }
          else {
               log(sessionId, "err", "DID NOT FIND chat nodeKey IN
nodeNameHashtable: " + chatNodeKeyKey);
               return chatNodeKey;
          }
          BonNode chatNode = getBonForumXML().getBonNode(chatNodeKey);
          String newChatAttributes = chatNode.nodeAttributes;
          newChatAttributes = newChatAttributes + " " + attrName + "=\"" +
attrValue + "\"";
          chatNodeKey = getBonForumXML().editBonNode(chatNodeKey, null,
newChatAttributes, null);
          return chatNodeKey;
     }
    /** Returns the nodeNameHashtable key for a chat node nodeKey in bonForumXML.
     *      NOTE: we must disallow '>[' in subject node names for this to work!
       *  For now, separator in incoming chat subject path is wired as '_'.
       *  Example of chatItem: "animals_fish_piranha_[first aid for fish
breeders]".
     *
     * @param chatItem String ("path_to_subject_[topic of chat]")
```

```
     *
     * @return String chatNodeKeyKey
     */
      protected String getBonForumChatNodeKeyKey(String chatItem) {
            String chatNodeKeyKey = "";
            BonNode chatItemNode = getChatItemNodeFromChatItem(chatItem);
            if(chatItemNode != null) {
                  String chatSessionId = chatItemNode.nodeName.substring(10);  //
10 is "sessionID_".length()
                  //sessionID_To1012mC7576871324604071At_985400336097:chat
                  chatNodeKeyKey = chatSessionId + ":chat";
            }
            return chatNodeKeyKey;
      }
    /** Returns a chatItem BonNode NodeKey from bonForumXML given a subject plus
topic string.
     *      NOTE: we must disallow '>[' in subject node names for this to work!
       *  For now, separator in incoming chat subject path is wired as '_'.
       *  Example of chatItem: "animals_fish_piranha_[first aid for fish
breeders]".
       *
     * @param chatItem String ("path_to_subject_[topic of chat]")
     *
     * @return NodeKey chatItemNode.nodeKey
     */
      protected NodeKey getBonForumChatItemNodeKey(String chatItem) {
            BonNode chatItemNode = getChatItemNodeFromChatItem(chatItem);
            if(chatItemNode != null) {
                  return chatItemNode.nodeKey;
            }
            return null;
      }
    /** Returns a chatItem BonNode from bonForumXML given a chatItem.
     *    NOTE: we must disallow '>[' in subject node names for this to work!
       *  For now, separator in incoming chat subject path is wired as '_'.
       *  Example of chatItem: "animals_fish_piranha_[first aid for fish
breeders]".
       *
     * @param chatItem String ("path_to_subject_[topic of chat]")
     *
     * @return BonNode chatItemNode
     */
      protected BonNode getChatItemNodeFromChatItem(String chatItem) {
            int topicIndex = chatItem.indexOf("[");
            // temp kludge until xsl to remove the '_' char before '[' is found!
            int adjuster = 1;
            int topicIndex2 = chatItem.indexOf("_[");
            if(topicIndex2 == topicIndex - 1) {
                  —topicIndex;
                  ++adjuster;
            }
```

```
                String pathToSubjectNode = chatItem.substring(0, topicIndex);
                // replace all '_' with '.' which is separator in pathNameHashtable
                pathToSubjectNode = pathToSubjectNode.replace('_', '.');
                topicIndex += adjuster;
                String chatTopic = chatItem.substring(topicIndex);
                // remove trailing ']'
                chatTopic = chatTopic.substring(0, chatTopic.length() - 1);
                //String chatSessionId = getChatSessionId(pathToSubject, chatTopic);
                NodeKey chatSubjectNodeKey =
this.subjectNodeKeyFromPathName(pathToSubjectNode,
getBonForumXML().getPathNameHashtable());
                if(chatSubjectNodeKey != null) {
                      BonNode chatItemNode =
getBonForumXML().getChildNodeFromAttributeValue(chatSubjectNodeKey, "chatTopic",
chatTopic);
                      return chatItemNode;
                }
                return null;
          }
      /** Returns the chatNode from bonForumXML using a chatNodeKeyKey.
       *  A chatNodeKeyKey is the nodeNameHashtable key for a chatNode nodeKey.
         *
       * @param chatNodeKeyKey String (host_session_id + ":" + creationTimeMillis +
":chat")
         *
       * @return BonNode chatNode
       */
          protected BonNode getBonForumChatNode(String chatNodeKeyKey) {
                BonNode chatNode = null;
                NodeKey chatNodeKey = null;
                // chatNodeKeyKey = sessionId + ":" + creationTimeMillis + ":chat";
                // NOTE cannot be simply done with guest sessionId!
                // It needs the *host* sessionId instead.
                if
(getBonForumXML().getNodeNameHashtable().containsKey(chatNodeKeyKey)) {
                      chatNodeKey =
(NodeKey)getBonForumXML().getNodeNameHashtable().get(chatNodeKeyKey);
                }
                else {
                      log(sessionId, "err", "DID NOT FIND chat nodeKey IN
nodeNameHashtable: " + chatNodeKeyKey);
                      return chatNode;
                }
                chatNode = getBonForumXML().getBonNode(chatNodeKey);
                return chatNode;
          }
      /** Returns the value of a BonNode attribute, given the BonNode and the
attribute name.
         *
       * @param bonNode BonNode
       * @param attributeName String
```

```
     *
     * @return String value of a BonNode attribute
     */
     protected String getBonForumAttributeValue(BonNode bonNode, String
attributeName) {
          String AttributeValue;
          return AttributeValue =
normalize(getBonForumXML().getAttributeValue(bonNode.nodeAttributes,
attributeName));
     }
    /** Changes the rating of a actor in a chat.
      *  Note: actorNicknames are unique in bonForum.
     * Uses session attribute chatGuest, or chatHost.
     * Uses session attribute chatNodeKeyKey.
     *
     * @param amount   String, amount to change (positive or negative integer as
string)
     * @param session   HttpSession (e.g., pageContext.getSession(), or session on
JSP)
     * @return String rating after change
     */
     public String changeChatActorRating(String amount, HttpSession session) {
          try {
               String chatNodeKeyKey =
(String)session.getAttribute("chatNodeKeyKey");
               if(chatNodeKeyKey == null) {
                    return null; // no chat
               }
               // is actor host?
               String chatActor = (String)session.getAttribute("chatHost");
               ArrayList actorKeys = null;
               if(chatActor == null) { // no, is actor guest?
                    chatActor = (String)session.getAttribute("chatGuest");
                    if(chatActor == null) {
                         return null;  // not host, not guest!
                    }
                    // actor is guest, get list of guests in chat
                    actorKeys = getGuestKeysInChat(chatNodeKeyKey);
               }
               else { // actor is host, get list of hosts in chat
                    actorKeys = getHostKeysInChat(chatNodeKeyKey);
               }
               // chatActor strings contain actorNickname, age:actorAge and
rating:actorRating
               // Here is an example:
               // John Doe age:12 rating:5
               // NOTE THIS DEPENDS ON XSL DOCUMENT RIGHT NOW!
               // strip off the age and rating
               int inx = chatActor.lastIndexOf("age:");
               String actorNickname = chatActor.substring(0, inx).trim();
               NodeKey actorNodeKey = getActorByNickname(actorKeys,
```

```
actorNickname);
                        NodeKey actorRatingNodeKey =
getActorRatingForActor(actorNodeKey);
                        return changeActorRating(actorRatingNodeKey, amount);
                }
                catch(Exception ee) {
                        return null;   //TEMP
                }
        }
    /** Changes integer-as-string content of actorRating, child of actor node.
       *  Note: actorRating nodes have no siblings.
     *
     * @param actorRatingNodeKey NodeKey
     * @param amount                  String  (negative or positive offset,
integer as string)
     *
     * @return String actorRating after increment
     */
      protected String changeActorRating(NodeKey actorRatingNodeKey, String
amount) {
                BonNode actorRatingNode =
getBonForumXML().getBonNode(actorRatingNodeKey);
                int rating = Integer.parseInt(actorRatingNode.nodeContent);
                int offset = Integer.parseInt(amount);
                rating = rating + offset;
                String nodeContent = Integer.toString(rating);
                NodeKey aRNK = getBonForumXML().editBonNode(actorRatingNodeKey, null,
null, nodeContent);
                if(aRNK != null) {
                        return nodeContent;
                }
                else {
                        return null;
                }
        }
    /** Returns NodeKey of actorRating, a child node of actor, given the
actorNodeKey.
       *  Note: actorRating nodes have no siblings.
     *
     * @param actorNodeKey    NodeKey
     *
     * @return NodeKey of actorRating BonNode, child of actor with given
actorNodeKey
     */
      protected NodeKey getActorRatingForActor(NodeKey actorNodeKey) {
                NodeKey nodeKey =
getBonForumXML().getChildNodeByNameAndContent(actorNodeKey, "actorRating", null);
                return nodeKey;
        }
    /** Returns NodeKey of actor BonNode, given an actorNickname.
       *  Note: actorNicknames are unique in bonForum.
```

```
     *
     * @param actorKeys ArrayList
     * @param actorNickname  String
     * @return NodeKey of actor BonNode with given actorNickname
     */
     protected NodeKey getActorByNickname(ArrayList actorKeys, String
actorNickname) {
            NodeKey nodeKey =
getBonForumXML().getNodeKeyByChildNameAndContent(actorKeys, "actorNickname",
actorNickname);
            return nodeKey;
     }
    /** Returns true if host is in a chat, given its nodeKey as a string, and a
chatNodeKeyKey.
      *  Note: hostKey element content values are unique in chat.
     *
     * @param hostNodeKeyValue    String
     * @param chatNodeKeyKey  String
     * @return boolean true if chat node for chatNodeKeyKey has hostKey child with
hostNodeKeyValue
     */
     protected boolean isHostInChat(String hostNodeKeyValue, String
chatNodeKeyKey) {
            ArrayList hostKeysInChat = getHostKeysInChat(chatNodeKeyKey);
            Iterator hostIterator = hostKeysInChat.iterator();
            while(hostIterator.hasNext()) {
                   if(hostNodeKeyValue.equals((String)hostIterator.next())) {
                          return true;
                   }
            }
            return false;
     }
    /** Returns true if guest is in a chat, given its nodeKey as a string, and a
chatNodeKeyKey.
      *  Note: guestKey element content values are unique in chat.
     *
     * @param guestNodeKeyValue    String
     * @param chatNodeKeyKey  String
     * @return boolean true if chat node for chatNodeKeyKey has guestKey child
with guestNodeKeyValue
     */
     protected boolean isGuestInChat(String guestNodeKeyValue, String
chatNodeKeyKey) {
            ArrayList guestKeysInChat = getGuestKeysInChat(chatNodeKeyKey);
            Iterator guestIterator = guestKeysInChat.iterator();
            while(guestIterator.hasNext()) {
                   if(guestNodeKeyValue.equals((String)guestIterator.next())) {
                          return true;
                   }
            }
            return false;
```

```
      }
    /** Returns array with contents of all guestKeys in a chat, given a
chatNodeKeyKey.
       *
     * @param chatNodeKeyKey  String
     * @return ArrayList of contents for all guestKey node children of chat node
     */
      protected ArrayList getGuestKeysInChat(String chatNodeKeyKey) {
            BonNode chatNode = getBonForumChatNode(chatNodeKeyKey);
            return getBonForumXML().getChildNodeContentsFromName(chatNode.nodeKey,
"guestKey");
      }
    /** Returns array with contents of all hostKeys in a chat, given a
chatNodeKeyKey.
       *
     * @param chatNodeKeyKey    String
     * @return ArrayList of contents for all hostKey node children of chat node
     */
      protected ArrayList getHostKeysInChat(String chatNodeKeyKey) {
            BonNode chatNode = getBonForumChatNode(chatNodeKeyKey);
            return getBonForumXML().getChildNodeContentsFromName(chatNode.nodeKey,
"hostKey");
      }
    /** Returns true if host is in a chat, given its chatNode.
       *  Note: hostKey element content values are unique in chat.
     *
     * @param hostNodeKeyValue    String
     * @param chatNode  BonNode
     * @return boolean true if chatNode has hostKey child with hostNodeKeyValue
     */
      protected boolean isHostInChatNode(String hostNodeKeyValue, BonNode
chatNode) {
            ArrayList hostKeysInChat = getHostKeysInChatNode(chatNode);
            Iterator hostIterator = hostKeysInChat.iterator();
            while(hostIterator.hasNext()) {
                  if(hostNodeKeyValue.equals((String)hostIterator.next())) {
                        return true;
                  }
            }
            return false;
      }
    /** Returns true if guest is in a chat, given its chatNode.
       *  Note: guestKey element content values are unique in chat.
     *
     * @param guestNodeKeyValue  String
     * @param chatNode  BonNode
     * @return boolean true if chatNode has guestKey child with guestNodeKeyValue
     */
      protected boolean isGuestInChatNode(String guestNodeKeyValue, BonNode
chatNode) {
            ArrayList guestKeysInChat = getGuestKeysInChatNode(chatNode);
```

```
        Iterator guestIterator = guestKeysInChat.iterator();
        while(guestIterator.hasNext()) {
            if(guestNodeKeyValue.equals((String)guestIterator.next())) {
                return true;
            }
        }
        return false;
    }
   /** Returns array with contents of all guestKeys in a chat, given a chatNode.
     *
    * @param chatNode  BonNode
    * @return ArrayList of contents for all guestKey node children of chat node
    */
    protected ArrayList getGuestKeysInChatNode(BonNode chatNode) {
        return getBonForumXML().getChildNodeContentsFromName(chatNode.nodeKey,
"guestKey");
    }
   /** Returns array with contents of all hostKeys in a chat, given a chatNode.
     *
    * @param chatNode  BonNode
    * @return ArrayList of contents for all hostKey node children of chat node
    */
    protected ArrayList getHostKeysInChatNode(BonNode chatNode) {
        return getBonForumXML().getChildNodeContentsFromName(chatNode.nodeKey,
"hostKey");
    }
   /** Returns true if there is a host actor with given actorNickname.
     *  Note: actorNicknames are unique in bonForum.
     *
     * @param nickname    String to look for in hosts' actorNickname contents
    * @return boolean true if actors has host node with actorNickname matching
argument
    */
    protected boolean isNicknameHost(String nickname) {
        ArrayList hostNicknames = getActorNicknames("host");
        if(hostNicknames.contains(nickname)) {
            return true;
        }
        else {
            return false;
        }
    }
   /** Returns true if there is a guest actor with given actorNickname.
     *  Note: actorNicknames are unique in bonForum.
     *
     * @param nickname     String to look for in guests' actorNickname contents
    * @return boolean true if actors has guest node with actorNickname matching
argument
    */
    protected boolean isNicknameGuest(String nickname) {
        ArrayList guestNicknames = getActorNicknames("guest");
```

```
                if(guestNicknames.contains(nickname)) {
                    return true;
                }
                else {
                    return false;
                }
            }
        /** Returns NodeKey of actor with given actorNickname.
          *  Note: actorNicknames are unique in bonForum.
          *
          * @param nickname          String      to look for in actors' actorNickname
contents
          * @param actorNodeName  String     , e.g., "host", "guest", "system"
        * @return NodeKey  of actor node with actorNickname matching argument, or
null
        */
        protected NodeKey getActorNicknameNodeKey(String actorNickname, String
actorNodeName) {
                NodeKey actorNicknameNodeKey = null;
                ArrayList actorNodeKeys =
                    getBonForumXML().getChildNodeKeysFromName(getActorsNodeKey(),
actorNodeName);
                Iterator iK= actorNodeKeys.iterator();
                while(iK.hasNext()) {
                    String nC = "";
                    NodeKey nodeKey =
getBonForumXML().getNodeKeyForString((String)iK.next());
                    NodeKey nicknameKey =
                        getBonForumXML().getChildNodeByNameAndContent(
                            nodeKey, "actorNickname", null);
                        if(nicknameKey != null) {
                        nC = getBonForumXML().getBonNode(nicknameKey).nodeContent;
                        if(nC == null) {
                            nC = "";
                        }
                        if(actorNickname.equals(nC)) {
                            return nicknameKey;
                        }
                    }
                }
                return null;
        }
        // LATER: factor out generic code and move to FH
        /** Returns ArrayList with all actor actorNickname node contents.
          *  Note: actorNicknames are unique in bonForum.
          *
          * @param orNodeName   String      act, e.g., "host", "guest", "system"
        * @return ArrayList of contents for all actorNickname node children of all
actorNodeName nodes
        */
        protected ArrayList getActorNicknames(String actorNodeName) {
```

```
            ArrayList actorNicknames = null;
            ArrayList actorNodeKeys =
                  getBonForumXML().getChildNodeKeysFromName(getActorsNodeKey(),
actorNodeName);
            Iterator iK= actorNodeKeys.iterator();
            while(iK.hasNext()) {
                  String nC = "";
                  NodeKey nodeKey =
getBonForumXML().getNodeKeyForString((String)iK.next());
                  NodeKey nicknameKey =
                        getBonForumXML().getChildNodeByNameAndContent(
                              nodeKey, "actorNickname", null);
                  if(nicknameKey != null) {
                        nC = getBonForumXML().getBonNode(nicknameKey).nodeContent;
                        if(nC == null) {
                              nC = "";
                        }
                        actorNicknames.add(nC);
                  }
            }
            return actorNicknames;
      }
    /** Normalizes the given string, replacing chars with entities.
     * (less than, greater than, ampersand, double quote, return and linefeed).
     * NOTE: replaces null string with empty string.
     *
     * @param s String
     * @return normalized string (not null)
     */
    protected static String normalize(String s) {
        StringBuffer str = new StringBuffer();
        str.append("");
            int len = (s != null) ? s.length() : 0;
            for (int i = 0; i < len; i++) {
                  char ch = s.charAt(i);
                  switch (ch) {
                        case '<': {
                             str.append("&lt;");
                             break;
                        }
                        case '>': {
                              str.append("&gt;");
                              break;
                        }
                        case '&': {
                              str.append("&amp;");
                              break;
                        }
                        case '"': {
                              str.append("&quot;");
                              break;
```

```
                    }
                    case '\r':
                    case '\n': {
                        str.append("&#");
                        str.append(Integer.toString(ch));
                        str.append(';');
                        break;
                    }
                    default: {
                        str.append(ch);
                    }
                }
            }
        return str.toString();
    }
}// end class BonForumStore
```

C.18 Filename: Projects\bonForum\src\de\tarent\forum\BonForumTagExtraInfo.java

```
package de.tarent.forum;
/*<Imports>*/
import javax.servlet.jsp.tagext.*;
/*</Imports>*/
/** BonForumTagExtraInfo creates page variables for bonForum JSP custom tags.
 * <br>The only variable now is a string named <code>output</code>.
 *
 * @author <A HREF="mailto://email@bonforum.org">Westy Rockwell</A>
 */
 public class BonForumTagExtraInfo extends TagExtraInfo {
    public VariableInfo[] getVariableInfo(TagData data) {
        return new VariableInfo[] {
            new VariableInfo("output",
                             "String",
                             true,
                             VariableInfo.NESTED),
                             // NESTED, AT_BEGIN or AT_END
        };
    }
}
```

C.19 Filename: Projects\bonForum\src\de\tarent\forum\BonForumUtils.java

```
/*
 * Note: This class is based in part on the source code for
 * the DOMFilter and DOMWriter classes, which are samples
```

```
 * provided with Apache Xerces.  The license for that source
 * code is either below (if this a file) or elsewhere in the
 * book (if this is printed).
 *
 * Note: This class is based in part on the source code for
 * the Clock2 applet, which is a sample provided with
 * Jakarta Tomcat.  The license for that source
 * code is either below (if this a file) or elsewhere in the
 * book (if this is printed).
 */

package de.tarent.forum;

/*<Imports>*/
import java.text.SimpleDateFormat;
import java.util.Date;
import java.util.Locale;
import java.util.Enumeration;
import org.w3c.dom.Attr;
import org.w3c.dom.NamedNodeMap;
import org.apache.xerces.readers.MIME2Java;
/*</Imports>*/

/** BonForumUtils has utility methods for the bonForum web application.
 * <p>For further information visit the open source.
 * <A HREF="http://www.bonForum.org">BonForum Project on SourceForge</A>.
 * @author <A HREF="mailto://email@bonforum.org">Westy Rockwell</A>.
 */
public class BonForumUtils {
      /* Code below here is based on Apache Software Foundation samples
        *     (see notice at file beginning)
        */
    /** Normalizes the given string, replacing chars with entities.
     * (less than, greater than, ampersand, double quote, return and linefeed).
     * NOTE: this replaces null string with empty string.
     *
     * @param s String
     * @return normalized string (not null)
     */
    public static String normalize(String s) {
        StringBuffer str = new StringBuffer();
        str.append("");
            int len = (s != null) ? s.length() : 0;
            for (int i = 0; i < len; i++) {
                  char ch = s.charAt(i);
                  switch (ch) {
                        case '<': {
                              str.append("&lt;");
                              break;
                        }
                        case '>': {
```

```
                        str.append("&gt;");
                        break;
                    }
                    case '&': {
                        str.append("&amp;");
                        break;
                    }
                    case '"': {
                        str.append("&quot;");
                        break;
                    }
                    case '\r':
                    case '\n': {
                        str.append("&#");
                        str.append(Integer.toString(ch));
                        str.append(';');
                        break;
                    }
                    default: {
                        str.append(ch);
                    }
                }
            }
        return str.toString();
    }
      /**  Default Encoding.
       * (taken from DOMFilter.java -
       * see notice at file beginning).
       */
      private static  String  PRINTWRITER_ENCODING = "UTF8";
      /**  Encodings available in Java.
       * (taken from DOMFilter.java -
       * see notice at file beginning).
       */
      private static String MIME2JAVA_ENCODINGS[] =
    { "Default", "UTF-8", "US-ASCII", "ISO-8859-1", "ISO-8859-2", "ISO-8859-3",
"ISO-8859-4",
      "ISO-8859-5", "ISO-8859-6", "ISO-8859-7", "ISO-8859-8", "ISO-8859-9", "ISO-
2022-JP",
      "SHIFT_JIS", "EUC-JP","GB2312", "BIG5", "EUC-KR", "ISO-2022-KR", "KOI8-R",
"EBCDIC-CP-US",
      "EBCDIC-CP-CA", "EBCDIC-CP-NL", "EBCDIC-CP-DK", "EBCDIC-CP-NO", "EBCDIC-CP-
FI", "EBCDIC-CP-SE",
      "EBCDIC-CP-IT", "EBCDIC-CP-ES", "EBCDIC-CP-GB", "EBCDIC-CP-FR", "EBCDIC-CP-
AR1",
      "EBCDIC-CP-HE", "EBCDIC-CP-CH", "EBCDIC-CP-ROECE","EBCDIC-CP-YU",
      "EBCDIC-CP-IS", "EBCDIC-CP-AR2", "UTF-16"
    };
      /** gets the default encoding.
       * method taken from Apache licensed source -
       * see license at end of source file).
```

```
 *
 * @return encoding as string
 */
public static String getWriterEncoding( ) {
    return (PRINTWRITER_ENCODING);
}
/** sets the default encoding.
 * method taken from Apache licensed source -
 * see license at end of source file).
 *
 * @param encoding String
 */
public static void  setWriterEncoding( String encoding ) {
if( encoding.equalsIgnoreCase( "DEFAULT" ) )
      PRINTWRITER_ENCODING  = "UTF8";
      else if( encoding.equalsIgnoreCase( "UTF-16" ) )
      PRINTWRITER_ENCODING  = "Unicode";
      else if( encoding.equalsIgnoreCase( "8859_2" ) )
            PRINTWRITER_ENCODING  = "8859_2";
      else
            PRINTWRITER_ENCODING = MIME2Java.convert( encoding );
}
/** returns true if encoding is valid for Java.
 * (method taken from Apache licensed source -
 * see license at end of source file).
 *
 * @param encoding String
 * @return boolean
 */
public static boolean isValidJavaEncoding( String encoding ) {
      for ( int i = 0; i < MIME2JAVA_ENCODINGS.length; i++ )
            if ( encoding.equals( MIME2JAVA_ENCODINGS[i] ) )
            return (true);
      return (false);
}
/** Returns a sorted list of attributes.
 * (method taken from Apache licensed source -
 * see license at end of source file).
 *
 * @param attrs NamedNodeMap with attributes
 * @return array of Attr with sorted attributes
 */
public static Attr[] sortAttributes(NamedNodeMap attrs) {
      int len = (attrs != null) ? attrs.getLength() : 0;
      Attr array[] = new Attr[len];
      for ( int i = 0; i < len; i++ ) {
            array[i] = (Attr)attrs.item(i);
      }
      for ( int i = 0; i < len - 1; i++ ) {
            String name  = array[i].getNodeName();
            int    index = i;
```

```
                    for ( int j = i + 1; j < len; j++ ) {
                          String curName = array[j].getNodeName();
                    if ( curName.compareTo(name) < 0 ) {
                          name  = curName;
                          index = j;
                    }
              }
              if ( index != i ) {
                    Attr temp    = array[i];
                    array[i]     = array[index];
                    array[index] = temp;
              }
              }
              return (array);
        }
        /** gets formatted current date for locale as a string.
         * (method taken from Apache licensed source -
         *  see license at end of source file).
         *
         * @return String with formatted current date for locale
         */
        public static String getLastDate() {
          SimpleDateFormat formatter = new SimpleDateFormat ("EEE MMM dd hh:mm:ss
yyyy", Locale.getDefault());
          Date currentDate = new Date();
          String lastdate = formatter.format(currentDate);
          return(lastdate);
        }
        /** gets time in milliseconds as a string.
         * (method taken from Apache licensed source -
         * see license at end of source file).
         *
         * @return String with formatted current time in milliseconds
         */
      public static String timeMillis() {
        return Long.toString(System.currentTimeMillis());
      }
}// end class BonForumUtils
```

C.20 Filename: Projects\bonForum\src\de\tarent\forum\BonLogger.java

```
package de.tarent.forum;
/*<Imports>*/
import java.io.*;
```

```
import java.util.*;
/*</Imports>*/
/** BonLogger is a (rough) information logger.
 * It is used by the bonForum web application.
 * <p>For further information visit the open source.
 * <A HREF="http://www.bonForum.org">BonForum Project on SourceForge</A>.
 * @author <A HREF="mailto://email@bonforum.org">Westy Rockwell</A>.
 */
public class BonLogger {
	private PrintWriter out = null;
	private Properties properties = null;
	private File tomcatHome = null;
	private String logFile = "";
	private String logFilePath = "";
	private String logging = "none";
	BonLogger(String logFileName, String logType) {
		properties = System.getProperties();
		tomcatHome = new File(System.getProperty("tomcat.home"));
		logFilePath = tomcatHome.getPath() +
				"/webapps/bonForum/WEB-INF/logs/";
		this.setLogFile(logFileName);
		if(logType == null) {
			logType = "none";
		}
		this.setLogging(logType);
	}
	public void setLogging(String newLoggingValue) {
		logging = newLoggingValue;
		boolean found = false;
		if(logging.equals("all") || logging.equals("std")) {
			System.err.println("BonForum Log File: " + logFile);
			found = true;
		}
		if(logging.equals("all") || logging.equals("file")) {
			found = true;
			if(out == null) {
				try {
					out = new PrintWriter(
							new BufferedOutputStream(
							new FileOutputStream(logFile)), true);
					out.println("BonForum Log File: " + logFile);
					properties.list(out);
				}
				catch(Exception ee) {
					ee.printStackTrace ();
					System.err.println(
					"Exception in BonLogger:" + logFile +
					     " newLoggingValue:" + newLoggingValue);
				}
			}
		}
```

```
            if(found == false && out != null) {
                  out.close();
                  //out = null;
            }
      }
      public String getLogging() {
            return logging;
      }
      public void setLogFile(String newLogFile) {
            logFile = logFilePath + newLogFile;
      }
      public String getLogFile() {
            return logFile;
      }
      public void logWrite(long timeMillis, String sessionId, String stdFile,
String info) {
            if(logging.equals("all") || logging.equals("std")) {
                  if(stdFile.equals("err")) {
                        System.err.println(Long.toString(timeMillis) + " " +
sessionId + "::" + info);
                  }
                  else if(stdFile.equals("out")) {
                        System.out.println(Long.toString(timeMillis) + " " +
sessionId + "::" + info);
                  }
            }
            if(logging.equals("all") || logging.equals("file")) {
                  try {
                        out.println(Long.toString(timeMillis) + " " + sessionId +
"::" + info);
                  //    out.close(); // finalize() not reliable!
                  }
                  catch(Exception e) {
                        //e.printStackTrace ();
                        System.err.println("Exception in BonLogger logWrite!");
                  }
            }
      }
}
```

C.21 Filename: Projects\bonForum\src\de\tarent\forum\BonNode.java

```
package de.tarent.forum;
/*<Imports>*/
import java.io.*;
```

```
/*</Imports>*/
/** BonNode implements an XML node in a ForestHashtable.
 * <pre>
 * public class BonNode {
 *    NodeKey nodeKey;  // ForestHashtable key
 *    NodeKey parentNodeKey;
 *    boolean deleted;  // flag as deleted, for quick deletes
 *    boolean flagged;   // general purpose state flag
 *    String nodeName;   // name of element
 *    String nodeAttributes;  // attributes of element
 *    String nodeContent;  // text between element opening and closing tags
 * }
 * </pre>
 * <p>For further information visit the open source.
 * <A HREF="http://www.bonForum.org">BonForum Project on SourceForge</A>.
 * @author <A HREF="mailto://email@bonforum.org">Westy Rockwell</A>.
 */
public class BonNode {
      NodeKey nodeKey;  // ForestHashtable key
      NodeKey parentNodeKey;
      boolean deleted;  // flag as deleted, for quick deletes
      boolean flagged;   // general purpose state flag
      String nodeName;   // name of element
      String nodeAttributes;  // attributes of element
      String nodeContent;  // text between element opening and closing tags
}
```

C.22 Filename: Projects\bonForum\src\de\tarent\forum\ForestHashtable.java

```
package de.tarent.forum;
/*<Imports>*/
import java.io.*;
import java.util.Iterator;
import java.util.Enumeration;
import java.util.Hashtable;
import java.util.ArrayList;
import javax.servlet.http.*;
/*</Imports>*/
/** ForestHashtable instance caches an XML document for fast processing.
 * Each element in a ForestHashtable can be cast to a BonNode, and each key to a
NodeKey.
 * The function of a NodeKey is to map the elements to nodes in one or more trees.
 * ForestHashtable design is based on triple-key database table design.
 * It is <b>only</b> a simulation of a relational database design.
 * which will be implemented with another database tool. Its purpose is
experimental.
 * NOTE: until this class is further developed, it works only for element nodes,
 * their attributes and text content. It provides only a subset of the full
```

```
 * XML document specification.
 * ForestHashtable is described fully in the book:
 * <i>XML, XSLT, Java and JSP - A Case Study in Developing a Web Application</i>,
 * by Westy Rockwell, published by
 * <A HREF="http://www.newriders.com">New Riders</A>.
 * Translation to German published by
 * <A HREF="http://www.galileocomputing.de">Galileo Press</A>.
 * <p>For further information visit the open source
 * <A HREF="http://www.bonForum.org">BonForum Project on SourceForge</A>
 * @author <A HREF="mailto://email@bonforum.org">Westy Rockwell</A>
 */
public class ForestHashtable extends java.util.Hashtable {
     private NodeNameHashtable nodeNameHashtable;
     private PathNameHashtable pathNameHashtable;
     private boolean lastRootNodeFound;
     private boolean lastChildOfRootNodeFound;
     // next one defined further down for recursion
     // private boolean lastChildOfNonRootNodeFound;
     private String currentRootNodeAKey;
     private String currentRootNodeBKey;
     private String currentRootNodeCKey;    // for debug only
     private String currentChildOfRootNodeAKey;
     private String currentChildOfRootNodeBKey;
     private String currentChildOfRootNodeCKey; // for debug only
     // next 3 defined further down for recursion
     // private String currentChildOfNonRootNodeAKey;
     // private String currentChildOfNonRootNodeBKey;
     // private String currentChildOfNonRootNodeCKey;
     private static BonLogger logFH = null;
     // Controls logger output.
     private static String logging = null;
     // False until logger ready.
     private static boolean loggingInitialized = false;
     // for logging output, when no sessionId available
     private static String sessionId = "0000000000";
     private static final int NO_NODEKEY_KEY_PREFIX = 0;
     private static final int SESSION_ID = 1;
     private static final int SESSION_ID_AND_CREATION_TIME = 2;
     private String uniqueNodeKeyKeyList = "message;messageKey";
   /** Sets uniqueNodeKeyKeyList of node names unique per session
    * in nodeNameHashtable.  Determines key prefix choice.
      * Node names in list can have one key per session
      * Node names not in list can have multiple keys per session
      * This saves space by not storing keys for unused nodeKey entries.
      * (Note: applies only adding children to non-root nodes.).
    *
    */
     protected void setUniqueNodeKeyKeyList(String newUniqueNodeKeyKeyList) {
          uniqueNodeKeyKeyList = newUniqueNodeKeyKeyList;
     }
   /** Gets uniqueNodeKeyKeyList setting.
```

```
     *  (see set method for details)
     *
     * @return String uniqueNodeKeyKeyList
     */
      public String getUniqueNodeKeyKeyList() {
            return uniqueNodeKeyKeyList;
      }
    /** Creates a ForestHashtable with the default capacity.
      */
      public ForestHashtable() {
            super();
            nodeNameHashtable = new NodeNameHashtable();
            pathNameHashtable = new PathNameHashtable();
      }
    /** Creates a ForestHashtable of a given capacity.
      *
      * @param capacity initialCapacity of parent java.util.Hashtable
      */
      public ForestHashtable(int capacity) {
            super(capacity);
            nodeNameHashtable = new NodeNameHashtable();
            pathNameHashtable = new PathNameHashtable();
      }
      private void log(String sessionId, String where, String what) {
            if(logging != null) {
                  logFH.logWrite(System.currentTimeMillis(), sessionId, where,
what);
            }
      }
    /** Gets logging setting.
      *
      * @return String logging
      */
      public String getLogging() {
            return logging;
      }
    /** Sets logging setting.
      *
      * @param String setting for logger logtype ("none","all","std","file")
      */
      protected void setLogging(String newLogging) {
            logging = newLogging;
            synchronized(this) {
                  if(!loggingInitialized) {
                        System.err.println("ForestHashtable init
loggingInitialized:" + loggingInitialized);
                        System.err.println("ForestHashtable init logging:" +
logging);
                        if(logging != null) {
                              logFH = new BonLogger("ForestHashtableLog.txt",
logging);
```

```
                                System.err.println("ForestHashtable init logFH:" +
logFH);
                                logFH.setLogging(newLogging);
                                loggingInitialized = true;
                                System.err.println("ForestHashtable init
loggingInitialized:" + loggingInitialized);
                            }
                        }
                    }
                }
    /** Gets nodeNameHashtable.
      * @return NodeNameHashtable nodeNameHashtable
      */
      protected NodeNameHashtable getNodeNameHashtable() {
            return nodeNameHashtable;
      }
    /** Gets pathNameHashtable.
      * @return PathNameHashtable pathNameHashtable
      */
      protected PathNameHashtable getPathNameHashtable() {
            return pathNameHashtable;
      }
    /** Returns nodeKey from a BonNode, as an object.
      *
      * @param bonNode  node whose key is returned
      * @return         nodeKey of BonNode cast to an Object
      */
      protected Object nodeKeyFromBonNode(BonNode bonNode) {
            return (Object)bonNode.nodeKey;
      }
    /** Provides a useable NodeKey with a unique default root key value.
      *
      * @return NodeKey instance with unique aKey, initialized as a root node key
      *                          (to use for non-root nodes, change bKey and
cKey values)
      */
      private NodeKey getNextAvailableNodeKey() {
            long temp = 0;
            long lastCurrentTimeMillis = System.currentTimeMillis();
            NodeKey nodeKey = new NodeKey();
            while (temp <= lastCurrentTimeMillis) {
                  temp = System.currentTimeMillis();
            }
            nodeKey.aKey = Long.toString(temp);
            // initialize other keys to first,
            // that makes node a root node by default
            nodeKey.bKey = nodeKey.aKey;
            nodeKey.cKey = nodeKey.aKey;
            return nodeKey;
      }
    /** Deletes a BonNode given its nodeKey value.
```

```
     *
     * @param keyOfNodeToDelete nodeKey of BonNode to delete
     * @return          boolean true if deleted, false otherwise
     */
    private boolean doDeleteNode(NodeKey keyOfNodeToDelete) {
        // LATER: this will just mark node as deleted,
        //        and a separate thread will scavenge deleted nodes.
        if (this.containsKey(keyOfNodeToDelete)) {
            this.remove(keyOfNodeToDelete);
            return true;
        }
        else {
            return false;
        }
    }
  /** Deletes a BonNode and its descendant nodes, given a nodeKey value.
     *
     * @param keyOfNodeToDelete    nodeKey of BonNode to delete
     * @return          boolean true if at least one node was deleted, false
otherwise
     */
    private boolean doDeleteNodeRecursive(NodeKey keyOfNodeToDelete) {
        // LATER: this will just mark node as deleted,
        // and a separate thread will scavenge deleted nodes.
        String parentAKey = keyOfNodeToDelete.aKey;
        NodeKey nodeKey = new NodeKey();
        BonNode bonNode = null;
        Enumeration enumeration = this.elements();
        if(!(enumeration.hasMoreElements())) {
            return false; // no elements to delete
        }
        while(enumeration.hasMoreElements()) {
            bonNode = (BonNode)enumeration.nextElement();
            nodeKey = bonNode.nodeKey;
            if(nodeKey.bKey.equals(parentAKey)) {  // found a child
                doDeleteNodeRecursive(nodeKey);
            }
        }
        bonNode = this.getBonNode(keyOfNodeToDelete);
        this.remove(keyOfNodeToDelete);
        return true;
    }
  /** Returns true if a BonNode has child nodes.
     *
     * @param parentNodeKey     the node being tested for children
     * @return          boolean true if at least one node was deleted, false
otherwise
     */
    protected boolean hasAtLeastOneChild(NodeKey parentNodeKey) {
        // in a ForestHashtable, children have nodeKey.bKey equal to the
parent's nodeKey.aKey
```

```
            BonNode bonNode = null;
            String parentAKey = parentNodeKey.aKey;
            Enumeration enumeration = this.elements();
            while(enumeration.hasMoreElements()) {
                  bonNode = (BonNode)enumeration.nextElement();
                  if(bonNode.nodeKey.bKey.equals(parentAKey)) {
                        return true;
                  }
            }
            return false;
      }
    /** Deletes a BonNode and possibly its descendant nodes, given a nodeKey
value.
      *
      * @param keyOfNodeToDelete   nodeKey of BonNode to delete
      * @param leafOnly boolean true to delete only if node has no children
      *                         false to delete node and any descendant nodes
      * @return   boolean true if at least one node was deleted, false otherwise
      */
      public boolean deleteNode(NodeKey keyOfNodeToDelete, boolean leafOnly) {
            // NodeKey is a three-valued key (ABCTable key).
            // if leafOnly is True, then Node not deleted if it has one or more
child nodes.
            // if leafOnly is False, then Node and all its descendants are
deleted!
            synchronized(this) {
                  if(this.containsKey(keyOfNodeToDelete)) {
                        if(leafOnly) {
                              if(hasAtLeastOneChild(keyOfNodeToDelete)) {
                                    return false;    // was not a leaf node, so
not deleted
                              }
                        }
                        // delete and report success or failure
                        return doDeleteNodeRecursive(keyOfNodeToDelete);
                  }
                  else {
                        return false;  // no such node
                  }
            }
      }
    /** Adds a BonNode (and optionally its nodeKey to another hashtable for fast
lookups).
      * To add nodes, user only calls addRootNode, addChildNodeToRootNode or
addChildNodeToNonRootNode.
      * If nodeKeyHashtableName is "nodeNameHashtable" then these nodeKeyKeyPrefix
values are possible:
      * <UL>
      *   <LI> NO_NODEKEY_KEY_PREFIX makes added node global, visible to all
HTTP Sessions,
      *   <LI> SESSION_ID makes node UNIQUE for nodeName in session, and visible
```

```
only to current session
        *   <LI> SESSION_ID_AND_CREATION_TIME allows multiple nodes with nodeName,
and visible only to current session
        * </UL>
        *
      * Note: more values of nodeKeyKeyPrefix will be defined in later versions!
      *
      * @param nodeName                    String naming this node
      * @param nodeAttributes         String containing all attributes concatenated
(name=value name=value ...)
      * @param nodeContent                 String containing text content of node
      * @param nodeKey                     NodeKey uniquely identifying and
positioning node to be added in hierarchy
      * @param parentNodeKey               NodeKey for parent of node to be added
      * @param nodeKeyHashtableName         String naming hashtable in which to
cache key of added node
      * @param nodeKeyKeyPrefix            int = NO_NODEKEY_KEY_PREFIX makes added
node global, visible to all HTTP Sessions,
      *                                                 = SESSION_ID makes
node UNIQUE for nodeName in session, and visible only to current session
      *                                                 =
SESSION_ID_AND_CREATION_TIME allows multiple nodes with nodeName, and visible only
to current session
      * @param sessionId                   String, ID of HTTP session calling the
method
      * @return BonNode that was added
      */
      private BonNode addNode(String nodeName, String nodeAttributes, String
nodeContent, NodeKey nodeKey, NodeKey parentNodeKey, String nodeKeyHashtableName,
int nodeKeyKeyPrefix, String sessionId) {
            BonNode node = new BonNode();
            node.deleted = false;
            node.flagged = false;
            node.nodeName = nodeName;
            if(nodeAttributes != null && nodeAttributes.length() > 0) {
                        node.nodeAttributes = "nodeKey=\""+ nodeKey + "\" " +
nodeAttributes;
            }
            else {
                  node.nodeAttributes = "nodeKey=\""+ nodeKey + "\"";
            }
            node.nodeContent = nodeContent;
            node.nodeKey = nodeKey;
            node.parentNodeKey = parentNodeKey;
            // put in this ForestHashtable
            // also optionally put nodeKey in nodeNameHashtable
            // but not if it is a subject element, etc.
            if(nodeKeyHashtableName.equals("nodeNameHashtable")) {
                  // Hashtable is synchronized, but we need to sync two together
here:
                  String nodeKeyKey = null;
```

```
                    synchronized(this) {
                        try {
                            this.put(nodeKey, node);
                        }
                        catch(Exception ee) {
                            log(sessionId, "err", "EXCEPTION in addNode():" +
ee.getMessage());
                            ee.printStackTrace();
                        }
                        if(nodeKeyKeyPrefix == SESSION_ID) {
                            // allows only one key per session
                            // use this option to reduce size of table
                            // by not storing key to nodeKeys not needed
                            // (examples: message keys, messageKey keys).
                            nodeKeyKey = sessionId + ":" + nodeName;
                        }
                        else if(nodeKeyKeyPrefix == SESSION_ID_AND_CREATION_TIME)
{
                            // the nodeKey.aKey acts as a timestamp
                            // allowing multiple keys per session in
nodeNameHashtable
                            // use to find multiple nodes with same name for one
session
                            // (example: chat keys, guest keys, host keys)
                            nodeKeyKey = sessionId + "_" + nodeKey.aKey +":" +
nodeName;
                        }
                        else if(nodeKeyKeyPrefix == NO_NODEKEY_KEY_PREFIX) {
                            // use no prefix for elements global to all sessions
                            nodeKeyKey = nodeName;
                        }
                        else {
                            nodeKeyKey = nodeName;  // unknown arg value, could
complain
                        }
                        // else ifs and/or else can add other prefixes here.
                        // Note: it replaces older entries, if any
                        this.nodeNameHashtable.put(nodeKeyKey, nodeKey);
                    }
                }
                // else ifs here can add other hashtables later
                else {
                    // Hashtable is synchronized, so if you change ancestor class
for this,
                    // be sure to sync addition to this here also.
                    this.put(nodeKey, node);
                }
                return node;
            }
        /** Adds a BonNode as a root node. (Names should be unique among siblings, if
nodeKeyHashtable is used)
```

```
     *
     * @param rootNodeName                     String naming this node
     * @param rootNodeAttributes          String containing all attributes
concatenated  (name=value name=value ...)
     * @param rootNodeContent                  String containing text content of
node
     * @param nodeKeyHashtableName        String naming hashtable in which to cache
key of added node
     * @return BonNode that was added
     */
     protected BonNode addRootNode(String rootNodeName, String
rootNodeAttributes, String rootNodeContent, String nodeKeyHashtableName) {
     // Node is an object that points to everything mapped to that node in the
tree.
     // In a table that holds objects, just stick Node in table.
     // OTW, you can extract info and write to fields in table.
             NodeKey nodeKey = getNextAvailableNodeKey(); // initially, nodeKey =
An.An.An;
         // When all three keys are equal, the row is a root node!
         // An empty parent node key means no parent, because it is a root node.
             NodeKey emptyParentNodeKey = new NodeKey();
             return addNode(rootNodeName, rootNodeAttributes, rootNodeContent,
nodeKey, emptyParentNodeKey, nodeKeyHashtableName, NO_NODEKEY_KEY_PREFIX, "");
     }
   /** Adds a BonNode as a child of a root node.(Names should be unique among
siblings, if nodeKeyHashtable is used)
     *
     * @param childNodeName                    String naming this node
     * @param childNodeAttributes         String containing all attributes
concatenated  (name=value name=value ...)
     * @param childNodeContent                 String containing text content of
node
     * @param childNodeKey                     NodeKey uniquely identifying a root
node
     * @param nodeKeyHashtableName                 String naming hashtable in which
to cache key of added node
     * @return BonNode that was added
     */
     protected BonNode addChildNodeToRootNode(String childNodeName, String
childNodeAttributes, String childNodeContent, NodeKey rootNodeKey, String
nodeKeyHashtableName) {
             NodeKey childNodeKey = getNextAvailableNodeKey(); // initially,
NodeKey = An.An.An;
             childNodeKey.bKey = rootNodeKey.aKey;
             childNodeKey.cKey = rootNodeKey.bKey;
             // when the second and third key are equal, it is child of a root
             return addNode(childNodeName, childNodeAttributes, childNodeContent,
childNodeKey, rootNodeKey, nodeKeyHashtableName, NO_NODEKEY_KEY_PREFIX, "");
     }
   /** Adds a BonNode as a child of a non-root node (and optionally its nodeKey
to another hashtable for fast lookups).
```

```
     * If "nodeNameHashtable" nodeKeyHashtable is used, sessionId must be passed
in to create session-related key for nodeKey.
     * (for now, caller is responsible for that!)
     *
     * @param childNodeName                   String naming this node
     * @param childNodeAttributes     String containing all attributes
concatenated  (name=value name=value ...)
     * @param childNodeContent                String containing text content of
node
     * @param nonRootNodeKey                NodeKey uniquely identifying a non-
root node
     * @param nodeKeyHashtableName       String naming hashtable in which to
cache key of added node
     * @param sessionId                     String id of callers session, if
nodeKeyHashtable is used.
     * @return BonNode that was added
     */
     protected BonNode addChildNodeToNonRootNode(String childNodeName, String
childNodeAttributes, String childNodeContent, NodeKey nonRootNodeKey, String
nodeKeyHashtableName, String sessionId) {
          NodeKey childNodeKey = getNextAvailableNodeKey();
          // when no keys are equal, its a root grandchild or deeper
          childNodeKey.bKey = nonRootNodeKey.aKey;
          childNodeKey.cKey = nonRootNodeKey.bKey;
          // Assume multiple keys per nodeKey allowed in "nodeNameHashtable"
nodeKeyHashtable
          int nodeKeyKeyPrefix = SESSION_ID_AND_CREATION_TIME;
          // unless node name to be added is in the "list".
          if(uniqueNodeKeyKeyList.trim().length() > 0) {
               if(uniqueNodeKeyKeyList.indexOf(childNodeName) > -1) {
                    nodeKeyKeyPrefix = SESSION_ID;
               }
          }
          return addNode(childNodeName, childNodeAttributes, childNodeContent,
childNodeKey, nonRootNodeKey, nodeKeyHashtableName, nodeKeyKeyPrefix, sessionId);
     }
    /** Counts the children of a BonNode.
     *
     * @param parentNodeKey               NodeKey of node whose children will be
counted
     * @return long number of child nodes
     */
     public long countChildren(NodeKey parentNodeKey) {
          // in a ForestHashtable, children have nodeKey.bKey equal to the
parent's nodeKey.aKey
          long counter = 0;
          BonNode bonNode = null;
          String parentAKey = parentNodeKey.aKey;
          Enumeration enumeration = this.elements();
          while(enumeration.hasMoreElements()) {
               bonNode = (BonNode)enumeration.nextElement();
```

```
            if(bonNode.nodeKey.bKey.equals(parentAKey)) {
                counter++;
            }
        }
        return counter;
    }
    /** Gets from NodeKey ArrayList the first one whose BonNode has a child with
given content.
     *
     * @param nodeKeys       ArrayList of NodeKeys to will be checked
     * @param childContent           String content of child node to look for
     * @return NodeKey of first BonNode with child node that has childContent as
content, or null
     */
    protected NodeKey getNodeKeyByChildNameAndContent(ArrayList nodeKeys, String
childName, String childContent) {
    Iterator iK= nodeKeys.iterator();
    while(iK.hasNext()) {
            NodeKey nodeKey = getNodeKeyForString((String)iK.next());
        NodeKey childNodeKey = getChildNodeByNameAndContent(nodeKey,
childName, childContent);
            if(childNodeKey != null) {
                return nodeKey;  // of parent whose child has content
            }
        }
        return null;
    }
    /** Gets a new NodeKey whose toString() method returns a given String.
     * Note: If argument string is empty or null method returns an empty
NodeKey.
     *
     * @param nodeKeyString String
     * @return NodeKey for the given nodeKeyString
     */
    protected NodeKey getNodeKeyForString(String nodeKeyString) {
        //log(sessionId, "", "getNodeKeyForString() nodeKeyString" +
nodeKeyString);
        NodeKey nodeKey = new NodeKey();
        int inx;
        if((nodeKeyString == null) || (nodeKeyString.equals(""))) {
            return nodeKey;
        }
        String keyString = nodeKeyString;
        // 984576125127.984576061235.984576061225
        //          1         2         3
        // 01234567890123456789012345678901234567
        inx = keyString.indexOf(".");
        if(inx > -1) {
            nodeKey.aKey = keyString.substring(0, inx);
            keyString = keyString.substring(inx + 1);
            inx = keyString.indexOf(".");
```

```
                    if(inx > -1) {
                          nodeKey.bKey = keyString.substring(0, inx);
                          String cKey = keyString.substring(inx + 1);
                          if(cKey.length() > 0) {
                                nodeKey.cKey = cKey;
                          }
                    }
              }
              if(nodeKey.toString().equals(nodeKeyString)) {
                    return nodeKey;
              }
              return null;
        }
      /** Gets ArrayList with contents of all child nodes with given name.
        *
        * @param parentNodeKey       NodeKey of node whose children will be checked
        * @param nodeName       String name of child nodes to look for
        * @return ArrayList of content of all child nodes with the given name
        */
        protected ArrayList getChildNodeContentsFromName(NodeKey parentNodeKey,
String nodeName) {
              // In a ForestHashtable, children have nodeKey.bKey equal to the
parent's nodeKey.aKey
              BonNode bonNode = new BonNode();
              ArrayList nodeContents = new ArrayList();
              if(parentNodeKey != null && nodeName != null) {
                    String parentAKey = parentNodeKey.aKey;
                    Enumeration enumeration = this.elements();
                    while(enumeration.hasMoreElements()) {
                          bonNode = (BonNode)enumeration.nextElement();
                          if(bonNode.nodeKey.bKey.equals(parentAKey)) { // it is
child node
                                if(nodeName.equals(bonNode.nodeName)) {

nodeContents.add(bonNode.nodeContent.toString());
                                }
                          }
                    }
                    return nodeContents;
              }
              return null;
        }
      /** Gets ArrayList with keys of all child nodes with given name.
        *
        * @param parentNodeKey       NodeKey of node whose children will be checked
        * @param nodeName       String name of child nodes to look for
        * @return ArrayList of NodeKeys of child nodes with the given name
        */
        protected ArrayList getChildNodeKeysFromName(NodeKey parentNodeKey, String
nodeName) {
              // In a ForestHashtable, children have nodeKey.bKey equal to the
```

```
parent's nodeKey.aKey
            BonNode bonNode = new BonNode();
            ArrayList nodeKeys = new ArrayList();
            if(parentNodeKey != null && nodeName != null) {
                  String parentAKey = parentNodeKey.aKey;
                  Enumeration enumeration = this.elements();
                  while(enumeration.hasMoreElements()) {
                        bonNode = (BonNode)enumeration.nextElement();
                        if(bonNode.nodeKey.bKey.equals(parentAKey)) { // it is
child node
                              if(nodeName.equals(bonNode.nodeName)) {
                                    nodeKeys.add(bonNode.nodeKey.toString());
                              }
                        }
                  }
                  return nodeKeys;
            }
            return null;
      }
    /** Gets first child node with given name and/or content.
      * <pre>
      * If nodeName is null, match by content only.
      * If nodeContent is null, match by name only.
      * If both null, or no match, or no children, returns null.
      * </pre>
      * @param parentNodeKey       NodeKey of node whose children will be checked
      * @param nodeName            String child name to look for
      * @param nodeContent         String child content to look for
      * @return NodeKey         for first (only!) child with the given name and/or
content
      */
      protected NodeKey getChildNodeByNameAndContent(NodeKey parentNodeKey, String
nodeName, String nodeContent) {
            // NOTE: only gets nodekey of first child with name and/or content
sought!
            //       It is used when argument value(s) must be unique among
sibling nodes.
            //       It can be easily changed to return a list of nodes instead,
when needed.
            // In a ForestHashtable, children have nodeKey.bKey
            //   equal to the parent's nodeKey.aKey
            BonNode bonNode = new BonNode();
            if(parentNodeKey != null && (nodeContent != null || nodeName != null))
{
                  String parentAKey = parentNodeKey.aKey;
                  Enumeration enumeration = this.elements();
                  while(enumeration.hasMoreElements()) {
                        bonNode = (BonNode)enumeration.nextElement();
                        if(bonNode.nodeKey.bKey.equals(parentAKey)) { // it is
child node
                              if(nodeName != null && nodeContent != null) {  //
```

```
match name and content
                                        if(nodeName.equals(bonNode.nodeName)) {

if(nodeContent.equals(bonNode.nodeContent)) {
                                                return bonNode.nodeKey;
                                            }
                                        }
                                }
                                else if(nodeName != null) { // match name only
                                        if(nodeName.equals(bonNode.nodeName)) {
                                            return bonNode.nodeKey;
                                        }
                                }
                                else if(nodeContent != null) { // match content only
                                        if(nodeContent.equals(bonNode.nodeContent)) {
                                            return bonNode.nodeKey;
                                        }
                                }
                            }
                        }
                }
                return null;
        }
    /** Gets first child node with given attribute name and value pair.
      *
      * @param parentNodeKey        NodeKey of node whose children will be checked
      * @param attributeName        String name of attribute to look for
      * @param attributeValue    String value of named attribute to look for
      * @return BonNode first child node (only!) with the given attribute name and
value
      */
      protected BonNode getChildNodeFromAttributeValue(NodeKey parentNodeKey,
String attributeName, String attributeValue) {
                // NOTE: only gets first child with value=name sought!
                //       It is used when attribute value must be unique among sibling
nodes.
                //       It can be easily changed to return a list of nodes instead,
when needed.
                // In a ForestHashtable, children have nodeKey.bKey equal
                //   to the parent's nodeKey.aKey
                BonNode bonNode = new BonNode();
                if(parentNodeKey != null && attributeName != null && attributeValue !=
null) {
                        String parentAKey = parentNodeKey.aKey;
                        Enumeration enumeration = this.elements();
                        while(enumeration.hasMoreElements()) {
                                bonNode = (BonNode)enumeration.nextElement();
                                if(bonNode.nodeKey.bKey.equals(parentAKey)) { // it is
child node

if(attributeValue.equals(getAttributeValue(bonNode.nodeAttributes,
```

```
attributeName))) {
                                                return bonNode;
                                        }
                                }
                        }
                }
                return null;
        }
        /** Finds out if a given attribute exists in a nodeAttributes string.
          *
          * @param allAttributes     String with format used in BonNode
nodeAttributes member
          *                                   (No spaces allowed between attributeName
and equals sign
          *                                   nor between equal sign and
attributeValue.)
          * @param attributeName     String naming attribute to look for in
          * <value>allAttributes</value>
          * @return boolean true if given attribute exists, false otherwise
          */
        public boolean attributeExists(String allAttributes, String attributeName) {
                if(allAttributes.indexOf(attributeName+"=\"") > -1) { // found name
                        return true;
                }
                else {
                        return false;
                }
        }
        /** Gets the value assigned to a given attribute in a nodeAttributes string.
          *
          * @param allAttributes String with format used in BonNode nodeAttributes
member
          *                                   (No spaces allowed between attributeName
and equals sign
          *                                   nor between equal sign and
attributeValue.).
          * @param attributeName     String naming attribute in
<value>allAttributes</value>
          * whose value is returned
          * @return null if value has no closing quote or if attributeName not
found,
          * else value as string.
          */
        protected String getAttributeValue(String allAttributes, String
attributeName) {
                String str1 = null;
                // type="tes\"ti\"ng" itemKey="961755688708.961755643923.961755643913"
dateStamp="Fri Jun 23 12:21:39 2000"
                int inx1 = allAttributes.indexOf(attributeName+"=\"");
                if(inx1 > -1) { // found name
                        int inx2 = inx1 + (attributeName+"=\"").length();
```

```
                    str1 = allAttributes.substring(inx2); // remove all up through
name, equals and opening quote
                    String str2 = new String(str1);
                    // tes\"ti\"ng" itemKey="961755688708.961755643923.961755643913"
dateStamp="Fri Jun 23 12:21:39 2000"
                    boolean findingClosingQuote = true;
                    int inxAcc = 0;
                    while(findingClosingQuote) {
                          int inx3 = str2.indexOf("\""); // find next quotation mark
                          if(inx3 < 0) {
                                str1 = null;
                                break;
                          }
                          // find next escaped quotation mark (if any)
                          int inx4 = str2.indexOf("\\\"");
                          if(inx4 > -1) {                 // found one
                               // te\"st\"ing" goal="961772451582"
                               //    ¦
                               //    inx3
                               //   ¦
                               //   inx4
                               if(inx3 == inx4 + 1) {  // same one again
                                     // accumulate an index relative to
                                     // beginning of attribute value
                                     inxAcc += inx3 + 1;
                                     // remove all up to and including escaped
quote

                                     str2 = str2.substring(inx3 + 1);
                                     // ti\"ng"
itemKey="961755688708.961755643923.961755643913" dateStamp="Fri Jun 23 12:21:39
2000"
                                     // ng"
itemKey="961755688708.961755643923.961755643913" dateStamp="Fri Jun 23 12:21:39
2000"
                                }
                                else {
                                     // 961772451582" type="te\"st\"ing"
                                     //               ¦           ¦
                                     //               inx3        inx4
                                     if(inxAcc > 0) {
                                           inx3 = inxAcc + ++inx3;
                                     }
                                     str1 = str1.substring(0, inx3);
                                     break; // success
                                }
                          }
                          else {
                                if(inxAcc > 0) {
                                     // ng"
itemKey="961755688708.961755643923.961755643913" dateStamp="Fri Jun 23 12:21:39
2000"
```

```
                                        //    ^
                                        inx3 = inxAcc + ++inx3;
                                }
                                str1 = str1.substring(0, inx3);
                                break; // success
                        }
                }
        }
        else {
                log(sessionId, "err", "ERROR in getAttributeValue()?
attributeName not found!?");
        }
        return str1;
    }
    /** Gets a BonNode given its nodeKey.
      *
      * @param nodeKey key of node to return
      * @return BonNode for the given key, or null if node non-existent
      * or <value>nodeKey</value> null
      */
    protected BonNode getBonNode(NodeKey nodeKey) {
        if(nodeKey == null) {
                return null;
        }
        if(this.containsKey(nodeKey)) {
                return (BonNode)this.get(nodeKey);
        }
        else {
                return null;
        }
    }
    /** Allows editing name, attributes and/or content of a BonNode given its
nodeKey.
      * Can use this for cross-HttpSession node edits, so later may have to
prevent that?
      * If no BonNode exists for nodeKey, silently does nothing.
      * If all String arguments are null, silently does nothing.
      *
      * @param nodeKey                      NodeKey of node to edit
      * @param newNodeName                  String name of node after editing
(unless null)
      * @param newNodeAttributes            String attributes of node after
      * editing (unless null)
      * @param newNodeContent               String content of node after editing
(unless null)
      * @return NodeKey of BonNode edited, or null if no such node or
      * <value>nodeKey</value> null
      */
    protected NodeKey editBonNode(NodeKey nodeKey, String newNodeName, String
newNodeAttributes, String newNodeContent) {
        NodeKey retval = null;
```

```
			synchronized(this) {
				BonNode bonNode = getBonNode(nodeKey);
				if(bonNode != null) {
					boolean putNew = false;
					if(newNodeName != null) {
						bonNode.nodeName = newNodeName;
						putNew = true;
					}
					if(newNodeAttributes != null) {
						bonNode.nodeAttributes = newNodeAttributes;
						putNew = true;
					}
					if(newNodeContent != null) {
						bonNode.nodeContent = newNodeContent;
						putNew = true;
					}
					if(putNew) {
						try {
							doDeleteNode(nodeKey);
						}
						catch(Exception ee) {
							log(sessionId, "err", "editBonNode() EXCEPTION
deleting node!:" + ee.getMessage());
						}
						try {
							retval = (NodeKey)this.put(nodeKey, bonNode);
						}
						catch(Exception ee) {
							log(sessionId, "err", "editBonNode() EXCEPTION
putting node!:" + ee.getMessage());
						}
					} // else silently do nothing
				} // else silently do nothing
			}
			return retval;
		}
		/** Gets BonNode as an XML element in a string.
		  *
		  * @param nodeKey    NodeKey of node to edit
		  * @return String containing an XML element, or empty if no such node
		  */
		protected String getXmlNode(NodeKey nodeKey) {
			String xml = "";
			BonNode bonNode = getBonNode(nodeKey);
			if(bonNode != null) {
				String name = bonNode.nodeName;
				String attributes = bonNode.nodeAttributes;
				String content = bonNode.nodeContent;
				if (attributes != null && attributes.trim().length() > 0) {
					xml = xml + "<" + name + " " + attributes;
				}
```

```
                else {
                      xml = xml + "<" + name;
                }
                if (content != null && content.trim().length() > 0) {
                      xml = xml + ">" + content + "<\\" + name + ">";
                }
                else {
                      xml = xml + "\\>";
                }
          }
          return xml;
    }
    /** Helps with debugging <b>only</b>, applying <value>getXMLNode</value> to
all elements.
      *
      * @return String containing entire ForestHashtable as XML elements
      */
    protected String getContent() {
          Enumeration ee = this.elements();
          String outString = "";
          while(ee.hasMoreElements()) {
                BonNode bonNode = (BonNode)ee.nextElement();
                NodeKey nodeKey = bonNode.nodeKey;
                outString = outString + this.getXmlNode(nodeKey);
          }
          return outString;
    }
    /** Returns a String containing all the trees in the ForestHashtable.
      * <pre>
      * NOTES: Depending on the application and its current state,
      *               that can be a large String object!
     *                More selectivity will be added later
     *                for extracting XML subsets from the entire content.
     *                This method assumes ForestHashtable includes
     *                zero or more well-formed XML SubTrees, or,
     *                more specifically, zero or more elements each
     *                either a leaf node, or else       the root of a
     *                well-formed tree of elements.
     * </pre>
      * @return String containing all the trees in the ForestHashtable.
     */
    protected String getXMLTrees() {
          BonNode bonNode;
          String xml = "";
          long elementCount;
          String nameRootNode = "";
          String nameChildOfRootNode = "";
          String name = "";
          String attributes = "";
          String content = "";
          synchronized(this) {
```

```
                        elementCount = unFlagAllFlaggedElements();  // unhide all hidden
elements
                        Enumeration enumerationRN = this.elements();
                        lastRootNodeFound = false;
                        while (!lastRootNodeFound) {
                            bonNode = getNextRootNode(enumerationRN);
                            if (bonNode == null) {
                                lastRootNodeFound = true;
                                break;
                            }
                            name = bonNode.nodeName;
                            nameRootNode = name;
                            attributes = bonNode.nodeAttributes;
                            content = bonNode.nodeContent;
                            // OUTPUT A ROOTNODE
                            if (attributes != null && attributes.trim().length() > 0)
{
                                xml = xml + "<" + name + " " + attributes;
                            }
                            else {
                                xml = xml + "<" + name;
                            }
                            if (content != null && content.trim().length() > 0) {
                                xml = xml + ">" + content;
                            }
                            else {
                                xml = xml + ">";
                            }
                            Enumeration enumerationCRN = this.elements();
                            lastChildOfRootNodeFound = false;
                            while (!lastChildOfRootNodeFound) {
                                bonNode = getNextChildOfRootNode(enumerationCRN);
                                if (bonNode == null) {
                                    lastChildOfRootNodeFound = true;
                                    break;
                                }
                                name = bonNode.nodeName;
                                nameChildOfRootNode = name;
                                attributes = bonNode.nodeAttributes;
                                content = bonNode.nodeContent;
                                // OUTPUT A CHILD OF A ROOTNODE
                                if (attributes != null && attributes.trim().length()
> 0) {
                                    xml = xml + "<" + name + " " + attributes;
                                }
                                else {
                                    xml = xml + "<" + name;
                                }
                                if (content != null && content.trim().length() > 0)
{
                                    xml = xml + ">" + content;
```

```
                                    }
                                    else {
                                        xml = xml + ">";
                                    }
                                    xml = getNextChildOfNonRootNodeRecursively(xml,
bonNode.nodeKey);
                                    xml = xml + "</" + nameChildOfRootNode + ">";
                                }
                                xml = xml + "</" + nameRootNode + ">";
                            }
                            elementCount = unFlagAllFlaggedElements();  // unhide all hidden
elements
                        }
                        return xml;
                    }
                    /** Makes <value>flagged</value> member false for all BonNodes.
                      *
                      * @return long count of all BonNodes
                      */
                    private long unFlagAllFlaggedElements() {
                        Enumeration enumerationALL;
                        BonNode bonNodeALL = null;
                        NodeKey nodeKeyALL = null;
                        long count = 0;
                        boolean foundNextRootNode;
                        foundNextRootNode = false;
                        enumerationALL = this.elements();
                        while(enumerationALL.hasMoreElements()) {
                            bonNodeALL = (BonNode)enumerationALL.nextElement();
                            nodeKeyALL = bonNodeALL.nodeKey;
                            if(nodeKeyALL != null) {
                                count++;
                                bonNodeALL.flagged = false;  // unhide each node, so we
can find it
                            }
                        }
                        return count;
                    }
                    /** Gets next root node in an enumeration of BonNode instances.
                      *  Sets its <value>flagged</value> member true so it will not be found
again.
                      *  Keeps its nodeKey.aKey in <value>currentRootNodeAKey</value>,
                      *  Keeps its nodeKey.bKey in <value>currentRootNodeBKey</value>,
                      *  Keeps its nodeKey.cKey in <value>currentRootNodeCKey</value>.
                      *
                      * @param enumerationRN Enumeration of nodes
                      * @return BonNode next root node in <value>enumerationRN</value> or null
                      */
                    protected BonNode getNextRootNode(Enumeration enumerationRN) {
                        // NOTE: This process is an extremely inefficient simulation for
database model!
```

```
            BonNode bonNodeRN = null;
            NodeKey nodeKeyRN = null;
            boolean foundNextRootNode;
            foundNextRootNode = false;
            while(enumerationRN.hasMoreElements()) {
                  bonNodeRN = (BonNode)enumerationRN.nextElement();
                  nodeKeyRN = bonNodeRN.nodeKey;
                  // this is a test for a root node
                  if((!bonNodeRN.flagged)
&&(nodeKeyRN.aKey.equals(nodeKeyRN.bKey)) &&
(nodeKeyRN.bKey.equals(nodeKeyRN.cKey))) {
                        foundNextRootNode = true;
                        bonNodeRN.flagged = true;  // hide this node, so we get it
only once
                        if(nodeKeyRN != null) {
                              currentRootNodeAKey = nodeKeyRN.aKey;
                              currentRootNodeBKey = nodeKeyRN.bKey;
                              currentRootNodeCKey = nodeKeyRN.cKey; // not needed,
just for debugging
                        }
                        break;
                  }
            }
            if (!foundNextRootNode) {
                  lastRootNodeFound = true;
                  bonNodeRN =  null;
            }
            return bonNodeRN;
      }
      /** Gets next child-of-root node in an enumeration of BonNode instances.
        *  Sets its <value>flagged</value> member true so it will not be found
again,
        *  Keeps its nodeKey.aKey in <value>currentChildOfRootNodeAKey</value>,
        *  Keeps its nodeKey.bKey in <value>currentChildOfRootNodeBKey</value>,
        *  Keeps its nodeKey.cKey in <value>currentChildOfRootNodeCKey</value>.
        *
        * @param enumerationCRN Enumeration of nodes
        * @return BonNode next child-of-root node in <value>enumerationCRN</value>
or null
        */
      protected BonNode getNextChildOfRootNode(Enumeration enumerationCRN) {
          // NOTE: This process is an extremely inefficient simulation for
database model!
            BonNode bonNodeCRN =  null;
            NodeKey nodeKeyCRN = null;
            boolean foundNextChildOfRootNode;
            foundNextChildOfRootNode = false;
            while(enumerationCRN.hasMoreElements()) {
                  bonNodeCRN = (BonNode)enumerationCRN.nextElement();
                  nodeKeyCRN = bonNodeCRN.nodeKey;
                  // this is a test for child of current root node
```

```
                    if((!bonNodeCRN.flagged) && (nodeKeyCRN.aKey != nodeKeyCRN.bKey)
&& (nodeKeyCRN.bKey == currentRootNodeAKey) && (nodeKeyCRN.cKey ==
currentRootNodeBKey)) {
                         foundNextChildOfRootNode = true;
                         bonNodeCRN.flagged = true;  // hide this node, so we get
it only once
                         if(nodeKeyCRN != null) {
                              currentChildOfRootNodeAKey = nodeKeyCRN.aKey;
                              currentChildOfRootNodeBKey = nodeKeyCRN.bKey;
                              currentChildOfRootNodeCKey = nodeKeyCRN.cKey; // for
debug only
                         }
                         break;
                    }
               }
               if (!foundNextChildOfRootNode) {
                    lastChildOfRootNodeFound = true;
                    bonNodeCRN =  null;
               }
               return bonNodeCRN;
          }
          /** Gets all descendants of a non-root node as one XML string.
            *     Applies <value>getNextChildOfNonRootNode</value> recursively.
            *
            * @param xml                         String that accumulates resulting
elements expressed in XML
            * @param nonRootNodeKey       NodeKey of non-root node whose descendants are
to be found
            * @return String that accumulated resulting elements expressed in XML
          */
          protected String getNextChildOfNonRootNodeRecursively(String xml, NodeKey
nonRootNodeKey) {
               String nameChildOfNonRootNode;
               String name;
               String attributes;
               String content;
               boolean lastChildOfNonRootNodeFound;
               BonNode bonNode;
               nameChildOfNonRootNode = "";
               bonNode = null;
               Enumeration enumerationCNRN = this.elements();
               lastChildOfNonRootNodeFound = false;
               while (!(lastChildOfNonRootNodeFound)) {
                    bonNode = getNextChildOfNonRootNode(enumerationCNRN,
nonRootNodeKey);
                    if (bonNode == null) {
                         lastChildOfNonRootNodeFound = true;
                         break;
                    }
                    name = bonNode.nodeName;
                    nameChildOfNonRootNode = name;
```

```
                    //log(sessionId, "", "Child of NonRoot: " + name);
                    attributes = bonNode.nodeAttributes;
                    content = bonNode.nodeContent;
                    // OUTPUT A CHILD OF A NON-ROOTNODE
                    if (attributes != null && attributes.trim().length() > 0) {
                         xml = xml + "<" + name + " " + attributes;
                    }
                    else {
                         xml = xml + "<" + name;
                    }
                    if (content != null && content.trim().length() > 0) {
                         xml = xml + ">" + content;
                    }
                    else {
                         xml = xml + ">";
                    }
                    xml = getNextChildOfNonRootNodeRecursively(xml,
bonNode.nodeKey);
                    xml = xml + "</" + nameChildOfNonRootNode + ">";
               }
               return xml;
          }
          /** Gets next child-of-non-root node in an enumeration of BonNode instances.
            *  Sets its <value>flagged</value> member true so it will not be found
again.
            *
            * @param enumerationCNRN    Enumeration of nodes
            * @param nonRootNodeKey     NodeKey of non-root node whose descendants are
to be found
            * @return BonNode next child-of-non-root node in
            * <value>enumerationCNRN</value> or null
          */
          protected BonNode getNextChildOfNonRootNode(Enumeration enumerationCNRN,
NodeKey nonRootNodeKey) {
               // NOTE: This process is an extremely inefficient simulation for
database model!
               BonNode bonNodeCNRN =  null;
               NodeKey nodeKeyCNRN = null;
               boolean foundNextChildOfNonRootNode;
               foundNextChildOfNonRootNode = false;
               while(enumerationCNRN.hasMoreElements()) {
                    bonNodeCNRN = (BonNode)enumerationCNRN.nextElement();
                    nodeKeyCNRN = bonNodeCNRN.nodeKey;
                    // this is a compound test for child of current non-root node
                    String currentChildOfNonRootNodeAKey = nonRootNodeKey.aKey;
                    String currentChildOfNonRootNodeBKey = nonRootNodeKey.bKey;
                    String currentChildOfNonRootNodeCKey = nonRootNodeKey.cKey;
                    boolean isChildOfNonRootNode;
                    isChildOfNonRootNode = false;
                    if(currentChildOfNonRootNodeAKey != null &&
currentChildOfNonRootNodeAKey.length() < 1) {  // then this is grandchild of a
```

```
root node
                        if((!bonNodeCNRN.flagged) && (nodeKeyCNRN.bKey ==
currentChildOfRootNodeAKey) && (nodeKeyCNRN.cKey == currentChildOfRootNodeBKey)) {
                            isChildOfNonRootNode = true;
                        }
                    }
                    else { // then this is great-grandchild or greater of a root
node
                        if((!bonNodeCNRN.flagged) && (nodeKeyCNRN.bKey ==
currentChildOfNonRootNodeAKey) && (nodeKeyCNRN.cKey ==
currentChildOfNonRootNodeBKey)) {
                            isChildOfNonRootNode = true;
                        }
                    }
                    if (isChildOfNonRootNode) {
                        foundNextChildOfNonRootNode = true;
                        bonNodeCNRN.flagged = true;  // hide this node, so we get
it only once
                        if(nodeKeyCNRN != null) {
                            currentChildOfNonRootNodeAKey = nodeKeyCNRN.aKey;
                            currentChildOfNonRootNodeBKey = nodeKeyCNRN.bKey;
                            // not needed, just for debugging
                            currentChildOfNonRootNodeCKey = nodeKeyCNRN.cKey;
                        }
                        break;
                    }
                }
                if (!foundNextChildOfNonRootNode) {
                    bonNodeCNRN = null;
                }
                return bonNodeCNRN;
        }
}
/** NodeNameHashtable only wraps java.util.Hashtable for access from JSP Custom
tag.
  * @author      Westy Rockwell (wrockwell@tarent.de)
  * @version     0.2
  */
class NodeNameHashtable extends java.util.Hashtable {
    // wrapped just for access from a tag
}

/** PathNameHashtable only wraps java.util.Hashtable for access from JSP Custom
tag.
  * @author      Westy Rockwell (wrockwell@tarent.de)
  * @version     0.2
  */
class PathNameHashtable extends java.util.Hashtable {
    // wrapped just for access from a tag
}
```

C.23 Filename: Projects\bonForum\src\de\tarent\forum\NodeKey.java

```
package de.tarent.forum;
/*<Imports>*/
import java.io.*;
/*</Imports>*/
/** NodeKey implements a three-part key in a ForestHashtable.
 * <pre>
 *    String aKey;
 *    String bKey;
 *    String cKey;
 * /<pre>
 * Note that in new NodeKey, no null xKey parts exist,
 * but any xKey can be set to null later.
 * Note also that toString returns:
 * <pre>
 * a ¦ a.b ¦ a.b.c ¦ .b ¦ .b.c ¦ a..c ¦ ..c
 * (where a, b, c can be null in toString return value,
 * but no trailing dots are allowed).
 * /<pre>
 * That allows using NodeKey for a.b.c and a.b type keys,
 * while still allowing partially filled keys to be used.
 *
 * <p>For further information visit the open source
 * <A HREF="http://www.bonForum.org">BonForum Project on SourceForge</A>
 * @author <A HREF="mailto://email@bonforum.org">Westy Rockwell</A>
 */
public class NodeKey{
      String aKey;
      String bKey;
      String cKey;
      /** Constructs a NodeKey.
       *  Sets aKey, bKey, cKey to empty strings.
       *
       */
      public NodeKey() {
            this.aKey = "";
            this.bKey = "";
            this.cKey = "";
      }
      /** Converts a NodeKey to a String.
       *  See doc comments for NodeKey class for details.
       *
       */
      public String toString() {
            String key = this.aKey + "." + this.bKey + "." + this.cKey;
            if(key.equals("..")) {
                  return("");
            }
```

```
            while(key.lastIndexOf(".") == key.length() - 1) {
                  key = key.substring(0, key.length() - 1);
            }
            return key;
      }
}
```

C.24 Filename: Projects\bonForum\src\de\tarent\forum\OutputChatMessages.java

```
package de.tarent.forum;
/*<Imports>*/
import java.util.*;
import javax.servlet.jsp.*;
import javax.servlet.jsp.tagext.*;
/*</Imports>*/
/** Outputs chat messages from a bonForum XML Document or ForestHashtable.
 * It has four attributes as follows:<p>
 * <OL>
 *    <LI> command    String ("bonForumXML" or "bonBufferXML", more to follow)
 *    <LI> attr1  String (reserved argument, available)
 *    <LI> attr2  String (reserved argument, available)
 *    <LI> attr3  String (reserved argument, available)
 * </OL>
 * <p>
 * Here are some notes about its use:
 * <OL>
 *    <LI> puts results into "option" scripting variable
 *    <LI> XML doc not yet implemented! Use forum or buffer only.
 *    <LI> attrN will later select chat messages by actor, date, etc.
 * </OL>
 * <p>For further information visit the open source
 * <A HREF="http://www.bonForum.org">BonForum Project on SourceForge</A>
 * @author <A HREF="mailto://email@bonforum.org">Westy Rockwell</A>
 */
 public class OutputChatMessagesTag
    extends BodyTagSupport
{
    TreeMap outputTable = null;
    Iterator iterator = null;
    private static BonForumStore bonForumStore = null;
    private static boolean loggingInitialized = false;
    private static BonLogger logOCMT = null;
    private static String logging = null;
    private String command = "";
    private String attr1 = "";
    private String attr2 = "";
    private String attr3 = "";
    private void log( String where, String what ) {
```

```
        if( logging != null ) {
            logOCMT.logWrite( System.currentTimeMillis( ), pageContext.getSession(
).getId( ), where, what );
        }
    }
    /** locates the BonForumStore instance for application
     */
    private void findBonForumStore( ) {
        if( bonForumStore == null ) {
            if ( pageContext.getServletContext( ).getAttribute( "bonForumStore" )
!= null ) {
                bonForumStore = ( BonForumStore )( pageContext.getServletContext(
).getAttribute( "bonForumStore" ) );
            }
            else {
                log( "err",  "ERROR? OutputChatMessagesTag DID NOT GET
bonForumStore." );
                log( "err", "pageContext.getSession( ).getId( ):" +
pageContext.getSession( ).getId( ) );
            }
        }
    }
    /** Sets value of the <code>command</code> attribute; also initializes
logging.
     *
     * @param value         string to which <code>command</code> attribute is
set
     */
    public void setCommand( String value ) {
        if( !loggingInitialized ) {
            logging = pageContext.getServletContext( ).getInitParameter( "Logging"
);
            logOCMT = new BonLogger( "OutputChatMessagesTagLog.txt", logging );
            loggingInitialized = true;
            System.err.println( "OutputChatMessagesTag init logging:" + logging );
        }
        if ( value.equals( null ) ) {
            value = "bonForumXML";
        }
        command = value;
    }
    /** Sets value of the <code>attr1</code> attribute.
     *
     * @param value         string to which <code>attr1</code> attribute is set
     */
    public void setAttr1( String value ) {
        if( value.equals( null ) ) {
            value = "";
        }
        attr1 = value;
    }
```

```
    /** Sets value of the <code>attr2</code> attribute.
      *
      * @param value          string to which <code>attr2</code> attribute is set
      */
    public void setAttr2( String value ) {
        if( value.equals( null ) ) {
            value = "";
        }
        attr2 = value;
    }
    /** Sets value of the <code>attr3</code> attribute.
      *
      * @param value          string to which <code>attr3</code> attribute is set
      */
    public void setAttr3( String value ) {
        if( value.equals( null ) ) {
            value = "";
        }
        attr3 = value;
    }
    /** Makes sure the body of the tag is evaluated.
      *
      * @returns EVAL_BODY_TAG          constant that causes tag body to be
evaluated
      * @throws JspException
      */
    public int doStartTag( ) throws JspException {
        return EVAL_BODY_TAG;
    }
    /** Initial tag body evaluation.
      * @throws JspException
      */
    public void doInitBody( ) throws JspException, JspTagException {
        findBonForumStore( );
        if( bonForumStore != null ) {
            try {
                outputTable = new TreeMap( bonForumStore.outputForumChatMessages(
command, attr1, attr2, attr3, pageContext.getSession( ) ) );
                if ( outputTable != null ) {
                    iterator = outputTable.values( ).iterator( );
                    if( iterator.hasNext( ) ) {
                        pageContext.setAttribute( "output", ( String
)iterator.next( ) );
                    }
                }
            } catch ( Exception ex ) {
                log( "err",  "caught Exception in OutputChatMessagesTag
doInitBody" );
                throw new JspTagException( "caught Exception in
OutputChatMessagesTag doInitBody" );
            }
```

```
        }
    }
    /** Iterates outputTable into "output" page attribute until done.
        *
        * @returns EVAL_BODY_TAG            constant that causes tag body to be
evaluated
        * @returns SKIP_BODY                constant that causes tag body to NOT be
evaluated (again)
        * @throws JspException
        */
    public int doAfterBody( ) throws JspException, JspTagException {
        if( bonForumStore != null && outputTable != null && iterator != null ) {
            try {
                if( iterator.hasNext( ) ) {
                    pageContext.setAttribute( "output", ( String )iterator.next( )
);
                    return EVAL_BODY_TAG;
                } else {
                    bodyContent.writeOut( bodyContent.getEnclosingWriter( ) );
                    return SKIP_BODY;
                }
            } catch ( java.io.IOException ex ) {
                log( "err",  "caught IOException in OutputChatMessagesTag
doAfterBody" );
                throw new JspTagException( "caught IOException in
OutputChatMessagesTag doAfterBody" );
            }
        }
        else {
            log( "err",  "ERROR: OutputChatMessagesTag doAfterBody no store ¦ no
table ¦ no iterator" );
            return SKIP_BODY;
        }
    }
}
```

C.24 Filename: Projects\bonForum\src\de\tarent\forum\OutputDebugInfoTag.java

```
package de.tarent.forum;
/*<Imports>*/
import java.util.*;
import javax.servlet.http.*;
import javax.servlet.jsp.*;
import javax.servlet.jsp.tagext.*;
/*</Imports>*/
/** OutputDebugInfoTag is JSP tag class to dump
```

```
 * debugging info into HTML output.
 * It has two attributes named "type" and "force".
 * Usage:<p>
 * <pre>
 * <bon:outputDebugInfo type="init"/>
 * <bon:outputDebugInfo type="init" force="yes"/>
 * <bon:outputDebugInfo force="yes"/>
 * <bon:outputDebugInfo/>
 * </pre><p>
 * The type attribute is not required except as follows:<p>
 * <OL>
 *    <LI> type="init"type="init" turns tags "on" for entire session,
 *  if a request parameter exists called "output_debug_info"
 *  that is equal to "yes".  Afterwards, a tag but no attribute
 *  is required to output debug info on page.
 *    <LI> type="init" turns tags "off", if no request parameter
 *  exists named "output_debug_info" that is equal to "yes".
 *    <LI> force="yes" turns that tag on only (can use on same page
 *  that sends request parameter output_debug_info="yes", or
 *  anywhere to use tag without tags being "on".)
 *    <LI> not force="yes" tags must be "on" for that tag to dump.
 * </OL>
 * <p>
 * <p>For further information visit the open source
 * <A HREF="http://www.bonForum.org">BonForum Project on SourceForge</A>
 * @author <A HREF="mailto://email@bonforum.org">Westy Rockwell</A>
 */
public class OutputDebugInfoTag extends BodyTagSupport
{
    private static BonLogger logODI = null;
    private static boolean loggingInitialized = false;
    private static String logging = null;
    private String type="";
    private String force="";
    private void log(String where, String what) {
        if(logging != null) {
            logODI.logWrite( System.currentTimeMillis( ), pageContext.getSession(
).getId( ), where, what );
        }
    }
    /** Sets value of the <code>type</code> attribute.
      * Currently, only "init" is available, turns tags on for session
      * if request parameter output_debug_info="yes", off otherwise.
      * First time called, sets up logger, using webapp context init param
      *
      * @param value    string to which <code>type</code> attribute is set
      */
    public void setType(String value) {
        if(!loggingInitialized) {
            logging = pageContext.getServletContext().getInitParameter("Logging");
            logODI = new BonLogger("OutputDebugInfoTagLog.txt", logging);
```

```
            loggingInitialized = true;
            System.err.println("OutputDebugInfoTag init logging:" + logging);
        }
        if (value.equals(null)) {
            value = "";
        }
        type = value;
    }
    /** Sets value of the <code>force</code> attribute.
      * Currently, only "yes" is available, outputs on page now
      *
      * @param value           string to which <code>force</code> attribute is set
      */
    public void setForce(String value) {
        if (value.equals(null)) {
            value = "";
        }
        force = value;
    }
    /** Sets "output_debug_info" request parameter value to session attribute
      * of the same name,  to switch the tag output on and off.
      * Also, forces tag body evaluation to happen
      *
      * @returns EVAL_BODY_TAG      constant that causes tag body to be evaluated
      */
    public int doStartTag() throws JspException {
        if(type.equals("init")) {
            if(pageContext.getRequest().getParameter(
                    "output_debug_info") != null) {
                if(((String)(pageContext.getRequest().getParameter(
                        "output_debug_info"))).equals("yes")
                  ) {
                    pageContext.setAttribute(
                        "output_debug_info", "yes", 4);
                        // 4 is application scope
                }
            }
            else {
                pageContext.setAttribute(
                    "output_debug_info", "no", 4);
            }
        }
        if(force.equals("yes")) {
            return EVAL_BODY_TAG;
        }
        if(pageContext.getAttribute(
                "output_debug_info", 4) != null) {
            if(((String)(pageContext.getAttribute(
                    "output_debug_info", 4))).equals("yes")) {
                return EVAL_BODY_TAG;
            }
```

```
        }
        return SKIP_BODY;
    }
    /** Outputs values of headers, parameters, attributes, etc. and ends tag
processing.
     *
     * @returns SKIP_BODY             constant that causes tag body to NOT be
evaluated (again)
     */
    public int doAfterBody() throws JspException, JspTagException {
        try {
            HttpServletRequest req =
                (HttpServletRequest)pageContext.getRequest();
            bodyContent.println("<H4>Request Headers: </H4>");
            Enumeration eh = req.getHeaderNames();
            while (eh.hasMoreElements()) {
                String name = (String)eh.nextElement();
                String value = (String)req.getHeader(name);
                bodyContent.println("\t<li>" + normalize(name) + " = " +
                    normalize(value) + "</li>");
            }
            bodyContent.println("<H4>Request Parameters: </H4>");
            Enumeration ep = req.getParameterNames();
            while(ep.hasMoreElements()) {
                    String name = (String)ep.nextElement();
                    String value = (String)req.getParameter(name);
                    bodyContent.println("\t<li>" + normalize(name) + " = " +
                        normalize(value) + "</li>");
            }
            bodyContent.println("<H4>Application Initialization Parameters:
</H4>");
            Enumeration eip =
pageContext.getServletContext().getInitParameterNames();
            while(eip.hasMoreElements()) {
                    String name = (String)eip.nextElement();
                    String value =

(String)pageContext.getServletContext().getInitParameter(name);
                    bodyContent.println("\t<li>" + normalize(name) + " = " +
                        normalize(value) + "</li>");

            }
            int scope;
            String title = null;
            for(scope = 4; scope >= 1; scope—) {
                switch(scope) {
                case 1:
                    title = "Page Attributes:";
                    break;
                case 2:
                    title = "Request Attributes:";
                    break;
```

```
                case 3:
                    title = "Session Attributes:";
                    break;
                case 4:
                    title = "Application Attributes:";
                    break;
                }
                bodyContent.println("<H4>" + title + "</H4>");
                Enumeration ea = pageContext.getAttributeNamesInScope(scope);
                    while(ea.hasMoreElements()) {
                        String name = (String)ea.nextElement();
                        String value =
                            (String)pageContext.getAttribute(
                                name, scope).toString();
                        bodyContent.println(
                            "\t<li>" + normalize(name) + " = " +
                            normalize(value) + "</li>");
                    }
            }
            bodyContent.writeOut(bodyContent.getEnclosingWriter());
            return SKIP_BODY;
        }
        catch(java.io.IOException ex) {
            log("err",  "OutputDebugInfoTag doInitBody caught IOException");
            throw new JspTagException("OutputDebugInfoTag doInitBody caught
IOException");
        }
    }
      /* Code below here is based on Apache Software Foundation samples
      */
    /** Normalizes the given string, replacing chars with entities.
      * (less than, greater than, ampersand, double quote, return and linefeed).
      * NOTE: replaces null string with empty string.
      *
      * @param s String
      * @return normalized string (not null)
      */
    protected String normalize(String s) {
        StringBuffer str = new StringBuffer();
        str.append("");
        int len = (s != null) ? s.length() : 0;
        for (int i = 0; i < len; i++) {
            char ch = s.charAt(i);
            switch (ch) {
                case '<': {
                    str.append("&lt;");
                    break;
                }
                case '>': {
                    str.append("&gt;");
                    break;
```

```
                }
                case '&': {
                    str.append("&amp;");
                    break;
                }
                case '"': {
                    str.append("&quot;");
                    break;
                }
                case '\r':
                case '\n': {
                    str.append("&#");
                    str.append(Integer.toString(ch));
                    str.append(';');
                    break;
                }
                default: {
                    str.append(ch);
                }
            }
        }
        return str.toString();
    }
}
```

C.25 Filename: Projects\bonForum\src\de\tarent\forum\OutputPathNamesTag.java

```
package de.tarent.forum;
/*<Imports>*/
import java.util.*;
import javax.servlet.jsp.*;
import javax.servlet.jsp.tagext.*;
/*</Imports>*/
/** Outputs pathNames from subTree of an XML tree or forest (except chatItems!).
<br>
 * It has four attributes as follows: <p>
 * <OL>
 *     <LI> docName is XML doc or ForestHashtable name ("bonForumXML" or
"bonBufferXML").
 *     <LI> pathToSubTreeRootNode selects starting node in XML or forest
("bonForum.things.subjects").
 *     <LI> ancestorReplacer [future] replaces all but last nodeName (*, nbsp, tab,
etc. in string).
 *     <LI> nodeSeparator [future] is separator char between node names (defaults
to "_").
 * </OL>
 * <p>The following notes apply to its use:
 * <OL>
```

```
 *    <LI> XML doc not yet implemented! Use forum or buffer only.
 *    <LI> chatItem nodes in bonForumXML are ignored and not output!
 * </OL>
 * <p>For further information visit the open source
 * <A HREF="http://www.bonForum.org">BonForum Project on SourceForge</A>
 * @author <A HREF="mailto://email@bonforum.org">Westy Rockwell</A>
 */
public class OutputPathNamesTag extends BodyTagSupport
{
    TreeMap outputTable = null;
    Iterator iterator = null;
    private static BonForumStore bonForumStore = null;
    private static BonLogger logOPNT = null;
    private static boolean loggingInitialized = false;
    private static String logging = null;
    private String docName = "";
    private String pathToSubTreeRootNode = "";
    private String ancestorReplacer = "";
    private String nodeSeparator = "";
    private void log( String where, String what ) {
        if( logging != null ) {
            logOPNT.logWrite( System.currentTimeMillis( ), pageContext.getSession(
).getId( ), where, what );
        }
    }
    /** locates the BonForumStore instance for application
     */
    private void findBonForumStore( ) {
        if( bonForumStore == null ) {
            if ( pageContext.getServletContext( ).getAttribute( "bonForumStore" )
!= null ) {
                bonForumStore = ( BonForumStore )( pageContext.getServletContext(
).getAttribute( "bonForumStore" ) );
            }
            else {
                log( "err",  "ERROR? OutputPathNamesTag DID NOT GET
bonForumStore." );
                log( "err", "pageContext.getSession( ).getId( ):" +
pageContext.getSession( ).getId( ) );
            }
        }
    }
    /** Sets value of the <code>docName</code> attribute; also initializes
logging.
      *
      * @param value          string to which <code>docName</code> attribute is
set
      */
    public void setDocName( String value ) {
        if( !loggingInitialized ) {
            logging = pageContext.getServletContext( ).getInitParameter( "Logging"
```

```
);
            logOPNT = new BonLogger( "OutputPathNamesTagLog.txt", logging );
            loggingInitialized = true;
            System.err.println( "OutputPathNamesTag init logging:" + logging );
        }
        if ( value.equals( null ) ) {
            value = "bonForumXML";
        }
        docName = value;
    }
    /** Sets value of the <code>pathToSubTreeRootNode</code> attribute.
        *
        * @param value          string to which <code>pathToSubTreeRootNode</code>
attribute is set
        */
    public void setPathToSubTreeRootNode( String value ) {
        if( value.equals( null ) ) {
            value = "";
        }
        pathToSubTreeRootNode = value;
    }
    /** Sets value of the <code>ancestorReplacer</code> attribute.
        *
        * @param value          string to which <code>ancestorReplacer</code>
attribute is set
        */
    public void setAncestorReplacer( String value ) {
        if( value.equals( null ) ) {
            value = "";
        }
        ancestorReplacer = value;
    }
    /** Sets value of the <code>nodeSeparator</code> attribute.
        *
        * @param value          string to which <code>nodeSeparator</code> attribute
is set
        */
    public void setNodeSeparator( String value ) {
        if( value.equals( null ) ){
            value = "";
        }
        nodeSeparator = value;
    }
    /** Makes sure the body of the tag is evaluated.
        *
        * @returns EVAL_BODY_TAG          constant that causes tag body to be
evaluated
        */
    public int doStartTag( ) throws JspException {
        return EVAL_BODY_TAG;
    }
```

```
    /** Gets bonforumStore, and outputTable with pathnames;
      * gets iterator.and outputs first pathname.
      */
    public void doInitBody( ) throws JspException, JspTagException {
        findBonForumStore( );
        if( bonForumStore != null ) {
            try {
                outputTable = new TreeMap( bonForumStore.outputForumPathNames(
docName, pathToSubTreeRootNode, ancestorReplacer, nodeSeparator ) );
                if ( outputTable != null ) {
                    // note that values iterator gives nodeKey.aKey for nodes, may
be useful to locate them
                    iterator = outputTable.keySet( ).iterator( );
                    if( iterator.hasNext( ) ) {
                        pageContext.setAttribute( "output", ( String
)iterator.next( ) );
                        // The rest of the Elements are set to output in
doAfterBody
                    }
                }
            } catch ( Exception ex ) {
                log( "err", "caught Exception in OutputPathNamesTag doInitBody"
);
                throw new JspTagException( "caught Exception in OutputPathNamesTag
doInitBody" );
            }
        }
    }
    /** Iterates outputTable into "output" page attribute until done.
      *
      * @returns EVAL_BODY_TAG           constant that causes tag body to be
evaluated
      * @returns SKIP_BODY               constant that causes tag body to NOT be
evaluated (again)
      */
    public int doAfterBody( ) throws JspException, JspTagException {
        if( bonForumStore != null && outputTable != null && iterator != null ) {
            try {
                if( iterator.hasNext( ) ) {
                    pageContext.setAttribute( "output", ( String )iterator.next( )
);
                    return EVAL_BODY_TAG;
                } else {
                    bodyContent.writeOut( bodyContent.getEnclosingWriter( ) );
                    return SKIP_BODY;
                }
            } catch ( java.io.IOException ex ) {
                log( "err", "caught IOException in OutputPathNamesTag
doAfterBody" );
                throw new JspTagException( "caught IOException in
OutputPathNamesTag doAfterBody" );
```

```
            }
        }
        else {
            //log( "",  "ERROR: OutputPathNamesTag doAfterBody no store ¦ no table
¦ no iterator" );
            return SKIP_BODY;
        }
    }
}
```

C.26 Filename: Projects\bonForum\src\de\tarent\forum\TransformTag.java

```
/*
  * Note: This class is based in part on the source code
  * provided with Jakarta Tomcat. The license for that source
  * code is either below (if this a file) or elsewhere in the
  * book (if this is printed in one).
  */
package de.tarent.forum;
/*<Imports>*/
import java.text.*;
import java.io.*;
import java.net.*;
import java.util.*;
import javax.servlet.jsp.*;
import javax.servlet.jsp.tagext.*;
/*</Imports>*/
/** TransformTag is a JSP custom tag class for XSLT processing.
 * It has four attributes named "type", "inXML", "inXSL" and "outDoc".
 * Use it as follows:<p>
 * <code>
 * &lt;bon:transform type=&quot;...&quot; inDoc=&quot;...&quot;
styleSheet=&quot;...&quot; outDoc=&quot;...&quot; />
 * </code><p>
 * <OL>
 *    <LI> The type attribute select the XSLT processor, and currently can
 * have three values: "Xalan Java 1", "Xalan Java 2", or "xalanVersion".
 * If type is "xalanVersion", the tag object looks for an application
 * attribute of the same name and uses its value to select processor.
 *    <LI> The inXML attribute can be a URI for an XML input source to XSLT.
 * Otherwise, it can be "bonForumXML" or "bonBufferXML" to use XML content
 * of the bonForum database object (currently a ForestHashtable).
 *    <LI> The inXSL attribute can be a URI for an XML input source to XSLT.
 * Otherwise it (will?) can be a string containing a valid XSL stylesheet.
 *    <LI> The outDoc attribute can be the URI of the file to write the output
 * of the XSLT process to. Otherwise, it can currently be set to either
 * "output" or "outputNormalized", in which case the output of the XSLT
 * process is put in a page attribute named "output", optionally normalized.
```

```
 * </OL>
 * <p>For further information visit the open source
 * <A HREF="http://www.bonForum.org">BonForum Project on SourceForge</A>
 * @author <A HREF="mailto://email@bonforum.org">Westy Rockwell</A>
 */
public class TransformTag extends BodyTagSupport
{
      private static BonForumStore bonForumStore;
      private static BonLogger logTT = null;
      private static boolean loggingInitialized = false;
      private static String logging = null;
      private String type = "";
      private String inXML = "";
      private String inXSL = "";
      private String outDoc = "";
      private void log( String where, String what ) {
            if(logging != null) {
                  logTT.logWrite(System.currentTimeMillis(),
pageContext.getSession().getId(), where, what);
            }
      }
      /** Locates the BonForumStore instance for application.
       */
      private void findBonForumStore( ) {
            if(bonForumStore == null) {
                  if
(pageContext.getServletContext().getAttribute("bonForumStore") != null) {
                        bonForumStore =
(BonForumStore)(pageContext.getServletContext().getAttribute("bonForumStore"));
                  }
                  else {
                        log("err", "TransformTag DID NOT GET bonForumStore.
Session ID:" + pageContext.getSession().getId());
                        // not a problem, as long as input is available to XSLT
                        // from file or string instead.
                  }
            }
      }
      /** Sets value of the <code>type</code> attribute to select an XSLT
processor.
        * Currently, three values: "Xalan Java 1", "Xalan Java 2", or
"xalanVersion".
        * If type is "xalanVersion", the tag object looks for an application
        * attribute of the same name and uses its value to select processor.
        *
        * @param value        String "Xalan-Java 1". "Xalan-Java 2" or
"xalanVersion".
        */
      public void setType( String value ) {
            if( !loggingInitialized ) {
                  logging = pageContext.getServletContext( ).getInitParameter(
```

```
"Logging" );
                    logTT = new BonLogger( "TransformTagLog.txt", logging );
                    loggingInitialized = true;
               }
               if( value.indexOf( "xalanVersion" ) > -1 ) {
                    try {
                         value = ( String )pageContext.getAttribute(
"xalanVersion", 4 ).toString( );  // 4 is application scope
                    }
                    catch( java.lang.NullPointerException ex ) {
                         value = "Xalan-Java 1";
                    }
               }
               if( value.equals( null ) ) {
                    value = "Xalan-Java 1";
               }
               type = value;
          }
     /** Sets <code>inXML</code> attribute value; determines input to XSLT
processing.
      * If inXML is "bonForumXML", will use contents of bonForum XML database.
        * If inXML is "bonBufferXML", will use contents of  XML buffer.
        * Otherwise, XSLT will assume inXML is a URI to an XML document.
        *
      * @param value             string to which <code>inXML</code> attribute is set.
      */
      public void setInXML( String value ) {
           inXML = value;
      }
     /** Sets <code>inXSL</code> attribute value; determines stylesheet to XSLT
processing.
      * The inXSL attribute can be a URI, or a complete XSL stylesheet in a
string.
      *
      * @param value             string to which <code>inXSL</code> attribute is set.
      */
      public void setInXSL( String value ) {
           inXSL = value;
      }
      /** Sets value of the <code>outDoc</code> attribute, determines output of
XSLT processing.
        * If outDoc is "output", result of XSLT process is put in "output" page
attribute.
        * If outDoc is "outputNormalized", same as "output" but result is
normalized.
        * If outDoc is "print", result of XSLT process is output in JSP out.
        * If outDoc is "printNormalized", same as "print" but result is
normalized.
        * OTW, XSLTResultTarget from a URI value.
        *
      * @param value            string to which <code>outDoc</code> attribute is set
```

```
	*/
	public void setOutDoc( String value ) {
		outDoc = value;
	}
    /** makes sure the body of the tag is evaluated
	 *
	 * @returns EVAL_BODY_TAG		constant that causes tag body to be
evaluated.
	 */
	public int doStartTag( ) throws JspException {
		return EVAL_BODY_TAG;
	}
	/** Apply XSLT transformation to XML with XSL stylesheet,
	 * input XML is from database or file, XSL is string or file,
	 * output document to browser, "output" page attribute, or file.
	 */
	public void doInitBody( ) throws JspException {
		if ( ( inXML != null ) && ( inXSL != null ) && ( outDoc != null ) ) {
			if( inXML.equals( "bonForumXML" ) ) {
				findBonForumStore( );
				if( bonForumStore != null ) {
					synchronized( bonForumStore ) {
						inXML = "<?xml version=\"1.0\" encoding=\"UTF-
8\"?>" + bonForumStore.getBonForumXML( ).getXMLTrees( );
					}
				}
			}
			else if( inXML.equals( "bonBufferXML" ) ) {
				findBonForumStore( );
				if( bonForumStore != null ) {
					synchronized( bonForumStore ) {
						inXML = "<?xml version=\"1.0\" encoding=\"UTF-
8\"?>" + bonForumStore. getBonBufferXML ( ).getXMLTrees( );
					}
				}
			}
			String param1 = ( String )pageContext.getSession(
).getAttribute( "param1" );
			if( param1 == null || param1.trim( ).length( ) < 1 ) {
				param1 = " ";
			}
			if( type.equals( "Xalan-Java 1" ) ) {
				try {
					synchronized( bonForumStore ) {
						Xalan1Transformer transformer = new
Xalan1Transformer( );
						if( outDoc.equals( "print" ) ) {
							bodyContent.println(
transformer.transform( inXML, inXSL, outDoc, param1 ) );
						}
						else if( outDoc.equals( "printNormalized" ) ) {
```

```
                                        bodyContent.println( normalize(
transformer.transform( inXML, inXSL, outDoc, param1 ) ) );
                                    }
                                    else if( outDoc.equals( "output" ) ) {
                                        pageContext.setAttribute( "output",
transformer.transform( inXML, inXSL, outDoc, param1 ) );
                                    }
                                    else if( outDoc.equals( "outputNormalized" ) )
{
                                        pageContext.setAttribute( "output",
normalize( transformer.transform( inXML, inXSL, outDoc, param1 ) ) );
                                    }
                                    else {
                                        transformer.transform( inXML, inXSL,
outDoc, param1 );
                                    }
                                }
                            }
                            catch ( Exception ex ) {
                                String mess = "Exception in TransformTag,
Xalan1Transformer process failed! \n" + ex.getMessage( );
                                log( "err", mess );
                                throw new JspException( mess );
                            }
                        }
                        else if ( type.equals( "Xalan-Java 2" ) ) {
                            try {
                                synchronized( bonForumStore ) {
                                    Xalan2Transformer transformer = new
Xalan2Transformer( );
                                    if( outDoc.equals( "print" ) ) {
                                        bodyContent.println(
transformer.transform( inXML, inXSL, outDoc, param1 ) );
                                    }
                                    else if( outDoc.equals( "printNormalized" ) )
{
                                        bodyContent.println( normalize(
transformer.transform( inXML, inXSL, outDoc, param1 ) ) );
                                    }
                                    else if( outDoc.equals( "output" ) ) {
                                        pageContext.setAttribute( "output",
transformer.transform( inXML, inXSL, outDoc, param1 ) );
                                    }
                                    else if( outDoc.equals( "outputNormalized" ) )
{
                                        pageContext.setAttribute( "output",
normalize( transformer.transform( inXML, inXSL, outDoc, param1 ) ) );
                                    }
                                    else {
                                        transformer.transform( inXML, inXSL,
outDoc, param1 );
```

```
                            }
                        }
                    }
                    catch ( Exception ex ) {
                        String mess = "Exception in TransformTag,
Xalan2Transformer process failed! \n" + ex.getMessage( );
                        log( "err", mess );
                        throw new JspException( mess );
                    }
                }
                else {
                    log( "err",  "Unsupported XSLT transformer type arg in
TransformTag!" );
                }
            }
            else {
                log( "err",  "Error: null arg( s ) in TransformTag!" );
            }
        }
        /** Puts XSLT results out to JSP, and ends processing.
          *
        * @returns EVAL_BODY_TAG           constant that causes tag body to be
evaluated.
        * @returns SKIP_BODY               constant that causes tag body to NOT be
evaluated (again).
        */
        public int doAfterBody( ) throws JspException {
            try {
                bodyContent.writeOut( bodyContent.getEnclosingWriter( ) );
                return SKIP_BODY;
            }
            catch ( Exception ex ) {
                String mess = "TransformTag doAfterBody caught Exception!" +
ex.getMessage( );
                log( "err", mess );
                throw new JspException( mess );
            }
        }
        /* Code below here is based on Apache Software Foundation samples.
        */
      /** Normalizes the given string, replacing chars with entities.
        * (less than, greater than, ampersand, double quote, return and linefeed).
        * NOTE: replaces null string with empty string.
        *
        * @param s String
        * @return normalized string (not null)
        */
        protected String normalize(String s) {
            StringBuffer str = new StringBuffer();
            str.append("");
            int len = (s != null) ? s.length() : 0;
```

```
            for (int i = 0; i < len; i++) {
                  char ch = s.charAt(i);
                  switch (ch) {
                        case '<': {
                              str.append("&lt;");
                              break;
                        }
                        case '>': {
                              str.append("&gt;");
                              break;
                        }
                        case '&': {
                              str.append("&amp;");
                              break;
                        }
                        case '"': {
                              str.append("&quot;");
                              break;
                        }
                        case '\r':
                        case '\n': {
                              str.append("&#");
                              str.append(Integer.toString(ch));
                              str.append(';');
                              break;
                        }
                        default: {
                              str.append(ch);
                        }
                  }
            }
            return str.toString();
      }
}
```

C.27 Filename: Projects\bonForum\src\de\tarent\forum\Xalan1Transformer.java

```
/*
 * Note: This class is based on example source code
 * provided with Apache Xalan-Java 1. The license for that source
 * code is either below (if this a file) or elsewhere in the
```

```
  * book (if this is printed in one).
  */
package de.tarent.forum;
/*<Imports>*/
import java.text.*;
import java.io.*;
import java.net.*;
import java.util.*;
import javax.servlet.jsp.*;
import javax.servlet.jsp.tagext.*;
import org.w3c.dom.*;
import org.xml.sax.*;
import org.apache.xerces.dom.*;
import org.apache.xerces.parsers.*;
import org.apache.xalan.xslt.*;
/*</Imports>*/
/** Xalan1Transformer is a class for XSLT processing using Xalan-Java 1.
 *
 * <p>For further information visit the open source
 * <A HREF="http://www.bonForum.org">BonForum Project on SourceForge</A>
 * @author <A HREF="mailto://email@bonforum.org">Westy Rockwell</A>
 */
public class Xalan1Transformer {
      /** XSLT of inXML to outDoc using inXSL stylesheet, with Xalan-Java 1.
       *
       * @param inXML  String: URL, or if begins as &quot;&lt;?xml&quot;, is XML
in a string.
       * @param inXSL String: URL, or XML string that contains
&quot;&lt;xsl:stylesheet&quot;.
       * @param outDoc String: &quot;print&quot;, &quot;printNormalized&quot;,
       * &quot;output&quot;, &quot;outputNormalized&quot;, or URL
       * <p>For further information visit the open source
       * <A HREF="http://www.bonForum.org">BonForum Project on SourceForge</A>
       * @author <A HREF="mailto://email@bonforum.org">Westy Rockwell</A>
       */
      public String transform(String inXML, String inXSL, String outDoc, String
param1)
      throws org.xml.sax.SAXException, Exception {
            XSLTProcessor processor = null;
            XSLTInputSource inputXML = null;
            XSLTInputSource inputXSL = null;
            XSLTResultTarget outputDoc = null;
            StringWriter stringWriter = null;
            try {
                  processor =
org.apache.xalan.xslt.XSLTProcessorFactory.getProcessor();
            }
            catch (org.xml.sax.SAXException ex) {
                  System.err.println("SAXException in Xalan1Transformer, cannot
create processor!");
                  throw ex;
```

```
          }
          try {
               // Set a param named "param1", that the stylesheet can obtain.
               processor.setStylesheetParam("param1",
processor.createXString(param1));
          }
          catch (Exception ex) {
               System.err.println("SAXException in Xalan1Transformer, cannot
set param1!");
               throw ex;
          }
          try {
               if(inXML.indexOf("<?xml") == 0) {
                    inputXML = new XSLTInputSource(new StringReader(inXML));
                    //System.out.println("StringReader to inputXML");
               }
               else {
                    inputXML = new XSLTInputSource(inXML);
               }
               if(inXSL.indexOf("<?xml") == 0) {
                    if(inXSL.indexOf("<xsl:stylesheet") > -1) {
                         inputXSL = new XSLTInputSource(new
StringReader(inXSL));
                    }
               }
               else {
                    inputXSL = new XSLTInputSource(inXSL);
               }
               if(outDoc.indexOf("output") == 0 || outDoc.indexOf("print") ==
0) {
                    stringWriter = new StringWriter();
                    outputDoc = new XSLTResultTarget(stringWriter);
               }
               else {
                    outputDoc = new XSLTResultTarget(outDoc);
               }
          }
          catch (Exception ex) {
               System.err.println("Exception in Xalan1Transformer, processor
prep failed!");
               throw ex;
          }
          try {
               //processor.reset();
               processor.process(inputXML, inputXSL, outputDoc);
               if(outDoc.indexOf("output") == 0 || outDoc.indexOf("print") ==
0) {
                    return outputDoc.getCharacterStream().toString();
               }
               else {
                    return null;
```

```
                    }
                }
                catch (org.xml.sax.SAXException ex) {
                    System.err.println("SAXException in Xalan1Transformer,
processing failed!");
                    throw ex;
                }
        }
}
```

C.28 Filename: Projects\bonForum\src\de\tarent\forum\Xalan2Transformer.java

```
/*
  * Note: This class is based on example source code
  * provided with Apache Xalan-Java 2. The license for that source
  * code is either below (if this a file) or elsewhere in the
  * book (if this is printed in one).
  */
package de.tarent.forum;
/*<Imports>*/
import java.text.*;
import java.io.*;
import java.net.*;
import java.util.*;
import javax.servlet.jsp.*;
import javax.servlet.jsp.tagext.*;
// Imported TraX classes
import javax.xml.transform.TransformerFactory;
import javax.xml.transform.Transformer;
import javax.xml.transform.stream.StreamSource;
import javax.xml.transform.stream.StreamResult;
import javax.xml.transform.TransformerException;
import javax.xml.transform.TransformerConfigurationException;
/*</Imports>*/
/** Xalan1Transformer is class for XSLT processing using Xalan-Java 2.
 *
 * <p>For further information visit the open source
 * <A HREF="http://www.bonForum.org">BonForum Project on SourceForge</A>
 * @author <A HREF="mailto://email@bonforum.org">Westy Rockwell</A>
 */
public class Xalan2Transformer {
      /** XSLT of inXML to outDoc using inXSL stylesheet, with Xalan-Java 2.
       *
       * @param inXML  String: URL, or if begins as &quot;&lt;?xml&quot;, is XML
in a string.
       * @param inXSL String: URL, or XML string that contains
&quot;&lt;xsl:stylesheet&quot;.
       * @param outDoc String: &quot;print&quot;, &quot;printNormalized&quot;,
```

```
     * &quot;output&quot;, &quot;outputNormalized&quot;, or URL
     * <p>For further information visit the open source
     * <A HREF="http://www.bonForum.org">BonForum Project on SourceForge</A>
     * @author <A HREF="mailto://email@bonforum.org">Westy Rockwell</A>
     */
    public String transform(String inXML, String inXSL, String outDoc, String
param1)
    throws TransformerException,
            TransformerConfigurationException,
            FileNotFoundException,
            IOException {
        String output = "";
        try {
            TransformerFactory factory = TransformerFactory.newInstance();
            Transformer transformer = null;
            if(inXSL.indexOf("<?xml") == 0) {
                if(inXSL.indexOf("<xsl:stylesheet") > -1) {
                    transformer = factory.newTransformer(
                                                        new
StreamSource(new StringReader(inXSL)));
                    transformer.setParameter("param1", param1);
                }
                System.err.println("ERROR: Xalan2Transformer No stylesheet
for inputXSL, thus no transformer!");
            }
            else {
                transformer = factory.newTransformer(new
StreamSource(inXSL));
              transformer.setParameter("param1", param1);
            }
            StreamSource inputXML = null;
            if(inXML.indexOf("<?xml") == 0) {
                inputXML = new StreamSource(new StringReader(inXML));
            }
            else {
                inputXML = new StreamSource(inXML);
            }
            StreamResult outputDoc = null;
            if(outDoc.indexOf("output") == 0 || outDoc.indexOf("print") ==
0) {
                outputDoc = new StreamResult(new StringWriter());
            }
            else {
                outputDoc = new StreamResult(new
FileOutputStream(outDoc));
            }
            transformer.transform(inputXML, outputDoc);
            if(outDoc.indexOf("output") == 0 || outDoc.indexOf("print") ==
0) {
                return outputDoc.getWriter().toString();
            }
```

```
                    else {
                        return null;
                    }
                }
                catch (TransformerConfigurationException ex) {
                    System.err.println("Xalan2Transformer transform caught
TransformerConfigurationException");
                    throw ex;
                }
                catch (TransformerException ex) {
                    System.err.println("Xalan2Transformer transform caught
TransformerException");
                    throw ex;
                }
                catch (FileNotFoundException ex) {
                    System.err.println("Xalan2Transformer transform caught
FileNotFoundException");
                    throw ex;
                }
                catch (IOException ex) {
                    System.err.println("Xalan2Transformer transform caught
IOException");
                    throw ex;
                }
        }
}
```

C.29 Filename: TOMCAT_HOME\webapps\bonForum\jsp\forum\actor_leaves_frameset_robot.jsp

```
<!doctype html public "-//w3c//dtd html 4.0 transitional//en">
<%@ taglib uri="http://www.bonForum.org/taglib/bonForum-taglib"
prefix="bon" %>
<%@ page errorPage="forum_error.jsp" %>
<html>
      <head>
            <meta http-equiv="Content-Type"
                  content="text/html;
                  charset=x-user-defined">
            </meta>
            <title>
                  bonForum
            </title>
      </head>
      <body bgcolor="#00FFFF">
      <%
      String target = (String)request.getAttribute("target");
```

```
      String document = (String)request.getAttribute("document");
      String refresh = (String)request.getAttribute("refresh");
      String increment = (String)request.getAttribute("increment");
      String limit = (String)request.getAttribute("limit");
      String message = (String)request.getAttribute("message");
      %>
      <%— message "debug" shows some info —%>
      <jsp:plugin type="applet" code="BonForumRobot.class"
            codebase="/bonForum/jsp/forum/applet"
            jreversion="1.3.0" width="0" height="0" >
        <jsp:params>
        <jsp:param name="target" value="<%=target%>"/>
        <jsp:param name="document" value="<%=document%>"/>
        <jsp:param name="refresh" value="<%=refresh%>"/>
        <jsp:param name="increment" value="<%=increment%>"/>
        <jsp:param name="limit" value="<%=limit%>"/>
        <jsp:param name="message" value="<%=message%>"/>
        </jsp:params>
        <jsp:fallback>Plugin tag OBJECT or EMBED
        not supported by browser.
        </jsp:fallback>
      </jsp:plugin>
      </body>
</html>
```

C.30 Filename: TOMCAT_HOME\webapps\bonForum\jsp\forum\bonForum.jsp

```
<!doctype html public "-//w3c//dtd html 4.0 transitional//en">
<%@ taglib uri="http://www.bonForum.org/taglib/bonForum-taglib"
prefix="bon" %>
<%@ page import="java.io.*" %>
<%@ page errorPage="forum_error.jsp" %>
<html>
      <head>
            <meta http-equiv="Content-Type"
                  content="text/html;
                  charset=x-user-defined">
            </meta>
            <title>
                  bonForum
            </title>
      </head>
      <body bgcolor="#00FFFF">
      <font face="Verdana">
      <a name="entry"></a>
      <h5>
      <p>
      Here are some links related to this bonForum.
```

```
Other bonForum sites can be listed here too!
</p>
<form method="POST"
      action="/bonForum/servlet/BonForumEngine">
<%—
Here we list links as created by the XSLT
Output can create a table, a list, or whatever is possible!
—%>
<p>
<bon:transform type="xalanVersion"
inXML=
      "bonForumXML"
inXSL=
      "..\\webapps\\bonForum\\mldocs\\bonForumLinks.xsl"
outDoc=
      "output">
      <%=output%>
</bon:transform>
</p>
<%—
Note that we here use actorStatus, actionStatus and
thingStatus instead of bonCommand to control the next
state of the web application.  That is just to test this
alternate destination control mechanism.
—%>
<p>
<input type="hidden" name="actorReturning"
      value="yes"></input>
<input type="hidden" name="actorStatus"
      value="visitor"></input>
<input type="hidden" name="actionStatus"
      value="executes"></input>
<input type="hidden" name="thingStatus"
      value="choice"></input>
<input type="submit" value="Back to last bonForum!"
      name="submit"></input>
</p>
</form>
<table border="0" rows="1" width="100%">
<tr>
<td align="center">
<a href="/bonForum/jsp/forum/license.jsp">
<img border="0" src="/bonForum/images/bonForumLogo.gif"
alt="BonForum open source license" width="50" height="50">
</a>
</td>
</tr>
</table>
<font face="Arial" color="blue">
<bon:outputDebugInfo/>
</font>
```

```
      <h5>
      </font>
      <%@ include file="../../mldocs/bonForumBottom.html" %>
      </body>
</html>
```

C.31 Filename: TOMCAT_HOME\webapps\bonForum\jsp\forum\forum_entry.jsp

```
<!doctype html public "-//w3c//dtd html 4.0 transitional//en">
<%@ taglib uri="http://www.bonForum.org/taglib/bonForum-taglib"
prefix="bon" %>
<%@ page import="java.io.*" %>
<%@ page errorPage="forum_error.jsp" %>
<%
String actorNickname = "";
try {
      actorNiokname =
            (String)session.getAttribute("actorNickname");
      if(actorNickname == null) {
            actorNickname = "";
      }
}
catch(java.lang.NullPointerException ex) {
      actorNickname = "";
}
%>
<%
String actorNicknameNotAvailable = "";
try {
      actorNicknameNotAvailable =
            (String)session.getAttribute("actorNicknameNotAvailable");
      if(!actorNicknameNotAvailable.equals("")) {
            actorNicknameNotAvailable =
            "Please try another nickname. " +
            actorNicknameNotAvailable +
            " is not available! " ;
      }
      if(actorNicknameNotAvailable == null) {
            actorNicknameNotAvailable = "";
      }
}
catch(java.lang.NullPointerException ex) {
      actorNicknameNotAvailable = "";
}
%>
<html>
      <head>
            <meta http-equiv="Content-Type"
```

```
                content="text/html;
                charset=x-user-defined">
            </meta>
            <title>
                bonForum
            </title>
        </head>
        <body bgcolor="#00FFFF">
        <font face="Verdana" color="black">
        <a name="entry"> </a>
        <h5>
        <form name="forum_entry" method="POST"
            action="/bonForum/servlet/BonForumEngine">
        <table border=0 cellspacing=0 cellpadding=0
            rows=4 cols=1 width=100% bgcolor=#00FFFF>
        <tr>
        <label for="actorNickname">Nickname: </label>
        <input type="text" name="actorNickname"
            value=<%=actorNickname%> ></input>
        </tr>
        <tr>
        <label for="actorAge">Your age: </label>
        <input type="text" name="actorAge"></input>
        </tr>
<%—
        <tr>
        <label for="actorAgeGroup">How old are you?
               </label>
        <input type="radio" name="actorAgeGroup"
            value="0-12">0 to 12   </input>
        <input type="radio" name="actorAgeGroup"
            value="13-17">13 to 17   </input>
        <input type="radio" name="actorAgeGroup"
            value="18-129+">21 to 129</input>
        </tr>
—%>
        <tr>
        <input type="hidden" name="actorReturning"
            value="yes"></input>
        <input type="hidden" name="bonCommand"
            value="visitor_executes_choice"></input>
        <input type="submit" value="continue" name="submit"></input>
        </tr>
        <tr>
        <font color="red">
        <%= actorNicknameNotAvailable %>
        </font>
        </tr>
        </table>
        </form>
        <font face="Arial" color="blue">
```

```
		<bon:outputDebugInfo/>
		</font>
		</h5>
		</font>
		<%@ include file="../../mldocs/bonForumSplash.html" %>
		</body>
	</html>
```

C.32 Filename: TOMCAT_HOME\webapps\bonForum\jsp\forum\forum_error.jsp

```
<!doctype html public "-//w3c//dtd html 4.0 transitional//en">
<%@ taglib uri="http://www.bonForum.org/taglib/bonForum-taglib"
prefix="bon" %>
<%@ page isErrorPage="true" %>
<%@ page import="javax.servlet.http.*" %>
<html>
<head>
	<meta http-equiv="Content-Type"
		content="text/html;
		charset=x-user-defined">
	</meta>
	<title>
		bonForum
	</title>
</head>
<body bgcolor="lime">
	<h3> Error! Please enter bonForum again!
	</h3>
	<h2>
	<%
		String errorMessage1 = "Error1";
		String errorMessage2 = "Error2";
		try {
	%>
	<jsp:useBean id="bonForumUtils"
		class="de.tarent.forum.BonForumUtils"
		scope="application"/>
	<p>
	Message: <%=bonForumUtils.normalize(exception.getMessage())%>
	</p>
	<%
		}
		catch(java.lang.NullPointerException ex) {
			String requestedSessionId = request.getRequestedSessionId();
			if(request.isRequestedSessionIdValid()) {
				errorMessage1 = requestedSessionId + " is valid session.";
			}
			else {
```

```
                    errorMessage1 = requestedSessionId + " is NOT valid
session.";
                }
                HttpSession maybeSession = request.getSession(false);
                if(maybeSession == null) {
                    errorMessage2 = "Session is null.";
                }
                else {
                    errorMessage2 = "Session not null.";
                }
        %>
                <%= errorMessage1 %><BR>
                <%= errorMessage2 %>
        <%
            }
        %>
        </h2>
        <h3>
        Try re-entering bonForum.  If the error
        keeps happening, you can copy this browser page
        and visit the BonForum Project
        website on SourceForge:
        <a href="http://www.bonforum.org">
            www.bonforum.org
        </a>. Check the bug tracker there.  You may find
        some info there, or if this problem is a new one,
        you can report it there, and paste this page into
        your bug report!
        </h3>
        <h2>
        <a href="UserMustLogin.tfe">
            bonForum re-login
        </a>
        </h2>
        <form name="forum_error" method="POST"
        action="/bonForum/servlet/BonForumEngine">
        <input type="hidden" name="actorReturning"
            value="no"></input>
        <input type="hidden" name="bonCommand"
            value="forum_error"></input>
        <p>
        <input type="submit" value="bonForum re-entry"
            name="submit"></input>
        </p>
        <label for="debug">debug</label>
        <input type="checkbox" id="debug"
            name="output_debug_info" value="yes"></input>
</form>
        <%
        try {
            exception.printStackTrace();
```

```
        }
        catch(Throwable ex) {
        }
        %>
        <font face="Arial" color="black">
        <bon:outputDebugInfo force="yes"/>
        </font>
</body>
</html>
```

C.33 Filename: TOMCAT_HOME\webapps\bonForum\jsp\forum\forum_error_robot.jsp

```
<!doctype html public "-//w3c//dtd html 4.0 transitional//en">
<%@ taglib uri="http://www.bonForum.org/taglib/bonForum-taglib"
prefix="bon" %>
<%@ page errorPage="forum_error.jsp" %>
<html>
        <head>
                <meta http-equiv="Content-Type"
                        content="text/html;
                        charset=x-user-defined">
                </meta>
                <title>
                        bonForum
                </title>
        </head>
        <body bgcolor="#00FFFF">
        <%
        String target = (String)session.getAttribute("target");
        String document = (String)session.getAttribute("document");
        String refresh = (String)session.getAttribute("refresh");
        String increment = (String)session.getAttribute("increment");
        String limit = (String)session.getAttribute("limit");
        String message = (String)session.getAttribute("message");
        %>
        <%— using message "debug" shows some info —%>
        <jsp:plugin type="applet" code="BonForumRobot.class"
                codebase="/bonForum/jsp/forum/applet"
                jreversion="1.3.0" width="0" height="0"  >
          <jsp:params>
          <jsp:param name="target" value="<%=target%>"/>
          <jsp:param name="document" value="<%=document%>"/>
          <jsp:param name="refresh" value="<%=refresh%>"/>
          <jsp:param name="increment" value="<%=increment%>"/>
          <jsp:param name="limit" value="<%=limit%>"/>
          <jsp:param name="message" value="<%=message%>"/>
          </jsp:params>
         <jsp:fallback>Plugin tag OBJECT or EMBED
```

```
            not supported by browser.
        </jsp:fallback>
      </jsp:plugin>
      </body>
</html>
```

C.33 Filename: TOMCAT_HOME\webapps\bonForum\jsp\forum\forum_login.jsp

```
<!doctype html public "-//w3c//dtd html 4.0 transitional//en">
<%@ page import="java.io.*" %>
<%@ taglib uri="http://www.bonForum.org/taglib/bonForum-taglib"
prefix="bon" %>
<%@ page errorPage="forum_error.jsp" %>
<html>
<head>
      <meta http-equiv="Content-Type"
            content="text/html;
            charset=x-user-defined">
      </meta>
      <title>
            bonForum
      </title>
</head>
<body bgcolor="#00FFFF">
<font face="Verdana">
<a name="entry"> </a>
<table border="0" rows="3" width="100%">
<tr>
<td align="center">
      <a href="/bonForum/jsp/forum/license.jsp">
      <img border="0" src="/bonForum/images/bonForumLogo.gif"
      alt="View BonForum License">
      </a>
</td>
</tr>
<tr>
<td align="center">
<form name="forum_login_enter" method="POST"
      action="/bonForum/servlet/BonForumEngine">
      <table border=0 cellspacing=0 cellpadding=0
            rows=3 cols=1 width=100% bgcolor=#00FFFF>
      <tr>
      <td align="center">
      <input type="hidden" name="actorReturning"
            value="no"></input>
      <input type="hidden" name="bonCommand"
            value="forum_entry"></input>
      <input type="submit" value="Enter bonForum"
```

```
            name="submit"></input>
        </td>
        </tr>
        </table>
</form>
</td>
</tr>
<tr>
<td align="left">
<form name="forum_login_system" method="POST"
        action="/bonForum/servlet/BonForumEngine">
        <table rows=1 cols=1 width=100% bgcolor=#00FFFF>
        <tr>
        <td align="center">
                <input type="hidden" name="actorReturning"
                        value="no"></input>
                <input type="hidden" name="bonCommand"
                        value="system_executes_command"></input>
                <p>
                <input type="submit" value="System Commands"
                        name="submit"></input></p>
        </td>
        </tr>
        </table>
</form>
</td>
</tr>
</table>
<font face="Arial" color="blue">
<bon:outputDebugInfo/>
<%—
<bon:outputDebugInfo force="yes"/>
—%>
<font>
</font>
<%@ include file="../../mldocs/bonForumSplash.html" %>
</body>
</html>
```

C.34 Filename: TOMCAT_HOME\webapps\bonForum\jsp\forum\forum_login_robot.jsp

```
<!doctype html public "-//w3c//dtd html 4.0 transitional//en">
<%@ taglib uri="http://www.bonForum.org/taglib/bonForum-taglib"
prefix="bon" %>
```

```
<%@ page errorPage="forum_error.jsp" %>
<html>
      <head>
            <meta http-equiv="Content-Type"
                  content="text/html;
                  charset=x-user-defined">
            </meta>
            <title>
                  bonForum
            </title>
      </head>
      <body bgcolor="#00FFFF">
      <%
      String target = (String)session.getAttribute("target");
      String document = (String)session.getAttribute("document");
      String refresh = (String)session.getAttribute("refresh");
      String increment = (String)session.getAttribute("increment");
      String limit = (String)session.getAttribute("limit");
      String message = (String)session.getAttribute("message");
      %>
      <%— using message "debug" shows some info —%>
      <jsp:plugin type="applet" code="BonForumRobot.class"
            codebase="/bonForum/jsp/forum/applet"
            jreversion="1.3.0" width="0" height="0"  >
        <jsp:params>
        <jsp:param name="target" value="<%=target%>"/>
        <jsp:param name="document" value="<%=document%>"/>
        <jsp:param name="refresh" value="<%=refresh%>"/>
        <jsp:param name="increment" value="<%=increment%>"/>
        <jsp:param name="limit" value="<%=limit%>"/>
        <jsp:param name="message" value="<%=message%>"/>
        </jsp:params>
        <jsp:fallback>Plugin tag OBJECT or EMBED
            not supported by browser.
        </jsp:fallback>
      </jsp:plugin>
      </body>
</html>
```

C.35 Filename: TOMCAT_HOME\webapps\bonForum\jsp\forum\guest_executes_chat.jsp

```
<!doctype html public "-//w3c//dtd html 4.0 transitional//en">
<%@ taglib uri="http://www.bonForum.org/taglib/bonForum-taglib"
prefix="bon" %>
```

```
<%@ page errorPage="forum_error.jsp" %>
<%
session.setAttribute("target", "display");
session.setAttribute("document", request.getScheme() + "://" +
      request.getServerName() + ":" +
      request.getServerPort() +
      "/bonForum/jsp/forum/guest_executes_chat_frame.jsp");
session.setAttribute("refresh", "true");
session.setAttribute("increment", "5000");
session.setAttribute("limit", "5000");
session.setAttribute("message", "refreshing...");
%>
<html>
      <head>
            <meta http-equiv="Content-Type"
                  content="text/html;
                  charset=x-user-defined">
            </meta>
            <title>
                  bonForum
            </title>
      </head>
<noframes>/bonForum/noframe/html.index</noframes>
<frameset rows="55%, 45%">
<frame src="/bonForum/jsp/forum/guest_executes_chat_frame.jsp.tfe"
      name="display"/>
<frameset cols="77%, 23%">
<frame src="/bonForum/jsp/forum/guest_executes_chat_controls.jsp.tfe"
      name="controls"/>
<frame src="/bonForum/jsp/forum/guest_executes_chat_robot.jsp.tfe"
      name="robot"/>
</frameset>
</frameset>
</html>
```

C.36 Filename: TOMCAT_HOME\webapps\bonForum\jsp\forum\guest_executes_chat_console.jsp

```
<!doctype html public "-//w3c//dtd html 4.0 transitional//en">
<%@ taglib uri="http://www.bonForum.org/taglib/bonForum-taglib"
prefix="bon" %>
<%@ page errorPage="forum_error.jsp" %>
<html>
      <head>
            <meta http-equiv="Content-Type"
                  content="text/html;
                  charset=x-user-defined">
```

```
            </meta>
            <title>
                  bonForum
            </title>
      </head>
      <body bgcolor="#00FFFF">
      <%— go via robot to leave frameset —%>
      <%
      request.setAttribute("target", "_top");
      request.setAttribute("document", request.getScheme() + "://" +
            request.getServerName() + ":" +
            request.getServerPort() +
            "/bonForum/jsp/forum/guest_executes_command.jsp");
      request.setAttribute("refresh", "true");
      request.setAttribute("increment", "100");
      request.setAttribute("limit", "1");
      request.setAttribute("message", "guest command console loading!");

      %>
      <jsp:forward page="actor_leaves_frameset_robot.jsp.tfe"/>
      </font>
      </body>
</html>
```

C.37 Filename: TOMCAT_HOME\webapps\bonForum\jsp\forum\guest_executes_chat_controls.jsp

```
<!doctype html public "-//w3c//dtd html 4.0 transitional//en">
<%@ taglib uri="http://www.bonForum.org/taglib/bonForum-taglib"
prefix="bon" %>
<%@ page errorPage="forum_error.jsp" %>
<%— greet guest by nickname: —%>
<%
      String actorNickname =
            ((String)session.getAttribute("actorNickname"));
      if(actorNickname == null ||
            actorNickname.trim().length() < 1) {
            actorNickname = "&lt;unknown visitor&gt;";
      }
      String chatWelcomeMessage = "" +
            actorNickname + "! Please make a choice:";
%>
<%—
Here we indicate to user if first or latest
messages will be displayed.  Note that previous
and next are one-shot actions so are left alone
—%>
```

```
<%
   String chatNavigatorFirst = "first";
   String chatNavigatorPrevious = "previous";
   String chatNavigatorNext = "next";
   String chatNavigatorLast = "latest";
   String chatMessagesNavigator = "";
   try {
      chatMessagesNavigator =
          (String)session.getAttribute("chatMessagesNavigator");
      if(!(chatMessagesNavigator.equals("first")) &&
           !(chatMessagesNavigator.equals("previous"))  &&
           !(chatMessagesNavigator.equals("next"))) {
           chatMessagesNavigator = "last";
      }
      if(chatMessagesNavigator.equals("first")) {
           chatNavigatorFirst = "FIRST";
      }
      else if(chatMessagesNavigator.equals("previous")) {
           chatNavigatorPrevious = "previous";
      }
      else if(chatMessagesNavigator.equals("next")) {
           chatNavigatorNext = "next";
      }
      else {
           chatNavigatorLast = "LATEST";
      }
   }
   catch (Exception ee) {
      chatMessagesNavigator = "last";
   }
%>
<html>
      <head>
            <meta http-equiv="Content-Type"
                  content="text/html;
                  charset=x-user-defined">
            </meta>
            <title>
                  bonForum
            </title>
      </head>
      <body bgcolor="#00FFFF">
      <font face="Verdana">
      <a name="entry"></a>
      <h5>
<table border=0 cellspacing=0 cellpadding=0
      rows=4 cols=1 width=100% bgcolor=#00FFFF>
<tr>
<%= chatWelcomeMessage %>
</tr>
<form method="POST" action="/bonForum/servlet/BonForumEngine">
```

```
<tr width=100%>
     <table border=0 cellspacing=0 cellpadding=0
          rows=1 cols=1 width=100% bgcolor=#00FFFF>
     <tr>
     <label for="chatMessage">chat message</label>
     <font face="Arial Narrow">
     <input type="text" name="chatMessage" size=50></input>
     </font>
     </tr>
     </table>
</tr>
<tr width=100%>
     <table border=0 cellspacing=0 cellpadding=0
          rows=4 cols=1 width=100% bgcolor=#00FFFF>
     <tr>
     <label for="bonCommand">send this message</label>
     <input type="radio" name="bonCommand"
          value="guest_executes_chat_controls"
          CHECKED></input>
     </tr>
     <tr>
     <label for="bonCommand">exit this chat</label>
     <input type="radio" name="bonCommand"
          value="guest_executes_chat_ready"></input>
     </tr>
     <tr>
     <label for="bonCommand">execute guest command</label>
     <input type="radio" name="bonCommand"
          value="guest_executes_chat_console"></input>
     </tr>
     <tr>
     <input type="hidden" name="actorReturning"
          value="yes"></input>
     <input type="submit" value="Do it!"
          name="submit"></input>
     </tr>
     </table>
</tr>
</form>
<tr width=10%>
     <table border=0 cellspacing=0 cellpadding=0
          rows=1 cols=4 width=10% bgcolor=#00FFFF>
     <%— here we display navigator buttons to
          page through chat messages —%>
     <label for="chatMessagesNavigator">page messages</label>
     <td width=10%>
     <form method="POST"
          action="/bonForum/servlet/BonForumEngine">
     <input type="hidden" name="chatMessagesNavigator"
          value="first"></input>
     <input type="hidden" name="actorReturning"
```

```
        value="yes"></input>
    <input type="hidden" name="bonCommand"
        value="guest_executes_chat_controls"></input>
    <input type="submit" value=<%=chatNavigatorFirst%>
        name="submit"></input>
    </form>
    </td>
    <td width=10%>
    <form method="POST"
        action="/bonForum/servlet/BonForumEngine">
    <input type="hidden" name="chatMessagesNavigator"
        value="previous"></input>
    <input type="hidden" name="actorReturning"
        value="yes"></input>
    <input type="hidden" name="bonCommand"
        value="guest_executes_chat_controls"></input>
    <input type="submit"
        value=<%=chatNavigatorPrevious%>
        name="submit"></input>
    </form>
    </td>
    <td width=10%>
    <form method="POST"
        action="/bonForum/servlet/BonForumEngine">
    <input type="hidden" name="chatMessagesNavigator"
        value="next"></input>
    <input type="hidden" name="actorReturning"
        value="yes"></input>
    <input type="hidden" name="bonCommand"
        value="guest_executes_chat_controls"></input>
    <input type="submit"
        value=<%=chatNavigatorNext%>
        name="submit"></input>
    </form>
    </td>
    <td width=10%>
    <form method="POST"
        action="/bonForum/servlet/BonForumEngine">
    <input type="hidden" name="chatMessagesNavigator"
        value="last"></input>
    <input type="hidden" name="actorReturning"
        value="yes"></input>
    <input type="hidden" name="bonCommand"
        value="guest_executes_chat_controls"></input>
    <input type="submit"
        value=<%=chatNavigatorLast%> name="submit"></input>
    </form>
    </td>
    </table>
</tr>
</table>
```

```
         <font face="Arial" color="blue">
        <bon:outputDebugInfo/>
        </font>
        </h5>
        </font>
        <%@ include file="../../mldocs/bonForumBottom.html" %>
        </body>
</html>
```

C.38 Filename: TOMCAT_HOME\webapps\bonForum\jsp\forum\guest_executes_chat_frame.jsp

```
<!doctype html public "-//w3c//dtd html 4.0 transitional//en">
<%@ taglib uri="http://www.bonForum.org/taglib/bonForum-taglib"
prefix="bon" %>
<%@ page errorPage="forum_error.jsp" %>
<%— here we get the chat subject and
     topic settings for later display —%>
<%
String chatSubject = (String)session.getAttribute("chatSubject");
String chatSubjectMessage = "";
if(chatSubject != null && chatSubject.trim().length() > 0) {
     chatSubjectMessage = "category: " + chatSubject;
}
String chatTopic = (String)session.getAttribute("chatTopic");
String chatTopicMessage = "";
if(chatTopic != null && chatTopic.trim().length() > 0) {
     chatTopicMessage = "topic: " + chatTopic;
}
%>
<html>
     <head>
          <meta http-equiv="Content-Type"
               content="text/html;
               charset=x-user-defined">
          </meta>
          <title>
               bonForum
          </title>
     </head>
     <body bgcolor="#00FFFF">
     <font face="Verdana">
     <a name="entry"></a>
     <h5>
     <table border=0 cellspacing=0 cellpadding=0
          rows=4 cols=1 width=100% bgcolor=#00FFFF>
     <tr>
```

```
<%=chatSubjectMessage%>
</tr>
<tr>
<%=chatTopicMessage%>
</tr>
<%-- here we get the number of lines per page
      for the chat messages display --%>
<%
String chatMessagesPageSize =
      (String)session.getAttribute("chatMessagesPageSize");
int size = 10;
try {
      size = Integer.parseInt(chatMessagesPageSize);
}
catch (NumberFormatException nFE) {
      chatMessagesPageSize = "10";
}
if(size > 99) {
      chatMessagesPageSize = "99";
}
else if(size < 1) {
      chatMessagesPageSize = "1";
}
session.setAttribute("chatMessagesPageSize",
                     chatMessagesPageSize);
%>
<%-- Here we list the messages in this chat --%>
<tr>
<form method="POST"
      action="/bonForum/servlet/BonForumEngine">
<select size="<%= chatMessagesPageSize %>"
      name="chatMessages">
      <font face="Arial Narrow">
      <bon:outputChatMessages command="bonForumXML">
            <option><%= output %></option>
      </bon:outputChatMessages>
      </font>
</select>
</form>
</tr>
<%-- here we get the page number and
      number of pages for later display --%>
<%
      (String)session.getAttribute("chatPageNumber");
String chatNumberOfPages =
      (String)session.getAttribute("chatNumberOfPages");
%>
<tr>
page: <%= chatPageNumber %>
       of <%= chatNumberOfPages %>
</tr>
```

```
        </table>
        <%— for debugging, we can display variables —%>
        <%— chatMessagesPageSize:<%= chatMessagesPageSize %>
            size:<%= size %>
        —%>
        <font face="Arial" color="blue">
        <bon:outputDebugInfo/>
        </font>
        </h5>
        </font>
        </body>
</html>
```

C.39 Filename: TOMCAT_HOME\webapps\bonForum\jsp\forum\guest_executes_chat_ready.jsp

```
<!doctype html public "-//w3c//dtd html 4.0 transitional//en">
<%@ taglib uri="http://www.bonForum.org/taglib/bonForum-taglib"
prefix="bon" %>
<%@ page errorPage="forum_error.jsp" %>
<html>
        <head>
              <meta http-equiv="Content-Type"
                    content="text/html;
                    charset=x-user-defined">
              </meta>
              <title>
                    bonForum
              </title>
        </head>
        <body bgcolor="#00FFFF">
        <%— go via robot to leave frameset —%>
        <%
        request.setAttribute("target", "_top");
        request.setAttribute("document",
              request.getScheme() + "://" +
              request.getServerName() + ":" +
              request.getServerPort() +
              "/bonForum/jsp/forum/guest_exits_chat.jsp");
        request.setAttribute("refresh", "true");
        request.setAttribute("increment", "100");
        request.setAttribute("limit", "1");
        request.setAttribute("message", "guest exiting chat!");
        %>
        <jsp:forward page="actor_leaves_frameset_robot.jsp.tfe"/>
        </body>
</html>
```

C.40 Filename: TOMCAT_HOME\webapps\bonForum\jsp\forum\guest_executes_chat_robot.jsp

```
<!doctype html public "-//w3c//dtd html 4.0 transitional//en">
<%@ taglib uri="http://www.bonForum.org/taglib/bonForum-taglib"
prefix="bon" %>
<%@ page errorPage="forum_error.jsp" %>
<%
String target = (String)session.getAttribute("target");
String document = (String)session.getAttribute("document");
String refresh = (String)session.getAttribute("refresh");
String increment = (String)session.getAttribute("increment");
String limit = (String)session.getAttribute("limit");
String message = (String)session.getAttribute("message");
%>
<%— message "debug" shows some info —%>
<html>
      <head>
            <meta http-equiv="Content-Type"
                  content="text/html;
                  charset=x-user-defined">
            </meta>
            <title>
                 bonForum
            </title>
      </head>
      <body bgcolor="#00FFFF">
      <font face="Verdana">
      <table>
      <tr>
      <img border="0" src="/bonForum/images/bonForumLogo.gif"
            alt="bonForum" width="112" height="112">
      </tr>
      <tr>
      <jsp:plugin type="applet" code="BonForumRobot.class"
            codebase="/bonForum/jsp/forum/applet"
            jreversion="1.3.0" width="400" height="160" >
        <jsp:params>
        <jsp:param name="target" value="<%=target%>"/>
        <jsp:param name="document" value="<%=document%>"/>
        <jsp:param name="refresh" value="<%=refresh%>"/>
        <jsp:param name="increment" value="<%=increment%>"/>
        <jsp:param name="limit" value="<%=limit%>"/>
        <jsp:param name="message" value="<%=message%>"/>
        </jsp:params>
         <jsp:fallback>Plugin tag OBJECT or EMBED
           not supported by browser.
        </jsp:fallback>
      </jsp:plugin>
```

```
        </tr>
        </table>
        <font face="Arial" color="blue">
        <bon:outputDebugInfo/>
        </font>
        </font>
        </body>
</html>
```

C.41 Filename: TOMCAT_HOME\webapps\bonForum\jsp\forum\guest_executes_command.jsp

```
<!doctype html public "-//w3c//dtd html 4.0 transitional//en">
<%@ taglib uri="http://www.bonForum.org/taglib/bonForum-taglib"
prefix="bon" %>
<%@ page errorPage="forum_error.jsp" %>
<%
session.setAttribute("target", "display");
session.setAttribute("document", request.getScheme() + "://" +
        request.getServerName() + ":" +
        request.getServerPort() +
        "/bonForum/jsp/forum/guest_executes_command_frame.jsp");
session.setAttribute("refresh", "false");
session.setAttribute("increment", "15000");
session.setAttribute("limit", "5000");
session.setAttribute("message", "hello");
%>
<html>
        <head>
                <meta http-equiv="Content-Type"
                        content="text/html;
                        charset=x-user-defined">
                </meta>
                <title>
                        bonForum
                </title>
        </head>
<noframes>/bonForum/noframe/html.index</noframes>
<frameset rows="59%, 41%">
<frame src="/bonForum/jsp/forum/guest_executes_command_frame.jsp.tfe"
        name="display"/>
<frameset cols="77%, 23%">
<frame src="/bonForum/jsp/forum/guest_executes_command_controls.jsp.tfe"
        name="controls"/>
<frame src="/bonForum/jsp/forum/guest_executes_command_robot.jsp.tfe"
        name="robot"/>
</frameset>
```

```
</frameset>
</html>
```

C.42 Filename: TOMCAT_HOME\webapps\bonForum\jsp\forum\guest_executes_command_controls.jsp

```
<!doctype html public "-//w3c//dtd html 4.0 transitional//en">
<%@ taglib uri="http://www.bonForum.org/taglib/bonForum-taglib"
prefix="bon" %>
<%@ page errorPage="forum_error.jsp" %>
<%-- here we get the number of lines per page
      for the chat messages display --%>
<%
String chatMessagesPageSize =
      (String)session.getAttribute("chatMessagesPageSize");
int size = 10;
try {
      size = Integer.parseInt(chatMessagesPageSize);
}
catch (NumberFormatException nFE) {
      chatMessagesPageSize = "10";
}
if(size > 99) {
      chatMessagesPageSize = "99";
}
else if(size < 1) {
      chatMessagesPageSize = "1";
}
session.setAttribute("chatMessagesPageSize", chatMessagesPageSize);
%>
<html>
      <head>
            <meta http-equiv="Content-Type"
                  content="text/html;
                  charset=x-user-defined">
            </meta>
            <title>
                  bonForum
            </title>
      </head>
      <body bgcolor="#00FFFF">
      <font face="Verdana">
      <a name="entry"></a>
      <h5>
      <%-- later, add commands and options for guests here! --%>
<table border=0 cellspacing=0 cellpadding=0
      rows=2 cols=1 width=100% bgcolor=#00FFFF>
```

```
<tr>
      <table border=0 cellspacing=0 cellpadding=0
            rows=1 cols=1 width="100%" bgcolor=#00FFFF>
      <tr>
      <p>
      Guest commands!
      </p>
      </tr>
      </table>
</tr>
<tr>
      <table border=0 cellspacing=0 cellpadding=0
            rows=4 cols=1 width="100%" bgcolor=#00FFFF>
      <form method="POST"
            action="/bonForum/servlet/BonForumEngine">
      <tr>
      <label for="bonCommand">exit guest commands</label>
      <input type="radio" name="bonCommand"
            value="guest_executes_command_ready" CHECKED></input>
      </tr>
      <tr>
      <input type="submit" value="Do it!" name="submit"></input>
      </tr>
      </form>
      <tr>
      </tr>
      <tr>
      <form method="POST"
            action="/bonForum/servlet/BonForumEngine">
      <input type="hidden" name="actorReturning"
            value="yes"></input>
      <label for="chatMessagesPageSize">show </label>
      <input type="text" name="chatMessagesPageSize"
            maxlength="2" size="2"
            value="<%= chatMessagesPageSize %>"></input>
      <input type="hidden" name="bonCommand"
            value="guest_executes_command_controls"></input>
      <label for="submit">messages per page</label>
      <input type="submit" value="set" name="submit"></input>
      </form>
      </tr>
      </table>
</tr>
</table>
      <font face="Arial" color="blue">
      <bon:outputDebugInfo/>
      </font>
      </h5>
      </font>
      <%@ include file="../../mldocs/bonForumBottom.html" %>
      </body>
```

```
</html>
```

C.43 Filename: TOMCAT_HOME\webapps\bonForum\jsp\forum\guest_executes_command_frame.jsp

```
<!doctype html public "-//w3c//dtd html 4.0 transitional//en">
<%@ taglib uri="http://www.bonForum.org/taglib/bonForum-taglib"
prefix="bon" %>
<%@ page errorPage="forum_error.jsp" %>
<html>
      <head>
            <meta http-equiv="Content-Type"
                  content="text/html;
                  charset=x-user-defined">
            </meta>
            <title>
                  bonForum
            </title>
      </head>
      <body bgcolor="#00FFFF">
      <font face="Verdana">
      <h5>
      <%— later add more according to
            guest commands developed later —%>
      <p>Check for new open source releases of bonForum!</p>
      <p>Mailing lists, discussion forums, bug reports,
            project news and more,
            are all hosted by SourceForge.</p>
      <p><a href="http://www.bonforum.org">
            www.bonforum.org
      </a></p>
      <font face="Arial" color="blue">
      <bon:outputDebugInfo/>
      </font>
      </h5>
      </font>
      </body>
</html>
```

C.44 Filename: TOMCAT_HOME\webapps\bonForum\jsp\forum\guest_executes_command_ready.jsp

```
<!doctype html public "-//w3c//dtd html 4.0 transitional//en">
<%@ taglib uri="http://www.bonForum.org/taglib/bonForum-taglib"
```

```
prefix="bon" %>
<%@ page errorPage="forum_error.jsp" %>
<html>
      <head>
            <meta http-equiv="Content-Type"
                  content="text/html;
                  charset=x-user-defined">
            </meta>
            <title>
                  bonForum
            </title>
      </head>
      <body bgcolor="#00FFFF">
      <%— go via robot to leave frameset —%>
      <%
      request.setAttribute("target", "_top");
      request.setAttribute("document",
            request.getScheme() + "://" +
            request.getServerName() + ":" +
            request.getServerPort() +
            "/bonForum/jsp/forum/guest_exits_command.jsp");
      request.setAttribute("refresh", "true");
      request.setAttribute("increment", "100");
      request.setAttribute("limit", "1");
      request.setAttribute("message",
            "Guest exiting command mode!");
      %>
      <jsp:forward page="actor_leaves_frameset_robot.jsp.tfe"/>
      </body>
</html>
```

C.45 Filename: TOMCAT_HOME\webapps\bonForum\jsp\forum\guest_executes_command_robot.jsp

```
<!doctype html public "-//w3c//dtd html 4.0 transitional//en">
<%@ taglib uri="http://www.bonForum.org/taglib/bonForum-taglib"
prefix="bon" %>
<%@ page errorPage="forum_error.jsp" %>
<%
String target = (String)session.getAttribute("target");
String document = (String)session.getAttribute("document");
String refresh = (String)session.getAttribute("refresh");
String increment = (String)session.getAttribute("increment");
String limit = (String)session.getAttribute("limit");
String message = (String)session.getAttribute("message");
%>
<%— message "debug" shows some info —%>
```

```
<html>
      <head>
            <meta http-equiv="Content-Type"
                  content="text/html;
                  charset=x-user-defined">
            </meta>
            <title>
                  bonForum
            </title>
      </head>
      <body bgcolor="#00FFFF">
      <font face="Verdana">
      <table>
      <tr>
      <img border="0" src="/bonForum/images/bonForumLogo.gif"
            alt="bonForum" width="112" height="112">
      </tr>
      <tr>
      <jsp:plugin type="applet" code="BonForumRobot.class"
            codebase="/bonForum/jsp/forum/applet"
            jreversion="1.3.0" width="400" height="160" >
        <jsp:params>
        <jsp:param name="target" value="<%=target%>"/>
        <jsp:param name="document" value="<%=document%>"/>
        <jsp:param name="refresh" value="<%=refresh%>"/>
        <jsp:param name="increment" value="<%=increment%>"/>
        <jsp:param name="limit" value="<%=limit%>"/>
        <jsp:param name="message" value="<%=message%>"/>
        </jsp:params>
        <jsp:fallback>Plugin tag OBJECT or EMBED
          not supported by browser.
        </jsp:fallback>
      </jsp:plugin>
      </tr>
      </table>
      <font face="Arial" color="blue">
      <bon:outputDebugInfo/>
      </font>
      </font>
      </body>
</html>
```

C.46 Filename: TOMCAT_HOME\webapps\bonForum\jsp\forum\guest_exits_chat.jsp

```
<!doctype html public "-//w3c//dtd html 4.0 transitional//en">
<%@ taglib uri="http://www.bonForum.org/taglib/bonForum-taglib"
prefix="bon" %>
<%@ page errorPage="forum_error.jsp" %>
```

```
<%—  here we can force actor
     to select from available chats
—%>
<%—
     session.setAttribute("chatItem", "NONE");
—%>
<html>
     <head>
          <meta http-equiv="Content-Type"
               content="text/html;
               charset=x-user-defined">
          </meta>
          <title>
               bonForum
          </title>
     </head>
     <body>
     <jsp:forward page="visitor_executes_choice.jsp.tfe"/>
     </body>
</html>
```

C.47 Filename: TOMCAT_HOME\webapps\bonForum\jsp\forum\guest_exits_command.jsp

```
<!doctype html public "-//w3c//dtd html 4.0 transitional//en">
<%@ taglib uri="http://www.bonForum.org/taglib/bonForum-taglib"
prefix="bon" %>
<%@ page errorPage="forum_error.jsp" %>
<html>
     <head>
          <meta http-equiv="Content-Type"
               content="text/html;
               charset=x-user-defined">
          </meta>
          <title>
               bonForum
          </title>
     </head>
     <body>
     <jsp:forward page="guest_executes_chat.jsp.tfe"/>
     </body>
</html>
```

C.48 Filename: TOMCAT_HOME\webapps\bonForum\jsp\forum\host_decreases_rating.jsp

```
<!doctype html public "-//w3c//dtd html 4.0 transitional//en">
```

```
<%@ taglib uri="http://www.bonForum.org/taglib/bonForum-taglib"
prefix="bon" %>
<%@ page errorPage="forum_error.jsp" %>
<jsp:useBean id="bonForumStore"
      class="de.tarent.forum.BonForumStore"
      scope="application"/>
<html>
      <head>
            <meta http-equiv="Content-Type"
                  content="text/html;
                  charset=x-user-defined">
            </meta>
            <title>
                  bonForum
            </title>
      </head>
      <body>
      <%—
      Here decrement the rating of the chosen chatGuest
      Later: will add code to remove guest from chat
      if rating is below some threshold, nominally 0
      —%>
      <%
      bonForumStore.changeChatActorRating("-1", session);
      %>
      <jsp:forward page="host_executes_command_controls.jsp.tfe"/>
      </body>
</html>
```

C.49 Filename: TOMCAT_HOME\webapps\bonForum\jsp\forum\host_executes_chat.jsp

```
<!doctype html public "-//w3c//dtd html 4.0 transitional//en">
<%@ taglib uri="http://www.bonForum.org/taglib/bonForum-taglib"
prefix="bon" %>
<%@ page errorPage="forum_error.jsp" %>
<%
session.setAttribute("target", "display");
session.setAttribute("document", request.getScheme() + "://" +
      request.getServerName() + ":" +
      request.getServerPort() +
      "/bonForum/jsp/forum/host_executes_chat_frame.jsp");
session.setAttribute("refresh", "true");
session.setAttribute("increment", "5000");
session.setAttribute("limit", "5000");
session.setAttribute("message", "refreshing...");
%>
      <html>
      <head>
```

```
                <meta http-equiv="Content-Type"
                      content="text/html;
                      charset=x-user-defined">
                </meta>
                <title>
                      bonForum
                </title>
          </head>
    <noframes>/bonForum/noframe/html.index</noframes>
    <frameset rows="55%, 45%">
    <frame src="/bonForum/jsp/forum/host_executes_chat_frame.jsp.tfe"
          name="display"/>
    <frameset cols="77%, 23%">
    <frame src="/bonForum/jsp/forum/host_executes_chat_controls.jsp.tfe"
          name="controls"/>
    <frame src="/bonForum/jsp/forum/host_executes_chat_robot.jsp.tfe"
          name="robot"/>
    <%—TESTING TEMP TEMP
    <frame src="/bonForum/jsp/forum/actor_refreshes_frame_robot.jsp.tfe"
          name="robot"/>
    —%>
    </frameset>
    </frameset>
    </html>
```

C.50 Filename: TOMCAT_HOME\webapps\bonForum\jsp\forum\host_executes_chat_console.jsp

```
<!doctype html public "-//w3c//dtd html 4.0 transitional//en">
<%@ taglib uri="http://www.bonForum.org/taglib/bonForum-taglib"
prefix="bon" %>
<%@ page errorPage="forum_error.jsp" %>
<html>
      <head>
            <meta http-equiv="Content-Type"
                  content="text/html;
                  charset=x-user-defined">
            </meta>
            <title>
                  bonForum
            </title>
      </head>
      <body bgcolor="#00FFFF">
      <%— go via robot to leave frameset —%>
      <%
      request.setAttribute("target", "_top");
      request.setAttribute("document",
```

```
            request.getScheme() + "://" +
            request.getServerName() + ":" +
            request.getServerPort() +
            "/bonForum/jsp/forum/host_executes_command.jsp");
      request.setAttribute("refresh", "true");
      request.setAttribute("increment", "100");
      request.setAttribute("limit", "1");
      request.setAttribute("message",
            "host command console loading!");
      %>
      <jsp:forward page="actor_leaves_frameset_robot.jsp.tfe"/>
      </font>
      </body>
</html>
```

C.51 Filename: TOMCAT_HOME\webapps\bonForum\jsp\forum\host_executes_chat_controls.jsp

```
<!doctype html public "-//w3c//dtd html 4.0 transitional//en">
<%@ taglib uri="http://www.bonForum.org/taglib/bonForum-taglib"
prefix="bon" %>
<%@ page errorPage="forum_error.jsp.tfe" %>
<%— greet guest by nickname: —%>
<%
      String actorNickname =
            ((String)session.getAttribute("actorNickname"));
      if(actorNickname == null ||
         actorNickname.trim().length() < 1) {
            actorNickname = "&lt;unknown visitor&gt;";
      }
      String chatWelcomeMessage = "" + actorNickname +
            "! Please make a choice:";
%>
<%—
Here we indicate to user if first
or latest messages will be displayed.
Note that previous and next are one-shot
actions so those are left alone.
—%>
<%
   String chatNavigatorFirst = "first";
   String chatNavigatorPrevious = "previous";
   String chatNavigatorNext = "next";
   String chatNavigatorLast = "latest";
   String chatMessagesNavigator = "";
   try {
      chatMessagesNavigator =
```

```
                    (String)session.getAttribute(
                    "chatMessagesNavigator");
                if(!(chatMessagesNavigator.equals("first")) &&
                    !(chatMessagesNavigator.equals("previous"))  &&
                    !(chatMessagesNavigator.equals("next"))) {
                    chatMessagesNavigator = "last";
                }
                if(chatMessagesNavigator.equals("first")) {
                    chatNavigatorFirst = "FIRST";
                }
                else if(chatMessagesNavigator.equals("previous")) {
                    chatNavigatorPrevious = "previous";
                }
                else if(chatMessagesNavigator.equals("next")) {
                    chatNavigatorNext = "next";
                }
                else {
                    chatNavigatorLast = "LATEST";
                }
            }
            catch (Exception ee) {
                chatMessagesNavigator = "last";
            }
%>
<html>
        <head>
                <meta http-equiv="Content-Type"
                        content="text/html;
                        charset=x-user-defined">
                </meta>
                <title>
                        bonForum
                </title>
        </head>
        <body bgcolor="#00FFFF">
        <font face="Verdana">
        <a name="entry"></a>
        <h5>
<table border="0" cellspacing="0" cellpadding="0"
        rows="4" cols="1" width="100%" bgcolor="#00FFFF">
<tr>
<%= chatWelcomeMessage %>
</tr>
<form method="POST" action="/bonForum/servlet/BonForumEngine">
<tr width=100%>
        <table border="0" cellspacing="0" cellpadding="0"
                rows="1" cols="1" width="100%" bgcolor="#00FFFF">
        <tr>
        <label for="chatMessage">chat message</label>
        <font face="Arial Narrow">
        <input type="text" name="chatMessage" size=50></input>
```

```
        </font>
        </tr>
        </table>
</tr>
<tr width=100%>
        <table border="0" cellspacing="0" cellpadding="0"
                rows="4" cols="1" width="100%" bgcolor="#00FFFF">
        <tr>
        <label for="bonCommand">send this message</label>
        <input type="radio" name="bonCommand"
                value="host_executes_chat_controls" CHECKED></input>
        </tr>
        <tr>
        <label for="bonCommand">exit this chat</label>
        <input type="radio" name="bonCommand"
                value="host_executes_chat_ready"></input>
        </tr>
        <tr>
        <label for="bonCommand">execute host command</label>
        <input type="radio" name="bonCommand"
                value="host_executes_chat_console"></input>
        </tr>
        <tr>
        <input type="hidden" name="actorReturning"
                value="yes"></input>
        <input type="submit" value="Do it!"
                name="submit"></input>
        </tr>
        </table>
</tr>
</form>
<tr width=100%>
        <table border="0" cellspacing="0" cellpadding="0"
                rows="1" cols="5" width="10%" bgcolor="#00FFFF">
        <%—here we display navigator buttons
                to page through chat messages —%>
        <label for="chatMessagesNavigator">page messages</label>
        <td width=10%>
        <form method="POST"
                action="/bonForum/servlet/BonForumEngine">
        <input type="hidden" name="chatMessagesNavigator"
                value="first"></input>
        <input type="hidden" name="actorReturning"
                value="yes"></input>
        <input type="hidden" name="bonCommand"
                value="host_executes_chat_controls"></input>
        <input type="submit" value=<%=chatNavigatorFirst%>
                name="submit"></input>
        </form>
        </td>
        <td width=10%>
```

```
        <form method="POST"
              action="/bonForum/servlet/BonForumEngine">
        <input type="hidden" name="chatMessagesNavigator"
              value="previous"></input>
        <input type="hidden" name="actorReturning"
              value="yes"></input>
        <input type="hidden" name="bonCommand"
              value="host_executes_chat_controls"></input>
        <input type="submit"
              value=<%=chatNavigatorPrevious%>
              name="submit"></input>
        </form>
        </td>
        <td width=10%>
        <form method="POST"
              action="/bonForum/servlet/BonForumEngine">
        <input type="hidden" name="chatMessagesNavigator"
              value="next"></input>
        <input type="hidden" name="actorReturning"
              value="yes"></input>
        <input type="hidden" name="bonCommand"
              value="host_executes_chat_controls"></input>
        <input type="submit" value=<%=chatNavigatorNext%>
              name="submit"></input>
        </form>
        </td>
        <td width=10%>
        <form method="POST"
              action="/bonForum/servlet/BonForumEngine">
        <input type="hidden" name="chatMessagesNavigator"
              value="last"></input>
        <input type="hidden" name="actorReturning"
              value="yes"></input>
        <input type="hidden" name="bonCommand"
              value="host_executes_chat_controls"></input>
        <input type="submit" value=<%=chatNavigatorLast%>
              name="submit"></input>
        </form>
        </td>
        </table>
</tr>
</table>
        <font face="Arial" color="blue">
        <bon:outputDebugInfo/>
        </font>
        </h5>
        </font>
        <%@ include file="../../mldocs/bonForumBottom.html" %>
        </body>
</html>
```

C.52 Filename: TOMCAT_HOME\webapps\bonForum\jsp\forum\host_executes_chat_frame.jsp

```
<!doctype html public "-//w3c//dtd html 4.0 transitional//en">
<%@ taglib uri="http://www.bonForum.org/taglib/bonForum-taglib"
prefix="bon" %>
<%@ page errorPage="forum_error.jsp" %>
<%--
The messages refresh problem - part I.
Try to use the robot applet without adding
the time value suffix to each showDocument
argument.  You will then need to prevent
caching of the output of this page, in order
to get refreshing of the dynamic messages display.
Problem is, if you put the following "no cache"
headers here as shown, and not on the "frameset" JSP,
(host_executes_chat.jsp), they will not prevent caching
of the output of this JSP (host_executes_chat_frame.jsp).
However, if you put the headers on the "frameset" JSP,
they will prevent caching - of both the display frame
and the "frameset" JSP.  Now, when the robot applet
refreshes the display frame, that will also refresh
the entire frameset and all the frames in it,
which is not pretty at all!
response.setHeader("Cache-Control", "no-cache");
response.setHeader("Pragma", "no-cache");
response.setDateHeader("max-age", 0);
response.setDateHeader("Expires", 0);
--%>
<%--
The messages refresh problem - part II.
If you put a Refresh header here as follows,
you will get refresh without using the robot
applet at all!  However, at least on IE5.X,
there is an unpleasant flashing of the message
display.  The flashing is much less with the applet
context showDocument method, so we used it instead
of this:
response.setIntHeader("Refresh", 5);
--%>
<%-- here we get the chat subject and
      topic settings for later display --%>
<%
String chatSubject = (String)session.getAttribute("chatSubject");
String chatSubjectMessage = "";
if(chatSubject != null && chatSubject.trim().length() > 0) {
      chatSubjectMessage = "category: " + chatSubject;
}
String chatTopic = (String)session.getAttribute("chatTopic");
```

```
String chatTopicMessage = "";
if(chatTopic != null && chatTopic.trim().length() > 0) {
     chatTopicMessage = "topic: " + chatTopic;
}
%>
<html>
     <head>
               content="text/html;
 action="/bonForum/servlet/BonForumEngine">
     <tr>
     <label for="bonCommand">increment rating of guest</label>
     <input type="radio" name="bonCommand"
          value="host_increases_rating"></input>
     </tr>
     <tr>
     <label for="bonCommand">decrement rating of guest</label>
     <input type="radio" name="bonCommand"
          value="host_decreases_rating"></input>
     </tr>
     <tr>
     <label for="bonCommand">exit host commands</label>
     <input type="radio" name="bonCommand"
          value="host_executes_command_ready" CHECKED></input>
     </tr>
     <tr>
     <input type="submit" value="Do it!"
          name="submit"></input>
     </tr>
     </form>
     <tr>
      
     </tr>
     <tr>
     <form method="POST"
          action="/bonForum/servlet/BonForumEngine">
     <input type="hidden" name="actorReturning"
          value="yes"></input>
     <label for="chatMessagesPageSize">show </label>
     <input type="text" name="chatMessagesPageSize"
          maxlength="2" size="2"
          value="<%= chatMessagesPageSize %>"></input>
     <input type="hidden" name="bonCommand"
          value="host_executes_command_controls"></input>
     <label for="submit">messages per page</label>
     <input type="submit" value="set"
          name="submit"></input>
     </form>
     </tr>
     </table>
</tr>
</table>
```

```
        <font face="Arial" color="blue">
        <bon:outputDebugInfo/>
        </font>
        </h5>
        </font>
        <%@ include file="../../mldocs/bonForumBottom.html" %>
        </body>
</html>
```

C.57 Filename: TOMCAT_HOME\webapps\bonForum\jsp\forum\host_executes_command_frame.jsp

```
<!doctype html public "-//w3c//dtd html 4.0 transitional//en">
<%@ taglib uri="http://www.bonForum.org/taglib/bonForum-taglib"
prefix="bon" %>
<%@ page import="java.io.*" %>
<%@ page errorPage="forum_error.jsp" %>
<%—
First we get the chatItem nodeKey value
and put it in the stylesheet parameter.
It is needed by the XSLT done by transform tag.
—%>
<%
String itemKey = (String)session.getAttribute("itemKey");
if(itemKey == null || itemKey.trim().length() < 1) {
     itemKey = "000000000000.000000000000.000000000000";
}
session.setAttribute("param1", itemKey);
%>
<html>
       <head>
              <meta http-equiv="Content-Type"
                     content="text/html;
                     charset=x-user-defined">
              </meta>
              <title>
                     bonForum
              </title>
       </head>
       <body bgcolor="#00FFFF">
       <font face="Verdana">
       <a name="entry"> </a>
       <h5>
       <%— TESTING TEMP
              <%=itemKey%>
         —%>
       <table border=0 cellspacing=0 cellpadding=0
```

```
      rows=2 cols=1 width=100% bgcolor=#00FFFF>
<tr>
<form method="POST"
      action="/bonForum/servlet/BonForumEngine">
<%— Here we list the guests and hosts in the chat
      in select boxes created by the XSLT.
—%>
<p>
<bon:transform type="xalanVersion"
      inXML="bonForumXML"
      inXSL=
            "..\\webapps\\bonForum\\mldocs\\bonChatGuests.xsl"
      outDoc="output">
      <%=output%>
</bon:transform>
</p>
<p>
<input type="hidden" name="actorReturning"
      value="yes"></input>
<input type="hidden" name="bonCommand"
      value="host_executes_command_frame"></input>
<input type="submit" value="choose selected chat guest"
      name="submit"></input>
</p>
</form>
</tr>
<tr>
<%—
Here we get the currently chosen option.
After posting the form, the BonForumEngine servlet
forwards us back to this same page, updating
the display with the last selected chatGuest.
—%>
<%
String chatGuest = (String)session.getAttribute("chatGuest");
String chatGuestMessage = "Chosen guest: &lt;none&gt;";
if(chatGuest != null && chatGuest.trim().length() > 0) {
      int inx = chatGuest.lastIndexOf("age:");
      if(inx > 0) {
            chatGuest = chatGuest.substring(0, inx);
      }
      chatGuestMessage = "Chosen guest: " + chatGuest;
}
%>
<%—
here we display the currently chosen guest
—%>
<p>
<%=chatGuestMessage%>
</p>
</tr>
```

```
        <font face="Arial" color="blue">
        <bon:outputDebugInfo/>
        </font>
        </h5>
        </font>
        </body>
</html>
```

C.58 Filename: TOMCAT_HOME\webapps\bonForum\jsp\forum\host_executes_command_ready.jsp

```
<!doctype html public "-//w3c//dtd html 4.0 transitional//en">
<%@ taglib uri="http://www.bonForum.org/taglib/bonForum-taglib"
prefix="bon" %>
<%@ page errorPage="forum_error.jsp" %>
<html>
        <head>
                <meta http-equiv="Content-Type"
                        content="text/html;
                        charset=x-user-defined">
                </meta>
                <title>
                        bonForum
                </title>
        </head>
        <body bgcolor="#00FFFF">
        <%— go via robot to leave frameset —%>
         <%
        request.setAttribute("target", "_top");
        request.setAttribute("document",
                request.getScheme() + "://" +
                request.getServerName() + ":" +
                request.getServerPort() +
                "/bonForum/jsp/forum/host_exits_command.jsp");
        request.setAttribute("refresh", "true");
        request.setAttribute("increment", "100");
        request.setAttribute("limit", "1");
        request.setAttribute("message",
                "Host exiting command mode!");
        %>
        <jsp:forward page="actor_leaves_frameset_robot.jsp.tfe"/>
</body>
</html>
```

C.59 Filename: TOMCAT_HOME\webapps\bonForum\jsp\forum\host_executes_command_robot.jsp

```
<!doctype html public "-//w3c//dtd html 4.0 transitional//en">
<%@ taglib uri="http://www.bonForum.org/taglib/bonForum-taglib"
prefix="bon" %>
<%@ page errorPage="forum_error.jsp" %>
<%
String target = (String)session.getAttribute("target");
String document = (String)session.getAttribute("document");
String refresh = (String)session.getAttribute("refresh");
String increment = (String)session.getAttribute("increment");
String limit = (String)session.getAttribute("limit");
String message = (String)session.getAttribute("message");
%>
<%— message "debug" shows some info —%>
<html>
      <head>
            <meta http-equiv="Content-Type"
                  content="text/html;
                  charset=x-user-defined">
            </meta>
            <title>
                  bonForum
            </title>
      </head>
      <body bgcolor="#00FFFF">
      <font face="Verdana">
      <table>
      <tr>
      <img border="0" src="/bonForum/images/bonForumLogo.gif"
            alt="bonForum" width="112" height="112">
      </tr>
      <tr>
      <jsp:plugin type="applet" code="BonForumRobot.class"
            codebase="/bonForum/jsp/forum/applet"
            jreversion="1.3.0" width="400" height="160" >
        <jsp:params>
        <jsp:param name="target" value="<%=target%>"/>
        <jsp:param name="document" value="<%=document%>"/>
        <jsp:param name="refresh" value="<%=refresh%>"/>
        <jsp:param name="increment" value="<%=increment%>"/>
        <jsp:param name="limit" value="<%=limit%>"/>
        <jsp:param name="message" value="<%=message%>"/>
        </jsp:params>
        <jsp:fallback>Plugin tag OBJECT or EMBED
            not supported by browser.
        </jsp:fallback>
      </jsp:plugin>
      </tr>
```

```
        </table>
        <font face="Arial" color="blue">
        <bon:outputDebugInfo/>
        </font>
        </font>
        </body>
</html>
```

C.60 Filename: TOMCAT_HOME\webapps\bonForum\jsp\forum\host_exits_chat.jsp

```
<!doctype html public "-//w3c//dtd html 4.0 transitional//en">
<%@ taglib uri="http://www.bonForum.org/taglib/bonForum-taglib"
prefix="bon" %>
<%@ page errorPage="forum_error.jsp" %>
<%-- here we can force actor
        to select new subject and topic
                for new chat
--%>
<%--
        session.setAttribute("chatSubject", "NONE");
        session.setAttribute("chatTopic", "NONE");
--%>
<%--
here we force engine to check
        for new subject and topic for new chat
--%>
<%
session.setAttribute("newChatSubject", "no");
session.setAttribute("newChatTopic", "no");
%>
<html>
        <head>
                <meta http-equiv="Content-Type"
                        content="text/html;
                        charset=x-user-defined">
                </meta>
                <title>
                        bonForum
                </title>
        </head>
        <body>
        <jsp:forward page="visitor_executes_choice.jsp.tfe"/>
        </body>
</html>
```

C.61 Filename: TOMCAT_HOME\webapps\bonForum\jsp\forum\host_exits_command.jsp

```
<!doctype html public "-//w3c//dtd html 4.0 transitional//en">
<%@ taglib uri="http://www.bonForum.org/taglib/bonForum-taglib"
prefix="bon" %>
<%@ page errorPage="forum_error.jsp" %>
<html>
      <head>
            <meta http-equiv="Content-Type"
                  content="text/html;
                  charset=x-user-defined">
            </meta>
            <title>
                  bonForum
            </title>
      </head>
      <body>
      <jsp:forward page="host_executes_chat.jsp.tfe"/>
      </body>
</html>
```

C.62 Filename: TOMCAT_HOME\webapps\bonForum\jsp\forum\host_increases_rating.jsp

```
<!doctype html public "-//w3c//dtd html 4.0 transitional//en">
<%@ taglib uri="http://www.bonForum.org/taglib/bonForum-taglib"
prefix="bon" %>
<%@ page errorPage="forum_error.jsp" %>
<jsp:useBean id="bonForumStore"
      class="de.tarent.forum.BonForumStore"
      scope="application"/>
<html>
      <head>
            <meta http-equiv="Content-Type"
                  content="text/html;
                  charset=x-user-defined">
            </meta>
            <title>
                  bonForum
            </title>
      </head>
      <body>
     <%—
      Here increment the rating of the chosen chatGuest
      Later: will add code to promote guest to host of chat
      if rating is above some threshold, nominally 10
      —%>
      <%
      bonForumStore.changeChatActorRating("1", session);
```

```
%>
        <jsp:forward page="host_executes_command_controls.jsp.tfe"/>
</body>
</html>
```

C.63 Filename: TOMCAT_HOME\webapps\bonForum\jsp\forum\license.jsp

```
<!doctype html public "-//w3c//dtd html 4.0 transitional//en">
<%@ taglib uri="http://www.bonForum.org/taglib/bonForum-taglib"
prefix="bon" %>
<%@ page errorPage="forum_error.jsp" %>
<html>
        <head>
                <meta http-equiv="Content-Type"
                        content="text/html;
                        charset=x-user-defined">
                </meta>
                <title>
                        bonForum License
                </title>
        </head>
        <body bgcolor="#00FFFF">
        <font face="Verdana" color="black">
<table border="0" rows="1" width="100%">
<tr>
<td align="center">
<a href="forum_login.jsp">
        <img border="0" src="/bonForum/images/bonForumLogo.gif"
        alt="bonForum" width="50" height="50">
</a>
</td>
</tr>
</table>
<pre>
BonForum Software License, version 1.1
Copyright (c) 2000, 2001 Westy Rockwell  All rights reserved.
Redistribution and use in source and binary forms, with or without
modification, are permitted provided the following conditions are met.
1. Redistributions of source code must retain the above copyright
   notice, these conditions, and the following disclaimer and note(s).
2. Redistributions in binary form must reproduce the above copyright
   notice, these conditions, and the following disclaimer and note(s)
   in the documentation and/or other materials with the distribution.
3. The end-user documentation included with the redistribution, if
   any, must include the following acknowlegement:
      "This product includes software developed by
       Westy Rockwell (http://www.bonForum.org/)."
   Alternately, this acknowlegement may appear in the software itself,
```

```
   if and wherever such third-party acknowlegements normally appear.
4. The names "bonForum", "BonForum", "BonForumEngine", "BonForumRobot",
   "BonForumStore" must not be used to endorse or promote products
   derived from this software without prior written permission.
   Permission info is at http://www.bonForum.org/.
5. Products derived from this software may not be called by the names
   listed in item 4, nor may these names appear in their names without
   written permission. Permission info is at http://www.bonForum.org/.
DISCLAIMER: THIS SOFTWARE IS PROVIDED "AS IS" AND ANY EXPRESSED OR
IMPLIED WARRANTIES, INCLUDING, BUT NOT LIMITED TO, THE IMPLIED
WARRANTIES OF MERCHANTABILITY AND FITNESS FOR A PARTICULAR PURPOSE
ARE DISCLAIMED.  IN NO EVENT SHALL THE AUTHORS OR CONTRIBUTORS TO
THIS SOFTWARE, NOR ITS PUBLISHERS IN WHATEVER FORM, BE LIABLE FOR ANY
DIRECT, INDIRECT, INCIDENTAL, SPECIAL, EXEMPLARY, OR CONSEQUENTIAL
DAMAGES (INCLUDING, BUT NOT LIMITED TO, PROCUREMENT OF SUBSTITUTE
GOODS OR SERVICES; LOSS OF USE, DATA, OR PROFITS; OR BUSINESS
INTERRUPTION) HOWEVER CAUSED AND ON ANY THEORY OF LIABILITY, WHETHER
IN CONTRACT, STRICT LIABILITY,OR TORT (INCLUDING NEGLIGENCE OR
OTHERWISE) ARISING IN ANY WAY OUT OF THE USE OF THIS SOFTWARE, EVEN
IF ADVISED OF THE POSSIBILITY OF SUCH DAMAGE.
NOTE: This software is part of bonForum, a web chat application
fully discussed in a book by Westy Rockwell, with the title:
"XML, XSLT, Java and JSP - A Case Study in Developing a Web Application",
published by New Riders.  (http://www.newriders.com).
The book is published in German translation as
"XML, XSLT, Java und JSP - Professionelle Web-Applikationen entwickeln"
by Galileo Press (http://galileocomputing.de/).
For further information, please visit: http://www.bonforum.org/.
</pre>
<table border="0" rows="1" width="100%">
<tr>
<td align="center">
<a href="forum_login.jsp">
      <img border="0" src="/bonForum/images/bonForumLogo.gif"
      alt="bonForum" width="50" height="50">
</a>
</td>
</tr>
</table>
      </body>
</html>
```

C.64 Filename: TOMCAT_HOME\webapps\bonForum\jsp\forum\system_dumps_xml.jsp

```
<!doctype html public "-//w3c//dtd html 4.0 transitional//en">
<%@ taglib uri="http://www.bonForum.org/taglib/bonForum-taglib"
prefix="bon" %>
<%@ page import="java.io.*" %>
```

```
<%@ page errorPage="forum_error.jsp" %>
<%—
For testing only, this JSP makes a dump of all
bonForumXML data as an XML file, and to browser.
This will later be done only by a "system" actor command.
This file also contains many commented-out examples
showing how to use and test the bonForum transform JSP custom tag,
with various combinations of input and output options.
First, we find out which version of Xalan to use:
—%>
<%
String xalanVersion = "";
try {
xalanVersion = (String)
     pageContext.getAttribute("xalanVersion", 4);
     if(xalanVersion == null) {
          xalanVersion = "";
     }
}
catch(java.lang.NullPointerException ex) {
     xalanVersion = "";
}
if(xalanVersion.equals("")) {
     xalanVersion = "Xalan-Java 1";
     pageContext.setAttribute("xalanVersion", "Xalan-Java 1", 4);
}
%>
<%—
Here, we get access to normalize method:
—%>
<jsp:useBean id="bonForumUtils"
     class="de.tarent.forum.BonForumUtils"
     scope="application"/>
<html>
     <head>
          <meta http-equiv="Content-Type"
               content="text/html;
               charset=x-user-defined">
          </meta>
          <title>
               bonForum
          </title>
     </head>
     <body bgcolor="#FFFF00">
     <table border="0" rows="1" width="100%">
     <tr>
     <td align="center">
     <form name="system_dumps_xml" method="POST"
          action="/bonForum/servlet/BonForumEngine">
          <input type="hidden" name="actorReturning"
               value="no"></input>
```

```
                <input type="hidden" name="bonCommand"
                     value="system_executes_command"></input>
                <p>
                <input type="submit" value="Return" name="submit"></input>
                     </p>
        </form>
        </td>
        </tr>
        </table>
<p><b>
This JSP demonstrates the bonForum "transform" custom tag <br/>
It does XSLT processing of XML data with XSL stylesheets. </b>
<li>The input XML data can come from the bonForumXML database,
from a file, or from a string custom tag attribute.</li>
<li>The input XSL data can come from a file or
a string custom tag attribute.</li>
<li>The XSLT output can be to a file (XML, HTML, etc.),
to the JSP output stream (browser), or to a page attribute.</li>
</p>
<p>
(The JSP source contains other commented-out examples showing
how to use input and output options not shown below.)
</p>
The examples below are now using <%=xalanVersion%>.
<HR/>
<p> EXAMPLE 1: XSLT of bonForumXML with identity.xsl</p>
<HR/>
<p>The JSP custom action:</p>
<small>
<%=bonForumUtils.normalize("<bon:transform ")%><BR/>
<%=bonForumUtils.normalize("type=\"xalanVersion\" ")%><BR/>
<%=bonForumUtils.normalize("inXML=\"bonForumXML\" ")%><BR/>
<%=bonForumUtils.normalize(
"inXSL=\"..\\webapps\\bonForum\\mldocs\\identity.xsl\" ")%><BR/>
<%=bonForumUtils.normalize(
"outDoc=\"..\\webapps\\bonForum\\mldocs\\bonForumIdentityTransform.xml\"/>")%><BR/
>
</small>
<p>Output is in the file: \bonForum\mldocs\bonForumIdentityTransform.xml<BR/>
<bon:transform
type="xalanVersion"
inXML="bonForumXML"
inXSL="..\\webapps\\bonForum\\mldocs\\identity.xsl"
outDoc="..\\webapps\\bonForum\\mldocs\\bonForumIdentityTransform.xml"/>
<HR/>
<p>The JSP custom action:</p>
<small>
<%=bonForumUtils.normalize("<bon:transform")%><BR/>
<%=bonForumUtils.normalize("type=\"xalanVersion\" ")%><BR/>
<%=bonForumUtils.normalize("inXML=\"bonForumXML\" ")%><BR/>
<%=bonForumUtils.normalize("inXSL=\"..\\webapps\\bonForum\\mldocs\\identity.xsl\"
```

```
")%><BR/>
<%=bonForumUtils.normalize("outDoc=\"printNormalized\"/>")%><BR/>
</small>
<p>Output is here (normalized):</p>
<bon:transform
type="xalanVersion"
inXML="bonForumXML"
inXSL="..\\webapps\\bonForum\\mldocs\\identity.xsl"
outDoc="printNormalized"/>
<HR/>
<HR/>
<p> EXAMPLE 2: XSLT of XML in a file,  with default2.xsl</p>
<HR/>
<p>The JSP custom action:</p>
<small>
<%=bonForumUtils.normalize("<bon:transform")%><BR/>
<%=bonForumUtils.normalize("type=\"xalanVersion\" ")%><BR/>
<%=bonForumUtils.normalize("inXML=\"..\\webapps\\bonForum\\mldocs\\bonForumIdentit
yTransform.xml\" ")%><BR/>
<%=bonForumUtils.normalize("inXSL=\"..\\webapps\\bonForum\\mldocs\\default2.xsl\"
")%><BR/>
<%=bonForumUtils.normalize("outDoc=\"..\\webapps\\bonForum\\mldocs\\bonForumTestTr
ansform.html\"/>")%><BR/>
</small>
<p>Output is in the file: \bonForum\mldocs\bonForumTestTransform.html</p>
<bon:transform
type="xalanVersion"
inXML="..\\webapps\\bonForum\\mldocs\\bonForumIdentityTransform.xml"
inXSL="..\\webapps\\bonForum\\mldocs\\default2.xsl"
outDoc="..\\webapps\\bonForum\\mldocs\\bonForumTestTransform.html"/>
<HR/>
<HR/>
<p> EXAMPLE 3: XSLT of XML in a string attribute,  with identity.xsl</p>
<HR/>
<p>The JSP custom action:</p>
<small>
<%=bonForumUtils.normalize("<bon:transform")%><BR/>
<%=bonForumUtils.normalize("type=\"xalanVersion\" ")%><BR/>
<%=bonForumUtils.normalize("inXML=\"<?xml version=\"1.0\" encoding=\"UTF-8\"?>
")%><BR/>
<%=bonForumUtils.normalize("    <hello> Hello, World!
<goodbye>Goodbye!</goodbye></hello>\" ")%><BR/>
<%=bonForumUtils.normalize("inXSL=\"..\\webapps\\bonForum\\mldocs\\identity.xsl\"
")%><BR/>
<%=bonForumUtils.normalize("outDoc=\"print\"/>")%><BR/>
</small>
<p>Output here (not normalized):</p>
<bon:transform
type="xalanVersion"
inXML="<?xml version=\"1.0\" encoding=\"UTF-8\"?>
      <hello> Hello, World! <goodbye>Goodbye!</goodbye></hello>"
```

```
inXSL="..\\webapps\\bonForum\\mldocs\\identity.xsl"
outDoc="print"/>
<HR/>
<p>The JSP custom action:</p>
<small>
<%=bonForumUtils.normalize("<bon:transform")%><BR/>
<%=bonForumUtils.normalize("type=\"xalanVersion\" ")%><BR/>
<%=bonForumUtils.normalize("inXML=\"<?xml version=\"1.0\" encoding=\"UTF-8\"?>
")%><BR/>
<%=bonForumUtils.normalize("     <hello> Hello, World!
<goodbye>Goodbye!</goodbye></hello>\" ")%><BR/>
<%=bonForumUtils.normalize("inXSL=\"..\\webapps\\bonForum\\mldocs\\identity.xsl\"
")%><BR/>
<%=bonForumUtils.normalize("outDoc=\"printNormalized\"/>")%><BR/>
</small>
<p>Output here (normalized):</p>
<bon:transform
type="xalanVersion"
inXML="<?xml version=\"1.0\" encoding=\"UTF-8\"?>
    <hello> Hello, World! <goodbye>Goodbye!</goodbye></hello>"
inXSL="..\\webapps\\bonForum\\mldocs\\identity.xsl"
outDoc="printNormalized"/>
<HR/>
<HR/>
<p> EXAMPLE 4: XSLT of XML in a string attribute, with XSL in a string
attribute</p>
<HR/>
<p>The JSP custom action:</p>
<small>
<%=bonForumUtils.normalize("<bon:transform")%><BR/>
<%=bonForumUtils.normalize("type=\"xalanVersion\" ")%><BR/>
<%=bonForumUtils.normalize("inXML=\"<?xml version=\"1.0\" encoding=\"UTF-8\"?>
")%><BR/>
<%=bonForumUtils.normalize("<hello> Hello, World!
<goodbye>Goodbye!</goodbye></hello>\" ")%><BR/>
<%=bonForumUtils.normalize("inXSL=\"<?xml version=\"1.0\"?>")%><BR/>
<%=bonForumUtils.normalize("<xsl:stylesheet
xmlns:xsl=\"http://www.w3.org/1999/XSL/Transform\" version=\"1.0\">")%><BR/>
<%=bonForumUtils.normalize("<xsl:output method=\"xml\" omit-xml-
declaration=\"yes\" indent=\"no\"/>")%><BR/>
<%=bonForumUtils.normalize("<xsl:param name=\"param1\" select=\"' '\"/> ")%><BR/>
<%=bonForumUtils.normalize("<xsl:template match=\"/\">")%><BR/>
<%=bonForumUtils.normalize("     <xsl:apply-templates
select=\"/hello/*\"/>")%><BR/>
<%=bonForumUtils.normalize("</xsl:template>")%><BR/>
<%=bonForumUtils.normalize("<xsl:template match=\"goodbye\">")%><BR/>
<%=bonForumUtils.normalize("<xsl:value-of select=\".\"/>")%><BR/>
<%=bonForumUtils.normalize("</xsl:template>")%><BR/>
<%=bonForumUtils.normalize("</xsl:stylesheet>")%><BR/>
<%=bonForumUtils.normalize("\" ")%><BR/>
<%=bonForumUtils.normalize("outDoc=\"print\"/>")%><BR/>
```

```
</small>
<p>Output here:</p>
<bon:transform type="xalanVersion"
inXML="<?xml version=\"1.0\" encoding=\"UTF-8\"?>
<hello> Hello, World! <goodbye>Goodbye!</goodbye></hello>"
inXSL="<?xml version=\"1.0\"?>
<xsl:stylesheet xmlns:xsl=\"http://www.w3.org/1999/XSL/Transform\"
version=\"1.0\">
<xsl:output method=\"xml\" omit-xml-declaration=\"yes\" indent=\"no\"/>
<xsl:param name=\"param1\" select=\"' '\"/>
<xsl:template match=\"/\">
     <xsl:apply-templates select=\"/hello/*\"/>
</xsl:template>
<xsl:template match=\"goodbye\">
     <xsl:value-of select=\".\"/>
</xsl:template>
</xsl:stylesheet>"
outDoc="print"/>
<HR/>
<%—
More examples using XML from a file
(file is the output of previous XSLT of bonForumXML)
—%>
<%—
<bon:transform
type="xalanVersion"
inXML="..\\webapps\\bonForum\\mldocs\\bonForumIdentityTransform.xml"
inXSL="..\\webapps\\bonForum\\mldocs\\identity.xsl"
outDoc="..\\webapps\\bonForum\\mldocs\\bonForumTestTransform.xml"/>
<HR/>
<bon:transform
type="xalanVersion"
inXML="..\\webapps\\bonForum\\mldocs\\bonForumIdentityTransform.xml"
inXSL="..\\webapps\\bonForum\\mldocs\\default2.xsl"
outDoc="print" />
<HR/>
<bon:transform
type="xalanVersion"
inXML="..\\webapps\\bonForum\\mldocs\\bonForumIdentityTransform.xml"
inXSL="..\\webapps\\bonForum\\mldocs\\identity.xsl"
outDoc="printNormalized" />
<HR/>
<bon:transform
type="xalanVersion"
inXML="..\\webapps\\bonForum\\mldocs\\bonForumIdentityTransform.xml"
inXSL="..\\webapps\\bonForum\\mldocs\\default2.xsl"
outDoc="output" >
<HR/><%= output %><HR/>
</bon:transform>
<bon:transform
```

```
type="xalanVersion"
inXML="..\\webapps\\bonForum\\mldocs\\bonForumIdentityTransform.xml"
inXSL="..\\webapps\\bonForum\\mldocs\\identity.xsl"
outDoc="outputNormalized" >
<HR/><%= output %><HR/>
</bon:transform>
—%>
<%—
These examples also use XML from a file
(an example file from Xalan-Java 2)
—%>
<%—
<bon:transform
type="xalanVersion"
inXML="..\\webapps\\bonForum\\mldocs\\birds.xml"
inXSL="..\\webapps\\bonForum\\mldocs\\default2.xsl"
outDoc="..\\webapps\\bonForum\\mldocs\\birds.html" >
</bon:transform>
<bon:transform
type="xalanVersion"
inXML="..\\webapps\\bonForum\\mldocs\\birds.xml"
inXSL="..\\webapps\\bonForum\\mldocs\\default2.xsl"
outDoc="print" >
</bon:transform>
<bon:transform
type="xalanVersion"
inXML="..\\webapps\\bonForum\\mldocs\\birds.xml"
inXSL="..\\webapps\\bonForum\\mldocs\\default2.xsl"
outDoc="printNormalized" >
</bon:transform>
bon:transform
type="xalanVersion"
inXML="..\\webapps\\bonForum\\mldocs\\birds.xml"
inXSL="..\\webapps\\bonForum\\mldocs\\birds.xsl"
outDoc="..\\webapps\\bonForum\\mldocs\\birdsView.html" >
</bon:transform>
<HR/>
<bon:transform
type="xalanVersion"
inXML="..\\webapps\\bonForum\\mldocs\\birds.xml"
inXSL="..\\webapps\\bonForum\\mldocs\\birds.xsl"
outDoc="print" >
</bon:transform>
<HR/>
<bon:transform
type="xalanVersion"
inXML="..\\webapps\\bonForum\\mldocs\\birds.xml"
inXSL="..\\webapps\\bonForum\\mldocs\\birds.xsl"
outDoc="printNormalized" >
</bon:transform>
—%>
```

```
<%—
More examples using bonForumXML database,
with a stylesheet from the web application
—%>
<%—
<HR/>
<bon:transform
type="xalanVersion"
inXML="bonForumXML"
inXSL="..\\webapps\\bonForum\\mldocs\\bonForumLinks.xsl"
outDoc="print">
</bon:transform>
<HR/>
<bon:transform
type="xalanVersion"
inXML="bonForumXML"
inXSL="..\\webapps\\bonForum\\mldocs\\identity.xsl"
outDoc="printNormalized">
</bon:transform>
<HR/>
<HR/>
<bon:transform
type="xalanVersion"
inXML="bonForumXML"
inXSL="..\\webapps\\bonForum\\mldocs\\bonForumLinks.xsl"
outDoc="output">
<%=output%>
</bon:transform>
<HR/>
<bon:transform
type="xalanVersion"
inXML="bonForumXML"
inXSL="..\\webapps\\bonForum\\mldocs\\identity.xsl"
outDoc="outputNormalized">
<%=output%>
</bon:transform>
<HR/>
<bon:transform
type="xalanVersion"
inXML="bonForumXML"
inXSL="..\\webapps\\bonForum\\mldocs\\bonForumLinks.xsl"
outDoc="output">
<%=output%>
</bon:transform>
<H1>The output scripting variable outside of any custom tag:</H1>
<%=output%>
—%>
<%—
These examples output to files, and then
include the file in the JSP output stream
—%>
```

```
<%—
<bon:transform
type="xalanVersion"
inXML="..\\webapps\\bonForum\\mldocs\\testing.xml"
inXSL="..\\webapps\\bonForum\\mldocs\\default2.xsl"
outDoc="..\\webapps\\bonForum\\mldocs\\bonForumView.html" >
</bon:transform>
<bon:transform
type="xalanVersion"
inXML="..\\webapps\\bonForum\\mldocs\\testing.xml"
inXSL="..\\webapps\\bonForum\\mldocs\\default2.xsl"
outDoc="..\\webapps\\bonForum\\mldocs\\bonForumView.xml" >
</bon:transform>
<%@ include file="../../mldocs/bonForumView.html"%>
<jsp:include page="../../mldocs/bonForumView.xml" flush="true" />
—%>
<font face="Arial" color="blue">
<bon:outputDebugInfo/>
</font>
</body>
</html>
```

C.65 Filename: TOMCAT_HOME\webapps\bonForum\jsp\forum\system_executes_command.jsp

```
<!doctype html public "-//w3c//dtd html 4.0 transitional//en">
<%@ taglib uri="http://www.bonForum.org/taglib/bonForum-taglib"
prefix="bon" %>
<%@ page errorPage="forum_error.jsp" %>
<%— TESTING
<jsp:forward page="forum_error.jsp.tfe"/>
—%>
<%— TESTING errorPage:
<%= 47/0 %>
—%>
<%— greet forum actor by nickname) —%>
<%
String actorNickname =
      ((String)session.getAttribute("actorNickname"));
   if(actorNickname == null ||
            actorNickname.trim().length() < 1) {
      actorNickname = "&lt;unknown visitor&gt;";
   }
String chatWelcomeMessage =
      "Hello, " + actorNickname + "! Execute commands:";
%>
<html>
```

```
    <head>
        <meta http-equiv="Content-Type"
            content="text/html;
            charset=x-user-defined">
        </meta>
    <title>
        bonForum
    </title>
    </head>
    <body bgcolor="#FFFF00">
    <font face="Verdana">
    <a name="entry"></a>
    <h5>
    <table border="0" cellspacing="0" cellpadding="0"
        rows="4" cols="1" width="100%" bgcolor="#00FFFF">
    <tr>
    <%= chatWelcomeMessage %>
    </tr>
    <tr>
     
    </tr>
    <tr>
    <form name="system_executes_command" method="POST"
        action="/bonForum/servlet/BonForumEngine">
<table border="0" cellspacing="0" cellpadding="0"
        rows="3" cols="1" width="100%" bgcolor="#00FFFF">
    <tr>
    <label for="dump">set max chat session inactivity</label>
    <input id="dump" type="radio" name="bonCommand"
        value="system_sets_timeout"></input>
    </tr>
    <tr>
    <label for="dump">output bonForum XML data</label>
    <input id="dump" type="radio" name="bonCommand"
        value="system_dumps_xml"></input>
    </tr>
    <tr>
    <label for="exit">exit system commands</label>
    <input id="exit" type="radio" name="bonCommand"
        value="UserMustLogin" CHECKED></input>
    </tr>
    <tr>
    <input type="hidden" name="actorReturning"
        value="yes"></input>
    <input type="submit" value="do it!"
        name="submit"></input>
    </tr>
    </table>
    </form>
    </tr>
    <tr>
```

```
<form method="POST"
action="/bonForum/servlet/BonForumEngine">
<table border="0" cellspacing="0" cellpadding="0"
      rows="3" cols="1" width="100%" bgcolor="#00FFFF">
<tr>
<label for="debug">enable debugging information:</label>
<%
String debug = "no";
try {
      debug = (String)
      request.getParameter("output_debug_info");
      if(debug == null) {
            debug = "no";
      }
}
catch(java.lang.NullPointerException ex) {
      debug = "no";
}
if(debug.equals("yes")) {
%>
<input type="checkbox" id="debug"
      name="output_debug_info" value="yes" CHECKED></input>
<%
}
else {
%>
<input type="checkbox" id="debug"
      name="output_debug_info" value="yes"></input>
<%
}
%>
</tr>
<tr>
<label for="xalanVersion">XSLT processor version: </label>
<%
String xalanVersion = "Xalan-Java 1";
try {
xalanVersion = (String)
      pageContext.getAttribute("xalanVersion", 4);
      if(xalanVersion == null) {
            xalanVersion = "Xalan-Java 1";
}
}
catch(java.lang.NullPointerException ex) {
      xalanVersion = "Xalan-Java 1";
}
if(xalanVersion.equals("Xalan-Java 1")) {
%>
<input id="xalan1" type="radio" name="xalanVersion"
      value="Xalan-Java 1" CHECKED>Xalan-Java 1 </input>
<input id="xalan2" type="radio" name="xalanVersion"
```

```
          value="Xalan-Java 2">Xalan-Java 2 </input>
     <%
     }
     else {
     %>
     <input id="xalan1" type="radio" name="xalanVersion"
          value="Xalan-Java 1">Xalan-Java 1 </input>
     <input id="xalan2" type="radio" name="xalanVersion"
          value="Xalan-Java 2" CHECKED>Xalan-Java 2 </input>
     <%
     }
     %>
     </tr>
     <tr>
     <input type="hidden" name="actorReturning"
          value="yes"></input>
     <input type="hidden" name="bonCommand"
          value="system_executes_command"></input>
     <input type="submit" value="set it!"
          name="submit"></input>
     </tr>
     </table>
     </form>
     </tr>
     </table>
     <font face="Arial" color="blue">
     <bon:outputDebugInfo type="init"/>
     </font>
<%— Examples of using a bean from JSP, discussed in chapter 8 of book
    (you can put these outside of comment block to try them out):
—%>
<%—
     <jsp:useBean id="bonForumStore"
          class="de.tarent.forum.BonForumStore"
          scope="application"/>
     <p>
     hitTimeMillis: <jsp:getProperty name="bonForumStore"
                    property="hitTimeMillis"/> <BR>
     initDate: <jsp:getProperty name="bonForumStore"
                    property="initDate"/> <BR>
     reset hitTimeMillis! <jsp:setProperty name="bonForumStore"
                    property="hitTimeMillis" value="HELLO!"/> <BR>
     </p>
     <p>
     hitTimeMillis: <%=bonForumStore.getHitTimeMillis()%> <BR>
     initDate: <%=bonForumStore.getInitDate()%> <BR>
     </p>
     <p>
     reset hitTimeMillis! <% bonForumStore.setHitTimeMillis("GOODBYE!"); %> <BR>
     </p>
     <% de.tarent.forum.BonForumStore bFS = (de.tarent.forum.BonForumStore)
```

```
            pageContext.getAttribute("bonForumStore", 4);
        %>
        <p>
        hitTimeMillis: <%= bFS.getHitTimeMillis()%> <BR>
        initDate: <%= bFS.getInitDate()%> <BR>
        </p>
<% bFS = (de.tarent.forum.BonForumStore)
            pageContext.getServletContext().getAttribute("bonForumStore");
            bFS.setHitTimeMillis(null);
        %>
        <p>
        reset hitTimeMillis!<BR>
        hitTimeMillis: <%= bFS.getHitTimeMillis()%> <BR>
        initDate: <%= bFS.getInitDate()%> <BR>
        </p>
        <% bFS = (de.tarent.forum.BonForumStore)
            application.getAttribute("bonForumStore");
        %>
        <p>
        hitTimeMillis: <%= bFS.getHitTimeMillis()%> <BR>
        initDate: <%= bFS.getInitDate()%> <BR>
        </p>
—%>
        </h5>
        </font>
        </body>
</html>
```

C.66 Filename: TOMCAT_HOME\webapps\bonForum\jsp\forum\system_sets_timeout.jsp

```
<!doctype html public "-//w3c//dtd html 4.0 transitional//en">
<%@ taglib uri="http://www.bonForum.org/taglib/bonForum-taglib"
prefix="bon" %>
<%@ page import="java.io.*" %>
<%@ page errorPage="forum_error.jsp" %>
<%—
This sets max inactivity timeout interval
for bonforum chat sessions
—%>
<html>
<head>
      <meta http-equiv="Content-Type"
            content="text/html;
            charset=x-user-defined">
      </meta>
      <title>
            bonForum
      </title>
```

```
</head>
<body bgcolor="#FFFF00">
<table border="0" rows="2" width="100%">
<tr>
<td align="left">
<form name="system_dumps_xml" method="POST"
      action="/bonForum/servlet/BonForumEngine">
      <input type="hidden" name="actorReturning"
            value="no"></input>
      <input type="hidden" name="bonCommand"
            value="system_executes_command"></input>
      <p>
      <input type="submit" value="Return" name="submit"></input>
      </p>
</form>
</td>
</tr>
<tr>
<td align="left">
<form method="POST"
      action="/bonForum/servlet/BonForumEngine">
<%
String sessionMaxInactiveMinutes = "";
try {
sessionMaxInactiveMinutes = (String)
      pageContext.getAttribute("sessionMaxInactiveMinutes", 4);
      if(sessionMaxInactiveMinutes == null) {
            sessionMaxInactiveMinutes = "-1";
      }
}
catch(java.lang.NullPointerException ex) {
      sessionMaxInactiveMinutes = "-1";
}
if(sessionMaxInactiveMinutes.equals("")) {
      sessionMaxInactiveMinutes = "-1";
      pageContext.setAttribute("sessionMaxInactiveMinutes", "-1", 4);
}
%>
<h4>
This JSP can be used to test and experiment with session lifetimes.
A setting of -1 means sessions do not timeout on the server.
If you set another value, the sessions will timeout if browser
inactivity exceeds that number of minutes.
When a session times out, the user
will be sent back to first page of webapp,
and their nickname will remain unavailable until bonForum restart.
Later, a user manager feature will be added to authenticate
users and restore their nicknames and other data.
Note that applet activity alone does not prevent session timeout.
</h4>
<p>Current Maximum Chat Inactivity in Minutes: <%=sessionMaxInactiveMinutes%></p>
```

```
<input type="text" id="timeout"
name="sessionMaxInactiveMinutes" value="<%=sessionMaxInactiveMinutes%>"
size="5" maxlength="9"></input>
<input type="hidden" name="actorReturning"
      value="yes"></input>
<input type="hidden" name="bonCommand"
      value="system_sets_timeout"></input>
<input type="submit" value="set"
      name="submit"></input>
</form>
</td>
</tr>
</table>
      <font face="Arial" color="blue">
      <bon:outputDebugInfo/>
      </font>
</body>
</html>
```

C.67 Filename: TOMCAT_HOME\webapps\bonForum\jsp\forum\visitor_executes_choice.jsp

```
<!doctype html public "-//w3c//dtd html 4.0 transitional//en">
<%@ taglib uri="http://www.bonForum.org/taglib/bonForum-taglib"
prefix="bon" %>
<%@ page errorPage="forum_error.jsp" %>
<%—
here we force engine to check
      for new subject and topic for new chat
—%>
<%
session.setAttribute("newChatSubject", "no");
session.setAttribute("newChatTopic", "no");
%>
<%—
here we can force actor to select
      from available chats
—%>
<%—
session.setAttribute("chatItem", "NONE");
—%>
<html>
      <head>
            <meta http-equiv="Content-Type"
                  content="text/html;
                  charset=x-user-defined">
            </meta>
      <title>
            bonForum
```

```
</title>
</head>
<body bgcolor="#00FFFF">
<font face="Verdana">
<a name="entry"></a>
<h5>
<%— greet forum actor by nickname) —%>
<%
String actorNickname =
      ((String)session.getAttribute("actorNickname"));
   if(actorNickname == null ||
      actorNickname.trim().length() < 1) {
      actorNickname = "&lt;unknown visitor&gt;";
   }
String chatWelcomeMessage =
      "Hello, " + actorNickname +
      "! Please make a choice:";
%>
<table border=0 cellspacing=0 cellpadding=0 rows=5 cols=1
      width="100%" bgcolor=#00FFFF>
<tr>
<%= chatWelcomeMessage %>
</tr>
<form name="visitor_executes_choice" method="POST"
      action="/bonForum/servlet/BonForumEngine">
<tr>
<label for="join">join a chat</label>
<input type="radio" id="join" name="bonCommand"
      value="visitor_joins_chat"></input>
</tr>
<tr>
<label for="start">start a chat</label>
<input type="radio" id="start" name="bonCommand"
      value="visitor_starts_chat" CHECKED></input>
</tr>
<tr>
<label for="exit">exit this forum</label>
<input type="radio" id="exit" name="bonCommand"
      value="bonForum"></input>
</tr>
<tr>
<input type="hidden" name="actorReturning"
      value="yes"></input>
<input type="submit" value="do it!" name="submit"></input>
</tr>
</form>
</table>
<font face="Arial" color="blue">
<bon:outputDebugInfo/>
</font>
</h5>
```

```
        </font>
        <%@ include file="../../mldocs/bonForumSplash.html" %>
        </body>
</html>
```

C.68 Filename: TOMCAT_HOME\webapps\bonForum\jsp\forum\visitor_joins_chat.jsp

```
<!doctype html public "-//w3c//dtd html 4.0 transitional//en">
<%@ taglib uri="http://www.bonForum.org/taglib/bonForum-taglib"
prefix="bon" %>
<%@ page errorPage="forum_error.jsp" %>
<%
session.setAttribute("target", "display");
session.setAttribute("document",
        request.getScheme() + "://" +
        request.getServerName() + ":" +
        request.getServerPort() +
        "/bonForum/jsp/forum/visitor_joins_chat_frame.jsp");
session.setAttribute("refresh", "true");
session.setAttribute("increment", "30000");
session.setAttribute("limit", "5000");
session.setAttribute("message", "refreshing...");
%>
<html>
        <head>
                <meta http-equiv="Content-Type"
                        content="text/html;
                        charset=x-user-defined">
                </meta>
                <title>
                        bonForum
                </title>
        </head>
<noframes>/bonForum/noframe/html.index</noframes>
<frameset rows="72%, 28%">
<frame src="/bonForum/jsp/forum/visitor_joins_chat_frame.jsp"
        name="display"/>
<frameset cols="77%, 23%">
<frame src="/bonForum/jsp/forum/visitor_joins_chat_controls.jsp"
        name="controls"/>
<frame src="/bonForum/jsp/forum/host_executes_chat_robot.jsp"
        name="robot"/>
<%— Note that all the bonForum states could share the same "refresh"
        "_robot" JSP.  For example, we tested the following one.  But that
        increases the interdependence of the frame contents in all states.
        <frame src="/bonForum/jsp/forum/actor_refreshes_frame_robot.jsp"
        name="robot"/>
—%>
```

```
</frameset>
</frameset>
```

C.69 Filename: TOMCAT_HOME\webapps\bonForum\jsp\forum\visitor_joins_chat_controls.jsp

```
<!doctype html public "-//w3c//dtd html 4.0 transitional//en">
<%@ taglib uri="http://www.bonForum.org/taglib/bonForum-taglib"
prefix="bon" %>
<%@ page errorPage="forum_error.jsp" %>
<%-- get actor nickname into a greeting: --%>
<%
String actorNickname =
    ((String)session.getAttribute("actorNickname"));
if(actorNickname == null ||
     actorNickname.trim().length() < 1) {
      actorNickname = "&lt;unknown visitor&gt;";
}
String chatJoinMessage =
      "Join a chat, " + actorNickname +
      "! First choose one from the list.";
%>
<html>
      <head>
            <meta http-equiv="Content-Type"
                  content="text/html;
                  charset=x-user-defined">
            </meta>
            <title>
                  bonForum
            </title>
      </head>
      <body bgcolor="#00FFFF">
      <font face="Verdana">
      <a name="entry"></a>
      <h5>
      <%-- a different frame lists the chats available --%>
      <form method="POST"
      action="/bonForum/servlet/BonForumEngine">
      <table border=0 cellspacing=0 cellpadding=0
            rows=2 cols=1 width=100% bgcolor=#00FFFF>
      <%-- greet forum actor by nickname: --%>
      <tr>
      <%= chatJoinMessage %>
      </tr>
      <tr>
      <input type="hidden" name="actorReturning"
```

```
            value="yes"></input>
        <input type="hidden" name="bonCommand"
            value="visitor_joins_chat_ready"></input>
        <input type="submit" value="join chat"
            name="submit"></input>
        </tr>
        </table>
        </form>
        <font face="Arial" color="blue">
        <bon:outputDebugInfo/>
        </font>
        </h5>
        </font>
        <%@ include file="../../mldocs/bonForumBottom.html" %>
        </body>
</html>
```

C.70 Filename: TOMCAT_HOME\webapps\bonForum\jsp\forum\visitor_joins_chat_frame.jsp

```
<!doctype html public "-//w3c//dtd html 4.0 transitional//en">
<%@ taglib uri="http://www.bonForum.org/taglib/bonForum-taglib"
prefix="bon" %>
<%@ page import="java.io.*" %>
<%@ page errorPage="forum_error.jsp" %>
<%—
Here we get the currently chosen option.
After posting the form, the BonForumEngine servlet
forwards us back to this same page, updating
the display with the last selected chatItem.
—%>
<%
String chatItem = (String)session.getAttribute("chatItem");
String chatItemMessage = "chat: &lt;none&gt;";
if(chatItem != null && chatItem.trim().length() > 0) {
  String subject = "";
  String topic = "";
  subject = chatItem.substring(0, chatItem.indexOf('[') - 1);
  subject = subject.replace('_', ' ');
  topic = chatItem.substring(chatItem.indexOf('[') + 1,
          chatItem.lastIndexOf(']'));
  chatItemMessage = "chat: " + subject + " —> " + topic;
}
%>
<%—
Here later we can get a flag to select subset of available chats
and passed it to the XSLT via an XSL parameter
```

```
Since chat selection based on flag is not yet implemented,
and XSLT needs one parameter, we pass an empty string for now.
--%>
<%
session.setAttribute("param1", "");
%>
<html>
      <head>
            <meta http-equiv="Content-Type"
                  content="text/html;
                  charset=x-user-defined">
            </meta>
            <title>
                  bonForum
            </title>
      </head>
      <body bgcolor="#00FFFF">
      <font face="Verdana">
      <a name="entry"></a>
      <h5>
      <form method="POST"
            action="/bonForum/servlet/BonForumEngine">
      <table border=0 cellspacing=0 cellpadding=0
            rows=3 cols=1 width=100% bgcolor=#00FFFF>
      <%-- Here we display the currently chosen chat --%>
      <tr>
      <%=chatItemMessage%>
      </tr>
      <%-- here we list the available chats
            in a select box created by the XSLT.
      --%>
      <tr>
      <bon:transform type="xalanVersion"
            inXML=
                  "bonForumXML"
            inXSL=
              "..\\webapps\\bonForum\\mldocs\\bonChatItems.xsl"
            outDoc=
                  "output">
            <%=output%>
      </bon:transform>
      </tr>
      <%-- LATER: chatModerated can filter the
            list of available chats
      <label for="chatModerated">Moderated chats only? </label>
      <input type="radio" name="chatModerated"
            value="yes">YES</input>
      <input type="radio" name="chatModerated"
            value="no">NO</input>
      --%>
      <tr>
```

```
            <input type="hidden" name="actorReturning"
                  value="yes"></input>
            <input type="hidden" name="bonCommand"
                  value="visitor_joins_chat_frame"></input>
            <input type="submit"
                  value="choose the selected chat"
                  name="submit"></input>
            </tr>
            </table>
            </form>
            <font face="Arial" color="blue">
            <bon:outputDebugInfo/>
            </font>
            </h5>
            </font>
            </body>
      </html>
```

C.71 Filename: TOMCAT_HOME\webapps\bonForum\jsp\forum\visitor_joins_chat_ready.jsp

```
<!doctype html public "-//w3c//dtd html 4.0 transitional//en">
<%@ taglib uri="http://www.bonForum.org/taglib/bonForum-taglib"
prefix="bon" %>
<%@ page errorPage="forum_error.jsp" %>
<html>
      <head>
            <meta http-equiv="Content-Type"
                  content="text/html;
                  charset=x-user-defined">
            </meta>
            <title>
                  bonForum
            </title>
      </head>
      <body bgcolor="#00FFFF">
      <%-- go via robot to leave frameset --%>
      <%--
      Notice that this page uses request not session attributes
      to send parameters to robot applet.  It can do that since
      the robot is acting as a "one-shot" and needs the attribute
      data only one time. Also, all the pages that use the robot
      to leave a frameset share the same robot.
      --%>
      <%--
      here we prefix the scheme, host and port
      of the web application server
```

```
        so the applet on the client can find it!
       --%>
        <%
        request.setAttribute("target", "_top");
        request.setAttribute("document",
              request.getScheme() + "://" +
              request.getServerName() + ":" +
              request.getServerPort() +
              "/bonForum/jsp/forum/guest_executes_chat.jsp");
        request.setAttribute("refresh", "true");
        request.setAttribute("increment", "100");
        request.setAttribute("limit", "1");
        request.setAttribute("message", "Joining a chat!");
        %>
        <%--These attributes become applet
              parameters in robot page--%>

        <jsp:forward page="actor_leaves_frameset_robot.jsp.tfe"/>

        </font>
        </body>
</html>
```

C.72 Filename: TOMCAT_HOME\webapps\bonForum\jsp\forum\visitor_joins_chat_robot.jsp

```
<!doctype html public "-//w3c//dtd html 4.0 transitional//en">
<%@ taglib uri="http://www.bonForum.org/taglib/bonForum-taglib"
prefix="bon" %>
<%@ page errorPage="forum_error.jsp" %>
<%
String target = (String)session.getAttribute("target");
String document = (String)session.getAttribute("document");
String refresh = (String)session.getAttribute("refresh");
String increment = (String)session.getAttribute("increment");
String limit = (String)session.getAttribute("limit");
String message = (String)session.getAttribute("message");
%>
<%-- message "debug" shows some info --%>
<html>
      <head>
            <meta http-equiv="Content-Type"
                  content="text/html;
                  charset=x-user-defined">
            </meta>
            <title>
                  bonForum
```

```
            </title>
        </head>
        <body bgcolor="#00FFFF">
        <font face="Verdana">

        <table>
        <tr>
        <img border="0" src="/bonForum/images/bonForumLogo.gif"
             alt="bonForum" width="112" height="112">
        </tr>
        <tr>
        <jsp:plugin type="applet" code="BonForumRobot.class"
             codebase="/bonForum/jsp/forum/applet"
             jreversion="1.3.0" width="400" height="160" >
          <jsp:params>
          <jsp:param name="target" value="<%=target%>"/>
          <jsp:param name="document" value="<%=document%>"/>
          <jsp:param name="refresh" value="<%=refresh%>"/>
          <jsp:param name="increment" value="<%=increment%>"/>
          <jsp:param name="limit" value="<%=limit%>"/>
          <jsp:param name="message" value="<%=message%>"/>
          </jsp:params>
          <jsp:fallback>Plugin tag OBJECT or EMBED
             not supported by browser.
          </jsp:fallback>
        </jsp:plugin>
        </tr>
        </table>
        <font face="Arial" color="blue">
        <bon:outputDebugInfo/>
        </font>
        </font>
        </body>
</html>
```

C.73 Filename: TOMCAT_HOME\webapps\bonForum\jsp\forum\visitor_starts_chat.jsp

```
<!doctype html public "-//w3c//dtd html 4.0 transitional//en">
<%@ taglib uri="http://www.bonForum.org/taglib/bonForum-taglib"
prefix="bon" %>
<%@ page errorPage="forum_error.jsp" %>
<%— LATER: uncomment these six lines and
      add a "robot" in a third frame below
      to auto refresh chat subject list.
      (See other examples elsewhere.)
<%
session.setAttribute("target", "display");
session.setAttribute("document",
      request.getScheme() + "://" +
```

```
        request.getServerName() + ":" +
        request.getServerPort() +
        "/bonForum/jsp/forum/visitor_starts_chat_frame.jsp");
session.setAttribute("refresh", "true");
session.setAttribute("increment", "5000");
session.setAttribute("limit", "5000");
session.setAttribute("message", "refreshing..."); %>
—%>
<html>
      <head>
            <meta http-equiv="Content-Type"
                  content="text/html;
                  charset=x-user-defined">
            </meta>
            <title>
                  bonForum
            </title>
      </head>
<noframes>/bonForum/noframe/html.index</noframes>
<frameset rows="65%, 35%">
<frame src="/bonForum/jsp/forum/visitor_starts_chat_frame.jsp.tfe"
      name="display"/>
<frame src="/bonForum/jsp/forum/visitor_starts_chat_controls.jsp.tfe"
      name="controls"/>
</frameset>
</html>
```

C.74 Filename: TOMCAT_HOME\webapps\bonForum\jsp\forum\visitor_starts_chat_controls.jsp

```
<!doctype html public "-//w3c//dtd html 4.0 transitional//en">
<%@ taglib uri="http://www.bonForum.org/taglib/bonForum-taglib"
prefix="bon" %>
<%@ page errorPage="forum_error.jsp" %>
<%— get actor nickname into a greeting: —%>
<%
String actorNickname =
      ((String)session.getAttribute("actorNickname"));
if(actorNickname == null ||
    actorNickname.trim().length() < 1) {
      actorNickname = "&lt;unknown visitor&gt;";
}
String chatStartMessage =
      "Start a chat, " + actorNickname +
      "!  First select a subject category from the list.";
%>
<%— get chat description, if any,
```

```
     displayed by input form element —%>
<% String chatTopic =
     (String)session.getAttribute("chatTopic");
   if(chatTopic == null || chatTopic.trim().length() < 1) {
     chatTopic = "";
   }
%>
<%
String chatSubjectAndTopic = "";
try {
      chatSubjectAndTopic =
            (String)session.getAttribute(
            "chatSubjectAndTopicTaken");
      if(!chatSubjectAndTopic.equals("")) {
            chatSubjectAndTopic =
            chatSubjectAndTopic + " is taken! " ;
      }
      if(chatSubjectAndTopic == null) {
            chatSubjectAndTopic = "";
      }
}
catch(java.lang.NullPointerException ex) {
      chatSubjectAndTopic = "";
}
%>
<html>
      <head>
            <meta http-equiv="Content-Type"
                  content="text/html;
                  charset=x-user-defined">
            </meta>
            <title>
                  bonForum
            </title>
      </head>
      <body bgcolor="#00FFFF">
      <font face="Verdana">
      <a name="entry"></a>
      <h5>
      <%— a different frame lists the subjects available—%>
      <form method="POST"
            action="/bonForum/servlet/BonForumEngine">
      <table border=0 cellspacing=0 cellpadding=0
            rows=4 cols=1 width=50% bgcolor=#00FFFF>
      <%— greet forum actor by nickname: —%>
      <tr>
      <%= chatStartMessage %>
      <font color="red">
      <%= chatSubjectAndTopic %>
      </font>
      </tr>
```

```
        <tr>
        <label for="chatTopic">
             Then enter a description for your new chat:</label>
        <input type="text" value = "<%=chatTopic%>"
             name="chatTopic"></input>
        </tr>
        <tr>
        <label for="chatModerated">Will you moderate this chat?
        </label>
        <input type="radio" name="chatModerated"
             value="yes">YES</input>
        <input type="radio" name="chatModerated"
             value="no" CHECKED>NO</input>
        <input type="hidden" name="actorReturning"
             value="yes"></input>
        <input type="hidden" name="bonCommand"
             value="visitor_starts_chat_ready"></input>
        <input type="submit" value="start chat"
             name="submit"></input>
        </tr>
        </table>
        </form>
        <font face="Arial" color="blue">
        <bon:outputDebugInfo/>
        </font>
        </h5>
        </font>
<%@ include file="../../mldocs/bonForumBottom.html" %>
        </body>
</html>
```

C.75 Filename: TOMCAT_HOME\webapps\bonForum\jsp\forum\visitor_starts_chat_frame.jsp

```
<!doctype html public "-//w3c//dtd html 4.0 transitional//en">
<%@ taglib uri="http://www.bonForum.org/taglib/bonForum-taglib"
prefix="bon" %>
<%@ page errorPage="forum_error.jsp" %>
<%-- here we get the chat subject and
     topic settings for later display --%>
<%
String chatSubject =
     (String)session.getAttribute("chatSubject");
String chatSubjectMessage = "category: &lt;none&gt;";
if(chatSubject != null && chatSubject.trim().length() > 0) {
     chatSubjectMessage = "category: " + chatSubject;
}
```

```
%>
<%
String chatTopic = (String)session.getAttribute("chatTopic");
String chatTopicMessage = "topic: &lt;none&gt;";
if(chatTopic != null && chatTopic.trim().length() > 0) {
      chatTopicMessage = "topic: " + chatTopic;
}
%>
<html>
      <head>
            <meta http-equiv="Content-Type"
                  content="text/html;
                  charset=x-user-defined">
            </meta>
            <title>
                  bonForum
            </title>
      </head>
      <body bgcolor="#00FFFF">
      <font face="Verdana">
      <a name="entry"></a>
      <h5>
      <%— here we list the chat categories available —%>
      <form method="POST"
            action="/bonForum/servlet/BonForumEngine">
      <table border=0 cellspacing=0 cellpadding=0
            rows=4 cols=1 width=50% bgcolor=#00FFFF>
      <tr>
      <%=chatSubjectMessage%>
      </tr>
      <tr>
      <%=chatTopicMessage%>
      </tr>
      <tr>
      <select size="12" name="chatSubject">
      <bon:outputPathNames
            docName="bonForumXML"
            pathToSubTreeRootNode="bonForum.things.subjects"
            ancestorReplacer="COMPLETE_PATHS"
            nodeSeparator="/">
            <option><%= output %></option>
      </bon:outputPathNames>
      </select>
      </tr>
      <tr>
      <input type="hidden" name="actorReturning"
            value="yes"></input>
      <input type="hidden" name="bonCommand"
            value="visitor_starts_chat_frame"></input>
      <input type="submit" value="choose selected chat subject"
            name="submit"></input>
```

```
        </tr>
        </table>
        </form>
        <font face="Arial" color="blue">
        <bon:outputDebugInfo/>
        </font>
        </h5>
        </font>
        </body>
</html>
```

C.76 Filename: TOMCAT_HOME\webapps\bonForum\jsp\forum\visitor_starts_chat_ready.jsp

```
<!doctype html public "-//w3c//dtd html 4.0 transitional//en">
<%@ taglib uri="http://www.bonForum.org/taglib/bonForum-taglib"
prefix="bon" %>
<%@ page errorPage="forum_error.jsp" %>
<html>
      <head>
            <meta http-equiv="Content-Type"
                  content="text/html;
                  charset=x-user-defined">
            </meta>
            <title>
                  bonForum
            </title>
      </head>
      <body bgcolor="#00FFFF">
      <%— go via robot to leave frameset —%>
      <%—
      Notice that this page uses request not session attributes
      to send parameters to robot applet.  It can do that since
      the robot is acting as a "one-shot" and needs the attribute
      data only one time. Also, all the pages that use the robot
      to leave a frameset share the same robot.
      —%>
      <%—
      here we prefix the scheme, host and port
      of the web application server
      so the applet on the client can find it!
      —%>
      <%
      request.setAttribute("target", "_top");
      request.setAttribute("document",
            request.getScheme() + "://" +
            request.getServerName() + ":" +
```

```
            request.getServerPort() +
            "/bonForum/jsp/forum/host_executes_chat.jsp");
        request.setAttribute("refresh", "true");
        request.setAttribute("increment", "100");
        request.setAttribute("limit", "1");
        request.setAttribute("message", "Preparing new chat!");
        %>
        <%—These attributes become applet
            parameters in robot page—%>
        <jsp:forward page="actor_leaves_frameset_robot.jsp.tfe"/>
        </font>
        </body>
</html>
```

C.77 Filename: TOMCAT_HOME\webapps\bonForum\jsp\forum\visitor_starts_chat_robot.jsp

```
<!doctype html public "-//w3c//dtd html 4.0 transitional//en">
<%@ taglib uri="http://www.bonForum.org/taglib/bonForum-taglib"
prefix="bon" %>
<%@ page errorPage="forum_error.jsp" %>
<%
String target = (String)session.getAttribute("target");
String document = (String)session.getAttribute("document");
String refresh = (String)session.getAttribute("refresh");
String increment = (String)session.getAttribute("increment");
String limit = (String)session.getAttribute("limit");
String message = (String)session.getAttribute("message");
%>
<%— message "debug" shows some info —%>
<html>
    <head>
        <meta http-equiv="Content-Type"
            content="text/html;
            charset=x-user-defined">
        </meta>
        <title>
            bonForum
        </title>
    </head>
    <body bgcolor="#00FFFF">
    <font face="Verdana">

    <table>
    <tr>
    <img border="0" src="/bonForum/images/bonForumLogo.gif"
        alt="bonForum" width="112" height="112">
```

```
      </tr>
      <tr>
      <jsp:plugin type="applet" code="BonForumRobot.class"
            codebase="/bonForum/jsp/forum/applet"
            jreversion="1.3.0" width="400" height="160" >
        <jsp:params>
        <jsp:param name="target" value="<%=target%>"/>
        <jsp:param name="document" value="<%=document%>"/>
        <jsp:param name="refresh" value="<%=refresh%>"/>
        <jsp:param name="increment" value="<%=increment%>"/>
        <jsp:param name="limit" value="<%=limit%>"/>
        <jsp:param name="message" value="<%=message%>"/>
        </jsp:params>
        <jsp:fallback>Plugin tag OBJECT or EMBED
            not supported by browser.
        </jsp:fallback>
      </jsp:plugin>
      </tr>
      </table>
      <font face="Arial" color="blue">
      <bon:outputDebugInfo/>
      </font>
      </font>
      </body>
</html>
```

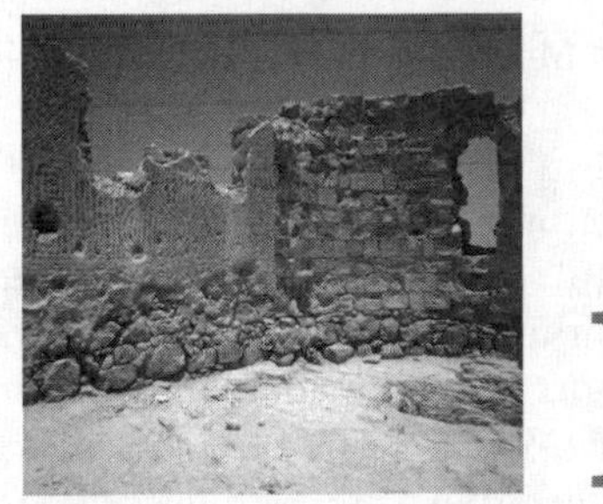

D

Sun Microsystems, Inc. Binary Code License Agreement

READ THE TERMS OF THIS AGREEMENT AND ANY PROVIDED SUPPLEMENTAL LICENSE TERMS (COLLECTIVELY "AGREEMENT") CAREFULLY BEFORE OPENING THE SOFTWARE MEDIA PACKAGE. BY OPENING THE SOFTWARE MEDIA PACKAGE, YOU AGREE TO THE TERMS OF THIS AGREEMENT. IF YOU ARE ACCESSING THE SOFTWARE ELECTRONICALLY, INDICATE YOUR ACCEPTANCE OF THESE TERMS BY SELECTING THE "ACCEPT" BUTTON AT THE END OF THIS AGREEMENT. IF YOU DO NOT AGREE TO ALL THESE TERMS, PROMPTLY RETURN THE UNUSED SOFTWARE TO YOUR PLACE OF PURCHASE FOR A REFUND OR, IF THE SOFTWARE IS ACCESSED ELECTRONICALLY, SELECT THE "DECLINE" BUTTON AT THE END OF THIS AGREEMENT.

1. LICENSE TO USE. Sun grants you a non-exclusive and non-transferable license for the internal use only of the accompanying software and documentation and any error corrections provided by Sun (collectively "Software"), by the number of users and the class of computer hardware for which the corresponding fee has been paid.

2. RESTRICTIONS Software is confidential and copyrighted. Title to Software and all associated intellectual property rights is retained by Sun and/or its licensors. Except as specifically authorized in any Supplemental License Terms, you may not make copies of Software, other than a single copy of Software for archival purposes. Unless enforcement is prohibited by applicable law, you may not modify, decompile, or reverse engineer Software. You acknowledge that Software is not designed, licensed or

intended for use in the design, construction, operation or maintenance of any nuclear facility. Sun disclaims any express or implied warranty of fitness for such uses. No right, title or interest in or to any trademark, service mark, logo or trade name of Sun or its licensors is granted under this Agreement.

3. LIMITED WARRANTY. Sun warrants to you that for a period of ninety (90) days from the date of purchase, as evidenced by a copy of the receipt, the media on which Software is furnished (if any and if provided by Sun) will be free of defects in materials and workmanship under normal use. Except for the foregoing, Software is provided "AS IS". Your exclusive remedy and Sun's entire liability under this limited warranty will be at Sun's option to replace Software media or refund the fee paid for Software, if any.

4. DISCLAIMER OF WARRANTY. **UNLESS SPECIFIED IN THIS AGREEMENT, ALL EXPRESS OR IMPLIED CONDITIONS, REPRESENTATIONS AND WARRANTIES, INCLUDING ANY IMPLIED WARRANTY OF MERCHANTABILITY, FITNESS FOR A PARTICULAR PURPOSE OR NON-INFRINGEMENT ARE DISCLAIMED, EXCEPT TO THE EXTENT THAT THESE DISCLAIMERS ARE HELD TO BE LEGALLY INVALID.**

5. **LIMITATION OF LIABILITY. TO THE EXTENT NOT PROHIBITED BY LAW, IN NO EVENT WILL SUN OR ITS LICENSORS BE LIABLE FOR ANY LOST REVENUE, PROFIT OR DATA, OR FOR SPECIAL, INDIRECT, CONSEQUENTIAL, INCIDENTAL OR PUNITIVE DAMAGES, HOWEVER CAUSED REGARDLESS OF THE THEORY OF LIABILITY, ARISING OUT OF OR RELATED TO THE USE OF OR INABILITY TO USE SOFTWARE, EVEN IF SUN HAS BEEN ADVISED OF THE POSSIBILITY OF SUCH DAMAGES.** In no event will Sun's liability to you, whether in contract, tort (including negligence), or otherwise, exceed the amount paid by you for Software under this Agreement. The foregoing limitations will apply even if the above stated warranty fails of its essential purpose.

6. Termination. This Agreement is effective until terminated. You may terminate this Agreement at any time by destroying all copies of Software. This Agreement will terminate immediately without notice from Sun if you fail to comply with any provision of this Agreement. Upon Termination, you must destroy all copies of Software.

7. Export Regulations. All Software and technical data delivered under this Agreement are subject to US export control laws and may be subject to export or import regulations in other countries. You agree to comply strictly with all such laws and regulations and acknowledge that you have the responsibility to obtain such licenses to export,re-export, or import as may be required after delivery to you.

8. U.S. Government Restricted Rights. If Software is being acquired by or on behalf of the U.S. Government or by a U.S. Government prime contractor or subcontractor (at any tier), then the Government's rights in Software and accompanying documentation will be only as set forth in this Agreement; this is in accordance with 48 CFR

227.7201 through 227.7202-4 (for Department of Defense (DOD) acquisitions) and with 48 CFR 2.101 and 12.212 (for non-DOD acquisitions).

9. Governing Law. Any action related to this Agreement will be governed by California law and controlling U.S. federal law. No choice of law rules of any jurisdiction will apply.

10. Severability. If any provision of this Agreement is held to be unenforceable, this Agreement will remain in effect with the provision omitted, unless omission would frustrate the intent of the parties, in which case this Agreement will immediately terminate.

11. Integration. This Agreement is the entire agreement between you and Sun relating to its subject matter. It supersedes all prior or contemporaneous oral or written communications, proposals, representations and warranties and prevails over any conflicting or additional terms of any quote, order, acknowledgment, or other communication between the parties relating to its subject matter during the term of this Agreement. No modification of this Agreement will be binding, unless in writing and signed by an authorized representative of each party.

For inquiries please contact: Sun Microsystems, Inc. 901 San Antonio Road, Palo Alto, California 94303

JAVATM 2 SOFTWARE DEVELOPMENT KIT STANDARD EDITION VERSION 1.3 SUPPLEMENTAL LICENSE TERMS

These supplemental license terms ("Supplemental Terms") add to or modify the terms of the Binary Code License Agreement (collectively, the "Agreement"). Capitalized terms not defined in these Supplemental Terms shall have the same meanings ascribed to them in the Agreement. These Supplemental Terms shall supersede any inconsistent or conflicting terms in the Agreement, or in any license contained within the Software.

1. Internal Use and Development License Grant. Subject to the terms and conditions of this Agreement, including, but not limited to, Section 2 (Redistributables) and Section 4 (Java Technology Restrictions) of these Supplemental Terms, Sun grants you a non-exclusive, non-transferable, limited license to reproduce the Software for internal use only for the sole purpose of development of your JavaTM applet and application ("Program"), provided that you do not redistribute the Software in whole or in part, either separately or included with any Program.

2. Redistributables. In addition to the license granted in Paragraph 1above, Sun grants you a non-exclusive, non-transferable, limited license to reproduce and distribute, only as part of your separate copy of JAVA(TM) 2 RUNTIME ENVIRONMENT STANDARD EDITION VERSION 1.3 software, those files specifically identified as redistributable in the JAVA(TM) 2 RUNTIME ENVIRONMENT STANDARD EDITION VERSION 1.3 "README" file (the "Redistributables") provided that: (a) you distribute the Redistributables complete and unmodified (unless otherwise specified in the applicable README file), and only bundled as part of the JavaTM applets and applications that you develop (the "Programs:); (b) you do not distribute addi-

tional software intended to supersede any component(s) of the Redistributables; (c) you do not remove or alter any proprietary legends or notices contained in or on the Redistributables; (d) you only distribute the Redistributables pursuant to a license agreement that protects Sun's interests consistent with the terms contained in the Agreement, and (e) you agree to defend and indemnify Sun and its licensors from and against any damages, costs, liabilities, settlement amounts and/or expenses (including attorneys' fees) incurred in connection with any claim, lawsuit or action by any third party that arises or results from the use or distribution of any and all Programs and/or Software.

3. Separate Distribution License Required. You understand and agree that you must first obtain a separate license from Sun prior to reproducing or modifying any portion of the Software other than as provided with respect to Redistributables in Paragraph 2 above.

4. Java Technology Restrictions. You may not modify the Java Platform Interface ("JPI", identified as classes contained within the "java" package or any subpackages of the "java" package), by creating additional classes within the JPI or otherwise causing the addition to or modification of the classes in the JPI. In the event that you create an additional class and associated API(s) which (i) extends the functionality of a Java environment, and (ii) is exposed to third party software developers for the purpose of developing additional software which invokes such additional API, you must promptly publish broadly an accurate specification for such API for free use by all developers. You may not create, or authorize your licensees to create additional classes, interfaces, or subpackages that are in any way identified as "java", "javax", "sun" or similar convention as specified by Sun in any class file naming convention. Refer to the appropriate version of the Java Runtime Environment binary code license (currently located at `http://www.java.sun.com/jdk/index.html`) for the availability of runtime code which may be distributed with Java applets and applications.

5. Trademarks and Logos. You acknowledge and agree as between you and Sun that Sun owns the Java trademark and all Java-related trademarks, service marks, logos and other brand designations including the Coffee Cup logo and Duke logo ("Java Marks"), and you agree to comply with the Sun Trademark and Logo Usage Requirements currently located at http://www.sun.com/policies/trademarks. Any use you make of the Java Marks inures to Sun's benefit.

6. Source Code. Software may contain source code that is provided solely for reference purposes pursuant to the terms of this Agreement.

7. Termination. Sun may terminate this Agreement immediately should any Software become, or in Sun's opinion be likely to become, the subject of a claim of infringement of a patent, trade secret, copyright or other intellectual property right.

License Agreement: Forte for Java, release 2.0, Community Edition for All Platforms

To obtain Forte for Java, release 2.0, Community Edition for All Platforms, you must agree to the software license below.

CAUSED REGARDLESS OF THE THEORY OF LIABILITY, ARISING OUT OF OR RELATED TO THE USE OF OR INABILITY TO USE SOFTWARE, EVEN IF SUN HAS BEEN ADVISED OF THE POSSIBILITY OF SUCH DAMAGES. In no event will Sun's liability to you, whether in contract, tort (including negligence), or otherwise, exceed the amount paid by you for Software under this Agreement. The foregoing limitations will apply even if the above stated warranty fails of its essential purpose.

6. Termination. This Agreement is effective until terminated. You may terminate this Agreement at any time by destroying all copies of Software. This Agreement will terminate immediately without notice from Sun if you fail to comply with any provision of this Agreement. Upon Termination, you must destroy all copies of Software.

7. Export Regulations. All Software and technical data delivered under this Agreement are subject to US export control laws and may be subject to export or import regulations in other countries. You agree to comply strictly with all such laws and regulations and acknowledge that you have the responsibility to obtain such licenses to export, re-export, or import as may be required after delivery to you.

8. U.S. Government Restricted Rights. If Software is being acquired by or on behalf of the U.S. Government or by a U.S. Government prime contractor or subcontractor (at any tier), then the Government's rights in Software and accompanying documentation will be only as set forth in this Agreement; this is in accordance with 48 CFR 227.7201 through 227.7202-4 (for Department of Defense (DOD)acquisitions) and with 48 CFR 2.101 and 12.212 (for non-DOD acquisitions).

9. Governing Law. Any action related to this Agreement will be governed by California law and controlling U.S. federal law. No choice of law rules of any jurisdiction will apply.

10. Severability. If any provision of this Agreement is held to be unenforceable, this Agreement will remain in effect with the provision omitted, unless omission would frustrate the intent of the parties, in which case this Agreement will immediately terminate.

11. Integration. This Agreement is the entire agreement between you and Sun relating to its subject matter. It supersedes all prior or contemporaneous oral or written communications, proposals, representations and warranties and prevails over any conflicting or additional terms of any quote, order, acknowledgment, or other communication between the parties relating to its subject matter during the term of this Agreement. No modification of this Agreement will be binding, unless in writing and signed by an authorized representative of each party.

JAVA(TM) DEVELOPMENT TOOLS FORTE(TM) FOR JAVA(TM), RELEASE 2.0, COMMUNITY EDITION SUPPLEMENTAL LICENSE TERMS

These supplemental license terms ("Supplemental Terms") add to or modify the terms of the Binary Code License Agreement (collectively, the "Agreement"). Capitalized terms not defined in these Supplemental Terms shall have the same meanings ascribed to them in the Agreement. These Supplemental Terms shall supersede any inconsistent or conflicting terms in the Agreement, or in any license contained within the Software.

1. Software Internal Use and Development License Grant. Subject to the terms and conditions of this Agreement, including, but not limited to Section 3 (Java(TM) Technology Restrictions) of these Supplemental Terms, Sun grants you a non-exclusive, non-transferable, limited license to reproduce internally and use internally the binary form of the Software complete and unmodified for the sole purpose of designing, developing and testing your [Java applets and] applications intended to run on the Java platform ("Programs").

2. License to Distribute Redistributables. In addition to the license granted in Section 1 (Redistributables Internal Use and Development License Grant) of these Supplemental Terms, subject to the terms and conditions of this Agreement, including but not limited to Section 3 (Java Technology Restrictions) of these Supplemental Terms, Sun grants you a non-exclusive, non-transferable, limited license to reproduce and distribute those files specifically identified as redistributable in the Software "README" file ("Redistributables") provided that: (i) you distribute the Redistributables complete and unmodified (unless otherwise specified in the applicable README file), and only bundled as part of your Programs, (ii) you do not distribute additional software intended to supersede any component(s) of the Redistributables, (iii) you do not remove or alter any proprietary legends or notices contained in or on the Redistributables, (iv) for a particular version of the Java platform, any executable output generated by a compiler that is contained in the Software must (a) only be compiled from source code that conforms to the corresponding version of the OEM Java Language Specification; (b) be in the class file format defined by the corresponding version of the OEM Java Virtual Machine Specification; and (c) execute properly on a reference runtime, as specified by Sun, associated with such version of the Java platform, (v) you only distribute the Redistributables pursuant to a license agreement that protects Sun's interests consistent with the terms contained in the Agreement, and (vi) you agree to defend and indemnify Sun and its licensors from and against any damages, costs, liabilities, settlement amounts and/or expenses (including attorneys' fees) incurred in connection with any claim, lawsuit or action by any third party that arises or results from the use or distribution of any and all Programs and/or Software.

3. Java Technology Restrictions. You may not modify the Java Platform Interface ("JPI", identified as classes contained within the "java" package or any subpackages of the "java" package), by creating additional classes within the JPI or otherwise causing the addition to or modification of the classes in the JPI. In the event that you create an additional class and associated API(s) which (i) extends the functionality of the Java platform, and (ii) is exposed to third party software developers for the purpose of developing additional software which invokes such additional API, you must promptly publish broadly an accurate specification for such API for free use by all developers. You may not create, or authorize your licensees to create, additional classes, interfaces, or subpackages that are in any way identified as "java", "javax", "sun" or similar con-

vention as specified by Sun in any naming convention designation.

4. Java Runtime Availability. Refer to the appropriate version of the Java Runtime Environment binary code license (currently located at `http://www.java.sun.com/jdk/index.html`) for the availability of runtime code which may be distributed with Java applets and applications.

5. Trademarks and Logos. You acknowledge and agree as between you and Sun that Sun owns the SUN, SOLARIS, JAVA, JINI, FORTE, STAROFFICE, STARPORTAL and iPLANET trademarks and all SUN, SOLARIS, JAVA, JINI, FORTE, STAROFFICE, STARPORTAL and iPLANET-related trademarks, service marks, logos and other brand designations ("Sun Marks"), and you agree to comply with the Sun Trademark and Logo Usage Requirements currently located at `http://www.sun.com/policies/trademarks`. Any use you make of the Sun Marks inures to Sun's benefit.

6. Source Code. Software may contain source code that is provided solely for reference purposes pursuant to the terms of this Agreement. Source code may not be redistributed unless expressly provided for in this Agreement.

7. Termination for Infringement. Either party may terminate this Agreement immediately should any Software become, or in either party's opinion be likely to become, the subject of a claim of infringement of any intellectual property right.

For inquiries please contact: Sun Microsystems, Inc. 901 San Antonio Road, Palo Alto, California 94303

JavaTM Plug-in HTML Converter Version 1.3 Binary Code License

SUN MICROSYSTEMS, INC. ("SUN") IS WILLING TO LICENSE THE JAVATM PLUG-IN HTML CONVERTER AND THE ACCOMPANYING DOCUMENTATION INCLUDING AUTHORIZED COPIES OF EACH (THE "SOFTWARE") TO LICENSEE ONLY ON THE CONDITION THAT LICENSEE ACCEPTS ALL OF THE TERMS IN THIS AGREEMENT. READ THE TERMS OF THIS AGREEMENT AND ANY PROVIDED SUPPLEMENTAL LICENSE TERMS (COLLECTIVELY "AGREEMENT") CAREFULLY BEFORE OPENING THE SOFTWARE MEDIA PACKAGE. BY OPENING THE SOFTWARE MEDIA PACKAGE, YOU AGREE TO THE TERMS OF THIS AGREEMENT. IF YOU ARE ACCESSING THE SOFTWARE ELECTRONICALLY, INDICATE YOUR ACCEPTANCE OF THESE TERMS BY SELECTING THE "ACCEPT" BUTTON AT THE END OF THIS AGREEMENT. IF YOU DO NOT AGREE TO ALL THESE TERMS, PROMPTLY RETURN THE UNUSED SOFTWARE TO YOUR PLACE OF PURCHASE FOR A REFUND OR, IF THE SOFTWARE IS ACCESSED ELECTRONICALLY, SELECT THE "DECLINE" BUTTON AT THE END OF THIS AGREEMENT.

1. LICENSE GRANT

(A) License To Use. Licensee is granted a non-exclusive and non-transferable no fee license to download, install and internally use the binary Software. Licensee may copy the Software, provided that Licensee reproduces all copyright and other proprietary notices that are on the original copy of the Software.

(B) License to Distribute. Licensee is granted a royalty-free right to reproduce and distribute the Software provided that Licensee: (i) distributes Software complete and unmodified only as part of Licensee's value-added applet or application ("Program"), and for the sole purpose of allowing customers of Licensee to modify HTML pages to access Sun's JavaTM Plug-in technology; (ii) does not distribute additional software intended to replace any component(s) of the Software; (iii) agrees to incorporate the most current version of the Software that was available 180 days prior to each production release of the Program; (iv) does not remove or alter any proprietary legends or notices contained in the Software; (v) includes the provisions of Sections 1(C), 1(D), 5, 7, 8, 9 in Licensee's license agreement for the Program; (vi) agrees to indemnify, hold harmless, and defend Sun and its licensors from and against any claims or lawsuits, including attorneys' fees, that arise or result from the use or distribution of the Program.

(C) Java Platform Interface. Licensee may not modify the Java Platform Interface ("JPI", identified as classes contained within the "java" package or any subpackage of the "java" package), by creating additional classes within the JPI or otherwise causing the addition to or modification of the classes in the JPI. In the event that Licensee creates any Java-related API and distributes such API to others for applet or application development, Licensee must promptly publish broadly, an accurate specification for such API for free use by all developers of Java-based software.

(D) License Restrictions. The Software is licensed to Licensee only under the terms of this Agreement, and Sun reserves all rights not expressly granted to Licensee. Licensee may not use, copy, modify, or transfer the Software, or any copy thereof, except as expressly provided for in this Agreement. Except as otherwise provided by law for purposes of decompilation of the Software solely for interoperability, Licensee may not reverse engineer, disassemble, decompile, or translate the Software, or otherwise attempt to derive the source code of the Software. Licensee may not rent, lease, loan, sell, or distribute the Software, or any part of the Software. No right, title, or interest in or to any trademarks, service marks, or trade names of Sun or Sun's licensors is granted hereunder.

(E) Nuclear Applications Restriction. SOFTWARE IS NOT DESIGNED OR INTENDED FOR USE IN THE DESIGN, CONSTRUCTION, OPERATION OR MAINTENANCE OF ANY NUCLEAR FACILITY. SUN DISCLAIMS ANY EXPRESS OR IMPLIED WARRANTY OF FITNESS FOR SUCH USES. LICENSEE REPRESENTS AND WARRANTS THAT IT WILL NOT USE THE SOFTWARE FOR SUCH PURPOSES.

2. CONFIDENTIALITY. The Software is the confidential and proprietary information of Sun and/or its licensors. The Software is protected by United States copyright law and international treaty. Unauthorized reproduction or distribution is subject to civil and criminal penalties. Licensee agrees to take adequate steps to protect the Software from unauthorized disclosure or use.

3. TRADEMARKS AND LOGOS. This Agreement does not authorize Licensee to use any Sun name, trademark, or logo. Licensee acknowledges that Sun owns the Java trademark and all Java-related trademarks, logos and icons including the Coffee Cup and Duke ("Java Marks") and agrees to: (i) comply with the Java Trademark Guidelines at `http://java.sun.com/trademarks.html`; (ii) not do anything harmful to or inconsistent with Sun's rights in the Java Marks; and (iii) assist Sun in protecting those rights, including assigning to Sun any rights acquired by Licensee in any Java Mark.

4. TERM, TERMINATION AND SURVIVAL

(A) The Agreement shall automatically terminate 180 days after production release of the next version of the Software by Sun.

(B) Licensee may terminate this Agreement at any time by destroying all copies of the Software.

(C) This Agreement will immediately terminate without notice if Licensee fails to comply with any obligation of this Agreement.

(D) Upon termination, Licensee must immediately cease use of and destroy the Software or, upon request from Sun, return the Software to Sun. (E) The provisions set forth in paragraphs 1 (D), 2, 5, 7, 8, 9, and 10 will survive termination or expiration of this Agreement.

5. NO WARRANTY. THE SOFTWARE IS PROVIDED TO LICENSEE "AS IS". ALL EXPRESS OR IMPLIED CONDITIONS, REPRESENTATIONS, AND WARRANTIES, INCLUDING ANY IMPLIED WARRANTY OF MERCHANTABILITY, SATISFACTORY QUALITY, FITNESS FOR A PARTICULAR PURPOSE, OR NON-INFRINGEMENT, ARE DISCLAIMED, EXCEPT TO THE EXTENT THAT SUCH DISCLAIMERS ARE HELD TO BE LEGALLY INVALID.

6. MAINTENANCE AND SUPPORT. Sun has no obligation to provide maintenance or support for the Software under this Agreement.

7. LIMITATION OF DAMAGES. TO THE EXTENT NOT PROHIBITED BY APPLICABLE LAW, SUN'S AGGREGATE LIABILITY TO LICENSEE OR TO ANY THIRD PARTY FOR CLAIMS RELATING TO THIS AGREEMENT, WHETHER FOR BREACH OR IN TORT, WILL BE LIMITED TO THE FEES PAID BY LICENSEE FOR SOFTWARE WHICH IS THE SUBJECT MATTER OF THE CLAIMS. IN NO EVENT WILL SUN BE LIABLE FOR ANY INDIRECT, PUNITIVE, SPECIAL, INCIDENTAL OR CONSEQUENTIAL DAMAGE IN CONNECTION WITH OR ARISING OUT OF THIS AGREEMENT (INCLUDING LOSS OF BUSINESS, REVENUE, PROFITS, USE, DATA OR OTHER ECONOMIC ADVANTAGE), HOWEVER IT ARISES, WHETHER FOR BREACH OR IN TORT, EVEN IF SUN HAS BEEN PREVIOUSLY ADVISED OF THE POSSIBILITY OF SUCH DAMAGE. LIABILITY FOR DAMAGES WILLBE LIMITED AND EXCLUDED, EVEN IF ANY EXCLUSIVE REMEDY PROVIDED FOR IN THIS AGREEMENT FAILS OF ITS ESSENTIAL PURPOSE.

8. GOVERNMENT USER. Rights in Data: If procured by, or provided to, the U.S. Government, use, duplication, or disclosure of technical data is subject to restrictions as set forth in FAR 52.227-14(g)(2), Rights in Data-General (June 1987); and for computer software and computer software documentation, FAR 52-227-19, Commercial Computer Software-Restricted Rights (June 1987). However, if under DOD, use, duplication, or disclosure of technical data is subject to DFARS 252.227-7015(b), Technical Data-Commercial Items (June 1995); and for computer software and computer software documentation, as specified in the license under which the computer software was procured pursuant to DFARS 227.7202-3(a). Licensee shall not provide Software nor technical data to any third party, including the U.S. Government, unless such third party accepts the same restrictions. Licensee is responsible for ensuring that proper notice is given to all such third parties and that the Software and technical data are properly marked.

9. EXPORT LAW. Licensee acknowledges and agrees that this Software and/or technology is subject to the U.S. Export Administration Laws and Regulations. Diversion of such Software and/or technology contrary to U.S. law is prohibited. Licensee agrees that none of this Software and/or technology, nor any direct product therefrom, is being or will be acquired for, shipped, transferred, or reexported, directly or indirectly, to proscribed or embargoed countries or their nationals, nor be used for nuclear activities, chemical biological weapons, or missile projects unless authorized by the U.S. Government. Proscribed countries are set forth in the U.S. Export Administration Regulations. Countries subject to U.S. embargo are: Cuba, Iran, Iraq, Libya, North Korea, Syria, and the Sudan. This list is subject to change without further notice from Sun, and Licensee must comply with the list as it exists in fact. Licensee certifies that it is not on the U.S. Department of Commerce's Denied Persons List or affiliated lists or on the U.S. Department of Treasury's Specially Designated Nationals List. Licensee agrees to comply strictly with all U.S. export laws and assumes sole responsibility for obtaining licenses to export or re-export as may be required. Licensee is responsible for complying with any applicable local laws and regulations, including but not limited to, the export and import laws and regulations of other countries.

10. GOVERNING LAW, JURISDICTION AND VENUE. Any action related to this Agreement shall be governed by California law and controlling U.S. federal law, and choice of law rules of any jurisdiction shall not apply. The parties agree that any action shall be brought in the United States District Court for the Northern District of California or the California Superior Court for the County of Santa Clara, as applicable, and the parties hereby submit exclusively to the personal jurisdiction and venue of the United States District Court for the Northern District of California and the California Superior Court of the County of Santa Clara.

11. NO ASSIGNMENT. Neither party may assign or otherwise transfer any of its rights or obligations under this Agreement, without the prior written consent of the other party, except that Sun may assign its right to payment and may assign this Agreement to an affiliated company.

12. OFFICIAL LANGUAGE. The official text of this Agreement is in the English language and any interpretation or construction of this Agreement will be based thereon. In the event that this Agreement or any documents or notices related to it are translated into any other language, the English language version will control.

13. ENTIRE AGREEMENT. This Agreement is the entire agreement between you and Sun relating to its subject matter. It supersedes all prior or contemporaneous oral or written communications, proposals, representations and warranties and prevails over any conflicting or additional terms of any quote, order, acknowledgment, or other communication between the parties relating to its subject matter during the term of this Agreement. No modification of this Agreement will be binding, unless in writing and signed by an authorized representative of each party.

JavaTM Media Framework (JMF) 2.1.1 Binary Code License Agreement

READ THE TERMS OF THIS AGREEMENT AND ANY PROVIDED SUPPLEMENTAL LICENSE TERMS (COLLECTIVELY "AGREEMENT") CAREFULLY BEFORE OPENING THE SOFTWARE MEDIA PACKAGE. BY OPENING THE SOFTWARE MEDIA PACKAGE, YOU AGREE TO THE TERMS OF THIS AGREEMENT. IF YOU ARE ACCESSING THE SOFTWARE ELECTRONICALLY, INDICATE YOUR ACCEPTANCE OF THESE TERMS BY SELECTING THE "ACCEPT" BUTTON AT THE END OF THIS AGREEMENT. IF YOU DO NOT AGREE TO ALL THESE TERMS, PROMPTLY RETURN THE UNUSED SOFTWARE TO YOUR PLACE OF PURCHASE FOR A REFUND OR, IF THE SOFTWARE IS ACCESSED ELECTRONICALLY, SELECT THE "DECLINE" BUTTON AT THE END OF THIS AGREEMENT.

1. License to Use. Sun Microsystems, Inc. ("Sun") grants you a non-exclusive and non-transferable license for the internal use only of the accompanying software and documentation and any error corrections provided by Sun (collectively "Software"), by the number of users and the class of computer hardware for which the corresponding fee has been paid.

2. Restrictions. Software is confidential and copyrighted. Title to Software and all associated intellectual property rights is retained by Sun and/or its licensors. Except as specifically authorized in any Supplemental License Terms, you may not make copies of Software, other than a single copy of Software for archival purposes. Unless enforcement is prohibited by applicable law, you may not modify, decompile, or reverse engineer Software. You acknowledge that Software is not designed or intended for use in the design, construction, operation or maintenance of any nuclear facility. Sun disclaims any express or implied warranty of fitness for such uses. No right, title or interest in or to any trademark, service mark, logo or trade name of Sun or its licensors is granted under this Agreement.

3. Limited Warranty. Sun warrants to you that for a period of ninety (90) days from the date of purchase, as evidenced by a copy of the receipt, the media on which Software is furnished (if any) will be free of defects in materials and workmanship under normal use. Except for the foregoing, Software is provided "AS IS". Your exclu-

sive remedy and Sun's entire liability under this limited warranty will be at Sun's option to replace Software media or refund the fee paid for Software.

4. DISCLAIMER OF WARRANTY. UNLESS SPECIFIED IN THIS AGREEMENT, ALL EXPRESS OR IMPLIED CONDITIONS, REPRESENTATIONS AND WARRANTIES, INCLUDING ANY IMPLIED WARRANTY OF MERCHANTABILITY, FITNESS FOR A PARTICULAR PURPOSE OR NON-INFRINGEMENT ARE DISCLAIMED, EXCEPT TO THE EXTENT THAT THESE DISCLAIMERS ARE HELD TO BE LEGALLY INVALID.

5. LIMITATION OF LIABILITY. TO THE EXTENT NOT PROHIBITED BY LAW, IN NO EVENT WILL SUN OR ITS LICENSORS BE LIABLE FOR ANY LOST REVENUE, PROFIT OR DATA, OR FOR SPECIAL, INDIRECT, CONSEQUENTIAL, INCIDENTAL OR PUNITIVE DAMAGES, HOWEVER CAUSED REGARDLESS OF THE THEORY OF LIABILITY, ARISING OUT OF OR RELATED TO THE USE OF OR INABILITY TO USE SOFTWARE, EVEN IF SUN HAS BEEN ADVISED OF THE POSSIBILITY OF SUCH DAMAGES. In no event will Sun's liability to you, whether in contract, tort (including negligence), or otherwise, exceed the amount paid by you for Software under this Agreement. The foregoing limitations will apply even if the above stated warranty fails of its essential purpose.

6. Termination. This Agreement is effective until terminated. You may terminate this Agreement at any time by destroying all copies of Software. This Agreement will terminate immediately without notice from Sun if you fail to comply with any provision of this Agreement. Upon termination, you must destroy all copies of Software.

7. Export Regulations. All Software and technical data delivered under this Agreement are subject to US export control laws and may be subject to export or import regulations in other countries. You agree to comply strictly with all such laws and regulations and acknowledge that you have the responsibility to obtain such licenses to export, re-export, or import as may be required after delivery to you.

8. U.S. Government Restricted Rights. If Software is being acquired by or on behalf of the U.S.

Government or by a U.S. Government prime contractor or subcontractor (at any tier), then the Government's rights in Software and accompanying documentation will be only as set forth in this Agreement; this is in accordance with 48 C.F.R. 227.7202-4 (for Department of Defense (DOD) acquisitions) and with 48 CFR 2.101 and 12.212 (for non-DOD acquisitions).

9. Governing Law. Any action related to this Agreement will be governed by California law and controlling U.S. federal law. No choice of law rules of any jurisdiction will apply.

10. Severability. If any provision of this Agreement is held to be unenforceable, this Agreement will remain in effect with the provision omitted, unless omission would frustrate the intent of the parties, in which case this Agreement will immediately terminate.

11. Integration. This Agreement is the entire agreement between you and Sun relating to its subject matter. It supersedes all prior or contemporaneous oral or written communications, proposals, representations and warranties and prevails over any conflicting or additional terms of any quote, order, acknowledgment, or other communication between the parties relating to its subject matter during the term of this Agreement. No modification of this Agreement will be binding, unless in writing and signed by an authorized representative of each party.

JavaTM Media Framework (JMF) 2.1.1 Supplemental License Terms

These supplemental license terms ("Supplemental Terms") add to or modify the terms of the Binary Code License Agreement (collectively, the "Agreement"). Capitalized terms not defined in these Supplemental Terms shall have the same meanings ascribed to them in the Agreement. These Supplemental Terms shall supersede any inconsistent or conflicting terms in the Agreement, or in any license contained within the Software.

1. Software Internal Use and Development License Grant. Subject to the terms and conditions of this Agreement, including, but not limited to Section 3 (Java_ Technology Restrictions) of these Supplemental Terms, Sun grants you a non-exclusive, non-transferable, limited license to reproduce internally and use internally the binary form of the Software, complete and unmodified, for the sole purpose of designing, developing and testing your Java applets and applications ("Programs").

2. License to Distribute Software. In addition to the license granted in Section 1 (Software Internal Use and Development License Grant) of these Supplemental Terms, subject to the terms and conditions of this Agreement, including but not limited to, Section 3 (Java_ Technology Restrictions) of these Supplemental Terms, Sun grants you a non-exclusive, non-transferable, limited license to reproduce and distribute the Software in binary code form only, provided that you:

i. distribute the Software complete and unmodified, except that you may omit those files specifically identified as "optional" in the Software "README" file, which include samples, documents, and bin files, or that are removable by using the Software customizer tool provided, only as part of and for the sole purpose of running your Program into which the Software is incorporated;

ii. do not distribute additional software intended to replace any components of the Software;

iii. do not remove or alter any proprietary legends or notices contained in the Software;

iv. only distribute the Software subject to a license agreement that protects Sun's interests consistent with the terms contained in this Agreement; and

v. agree to defend and indemnify Sun and its licensors from and against any damages, costs, liabilities, settlement amounts or expenses, including attorneys' fees, incurred in connection with any claim, lawsuit or action by any third party that arises or results from the use or distribution of any and all Programs or Software.

3. Java_ Technology Restrictions. You may not modify the Java Platform Interface

("JPI", identified as classes contained within the "java" package or any subpackages of the "java" package), by creating additional classes within the JPI or otherwise causing the addition to or modification of the classes in the JPI. In the event that you create an additional class and associated API's, which:
i. extends the functionality of the Java platform, and
ii. is exposed to third party software developers for the purpose of developing additional software which invokes such additional API, you must promptly publish broadly an accurate specification for such API for free use by all developers. You may not create, or authorize your licensees to create additional classes, interfaces, packages or subpackages that are in any way identified as "java", "javax", "sun" or similar convention as specified by Sun in any class file naming convention designation.
4. JavaTM Runtime Availability. Refer to the appropriate version of the Java_ Runtime Environment binary code license (currently located at http://www.java.sun.com/jdk/index.html) for the availability of runtime code which may be distributed with Java_ applets and applications.
5. Trademarks and Logos. You acknowledge and agree as between you and Sun that Sun owns the SUN,
SOLARIS, JAVA, JINI, FORTE, STAROFFICE, STARPORTAL and iPLANET trademarks and all SUN, SOLARIS, JAVA, JINI, FORTE, STAROFFICE, STARPORTAL and iPLANET-related trademarks, service marks, logos and other brand designations ("Sun Marks"), and you agree to comply with the Sun Trademark and Logo Usage Requirements currently located at `http://www.sun.com/policies/trademarks`. Any use you make of the Sun Marks inures to Sun's benefit.
6. Source Code. Software may contain source code that is provided solely for reference purposes pursuant to the terms of this Agreement. Source code may not be redistributed unless expressly provided for in this Agreement.
7. Termination for Infringement. Either party may terminate this Agreement immediately should any Software become, or in either party's opinion be likely to become, the subject of a claim of infringement of any intellectual property right.

Index

A

C

E

F

G

H

I

K–L

M

N

Q–R

S

T

U-V

W

X - Y - Z

HOW TO CONTACT US

VOICES THAT MATTER

VISIT OUR WEB SITE

WWW.NEWRIDERS.COM

On our web site, you'll find information about our other books, authors, tables of contents, and book errata. You will also find information about book registration and how to purchase our books, both domestically and internationally.

EMAIL US

Contact us at: **nrfeedback@newriders.com**

- If you have comments or questions about this book
- To report errors that you have found in this book
- If you have a book proposal to submit or are interested in writing for New Riders
- If you are an expert in a computer topic or technology and are interested in being a technical editor who reviews manuscripts for technical accuracy

Contact us at: **nreducation@newriders.com**

- If you are an instructor from an educational institution who wants to preview New Riders books for classroom use. Email should include your name, title, school, department, address, phone number, office days/hours, text in use, and enrollment, along with your request for desk/examination copies and/or additional information.

Contact us at: **nrmedia@newriders.com**

- If you are a member of the media who is interested in reviewing copies of New Riders books. Send your name, mailing address, and email address, along with the name of the publication or web site you work for.

BULK PURCHASES/CORPORATE SALES

If you are interested in buying 10 or more copies of a title or want to set up an account for your company to purchase directly from the publisher at a substantial discount, contact us at 800-382-3419 or email your contact information to `corpsales@pearsontechgroup.com`. A sales representative will contact you with more information.

WRITE TO US

New Riders Publishing
201 W. 103rd St.
Indianapolis, IN 46290-1097

CALL/FAX US

Toll-free (800) 571-5840
If outside U.S. (317) 581-3500
Ask for New Riders
FAX: (317) 581-4663

WWW.NEWRIDERS.COM

RELATED NEW RIDERS TITLES

ISBN 0735711127
400 pages
US $44.99

XML and SQL Server 2000

John Griffin

XML and SQL Server 2000 enables SQL developers to understand and work with XML, the preferred technology for integrating eBusiness systems. SQL Server 2000 has added several new features that SQL Server 7 never had that make working with and generating XML easier for the developer. *XML and SQL Server 2000* provides a comprehensive discussion of SQL Server 2000's XML capabilities.

ISBN 0735711178
300 pages
US $34.99

ebXML: The New Global Standard for Doing Business on the Internet

Alan Kotok
David Webber

To create an e-commerce initiative, managers need to understand that XML is the technology that will take them there. Companies understand that to achieve a successful Internet presence their company needs an e-commerce methodology implemented. Many department managers (the actual people who design, build, and execute the plan) don't know where to begin. *ebXML* will take them there.

ISBN 0735711364
640 pages
US $49.99

Inside XSLT

Inside XSLT is designed to be a companion guide to the highly succesful Inside XML. This example oriented book covers XML to HTML, XML to Music, XML with Java, style sheet creation and usage, nodes and attributes, sorting data, creating Xpath expressions, using Xpath and XSLT functions, namespaces, names templates, name variables, designing style sheets and using XSLT processor API's, the 56 XSL formatting objects, the XSLT DTD, and much much more.

ISBN 073571052X
with CD-ROM
330 pages
US $39.99

C++ XML

Fabio Arciniegas

The demand for robust solutions is at an all-time high. Developers and programmers are asking the question, "How do I get the power performance found with C++ integrated into my web applications?" Fabio Arciniegas knows how. He has created the best way to bring C++ to the web. Through development with XML and in this book, he shares the secrets developers and programmers worldwide are searching for.

ISBN 0735710201
1152 pages
US $49.99

Inside XML

Steven Holzner

Inside XML is a foundation book that covers both the Microsoft and non-Microsoft approach to XML programming. It covers in detail the hot aspects of XML, such as DTD's vs. XML Schemas, CSS, XSL, XSLT, XLinks, XPointers, XHTML, RDF, CDF, parsing XML in Perl and Java, and much more.

ISBN 0735710430
368 pages
US $45.00

Advanced Linux Programming

CodeSourcery, LLC

An in-depth guide to programming Linux from the most recognized leaders in the Open Source community, this book is the ideal reference for Linux programmers who are reasonably skilled in the C programming language and who are in need of a book that covers the Linux C library (glibc).

Colophon

The image on the cover of this book, captured by photographer Ian Cartwright, is that of the Ruins of Masada, situated on top of a twenty-three acre mesa ten miles south of Ein Gedi and a couple miles off the west shore of the Dead Sea. While accounts of its origination vary, consensus suggests it was first established by "Jonathan the High Priest" as a royal retreat during the second century BC. It would later be occupied by Herod the Great who used it both as a retreat and place to escape attack by either Cleopatra of Egypt, or the Jewish people.

Herod is said to have transformed this refuge into a luxurious fortress. His improvements included two palaces, Roman style bathhouses, administrative buildings, villas, storehouses, a sophisticated water system, and defensive structures. Historical accounts suggest that after Herod's death in 4 BC, Masada fell under Roman occupation until about 66 AD at which time it came under attack during a Jewish Revolt. It is believed the Zealots fought against Rome for three years at Masada and ultimately chose mass suicide over surrender to the Romans. Today Masada is considered a symbol of Jewish freedom and is frequently visited by Israeli school children who study its history as part of their curriculum. It is one of Israel's most popular tourist attractions.

This book was written and edited in Microsoft Word, and laid out in QuarkXPress. The font used for the body text is Bembo and MCPdigital. It was printed on 50# Husky Offset Smooth paper at R.R. Donnelley & Sons in Crawfordsville, Indiana. Prepress consisted of PostScript computer-to-plate technology (filmless process). The cover was printed at Moore Langen Printing in Terre Haute, Indiana, on Carolina, coated on one side.